Elements of a Cha

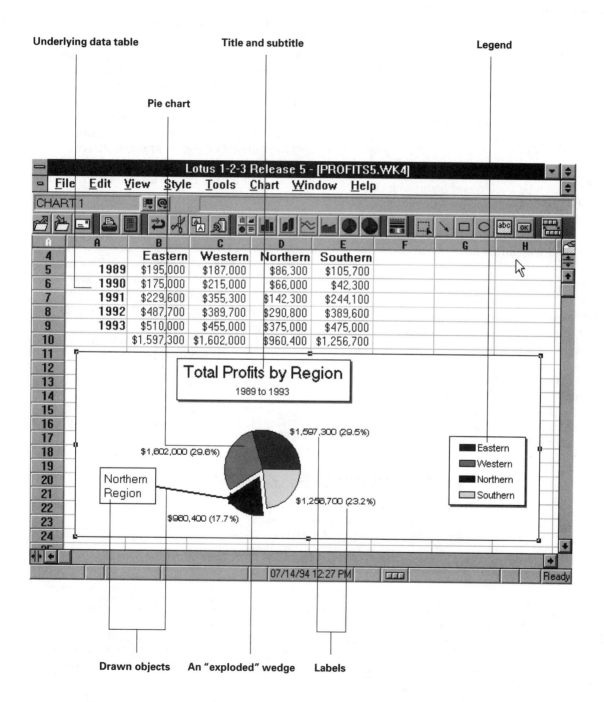

Underlying data table

Title and subtitle

Legend

Pie chart

Drawn objects   **An "exploded" wedge**   **Labels**

FOR EVERY COMPUTER QUESTION,
THERE IS A SYBEX BOOK THAT HAS THE ANSWER

Each computer user learns in a different way. Some need thorough, methodical explanations, while others are too busy for details. At Sybex we bring nearly 20 years of experience to developing the book that's right for you. Whatever your needs, we can help you get the most from your software and hardware, at a pace that's comfortable for you.

We start beginners out right. You will learn by seeing and doing with our **Quick & Easy** series: friendly, colorful guidebooks with screen-by-screen illustrations. For hardware novices, the **Your First** series offers valuable purchasing advice and installation support.

Often recognized for excellence in national book reviews, our **Mastering** titles are designed for the intermediate to advanced user, without leaving the beginner behind. A **Mastering** book provides the most detailed reference available. Add our pocket-sized **Instant Reference** titles for a complete guidance system. Programmers will find that the new **Developer's Handbook** series provides a more advanced perspective on developing innovative and original code.

With the breathtaking advances common in computing today comes an ever increasing demand to remain technologically up-to-date. In many of our books, we provide the added value of software, on disks or CDs. Sybex remains your source for information on software development, operating systems, networking, and every kind of desktop application. We even have books for kids. Sybex can help smooth your travels on the **Internet** and provide **Strategies and Secrets** to your favorite computer games.

As you read this book, take note of its quality. Sybex publishes books written by experts—authors chosen for their extensive topical knowledge. In fact, many are professionals working in the computer soft-ware field. In addition, each manuscript is thoroughly reviewed by our technical, editorial, and production personnel for accuracy and ease-of-use before you ever see it—our guarantee that you'll buy a quality Sybex book every time.

To manage your hardware headaches and optimize your software potential, ask for a Sybex book.

FOR MORE INFORMATION, PLEASE CONTACT:

Sybex Inc.
2021 Challenger Drive
Alameda, CA 94501
Tel: (510) 523-8233 • (800) 227-2346
Fax: (510) 523-2373

Let us hear from you.

 Talk to SYBEX authors, editors and fellow forum members.

 Get tips, hints and advice online.

 Download magazine articles, book art, and shareware.

Join the SYBEX Forum on  **CompuServe**®

Understanding 1-2-3® Release 5 for Windows™

Douglas Hergert with Guy Hart-Davis

SYBEX®

SAN FRANCISCO • PARIS • DÜSSELDORF • SOEST

Acquisitions Editor: Joanne Cuthbertson
Developmental Editor: Richard Mills
Editor: Peter Weverka
Project Editor: Valerie Potter
Technical Editor: Adebisi Oladipupo
Book Designer: Suzanne Albertson
Production Artist: Helen Bruno
Screen Graphics Artist: Dan Schiff
Page Layout/Typesetters: Alissa Feinberg and Stephanie Hollier
Proofreaders/Production Assistants: Stephen Kullmann and Rhonda Holmes
Indexer: Nancy Guenther
Cover Designer: Joanna Kim Gladden

SYBEX is a registered trademark of SYBEX Inc.

1-2-3 is a registered trademark of Lotus Development Corporation.

Library of Congress Card Number: 94-67534
ISBN: 0-7821-1579-9

Manufactured in the United States of America
10 9 8 7 6 5

To Boubacar Diatta and Azeb Mengistab

ACKNOWLEDGMENTS

This book represents the talents of many able contributors. Guy Hart-Davis developed and wrote Part Four, a complete reference guide to 1-2-3's built-in functions. Richard Mills made many helpful suggestions at the outset. Peter Weverka edited the book with expertise and good humor. Val Potter skillfully and patiently guided the book through the editorial process. Adebisi Oladipupo kept an eye on technical accuracy. Claudette Moore of Moore Literary Agency offered advice and encouragement. The SYBEX production team of Stephanie Hollier, Alissa Feinberg, Stephen Kullmann, Rhonda Holmes, Helen Bruno, and Dan Schiff put it all together.

In addition, the following people worked on the book's earlier incarnations: Maryann Brown, David Clark, Sharon Crawford, Christian Crumlish, Sheila Dienes, Alissa Feinberg, Brenda Kienan, Dianne King, Erik Ingenito, Lisa Jaffe, Cuong Le, Janet MacEachern, Deborah Maizels, and Savitha Varadan. My sincere thanks to all.

CONTENTS
AT A GLANCE

TABLE OF CONTENTS

PART THREE   ADVANCED FEATURES OF 1-2-3

PART FOUR   FUNCTIONS AND MARCO LANGUAGE REFERENCE

INTRODUCTION

1-2-3 for Windows Release 5 is the latest version of the popular and enduring spreadsheet software from Lotus. This book guides you through the stages of mastering this powerful program. In a sequence of tutorial-style chapters, you'll learn all the essential details of 1-2-3 while you work through complete business examples on your own computer. In these hands-on exercises you'll learn to:

- Produce clear, accurate, and flexible worksheet documents
- Generate presentation-quality charts from worksheet data
- Build accessible databases and perform varieties of query operations on data
- Create custom macro tools, adapting 1-2-3 to your own work patterns

Each chapter begins with several *fast tracks*, which are short instructions that give you a preview of the material to come and a quick-reference guide to essential 1-2-3 procedures. In addition, you'll find hundreds of screen illustrations that show you exactly what happens in 1-2-3 when you perform specific worksheet, chart, and database operations. Tips, Notes, and Warnings provide added advice and instructions to help you master 1-2-3.

How This Book Is Organized

The book is divided into four parts. The two chapters of Part One give you an introductory overview of 1-2-3.

Chapter 1, "Working with Lotus 1-2-3 for Windows," presents an application that illustrates the spreadsheet, charting, and database components of 1-2-3. This application serves as a preview of the features you'll be studying individually in later chapters. In the hands-on portion of Chapter 1, you'll begin working with a few of the features that make 1-2-3 easier to use than ever before, including SmartIcons, quick menus, the "live" status bar, and worksheet tabs.

Chapter 2, "Lotus 1-2-3 and the Windows Interface," explores the elements of 1-2-3 in the Windows environment. In particular, you'll learn to work with menus, dialog boxes, and tools that are common to all Windows applications. You'll practice mouse and keyboard techniques for selecting and using these tools. Finally, you'll learn to take advantage of the comprehensive Windows-style Help system that is an integral part of 1-2-3 for Windows.

Part Two contains seven chapters that introduce the basics of 1-2-3—the spreadsheet, the charting and mapping capabilities, the database, and macros.

Chapter 3, "Worksheet Essentials," takes you through the initial steps of building a worksheet for a business application. You'll learn how to enter labels and numeric data into a worksheet, to calculate totals, to perform important range operations such as assigning range names and moving data, and to write formulas and copy them from one location to another in a worksheet. Along the way, you'll master the essential distinctions between absolute, relative, and mixed references in formulas, and you'll learn how to develop a worksheet in order to make it an effective "what-if" analysis tool. You'll also learn to save your worksheet to disk. Throughout this chapter, you'll concentrate on using 1-2-3's SmartIcons, along with other efficient tools and techniques such as quick menus, the "live" status bar, the Navigator button, the New Sheet button, and drag-and-drop mouse actions.

Chapter 4, "Worksheet Formatting and Printing," continues your introduction to basic spreadsheet operations. You'll learn to apply formats and type styles to numbers and labels on a worksheet, and to make adjustments in the appearance of a worksheet itself to accommodate your data. You'll also begin working with date and time values, and you'll learn the tools and techniques of date and time arithmetic. Finally, you'll work through the steps of printing a worksheet, producing effective presentations of your data on paper.

Chapter 5, "Worksheet Formulas and Functions," guides you further into the large library of calculation tools that 1-2-3 provides for your use in worksheets. First you'll expand your understanding of numeric, chronological, logical, and text formulas. Then you'll begin studying 1-2-3's collections of built-in @functions for use in specific applications—including statistical, financial, mathematical, chronological, logical, string, and lookup functions. Chapter 5 includes dozens of worksheet exercises for you to examine and work with as you master the use of these important spreadsheet tools. Along the way, you'll learn to use new features such as fill-by-example and the Function selector button.

Chapter 6, "Charts, Maps, and Graphics," introduces the second component of the 1-2-3 package. In this chapter you'll learn to create varieties of charts and graphs from numeric data—including bar graphs, line graphs, area graphs, pie charts, and other pictorial formats for presenting information. You'll also explore the important tools available for editing and manipulating chart objects. In particular, you'll discover a new set of SmartIcons and menu commands dealing specifically with charts. You'll find out how to add drawn objects such as arrows and boxes to a chart. Along the way, you'll learn to use a chart as a tool for exploring "what-if" scenarios. Finally, you'll learn to use 1-2-3's new mapping feature to create visual representations of geographical data.

Chapter 7, "Database Essentials," takes up the third major component in 1-2-3, the database-management tools. This chapter introduces you to essential database concepts, and guides you through a series of hands-on exercises in which you create and work with a database. In particular, you'll learn to define fields, enter records, and create calculated fields. Then you'll begin mastering a variety of tools for sorting, finding, and changing the information in databases. You'll learn to create a query table for extracting a subset of records and fields and for joining information from two or more database tables.

Chapter 8, "Database Calculations and Operations," teaches you more about 1-2-3's database capabilities. You'll begin by learning to use the special library of statistical functions designed for database queries, including @DCOUNT, @DSUM, @DAVG, and @DSTD. You'll also learn the steps for creating computed columns, aggregate columns, and crosstab tables. Finally, you'll explore 1-2-3's special DataLens drivers that allow you to establish connections between an external worksheet and a 1-2-3 worksheet. Specifically, you'll learn to create a query table from an external database.

Chapter 9, "Macros," shows you how to create your own library of 1-2-3 macro tools to streamline your work with worksheets, charts, and databases. The macros you'll create in this chapter are shortcuts for specific operations you perform frequently in 1-2-3. By creating a macro, you can reduce the steps for almost any 1-2-3 procedure to a simple pair of keystrokes. For example, you'll learn to create macros to enter a company name and address instantly into a range of worksheet cells and to choose options from the 1-2-3 menu commands. You'll also learn to create your own icons to represent macros in the SmartIcon set. After completing this step, you can perform a macro simply by clicking a custom SmartIcon with the mouse. The topic of macro programming is continued in Chapter 12.

Part Three introduces advanced worksheet tools, links between files, and macro programming. This section of the book comprises three chapters.

Chapter 10, "Advanced Worksheet Tools," helps you master some of 1-2-3's most sophisticated features. You'll take a look at the new collection of SmartMasters, which are professionally designed templates for streamlining the production of standard business worksheets. You'll also learn to use 1-2-3's powerful Version Manager to maintain multiple versions of data in the context of a single worksheet. Finally, you'll take a tour of the powerful features available in the Range ➤ Analyze menu. These include the What-If Table command for performing multiple what-if calculations in a single operation, the Solver command for examining scenarios that match specific constraints in worksheet problems that you define, the Backsolver command for finding an input value that produces a desired bottom-line calculation, the Distribution command for examining the frequency of values on a worksheet, the Regression command for exploring the correlation between numeric data sets, and the Matrix commands for solving simultaneous equations. The details of these valuable worksheet tools are all illustrated in step-by-step hands-on exercises.

Chapter 11, "Links between Files," shows you how to work with multiple-file applications in 1-2-3 and Windows. Lotus 1-2-3 allows you to open more than one worksheet file at a time and to write special formulas to create links between worksheets. With a link formula, one worksheet can read data from another, whether the source worksheet is open or not. In an example presented in this chapter, you'll learn to take advantage of worksheet links to create a business summary from data contained in four different worksheets. In addition, 1-2-3 supports the important Windows features known as Dynamic Data Exchange (DDE) and Object Linking and Embedding (OLE), which allow you to transfer data and objects between documents in different Windows applications. Chapter 11 helps you explore these links.

Chapter 12, "Macro Programming," is an introduction to 1-2-3's complete macro language. You'll learn to use a variety of macro commands for programming operations such as loops, decisions, subroutines, and branches of control. You'll also learn to write interactive macro programs that display dialog boxes on the screen to elicit input from the user. Along the way, you'll explore the Lotus Dialog Editor, a tool for designing custom dialog boxes. The sample programs in this chapter include macros that create daily appointment worksheets and produce mailing labels from an address database.

Part Four, "Functions and Macro Language Reference," is a reference guide to the entire library of built-in functions available in 1-2-3. Chapter 13 lists all the functions in alphabetical order and tells you which page to turn to for detailed information about each function. At the start of Chapters 14 through 20, you'll find alphabetical lists of the functions covered in these chapters along with the page numbers to turn to. Function descriptions include syntax descriptions, explanations, tips, notes, warnings, and examples. Chapter 21 explains 1-2-3's macro commands.

LOTUS 1-2-3 IN THE WINDOWS ENVIRONMENT

CHAPTER 1

Working

with

Lotus 1-2-3

for Windows

fast TRACK

To choose a command from a quick menu,   **21**

position the mouse pointer over the object whose quick menu you want to view, and click the right mouse button. Then click the command you want to carry out.

To choose an option from the live status bar,   **22**

click one of the live panels on the status bar (at the bottom of the screen), and then choose an option from the resulting pop-up menu.

To view the 1-2-3 Classic window,   **24**

press the slash key on the keyboard.

To determine whether 1-2-3 is accepting a cell entry as a label or as a value,   **25**

look at the mode indicator (located in the lower-right corner of the screen, on the right side of the status bar) after you begin the entry. You will see either the word *Label* or *Value*.

To exit from 1-2-3,   **27**

choose File ➤ Exit.

LOTUS 1-2-3 for Windows offers you three interrelated software components, known by the familiar terms spreadsheet, graphics, and database:

- The *spreadsheet* provides efficient tools for organizing and working with tables of labels and numbers.

- The *graphics* component lets you create and print visual representations of numeric data. For example, you can create bar graphs and pie charts.

- The *database* gives you simple but effective techniques for storing and managing records of information.

Lotus 1-2-3 now combines the familiar elements of Microsoft Windows' *graphical user interface* with new tools that make the application easier to use than ever before. If you're upgrading from a DOS version of the spreadsheet program, you'll find many important advantages in the Windows version:

- Like other major Windows programs, Lotus 1-2-3 has pull-down menus, dialog boxes, special-purpose keyboard functions, mouse control, a set of elaborate Help features, and a large collection of buttons—called SmartIcons in 1-2-3—that allow you to perform important tasks at the click of a mouse.

- Within the Windows environment you can run 1-2-3 at the same time that you're using other programs—a word processor, a desktop publishing program, and even a programming language. Switching back and forth from one program to another is easy.

- You can exchange data between Lotus 1-2-3 and other applications in a variety of simple ways. For example, you can use the Clipboard to copy data or graphs from Lotus 1-2-3 to other Windows

This chapter introduces you to the three major components of 1-2-3 for Windows—spreadsheet, graphics, and database—and shows you how they interact with one another. You'll take a first look at what the program can do, and then you'll start thinking about ways to use 1-2-3 in your own work. You'll also begin learning how Lotus 1-2-3 operates in Windows. Exercises in this chapter will help you master the keyboard and the mouse, and explore the dimensions, features, and appearance of Lotus 1-2-3 for Windows.

Lotus 1-2-3: The Basics

A *worksheet* is a large grid of individual cells, ideal for organizing and analyzing tables of information. In 1-2-3, a single worksheet file may contain as many as 256 "pages" of worksheets, each represented by a *tab* displayed at the top of the worksheet window. This three-dimensional worksheet arrangement gives you the opportunity to arrange many interrelated tables of data in one convenient location.

Figure 1.1 identifies many parts of the 1-2-3 screen as it appears when you run the program in Windows. (If you see a Welcome window when you first start 1-2-3, simply click the Cancel button with the mouse or press Esc at the keyboard to close the window and view the spreadsheet.) At first glance the screen may seem to contain a bewildering assortment of elements, but you'll quickly learn to use each category of tools to create efficient and effective worksheets in Lotus 1-2-3.

At the top of the screen you see the 1-2-3 *title bar*, the *menu bar*, and the *edit line*. These three lines together are known as the *control panel*. Beneath the control panel is a row of *SmartIcons,* which provide fast access to important 1-2-3 operations. (This row is sometimes called the SmartIcon *palette.*) The fifth row of the screen displays the tabs of the active worksheet file. Initially a worksheet contains only one page, identified by a tab labeled A, but you'll find that you can easily add new sheets to a file and change the label on a tab. The worksheet window itself, organized in rows and columns, takes up most of the screen area. At the bottom of the worksheet you see the *status bar,* which provides additional techniques for changing the appearance of a worksheet.

FIGURE 1.1

A Lotus 1-2-3
worksheet

The 1-2-3 window and the active worksheet window display the familiar features of the Windows environment, including Control menus, Maximize and Minimize buttons, scroll bars, and title bars. If you're new to Windows, you can learn more about all these features in Chapter 2.

The Worksheet

Worksheets are divided into rows and columns of cells. Each row is identified by a number, and each column by a letter. A cell has an *address* made up of its column letter and row number. For example, the cell at the intersection of column D and row 9 has the address D9.

To develop a worksheet table, you simply begin typing numbers and labels into individual cells. The *current cell*—the cell ready to receive a data entry—is marked by a bold frame called the *cell pointer*. As you can see in

Figure 1.1, cell A1 is the current cell when you begin working in Lotus 1-2-3 or when you open a new worksheet. Notice that the column and row headings of the current cell—initially A and 1—have a *sunken* appearance; this visual feature makes it easy to identify the address of the current cell. In addition, the current cell address is displayed in the first panel of the edit line, near the upper-left corner of the screen.

Every worksheet has a title. When a worksheet window is *maximized*—enlarged to is maximum size within the 1-2-3 application window—the title appears in the 1-2-3 title bar at the top of screen.

NOTE *Untitled* is the default name of the first worksheet window displayed on the screen. As you begin developing a data table, you'll save your worksheet as a file on disk, and you'll give the file a name that you choose yourself. Until then, the default name *Untitled* appears on the title bar.

Moving Around the Worksheet

When a worksheet window is maximized, two special buttons appear on each end of the 1-2-3 menu bar. The worksheet's *Control-menu box* is displayed at the left side of the menu bar, and the *Restore* button, a two-headed arrow icon, appears at the right. Clicking the Restore button reduces the worksheet window to a smaller size within the 1-2-3 application window. Along the right side of the window is a *vertical scroll bar* for navigating up and down the rows of the worksheet. Along the lower border of the window you see a *horizontal scroll bar* for navigating left and right across the columns of the worksheet.

NOTE The mouse pointer initially appears on the screen as a white arrow, pointing up and to the left. *Clicking* the mouse means moving the pointer to a particular object on the screen and clicking the left mouse button once.

In the following exercise, you'll use these buttons and scroll bars to explore the dimensions of the worksheet:

1. Click the Restore button at the right side of the menu bar to reduce the size of the active worksheet window. (Alternatively, press Alt+hyphen from the keyboard to pull down the window's Control menu, and then press R to choose the Restore command.)

As you can see in Figure 1.2, several changes take place in the appearance of the worksheet window. The window now has its own title bar, which displays the name *Untitled*. The Control-menu box appears at the left side of the title bar, and two arrow icons known as the Minimize and Maximize buttons appear at the right.

FIGURE 1.2

The result of clicking
the Restore button

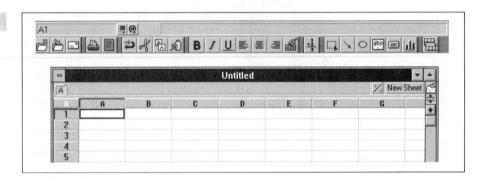

2. Restore the window's original appearance by clicking the Maximize button (or by pressing Alt+hyphen and then X).

3. Press → once on your keyboard. The cell pointer moves one cell to the right, to address B1. Repeat this action six times to move the cell pointer to H1. Column H is at the right side of the current worksheet window.

4. Now move the cell pointer one more column to the right and watch what happens to the worksheet. Column A disappears from the left side of the window to make room for column I on the right side. As this action demonstrates, the worksheet contains many more columns and rows than can be displayed in the window at one time.

5. Press the ↓ key on the keyboard. The cell pointer moves down one position, to cell I2. Press ↓ repeatedly until the cell pointer reaches I20, and then move the pointer down one more cell. Row 1 disappears from the worksheet window to make room for row 21.

6. Position the mouse pointer over the small gray *scroll box* that appears at the left side of the horizontal scroll bar. Hold down the left mouse button and drag the box part way across the bar. A new sequence of columns now appears in the worksheet window.

N O T E

Dragging is another common mouse operation. To drag an object from one place to another on the screen, you position the mouse pointer over the object, hold down the left mouse button, and move the pointer to the target position. The object moves with the mouse pointer. Release the mouse button to complete the move.

7. Press End and then →. On this empty worksheet, the cell pointer moves to column IV, the last column in the worksheet.

The first 26 columns of the worksheet are identified by the letters A through Z, the next 26 by AA though AZ, the next 26 by BA through BZ. IA through IV are the last columns. Under this lettering scheme, the worksheet has a total of 256 columns.

8. Press End and then ↓ to move to the final row on the worksheet, row 8192. The cell at the bottom-right corner of the worksheet has the address IV8192, as shown in Figure 1.3.

9. Press the Home key on the keyboard. Pressing Home moves the cell pointer back to its beginning position, cell A1.

As you've seen, a Lotus 1-2-3 worksheet is a huge grid of over 2 million cells (256 columns × 8192 rows). The worksheet window can show only a small part of the worksheet at a time, but you can scroll the worksheet to view any group of cells that you want to work with.

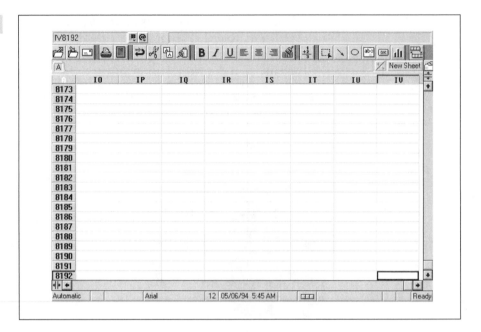

As you've learned, a 1-2-3 file can contain many pages of tabbed worksheets in which you can organize tables of interrelated data. By writing formulas that refer to data values in more than one worksheet, you can establish relationships among the multiple sheets of a file. In the following exercises, you'll explore three-dimensional worksheets. Along the way you'll have your first opportunity to work with 1-2-3 menu commands.

The Menu Bar

As in most Windows applications, the menu bar is the horizontal row of commands at the top of the screen, just below the title bar:

File   Edit   View   Style   Tools   Range   Window   Help

When you choose one of these commands, a *pull-down menu* appears with a list of options. For example, Figure 1.4 shows the commands on the File menu displayed when you choose File on the menu bar.

FIGURE 1.4

The File menu

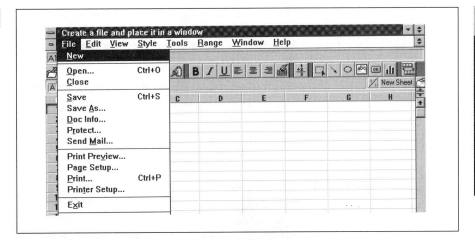

> **TIP**
>
> Below the Exit command, the File menu also lists as many as five of the worksheet files you've opened most recently. The list gives you a quick way to reopen files that you've been working on in previous sessions with 1-2-3.

Mastering this system of menus and the commands they offer is a large part of learning Lotus 1-2-3 for Windows. In Release 5.0, the menu structure has been simplified and streamlined in a couple of ways. For one thing, it is now *context-sensitive*. This means different menus may appear that apply specifically to the task you're currently working on. In addition, a number of menu commands have been consolidated into single options and multi-use dialog boxes, so that interrelated operations are all available to you at once. Thanks to these characteristics, you'll find the menu system easy and efficient to use.

Choosing Menu Commands

Several mouse and keyboard techniques are available for choosing commands from the 1-2-3 menu system:

- Press the Alt key or the F10 key to activate the menu bar. With the menu bar active, you can press → or ← to highlight one of the Main menu commands and ↵ to pull down the menu.

- A keyboard shortcut for selecting a menu command is simply to press the Alt key followed by the underscored letter in the menu command's name. For example, pressing Alt+F pulls down the File menu.

- With the mouse, pull down a menu by clicking the corresponding command in the menu bar. For example, to pull down the File menu, position the mouse pointer over File in the menu bar and click the left mouse button.

TIP

When you highlight an entry on the menu bar or a command in a pull-down menu, a brief description appears at the top of the Lotus 1-2-3 window, temporarily replacing the title bar (see Figure 1.4).

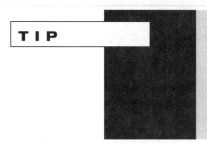

TIP

To back out of the menu system and return to your work in the worksheet window, use the Escape key. Press Escape once if the menu bar is active but no pull-down menu is displayed. Press Escape twice to back out of a pull-down menu. Alternatively, click anywhere inside the worksheet window with the mouse.

Mode indicator As you switch between menus and worksheets, you'll notice changes in the *mode indicator*, the panel at the far right side of the status bar. When the worksheet is active, the mode indicator displays the word *Ready* (see Figure 1.3), but when a menu is active, the mode indicator displays the word *Menu*. Ready and Menu are two of several different *modes* that 1-2-3 operates in. You'll see other changes in the mode indicator later in this chapter (see page 25). By the way, another way to back out of a pull-down menu—and switch back to Ready mode—is to click the mode indicator with the mouse.

Working with 1-2-3 **1**

Creating a Three-Dimensional Worksheet

In the following exercise, you'll learn to add new sheets to a worksheet window and to change the way you view multiple sheets on the screen. Along the way, you'll try your hand at choosing menu commands and using dialog boxes.

New Sheet

1. Find the New Sheet button, located at the right side of the screen on the line between the SmartIcons and the worksheet window. Click this button twice with the mouse.

With each click, 1-2-3 adds a new sheet to the current worksheet file. After the second click, you'll see three worksheet tabs—labeled A, B, and C—just above the worksheet window at the left side of the screen, as shown in Figure 1.5. Each tab represents one sheet, or "page," in the current worksheet. To activate a sheet, you simply click the corresponding tab with the mouse.

FIGURE 1.5

Adding sheets to a worksheet file. Click the New Sheet button to add a new sheet to the current worksheet.

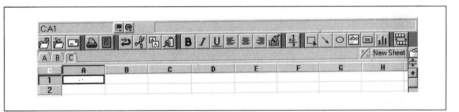

2. Pull down the View menu by pressing Alt+V or clicking View on the menu bar, and then choose the Split command. This brings up the Split dialog box, with options for changing the appearance of the worksheet window:

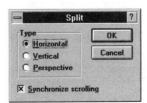

3. Select Perspective by clicking the option with the mouse or pressing P from the keyboard. This option allows you to view multiple worksheets inside the current window. When you make the selection, the option button is filled with a black circle.

4. To confirm the new option and close the dialog box, press ↵ or click the OK button with the mouse.

When you complete these steps, the worksheet window appears as shown in Figure 1.6. It's now divided into sections displaying the three sheets. The sheets are still identified by the letters A, B, and C. Sheet C is currently active; the cell pointer appears in cell A1 of sheet C.

5. Press Ctrl+PgDn twice to activate each of the other sheets in turn. Then press Ctrl+PgUp twice to activate sheet C again. As you activate each window, you'll see the *current cell address* displayed as A:A1, B:A1, or C:A1 on the edit line, just above the SmartIcons.

6. Now return to the original tabbed view of the worksheet by pulling down the View menu and choosing the Clear Split command.

FIGURE 1.6

The Perspective view of the worksheet window. To switch to the Perspective view, choose View ➤ Split and click the Perspective option.

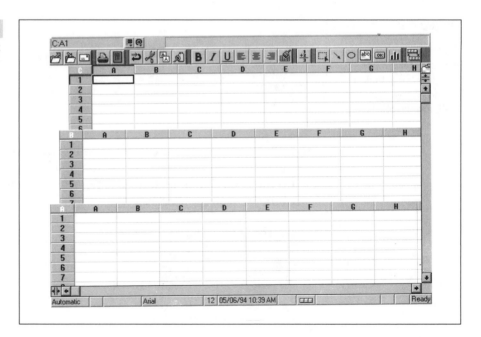

Reviewing What You've Learned So Far

Take a moment to review what you've learned in these initial hands-on exercises.

Worksheets A worksheet file can contain multiple sheets—as many as 256. Every new worksheet window starts out with only one worksheet. The simplest way to add new sheets is to click the New Sheet button one or more times. Each new sheet is represented by a tab displayed just above the worksheet window; you activate a sheet by clicking its tab. In the Perspective view, you can view three worksheets at once; press Ctrl+PgUp or Ctrl+PgDn to activate each sheet in turn.

Multiple sheets in a file are identified by letters of the alphabet, from A, B, and C for the first three worksheets, up to IV for worksheet 256. These letters initially appear on the sheet tabs, but you can change the label on any tab, as you'll learn in Chapter 2 (see page 94).

Cells A *complete cell address* consists of three elements:

- The sheet letter, followed by a colon
- The column letter
- The row number

For example, C:E29 refers to the cell at the intersection of column E and row 29 on sheet C.

You've used menu commands and their resulting dialog boxes to make changes to the appearance and content of a worksheet window. To streamline your work, 1-2-3 offers several kinds of alternative tools for accomplishing particular tasks. Depending on how you prefer to work, these alternatives can be quicker and simpler than the standard menu commands. You'll examine some of these tools in the upcoming sections of this chapter.

SmartIcons, Quick Menus, and the Live Status Bar

SmartIcons—the row of buttons displayed above the worksheet area in the 1-2-3 window—are one-step shortcuts for accomplishing common operations, including file storage, printing, copying, graphing, and formatting. To perform the action that an icon represents, you simply click a SmartIcon with the mouse. But SmartIcons are not the only shortcuts available to you in Release 5.0. Lotus also has special lists of context-sensitive commands known as quick menus, along with a variety of "live" tools on the status bar at the bottom of the screen. You can use all these tools to carry out worksheet operations quickly and efficiently. You'll take a first look at these features in this section.

NOTE You can't access SmartIcons, quick menus, or the live status bar with the keyboard. All of these features require the use of the mouse.

SmartIcons

Lotus 1-2-3 initially displays a line of the two dozen SmartIcons that you're likely to use most commonly as you develop worksheets. The graphic displayed on each of these buttons generally gives you a clear idea of what the SmartIcon does. For example, the first two buttons—each showing an image of a folder, with an arrow pointing out of or into the folder—are for opening and saving files, respectively. Likewise, the button that contains a small picture of a printer is for printing the active worksheet; the buttons displaying scissors and a pot of glue are for cut-and-paste operations; the button with a bar graph image is for adding a graph to your worksheet; and so on.

If you forget what a particular button does, 1-2-3 offers a simple technique for finding out the use of each SmartIcon. Simply position the mouse pointer over the icon you want to learn about. In response, 1-2-3 displays a *bubble* that gives a brief description of the tool. For example, if you position the mouse pointer over the fourth button in the row of

SmartIcons, the description "Displays the Print dialog box" appears in the bubble:

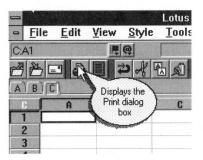

Take a moment to read the description of each button in the initial row of SmartIcons. Here's a list of the descriptions you'll see in the bubbles:

SMARTICON	DESCRIPTION
	Open an existing file
	Save the current file
	Send data by electronic mail
	Displays the Print dialog box
	Preview the print selection
	Undo the last command or action
	Cut to the Clipboard
	Copy to the Clipboard
	Paste Clipboard contents

SMARTICON	DESCRIPTION
B	Bold data
I	Italicize data
U	Underline data
≣	Align data to the left
≣	Center data
≣	Align data to the right
	Copy a range's styles to other ranges
+½₃	Sum values above or to the left
	Select several objects
↘	Draw a forward-pointing arrow
○	Draw an ellipse or circle
abc	Draw a text block
ok	Draw a macro button
▮▮	Draw a chart using the selected range
	Select the next set of SmartIcons

You'll be interested to learn that this group is only one of *eight* sets of SmartIcons available for your use in 1-2-3. Other sets are just a mouse-click away. Notice that the very last icon in the row is designed for switching from one set of SmartIcons to another. Try clicking this last icon now. When you do so, a new set of SmartIcons appears on the screen. Click the button seven more times to step through all the available sets and to return to the original set of SmartIcons.

Lotus 1-2-3 also allows you to *customize* each SmartIcon set. The Smart-Icons command in the Tools menu gives you simple ways to rearrange, insert, and delete the icons in a selected set. You'll learn more about customizing the SmartIcon sets in Chapter 2 (see page 90).

Quick Menus

Sometimes you may want to see a short list of menu commands that relate to a specific object on the screen. Like many recently developed Windows applications, 1-2-3 now offers *quick menus* for just this purpose. A quick menu is a context-sensitive command set that you can view for a particular item in a worksheet. To bring up a quick menu, you simply position the mouse pointer over an item and click the *right* mouse button. The resulting selection of commands are the ones you're most likely to want to use on your selection.

For example, try positioning the mouse pointer over any cell in the active worksheet, and then click the right mouse button. As you can see in Figure 1.7, the resulting quick menu contains commands for cutting and pasting, copying, formatting, and naming the cell that you've selected. To choose a command, you can press arrow keys at the keyboard or click a command with the mouse. (To close the quick menu without choosing a command, press Escape or click on the worksheet with the left mouse button.)

Quick menus allow you to perform common worksheet operations without having to memorize the menu locations of specific commands. You'll find lots of good uses for quick menus as you work through the exercises in this book.

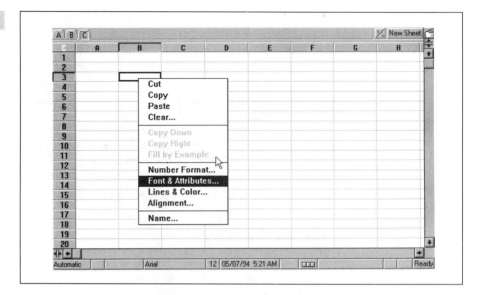

The Live Status Bar

In most Windows applications, the status bar simply supplies information about the file or object that you're currently working on. Because this information is located at the very bottom of the screen, it's seldom the focus of your attention. But Lotus 1-2-3 gives you some important new uses for this line. The status bar is "live," which means it not only *displays* information, but also gives you some simple ways to *change* the settings of your work.

Take a first look at the status bar as it initially appears on the screen. For a selected cell, individual panels on the bar show you the settings that determine how a data entry will be displayed—the numeric format, the font, and the point size. You can click the panels shown in Figure 1.8 with the mouse to view a complete list of the available settings in each category. (Notice that some panels remain blank until you've chosen a relevant setting.) These lists can save you lots of time when you want to change the appearance of data on your worksheet.

FIGURE 1.8

Information on the status bar

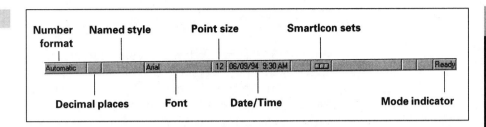

The status bar also shows the current date and time. Then, two panels to the right of the date/time display, you can see an icon consisting of three small squares. Try clicking this panel; as shown in Figure 1.9, the resulting pop-up list contains the names of the eight SmartIcon sets available in 1-2-3. You can choose any entry in the list to display a new set of buttons on the SmartIcon row at the top of the screen.

In short, 1-2-3 often gives you several different ways to carry out a given operation on a worksheet. SmartIcons, quick menus, and the live status bar present you with convenient alternatives for completing your work. It's always up to you to decide which technique is the easiest and most efficient.

Another special feature is the 1-2-3 Classic window, the subject of the next section of this chapter.

FIGURE 1.9

The list of SmartIcons in the "live" status bar

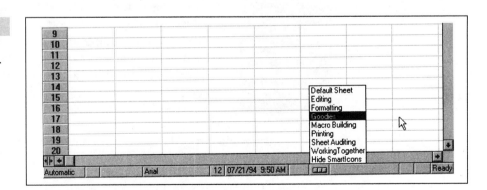

The 1-2-3 Classic Window

The 1-2-3 Classic window is an alternate menu system for users who are upgrading from an earlier DOS release of the program. This menu system appears on the screen when you press the slash key (/), the key that has traditionally accessed menus in previous versions of Lotus 1-2-3. (Alternatively, you can press Shift+<.) Press the slash key now, and you'll see the 1-2-3 Classic window at the top of the screen, as in Figure 1.10. If you've worked with a previous version of 1-2-3, the commands in the Classic window will be comfortingly familiar. This alternate menu system is accessible only from the keyboard, not with the mouse.

FIGURE 1.10

The 1-2-3 Classic window

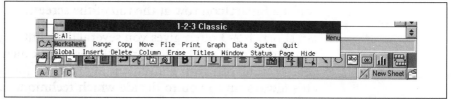

TIP

Use the 1-2-3 Classic window while you're first adjusting to the 1-2-3 for Windows interface, but try to wean yourself from it as quickly as possible. Learn to use the standard menu bar, the SmartIcons, quick menus, and the live status bar to accomplish tasks in this new environment. In the long run, you'll become a much more efficient 1-2-3 user if you adjust yourself to these new features.

As an exercise with the Classic menu system, try switching between the Perspective view and the single-worksheet view in the current window:

1. Press **/** if you haven't done so already to bring up the 1-2-3 Classic menu. With the menu displayed on the screen, choose the **Work**sheet command.

2. Choose **Window**.

3. Choose **P**erspective. The result is the same as choosing View ➤ Split ➤ Perspective from 1-2-3's standard menu bar: the current window displays three worksheets. Notice that the 1-2-3 Classic menu disappears after you select the commands.

4. Press the following four keys in sequence: **/WWC**. (This is the traditional notation for representing command selections in DOS versions of 1-2-3. In this case, the notation represents the **/W**orksheet **W**indow **C**lear command from the 1-2-3 Classic menu.) The current window once again displays a single worksheet.

By the way, if you press Shift+colon (:), another part of the 1-2-3 Classic menu appears on the screen. This second Classic menu offers commands for formatting and preparing a worksheet for printing and publication.

As a final introductory exercise, you'll enter data values into some of the cells of the worksheet you've been examining.

Data Entry and the Mode Indicator

Lotus 1-2-3 recognizes two general types of data for entry into the cells of a worksheet: *labels* and *values*.

- A label is a non-numeric entry beginning with a letter of the alphabet or with one of several special symbols that 1-2-3 recognizes as the first character in a label.

- A value is a number or the numeric result of a formula. (Actually, Lotus also recognizes date and time entries, and translates them into numeric values.)

Entering Data in Cells

Several interesting changes take place in the 1-2-3 window when you begin entering data into cells. You'll explore these changes in the following brief exercise, as you enter the word *Profit* as a label in cell A1 and the value 9876 in cell A2.

1. Press the Home key, if necessary, to select cell A1 on the active worksheet.

2. From the keyboard, hold down the Shift key and type the letter **P**.

Notice the mode indicator in the status bar; it shows the word *Label*, which means that 1-2-3 is accepting your entry as a non-numeric data item:

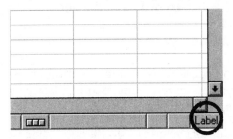

The uppercase *P* that you've typed appears in two places: on the edit line (just below the menu bar) and in the cell itself. Unlike older spreadsheet programs, Lotus 1-2-3 supports an important new feature known as *in-cell editing*. You no longer have to look up at the edit line when you're entering or editing data in a worksheet; rather, you can focus you attention directly at the cell where you're working, and complete the entry or edit operation in place. You'll learn more about in-cell editing as you continue through this book.

3. Complete the label by typing the remaining letters of the word *Profit*. If you make a mistake, you can press the Backspace key to erase the last character you typed.

4. Confirm the entry by pressing ↵.

The label you've just entered is left-justified inside the cell, following the default *alignment* for labels in 1-2-3. The mode indicator now displays the word *Ready*.

5. Press ↓ to select cell A2.

6. Type the four digits **9876** from the keyboard. This time the mode indicator displays the word *Value*, which means that 1-2-3 is

accepting your data entry as a numeric value:

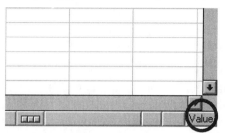

As before, the entry appears both on the edit line and in the cell itself.

7. Press ↓ once. This action accomplishes two steps at once: it completes the data entry and moves the cell pointer down to cell A3.

Notice that the value 9876 is displayed right-justified inside cell A2. Numeric values are right-justified by default, although you can change their alignment just as you can do with labels.

8. In cell A3, begin the following label entry: **ABC**. (Do not press ↵.) Now cancel the entry by pressing Escape.

T I P   You can always check the mode indicator during data entry to make sure that 1-2-3 is accepting your data the way you are expecting it to—that is, as a label or a value.

In short, you can complete an entry by pressing ↵ or by pressing a direction key (such as ↑, ↓, ←, or →). Cancel an entry by pressing the Escape key.

Exiting 1-2-3

This is the end of the hands-on portion of this chapter. If you wish to exit 1-2-3 before you continue reading, here are the steps:

1. Choose File ➤ Exit from the menu bar (or press Alt+F4).

2. In the Exit dialog box, click No to indicate that you wish to exit without saving your current worksheet.

After these steps, you remain in Windows, but the 1-2-3 application window is no longer open.

In the remainder of this chapter, you'll examine a set of sample applications designed to illustrate the three major 1-2-3 components—spreadsheet, graphics, and database.

Planning, Developing, and Creating a Worksheet

You can enter labels, numbers, and chronological values (dates and times) as the data values on a worksheet. You can also enter *formulas* that instruct Lotus to perform arithmetic operations on your data. Given a table of raw data, a worksheet simplifies all kinds of calculations, from finding bottom-line numeric totals to performing complex statistical and financial formulas.

Perhaps the single most important feature of the Lotus spreadsheet is this: *Worksheets automatically recalculate totals and other formulas whenever you change the data that the formulas work with.* This essential characteristic is what distinguishes an "electronic spreadsheet" from manual calculations with paper and pencil. You can change underlying data values whenever you want without having to face the prospect of redoing the rest of your work. If you plan and write your formulas appropriately, Lotus recalculates all the results that depend on the raw data you've changed.

Spreadsheet users sometimes refer to this essential characteristic as 1-2-3's "what-if" capability. You can instantly find out what happens to a specific set of calculations when numeric information changes. "What-if" questions come up in an infinite variety of common business applications.

Consider the following examples:

- What is the new break-even point in the projected sales of a product if costs increase by a specific amount per unit?

- What happens to a company's projected tax rate this year if it purchases a major depreciable asset, such as a new computer?

- What is the new monthly payment on a business loan if the term of the loan is doubled and the interest rate decreased by 1 percent?

In calculations that are done by hand, finding the answers to questions like these can take a lot of time and effort. But in Lotus 1-2-3 you simply change the appropriate data entries in your worksheet, and the rest of the work is done for you. As you gain experience with worksheets, you'll quickly learn to organize your work to take full advantage of this important feature.

The worksheet examples you're about to examine are designed to illustrate the "what-if" power of Lotus 1-2-3. Here is the imaginary situation for these examples: A company has invited a nutritionist named Barbara Johnson to conduct a series of lunchtime seminars for its employees on the subject of good nutrition for working people. In particular, some employees have expressed interest in a confusing diet-related subject that has been in the news lately: the fat content of typical fast-food meals. There's been a lot of talk about the so-called 30-percent fat diet; many of the employees would like to know more about it.

Johnson is using Lotus 1-2-3 to prepare a series of handouts on which to base her discussion of this subject. These handouts will take the form of worksheets, graphs, and databases. She begins her preparations by designing some worksheets that analyze the caloric and fat content of what she imagines are typical lunches eaten by the employees in her audience.

As you examine Johnson's work, keep in mind your main goals in this chapter—to gain a general understanding of the components of 1-2-3, and to begin imagining uses for the spreadsheet in your own work. For the moment, focus on capabilities and features; you'll master specific techniques in later chapters.

Developing a Worksheet

Most of the worksheets you create will likely become tools for presenting information to other people. Whether you're sharing data with the person in the next office or exchanging ideas with a room full of professionals, your data should not only be accurate, but also clearly organized, attractively presented, and easy to understand. Lotus 1-2-3 includes a great many tools designed to help you meet these requirements.

Creating a successful worksheet typically involves several detailed tasks:

1. Place a descriptive title near the top of the worksheet.

2. Enter column headings and row labels that describe the categories of numeric data that you'll include in the worksheet table.

3. Enter the numeric data values themselves.

4. Write formulas that perform specific calculations on the numeric data. When appropriate, copy these formulas to other cells on the worksheet to perform the same calculations on other columns or rows of data.

5. Improve the appearance of the data—both the labels and numbers—by changing display formats and styles in particular cells. For example, you could display certain numbers in a currency or percentage format. Titles, labels, and numbers can also be displayed in special type styles for clarity and emphasis. You can display data in boldface, italic, and underlined styles.

This sequence of tasks is illustrated in Barbara Johnson's worksheet examples. Her initial goal is to explain the significance of the 30-percent fat diet, and, in the context of this diet, to analyze typical lunches that employees eat in fast-food restaurants or bring to work themselves.

Entering the Labels and Data

As the starting point for her research, Johnson visits the fast-food restaurant located across the street from the company's offices. She knows that lots of the employees come here for quick, inexpensive lunches. She asks for nutritional information about several items on the menu and is given a printed nutritional report. A quick glance at the report tells Johnson that the report has the data she will need for her presentation. It lists the calories and fat content of each item on the menu.

Back at her office, she imagines the typical lunch served by this restaurant: a hamburger, an order of French fries, some cookies, and a diet soda. She starts up 1-2-3 and begins designing a worksheet on which to present nutritional information about this particular meal.

She begins by entering a title for the worksheet in cells A3 and B3:

Lunch #1   Fast-Food Restaurant

Because she's planning to create additional worksheets for other menus, she identifies this one as Lunch #1.

Her purpose in this worksheet is to analyze the fat content of a meal and compare it with the recommended fat intake for a healthy adult. Secondarily, she wants to translate nutritional information into meaningful data that employees will find useful when they choose what to eat for lunch. The two major nutritional facts she'll present in her seminar are the following:

- Nutritionists recommend that the daily fat intake of healthy adults be 30 percent or less of their total daily caloric consumption (hence the term "30-percent fat diet").
- One gram of fat is equivalent to nine calories.

The nutritional panels on food packages usually list the fat content per serving in grams, but not as a percentage of total calories. For this reason, the health-conscious consumer needs to do some arithmetic to figure out whether a food item is a reasonable part of a 30-percent fat diet. Johnson will eventually express this arithmetic in formulas that she enters on her worksheet.

She continues her work by entering labels for four columns in rows 5 and 6:

Item	Total Calories	Fat in grams	% Fat Calories

The first column, "Item," is for the name of the food item. The second and third columns, "Total Calories" and "Fat in grams," will list data acquired from the nutritional report she picked up at the restaurant. The final column, "% Fat Calories," is for values that will be calculated from the available nutritional data: the percent of total calories represented by the fat content in each food item.

Next, Johnson types rows of information for the four food items she's including in her sample menu. She enters the name of each food item, the number of calories, and the fat content in grams. She also places a "Total" line at the bottom of the table for the total figures of each column. For the moment, she leaves the totals row and the percent fat column blank.

Figure 1.11 shows Johnson's work up to this point. Notice two interesting features of this worksheet: she has widened column A to accommodate the names of the food items, and she has removed the grid lines—the vertical and horizontal lines that separate columns and rows in a worksheet. These are two ways in which Lotus 1-2-3 gives you control over the appearance of a worksheet.

FIGURE 1.11

The first stage of the Lunch #1 worksheet

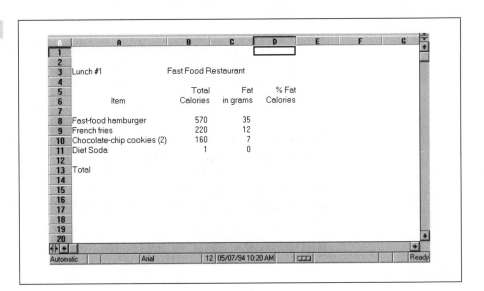

N O T E

You'll learn how to widen columns and remove grid lines in Chapter 4 (see page 198).

Now the nutritionist has completed the first few steps of designing her worksheet. She has created a title, entered descriptive column headings and row labels to identify the numeric data in the table, and copied the basic numeric data into the table. Her next step is to write formulas to perform calculations. She'll enter formulas at two different locations on the worksheet, the Total line at the bottom of the table and the % Fat Calories column on the right side.

Writing Formulas

The purpose of a formula in a worksheet is to calculate a value, usually from existing data on the worksheet. When you complete a formula entry, 1-2-3 displays the *result* of the formula in the cell where the formula is located. To view the formula itself, you can select the cell where the result is displayed and look up at the edit line.

Lotus 1-2-3 enforces precise rules about the format and content of formulas. Here are some of the most common elements you'll include in formulas:

- Literal numeric values, such as 9 and 365.

- Cell addresses, such as D5 or B4. In a formula, an address represents the value that is currently stored in the corresponding cell.

- Arithmetic operators, such as + (addition), – (subtraction), * (multiplication), and / (division).

- Functions from 1-2-3's large function library. A *function* is a built-in tool designed to perform a specific calculation. The names of functions begin with the @ character in 1-2-3. For example, the @SUM function—one of the simplest and most commonly used of all—finds the sum of a group of numbers. (Chapter 5 presents a survey of 1-2-3 worksheet functions.)

You'll find examples of all these elements in the formulas Barbara Johnson enters into her Lunch #1 worksheet.

Entering Formulas and Values in Cells

Johnson's first task is to find the total calories and the total grams of fat in the meal. To accomplish this, she begins by creating the following formula in cell B13:

@SUM(B8..B11)

To enter this formula, Johnson uses the convenient *Function selector* represented by the @ button on the edit line. When she clicks this button, a short list of commonly used functions appears on the screen, as shown in Figure 1.12. She selects the @SUM function, and then specifies the range of values that she wants to include in the summation. As you might guess, B8..B11 inside parentheses of this formula tells the @SUM function to find the total of all values stored in cells B8, B9, B10, and B11.

An expression like B8..B11 represents a *range* of cells. The two periods tell 1-2-3 to include all cells between the two listed cells in the calculation. You'll find many contexts in which ranges are important during your work with 1-2-3.

The result of the @SUM function, displayed in cell B13, is 951. Similarly, Johnson enters an @SUM expression in cell C13 to find the total grams of fat in the meal. (Actually, she has the option of entering a new version of the

FIGURE 1.12

Using the Function selector

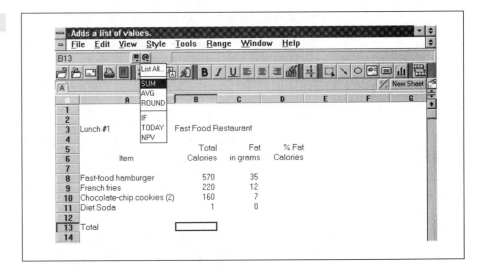

formula directly from the keyboard, as she did before, or *copying* the formula from cell B13 to cell C13. You'll learn several ways to copy formulas in Chapter 3.) The resulting value in cell C13 is 54.

Next Johnson has to devise a formula to calculate the fat calories in each food item as a percentage of the total calories. Given that there are nine calories in each gram of fat, here is the formula for finding the ratio of fat calories to total calories:

(Fat Grams × 9) ÷ Total Calories

Johnson's task is to translate this into a formula that 1-2-3 can accept and perform. She moves to cell D8 and enters the following:

+C8*9/B8

- Cell C8 contains the number of grams of fat in a hamburger.

- Multiplying this value by 9 gives the total calories of fat.

- Dividing the product by the total calories (stored in cell B8) gives the ratio.

When Johnson first enters this formula into cell D8, this calculated value appears in the cell: 0.552632.

NOTE Keep in mind that * represents multiplication in a 1-2-3 formula.

Changing number formats This number is the decimal format of the ratio, but Johnson wants to display the ratio as a percentage. With the cell pointer still in D8, she clicks the Number Formats panel, the first "live" area of the status bar at the bottom of the screen. From the resulting pop-up menu list, she chooses the Percent format, as shown in Figure 1.13. She then clicks the Decimal Places panel in the status bar and chooses 0 for the number of decimal places in her percentage figure, as shown in Figure 1.14. As a result of her selections, the percentage is displayed simply as 55%.

FIGURE 1.13

The Number Formats
list in the status bar

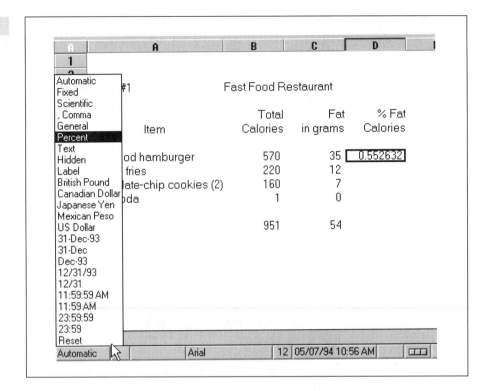

Johnson has written a successful formula. The fat calories account for 55
percent of total calories in the hamburger. Now she copies this formula
down column D—first to find the percent of fat calories for the other food
items on the menu, and then to find the total percent of fat calories for
the entire meal. Figure 1.15 shows the results of her work. Notice that fat
calories for the meal amount to 51 percent of total calories—far above the
recommended 30 percent. As Johnson notes with satisfaction, this worksheet will easily prove a point about the nutritional value of fast-food
lunches!

FIGURE 1.14

The Decimal Places list in the status bar

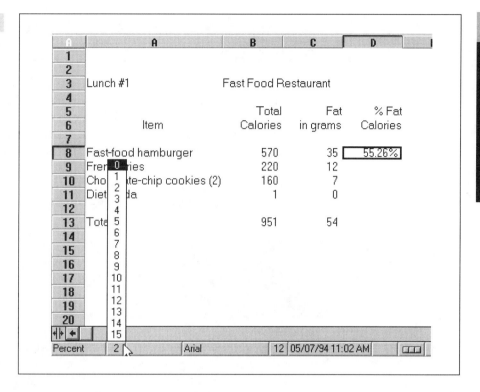

FIGURE 1.15

Adding formulas to the worksheet

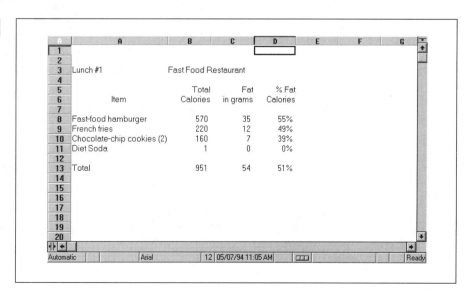

Preparing the Worksheet for Presentation

Up to now, Barbara Johnson has concentrated on entering data and writing formulas, without worrying much about the appearance of her worksheet. With two exceptions, she's left data items in their default formats, alignments, and display styles. One exception is the percent format that she applied to the fourth column (column D) in her data table; the second is the alignment of the four column headings. Can you see in Figure 1.15 that the four column heading labels are not displayed in their default, left-justified positions? These heading labels are right-justified.

N O T E
Left-justified means that text is aligned with the left side of the cell. *Right-justified* means that it is aligned along the right side.

Now the nutritionist is ready to give some thought to the appearance of her worksheet. 1-2-3 offers a rich variety of options for changing appearances. For example, she can change formats of numeric values, displaying them in the currency, decimal, or percentage format. Values and labels can be displayed in different *styles*—in bold, italics, or underlined characters—to provide emphasis in a worksheet. Furthermore, 1-2-3 (like all Windows applications) offers a selection of type fonts and font sizes for displaying and printing the information in a worksheet.

Changing Styles and Type Size

Johnson decides to use combinations of bold, italic, and underlined styles—along with larger type sizes for selected data items—to prepare her worksheet for presentation. You can see the result of her work in Figure 1.16.

Changes in style and size can be accomplished with the click of a mouse, thanks to 1-2-3's SmartIcons and live status bar. For example, here are

FIGURE 1.16

New type styles for the worksheet

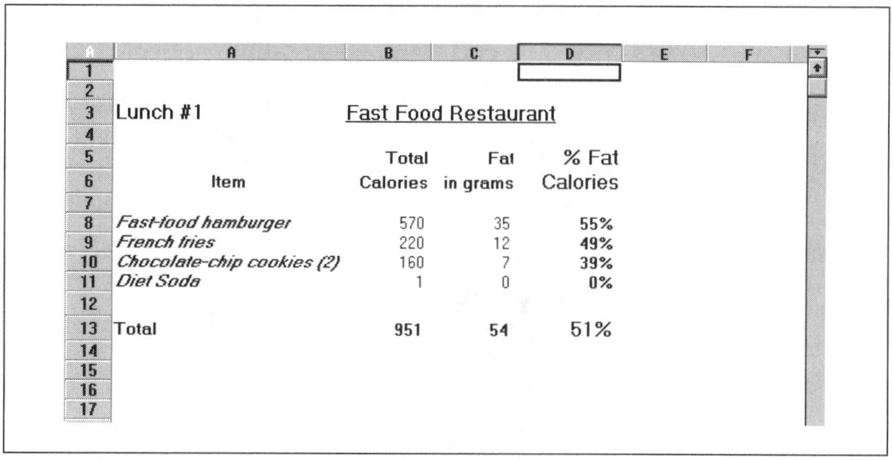

	A	B	C	D	E	F
1						
2						
3	Lunch #1		Fast Food Restaurant			
4						
5		Total	Fat	% Fat		
6	Item	Calories	in grams	Calories		
7						
8	Fast-food hamburger	570	35	55%		
9	French fries	220	12	49%		
10	Chocolate-chip cookies (2)	160	7	39%		
11	Diet Soda	1	0	0%		
12						
13	Total	951	54	51%		
14						
15						
16						
17						

the steps Johnson takes to change the column of food items (A8 to A11) to bold italic type style:

1. Select the target range of cells—in this case, A8 down to A11—by positioning the mouse pointer at A8 and dragging the mouse down to A11. Lotus 1-2-3 highlights the entire range.

2. Click the Bold SmartIcon. The bold style is applied to all the labels in the range.

3. Click the Italicize SmartIcon. The italic style is applied to the labels.

Notice how these actions are accomplished. First you select a range of cells on which to perform the action, and then you choose an option to apply to the range. This is a typical way of accomplishing many kinds of tasks in a worksheet. Conveniently, Lotus 1-2-3 for Windows often lets you choose between the following two approaches:

- Select a range first, and then choose a command that applies to the range.

- Choose a command, and then use the command's dialog box to specify the range over which the command will act.

Which method you choose is a matter of personal preference and convenience. The end result is the same.

The nutritionist has now completed her first version of the lunch worksheet. She saves her work to disk by pulling down the File menu and choosing the Save As command. She supplies the name Lunches for her worksheet, and 1-2-3 saves the file under the name LUNCHES.WK4.

N O T E .WK4 is the default extension name for worksheets.

She's now ready to begin formulating other lunch menus to include in her presentation on fat in diet. Clearly there's nothing particularly healthy about this first menu. She decides to prepare two more menus, the first a combination of items purchased from the fast-food restaurant and food prepared at home, and the second a "brown bag" lunch brought from home.

This is where 1-2-3's "what-if" facility becomes central to her work. As you'll see, the nutritionist can create the two new lunch worksheets simply by changing a few data items in the original worksheet. Whenever she enters new numeric data values to describe a particular food item, 1-2-3 automatically recalculates the applicable formulas.

Making Changes in the Data

For Lunch #2, Johnson decides to make two changes in the menu. She substitutes a turkey sandwich for the fast-food hamburger and a carton of low-fat milk for the diet soda. She begins by entering the names of the two new food items in cells A8 and A11, as follows:

A8	**Turkey sandwich (with mayo)**
A11	**Low-fat milk (1/2 pint)**

To change the contents of a cell in a worksheet, you can simply select the cell and enter a new label or value. When you confirm the entry by pressing ↵, the previous data item disappears and the new item takes its place. If you've applied a display style to the cell, it is retained. In this case the two new food items are still displayed in bold italic type.

Next, Johnson determines the approximate caloric and fat contents of these two new menu items. She enters the calories into column B (cell B8 for the turkey sandwich and B11 for the milk). She enters the fat content, in grams, into column C (cell C8 for the sandwich and C11 for the milk).

Automatic Recalculations

Each time Johnson enters a new numeric data value, three changes take place instantly:

- A new column total appears in the Total row at the bottom of the worksheet (row 13).

- A new fat percentage appears in the final column of the worksheet (column D).

- The new total fat percentage for the meal appears in cell D13.

In effect, these are the "what-if" factors for her worksheet. What happens to the total calories, the total fat content, and the fat percentages if she changes an item in the menu? Because 1-2-3 recalculates formulas instantly, the answers appear as soon as the nutritionist makes changes to the worksheet data. Figure 1.17 shows the second lunch menu, with the revised nutritional information. (Notice that the title of the worksheet has also been changed.)

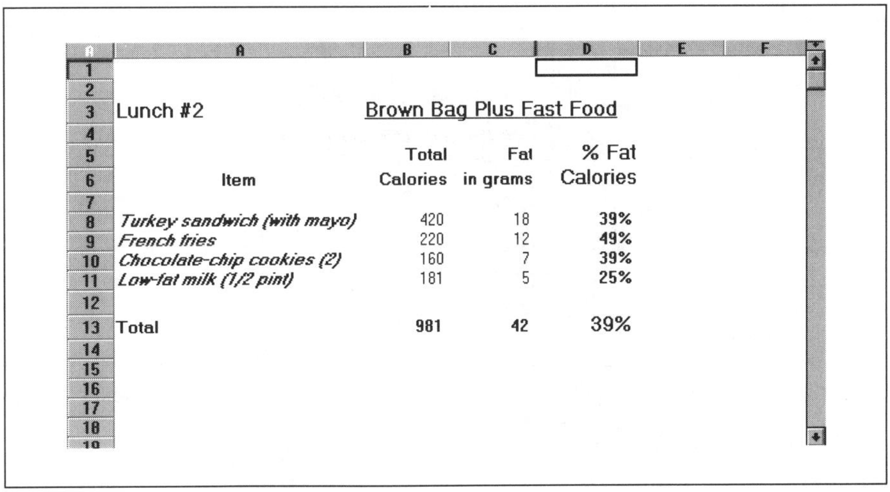

FIGURE 1.17

Revised data and recalculated formulas

	A	B	C	D	E	F
1						
2						
3	Lunch #2		Brown Bag Plus Fast Food			
4						
5		Total	Fat	% Fat		
6	Item	Calories	in grams	Calories		
7						
8	Turkey sandwich (with mayo)	420	18	39%		
9	French fries	220	12	49%		
10	Chocolate-chip cookies (2)	160	7	39%		
11	Low-fat milk (1/2 pint)	181	5	25%		
12						
13	Total	981	42	39%		
14						
15						
16						
17						
18						
19						

In terms of fat calories, this meal is an improvement over the first one, but it still does not meet the goal of the 30-percent fat diet.

For her third menu, the nutritionist wants to illustrate the importance of making simple but careful dietary decisions. After revising the title again, she makes two more changes to the menu. She removes the mayonnaise from the turkey sandwich and substitutes an apple for the french fries. She enters the new calorie and fat data into columns B and C. Once again, 1-2-3 recalculates her formulas as she changes nutritional data. The final result, shown in Figure 1.18, is a dramatically reduced fat percentage, well below the 30-percent goal.

For convenience, Barbara Johnson decides to save all three of the lunch worksheets in a single file. She clicks the New Sheet button twice to add two worksheets to the current window, and copies the current version of the lunch menu to each of the two new worksheets. She reformulates the first two menus in worksheets A and B, and retains the final menu in worksheet C. When she saves her work to disk, LUNCHES.WK4 contains three worksheets, one for each lunch menu she will present in her seminar. Figure 1.19 shows how these worksheets appear in the Perspective view.

FIGURE 1.18

The final lunch menu

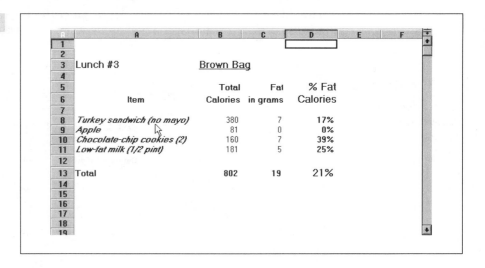

FIGURE 1.19

The three lunch worksheets in a single file. Here they are shown in Perspective view.

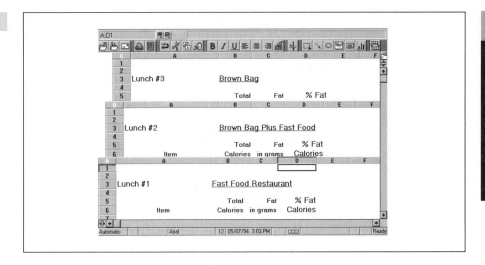

Creating Graphs from a Worksheet

The graphics component of 1-2-3 gives you efficient tools for creating graphs and charts from your worksheet data. Lotus 1-2-3 supports an impressive variety of two- and three-dimensional graph types, including line graphs, bar graphs, and pie charts. The initial steps for creating a graph are simple:

1. Select a worksheet range with the titles, numbers, and labels you want represented in your graph.

2. Click the Chart SmartIcon.

3. Click inside your worksheet at the location where you want to graph to appear.

N O T E   For a detailed look at creating graphs, see Chapter 6.

After you have created the initial graph from a table of data, you can change the graph type and revise the graph's titles, labels, and legend if you wish. You can also add other graphic objects, including arrows and frames. Menu commands and SmartIcons offer options for all these features. You can make other revisions directly on the graph itself.

Like the formulas in a worksheet, graphs are dependent upon the original raw data. When you make changes to the raw data that a graph represents, 1-2-3 automatically redraws the graph.

Designing a Graph

Barbara Johnson now turns her attention to a new topic that she wants to cover in her seminar. She realizes that many people have trouble interpreting the nutritional information that appears on food labels. Regarding fat content, the problem is simple: labels often disclose the number of grams of fat per serving, whereas the important factor to consider is the percent of fat calories in the serving. For example, Johnson has found the following information on a package of bologna:

Serving size:	1 slice (30 grams)
Calories per serving:	90
Fat per serving:	8 grams

In this example, the fat content (8 grams) is less than a third of the total weight of a serving (30 grams). However, the significant factor is not the weight of the fat, but rather the fat calories in proportion to the total calories. The 8 grams of fat are equivalent to 72 calories, or more than three-quarters of the total caloric content of a serving.

To underscore the importance of this distinction, Johnson decides to create some simple graphics and hand them out at the seminar. The graphs should illustrate clearly the discrepancy between the weight content and the caloric content of fat in a particular food item.

For this second topic, the nutritionist will take advantage of the graphics component of 1-2-3. She begins by creating a small worksheet table with the information about a slice of bologna. As shown in Figure 1.20, the worksheet has two rows of numeric data, one to record the weight and one

FIGURE 1.20

The Bologna worksheet

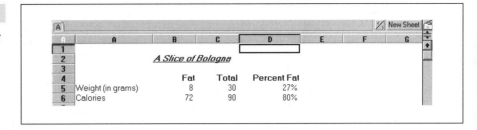

to record caloric content of the food serving. There are three columns of numbers. The first two columns display the fat content and the total serving data. The final column is a calculation of the percentage of fat. While the fat is only 27 percent of the weight of a serving, it is a full 80 percent of the caloric content.

Creating a Graph

After completing this worksheet, the nutritionist follows a quick and easy sequence of steps to create her graphs. She decides to create one graph to represent the relationship between the total weight of a serving and the fat weight in the serving. She'll then create a second graph to represent the relationship between total calories and fat calories.

She bases each graph on a particular range of numeric data: B5..C5 for the weight and B6..C6 for the calories. To create a graph, she clicks the Chart SmartIcon and then clicks the location on the Bologna worksheet where she wants the graph to appear. Then she can make any adjustments she wants in the style and appearance of the graph.

NOTE   When a chart is the object currently selected on the screen, the Chart menu option appears in the menu bar in place of the Range menu option.

The entire job of creating the graphs takes only a few minutes. The result of Johnson's work appears in Figure 1.21. Each graph contains two bars. The first graph shows the relationship between the fat weight and the total weight of a serving, and the second graph shows the relationship between

FIGURE 1.21

The bologna graphs

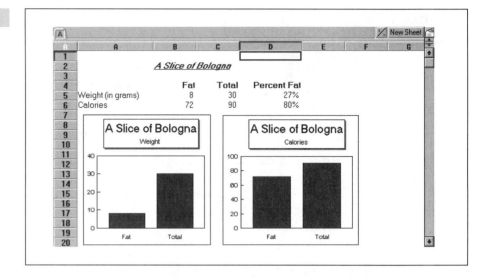

fat calories and total calories. The contrast between these two relationships is dramatic, and the nutritionist is satisfied that this handout will adequately illustrate her point to the seminar participants.

For the final topic in her nutrition seminar, Barbara Johnson wants to apply the 30-percent fat diet to a group of people with different nutritional needs. For this purpose, she has created a database of imaginary, but representative, individuals whose daily caloric and fat requirements vary. She wants to compare these individual requirements with the nutritional content of one of the lunch menus she devised earlier. Her goal is to demonstrate the suitability—or inadequacy—of this menu for meeting specific nutritional needs.

Performing Database Operations

A *database* in 1-2-3 is a collection of *records* stored in the rows and columns of a worksheet—for example, a client address directory, a group of employee records, or a list of inventory items. Each row in the database contains one record of information. The worksheet columns contain the *fields* of the database—that is, the categories of information within each record. The *field names* are column headings that describe each category of information, or field. An inventory database might include the following fields:

| Item | Quantity | Reorder Date | Reorder Amount | Price |

Usually a record in the database includes a data entry for each field. Some field items are labels or numbers that you enter directly from the keyboard. Others field items may be *calculated fields*—that is, numeric or chronological items that are calculated from the data in other fields.

N O T E   Databases are discussed in detail in Chapters 7 and 8.

The length of a database is equal to the number of records currently stored in the table. For example, an inventory database might have a length of a few dozen, or a few thousand, records. Over time, the length of a database might change, as you insert or append new records, or as you perform operations that delete records.

After you've developed a database, you can perform a variety of operations on the information it contains. For example, a *query* is an important database operation that locates records matching specific *criteria*. Lotus 1-2-3 supplies database commands designed to simplify the query process, regardless of the length of your database.

Lotus 1-2-3 offers other important database operations. For example, you can rearrange, or *sort*, the database records in alphabetical, numerical, or chronological order. You can also apply statistical functions to selected records. Lotus 1-2-3 offers a complete set of built-in functions that work on databases.

For the purposes of this introduction, you'll examine a short (and imaginary) database that nutritionist Barbara Johnson might develop to describe the nutritional requirements of a specific group of individuals.

Defining a Database

The first step in designing a database is to determine the number and types of data fields for the table and to choose a name for each field. Field names play several important roles in query operations and criteria.

The nutritionist wants to include seven fields in her database of imaginary clients. On the first row of her database table, she enters seven field names. The first four names— Name, Age, Sex, and Weight—will have personal information about each client. The final three fields—Total Calories, Fat Calories, and Fat Grams—will represent nutritional guidelines:

Total Calories   is the recommended daily caloric intake needed to maintain a person's current weight. The nutritionist will enter this value directly from the keyboard for each client.

Fat Calories   is the recommended maximum daily fat consumption for a person. To calculate the value of this field for each client, Johnson will write a formula that yields 30 percent of each entry in the Total Calories column.

Fat Grams   is the recommended maximum daily fat consumption in grams. This will also be a calculated field and will be found by dividing the entries in the Fat Calories column by 9. (You'll recall that a gram of fat is equal to nine calories.)

Entering the Records

After creating the field names, Johnson begins entering the individual records of the database. Each client record occupies one row of the table. She begins by entering data in the fields that are not calculated—Name, Age, Sex, Weight, and Total Calories. When these fields are entered for each record, she writes and copies formulas for the two calculated fields, Fat Calories and Fat Grams.

Her completed database appears in Figure 1.22. Notice that the records are entered in alphabetical order by client name. To work more effectively with the information, she may want to view the database in a different order. 1-2-3 has an efficient Sort command that she can use to rearrange the records quickly. She'll also want to perform other database operations to create a meaningful handout for the seminar participants.

FIGURE 1.22

The database of nutritional guidelines for individual clients

	Name	Age	Sex	Weight	Total Calories	Fat Calories	Fat Grams
	Allen, N.	41	M	135	1650	495	55
	Barnes, J.	32	F	120	1350	405	45
	Byron, A.	23	M	185	2250	675	75
	Everette, Y.	39	F	140	1550	465	52
	Giles, C.	25	M	225	2700	810	90
	Hall, N.	52	M	160	1950	585	65
	Johnson, C.	35	F	155	1700	510	57
	Lange, G.	27	F	115	1250	375	42
	Paulson, G.	45	M	145	1750	525	58
	Ralston, T.	59	F	130	1450	435	48

Daily Calories and Maximum Fat Consumption

Performing Sort and Search Operations in a Database

Sorting a database requires several simple steps:

1. Select the range of database records you want to sort, but *not* the database field names.

2. Choose Range ➤ Sort.

3. In the Sort dialog box, specify a *key* field by which the records will be reordered. Enter the address of the field in the Sort by text box.

4. Specify whether you want to sort this field in Ascending or Descending order.

5. If you want to sort by additional fields, click the Add Key button to add the current key to the All Keys list. Then define the next key. When you have created all of the keys you want, click on OK to complete the Sort operation.

For example, here is what the Sort dialog box looks like for a two-key sort:

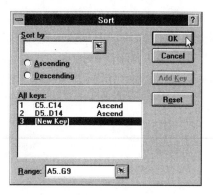

The nutritionist begins her work by performing the steps to arrange the clients from youngest to oldest—in other words, to sort the database in ascending order by the Age field. Figure 1.23 shows the result of the sort operation.

Daily Calories and Maximum Fat Consumption

Name	Age	Sex	Weight	Total Calories	Fat Calories	Fat Grams
Byron, A.	23	M	185	2250	675	75
Giles, C.	25	M	225	2700	810	90
Lange, G.	27	F	115	1250	375	42
Barnes, J.	32	F	120	1350	405	45
Johnson, C.	35	F	155	1700	510	57
Everette, Y.	39	F	140	1550	465	52
Allen, N.	41	M	135	1650	495	55
Paulson, G.	45	M	145	1750	525	58
Hall, N.	52	M	160	1950	585	65
Ralston, T.	59	F	130	1450	435	48

Johnson realizes that there might be other useful ways to order the records. For example, she could divide the database into male and female clients, and sort by weight within the two groups. In effect, this sort requires *two* key fields: the Sex field is the *primary key* and the Weight field is the *secondary key*. Figure 1.24 shows the database after this two-key sort has been completed.

FIGURE 1.24

Sorting the database by two key fields, in this case by sex and weight

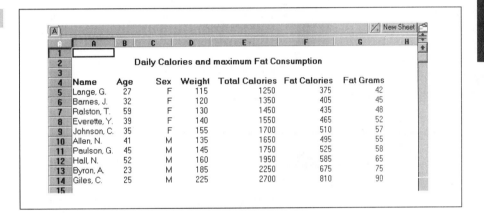

Formulating Selection Criteria

Finally, the nutritionist would like to query the database to find a specific subset of the records from the original table. In the query she wants to extract client records that meet a particular selection criterion. To formulate this criterion, she'll use data from her Lunches worksheet to answer the following question: Which clients can use the menu from Lunch #3 as a satisfactory way of staying within their maximum fat guidelines?

The nutritionist starts with the assumption that fat consumed at lunch should total no more than one-third of the total daily fat consumption. She pulls down the Tools menu and chooses the Database command; then chooses the New Query command from the resulting cascade menu. The resulting dialog box provides all the tools she needs to define her query. She creates the query table on a separate sheet in her database file, as shown in Figure 1.25.

As you can see, only half of the clients in the sample database meet this particular selection criterion. Barbara Johnson will use this query table to illustrate a final point to her seminar participants: Each client must look at his or her total caloric and fat intake in relation to nutritional requirements and personal weight goals.

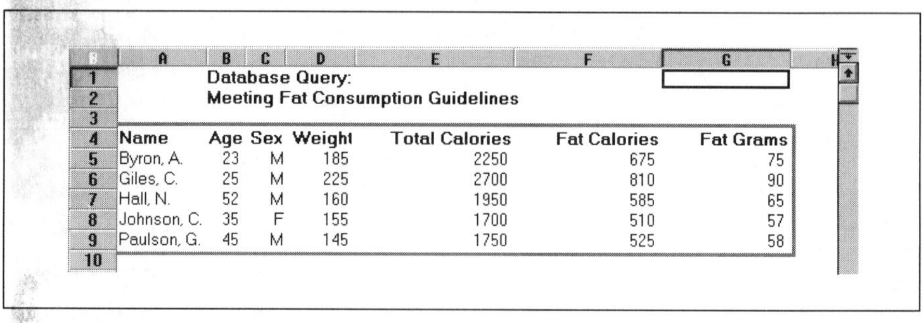

FIGURE 1.25

Querying the database

Database Query:
Meeting Fat Consumption Guidelines

Name	Age	Sex	Weight	Total Calories	Fat Calories	Fat Grams
Byron, A.	23	M	185	2250	675	75
Giles, C.	25	M	225	2700	810	90
Hall, N.	52	M	160	1950	585	65
Johnson, C.	35	F	155	1700	510	57
Paulson, G.	45	M	145	1750	525	58

Summary

The three components of Lotus 1-2-3 for Windows—spreadsheet, graphics, and database—are designed to work smoothly together in an integrated environment. In many business applications, you may find yourself using the three components together to create interrelated tables and documents. Perhaps the single most important characteristic of a 1-2-3 worksheet is its ability to recalculate formulas based on changes to raw data. This "what-if" capability is a feature you'll be seeing in many different forms and contexts throughout this book.

In Part Two of this book you'll begin examining the three components in detail. But first, Chapter 2 will introduce you some additional features of 1-2-3 in the Windows environment.

Lotus 1-2-3

and the

Windows

Interface

f a s t   **TRACK**

WINDOWS applications work in consistent and predictable ways, always providing familiar techniques to perform important tasks. Because Windows programs have many elements in common, you naturally apply much of what you know about one program to the other applications you learn. For this reason, each new Windows application is easier to master than the previous one.

In this chapter you'll review a variety of features that Windows applications have in common, and you'll see how these features appear in Lotus 1-2-3. In particular, you'll examine:

- The 1-2-3 application window
- Menus, dialog boxes, and SmartIcons
- Worksheet windows—and mouse and keyboard techniques for manipulating windows
- The Windows-style Help system

TIP

If you're a veteran Windows user, you'll move quickly through this chapter, focusing only on details that are new and unfamiliar to you. But if Lotus 1-2-3 is your first Windows application, you'll want to read this chap-ter from beginning to end and carefully work through each exercise.

Exploring the 1-2-3 Application Window

Two windows appear initially on the screen when you start Lotus 1-2-3:

- The 1-2-3 application window.

- A worksheet window, displayed inside the application window. This window is initially *maximized* so that you can see as much of its contents as possible.

In Chapter 1 you worked with both the 1-2-3 window and the worksheet window. Now you'll examine these two windows in greater detail.

Figure 2.1 shows the various parts of the 1-2-3 application window. Take another look at the lines located above and below the worksheet window:

- The title bar

- The menu bar

- The edit line

- The row of SmartIcons

- The row of worksheet tabs, initially displaying one tab labeled A (this line also contains the New Sheet button)

- The "live" status bar at the bottom of the screen

tools displayed on these lines give you a variety of ways to carry out operations on 1-2-3 worksheets. There's an intentional redundancy built into all these tools; you can often choose among two or three different techniques for accomplishing the same task. Accordingly, 1-2-3 also lets you rearrange the application window itself to suit your own work patterns. For example, you can move the row of SmartIcons to other places on the screen. You can also remove several of these lines from the screen altogether to make more space for displaying the contents of the worksheet window. The lines you can hide from view include the edit line, the row of SmartIcons, the worksheet tabs, and the status bar.

Throughout this chapter you'll examine these lines and the features they offer. For now, concentrate on recognizing the variety of tools displayed on these lines. In later chapters, you'll focus on what these tools actually do as you create worksheets, graphs, and databases.

FIGURE 2.1

The 1-2-3 application window

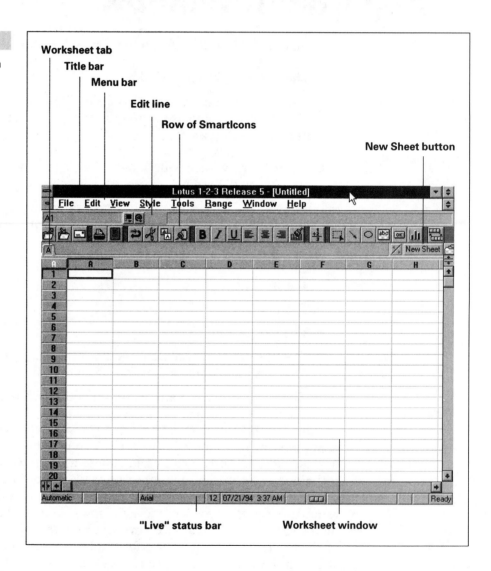

The 1-2-3 Window Title Bar

At the beginning of a session with 1-2-3, the caption in the title bar identifies the version of the program and the temporary name of the active worksheet:

Lotus 1-2-3 Release 5 - [Untitled]

When you save a worksheet to disk and assign it a name, the title bar gives the name of the file; for example:

Lotus 1-2-3 Release 5 - [LUNCHES.WK4]

Depending on your current activity, the title bar may provide other information. For example, when you choose a menu or highlight a command, the title bar provides a brief description. To review this feature, try this exercise:

1. Press the Alt key to activate the menu bar, and press → a few times. Each time you highlight a new command in the menu bar, the description in the title bar changes accordingly. For example, when you highlight the View menu, the title bar provides a general-purpose description of the tools in the View menu:

   Control the display settings for the worksheet and 1-2-3

2. Now highlight the Tools menu and press ↵ to pull down the menu. Press ↓ several times and notice the descriptions in the title bar. For example, the description of the SmartIcons command is:

   Select a new set of icons; reposition and customize icons

3. Press the Esc key twice to close the menu and deactivate the menu bar. Now the application name reappears in the title bar.

Minimize, Maximize, and Restore Buttons—Sizing and Moving the Window

On the right side of the title bar are two buttons:

- The Minimize button, an arrowhead icon pointing down. Clicking this button reduces the application to an icon on the Windows desktop.

- The Restore button, a double-arrowhead icon. Clicking this button reduces the size of the 1-2-3 application window.

Experiment with these buttons in the following exercise:

1. Click the Restore button. The 1-2-3 window shrinks to a smaller size. The Restore button is replaced by the Maximize button—an arrowhead pointing up.

2. Place the mouse pointer over the right border of the 1-2-3 window. The mouse pointer becomes a double arrowhead, pointing left and right.

3. Drag the border to the left, toward the center of the screen, and release the mouse button.

You've reduced the 1-2-3 window to about half its horizontal width. Notice how 1-2-3 rearranges the menu bar so that you can still see all of the commands.

4. Position the mouse pointer over the bottom border of the window.

5. Drag the border up toward the center of the screen.

You've now reduced the vertical length of the window by about half.

6. Position the mouse pointer over the 1-2-3 window's title bar, hold down the left mouse button, and drag the window toward the center of the screen. When you complete this action, your screen should look approximately like Figure 2.2.

TIP

Reducing the size of the application window gives you the opportunity to view more than one application at a time in the Windows environment.

7. Click the Maximize button, the up-arrow button at the right side of the title bar. The 1-2-3 window returns to its full-screen dimensions.

FIGURE 2.2

Moving and changing
the size of the 1-2-3
window

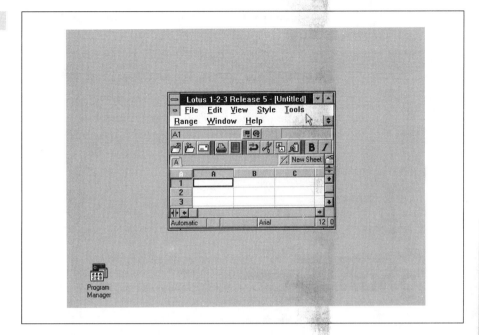

2

1-2-3 and Windows

8. Click the Minimize button. The 1-2-3 window disappears altogether and is represented by the 1-2-3 icon near the bottom of the Windows screen.

9. Double-click the 1-2-3 icon. The 1-2-3 window reappears in its original dimensions.

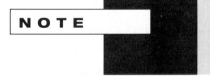

NOTE

Double-clicking means placing the mouse pointer over an object and clicking the left mouse button twice in quick succession.

Everyone who runs major applications in Windows should have a mouse, because many Windows operations are simpler and more efficient with the mouse than with the keyboard. All the same, an application's Control menu provides keyboard alternatives for certain Windows operations. Even if you rarely use the Control menu, its arrangement of commands can prove convenient from time to time. You'll learn how to use the 1-2-3 Control menu in the next section.

The 1-2-3 Window Control Menu

The Control-menu box is on the left side of the title bar. You can pull down the application's Control menu by clicking the Control-menu box with the mouse or by pressing Alt+spacebar at the keyboard. The Control menu contains the following commands:

Restore

Move

Size

Minimize

Maximize

Close

Switch to…

Some of these commands are dimmed in certain contexts; that is, they appear in light gray text. A *dimmed* entry in any menu simply means that the command isn't available for use in your current activity.

The Restore, Minimize, and Maximize commands are equivalent to the buttons that appear on the right side of the title bar. The Move and Size commands are tools you can use to move and size the application window.

Try working with these commands in the following exercise:

1. Press Alt+spacebar to pull down the 1-2-3 Control menu.

2. Press **R** to choose the Restore command. The 1-2-3 window returns to the location and size you gave it in the previous exercise (see Figure 2.2).

3. Pull down the Control menu again and press **M** to choose the Move command. A four-headed pointer appears over the window.

4. Press ↑ on your keyboard. A shadow border appears above the 1-2-3 window. Keep pressing ↑ until the top of the shadow border

is near the top of the screen.

5. Press ← until the left side of the shadow border approaches the left side of the screen.

6. Press ↵ to complete the move operation.

7. Pull down the Control menu again and press **S** to choose the Size command.

8. Press → and ↓ repeatedly to extend the right and bottom borders, until the 1-2-3 window takes up almost the full dimensions of the screen. As you perform the size operation, a shadow border extends beyond the window itself and the pointer becomes a two-headed arrow.

9. Press ↵ to complete the Size operation.

10. Pull down the Control menu again and press **X** to choose the Maximize command. The window returns to its original, full-screen dimensions.

The Close command in the Control menu closes the 1-2-3 window and ends your current session with the application. Choosing Close is the same as choosing File ➤ Exit. In fact, you can use any of the following mouse or keyboard techniques to exit from 1-2-3 for Windows:

- Choose File ➤ Exit.
- Pull down the 1-2-3 Control menu and choose Close.
- Press Alt+F4 (the keyboard shortcut for the Close command).
- Double-click on the 1-2-3 Control-menu box.

Before an exit 1-2-3 checks all open worksheets to see if you've made any changes without saving them to disk. If any unsaved worksheets are found, an Exit dialog box appears on the screen, giving you the options of saving or abandoning your work:

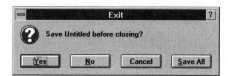

You can click the Cancel button to cancel the Exit and return to your worksheet.

The Switch to command in the Control menu is a tool for activating another application in Windows. When you choose this command, the Task List dialog box appears on the screen, listing all the programs you're currently running on the Windows desktop:

To switch to another application, highlight the program's name in the list and press ↵. Or, instead of choosing the Switch command, you can simply press Alt+Tab repeatedly at the keyboard until you see the name of the program you want to switch to. Release the Alt key to make the switch.

As you saw in Chapter 1 (see page 9), worksheet windows have their own Control menus whose commands are similar to the commands in the 1-2-3 Control menu. You'll learn more about worksheet windows later in this chapter.

The Menu Bar

The menu bar is located just below the 1-2-3 title bar. To activate the menu bar, press Alt or F10, or click one of the menus with the mouse.

When a worksheet is active, the menu bar contains eight items, each representing a pull-down menu:

MENU	DESCRIPTION
File	Offers commands for saving worksheets to disk, opening files from disk, printing worksheets, and previewing your work before you print it. Other useful commands are also available; for example, the Doc Info command allows you to record notes and comments about a particular file. The list of file names at the end of the File menu gives you quick access to files you've recently worked on; to open a file, simply choose its name in the menu list.
Edit	Offers the Undo command for reversing an action in 1-2-3. It also provides commands for cut-and-paste and copy-and-paste operations (via the Windows Clipboard); for creating links between 1-2-3 worksheets and documents from other applications; for copying formulas across ranges of worksheet cells; for inserting and deleting rows, columns, and sheets; for performing search-and-replace operations; and for inserting and arranging objects.
View	Provides ways of controlling a worksheet's appearance on the screen. With the commands in this menu, you can zoom to larger or smaller views of the worksheet; freeze rows or columns of titles in view on the current sheet; split the screen into panes; switch to perspective view; and specify preferences for the appearance of a sheet and the 1-2-3 window itself.

2

1-2-3 and Windows

MENU	DESCRIPTION
Style	Furnishes options for changing the appearance of data on the screen and on the printed page, including numeric format, font, point size, style, alignment, color, border style, shading options, column width, and row height. The Gallery command offers a list of predefined style templates that you can apply to a table you've developed on a worksheet. These templates are simple to use, but can greatly enhance the appeal and clarity of a worksheet.
Tools	Provides the access point for several major components of 1-2-3, including charting, the new mapping feature, object drawing, database operations, and macro recording. This menu also provides several miscellaneous features, such as a spelling checker, a formula auditor, and setup commands for customizing SmartIcon sets and other spreadsheet characteristics.
Range	This menu's Version ommand opens a major feature called the *Version Manager*, designed to expand the power of what-if analysis on a worksheet. In addition, the Range menu contains commands for filling ranges with series of data, sorting records of data, parsing long labels, transposing the dimensions of tables, and defining names on a worksheet. Finally, the Analyze cascade menu provides a host of advanced analysis tools.
Windows	Contains the Tile and Cascade commands for arranging multiple open worksheet windows within the 1-2-3 work area. This menu also lists all open files and gives you a convenient way to activate the file you want to work with.

MENU	DESCRIPTION
Help	Provides a variety of entry points into the 1-2-3 Help system, as well as a tutorial for beginners and an overview of new features for experienced users.

Before reading on, take a few minutes to browse through the menu system and examine the brief descriptions that 1-2-3 displays in the title bar for each command in the pull-down menus.

Context-Sensitive Menus

In some contexts, 1-2-3 replaces the Range menu with one of three other menus designed to provide commands for specific tasks:

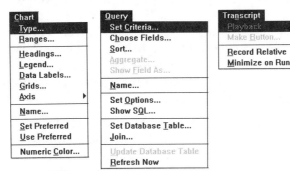

Chart	When you activate a chart or graph, 1-2-3 replaces the Range menu with the Chart menu. As you'll learn in Chapter 6, this menu gives you commands for changing the chart type and many other visual characteristics of the active chart.
Query	When you activate a database query, the Query menu provides commands for modifying and working with the query. You'll learn to work with databases and queries in Chapters 7 and 8.

Transcript When you open the Transcript window to record actions for a macro, the Transcript menu contains commands for controlling the recording process. You'll learn to create macros and work with the Transcript window in Chapter 9.

Cascade Menus and Dialog Boxes

As you've seen, each entry in the menu bar represents a pull-down list of commands. Some of the commands in these menu lists produce immediate actions. Others display additional options and selections on the screen, prompting you to specify the action you want to carry out:

- A *cascade menu* appears on the screen when you select a command that is followed by a right-pointing arrowhead (➤) in the menu list. Examples of commands that produce cascade menus are Database and Macro in the Tools menu, and the Analyze command in the Range menu.

- A *dialog box* of additional options results from any command that is followed by ellipses (...) in the menu list—for example, the Open command in the File menu, the Number Format command in the Style menu, and the Sort command in the Range menu.

In the sections ahead you'll learn to use cascade menus and dialog boxes.

Cascade Menus

Follow these steps to see an example of a cascade menu:

1. Click Tools on the menu bar. In the resulting pull-down menu, notice the right-pointing arrowhead (➤) next to the Database command:

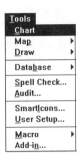

2. Click the Database command. A cascade menu appears with additional commands:

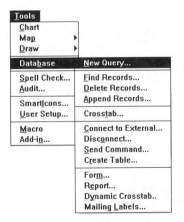

You can select a command from a cascade menu in the same ways you would choose commands from pull-down menus: click a command with the mouse, press the underlined letter on the keyboard, or highlight a command and press ⏎.

Dialog Boxes

Dialog boxes prompt you for detailed information so you can carry out operations in 1-2-3. For example, Figure 2.3 shows the dialog box that appears when you choose Style ➤ Number Format. A dialog box is a window with its own title bar, and a name that comes from the corresponding menu command.

Dialog boxes in 1-2-3 have several important features in common:

- A dialog box initially appears near the center of the screen, but can be moved to another location if necessary. To move a dialog box, drag its title bar.

- A dialog box has its own Control menu, represented by the small box at the upper-left corner of the window.

FIGURE 2.3

The Number Format dialog box

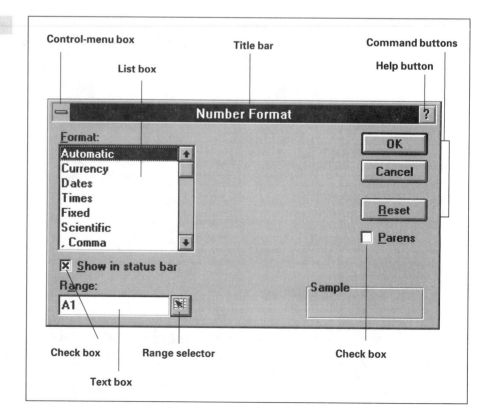

- At the upper-right corner of each dialog box is a Help button. Click this button to get detailed help about the purpose and procedures of a particular dialog box. (You'll read more about 1-2-3's Help system later in this chapter.)

- Inside all dialog boxes are standard *controls* that operate in familiar and intuitive ways. These include labels, command buttons, text boxes, check boxes, list boxes, frames, option buttons, combo boxes, file list boxes, directory list boxes, and drive list boxes. A given dialog box may contain any combination of these controls, depending on the options that are relevant to the task at hand. As Figure 2.3 shows, the Number Format dialog box contains command buttons, a text box, a list box, two check boxes, and a framed Sample box. Sometimes new controls may appear interactively in a dialog box as a result of the options you select.

- When a particular command requires you to choose a range of cells over which the command will operate, you can select the range before or after you choose the command. If you select the range first, the range address automatically appears in the Range box inside the dialog box. But if you need to select or modify the range after the dialog box has already appeared, you can click the *range selector* button located at the right side of the Range text box. (See Figure 2.3 for an example of this button.) When you do so, the dialog box temporarily disappears from the screen so you can select a range on the worksheet. As soon as you complete your selection, the dialog reappears.

In the sections ahead, you'll look briefly at a variety of controls that may appear in 1-2-3 dialog boxes. You'll see that only one control in a dialog box is active for use at a time. (Another way to say this is that only one control *has the focus* at a time.) Special visual effects show you which control is active. For example, when a command button is active, its name is enclosed by a dotted box and its border is darkened. When a text box is active, its contents may be highlighted. You'll quickly learn to recognize these effects inside a dialog box.

Activating a control There are a number of ways to activate a particular control in a dialog box:

- **Press Tab.** Press the Tab key to move forward through the dialog box from one control to the next. Pressing the Tab key is a neutral way of activating an element without completing a particular action.

- **Press Shift+Tab.** Press Shift+Tab to move backward through the elements of the dialog box.

- **Click.** In some cases you can activate an element by clicking it with the mouse. However, a mouse-click can mean different things to different controls, as you'll learn in the sections ahead.

- **Use the keyboard shortcut.** Press Alt and the underlined letter in a label or caption in the dialog box. (Sometimes this action simply activates a control; in other cases it actually selects the option that the control represents.) For example, in the Number Format dialog box you can press Alt+P to activate the Parens check box and change its status from checked to unchecked or from unchecked to checked. Pressing Alt+F activates the Format box so you can select a new format. By contrast, pressing Alt+R is the equivalent of clicking the Reset command button, which in this case closes the dialog box. An Alt+key shortcut is sometimes known as an *access key*.

In the following paragraphs you'll learn how specific controls are used.

Command buttons A *command button* is one of the simplest and most common controls you'll find in dialog boxes. Command buttons present actions you can carry out with a click of the mouse. For example, the Number Format dialog box (see Figure 2.3) has three command buttons, labeled OK, Cancel, and Reset. Click one of these buttons and 1-2-3 immediately carries out the action that the button represents.

NOTE OK and Cancel buttons are found on most dialog boxes. Choosing OK confirms the choices you've made and closes the dialog box. Choosing Cancel closes the dialog box without carrying out any action.

There are several techniques for choosing a command button with the keyboard:

- Press Alt and the corresponding access key.
- Press Tab (or Shift+Tab) until the target button is active, and then press ↵.
- Press ↵ to choose the OK button in a dialog box (except when another command button is active), or press Esc to choose the Cancel button.

As an exercise in using command buttons, follow these steps:

1. Choose File ➤ Print. The Print dialog box appears, as shown in Figure 2.4.

2

1-2-3 and Windows

FIGURE 2.4

The Print dialog box

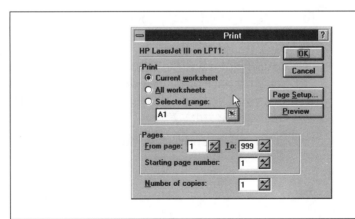

2. Click the Page Setup button with the mouse, or press Alt+S to choose Page Setup from the keyboard. (Notice the graphic push-button effect that takes place on the screen as you click the mouse.) A new dialog box named Page Setup appears over the Print dialog box.

3. Click the Close button or press Esc. The Page Setup dialog box disappears and you once again see the Print dialog box.

4. Click Cancel or press Esc to close the Print dialog box as well.

Text boxes A *text box* is a rectangular control in which you enter information from the keyboard. You might enter a number, a text value, or a range, depending on the requirements of the particular dialog box. For example, the Number Format dialog box (see Figure 2.3) has a Range text box for specifying a range of cells where you want to apply a selected format.

TIP

When a dialog box first appears, a text box may contain a *default value*. This value applies if you make no changes in the text box.

To enter a value into a text box:

1. Activate the box by clicking it with the mouse or by pressing Tab until the box has the focus. (If a text box already contains a value, you may have to *double-click* the box to highlight the contents. Once you've taken this action, any new entry in the box replaces the existing entry.)

2. Enter information from the keyboard.

T I P

A numeric text box is sometimes accompanied by an increase/decrease button. (See the Print dialog box in Figure 2.4 for examples.) If this button is available, you can use your mouse to increase or decrease the value in the box. Click the up-pointing arrowhead (▲) to increase the value, or the down-pointing arrowhead (▼) to decrease it.

Range boxes   As you've learned, a *range box* is a special kind of text box. If you select a range of cells in the current worksheet before selecting a menu command that applies to a range, the range box displays your se-lected range as its default value. Alternatively, if you want to enter a new range into a text box when a dialog box is already displayed on the screen, you simply click the range selector button displayed to the right of the range box.

As an introduction to range boxes, try this exercise with the Print dialog box:

1. Press the Home key, if necessary, to select cell A1 in the active worksheet.

2. Choose File ➤ Print. The address A1 is displayed inside the Se-lected range box.

3. Click the range selector button at the right side of the Selected range box.

The Print dialog box disappears temporarily. On the worksheet, the mouse pointer takes the shape of a white arrow superimposed over a range-selection icon.

4. Position the mouse pointer over cell A1, hold down the left mouse button, and drag the pointer down to cell F6.

Several changes take place on the screen as you select the range. The range of cells from A1 to F6 is highlighted on the worksheet, and the no-tation A1..F6 appears on the edit line. The word *Point* appears in the mode indicator, indicating that you are currently selecting a range. Figure 2.5 illustrates all these visual effects. (Also notice the shape of the mouse pointer.)

FIGURE 2.5

Selecting a range
of cells

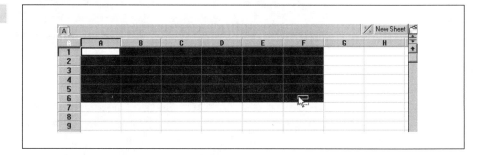

5. Release the mouse button.

The Print dialog box returns to the screen and the Selected range box shows the address of the range you've selected in the worksheet. (Also notice that the Selected range option button is now selected.) If you were actually ready to print your worksheet, this is the range that 1-2-3 would send to the printer.

6. For now, click the Cancel button or press Esc to cancel the operation and close the Print dialog box.

NOTE

You can also use the keyboard to point to a range, or you can type a range address directly into a Range text box. You'll learn much more about ranges and the techniques for selecting them in Chapter 3.

List boxes A *list box* control contains a list from which you select an option. When the list is too long to be displayed all at once, a vertical scroll bar appears on the right side of the list box.

For example, the Number Format dialog (see Figure 2.3) displays a list box labeled Format. This box contains a list of predefined formats you can choose from to change the appearance of a range of values on a worksheet.

Here are the general steps for using a list box:

1. Activate the list box.

2. If necessary, scroll up or down the list until the item you want is displayed in the box. To scroll through the box, click the up- or down-arrow on the scroll bar, or drag the scroll box up or down the length of the bar.

3. Click the item you want to select. Lotus 1-2-3 highlights it in the list. (Alternatively, press ↑ or ↓ repeatedly from the keyboard to scroll through the list and select the item you want.)

Most list boxes contain lists of predefined options supplied by 1-2-3. But some contain names or other items that you've defined yourself. For example, the Name dialog box contains a list of names defined to identify areas of the active worksheet (you'll learn how to use range names in Chapter 3):

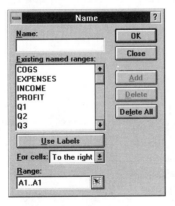

Check boxes *Check boxes* present options that you can turn on or off:

● When the option is on, the check box contains an *X*.

● When the option is off, the box is empty.

• When 1-2-3 cannot determine the current status of an option—or when the status is ambiguous for the current range selection—the box is filled with a gray background.

The Number Format dialog box (see Figure 2.3) has two check boxes, labeled Parens and Show in status bar. When you check the Parens box, 1-2-3 puts parentheses around numeric values in your worksheet. The Show option specifies whether a format will appear in the pop-up format list accessed from the status bar.

When a check box is active, the label next to the box is enclosed in dotted lines. At this point you can toggle the control's status between on and off by pressing the spacebar or by clicking the check box with the mouse.

In some dialog boxes you'll find lists of check boxes that are grouped together. For example, the Font & Attributes dialog box, shown in Figure 2.6, has Attributes check boxes labeled Normal, Bold, Italics, and Underline. With one exception, the check boxes in this group operate independently of one another. You can choose any combination of on or off values for the Bold, Italics, and Underline check boxes. If you click Normal, however, 1-2-3 automatically clears the other three check boxes. Although the value of one check box usually has no effect on other check boxes, the Normal option in this case means that the other options are turned off.

FIGURE 2.6

The Attributes controls in this dialog box—Normal, Bold, Italics, Underline—are check boxes

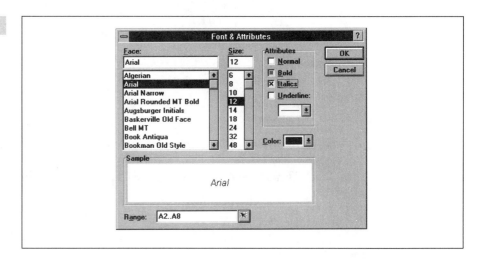

Try this exercise with the check boxes in the Font & Attributes dialog box:

1. Choose Style ➤ Font & Attributes. The dialog box appears.

2. Press Alt+B to move the focus to the Bold check box and to turn this option on. Notice that a dotted box encloses the Bold label, and an *X* appears in the box.

3. Press the spacebar several times to toggle this option between its on and off values.

4. Press the Tab key to move the focus to the Italics check box.

5. Press the spacebar several times, this time changing the setting of the Italics check box. Notice that changing the status of Italics has no effect on the current settings of the other check boxes.

6. Press Alt+N to select the Normal option. An *X* appears in the Normal check box, and the other check boxes are cleared.

7. Click the Cancel button or press Esc to close the dialog box.

Option buttons Unlike check boxes, a group of option buttons always represents mutually exclusive options in a dialog box. When you select an option button, the previous selection is automatically switched off. Each option button appears as a small circle with an attached label. When an option is *on*, the circle is filled with a bold black dot; when it is *off*, the circle is empty. On and off are the only settings for option buttons.

When a group of option buttons has the focus, you can select a new option in the group by pressing ↑ or ↓. Alternatively, you can use either of these techniques:

- Click an option button with the mouse, or
- Press the corresponding Alt+key combination.

The Spell Check dialog box has a group of option buttons for specifying where you want the spelling to be checked:

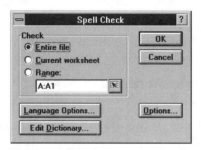

The default option is Entire file; unless you choose another option, 1-2-3 checks the spelling in all the sheets of the active worksheet file. Try this brief exercise with the Spell Check command:

1. Choose Tools ➤ Spell Check to view the dialog box.

2. Press ↓ to choose the Current worksheet option button.

3. Press Alt+E. This switches the Entire file option on again.

4. Click the Cancel button or press Esc to close the dialog box.

Frames When a dialog box contains more than one group of option buttons, each separate group is usually enclosed in a frame. A *frame* is a rectangular box with a label displayed along its top border. For example, the Alignment dialog box presents two groups of option buttons, Horizontal and Vertical, each inside a frame:

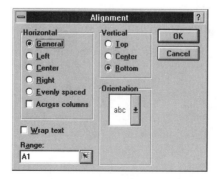

In this case, each option group is independent of the other; you can select one option in the Horizontal group and one in the Vertical group.

Drop-down boxes A text box with an attached pull-down list is called a *drop-down box*. When you see a small down-arrow button on the right side of a text box, you know that the box has an attached drop-down list. In general, there are two ways to enter a value in a drop-down box:

- Type the entry directly from the keyboard.

- Pull down the list and select an entry. To pull down the list, either click the down-arrow button with the mouse or press Alt+↓. When you complete your selection, the list entry is automatically copied to the text box.

Two examples of drop-down boxes appear in the Open File dialog box shown in Figure 2.7. The Drives box is for choosing the name of the drive (A:, B:, C:, and so on) that stores the file you want to open. The other drop-down box in the Open dialog box is labeled File type. It contains a list of applications from which you may want to import data into 1-2-3. (Notice that the default selection is the 1-2-3 worksheet file.)

2

1-2-3 and Windows

FIGURE 2.7

The Open File dialog box has two drop-down boxes, File type and Drives.

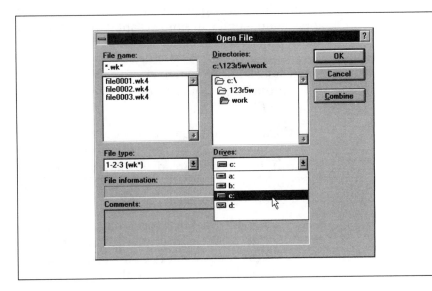

File name, Directories, and Drives list boxes Several 1-2-3 commands require you to identify a file that becomes the object of a disk operation. For example, to carry out the File ➤ Open command, 1-2-3 needs the name and location of the worksheet file you want to open. One way to specify a file is to enter its complete path and file name in the File name text box. But this entry can be long and detailed if the file you want to open is located somewhere other than the current disk and directory. For example, you might find yourself typing a complete path and file name such as:

D:\BUDGETS\WORK94\BUDG94.WK4

To simplify the task of selecting a worksheet file on disk, Windows supplies three dialog box controls, known as the file list, directory list, and drive list boxes. You can see examples of these three controls in the Open File dialog box (see Figure 2.7). They are always logically linked together in a given dialog box, so that they operate in a coordinated manner. When you select a new drive in the Drives list box, the Directories list box automatically lists directories in the new drive. Likewise, when you select a new directory in the Directories list box, the File name list box automatically lists the worksheet files in the new directory.

Opening and saving files are basic operations in almost all Windows applications. If you've worked before in Windows, you already know how to select a file in an Open File dialog box. But if 1-2-3 is your first Windows application—or if you simply want to review the use of disk, directory, and file controls—try the following exercise:

1. Choose File ➤ Open, or click the Open File SmartIcon, the first button in the default icon set. The Open File dialog box appears (see Figure 2.7).

2. Click the small down-arrow button at the right side of the Drives box to view a list of the drives available on your system. If the correct drive is not already displayed in the box, choose the drive where Lotus 1-2-3 is installed. Otherwise, click the down-arrow button again to close the list.

3. Click inside the Directories box. At the top of the box is a file folder icon labeled with the current drive name. This folder represents the root directory of the disk. As an experiment, double-click the folder to move to the top of the directory path. In the

resulting list you'll see the names of all the directories on your disk, including 123R5W, where 1-2-3 is installed by default.

4. Double-click the 123R5W folder. The directory list now shows all the 1-2-3 subdirectories.

5. Double-click the SAMPLE subdirectory and then the TUTO-RIAL subdirectory. As a result, the file list box displays the names of all 1-2-3 worksheet files stored in the path \123R5W\SAM-PLE\TUTORIAL\, as in Figure 2.8. These worksheet files are part of the introductory tutorial.

6. Click any one of the names in the file list. Your selection is auto-matically copied to the File name text box, indicating that 1-2-3 is ready to open the file when you click OK. In addition, the File in-formation box displays the date and time when the file was last saved, along with the size of the file in bytes.

7. For now, click Cancel to close the dialog box without opening a file.

Next you'll look at the third line of the control panel, the edit line.

FIGURE 2.8

Using the drive, directory, and file list controls

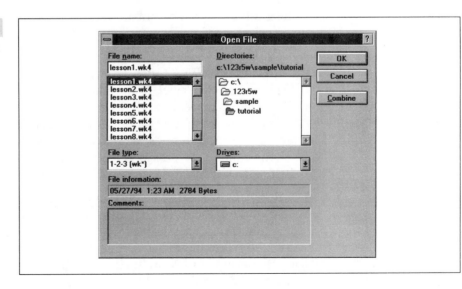

2

1-2-3 and Windows

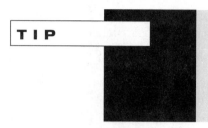

TIP

You can use the File ➤ Open command to open two or more worksheet files in one operation. To do so, hold down the Ctrl key and click two or more entries in the File name list, or drag your mouse over a sequence of entries. Then click OK. 1-2-3 opens all the files you've selected.

The Edit Line

The edit line contains two main parts, the *selection indicator* and the *contents box*. In addition it displays two important buttons, called the Navigator and the Function selector.

- **Selection indicator.** On the left side of the edit line, the selection indicator gives the address of the current cell in the active worksheet, as shown in Figure 2.9. If the current worksheet file contains only one sheet, this address is displayed as a column letter and a row number, such as A1. But if the file contains multiple sheets, the complete address includes the letter name of the active sheet followed by a colon and the cell address, as in A:A1. When you select a cell or range for which you've defined a name, the selection indicator displays the name rather than the address.

- **Contents box.** The contents box at the right side of the edit line displays the value, label, or formula that is stored in the current cell. The contents box shows what is actually *stored* in the cell, rather than what is *displayed* in the cell. For example, cell E8 in Figure 2.9 contains a formula that finds the sum of the values in row 8. As you can see, the contents box displays the formula @SUM(B8..D8), while the cell itself displays the result of the formula.

- **Navigator button.** The Navigator button, located just to the right of the selection indicator, is a useful tool for jumping to any named area on a worksheet. For example, the worksheet in Figure 2.10 contains ranges named North, South, East, West, January, February, and March. Clicking the Navigator button results in a drop-down list of all these names. To select a corresponding range on the worksheet, you can simply click one of the names in

FIGURE 2.9

The elements of the edit line

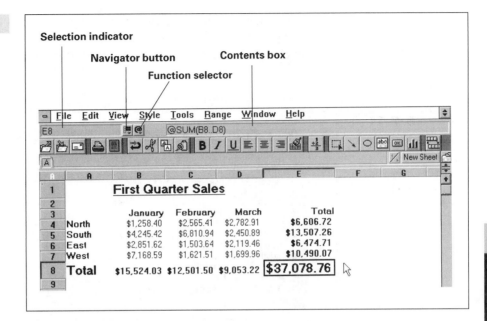

FIGURE 2.10

A drop-down list of range names from the Navigator

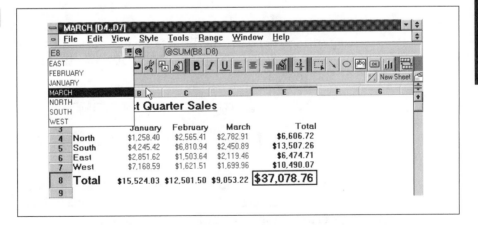

the list. You'll learn much more about range names in Chapter 3 (see page 134).

- **Function selector.** The Function selector, located to the right of the Navigator button, provides a list of commonly used @ functions, such as @SUM, @AVERAGE, and @ROUND, as shown in Figure 2.11. As you learned in Chapter 1 (see page 33), functions are built-in tools for performing calculations in a 1-2-3 worksheet. Chapter 5 covers functions in detail, and Part Four of this book is a reference guide to the entire function library.

FIGURE 2.11

The drop-down list of commonly used @functions available from the Function selector

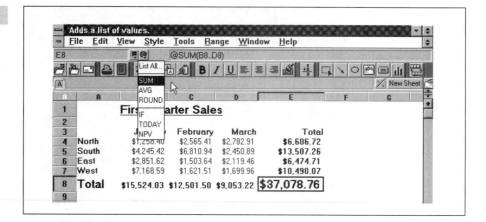

When you begin a new entry in any cell, 1-2-3 displays two additional buttons between the Function selector and the contents box; these buttons are known as the Cancel button (a boldface *X*) and the Confirm button (a ✓):

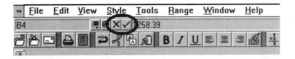

You can click the Cancel button to back out of the current data entry without changing the contents of the active cell; or you can click the Confirm button to complete a data entry.

In-Cell Editing

But 1-2-3's *in-cell editing* capability makes it unlikely that you'll use the edit line as frequently as in previous versions of the spreadsheet programming. Now you can type and revise a value directly in the cell where you're entering it. While you are first entering a value, you can press the

F2 function key to switch into Edit mode; then you can use keys such as Home, End, →, and ← to move the cursor to a new position within your entry in the cell. You can insert, delete, or overwrite existing characters, just as you would in any Windows text box. To complete an entry, press ↵; to cancel it, press the Escape key.

Here is a brief exercise that demonstrates in-cell editing:

1. Select cell A1 in the active worksheet, and type the word **Spread-sheet**. (Don't press ↵ yet.)

As you type, your entry appears both in the cell and in the contents box of the edit line. The mode indicator, at the lower-right corner of the screen, displays the word *Label*, telling you that 1-2-3 is accepting your entry as text rather than a numeric value. The Cancel and Confirm buttons appear on the edit line.

2. Press F2. The mode indicator changes to *Edit*.

3. Press the Home key. In the cell itself, the flashing cursor jumps to the beginning of your text entry, just before the *S*.

4. Now type **Lotus 1-2-3,** followed by a space. This new text is inserted before the existing text.

5. Complete the entry by pressing ↵. 1-2-3 returns to Ready mode.

When you complete these steps, the label "Lotus 1-2-3 Spreadsheet" appears in cell A1.

You can also edit an *existing* entry in any cell of a worksheet:

1. Position the mouse pointer over the cell you want to edit. (Make sure the pointer has the shape of a white arrow pointing up and to the left; if it has some other shape, move the pointer to the center of the cell.)

2. Double-click the left mouse button. The mode indicator displays the word *Edit*.

3. Use the Home, End, ←, or → keys to move the cursor to the position where you want to change the entry. You can also use the

Backspace key to delete the character just before the cursor, or Del to delete the character after the cursor.

4. Press the Ins key one or more times to toggle between Insert and Typeover modes. In the Insert mode, the edit cursor is a thin flashing vertical line; in Typeover mode, the flashing cursor is preceded by a solid block, one character in width.

5. Make any necessary changes in the entry, and press ↵ to confirm.

Before you read on, you might want to practice this technique on the label you've entered in cell A1.

Removing the edit line Because of the in-cell editing feature, the edit line is likely to become less central to your work than in previous versions of 1-2-3. Accordingly, 1-2-3 allows you to remove the edit line from the screen altogether if you want to. To do so:

1. Choose View ➤ Set View Preferences to display the Set View Preferences dialog box:

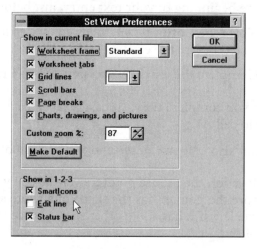

2. Near the bottom of the dialog box, click the Edit line option to remove the *X* from the corresponding check box.

3. Click OK.

In response, 1-2-3 removes the edit line from the control panel, giving you an extra line of space for your worksheets. The disadvantage of removing the edit line, however, is that you no longer have access to the new Navigator and Function selector buttons. Decide for yourself whether or not the edit line tools are important to your work. (To restore the Edit line, choose View ➤ Set View Preferences and toggle the Edit line option on again.)

The SmartIcons

The next line in the application window displays the SmartIcons, the one-click shortcuts for performing common operations in 1-2-3. You can customize SmartIcons in several interesting ways:

- Display a new set of SmartIcons for use in a particular task.
- Move the SmartIcons to a different position on the screen.
- Create new SmartIcons and write *macros* to define the corresponding action.

As you learned in Chapter 1 (see page 18), there are two quick ways to choose any one of the predefined SmartIcon sets available in 1-2-3. Click the last SmartIcon in the row to scroll to the next set of SmartIcons; or, click the SmartIcon selector on the status bar to view a pop-up list of all the sets. Then click the name of the set you want to view:

Lotus 1-2-3 automatically switches to a new SmartIcon set when you select certain kinds of objects. For example, when you're working with a chart, a database query, or a graphic object, 1-2-3 displays the icon set that's most likely to prove useful to you with the current selection.

You can also change the selection of icons in any predefined set—producing a set that suits your own work patterns. The following section shows you how to do this, and how to move the SmartIcons to new positions on the screen, using the SmartIcons dialog box. Creating new SmartIcons and macros is an advanced subject that you'll read about in Chapter 9.

Creating a Custom SmartIcon Set

To customize a set of SmartIcons, begin by choosing the Tools ➤ SmartIcons command. The SmartIcons dialog box appears as shown in Figure 2.12. At the left side of this dialog box you see a scrollable list of all the available SmartIcons. In the center of the dialog box is a list of all the icons that are part of a particular set. Above this central list is a drop-down list of all the predefined sets, from which you can select the set you want to modify. To remove an icon from a particular set, you select the set and then drag the icon out of the set list. To add a new icon to a set, you select the icon from the Available icons box and drag it to the current set list.

For example, suppose you want to delete the Mail SmartIcon from the default icon set and replace it with a SmartIcon that closes the active worksheet window. Here are the steps:

1. Choose Tools ➤ SmartIcons. The SmartIcons dialog box appears on the screen.

FIGURE 2.12

The SmartIcons
dialog box

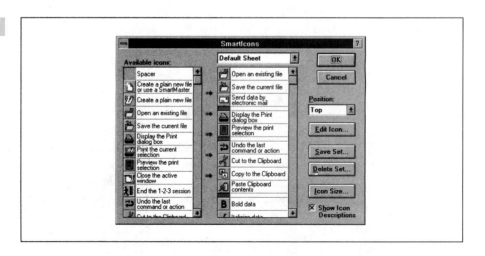

2. Make sure the Default Sheet icon set is displayed as the current set. If it isn't, pull down the list at the top of the dialog box, and choose the Default Sheet option.

3. Move the mouse pointer to the SmartIcon labeled "Close the active window" in the Available icons box. (The graphic on this icon is a window shade partly closed over a window.) Hold down the left mouse button and drag this icon to a position just above the Mail icon in the Default Sheet box. Release the mouse button, and 1-2-3 makes a copy of the icon in the Default Sheet set.

4. Now position the mouse pointer over the Mail SmartIcon in the Default Sheet set. Hold down the left mouse button and drag the icon outside of the Default Sheet box. When you release the mouse button, 1-2-3 removes the icon from the set.

5. Click OK to complete the change.

When you complete these steps, the new SmartIcon appears in the default icon set:

To go back to the original icon set, choose Tools ➤ SmartIcons, drag the Mail SmartIcon back into the default set, and drag the Close window icon out again.

Changing the Position of the SmartIcon Palette

You can also use the Tools ➤ SmartIcons command to change the position of the SmartIcon palette on the screen. Here are the steps:

1. Choose Tools ➤ SmartIcons.

2. Pull down the Position list at the right side of the SmartIcons dialog box (see Figure 2.12). The options in this list are Floating, Left, Top, Right, and Bottom. (Top is the default.)

3. Choose a position from the list.

4. Click OK.

Figure 2.13 shows what happens when you move the SmartIcons to the bottom of the application window. The horizontal set of SmartIcons is arranged just above the status bar.

If you want even more control over the position and shape of the SmartIcons, choose the Floating option in the Position list. The SmartIcons will appear in a free-floating window that you can resize and move anywhere in the 1-2-3 window. Figure 2.14 shows one possible arrangement for a free-floating SmartIcons window.

FIGURE 2.13

Moving the SmartIcons to the bottom of the 1-2-3 window

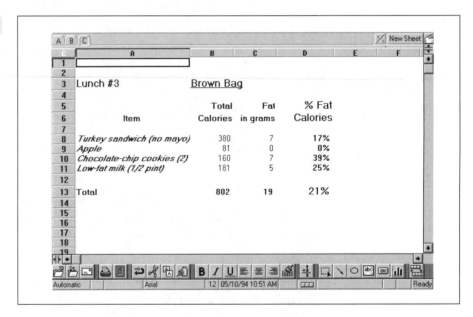

FIGURE 2.14

A free-floating
SmartIcon window

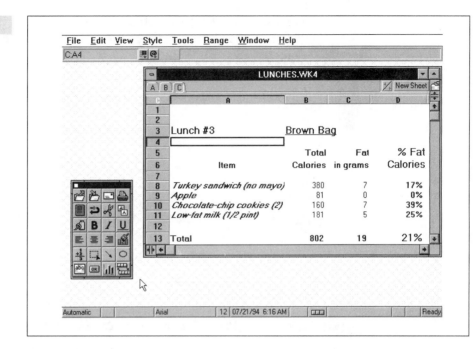

Worksheet Tabs

Just above the worksheet window is the *tab line*. This line displays a tab
for each sheet in a worksheet file. Figure 2.15 identifies the various tools
on this line. Here are brief descriptions of what these tools do:

- **Worksheet tabs.** The worksheet tabs themselves identify the
  sheets in a file. Tabs are initially labeled with letters of the alphabet, from A to Z, AA to AZ, BA to BZ, and so on. Each new file
  starts out with only one sheet, labeled A; but you can store as
  many as 256 sheets in a given worksheet file.

- **Tab-scroll arrows.** The *tab-scroll arrows* are for scrolling through
  the tabs of a worksheet if there are too many tabs to be displayed
  at once on the tab line.

- **New sheet button.** The New Sheet button adds a new sheet to
  the active file. Each time you click this button, 1-2-3 adds one
  new sheet immediately after the active sheet.

2

1-2-3 and Windows

• **Tab button.** The Tab button hides or redisplays the tab line itself. This button is a toggle. Click it once to hide the tab line; click it again to redisplay the line.

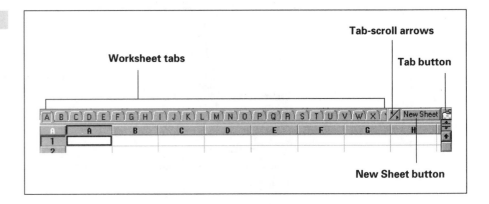

Changing the Name on a Sheet Tab

You can easily change the labels on tabs to assign meaningful names to the sheets of a file. For example, Figure 2.16 shows a file containing eight sheets. The tab for each sheet has a name that clearly identifies the contents of the sheet itself.

FIGURE 2.16

Changing the names displayed on tabs

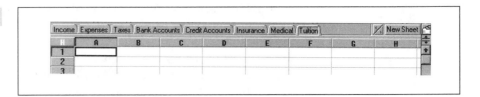

Here are the steps for changing the name displayed on a tab:

1. Double-click the tab belonging to the sheet you want to rename.

2. Type a new name for the sheet.

3. Press ↵.

After you change the name of a sheet, you can use either the new name or the original letter name to refer to the sheet. For example, in Figure 2.16 you can use A:A1 or Income:A1 to refer to the upper-left corner cell in the first sheet.

The Status Bar

As you saw in Chapter 1 (see page 22), the 1-2-3 status bar is much more than a source of information about your current work: it's one of several dynamic new tools you can use to change the appearance of a worksheet. Across the length of the status bar there are a dozen panels of information. Of these, six are "live," meaning that you can click them with the mouse to view pop-up lists of options for your current work.

Figure 2.17 identifies the live panels on the status bar. The first five give you quick ways to apply formats and styles to entries on a worksheet. To use them you begin by selecting the range of cells, and then you click the appropriate panel to view the pop-up list of options. Here are brief descriptions of the live panels:

PANEL	DESCRIPTION
Format selector	Supplies a pop-up list of all the numeric formats available in 1-2-3, including currency, percentage, date, and time formats.
Decimal selector	Allows you to change the number of digits displayed after the decimal point in a range of numeric values.
Style selector	Gives you a list of *named styles* defined for the current worksheet, and allows you to apply one of these styles to a range of data.
Font selector	Lists all the fonts available in your installation of Windows and gives you a quick way to select a font for a range of cells.

2

1-2-3 and Windows

PANEL	DESCRIPTION
Point-Size selector	Provides a list of type sizes for a given font selection.
SmartIcons selector	As you've seen already, lists the predefined icon sets available in 1-2-3 so that you can switch easily from one set to another.

FIGURE 2.17

The "live" panels on the status bar

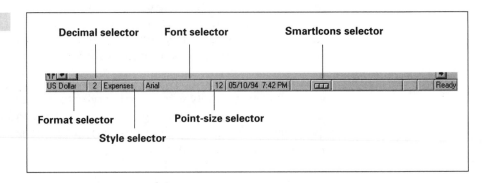

The Mode Indicator

The last item at the right side of the status bar is the mode indicator, which identifies your current activity. Here's a review of several common modes:

MODE	MEANING
Ready	1-2-3 is ready for your next action—for example, a data entry or a menu selection.
Label	1-2-3 recognizes your current entry as text.
Value	1-2-3 recognizes your current entry as a numeric value.
Menu	You are in the process of choosing a menu command or selecting options from a 1-2-3 dialog box.

MODE	MEANING
Point	You are pointing to a range of cells.
Edit	You are ready to edit the contents of a cell.

TIP

You'll quickly learn to recognize the most common modes. Check the mode indicator whenever you're confused about what is happening in your work. Sometimes you'll find that 1-2-3 is in a different mode than you thought. In many cases, pressing Esc or Ctrl+Break takes you back to Ready mode.

2

1-2-3 and Windows

A Review

You've now examined the title bar, menu bar, edit line, SmartIcon set, worksheet tabs, and status bar. Take a moment to review what you've learned:

Title bar	Displays the application name, the current worksheet name, or a brief description of a selected menu command or icon.
Menu bar	Provides access to the system of pull-down menus and dialog boxes in the 1-2-3 command set.
Edit line	Contains the selection box and contents box, along with the Navigator and Function selector buttons.
SmartIcon set	Displays a versatile set of tools for streamlining your work with worksheets, graphs, and databases.

Worksheet tab line	Identifies the multiple sheets in a file, and provides buttons for scrolling through the tabs, adding new sheets, and hiding the tab line.
Status bar	Contains several "live" panels that you can use to change the format and style of a range of worksheet data.

In the next part of this chapter, you'll focus on the worksheet window.

Performing Operations on the Worksheet Window

As you know, the worksheet window is initially maximized; its Control-menu box and Restore button appear on either end of the menu bar. You can pull down a worksheet window's Control menu by clicking the Control-menu box or by pressing Alt+hyphen (recall that pressing Alt+space-bar pulls down the 1-2-3 window's Control menu):

When you choose the Restore command (or simply click the window's Restore button) you see that the worksheet has its own title bar, with Maximize and Minimize buttons. To move the worksheet window to a new position within the work area, drag it by its title bar. To change the dimensions of the window, position the mouse pointer on a vertical or horizontal border, or on a corner, and drag the border. Minimize a worksheet window by clicking the Minimize button or by choosing Minimize in the Control menu. When you do so, the window is represented by an icon in the 1-2-3 work area. To restore a minimized window to its previous size, double-click its icon:

Close the active worksheet window by choosing File ➤ Close. (Alternatively, double-click the Control-menu box.) If you've made unsaved changes in the worksheet, 1-2-3 gives you the opportunity to save or abandon the changes, or to cancel the Close operation. When you close the last open worksheet window, 1-2-3 automatically opens a new window named "Untitled."

In Chapter 1 you learned how to switch to the Perspective view so you can see three sheets at once from the same worksheet file. (Choose View ➤ Split and select the Perspective option, as explained on page 15.) In the next section you'll see another kind of split view, in which you can examine two different parts of the same sheet.

Dividing a Worksheet Window into Panes

By splitting a sheet into *panes*, you can look at two noncontiguous ranges at the same time. For example, consider the Lunches worksheet that you examined in Chapter 1. As shown in Figure 2.18, the Lunches worksheet has four columns: the labels in column A, numeric data entries in columns B and C, and calculated percentages in column D. Suppose you want to view columns A and D side by side. One way to do so is to split the worksheet into vertical panes, where column A appears in the first pane and column D is in the second pane. The result might look like Figure 2.19.

FIGURE 2.18

The Lunches worksheet before its division into panes

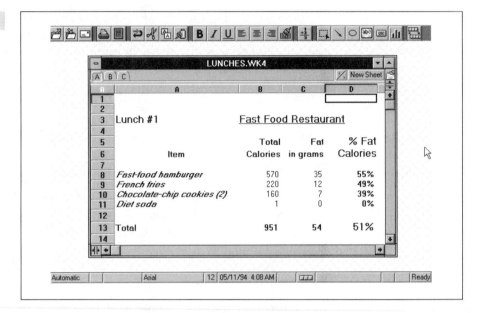

FIGURE 2.19

The Lunches worksheet divided vertically into panes

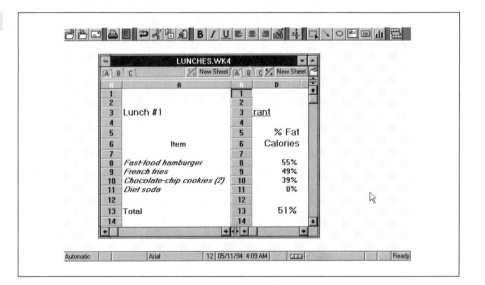

In this particular illustration the worksheet contains only a small table of data, all of which can be viewed at once in a single pane. But you can imagine how useful panes are in a very large worksheet, when you want to examine and compare columns or rows of data that are far away from one another. There are two ways to split a worksheet into panes, one with the mouse and one with the View ➤ Split command.

Splitting a window with the mouse Using the mouse technique, you select and drag one of two *splitter* icons:

- The vertical splitter is located to the immediate left of the horizontal scroll bar. It appears as a pair of left- and right-pointing arrowheads attached to two short vertical lines. To produce a vertical split like the one shown in Figure 2.19, drag this splitter across the horizontal scroll bar. (While you drag, the mouse pointer is a solid black version of the splitter.)

- The horizontal splitter is located just above the vertical scroll bar. It appears as a pair of up- and down-pointing arrowheads attached to horizontal lines. To create a horizontal split, drag this splitter down the vertical scroll bar.

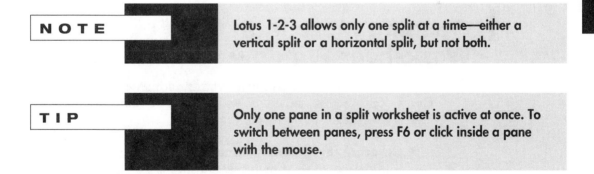

NOTE Lotus 1-2-3 allows only one split at a time—either a vertical split or a horizontal split, but not both.

TIP Only one pane in a split worksheet is active at once. To switch between panes, press F6 or click inside a pane with the mouse.

Splitting a window with View ➤ Split You can also choose View ➤ Split to split a sheet into panes. Here are the steps:

1. On the active sheet, select a cell in the column or row where you want to create the split.

2. Choose View ➤ Split. The Split dialog box appears:

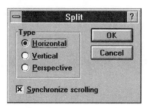

3. Select the Horizontal or Vertical option, and then click OK or press ⏎.

Notice the Synchronize scrolling check box in the Split dialog box. This option determines whether scrolling takes place simultaneously in the two panes of the window. The option is checked by default: in a vertically split worksheet, both panes always display the same range of rows; in a horizontally split worksheet, both panes always display the same range of columns. If you uncheck the Synchronize option, scrolling is independent in each pane.

To remove a split, choose View ➤ Clear Split, or drag the splitter back to its original position at the beginning of the scroll bar.

Opening More than One Worksheet Window

In 1-2-3 you can open and work with multiple worksheet files at once. Don't confuse this capability with the three-dimensional worksheets. Here's a summary of both features:

- **Creating three-dimensional worksheets.** A single worksheet window can have as many as 256 sheets. To insert new worksheets in a window, you click the New Sheet button. When you save the worksheet, all the sheets are saved in one file. In the Perspective view, you can examine three sheets at a time inside the same window.

- **Opening multiple worksheet files.** Two or more worksheet *files* can be open concurrently in the 1-2-3 environment. The File ➤

New command creates a new worksheet window, and the File ➤ Open command opens an existing worksheet from disk. Either way, each open file occupies its own window. To view multiple open windows, you can choose *tiled* or *cascading* arrangements.

To experiment with multiple worksheet files, try the following exercise:

1. Choose File ➤ New. If the New File dialog box appears, check the option labeled Create a plain worksheet, and then click OK. A new worksheet window opens over the existing worksheet.

2. Choose File ➤ New two more times to create two more new files.

3. Pull down the Window menu to see a list of open files. To activate a file, choose a name from this menu. (Alternatively, press Ctrl+PgUp or Ctrl+PgDn in the Ready mode.)

4. Choose Window ➤ Tile. This command arranges the open worksheets as windows of equal size, as in Figure 2.20.

5. Choose Window ➤ Cascade. Now the open worksheet files are arranged in windows that overlap, as in Figure 2.21.

FIGURE 2.20

A tiled view of four worksheet windows

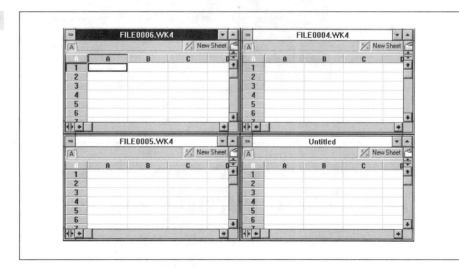

FIGURE 2.21

FIGURE 2.21

A cascade view of four
worksheet windows

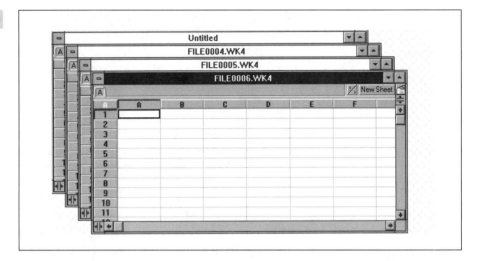

TIP

By default, the File ➤ New command displays the
New File dialog box, offering you a selection of
SmartMasters—templates for common spreadsheet tasks.
(You'll learn more about SmartMasters in Chapter 10.) If
you want to skip the dialog box, choose Tools ➤ User
Setup and check the option labeled Skip New File dialog
box. Then click OK. Next time you choose File ➤ New, a
new worksheet file will be created immediately, without
an intervening dialog box.

Getting Help in Lotus 1-2-3 for Windows

A complete and systematic Help system is a standard part of any Windows application. Lotus 1-2-3 for Windows meets the highest standards
for providing help, giving you clear and relevant on-screen help for any

task you need to perform. While you're working in 1-2-3, you can bring up detailed information about virtually any topic, command, function, procedure, tool, or technique.

If 1-2-3 is your first Windows application, you should take the time to explore the Help system early in your work with the program. One way to begin is simply to examine the Help menu, which provides several entry points into the Help system:

Some commands in the Help menu open a special Help window. From this window you can get help with specific topics and view lists of cross-referenced help categories.

Exploring the Help Menu

Here is a summary of the eight commands in the Help menu:

COMMAND	DESCRIPTION
Contents	Displays a collection of icons representing major help categories, as shown in Figure 2.22. Click an icon to jump directly to a help topic.
Search	Opens a dialog box in which you can search for specific help topics by key words.
Using Help	Provides a general-purpose introduction to the Help system, a topic that is worth studying carefully.

FIGURE 2.22

The Help Contents window

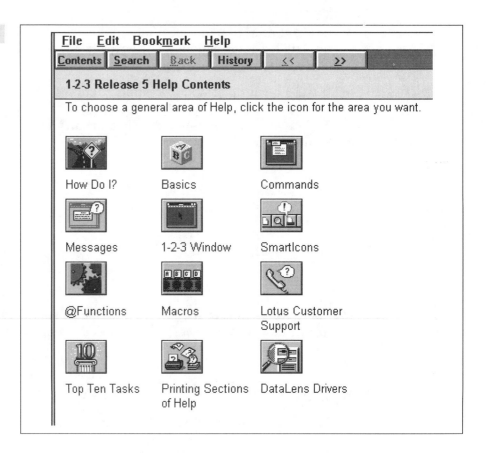

COMMAND	DESCRIPTION
Keyboard	Provides a list of cross-reference topics that show you how to use special keyboard techniques in 1-2-3.
How Do I?	Gives useful lists of general-purpose procedures. Each procedure contains extensive cross-referencing to other relevant topics. The How Do I? command is a good place to start whenever you need to review a particular task involving worksheets, graphs, or databases.

COMMAND	DESCRIPTION
For Upgraders	Supplies an orientation for users of previous 1-2-3 releases. If you want to find out what's new in this latest release, choose this command.
Tutorial	Starts the on-line 1-2-3 tutorial, where you can choose lessons that will help you learn all the components of 1-2-3.
About 1-2-3	Displays a dialog box with information about the current release of 1-2-3 for Windows.

Finding Context-Sensitive Help

Context-sensitive help is one of the most useful features of the Help system. You can get help relevant to your current activity by pressing the F1 function key at almost any time during your work in 1-2-3.

For example, imagine that you are selecting options in a dialog box, but you can't recall exactly how to use some aspect of the command in question. To get help you press F1—or you click the Help button at the upper-right corner of the dialog box. A Help window appears with specific information about the command you're working with.

Here is a brief exercise to demonstrate this help feature:

1. Choose Tools ➤ SmartIcons. The SmartIcons dialog box appears.

2. Press F1 or click the Help button at the upper-right corner of the dialog box. The help topic for the SmartIcons command immediately appears. You can resize the Help window so that you can read its contents and view your work in 1-2-3 at the same time, as shown in Figure 2.23.

3. Scroll through the Help window to read the information it contains.

4. Press Escape to return to the SmartIcons dialog box. (For now, press Escape again to close the dialog box and end this exercise.)

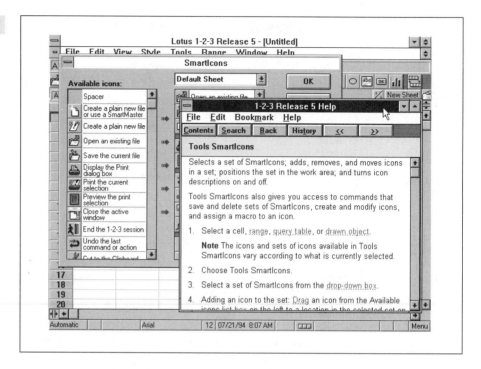

The Help Window

As you saw in the previous exercise, the Help window has its own title bar, Control-menu box, and Minimize and Maximize buttons. These features work the same way as in other windows. For example, if you need to enlarge a Help window so you can see more information at once, click the Maximize button.

The menu bar in the Help window offers four commands with pull-down menus:

COMMAND	DESCRIPTION
File	Contains commands for printing the current help topic, for opening the help system files for other Windows applications, and for exiting the Help system.

COMMAND	DESCRIPTION
Edit	Allows you to copy the current help topic to the Clipboard or to add your own annotations to a help topic.
Bookmark	Lets you mark passages in the Help system so you can find them quickly.
Help	Provides access to a general description of the Windows Help facility.

Finally, the Help window provides six special command buttons (see Figure 2.23), located below the Help menu bar:

HELP BUTTON	DESCRIPTION
Contents	Takes you to the Help Contents window (see Figure 2.22).
Search	Opens the Search dialog box, where you can quickly search by name for any topic that you want to read about.
Back	Returns you to the previous Help topic.
History	Displays a list of Help topics you've accessed recently. You can return to any topic by double-clicking its name in the list.
<<	Scrolls backward through help topics.
>>	Scrolls forward through help topics.

Here's a brief exercise that will introduce you to the Search dialog box:

1. With the 1-2-3 application window displayed on the screen, press F1.

2. Click the Search button. The Search dialog box appears.

3. In the text box at the top of the window, enter the words **control panel**. As you do so, the index list beneath the text box automatically scrolls to the Control panel topic.

4. Press ↵. Topics related to the control panel are listed at the bottom of the dialog box, as in Figure 2.24.

5. Select a topic and click the Go To button. The topic appears in the Help window.

6. When you've finished reading the help topic, press Escape to return to your work in 1-2-3.

FIGURE 2.24

The Search dialog box

Summary

The 1-2-3 application window displays several lines of important tools—the title bar, menu bar, edit line, SmartIcons, sheet tabs, and the status bar. As you learn to take advantage of these tools, your work in 1-2-3 becomes more efficient and more effective.

1-2-3 gives you two versatile ways to work with multiple worksheets. A single window can hold as many as 256 worksheets. In addition, you can open and work with multiple worksheet files concurrently in the 1-2-3 environment. You can also divide a given worksheet window into panes in order to view two distant portions of a worksheet at the same time.

One of the most important resources in 1-2-3 is its Help system. The Help menu and the Help window each give you many ways to search for a topic that you need information about. Learn to take advantage of the 1-2-3 for Windows Help window as a guide to understanding worksheets, graphs, and databases.

2

1-2-3 and Windows

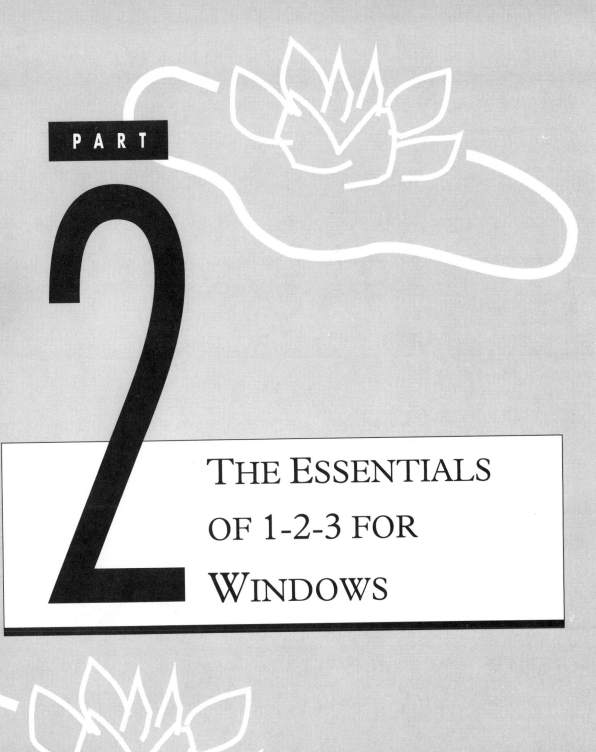

2

THE ESSENTIALS OF 1-2-3 FOR WINDOWS

Worksheet

Essentials

fast TRACK

ONE of the most remarkable qualities of the Lotus 1-2-3 spreadsheet is its flexibility. Rather than providing a single set of fixed techniques for performing spreadsheet tasks, 1-2-3 offers you a multitude of tools and options so you can do your work in your own way. As soon as you begin entering data onto a worksheet, the results reflect your own requirements, preferences, and style.

In this chapter you'll practice the basic procedures for entering and calculating data in a worksheet window. You'll learn how to:

- Enter labels and values
- Select ranges on a worksheet
- Calculate totals
- Assign names to ranges
- Copy data ranges
- Save a worksheet to disk
- Insert, delete, and move blocks of data
- Develop formulas and copy them to new ranges
- Select the appropriate reference type—absolute or relative—for addresses in formulas
- Use parentheses to establish the order of operations in formulas
- Explore "what-if" scenarios

Throughout this chapter and Chapter 4 you'll develop a sample worksheet for an imaginary company named Computing Conferences, Inc. This company organizes and conducts one-day training conferences that focus on the computing needs of different businesses. Your sample worksheet will compute the projected revenues, expenses, and profits of a one-day conference.

Figure 3.1 shows a sample of the worksheet, similar to the way it will appear when you finish the exercises in Chapters 3 and 4. The worksheet is divided into sections. The top section gives general information about a one-day conference: the name, location, date, price of admission, and two attendance estimates, a minimum and a maximum. The next two sections show projected revenues and expenses, based on attendance. The two columns on the right side of the worksheet display financial figures based on the minimum and maximum attendance estimates, respectively. The bottom line gives the anticipated profit, again with projections based on the two different attendance estimates.

FIGURE 3.1

The conference worksheet

Computing Conferences, Inc.
Profit Projection for a One-Day Conference

Conference:	*Computing for Video Stores*		
Place:	St. Louis		
Date:	15-Oct-94		

		Expected Attendance	
		Minimum	*Maximum*
Price: $195.00		80	150

	Per Person	Min.Total	Max.Total
Projected Revenues:			
Attendance		$15,600.00	$29,250.00
Video Sales	**$35.00**	$1,400.00	$2,625.00
Total Revenues		**$17,000.00**	**$31,875.00**
Projected Expenses -- Fixed			
Conference Room		$1,500.00	$2,000.00
Video Production		$1,000.00	$1,000.00
Promotion		$3,500.00	$3,500.00
Travel		$800.00	$800.00
Total Fixed Expenses		$6,800.00	$7,300.00
Projected Expenses -- Variable by Attendance			
Conference Materials	$8.25	$660.00	$1,237.50
Coffee and Pastries	$3.25	$260.00	$487.50
Box Lunch	$4.75	$380.00	$712.50
Total Variable Expenses		$1,300.00	$2,437.50
Projected Profit		**$8,900.00**	**$22,137.50**

3

Worksheet Essentials

This version of the worksheet contains projected data for a particular training conference. But at the same time, the sheet is carefully designed as a general-purpose *template* for any event that Computing Conferences is planning. It can easily be reused to display the expenses, revenues, and profits of other conferences. The five areas that are shaded in light gray are the input ranges for information about a given conference. All the other numeric values are calculated from the input data. When new values are entered into the input areas, 1-2-3 recalculates the formulas in the worksheet and displays new results in other ranges. You'll see exactly how this works as you proceed with this exercise.

This general-purpose template represents an important approach to developing worksheets in 1-2-3. You can simplify and streamline your work if you think of each new worksheet you develop as a template for similar tasks you might need to accomplish in the future. To be sure, not all worksheets lend themselves to this kind of planning. But each time you start a new worksheet, you should ask yourself whether you're likely to perform a similar job again, on a daily, weekly, monthly, quarterly, or even yearly basis. If so, you should carefully organize your work so that you can reuse the worksheet for future computational tasks.

Start up 1-2-3 now if you haven't already done so. In the hands-on exercises you'll work on in this chapter, you'll enter a variety of labels, values, and formulas onto the worksheet.

Developing a Worksheet

As you begin creating a worksheet, you may sometimes find yourself entering data in a temporary position on the sheet. Because 1-2-3 gives you simple ways to move blocks of data from one place to another and to insert new blank rows and columns, you're free to perform initial data-entry tasks in any way that's convenient. You can easily reorganize your work later. Accordingly, you'll begin your work in the following exercise by entering the data for fixed expenses at the top of the worksheet. Then, when you're ready to develop other parts of the worksheet, you'll make room by moving the fixed-expense section down to its correct position.

Entering Labels

You'll recall that a label is a non-numeric data entry in a cell. Labels typically appear on worksheets as titles, column headings, and row descriptions. When you begin entering a label, 1-2-3 switches into Label mode. By default, 1-2-3 left-justifies labels, but you can change label alignments in several ways, as you'll learn in Chapter 4.

Lotus 1-2-3 has an interesting way of displaying *long* labels. When a label entry has more characters than will fit in a cell, the label extends across adjacent cells to the right if those cells are empty. But if the cells to the right already contain data, the long label display is cut short within its own cell. To see how this works, enter the two title lines at the top of the conference worksheet:

1. Select cell B1 and type the company name, **Computing Conferences, Inc.**

As you type, your entry appears in the cell itself and also in contents box near the top of the screen. The mode indicator (at the right side of the status bar) displays the word *Label*.

2. Press ↵ to complete your entry. The entry extends across row 1, into cells C1 and D1, as shown in Figure 3.2.

3. Press ↓ to select cell B2, and enter the worksheet title in this cell: **Profit Projection for a One-Day Conference**.

4. Press ↵ to complete the entry. Again, the long label crosses empty cells C2, D2, and E2.

Worksheet Essentials **3**

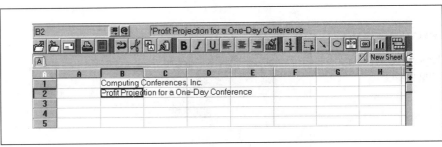

By examining the selection indicator and the contents box on the edit line (see Figure 3.2), you can see how 1-2-3 identifies the entry in cell B2:

'Profit Projection for a One-Day Conference

Even though this label is *displayed* across cells B2 through E2, its actual storage location is cell B2 alone.

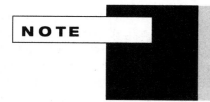

NOTE In the contents box, a single quotation mark (') at the beginning of a label means that the label is left-aligned. You'll learn about other alignment symbols starting on page 191 in Chapter 4.

What happens to a long label if you enter data in the cell to its immediate right? To answer this question, try the following exercise:

1. Press → to select cell C2. Notice that the contents box shows no entry for this cell. Cell C2 is empty, even though the display of the label in B2 extends into C2.

2. Type **abc** as a temporary label in cell C2.

3. Press ↵ to complete the entry. Notice what happens to the long label display in cell B2. It's cut off within the width of its own cell, and C2 now displays the new label.

4. Press ← to select cell B2 again.

As shown in Figure 3.3, the contents box displays the entire long label that you originally entered in cell B2, even though the worksheet displays only the first several letters of the label.

FIGURE 3.3

Experimenting with a long label

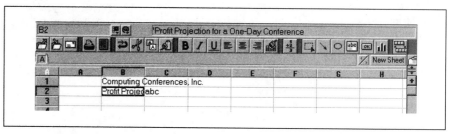

In summary, the display of a long label extends into the cells to the right if those cells are empty. But the long label display is *truncated* if a cell to the right contains an entry of its own.

As a result of this experiment, you now have an unwanted label entry in cell C2. Deleting this entry is a simple step.

Deleting a Label or Value

To delete a label or value in a cell, you can simply select the cell and press the Delete key on your keyboard. For example, follow these steps to delete the "abc" label in cell C2:

1. Select C2.

2. Press the Delete key.

When you delete the label in cell C2, the long label in cell B2 is displayed once again across cell C2, D2, and E2. There's no entry in cell C2 to interrupt the display.

Now pull down the Edit menu, shown in Figure 3.4, to look briefly at commands you can use for deleting the contents of a cell or range of cells. The Cut command deletes an entry and copies it to the Windows Clipboard; this is the first step in a *cut-and-paste* procedure. By contrast, the Clear command gives you the options of clearing the contents of a cell, the style applied to a cell, or both, as you can see in the Clear dialog box:

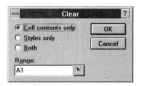

3

Worksheet Essentials

TIP

The Cut and Clear commands are also available in the quick menu that appears when you click a cell or range with the right mouse button.

FIGURE 3.4

The Edit menu

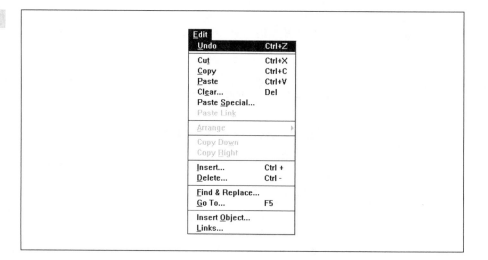

Because the Delete key is so readily available for deleting the contents of a cell or range of cells, you might sometimes perform deletions unintentionally. If this happens—or if you make any other mistakes during your work in 1-2-3—you can use the Undo command to restore your worksheet to its state before the last action.

Using the Undo Command

To undo the effect of your last action at the keyboard or with the mouse, you can pull down the Edit menu and choose Undo, the first command on the menu, or use one of two keyboard shortcuts, Ctrl+Z or Alt+Backspace. Or, simplest of all, you can click the Undo SmartIcon.

Here is an exercise with the Undo command:

1. Press ← to select cell B2. This is the cell that currently contains the second line of the worksheet title ("Profit Projection for a One-Day Conference").

2. Press the Delete key. The entry in the cell disappears. Imagine that you've performed this action by mistake. You now want a quick way to correct your error.

3. Click the Undo SmartIcon. The label entry in cell B2 reappears.

WARNING

To use Undo successfully, you have to correct a mistake before you perform another action. Undo operates only on an action you perform just previous to choosing the command.

Next you'll continue entering labels into the conference worksheet, to produce the sheet shown in Figure 3.5. As you do so, keep in mind that you can press an arrow key (right, left, up, or down) instead of the ⏎ key to complete an entry. An arrow key performs two actions at once: it completes your entry in the current cell and selects a new cell for the next entry. This can streamline the process of entering a column or row of data into a worksheet.

FIGURE 3.5

Entering labels into the conference worksheet

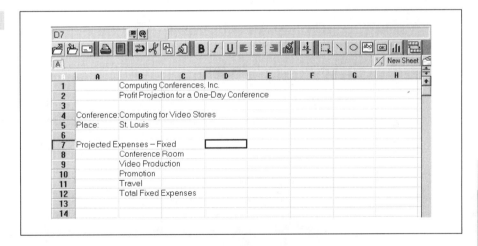

Follow these steps to enter the labels:

1. Enter **Conference:** into cell A4 and **Place:** into A5.

2. At the right of these entries, enter the name and place of the current conference: **Computing for Video Stores** in B4, and **St. Louis** in B5.

3. Enter the subtitle **Projected Expenses–Fixed** into cell A7.

3

Worksheet Essentials

4. Finally, enter these column labels, representing the fixed-expense categories, into the range of cells from B8 to B12:

CELL	ENTER
B8	**Conference Room**
B9	**Video Production**
B10	**Promotion**
B11	**Travel**
B12	**Total Fixed Expenses**

These categories represent the expenses that remain unchanged regardless of the number of people who attend the conference—the rental price for the conference room, the cost of producing a video of the conference, the pre-conference promotion costs, and the amount spent on travel to the conference site. Later you'll enter a group of *variable expenses* that depend directly on attendance.

The next step is to begin entering numeric values for the fixed expenses.

Entering Values

As you'll recall from Chapter 1, a *value* is an entry that 1-2-3 accepts as a number (see page 25). A value can become part of an arithmetic formula in your worksheet.

TIP

Whenever you begin an entry with a digit, 1-2-3 assumes you're beginning a numeric value. Accordingly, the mode indicator displays the word *Value*. But sometimes you may enter a label that happens to begin with a digit—for example, in an address entry such as 456 Flower Street. When you complete a label entry like this one, 1-2-3 automatically recognizes the switch in data type, and accepts your entry as a label rather than a value. In the contents box, a single quote character (') appears just before your entry: '456 Flower Street.

NOTE Previous versions of 1-2-3 (before Release 4.0) required you to type a single quote character (') before a label entry beginning with a digit. This is no longer necessary in an entry consisting of digits followed by non-numeric characters. But if you want to enter a sequence of digits alone as a label, you still need to begin the entry with a single quote character. For example, to enter 1994 as a label, type the entry as '1994.

In the following exercise you'll begin entering numeric values into the worksheet.

1. Select cell D8, the top cell of the column range where you'll enter the expense figures.

2. Type **1500** into D8. Notice that the word Value appears in the mode indicator as soon as you type the first digit of this number. To complete the entry and select the next cell down, press ↓.

3. Type **1000** into cell D9 and press ↓.

4. Type **3500** into cell D10 and press ↓.

5. Type **800** into cell D11 and press ↵.

Computing Totals

Now that you've entered an entire column of numbers, you'll want to compute the total and display it in cell D12. Calculating the total of a column or row of numbers is a common spreadsheet operation—so common that 1-2-3 provides a Sum SmartIcon that makes the process automatic.

To use this tool you simply select a cell at the bottom of a column of numbers or to the right of a row of numbers; then you click the Sum Smart-Icon. In response, 1-2-3 enters a formula that finds the total of all the numbers. Try it now:

1. Press ↓ to select cell D12.

2. Click the Sum SmartIcon.

As you see in Figure 3.6, the result is displayed as 6800. The contents box shows the formula that carries out this calculation:

@SUM(D8..D11)

FIGURE 3.6

Using the Sum
SmartIcon

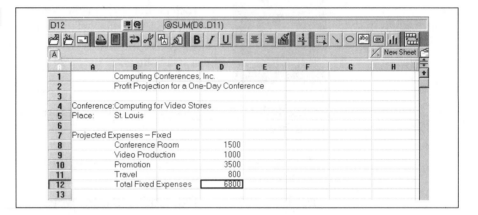

@SUM is one of the tools in 1-2-3's large library of *built-in functions*. In this case, 1-2-3 has entered a formula that finds the sum of the numeric values stored in the range D8..D11. You'll study this and other functions in Chapter 5.

NOTE

Part Four of this book is a complete reference to 1-2-3's function library.

Of course, you can enter the @SUM function into cell D12 directly from the keyboard if you prefer. To try this exercise, select D12 and press Delete to erase the cell's current contents. Then follow these steps:

1. Begin the summation formula by entering @**sum(** from the keyboard. When you do so, 1-2-3 switches into the Value mode.

2. Press ↑ four times, selecting cell D8. 1-2-3 switches into the Point mode and automatically enters the cell address into the summation formula you're building.

3. Press the period key (.) to *anchor* the range. In this case, D8 is the starting point for the range.

4. Press ↓ three times to highlight the range D8..D11. This range notation appears in the summation formula. At this point the screen looks like Figure 3.7.

5. Press ↵ to enter the formula. 1-2-3 automatically appends a) character after the range notation, for a correct use of the @SUM function.

FIGURE 3.7

Entering the @SUM formula from the keyboard

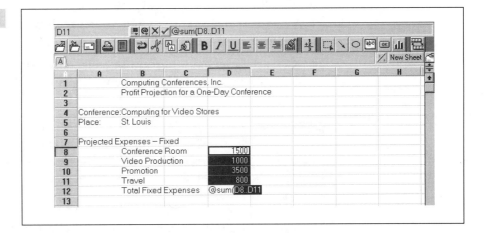

The calculated result is the same as before. After trying both techniques, you can see how much time you save by using the Sum SmartIcon. All the same, entering the formula manually is an instructive exercise. You've learned to use a pointing technique for incorporating a range in a formula. In the next section you'll expand your understanding of worksheet ranges, and you'll learn additional ways to select a range.

3

Worksheet Essentials

TIP

You can also select the @SUM function from the Function selector list on the edit line. You'll learn more about this feature later in this chapter, and in Chapter 5.

Selecting Ranges

As you know, a range is a rectangular area of worksheet cells that you select for a particular operation. Many of 1-2-3's menu commands and functions work with ranges. A range consists of any of the following arrangements of cells in a worksheet window:

- A single cell

- A group of contiguous cells contained within one row or one column

- A two-dimensional rectangle of cells within multiple rows and columns in a worksheet

- A three-dimensional group of cells, consisting of identically addressed ranges from adjacent sheets in a file

TIP

1-2-3 also allows you to select multiple ranges at once, which is known as a *collection*. You'll learn how to use a collection in Chapter 4 (see page 226).

The familiar notation for a range in 1-2-3 consists of two cell addresses separated by two dots. For a range on a single sheet, this notation can appear with or without the sheet name. For instance, a range of cells on worksheet A might be identified either as A:B2..A:F6, or simply as B2..F6 if there is no possibility of confusing this range with the same ranges on other worksheets.

Here are some examples of ranges, as illustrated in Figures 3.8 through 3.12:

- **B4..B4** is a range consisting of a single cell on a worksheet, at address B4 (see Figure 3.8).

- **C5..C10** is a column range—that is, a range of cells all contained within a single worksheet column, C in this case (see Figure 3.9). C5 is the top of the range and C10 is the bottom.

FIGURE 3.8

A range consisting of
a single cell, B4..B4

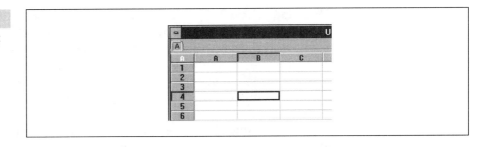

FIGURE 3.9

A column range,
C5..C10

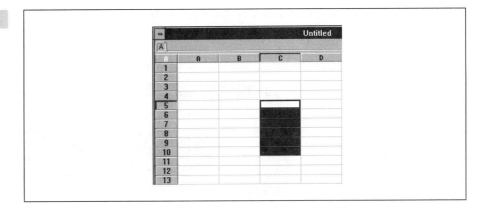

- **A6..E6** is a row range—a range of cells contained within row 6
  (see Figure 3.10). A6 at the left is the first cell and E6 at the right
  is the last cell.

- **B2..F6** is a two-dimensional range (see Figure 3.11). B2 is the
  upper-left corner of the range, and F6 is the lower-right corner.

3

Worksheet Essentials

FIGURE 3.10

A row range, A6..E6

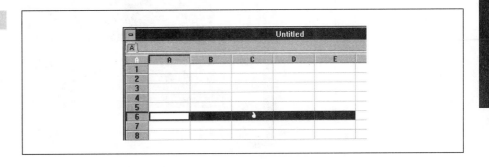

- **A:B2..C:F6** is a three-dimensional range, consisting of cells from three different worksheets in a window—that is, the range B2..F7 in worksheets A, B, and C (see Figure 3.12).

You can select a range for a particular operation either before or after you choose a menu command. When you choose a command that operates over a range, the command's dialog box has a text box in which you specify the target range. Displayed just to the right of the Range text box is the range selector button, as you saw in Chapter 2 (see page 71.) When you click this button, the dialog box disappears temporarily so you can select a range. After you complete the selection, the dialog box reappears and the range is displayed in the Range text box.

FIGURE 3.11

A two-dimensional range, B2..F6

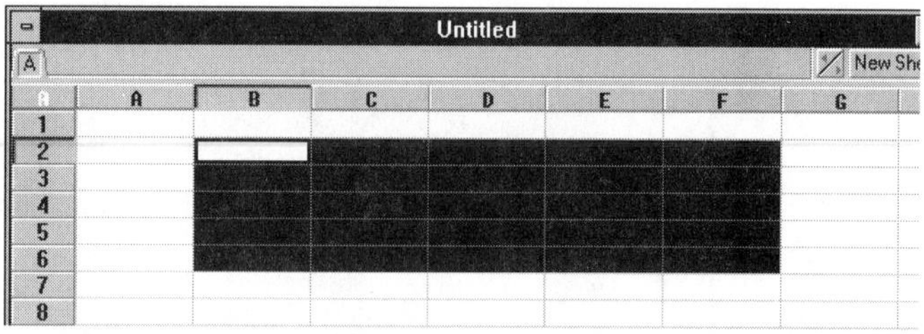

FIGURE 3.12

A three-dimensional range, A:B2..C:F6

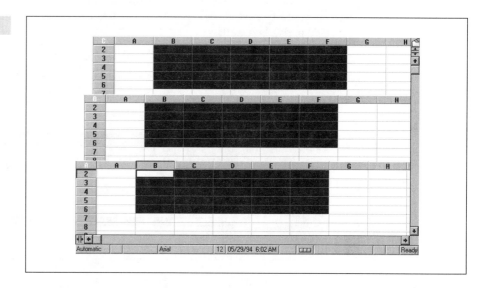

Selecting a range before you choose a menu command is sometimes called *preselecting*. Some of the 1-2-3 SmartIcons require a preselected range. You can preselect a range with the mouse or the keyboard; in either case, 1-2-3 switches from the Ready mode to the Point mode, indicating that you are in the process of pointing to a range of cells. As you carry out the action, 1-2-3 highlights your selection.

Here are the steps for preselecting a worksheet range with the mouse:

1. Position the mouse pointer over the first cell in the range.

2. Hold down the left mouse button and drag the pointer down and/or across to the last cell in the range.

3. Release the mouse button when the target range is highlighted.

From the keyboard, the F4 function key switches 1-2-3 from the Ready mode to the Point mode. Here are the steps for preselecting a range with the keyboard:

1. Select the cell that is to become the first cell in the range.

2. Press the F4 function key. This anchors the current cell as the starting point of the range, and switches 1-2-3 into the Point mode.

3. Press arrow keys to highlight the target range—for example, the ↓ key for a column range and/or the → key for a row range.

4. To select a three-dimensional range over adjacent worksheets in a file, press Ctrl+PgUp or Ctrl+PgDn while you are in the Point mode. (The current file must already contain two or more sheets. You'll recall that you click the New Sheet button to add sheets to a file.)

5. Press ↵ to complete the range selection. This final step switches you back into the Ready mode, but leaves the selected range highlighted.

Here is a second keyboard technique for preselecting a range:

1. Select the first cell of the range.

2. Hold down the Shift key as you press the →, ←, ↑, or ↓ keys to define a range on the active worksheet.

3. Press Ctrl+Shift+PgUp or Ctrl+Shift+PgDn to select a three-dimensional range over multiple sheets in the active file.

4. Release the Shift key—and the Ctrl key if applicable—to complete the selection.

You'll have the opportunity to practice these techniques as you continue developing the Conference worksheet.

TIP

A preselected range can be a convenient shortcut when you're preparing to enter data into specific rows and columns of a worksheet. To streamline the process, select the entire range first and then simply press ⅃ at the end of each data entry. Within the preselected range, pressing ⅃ automatically moves the cell pointer to the next cell in the range. (Pressing ⅃ at the last cell in the range moves you back up to the first cell in the range.) This technique works in a one-row or one-column range, or in a range of multiple rows and columns.

Creating Range Names

Formulas that contain the addresses of cells and ranges are sometimes difficult to read and understand. For example, consider the summation formula you entered into the Conference worksheet. If you return to this worksheet some weeks or months from now, you may not immediately see the significance of this formula:

@SUM(D8..D11)

But if the range notation D8..D11 were replaced with a meaningful name—such as EXPENSES—you would have an easier time recognizing the purpose of the formula:

@SUM(EXPENSES)

For this reason, 1-2-3 gives you the option of assigning names to individual cells or to ranges of cells on a worksheet. To do so, you select the range, choose the Name command from the Range menu, and enter a name in the Name dialog box, which is shown in Figure 3.13.

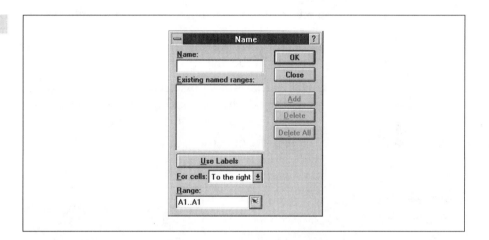

A range name may contain as many as fifteen characters. 1-2-3 automatically converts a range name entry to all uppercase letters. As a first exercise with range names, try assigning the name EXPENSES to the range of fixed expenses on the conference worksheet:

1. Select the range of expense values, D8..D11.

2. Choose Range ➤ Name.

3. Enter the name EXPENSES.

4. Click the OK button or press ↵ to confirm your entry.

This new definition doesn't change the appearance of your worksheet. But the next time you need to write a formula involving the column of fixed expenses, you can use the name EXPENSES to represent the range.

Using the Navigator Button

In fact, 1-2-3 provides a convenient list of all the existing range names defined for the current worksheet. View the list by clicking the Navigator

3

Worksheet Essentials

button on the edit line. You can select from this list while you're in the process of building a formula.

In the following exercise you'll reenter the summation formula into cell D12, this time using the new range name you have defined. This exercise gives you the chance to practice using *both* of the important buttons on the edit line—the Navigator and the Function selector:

1. Select cell D12 and press the Delete key to erase the formula currently in the cell.

2. Click the Function selector, the button labeled with a @ character on the edit line. As in Figure 3.14, the resulting list shows a selection of 1-2-3's built-in functions.

3. Click the SUM function near the top of the list.

FIGURE 3.14

The Function selector list.

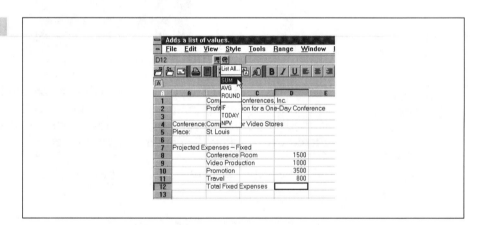

In response, 1-2-3 closes the Function selector list, and enters @SUM(list) in the current cell. The word *list* is highlighted in the formula, ready to be replaced by an actual range. Notice that you're in the Edit mode at this point.

4. Click the Navigator button, located just to the left of the Function selector on the edit line.

1-2-3 displays a drop-down list of the range names defined on the current worksheet. In this case, you've defined only one name, EXPENSES, as shown here:

5. Click EXPENSES in the list. The Navigator list disappears, and the name EXPENSES appears in the SUM formula:

@SUM(EXPENSES)

6. Press ⏎ to complete the entry. The result is the same as for the previous entries you've made in cell D12.

You'll work with other range names later in this chapter.

Next you'll copy the fixed-expense figures from column D to column E in the conference worksheet. Looking back at Figure 3.1 (see page 119), you can see that the fixed expenses are almost the same in the two columns. Rather than reenter the figures in the second column, you can quickly copy them and then revise the data in column E as necessary.

Copying a Range of Values

There are several ways to copy a range of data from one place to another in a worksheet. Probably the fastest and simplest technique is 1-2-3's drag-and-drop action, in which you use your mouse to drag a copy of a selected range to a new location. Other techniques employ the Windows Clipboard as a temporary storage place for the range of data you want to copy.

In the following exercises you'll try three different techniques that produce identical results on the worksheet itself—drag-and-drop, copy-and-paste with SmartIcons, and copy-and-paste from the keyboard. After each of the first two exercises you'll delete the copy so you can try the next technique. In each copy procedure you begin your work by selecting the range of cells that you want to copy. Make this range selection using either the mouse or the keyboard.

The Drag-and-Drop Action

Here's how you use the drag-and-drop operation to copy the range of expense data:

1. Select D8..D12, the range you want to copy.

2. Position the mouse pointer anywhere around the perimeter of the selection (except at the right bottom border) and watch for the pointer to take the shape of an open hand:

3. Hold down the Ctrl key on the keyboard. A small plus sign appears inside the hand pointer on the screen (this sign indicates that you are about to perform a *copy* operation, rather than a *move*):

4. Hold down the left mouse button and drag the selection one column to the right. While you drag, the mouse pointer takes the shape of a closed fist with a plus sign, and a dotted outline appears around the range E8..E12:

5. Release the mouse button and then release the Ctrl key. A copy of the entries in D8..D12 now appears in the new target range:

Projected Expenses – Fixed		
Conference Room	1500	1500
Video Production	1000	1000
Promotion	3500	3500
Travel	800	800
Total Fixed Expenses	6800	6800

Because the source range is a column of values, 1-2-3 assumes you want to copy the same arrangement of values to the destination, starting at E8.

There is another very important point to notice in the result of this copy operation. Move the cell pointer down to E12 and look at the contents box to examine the formula that 1-2-3 has copied to the cell:

@SUM(E8..E11)

This formula was copied from the equivalent formula in cell D12. In the copy, 1-2-3 has adjusted the range of the @SUM function to E8..E11. Thanks to this adjustment, the formula in cell E12 produces the total of the expense figures in column E. Furthermore, this formula will be recalculated if you make any changes in those figures. To see that this is true, move the cell pointer to E8 now and enter 2000 as the cell's new value. In response to this new entry, 1-2-3 instantly recalculates the formula in cell E12, giving a new result of 7300. Later in this chapter you'll learn much more about the adjustments 1-2-3 makes in formulas that you copy from one location to another in a worksheet.

To prepare for the next copy exercise, delete the copy you've just made. Select the range E8..E12 and press the Delete key at the keyboard. Delete has the same effect on a range of cells as it does on a single cell: All the data is cleared away. In the steps ahead you'll use SmartIcons to perform an operation known as *copy-and-paste.*

Performing a Copy-and-Paste Operation

If you're an experienced Windows user, you're familiar with the Copy and Paste commands. They appear in the Edit menus of most major Window applications, and they operate in much the same way from one application to the next. The Copy command copies the currently selected data to the Windows Clipboard without deleting or otherwise changing the original version of the data. The Paste command copies the current contents of the Clipboard to a specified location in the current document.

 Because these operations are used so commonly, 1-2-3 provides SmartIcons for them. The Copy SmartIcon appears as a pair of overlapping squares, each containing the letter A, and the Paste SmartIcon is depicted as a jar of paste.

 Here's how to use these SmartIcons to perform a copy-and-paste operation on the Conference worksheet:

1. Select the range D8..D12.

2. Click the Copy SmartIcon.

3. Select cell E8.

4. Click the Paste SmartIcon.

Once again examine the formula stored in cell E12 after the copy operation is complete. You'll see the same adjustment as before: The @SUM function applies to the data in column E.

Other ways to perform a copy-and-paste operation are to choose the Copy and Paste commands directly from the Edit menu, or to choose the same commands from a quick menu. To use a quick menu, select the range that you want to copy, click the selection with the right mouse button, and choose the Copy command, as shown in Figure 3.15. Then click the destination with the right mouse button, and choose the Paste command from the quick menu.

Finally, if you prefer to keep your hands on the keyboard as much as possible, you can use keyboard shortcuts to complete a copy-and-paste operation. Before trying the next exercise, you should once again select the range E8..E12 and press the Delete key to erase the data you've just copied.

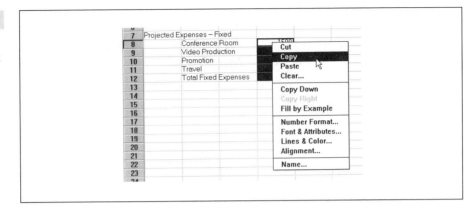

Using Keyboard Shortcuts to Perform a Copy-and-Paste

The keyboard shortcuts for the Copy and Paste commands are Ctrl+C and Ctrl+V, respectively. (These shortcuts are available almost universally in Windows applications.) Here is the keyboard technique for copying the expense data from column D to column E:

1. Use arrow keys to select cell D8.

2. Hold down the Shift key and press ↓ four times to select the range D8..D12.

3. Press Ctrl+C to copy this range to the Clipboard.

4. Press → once to select cell E8.

5. Press Ctrl+V to paste a new copy of the expense data to the range E8..E12.

As the final step in this first stage of worksheet development, enter 2000 as the conference room expense in cell E8. Your worksheet appears as shown in Figure 3.16. In sections ahead you'll change the worksheet in several ways to make room for additional data. But first, it's time to save the worksheet as a file on disk.

FIGURE 3.16

The first stage of development for the conference worksheet

	A	B	C	D	E	F	G	H
1		Computing Conferences, Inc.						
2		Profit Projection for a One-Day Conference						
3								
4	Conference:	Computing for Video Stores						
5	Place:	St. Louis						
6								
7	Projected Expenses – Fixed							
8		Conference Room		1500	2000			
9		Video Production		1000	1000			
10		Promotion		3500	3500			
11		Travel		800	800			
12		Total Fixed Expenses		6800	7300			
13								
14								

Saving the Worksheet

As in any other program, you should perform frequent save operations during your work in 1-2-3. If you experience a hardware or software problem you can lose any data you have entered since the last save. The correct length of time between save operations therefore depends upon how much data you are willing to risk losing. Fortunately, 1-2-3 saves your worksheet at the click of a SmartIcon—so it's easy to save worksheets at regular intervals.

The first time you save a worksheet to disk, the Save As dialog box appears on the screen, giving you the opportunity to supply a name for the file. The file name you enter can contain up to eight characters, consisting of letters, digits, underscore characters, and hyphens. When you save a worksheet, 1-2-3 supplies a default extension name of WK4 for the worksheet file. The Save As command also has a password option you can select if you want to restrict access to the file.

After the first save operation, you can simply choose the Save command to save new versions of your worksheet to disk under the same file name.

NOTE

Previous versions of 1-2-3 have automatically created *two* files—a worksheet file and a format file—to save all the information about a worksheet. But Release 5 saves everything in a single file.

Using the Save As Command

To save a worksheet for the first time, you can pull down the File menu and choose the Save As command or you can simply click the Save Smart-Icon. Either way, the dialog box shown in Figure 3.17 appears on the screen. You use the Drives and Directories boxes to navigate to the path location where you want to save your worksheet file. The Files box shows you a list of the worksheet files currently saved in the directory you select. 1-2-3 suggests a default file name such as FILE0001.WK4 for your file. Replace this default by entering a new name in the File name text box. Then click the OK button to complete the save operation.

FIGURE 3.17

The Save As dialog box

3

Worksheet Essentials

WORKSHEET ESSENTIALS

Follow these steps now to save the Conference worksheet for the first time:

1. Click the Save SmartIcon. You can save your worksheet file in the current directory, or select another location.

2. Enter the file name **CONF** into the File name text box.

3. Click OK or press ↵ to save the file.

As a result of these steps, the worksheet is saved as CONF.WK4.

The Save As dialog box allows you to select an existing file name from the File name list box as the name for the current save operation. If you do so, a second dialog box appears on the screen prompting you for specific instructions. The box displays the message "File already exists" and offers you three choices in the form of command buttons:

Replace   Click this button to replace the existing file with the new file you are now saving.

Backup   Click this button to retain the existing file on disk as a backup for the current worksheet. The worksheet you are saving receives the extension name WK4, and the extension of the existing worksheet on disk is changed to BAK.

Cancel   Click this button to cancel the save operation under the name you have selected.

Assigning a Password to a File

Finally, you can save a file with password protection to restrict the number of people who are allowed to open it. When you attempt to open a password-protected file, 1-2-3 prompts for the password—and denies access to the file if you can't supply the password correctly.

WARNING — Keep in mind the inevitable liability of password protection: If you forget the password you've created, you won't be able to open your own file.

Here are the general steps for saving a file with a password:

1. Choose the Save As command from the File menu.

2. After supplying a file name, click the With password option near the bottom of the Save As dialog box (see Figure 3.17). An *X* appears in the option box.

3. Click OK. The Set Password dialog box appears on the screen prompting you for the password that will be assigned to the file:

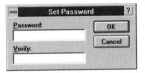

Enter the password twice, first in the Password box and then in the Verify box.

Asterisks appear in both boxes as you enter the characters of the password. The password may be up to fifteen characters long. Alphabetic case *is* significant; whatever combination of uppercase and/or lowercase letters you create in a password, 1-2-3 will require exactly the same combination when you try to open the file.

4. Click the OK button in the second dialog box to confirm the password, or click Cancel if you change your mind.

When you attempt to open a password-protected worksheet file, the Get Password dialog box appears first on the screen, prompting you to enter

3

Worksheet Essentials

the file's password:

As you type the password, 1-2-3 displays a string of asterisks in the Enter password text box. Click OK; if your password is correct, 1-2-3 opens the file.

You can change a file's password—if you know the original password—by opening the file and selecting the Save As command to resave the file.

Using the Save Command

After you save a file for the first time, you can update the file by choosing the Save command from the File menu or by clicking the Save SmartIcon. *Updating* means storing the current version of the worksheet under its existing file name. As you make significant changes in data, formatting, or organization during the development of a worksheet, you should update your file regularly.

Here are the steps for updating a file:

1. Activate the window containing the worksheet you want to save.

2. Pull down the File menu and choose the Save command, or simply click the Save SmartIcon.

The next step in the development of the Conference worksheet is to enter the projected revenues. As you anticipated at the beginning, you'll have to move the range of expense data down several rows below its current position to make room for the revenues data. In the next section of this chapter you'll learn how to move a range of data and to insert blank columns and rows at specified locations in the worksheet—and you'll continue entering data into the worksheet.

Changing the Worksheet

You've seen how to use a drag-and-drop operation to copy a range of data (see page 138). Now you'll learn to use a similar mouse action to *move* data from one place to another in your worksheet. You'll also experiment with alternative techniques for achieving the same effect—using the cut-and-paste operation, and inserting blank rows or columns at selected locations.

Moving Ranges of Data

To move a range of data, you simply select it and drag it to its new location. For example, in the following steps you'll move the range of expense data down the worksheet by several rows:

1. Select the range A7..E12.

2. Position the mouse pointer over the border of the selection, and watch for the pointer to take the shape of an open hand.

3. Hold down the left mouse button and drag the top of the selection down to row 15, as shown in Figure 3.18. The mouse pointer changes to a closed fist while you drag.

4. Release the mouse button to complete the move.

Figure 3.19 shows the result of the drag-and-drop operation.

You might wonder what has happened to the two summation formulas that are included in the range of data that you just moved. To find out, select cells D20 and E20 in turn and examine their formulas in the contents box at the top of the 1-2-3 window. You'll see that 1-2-3 has automatically adjusted the ranges in the cells in response to the move. For example, the formula in cell E20 is now

@SUM(E16..E19)

In the case of cell D20, 1-2-3 has adjusted the range represented by the name EXPENSES. Accordingly, the values displayed in D20 and E20 still correctly represent the total fixed expenses for the low- and high-attendance estimates.

3

Worksheet Essentials

FIGURE 3.18

Performing a
drag-and-drop
operation

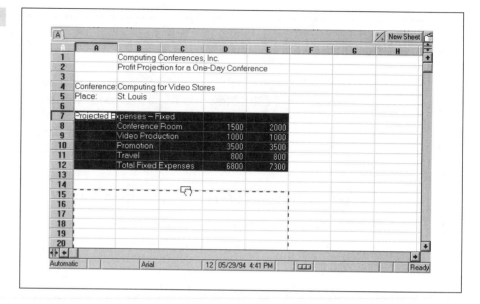

FIGURE 3.19

Moving a range of
data

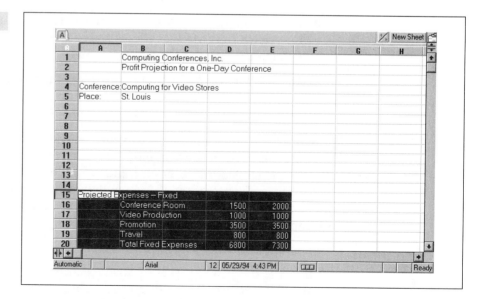

Using the Cut-and-Paste Operation

The cut-and-paste technique is an alternative to drag-and-drop. To perform a cut-and-paste operation, you select the range that you want to move and choose the Cut command to copy the selection to the Clipboard. Then you select the destination of the move and choose the Paste command. You can access the Cut and Paste commands by any of these methods:

- Click the Cut and Paste SmartIcons.

- Choose Cut and then Paste from the Edit menu.

- Click a selection with the right mouse button and choose Cut or Paste from the resulting quick menu.

- Use keyboard shortcuts: Ctrl+X for Cut, and Ctrl+V for Paste.

If you want to try a cut-and-paste operation, follow these steps:

1. Click the Undo SmartIcon to undo the result of your previous drag-and-drop action.

2. Select the range of expense data, A7..E12.

3. Click the Cut SmartIcon. The data disappears and is copied to the Clipboard.

4. Select cell A15.

5. Click the Paste SmartIcon. The data reappears at its new location.

In the area that has been opened up by the move, you can now enter the new labels and values that you see in Figure 3.20.

1. Starting in column A, enter the following three labels:

A6	**Date:**
A8	**Price:**
A10	**Projected Revenues**

FIGURE 3.20

FIGURE 3.20

Entering new data into
the Conference
worksheet

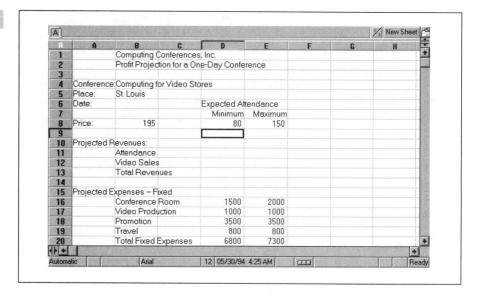

2. Enter the following revenue categories into column B:

B11	**Attendance**
B12	**Video Sales**
B13	**Total Revenues**

Notice that Computing Conferences, Inc. earns revenue both
from the price of attendance and from sales of a video that is produced during the conference.

3. Enter a value of **195** in cell B8. This is the per-person attendance
price for this particular conference.

4. Enter **Expected Attendance** into cell D6. Notice that the label is
displayed across two columns of the worksheet.

The labels in cells D7 and E7 should be right-aligned in their respective
cells, to match the alignment of the numeric values that will appear immediately beneath them. To achieve right-alignment you can use a simple
technique at the time you enter a label into its cell: Start the label with a
double-quotation mark character.

5. Try this technique as you enter labels into cells D7 and E7:

D7	**"Minimum**
E7	**"Maximum**

As you'll learn in Chapter 4, there are several other ways to control label alignment in 1-2-3 (see page 191).

6. Enter a value of **80** as the low estimate for the number of people who will attend the conference (cell D8).

7. Enter a value of **150** as the high estimate (cell E8).

Now if you compare Figure 3.20 with Figure 3.1 (see page 119), you'll notice that you need additional space on the worksheet for information that you haven't entered yet. Specifically, you need a blank row for column headings just above the Projected Revenues label; and you need a blank column for the per-person revenue and expense figures, just to the right of column C. One way to open up these ranges would be to move the appropriate ranges of data, using the drag-and-drop or copy-and-paste operation. But in this case you can accomplish the task more easily by inserting a blank row and a blank column at selected positions on the worksheet. You'll learn how to do this in the next section.

Inserting Rows and Columns

The Edit ➤ Insert command contains options for inserting new sheets in an open worksheet file, or inserting new rows or columns in an active sheet:

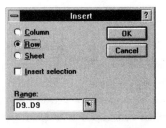

As you've learned, the New Sheet button is a shortcut for adding sheets; 1-2-3 also provides shortcuts for inserting rows or columns.

3

Worksheet Essentials

To add a single new row or column to the active worksheet, you can use the Edit ➤ Insert command in the following way:

1. Select a cell that's located in the row or column position where you want to make the insert.

2. Choose Edit ➤ Insert.

3. Click either the Column or Row option.

4. Click the OK button or press ↵ to complete the insert operation.

To insert more than one row at a time, select a range of consecutive cells in a single column—one cell for each row that you want to insert. Conversely, to insert multiple columns, preselect a range of adjacent cells in a row—one cell for each column you want to insert. Choose Edit ➤ Insert and click the Row or Column option after you've selected the range.

1-2-3 also provides Insert Row and Insert Column SmartIcons, but you have to switch to a new set of SmartIcons to find them. If you're planning to make several insertions in a particular worksheet, you can save time by making this switch. Click the SmartIcons selector on the status bar and choose Editing, the second SmartIcon set in the list:

TIP

Another way to page through 1-2-3's SmartIcon sets is to click the Next Set SmartIcon, which is always dis-played as the last button in the current set of Smart-Icons. Once you become familiar with the tools available in the various SmartIcon sets, this is a convenient way to switch from one set to the next. But initially you may prefer to choose a set by name from the SmartIcons selector list.

As you can see, the Insert Row and Insert Column SmartIcons are located near the right side of the new SmartIcon set:

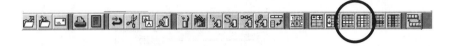

You'll use these tools to make insertions in your worksheet.

In the current version of the Conference worksheet you can select cell D9 as the insert position for both the new row and the new column. Follow these steps to make the insertions:

1. Select cell D9 on the worksheet.

2. Click the Insert Row SmartIcon.

3. Click the Insert Column SmartIcon.

4. Click the SmartIcons selector on the status bar and choose Default Sheet from the resulting list. This returns you to the original SmartIcon set.

After these insertions you might once again want to examine the summation formulas, now located in cells E21 and F21. As before, 1-2-3 has adjusted the ranges in these formulas in response to the changes you have made in the worksheet.

Now you're ready to enter column headings in row 10 and the per-unit price of the conference video in column D. As you complete this second stage of data entry into the worksheet, you'll also assign range names to cells containing important values on the sheet:

1. Enter the following three labels in row 10, again starting each label with a double quotation character for right alignment:

D10	**"Per Person**
E10	**"Min. Total**
F10	**"Max. Total**

2. Enter a value of **35** into cell D13. This is the retail price of the conference video.

3. Select cell B8 and choose Range ➤ Name. The Name dialog box appears:

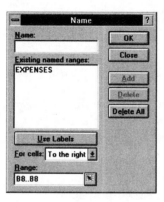

4. Enter **Price** as the name for cell B8 and press ↵.

5. Likewise, select cell D13, choose Range ➤ Name, and enter **Video** as the name for this cell.

6. Preselect the range E7..F7, containing the Minimum and Maximum labels.

7. Choose Range ➤ Name.

8. Near the bottom of the Name dialog box, click the down-arrow button next to the For cells box, and select Below from the resulting drop-down list, as shown in Figure 3.21.

9. Click the Use Labels button and click OK to confirm.

This action instructs 1-2-3 to assign the labels in cells E7 and F7 as the names for cells E8 and F8. Specifically, you've just assigned the name MINIMUM to cell E8, and the name MAXIMUM to cell F8. You can now use these two names to represent the two attendance estimates in formulas you'll write for the worksheet.

FIGURE 3.21

Assigning worksheet
labels as range names

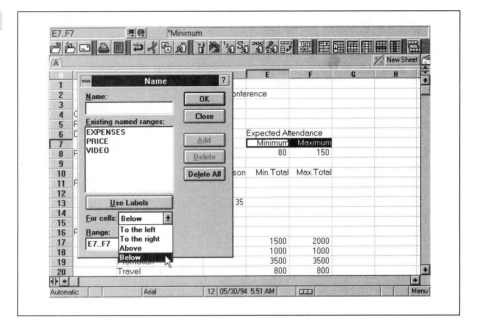

10. Pull down the File menu and choose the Save command—or simply click the Save SmartIcon. This saves your latest version of the
conference worksheet to disk, still under the file name
CONF.WK4.

When you complete these steps, your worksheet appears as shown in Figure 3.22.

The next step in the worksheet development is to enter formulas for calculating the minimum and maximum revenue projections, based on expected attendance. When you enter these formulas, you'll use the range
names you've created for several individual cells on the worksheet. To review the five names you've defined, click the Navigator button on the edit

FIGURE 3.22

Reorganizing the
Conference worksheet

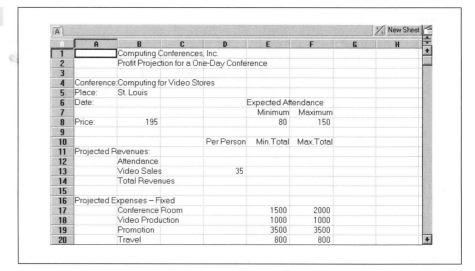

	A	B	C	D	E	F	G	H
1		Computing Conferences, Inc.						
2		Profit Projection for a One-Day Conference						
3								
4	Conference:	Computing for Video Stores						
5	Place:	St. Louis						
6	Date:				Expected Attendance			
7					Minimum	Maximum		
8	Price:	195			80	150		
9								
10				Per Person	Min.Total	Max.Total		
11	Projected Revenues:							
12		Attendance						
13		Video Sales	35					
14		Total Revenues						
15								
16	Projected Expenses – Fixed							
17		Conference Room			1500	2000		
18		Video Production			1000	1000		
19		Promotion			3500	3500		
20		Travel			800	800		

line. You'll see the following list:

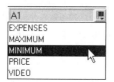

When you highlight an entry in this list, the title bar identifies the cell or range that the name represents.

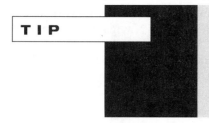

TIP

A quick way to go to a named cell or range in a worksheet is to click the Navigator button and then select a name. If the name represents a single cell, 1-2-3 moves the pointer to that cell. If the name represents a range, 1-2-3 highlights the range.

Working with Formulas in a Worksheet

By writing formulas, you transform a worksheet from a static collection of data to a dynamic calculation tool. As you first saw in Chapter 1, formulas are made up of a variety of elements, including

- Arithmetic operations, such as +, −, *, and /
- Literal numeric values such as 2 or 5280
- Cell addresses—or alternatively, range names—that represent the values stored in those cells
- Worksheet functions like @SUM

When you enter a formula into a cell, 1-2-3 immediately evaluates it and displays its numeric result in the cell. Furthermore, 1-2-3 recalculates a formula whenever you change the value of a cell that is part of the formula. This is what users sometimes refer to as the "what-if" feature of a spreadsheet.

As a quick demonstration of this feature, follow the steps of this exercise:

1. Click the New Sheet button to add sheet B temporarily to the CONF.WK4 file. (You'll delete this sheet when you've finished with this exercise.)
2. Enter a value of **92** in cell A1 of the new sheet B.
3. Select cell B1 and enter the formula **2*A1.**

For this exercise, you can simply enter the entire formula directly from the keyboard. (Later you'll use the *pointing* technique to enter a cell address into a formula.) The formula multiplies the value stored in A1 by 2. The result displayed in B1 is 184.

4. Select A1 again and enter **32** as the cell's new value. In response, 1-2-3 instantly recalculates the value in B1, displaying the result as 64.

3

Worksheet Essentials

5. Try several more new values in A1, one at a time: **5, 3212, 19, 543,** and **27**. Each time you enter a new value into A1, 1-2-3 instantly recalculates the value in B1. The values 10, 6424, 38, 1086, and 54 appear in turn in cell B1.

6. When you are finished experimenting, click the B tab (on the line above the worksheet) with the right mouse button, and choose Delete from the resulting quick menu.

Sheet B is removed, leaving CONF.WK4 with its original sheet A.

The idea is the same on complex worksheets designed to perform business calculations: Given a formula containing a cell reference, 1-2-3 recalculates the formula whenever you change the value in the cell.

Return now to the Conference worksheet for a more interesting illustration of this feature. In an upcoming exercise you'll enter formulas into cells E12 and F12 to calculate the projected attendance revenue from the conference.

Entering Formulas

The attendance revenue is calculated by multiplying the price per person by the number of people attending the conference. The price per person is stored in cell B8 and the first of the two attendance estimates (the minimum attendance) is stored in cell E8. Furthermore, you know that multiplication is represented by the asterisk character (*) in 1-2-3. Given all this information, you might expect to enter the following formula into cell E12 to calculate the minimum projected revenue from attendance fees:

    B8*E8

But there is a problem here. If you type the first character, *B*, of this formula into the cell, 1-2-3 switches into the Label mode, whereas the correct mode for entering a formula is Value. You clearly need to start the formula with a character that triggers the Value mode.

The general-purpose character for starting a formula in 1-2-3 is the plus sign (+). This character is not needed in all formulas—for example, when a formula begins with a number or with the @ symbol of a function. But when the first element of a formula is a cell address, the plus sign is a good way to begin in the Value mode. Here, then, is the correct format for the projected revenue formula:

    +B8*E8

Using the Pointing Technique

You can enter a formula like this one directly from the keyboard if you want to. But there is an easier way. As you are entering the formula, you can use the mouse or the keyboard to *point* to cells that you want to include in the formula. You'll see how this works as you enter the first revenue formula into cell E12:

1. Select cell E12 in the conference worksheet.

2. Enter the plus sign (+) to begin the formula. The + appears in the cell, and the mode indicator displays the word *Value*.

3. To point to the first cell address in the formula, B8, press ↑ four times and ← three times. The mode switches to Point while you are pointing to the cell. Cell E12 now displays the formula as +B8.

4. Enter the asterisk character (*), for multiplication. 1-2-3 switches back to the Value mode.

5. To point to the second cell address in the formula, E8, press ↑ four times. When the cell is selected, the formula is displayed as +B8*E8.

6. Now press ↵ to complete the formula entry. When you do so, 1-2-3 immediately calculates the result of the formula and displays it in cell E12 as 15600.

Take a close look at the contents box on the edit line. Because both of the references in your formula identify *named* cells, 1-2-3 automatically uses those names to express the formula as +PRICE*MINIMUM. This convenient feature makes your formula a lot easier to understand.

3

Worksheet Essentials

Using Range Names

You now need to enter a similar formula into cell F12 to calculate the revenue projection from the maximum attendance estimate. This time try expressing the formula with range names. Recall that cell B8 is named PRICE and cell F8 is named MAXIMUM. You can therefore write the formula as:

+PRICE*MAXIMUM

Notice that the formula must still begin with a plus sign to start the entry correctly in the Value mode. You can type this formula directly into cell F12 from the keyboard, or you can use the Navigator button to display a list of defined names from the worksheet. Alternatively, you can press the F3 function key to view a special Range Names dialog box, from which you can select a name. Here are the steps of this final approach:

1. Select cell F12.

2. Type + from the keyboard to start the formula.

3. Press F3. Select PRICE from the list of range names and then press ↵ or click OK:

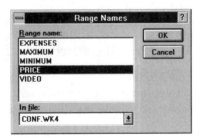

4. Type * to continue the formula.

5. Press F3 again, select MAXIMUM from the name list. Press ↵ or click OK to confirm.

6. Press ↵ to complete the formula entry.

When you finish these steps, 1-2-3 enters the result of your formula into cell F12. The revenue projection is displayed as 29250.

Now you've seen two distinct ways of expressing and entering formulas into the conference worksheet. You can identify cells by their addresses or by the range names you have assigned to the cells.

There are two more formulas to enter into the revenue section of the worksheet. In cells E13 and E14 you need formulas to calculate projected revenues from sales of the conference video. The planners at Computing Conferences, Inc., know from experience that they can count on approximately half of the participants of a given conference to order the video tape. Given this expectation, the estimated revenue is equal to the retail video price times one-half the number of participants.

You'll recall that you assigned the range name VIDEO to cell D13, where the unit retail price of the video is stored. The formula you can enter into cell E13 is therefore +VIDEO*MINIMUM/2. Likewise, the formula for cell F13 is +VIDEO*MAXIMUM/2. Enter these two formulas into their respective cells now, using any entry technique you choose. The result is 1400 for the minimum revenue projection (E13) and 2625 for the maximum (F13).

Finally, you need to enter summation formulas into row 14 to find the two total revenue projections. You may be surprised to learn that you can enter both formulas in a single action. Here are the steps:

1. Select the range E14..F14.

2. Click the Sum SmartIcon.

When you click the SmartIcon, 1-2-3 enters the two summation formulas into cells E14 and F14. The results of the formulas are displayed as 17000 and 31875, respectively. Figure 3.23 shows what the worksheet looks like at this stage of your work.

3. Click the Save SmartIcon now to save your work to disk.

You still have two sections of information to enter into the Conference worksheet—the variable expenses and the bottom-line profit. As you work on these sections you'll explore another important worksheet topic, the techniques for copying formulas from one range to another.

3

Worksheet Essentials

FIGURE 3.23

Entering the formulas
for projected revenue

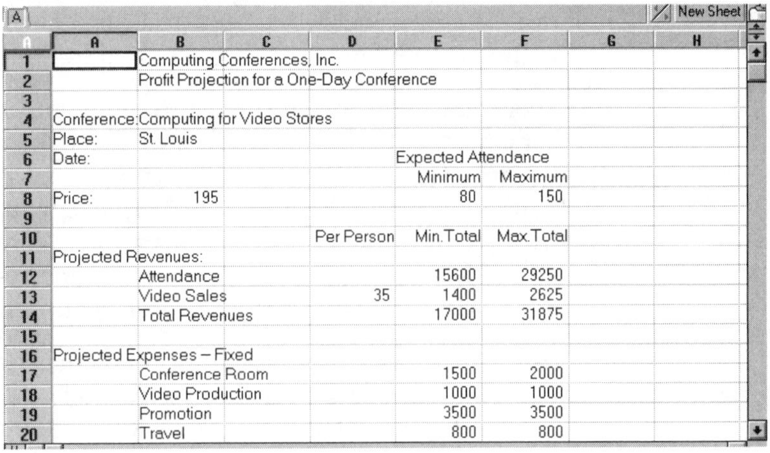

	A	B	C	D	E	F	G	H
1		Computing Conferences, Inc.						
2		Profit Projection for a One-Day Conference						
3								
4	Conference:	Computing for Video Stores						
5	Place:	St. Louis						
6	Date:				Expected Attendance			
7					Minimum	Maximum		
8	Price:	195			80	150		
9								
10				Per Person	Min.Total	Max.Total		
11	Projected Revenues:							
12		Attendance			15600	29250		
13		Video Sales		35	1400	2625		
14		Total Revenues			17000	31875		
15								
16	Projected Expenses – Fixed							
17		Conference Room			1500	2000		
18		Video Production			1000	1000		
19		Promotion			3500	3500		
20		Travel			800	800		

Copying Formulas

In many worksheets, a formula in one cell may be identical in *structure* to formulas you need to enter into other cells. Rather than entering these similar formulas one by one, you can copy the original formula to other locations on the worksheet. 1-2-3 handles this copy operation in a logical manner, taking care to adjust cell references and range addresses as necessary.

You've already seen an example. Earlier in this chapter you copied the summation formula for fixed expenses from one column to an adjacent column (see page 138). At the time of the copy operation, the expense figures were located in column D and the summation formula in cell D12 was @SUM(D8..D11). When you copied this formula to cell E12, 1-2-3 automatically adjusted the range reference, producing the formula @SUM(E8..E11).

The logic that 1-2-3 follows to make this adjustment is simple: In a formula copied from column D to column E, a reference to a range in D becomes a reference to the adjacent range in E. The range address in this copy operation is an example of a *relative reference*. When you copy a formula containing a relative reference, 1-2-3 adjusts the cell or range address *relative to the location of the copy*.

A similar adjustment occurs when you copy a formula from one row to another. For example, imagine that you have entered the following formula into cell C3:

+A3+B3

This formula adds the contents of the two cells located to the left of C3 in row 3. If you copy this formula down to cell C4, 1-2-3 adjusts the formula as follows:

+A4+B4

The logic is the same: A formula copied to row 4 should contain references to the data stored in row 4. Accordingly, 1-2-3 adjusts the address references relative to the row to which the formula is copied.

Unless you specify otherwise, 1-2-3 treats cell and range addresses as relative references whenever you copy a formula from one place to another. In short, relative references are the default in copy operations.

But in some contexts you will want to override this default. A formula may contain a reference to a fixed cell address—that is, an address that you want to remain unchanged when you copy the formula to other locations. In this case, you express the address as an *absolute reference*. You'll learn how to do this in upcoming exercises.

Understanding Reference Types

The distinction between relative and absolute references is perhaps the single most important concept for you to master now as you continue your work in 1-2-3. The concept itself is not difficult or subtle, but it does force you to make a variety of decisions while you're writing a formula. In effect, you must think carefully about *two* characteristics of each formula you create:

- The arithmetic structure of the formula—the specific operations and operands that ultimately produce the correct result in the original formula.

- The types of address references in the formula—the directions that specify how the formula will be copied to other locations in the worksheet.

3

Worksheet Essentials

Of course, relative and absolute reference types are relevant only in formulas that you intend to copy. If you write a formula that applies to only one location on a worksheet—a formula that will not be copied elsewhere—then you don't have to worry about relative and absolute references. But as you develop your own worksheets you may be surprised at how often you find yourself copying formulas.

Absolute and relative references Lotus 1-2-3 has a simple notation that you use to distinguish between relative and absolute references—and a simple technique for changing an address from one reference type to another. The default address format that you've been using in all your work up to now is the relative reference format. For example, the following address is a relative reference:

B8

To change this address to an absolute reference, you insert a dollar-sign character ($) before each element of the address. Here is the absolute reference to this same address:

$B$8

You can also create an absolute reference from a range name. Place a $ character just before the name:

$PRICE

While you are entering a formula, you can create absolute references by typing $ characters at the appropriate locations. But 1-2-3 offers an easier technique for transforming a reference from relative to absolute. In the Point, Edit, or Value modes, you can press the F4 function key to change a reference type.

NOTE   You'll recall that F4 has an additional use: When you are in the Ready mode, pressing F4 switches you into the Point mode so you can preselect a range.

In the following exercise you'll explore the significance of absolute references, and you'll practice the mechanical details of changing an address from relative to absolute. For the purposes of this exercise, you're going to backtrack a little in the Conference worksheet and redo some work that you completed earlier. Specifically, you'll reenter the formula for projected attendance revenues in cell E12; then you'll copy this formula to cell F12. Keep in mind that the formulas in these cells are both designed to multiply the attendance price per person by the anticipated number of people attending the conference. You'll make no change in the *structure* of these formulas—and the end result will remain the same. What you'll change is the reference type that allows you to copy the formula successfully from E12 to F12.

To prepare for this exercise begin by deleting the current contents of these two cells. Select the range E12..F12 and press the Delete key. Now you have an empty range in which to perform the following steps:

1. Select cell E12 and enter the + character to begin the formula entry. This switches 1-2-3 into the Value mode.

2. To point to cell B8, press ↑ four times and ← three times. The mode changes to Point and the reference +A:B8 is displayed in cell E12.

3. Press the F4 function key one time.

This transforms the address to an absolute reference, $A:$B$8. Notice that 1-2-3 places a $ character in front of all three elements of the address—the sheet letter, the column letter, and the row number.

4. Now type the * sign, representing multiplication. The mode switches back to Value.

5. Press ↑ four times to point to cell E8.

The formula now appears as +$A:$B$8*A:E8. Don't change the reference type of this second address. It remains a relative reference for the purposes of copying the formula.

6. Press ↵. The value 15600 appears in cell E12.

This is the same as the value produced by the previous version of the formula, but now the contents box displays the formula as +$PRICE*MINIMUM. Once again, 1-2-3 automatically substitutes names for the addresses in the formula, but now the first name is preceded by a $ sign, representing an absolute reference. The second name is a relative reference.

Now you're ready to copy the formula in cell E12 to cell F12. To do so, you can use any of the copying techniques you've already learned, including the drag-and-drop action or the various mouse and keyboard approaches to a copy-and-paste operation (see page 137 to review copying methods if necessary). Alternatively, try this new method, using the Copy Right command:

1. Select the range E12..F12.

2. Click the selection with the right mouse button, to view the corresponding quick menu.

3. Choose the Copy Right command from the quick menu:

The same value as before appears in cell F12—a projected attendance revenue of 29250.

To see exactly what has happened in this exercise, you should now examine the new formulas in cells E12 and F12. At E12 you see the formula you've entered, with an absolute reference to $PRICE (equivalent to $B$8, the address of the attendance price) and a relative reference to MINIMUM (equivalent to E8, the address of the minimum expected attendance level):

    +$PRICE*MINIMUM

Then at F12 you find the copied formula:

    +$PRICE*MAXIMUM

In copying the formula, 1-2-3 has made no change in the absolute reference but has adjusted the relative reference appropriately. This is exactly
what you wanted to happen: The original formula in cell E12 calculates
the *minimum* expected attendance revenue and the formula copied to cell
F12 gives the *maximum* revenue.

In summary, you write absolute and relative references to instruct 1-2-3
exactly how to copy a formula:

- An absolute reference is copied without change.

- A relative reference is adjusted according to the row or column to
  which it is copied.

But this isn't the complete picture. In some worksheets you might plan to
copy a particular formula in *two* directions—both down a column and
across a row. To anticipate this double copy operation, you'll find yourself
working with a third type of address format—the *mixed reference*. You'll
learn about mixed references as you complete the final sections of the
Conference worksheet.

To prepare for the remaining exercises of this chapter, perform the following data-entry tasks:

1. Enter **Projected Expenses – Variable by Attendance** in cell A23.

2. In cells B24 to B27, enter the variable-expense categories. These
represent the materials and meals given to each participant in the
conference:

B24	**Conference Materials**
B25	**Coffee and Pastries**
B26	**Box Lunch**
B27	**Total Variable Expenses**

3. Enter the corresponding per-person costs for these items in cells
D24, D25, and D26:

D24	**8.25**
D25	**3.25**
D26	**4.75**

4. Finally, enter **Projected Profit** in cell A29.

When you complete these entries, your worksheet appears as shown in Figure 3.24.

FIGURE 3.24

Preparing the final sections of the worksheet

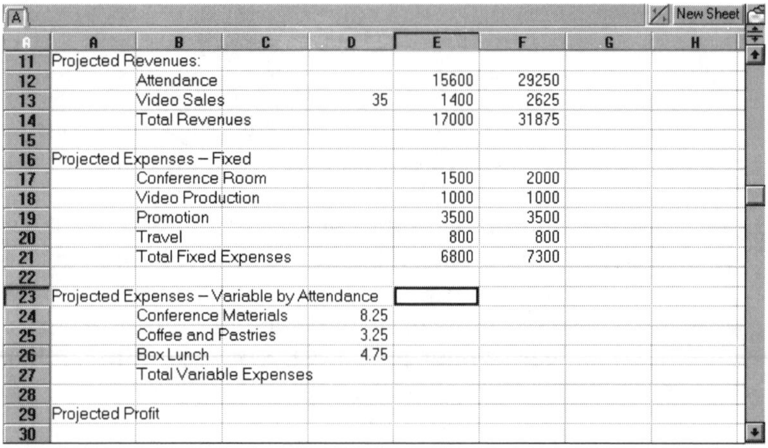

	A	B	C	D	E	F	G	H
11	Projected Revenues:							
12		Attendance			15600	29250		
13		Video Sales		35	1400	2625		
14		Total Revenues			17000	31875		
15								
16	Projected Expenses – Fixed							
17		Conference Room			1500	2000		
18		Video Production			1000	1000		
19		Promotion			3500	3500		
20		Travel			800	800		
21		Total Fixed Expenses			6800	7300		
22								
23	Projected Expenses – Variable by Attendance							
24		Conference Materials		8.25				
25		Coffee and Pastries		3.25				
26		Box Lunch		4.75				
27		Total Variable Expenses						
28								
29	Projected Profit							
30								

Mixed references A mixed reference instructs 1-2-3 to adjust one part of an address and leave another part unchanged when the address is copied from one cell to another. In the notation for a mixed reference, a $ character appears to the left of one address element but not the other. For example, in the following reference the column is absolute and the row is relative:

$D24

When you copy a formula containing this address, 1-2-3 retains a fixed reference to column D but adjusts the row reference to match the row of the copy.

Conversely, the following example contains a relative column reference and an absolute row reference:

E$8

In copies of this address, 1-2-3 adjusts the column reference to match the column location of the copy, but retains a fixed reference to row 8.

You can use the F4 function key to create mixed references just as you did to create absolute references. In the Point, Value, and Edit modes, you press F4 *multiple times* to cycle through the various reference types. As you have seen, the first keypress gives an absolute reference. When you press F4 additional times, the address switches between forms of the mixed reference. You'll see how this works shortly.

The variable-expense section of the conference worksheet (see Figure 3.24) presents a perfect opportunity to experiment with mixed references. In the range E24..F26, you need to enter six instances of essentially the same formula. The formula should calculate the total expense amounts for each variable-expense category—that is, the per-person expense amount times the number of participants. Using mixed references, you can enter this formula once into cell E24. Then you can copy the formula in two directions: down column E and across to rows 24, 25, and 26. Here are the steps:

1. Select cell E24 and enter the + character to start the formula.

2. Press ← once to point to cell D24, the first of the per-person expense figures.

3. Press the F4 function key three times.

With each keypress, the address displayed in the contents box changes its format—from an absolute reference to various forms of mixed reference. The third time you press F4, the address appears as $A:$D24. When you later copy the formula to other rows, column D will remain fixed but the row number will change.

4. Press the * character.

5. Press ↑ sixteen times to point to cell E8, the minimum attendance estimate.

6. Press the F4 function key two times to produce the mixed reference $A:E$8. When you copy the formula, the column letter will change but row 8 will remain fixed.

7. Press ↵ to complete the formula entry.

3

Worksheet Essentials

The value 660 appears in cell E24. The cell's formula appears in the contents box as +$A:$D24*MINIMUM. 1-2-3 has substituted the range name for the mixed reference to cell $A:E$8.

There's nothing arbitrary about the formula you've just created. It contains the exact reference formats that allow you to copy the formula successfully in two directions. Here are the steps for copying the formula:

1. Select the range E24..F24.

2. Click the selection with the right mouse button, and choose Copy Right from the resulting quick menu. 1-2-3 copies the formula from cell E24 to F24.

3. Select the range E24..F26.

4. Click the selection with the right mouse button, and choose Copy Down from the quick menu. 1-2-3 copies the selected formulas from row 24 down to the cells in rows 25 and 26.

5. As a final step, produce the total variable-expense projections. Select the range E27..F27 and then click the Sum SmartIcon.

Figure 3.25 shows the result of your work. The best way to see the effect of mixed references on the copy operations you have just performed is to examine the six formulas in the range E24..F26:

+$A:$D24*MINIMUM	+$A:$D24*MAXIMUM
+$A:$D25*MINIMUM	+$A:$D25*MAXIMUM
+$A:$D26*MINIMUM	+$A:$D26*MAXIMUM

For each row, 1-2-3 has adjusted the row portion of the first reference ($A:$D24, $A:$D25, $A:$D26). Likewise, the second reference has been adjusted appropriately from MINIMUM in the first column to MAXIMUM in the second column.

Now you are ready to enter the formula for the projected profit. As you do so, you'll learn how to control the order in which operations are performed.

FIGURE 3.25

Copying a formula in
two directions

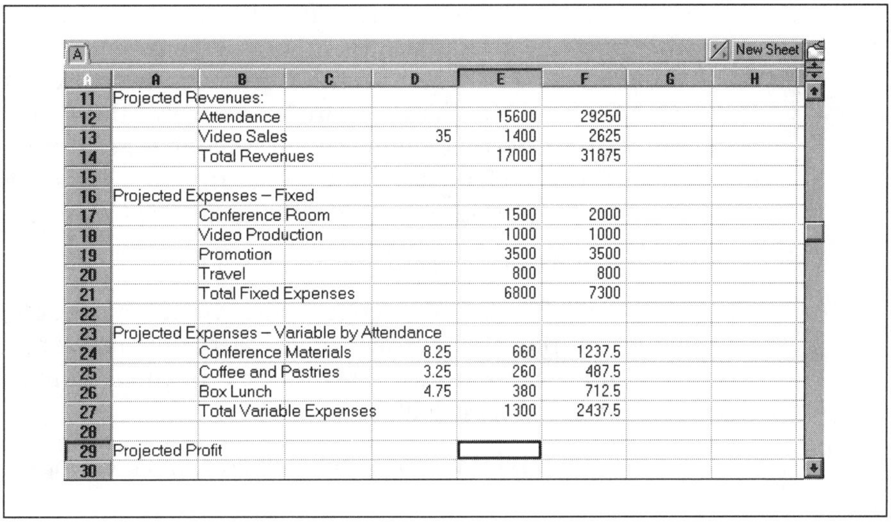

	A	B	C	D	E	F	G	H
11	Projected Revenues:							
12		Attendance			15600	29250		
13		Video Sales		35	1400	2625		
14		Total Revenues			17000	31875		
15								
16	Projected Expenses – Fixed							
17		Conference Room			1500	2000		
18		Video Production			1000	1000		
19		Promotion			3500	3500		
20		Travel			800	800		
21		Total Fixed Expenses			6800	7300		
22								
23	Projected Expenses – Variable by Attendance							
24		Conference Materials		8.25	660	1237.5		
25		Coffee and Pastries		3.25	260	487.5		
26		Box Lunch		4.75	380	712.5		
27		Total Variable Expenses			1300	2437.5		
28								
29	Projected Profit							
30								

Controlling the Order of Operations

By default, 1-2-3 follows standard mathematical rules for the *order of precedence*—that is, for deciding the order of operations in a formula that contains more than one operation. For example, here are the two rules governing the most common arithmetic operations:

- Multiplication and division are performed before addition and subtraction.

- Given operations of equal precedence, 1-2-3 performs the operations from left to right.

You can override the precedence rules by inserting pairs of parentheses in a formula. Operations enclosed in parentheses are performed before others. Furthermore, one pair of parentheses can be *nested* inside another pair; in this case, 1-2-3 begins with the operation inside the innermost parentheses.

3

Worksheet Essentials

The formula for calculating the bottom-line profit in the Conference worksheet requires parentheses. The profit is calculated as revenues minus expenses. But in this worksheet there are two groups of expenses, fixed and variable. To make sure that the two expense categories are added together before the subtraction is performed, you must enclose the expense references in parentheses. For example, here is the formula that you'll enter into cell E29 for the first profit projection:

    +E14-(E21+E27)

Cells E21 and E27 contain the two expense subtotals and cell E14 contains the total revenues. If you were to omit the parentheses from this formula, 1-2-3 would perform the operations from left to right, resulting in an incorrect calculation.

Enter this formula into cell E29 now, and then copy the formula over to F29:

1. Select cell E29 and enter the + character to begin the formula.

2. Use the mouse or the arrow keys on the keyboard to point to the total revenue figure in cell E14.

3. Type the minus sign and then the open parenthesis character, (. At this point the formula appears as +A:E14-(.

4. Point to the total fixed expense figure in cell E21.

5. Type the plus sign.

6. Point to the total variable-expense figure in cell E27.

7. Type the close-parenthesis character,).

In the contents box the formula now appears as +A:E14-(A:E21+A:E27). Notice that all the address references are relative. There is no need for absolute or mixed references for the upcoming copy operation.

8. Press ↵ to confirm the formula entry.

9. Use any of the copy techniques you've learned to copy the formula from cell E29 to cell E30.

10. Click the Save SmartIcon to save this version of the worksheet to disk.

The final version of the worksheet for this chapter appears in Figure 3.26.

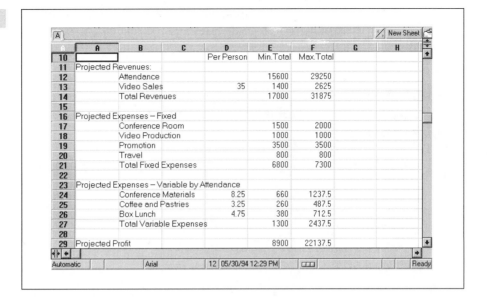

Examining "What-If" Scenarios

The Conference worksheet presents many opportunities for exploring variations in the plans and projections. For example, imagine that Computing Conferences, Inc., is considering the possibility of increasing the price of attendance from $195 to $225. In so doing, they anticipate a possible 15 percent decrease in attendance. They would like to see what happens to the projected profit under these combined circumstances.

To view the results of this scenario, revise three values in the worksheet:

1. Enter a value of 225, the new fee, in cell B8.

2. Enter a value of 68, the new minimum attendance, in cell E8.

3. Enter a value of 128, the new maximum attendance, in cell F8.

Each time you enter a new value, 1-2-3 instantly recalculates all the formulas that contain references to the revised cell. The split worksheet in Figure 3.27 shows the three revised values, and the new profit projections. Comparing this worksheet with Figure 3.26, you can see that the range

3

Worksheet Essentials

of profits in this scenario is down from the original projection. The company therefore decides against raising the price at this time.

	A	B	C	D	E	F	G	H
1		Computing Conferences, Inc.						
2		Profit Projection for a One-Day Conference						
3								
4	Conference:	Computing for Video Stores						
5	Place:	St. Louis						
6	Date:				Expected Attendance			
7					Minimum	Maximum		
8	Price:	225			68	128		
9								
10				Per Person	Min. Total	Max. Total		
11	Projected Revenues:							
12		Attendance			15300	28800		
13		Video Sales		35	1190	2240		
14		Total Revenues			16490	31040		

	A	B	C	D	E	F	G	H
27		Total Variable Expenses			1105	2080		
28								
29	Projected Profit				8585	21660		
30								
31								
32								

You might want to try other changes in the worksheet to see what happens to profits. For example, make the changes corresponding to each of these situations:

- The company is notified of a 10 percent price increase for the use of the conference room.

- Due to last-minute revisions in the curriculum, some conference materials have to be redone—increasing the cost of materials by $5 per person.

- The company decides to produce a radio commercial promoting the conference. The commercial adds $2,500 to promotion costs, but the company anticipates a possible 25 percent increase in attendance.

These and other experiments demonstrate the flexibility of the worksheet as a tool for exploring the variations and unknowns in any business projection.

When you finish these exercises, exit from 1-2-3 *without* saving the latest revisions to disk. You'll continue working with the Conference worksheet in Chapter 4, using the original data that you've already saved in the CONF.WK4 file. Specifically, you'll begin exploring the variety of formatting and style options available in 1-2-3, and you'll see the results of these options on the printed worksheet.

Summary

In the first steps of creating a new worksheet you're normally preoccupied with data entry and organization. To help you with these tasks, 1-2-3 has a variety of tools you can use to move and copy data from one location on the worksheet to another, or to delete entries from a cell or a range. You perform these procedures by choosing menu commands, clicking SmartIcons, or performing special mouse actions such as drag-and-drop.

When a command operates over a range of data, you often have the choice of preselecting the range before you choose the command, or of pointing to the range after the command's dialog box has appeared on the screen.

Once you've begun investing your time in a worksheet, you'll want to save your work to disk without much delay. The Save As command in the File menu gives you the opportunity to name your file and to add password protection if you wish. For subsequent updates of your worksheet file you can simply click the Save SmartIcon.

As you complete sections of numeric data in your worksheet, you can begin adding formulas to display calculated values. For producing totals at the bottom of a column or at the end of a row, 1-2-3 provides the convenient Sum SmartIcon. This tool automatically enters @SUM formulas onto your worksheet to calculate the totals of specified ranges of numbers.

3

Worksheet Essentials

In formulas that you write yourself, the use of range names can often make your work simpler and clearer. When you write a formula that you intend to copy to other locations on your worksheet, you must choose carefully among relative, absolute, and mixed address references. (While you are entering a formula, pressing the F4 function key cycles you through these reference types.) References determine how 1-2-3 ultimately copies your formula to other cells.

A well-organized worksheet becomes an ideal tool for investigating what-if questions. By making changes in key data items, you can find out what happens to totals and other calculated values under new assumptions.

Worksheet Formatting and Printing

fast TRACK

To change the width of a column on the worksheet,   183

use the mouse to drag the column's right border in the row of column letters at the top of the worksheet. Alternatively, double-click the border to find the best fit.

To left-align, center, or right-align the labels in a range of cells,   191

select the range and click one of the three alignment Smart-Icons—Left, Right, or Center.

To center a label over a horizontal range of cells,   191

select a horizontal range, where the first cell in the range contains the label that you want to center; then choose Style ➤ Alignment and select the options labeled Center and Across columns.

To apply a format globally to the numeric values on a worksheet,   201

choose Style ➤ Worksheet Defaults and select an option from the Format list.

To apply a format to a selected range on the worksheet,   203

select the range, choose Style ➤ Number Format, and select an option in the Format list. Alternatively, select an entry from the Format selector, the first panel on the status bar.

To display a date value in a cell,   210

> enter the date in a format that 1-2-3 recognizes (such as 10/15/94 or 15-Oct-94). 1-2-3 stores your entry as a date number, but displays it in a date format.

To display a time value in a cell,   218

> enter the time in a format that 1-2-3 recognizes (such as 7:00 PM or 19:00). 1-2-3 stores your entry into a decimal time value, but displays it in a time format.

To establish a protection scheme for a worksheet,   226

> choose Style ➤ Protection to establish one or more ranges that you want to remain unprotected. Then choose File ➤ Protect to seal the file.

To change the font or type size of a range on the worksheet,   230

> select the range and choose a new font and size in the Font and Point-size selectors from the status bar.

To define a print range,   238

> click the Print SmartIcon and enter the range into the resulting dialog box.

To see a preview of the printed worksheet,   238

> click the Preview SmartIcon, select a print range, and click OK.

AFTER you create a working table of data and formulas, your next task is to refine the appearance of your worksheet. You'll want to present information as clearly and attractively as possible—both for your own benefit as you work with data on the screen, and for other people who later see your work as a printed document. Lotus 1-2-3 for Windows gives you a wealth of choices for controlling the appearance of values and labels on a worksheet.

In this chapter you'll concentrate primarily on commands that affect the way your worksheet looks and functions. Specifically, you'll learn to accomplish the following tasks:

- Change column widths, both for the entire worksheet and for individual columns.

- Control the alignment of labels on the worksheet.

- Hide columns and ranges of data.

- Select numeric formats for the whole worksheet and for ranges on the worksheet.

- Enter date and time values in their appropriate formats—and then perform arithmetic operations with these values.

- Protect the worksheet from accidental revisions.

- Select styles, fonts, shadings, colors, and borders.

- Print the worksheet.

To practice these procedures, you'll return to the Conference worksheet you began developing in Chapter 3. In its current version, the worksheet is already a functioning tool for projecting the revenues, expenses, and profit of a future business event. Now you'll transform it into a lucid document that places appropriate emphasis on specific parts of the information.

Resuming Work on an Existing Worksheet

The first step is to reopen the Conference worksheet that you saved at the end of Chapter 3. Pull down the File menu and choose CONF.WK4 from the list of file names at the end of the menu. The Conference worksheet reappears on the screen, with all the work that you completed in the last chapter.

In upcoming exercises you'll be moving back and forth to specific ranges and cells on the Conference worksheet to change formats and styles. A tool that can speed you on your way to a specified location on the worksheet is the Go To command from the Edit menu.

Using the Go To Command

In response to the Go To command, the cell pointer jumps to a cell or range that you specify. To perform the command, pull down the Edit menu and choose Go To, or simply press the F5 function key. Either way, the Go To dialog box appears on the screen:

In this box you can enter the address of the cell to which you want to move, or you can select a range name from a list box that the command displays.

In the Go To box you can see the list of range names you've defined on the Conference worksheet. To jump to the cell or range represented by one of these names, highlight the name and press ↵, or double-click the selected name in the list. If you select a name that represents a range of cells, 1-2-3 highlights the range.

Now that the Conference worksheet is open, try the following exercise with the Go To command:

1. Press F5 to choose the command.

2. Highlight the EXPENSES name in the Range name list. (When the Go To dialog box first appears, you can press the Tab key and then the down-arrow key to highlight the first name in the list.)

3. Click the OK button or press ↵.

In response, 1-2-3 highlights the range E17..E20, the range you've named EXPENSES.

As you work through the exercises in this chapter, you'll find that the F5 function key—representing the Go To command—is a quick and convenient tool for moving to a particular location in the current worksheet window. In addition, you might also press F5 if you simply want to review a list of all the range names you have defined for your worksheet.

TIP

Keep in mind two similar tools that you've already learned about. You can click the Navigator button on the edit line to see a drop-down list of all the names defined for a worksheet. In addition, you can press the F3 function key while you are building a formula (in the Value, Edit, or Point modes) to view the Range Names dialog box, which also lists the names defined on a sheet. Note that the F3 key will not work unless at least one range name is already defined in the worksheet.

Making Adjustments in the Worksheet

While refining the appearance of your worksheet, you'll find that some worksheet properties can be changed in two ways:

- Globally for the entire worksheet.
- Selectively for one or more ranges on the worksheet.

Before modifying a given property, you have to decide whether you want to make the change for the whole worksheet or for a range on the worksheet. The Style menu provides commands for both of these options.

Changing Column Widths

Column width is an example of a visual property that you can change globally for the whole worksheet or individually for specific columns.

To increase or decrease the width of all columns, you choose the Style ➤ Worksheet Defaults command. In the resulting dialog box, shown in Figure 4.1, the Column width box has a default setting of 9. Under this default, each column in the worksheet is wide enough to display a nine-digit number in the default font, 12-point Arial. In the Column width box you can enter any value from 1 to 240 for the worksheet's global column width.

Take the following steps now to increase the global column width of the Conference worksheet to 11:

1. Choose Style ➤ Worksheet Defaults.

2. Change the Column width setting to 11. (You can enter the new value directly from the keyboard, or you can click the up-arrow icon twice with the mouse to increment the setting from 9 to 11.)

3. Click OK or press ↵.

FIGURE 4.1

The Worksheet
Defaults dialog box

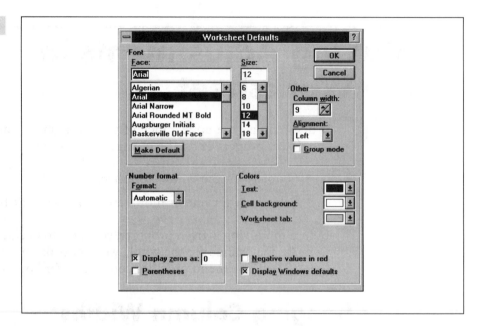

After you widen the columns, the data on your worksheet spreads out over almost the entire width of the screen area.

Changing the Width of a Single Column

The Style menu also has a Column Width command for changing the width of a single column or a range of columns. You can use this command to set the width numerically, to adjust a width appropriately to the contents of a column, or to restore column to the global width setting. As you can see in Figure 4.2, these choices are represented as option buttons

FIGURE 4.2

The Column Width
dialog box

in the Column Width dialog box.

To experiment with the Column Width dialog box, follow these steps to widen columns E and F to a setting of 13 characters:

1. Select the range E1..F1.

2. Pull down the Style menu and choose Column Width. In the resulting dialog box, the selected range appears in the Column(s) text box, as shown in Figure 4.2.

3. Enter a value of **13** in the Set width to text box.

4. Click OK or press ↵ to complete the operation.

Finally, there are two fast and convenient mouse techniques for changing the width of one column at a time. In both techniques, you change a width by moving the vertical border line between column headings at the very top of the worksheet. For example, to change the width of column C, you drag the line between the C and D headings. When you position the mouse pointer over this line, it changes to a double-headed arrow icon:

Here are the two ways you can use this mouse pointer:

- You can drag a column's border to the right to increase the column width, or the left to decrease it. This technique allows you to change a column visually. While you make the change, the Selection indicator box at the left side of the edit line shows you the numeric setting of the column width.

- You can double-click the left mouse button when the pointer is positioned over a border between two columns. In response, 1-2-3 resizes the column to its *best fit*—that is, the ideal width for the current contents of the column.

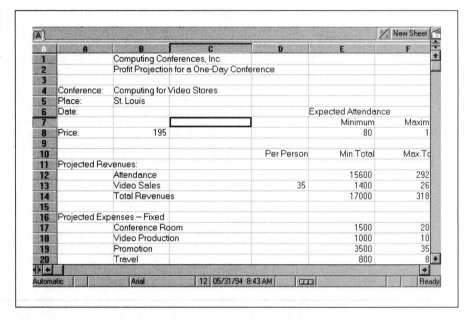

Try using the first of these two techniques to increase the width of column C:

1. Position the mouse pointer over the vertical border line between the C and D headings at the top border of the worksheet.

2. Drag the border to the right. As you do so, a moving border shows you where the new border will be when you release the mouse button. Move this border to a position just to the left of the D heading. (The Selection indicator on the edit line displays the setting as 16 characters.)

3. Release the mouse button.

Figure 4.3 shows the 1-2-3 window at this point in your work. Column F is now partly out of view because of the increased column widths.

Resizing a Column to Its "Best Fit"

In the Conference worksheet, changing the column widths is merely a first step in the process of improving the presentation of your data. In other cases, you may need to increase the widths of columns for a more basic reason—to enable your worksheet to display all of its numeric data. If a number in a cell is too long to fit in the width of the corresponding column, 1-2-3 replaces the numeric display with a string of asterisks. These asterisks tell you that you have to increase the column width in order to display the number itself.

Experiment with this effect in the following exercise:

1. Click the New Sheet button to add a temporary sheet B to the CONF.WK4 file.

2. With the cell pointer positioned at cell A1, click the Format selector, the first panel on the status bar. In the resulting pop-up list, choose the US Dollar option.

3. Type the value 123456789 in cell A1. When you press ↵, the cell fills with a string of asterisks:

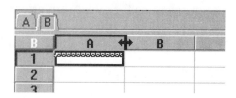

4. Now position the mouse pointer over the border between the A and B column headings, and double-click the left mouse button. 1-2-3 adjusts the column width appropriately, and you now see the number displayed as $123,456,789.00:

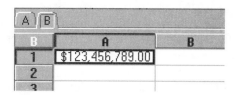

5. After you have examined the result of this exercise, click the sheet's B tab with the right mouse button, and choose the Delete command from the resulting quick menu. CONF.WK4 once again has only one sheet, labeled A.

In this experiment, the number in A1 wasn't displayed until you increased the column width appropriately.

Another interesting adjustment you can make in a worksheet is to *hide* a column completely.

Hiding Columns

You may want to hide one or more columns temporarily so that you can concentrate on other columns of data on your worksheet. Or you may have other reasons for hiding columns. If you're planning to distribute a particular worksheet to many people, you might decide to hide a column of sensitive or private information.

Whatever your reasons, you use the Hide command in the Style menu to hide a column. For example, imagine that you've decided to focus temporarily on the projections for maximum attendance on your Conference worksheet. You want to hide the column containing the minimum estimate, column E. Here are the steps for accomplishing this:

1. Move the cell pointer to E1.

2. Choose Style ➤ Hide. The Hide dialog box appears:

The Hide dialog box contains options for hiding a column or an entire sheet in a file; Column is the default. A reference to the cell E1 appears in the Range text box.

3. Click OK or press ↵ to complete the Hide operation. Press the Home key to move the cell pointer to A1.

At the end of these steps, column E disappears from the worksheet, as you can see in Figure 4.4. You can now concentrate on the data in column F.

FIGURE 4.4

Hiding a column

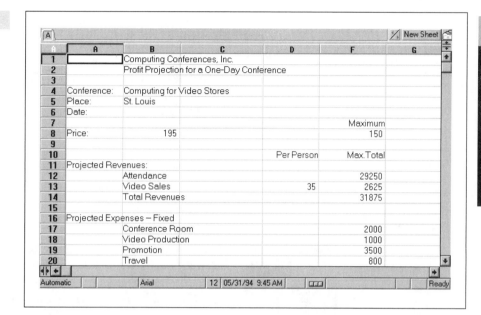

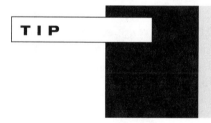

TIP

You can also use a mouse techique to hide a column: Drag the column's border to the left until you reach the right border of the previous column. Release the mouse button, and the column disppears. The effect is the same as choosing the Style ➤ Hide command.

At some point you'll want to restore the hidden data in column E. There are several ways to do this. You can choose Style ➤ Hide, enter a reference to a cell in the hidden column, and click Show. Alternatively, you can pre-select the range in which a column is hidden before you choose the command; for example, select D1..F1 and choose Style ➤ Hide ➤ Show to unhide column E.

Or you can postpone selecting the range until after choosing the command itself, as in the following steps:

1. Choose Style ➤ Hide.

2. Click the Range selector button, located just to the right of the Range text box in the Hide dialog box. The dialog box disappears temporarily.

3. Use the mouse to select the range D1..F1. (The hidden column E is located inside this range.) When you release the mouse button, the Hide dialog box returns to the screen.

4. Click the Show button to complete this operation.

The worksheet is restored to its original state, with all its columns in view. Column E has the column width setting you assigned it before the Hide operation.

NOTE

In a nutshell, here's a review of the various ways to select a target range for use in a 1-2-3 command. Select the range first and then choose the command. In the resulting dialog box, the Range box will contain a reference to the range you've preselected. You can also choose the command, and then enter a reference to a target range in the Range text box. Another way is to choose the command and then click the range selector button at the right side of the Range text box. The dialog box then disappears temporarily so you can select a target range on the worksheet itself.

You can also use the mouse to unhide a column, by dragging the border of the missing column. For example, to restore a hidden column E, you position the mouse pointer on the border between the letter headings for columns D and F and drag the border to the right. Column E reappears.

Once you've arranged the column widths the way you want them, you'll start formatting the data in specific ranges on the worksheet. One property that you've already begun to learn about is label alignment. In Chapter 3 you used double quotation mark prefixes to right-align the label entries Maximum and Minimum in their cells. Often it's easier to apply alignment properties to a range of entries *after* you enter the data onto the worksheet.

Aligning Data in Cells

 In Release 5, you can control the alignment of both numeric values and label entries. By default, labels are left-aligned in their cells and numbers are right-aligned; but you can apply left-, center-, or right-alignment options to any entry or range of entries in a worksheet.

 You can choose the Alignment command in the Style menu (or in the quick menu for a cell or range) to change data alignment, or you can simply select the data you want to realign and then click the Left, Center, or Right SmartIcon. (You can also apply a new default alignment for the entire worksheet by choosing Style ➤ Worksheet Defaults and selecting an option from the Alignment box; but this default setting applies only to labels, not to numeric entries.)

 When you set the alignment of a label, 1-2-3 automatically changes the label's prefix in the contents box. Three prefixes indicate a label's alignment:

PREFIX	ALIGNMENT
'	A single-quotation mark produces left-alignment, the default.
^	A caret symbol centers a label in its cell.
"	A double quotation mark produces right-alignment.

As a quick experiment with alignments, try changing the alignments of the labels in the range A4..A8 on the Conference worksheet. This range contains the labels Conference:, Place:, Date:, and Price:, all of which are initially left-aligned by default. Notice that a single quote appears as the prefix for each label in the contents box; for example:

　'Conference:

Here are the steps for examining the other possible alignments:

1. Preselect the range A4..A8.

2. Click the Center SmartIcon. The four labels are centered in their cells, and the prefix in the contents box changes to a caret symbol,

^Conference:

4	Conference:	Computing for Video Stores
5	Place:	St. Louis
6	Date:	
7		
8	Price:	195
9		

3. Click the Right SmartIcon. The labels are right-aligned, and the prefix changes to a double quote character:

4	Conference:	Computing for Video Stores
5	Place:	St. Louis
6	Date:	
7		
8	Price:	195
9		

4. As a demonstration of numeric alignment, select cell B8 (which currently contains the value 195) and click the Left SmartIcon. The numeric entry moves to the left side of the cell.

5. Right-alignment is a good choice for the labels in A4..A8, but a small adjustment is now necessary. Double-click the label in cell A4 to toggle into the Edit mode. Press the spacebar once to append a space to the end of the label, and then press ↵ to complete the edit.

6. Repeat this step for the other three labels, in cells A5, A6, and A8. On the printed worksheet this space will serve to separate the right-aligned labels in column A from the left-aligned data in column B.

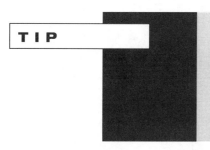

The previous exercise served as a reminder that 1-2-3 now allows in-cell editing. To edit any entry in a cell, you simply double-click the cell with the mouse, or select the cell and press F2. The contents box on the edit line is also available as a location for editing, but in-cell editing is generally more convenient.

You can change the alignment of long labels in two different ways—around a single cell or over a horizontal range of adjacent cells. For example, consider the two title lines of the Conference worksheet, in cells B1 and B2. If you select B1..B2 and click the Center SmartIcon, 1-2-3 centers the labels horizontally around the cells that contain them. Each centered label is displayed from column A to column C:

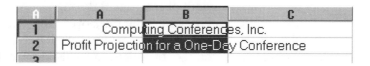

But 1-2-3 also gives you a simple way to center these titles horizontally over the worksheet. To do so, you begin by selecting a range for the centering operation and then you choose the Style ➤ Alignment command:

1. Select the range B1..E2 on the Conference worksheet.

2. Choose Style ➤ Alignment. In the Alignment dialog box, the Range text box contains a reference to the range you've selected.

3. Click the Across columns option, placing an *X* in the corresponding check box.

4. Click the Center option:

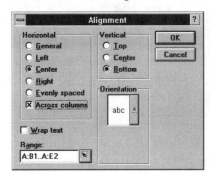

5. Click OK or press ↵ to complete the centering operation.

When you complete this procedure, 1-2-3 centers the two title labels horizontally within the width of columns B through E. As you can see in Figure 4.5, this approximately centers the titles over the worksheet area. However, the titles themselves are still contained in cells B1 and B2. Selecting each of these cells in turn, you see the following labels in the contents box:

    ^Computing Conferences, Inc.
    ^Profit Projection for a One-Day Conference

Notice that 1-2-3 uses the caret prefix for centering within either a single cell or a horizontal range of cells.

FIGURE 4.5

Centering titles over a horizontal range of cells

Repeating Characters

Lotus 1-2-3 has another label prefix that's not related to alignment. The backslash prefix (\) instructs 1-2-3 to fill a cell with a single repeating character or with a pattern of repeating characters. You can use this feature to create division lines or other visual effects in a cell or a row of cells.

Here is an exercise with the backslash prefix:

1. Click the New Sheet button to add a temporary sheet B to the CONF.WK4 worksheet.

2. Use the mouse to expand the width of column A to a setting of 50 (as shown in the Selection indicator box at the left side of the edit line).

3. Enter the following labels, one each into cells A1 through A6:

CELL	ENTER
A1	\( )
A2	\#!
A3	\.
A4	\-
A5	\ Lotus 1-2-3

Here's the result of these five entries:

When you've finished examining these visual effects, click the tab of sheet B with the right mouse button and choose Delete from the resulting quick menu. This action removes sheet B from the CONF.WK4 worksheet.

Holding Worksheet Titles on the Screen

As you know, you can scroll down the worksheet by pressing the PgDn key at the keyboard or by clicking in the vertical scroll bar. Normally when you scroll down by a window's length, the rows at the top of the worksheet disappear from view. Likewise, when you scroll to the right—by pressing Ctrl+→ or by clicking in the horizontal scroll bar—you normally lose sight of the columns located at the left of your worksheet. Sometimes you might want a way to hold a range of rows or columns on the screen, even when you scroll down or across the worksheet. The View ➤ Freeze Titles command "freezes" the top rows and/or left-hand columns on the worksheet, so that the information in these ranges always remains in view.

For example, on the Conference worksheet it would be convenient to freeze the first ten rows in the worksheet—the rows containing the worksheet title, the general information about the planned conference, and the column headings. In other words, you might like to have all this information stay in view as you scroll down the worksheet. Here are the steps for freezing these rows on the worksheet:

1. Move the cell pointer to cell A11. This is the row just below the range of rows that you want to freeze onto the screen.

2. Choose View ➤ Freeze Titles. The Freeze Titles dialog box appears:

The Freeze Titles dialog box gives you options for freezing a range of rows at the top of the worksheet, a range of columns at the left side of the worksheet, or both at once. On the Conference worksheet you want the Rows option, which is selected by default.

3. Click OK or press ↵ to complete the operation.

Now press the PgDn key to scroll down the worksheet. When you do so, the first ten rows remain in view, and scrolling takes place only in the lower half of the worksheet. For example, in Figure 4.6 the worksheet has been scrolled all the way down to the projected profit line, giving you a juxtaposed view of the summary information in the first ten rows along with the bottom-line profit. Notice that rows 11 through 27 do not appear on screen.

FIGURE 4.6

A range of frozen
rows at the top of the
worksheet

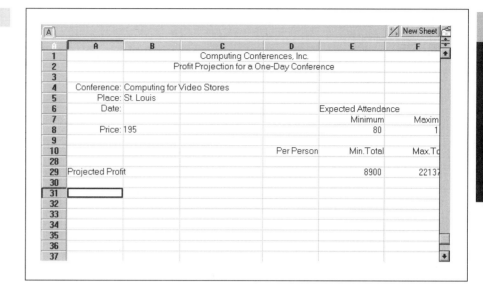

Interestingly enough, you can't use arrow keys or the mouse to move the
cell pointer into a frozen range. When you press the Home key the cell
pointer now jumps to cell A11 instead of A1. Furthermore, clicking the
mouse inside the frozen range has no effect. If you want to access the frozen range and edit some information there, you have two choices:

- Choose View ➤ Clear Titles to "unfreeze" the titles range.

- Press the F5 function key to open the Go To dialog box, and enter
  a reference to a cell within the frozen range.

Try pressing F5 now. Type a reference to cell A1 and click OK. 1-2-3 presents you temporarily with a second view of the frozen titles, as shown in
Figure 4.7. Inside this second view you can now edit entries in the range.
When you scroll down the worksheet, however, the second view is lost and
the top rows remain frozen.

Now choose View ➤ Clear Titles to clear the frozen rows. You can once
again move the cell pointer to any position within the first ten rows. Before you read on, you might want to try freezing columns at the left side
of the worksheet. For example, try establishing columns A and B as a titles

FIGURE 4.7

Using the Go To dialog box to access the frozen rows

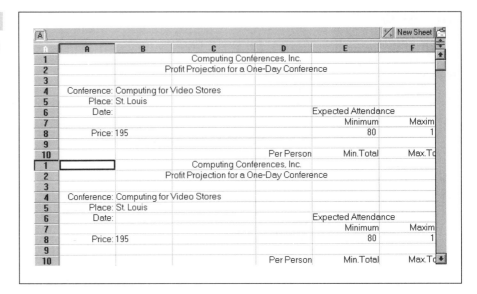

range. Then scroll toward the right side of the worksheet. What happens as you do so? What's the advantage of freezing these columns? Clear the frozen columns again when you are finished with this exercise.

Changing the View Preferences

Another significant change you can make in the appearance of the worksheet is removing the grid lines. Working with or without grid lines is a matter of personal preference; this option does not affect any other aspect of operations inside the worksheet.

To remove the grid lines, you switch off the Grid lines option in the Set View Preferences dialog box:

1. Choose View ➤ Set View Preferences. The Set View Preferences dialog box appears as shown at the top of the next page.

The Set View Preferences dialog box contains a variety of check-box options, representing visual components of the 1-2-3 window that you can switch on or off.

2. Click the Grid lines check box or press Alt+G from the keyboard. This removes the *X* from the check box.

3. Click OK or press ↵.

In response, 1-2-3 removes the grid lines from the worksheet window, as you can see in Figure 4.8. You can restore them by choosing View ➤ Set View Preferences again and checking the Grid lines box.

FIGURE 4.8

Removing the grid lines from the worksheet window

	A	B	C	D	E	F
1			Computing Conferences, Inc.			
2			Profit Projection for a One-Day Conference			
3						
4	Conference: Computing for Video Stores					
5	Place: St. Louis					
6	Date:				Expected Attendance	
7					Minimum	Maxim
8	Price: 195				80	1
9						
10				Per Person	Min.Total	Max.To
11	Projected Revenues:					
12		Attendance			15600	292
13		Video Sales		35	1400	26
14		Total Revenues			17000	318
15						
16	Projected Expenses – Fixed					
17		Conference Room			1500	20
18		Video Production			1000	10
19		Promotion			3500	35
20		Travel			800	8

Other Set View Preferences options allow you to remove or display a variety of standard objects in the current worksheet window, including the frame row and column headings around the worksheet, the row of tabs above the worksheet, and the scroll bars. The Custom zoom text box allows you to change the size of cells as they are displayed on the screen—increasing the size by as much as 400 percent, or decreasing it by as much as 25 percent. For example, here is a detail of the worksheet, zoomed up to 200 percent:

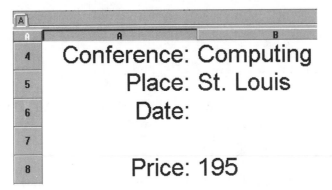

And here is the worksheet zoomed down to 40 percent:

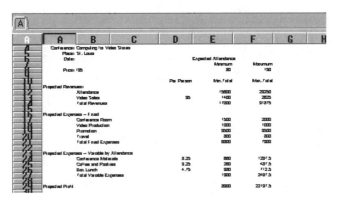

TIP

The Zoom In, Zoom Out, and Custom commands in the View menu provide additional methods to change the zoom view of the current worksheet. Zoom In increases the view size by 10 percent each time you choose the command, and Zoom Out decreases the view size by 10 percent. The Custom command returns to the view size specified in the Set View Preferences dialog box.

Finally, the View ➤ Set View Preferences command has three options that apply to the elements of the 1-2-3 window rather than to the current worksheet. You can hide or display the SmartIcon line, the edit line, and the status bar by clicking options located at the bottom of the dialog box. You might occasionally want to turn these elements off in order to increase the visible area of a particular worksheet. Turn them on again by choosing View ➤ Set View Preferences and clicking the appropriate check boxes.

Formatting Values on a Worksheet

One way to give meaning to a numeric value on your worksheet is to pair the value with a descriptive label. A number and an adjacent label together form a clearly identified item of information; for example:

Price: 195

But another important technique for establishing the meaning of numbers—and to improve the general readability of your worksheet—is to apply appropriate formats to numeric values:

Price: $195.00

Lotus 1-2-3 provides standard numeric formats that you can assign to the numbers on your worksheet. Like other worksheet properties, you can apply formats globally to the entire worksheet, or selectively to particular cells or ranges. A format does not change the numeric value entered into a cell, only the way the number is displayed in the cell.

You can apply most formats either before or after you enter values onto your worksheet. The Style ➤ Worksheet Defaults command establishes formats for the entire worksheet. As shown in Figure 4.9, the Number format group in the lower-left quadrant of the Worksheet Defaults dialog box contains a pull-down Format list.

FIGURE 4.9

The Format list in the Worksheet Defaults dialog box

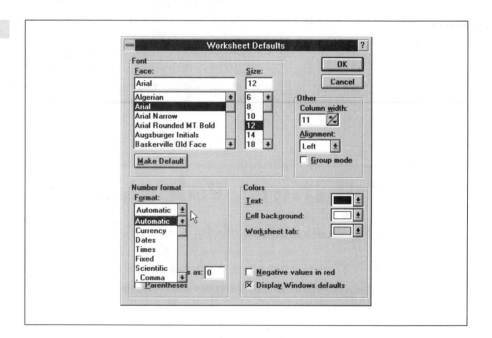

When you select a format from the list, additional options may appear in the dialog box. For example, when you choose the Currency format, 1-2-3 supplies a Decimals box for specifying the number of digits that will appear after the decimal point; a Currency list for selecting an international currency format; and a Modify Symbol button for changing the symbol or format for a selected currency:

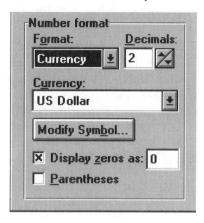

The Style ➤ Number Format command supplies a similar arrangement of options, designed for applying formats to a selected range on the worksheet rather than the entire worksheet. As shown in Figure 4.10, the Number Format dialog box also has a Reset command button (below the Cancel button); clicking this button resets the format to the current default for the worksheet.

FIGURE 4.10

The Number Format dialog box

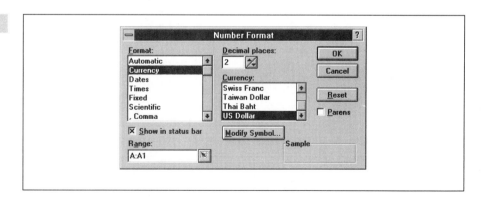

TIP

Notice the check box labeled "Show in status bar" in the Number Format dialog box. This check box gives you the opportunity to modify the list of formats that appear in the number format list that you access from the Format selector, the first panel in the status bar. To include or exclude a format, select its name in the Format box, and click the Show check box.

Using Common Numeric Formats

The worksheet in Figure 4.11 shows examples of commonly used formats. Column C on this worksheet displays the six available numeric formats:

FORMAT	DESCRIPTION
Fixed	Displays values with a specified number of decimal places, up to fifteen.
Scientific	Displays numbers in an exponent notation, where the digits after the letter E represent the power of 10 by which the base value is multiplied.
US Dollar Currency	Displays a dollar sign at the beginning of the number, and a comma before every third digit at the left of the decimal point.
Comma	Displays a comma before every third digit at the left of the decimal point.
General	Displays a value without special formatting.
Percent	Multiplies the displayed value by 100 and appends a percent sign.

FIGURE 4.11

Examples of numeric formats

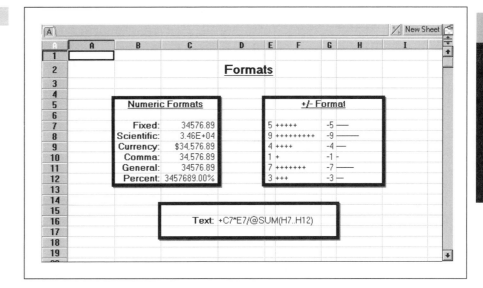

Examples of two other formats appear in Figure 4.11. The +/- format transforms the display of a value into a string of plus or minus signs. This format is useful for creating simple character-based horizontal bar graphs on a worksheet. (In Figure 4.11, the +/- format has been applied in columns F and H. Column F contains the same positive numbers as are displayed in column E. Likewise, column H contains the same negative values displayed in column G.)

Finally, the Text format operates on a cell that contains a formula. Under this format, the cell displays the text of the formula itself rather than the formula's numeric result, as you can see in cell D16 of Figure 4.11. If you want to examine all the formulas on your worksheet at once, choose Style ➤ Worksheet Defaults and select Text as the global format.

You'll recall that first panel of the "live" status bar gives you a useful shortcut for changing the number formats for a selected range of values on a worksheet (see page 95). The Format selector considerably simplifies the process of formatting values:

1. Select a cell or range of cells containing numeric entries.

2. Click the first panel in the status bar. The Format selector list pops up on the screen, as shown on the next page.

```
Automatic
Fixed
Scientific
, Comma
General
Percent
Text
Hidden
Label
British Pound
Canadian Dollar
Japanese Yen
Mexican Peso
US Dollar
31-Dec-93
31-Dec
Dec-93
12/31/93
12/31
11:59:59 AM
11:59 AM
23:59:59
23:59
Reset
```

3. Select a format from the list.

You'll have a chance to practice using this technique as you change the numeric formats on the Conference worksheet.

Selecting Global and Range Formats

Because most of the values on the Conference worksheet are dollar-and-cent figures, it is convenient to assign a global Currency format to the worksheet and then go back and change the formats of figures that are not dollars and cents. Here are the steps:

1. Choose Style ➤ Worksheet Defaults.

2. In the Worksheet Defaults dialog box (see Figure 4.9), pull down the Format list.

3. Select the Currency format in the list. (Don't change the default settings of 2 in the Decimals box or US Dollar in the Currency box.)

4. Click OK or press ↵ to confirm the default format selection.

As a result, all of the values on the worksheet are displayed as dollar-and-cent values. But the worksheet currently contains two values that should be displayed as simple integers: the minimum and maximum attendance estimates in cells E8 and F8. You can use the Format selector from the status bar to change these two values to an appropriate format:

1. Select the range E8..F8.

2. Click the Format selector, the first panel on the status bar.

3. Select the Automatic option in the list.

In Figure 4.12 you can see the changes that take place in your worksheet when you complete these formatting operations.

FIGURE 4.12

Formatting values on the Conference worksheet

	E	F
6	Expected Attendance	
7	Minimum	Maximum
8	80	150
9		
10	Min.Total	Max.Total
11		
12	$15,600.00	$29,250.00
13	$1,400.00	$2,625.00
14	$17,000.00	$31,875.00
15		
16		
17	$1,500.00	$2,000.00
18	$1,000.00	$1,000.00
19	$3,500.00	$3,500.00
20	$800.00	$800.00
21	$6,800.00	$7,300.00
22		

The Number Format dialog box offers a great variety of international currency formats—for example, British Pound (£), French Franc (FF), and Japanese Yen (¥), along with the US Dollar ($). (The Format selector list from the status bar also includes a selection of these formats.) If you're building a worksheet that displays international currencies, you may want to reverse the roles of commas and periods, as is the common notation in some currencies. For example, you may want to change FF 1,234.50 to FF 1.234,50. To make this change, choose the Tools ➤ User Setup command and click the International button. Then make a new selection in the Punctuation list:

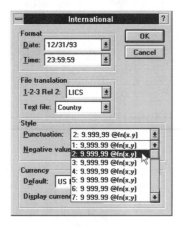

Using the Automatic Format

Two additional formats—Label and Automatic—determine how 1-2-3 will accept new data entries on a worksheet. In effect, these formats represent special data-entry modes:

- **Label.** Label accepts all new entries on the worksheet as labels, even if they begin with digits or other characters that would normally trigger the Value entry mode.

- **Automatic.** Automatic applies a format according to the way you initially enter a value into a cell. For example, if you enter a value as a currency, a date, or a percentage, 1-2-3 automatically applies the corresponding numeric format to the cell. If you subsequently enter a different value into the same cell, the new value is displayed in the existing format. Automatic is the default format in new worksheets.

In the following exercise you'll experiment with the effect of the Automatic format. You'll begin by using the File ➤ New command to open a new worksheet file.

TIP

Keep in mind the distinction between the New Sheet button and File ➤ New command. The New Sheet button adds an additional sheet—labeled B, C, D, and so on—to the current file. The File ➤ New command opens a new worksheet file. (As you learned in Chapter 2 on page 102, Lotus 1-2-3 allows you to work with multiple open files concurrently.) Depending upon the status of a specific User Setup option, the File ➤ New command works in one of two ways: it opens a new worksheet file immediately, or it displays the New File dialog box. If you want to skip this dialog box, choose Tools ➤ User Setup and place an *X* in the option box labeled "Skip New File dialog box." Click OK to confirm. Next time you choose the File ➤ New command, 1-2-3 will create a new worksheet immediately without displaying a dialog box.

1. Choose File ➤ New. (If the New File dialog box appears, make sure there's an *X* in the check box labeled "Create a plain worksheet." Then click OK.)

1-2-3 opens a new worksheet file. As you can see in the first panel of the status bar, Automatic is the default format in this new file.

2. Type **$1234.56** into cell A1. You haven't included a comma in your entry, but the initial dollar sign is enough to assign the US Dollar currency format to the cell. Press ↵ and note the results. The cell displays the new entry as $1,234.56, and the status bar reports the cell's format as US Dollar.

3. Enter a new numeric value, **6543.21**, into the same cell. The US Dollar format applies to this new entry, which is displayed as $6,543.21.

4. Now select cell A2 and enter **27%**. The status bar identifies the automatic format as Percent.

5. Try entering a new value in A2, such as **.88**. The value is displayed as 88%.

6. Select cell A3 and enter a date: **15-Apr-95**. As you can see in the status bar, 1-2-3 automatically applies a date format to the cell. You'll learn more about date entries in the next section of this chapter.

7. When you've finished examining the results of this exercise, choose File ➤ Close and click the No button on the resulting dialog box to close the worksheet window without saving it.

Entering Dates in a Worksheet

Lotus 1-2-3 has a versatile collection of tools for working with calendar dates. You can enter dates on your worksheet as specially formatted values. Then you can use date entries in operations known as *date arithmetic*. For example, you can:

- Find the number of days between any two dates.

- Find the date that is a specified number of days forward or backward from another date.

Performing these two operations is a complicated programming task in some software environments, but in 1-2-3 you can accomplish them with simple arithmetic formulas, as you'll see shortly.

A date can be recorded as a label or a value in a 1-2-3 worksheet. If you want to display a date, but you have no plans to use the date in arithmetic operations, a label entry is probably the simpler option. 1-2-3 generally accepts a date entry as a label when you begin the date with the name of a month, for example:

October 15, 1994

But if you anticipate working with the date entry in any calendar-related calculations, you must enter the date as a value. To use date values successfully, it's important to understand the date system used in Lotus 1-2-3. The system relies on 1-2-3's ability to convert date entries into *date numbers*, assigning an integer equivalent to any date between January 1, 1900 and December 31, 2099. The first of these dates, January 1, 1900, is day 1 in the date number system, and each date forward is numbered consecutively—that is, 1 greater than the previous date. Here is a sampling of date numbers in this system:

DATE	DATE NUMBER
January 1, 1900	1
January 2, 1900	2
May 10, 1910	3783
December 1, 1945	16772
March 2, 1976	27821
October 15, 1992	33892
December 31, 2099	73050

When you enter a value in one of the five formats that 1-2-3 recognizes as a date, the entry is stored as a date number. Here's how these five formats are represented in the Format selector from the status bar:

The first three formats use a three-character month abbreviation, along with two digits each for the month and/or year; for example:

15-Jun-95

15-Jun

Jun-95

The second two formats—named *Long International Date* and *Short International Date*—have defaults corresponding to these examples:

06/15/95

06/15

TIP You can select a different setting for the two international date formats. Choose Tools ➤ User Setup, click the International button, and choose a new setting in the Date list.

In summary, to create a date entry in a worksheet cell you simply enter the date in a format that 1-2-3 recognizes. Lotus 1-2-3 converts your entry into the corresponding date number. To practice this technique, return now to the Conference worksheet. Cell B6 is set aside for the date of the conference, but the cell is still empty. Here are the steps for entering this date:

1. Select cell B6 and type the date of the conference as follows:

   15-Oct-94

   Press ↵ and then examine the contents box.

The corresponding date number is displayed as 34622. This same value is displayed in the cell itself, incongruously in the worksheet's default US Dollar format, $34,622.00. Obviously, you need to change the cell's format to display the date.

2. Click the Format selector, the first panel of the status bar, and choose the first date format on the list, represented as 31-Dec-93. The entry in cell B6 is now displayed correctly as a date.

3. Click the Left SmartIcon to change the alignment of the date displayed in the cell.

Now the date is displayed in the format you've selected:

4	Conference: Computing for Video Stores
5	Place: St. Louis
6	Date: 15-Oct-94
7	
8	Price: $195.00

You can save time by using the default Automatic format, especially in a worksheet that requires many date entries. Under this format you can enter a date that 1-2-3 recognizes, and the date format will automatically be assigned to the cell. Try this technique in the following exercise:

1. Click cell B6 with the right mouse button, and choose Clear from the resulting quick menu. Select the Both option in the Clear dialog box, and click OK:

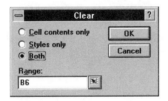

This action clears both the contents and the format of the cell. (The cell's format is now US Dollar, the default format for the entire worksheet.)

2. Click the Format selector, the first panel in the status bar, and choose the Automatic option from the pop-up list of number formats.

3. In cell B6, reenter the date in the same format as before: **15-Oct-94**.

This time the date value retains the format in which you entered it. The contents box on the edit line displays the date number equivalent, 34622.

4. Click the Left SmartIcon to realign the entry.

5. Click the Save SmartIcon to save the work you have done on the worksheet up to now in this chapter.

Now that you have learned how to enter and format a date value, the following section will guide you through a brief exercise in date arithmetic. Along the way, you'll learn to use a SmartIcon that copies formatting instructions from one range to another.

Performing Date Arithmetic

Computing Conferences, Inc., has decided to offer discounts to participants who enroll and pay in advance for admission to the conference. There will be a 10 percent discount for payments received 45 days in advance, and a 20 percent discount for payments received 90 days in advance. Accordingly, the conference organizers want to develop a small worksheet that formulates and displays the discount schedule.

In the following steps you begin developing this schedule by adding a second sheet to the CONF.WK4 file. You've temporarily added new sheets to this file in previous exercises, but this time you'll save the new sheet as a permanent part of the file.

1. Click the New Sheet button. Sheet B is added to the window, and becomes the current worksheet.

2. To simplify the data-entry task ahead of you, restore the gridlines to the worksheet. (You can remove them again later if you want.) Choose View ➤ Set View Preferences, and click the Grid lines option. An *X* appears in the corresponding check box. Click OK to confirm.

3. Choose View ➤ Split and select the Perspective option. Then click OK. You can now see sheets A and B in a single window.

4. In cell B:A2 enter the title **Discount Schedule for Advance Enrollment**.

5. In worksheet A, select the range A:A4..A:B8, which contains the basic information about the conference. Press Ctrl+C to copy this information to the Clipboard.

6. In sheet B, select cell B:A4 and press Ctrl+V. A copy of the conference information appears in worksheet B. Choose View ➤ Clear Split to toggle back into a view of worksheet B alone.

4

Formatting and Printing

7. Select cell B:B8, click the Format selector, the first panel in the status bar, and choose US Dollar from the pop-up list of numeric formats.

8. Enter the following three headings:

CELL	ENTER
B:B10	**If paid by:**
B:C10	**Discount**
B:D10	**Price**

9. Select the range B:B10..B:D10 and click the Right SmartIcon. The alignment of the column headings in these three cells will now match the alignment of the numeric values that will appear beneath them.

At this point in the process, worksheet B appears as shown in Figure 4.13.

FIGURE 4.13

Creating a discount schedule on sheet B

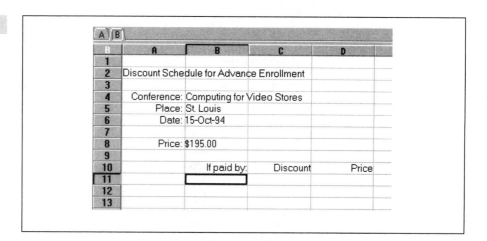

The next step is to write formulas in cells B:B11 and B:B12 to display the deadline dates for the two discount rates. Because cell B:B6 contains an entry representing the date of the conference, you'll create formulas that subtract the appropriate number of days from this date.

Enter the following formula in B:B11:

+B:B6–90

As you can see, this formula subtracts a value of 90 (representing 90 days) from the date number stored in cell B6. The result displayed in cell B6 is 34532. Now enter the following formula into cell B:B12 to subtract 45 days from the conference date:

+B:B6–45

The result is 34577.

Now you have to format these two cells so they'll appear as dates. You can use the Copy Styles SmartIcon to duplicate the format that is already applied to the date in cell B6:

1. Select cell B:B6, which has the format that you want to copy.

2. Click the Copy Styles SmartIcon. When you move the mouse pointer over the worksheet, the pointer takes on the form of a paint brush icon.

3. Select cells B:B11..B:B12, the range over which you want to apply the specified format. When you release the mouse button, the two entries in this range are displayed as dates.

4. Click the Right SmartIcon to right-justify these entries in their cells.

As you can see, the Copy Styles SmartIcon is an extremely convenient way to apply an existing format to a new range of cells.

Now follow these steps to complete the discount schedule worksheet:

1. Enter a value of **20%** in cell B:C11 and a value of **10%** in B:C12.

2. Select cell B:D11 and enter the following formula:

+$B:$B$8*(1–B:C11)

(Use the pointing technique to create the formula. Type a plus sign and then click cell B8 with the mouse. Press F4 to change the address to an absolute reference. Then continue the formula. Notice that the reference to cell C11 remains as a relative reference.)

3. Use the drag-and-drop technique to copy this formula into cell B:D12. The copied formula—adjusted for its position relative to the original formula—appears as +$B$8*(1–C12).

4. Select the range B:D11..B:D12, click the Format selector, the first panel of the status bar, and choose the US Dollar format from the resulting list.

Changing the labels on worksheet tabs Now that the CONF.WK4 file contains two sheets, you should take this opportunity to change the tab labels for each sheet. As you know, the initial names for multiple sheets in a worksheet file are letters of the alphabet (A, B, C, and so on). But you can easily change these names. To do so you simply double-click a tab, type a new name, and press ⏎. Try changing the names sheets A and B now:

1. Double-click tab A, type **Conference** as the new sheet name, and press ⏎.

2. Double-click tab B, type **Discounts** as the name, and press ⏎.

Figure 4.14 shows the result of your work in sheet B, now called Discounts.

FIGURE 4.14

Completing and naming the discount sheet

	A	B	C	D
1				
2	Discount Schedule for Advance Enrollment			
3				
4	Conference:	Computing for Video Stores		
5	Place:	St. Louis		
6	Date:	15-Oct-94		
7				
8	Price:	$195.00		
9				
10		If paid by:	Discount	Price
11		17-Jul-94	20%	$156.00
12		31-Aug-94	10%	$175.50
13				

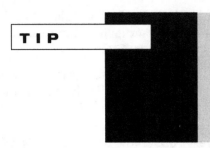

T I P

For an even clearer way to distinguish between different sheets in a file, you can display sheet tabs in color. Select the sheet whose tab you want to change, choose Style ➤ Worksheet Defaults, and click the down-arrow button next to the Worksheet tab box. Select a color from the resulting palette and then click OK.

Entering Time Values into a Worksheet

You can also use a worksheet to work with chronological values—that is, time values during a 24-hour day. Like a date, a time value is stored in a cell as a number. To display the value as a time you use one of the time formats that 1-2-3 recognizes. Then you can perform a variety of *time arithmetic* operations, such as:

- Finding the number of minutes between two time values in a 24-hour day.

- Finding the point in time that is a specified number of minutes forward or backward from another time value.

Once again, it's useful to learn how 1-2-3 translates time values into numbers before you try to perform operations like these. A time number is a fractional value, expressed as a decimal. Specifically, the fraction expresses the portion of the 24-hour day that has gone by at a particular time. For example, the time value for 12:00 noon is .5, because one-half of the day has elapsed at noon. Here is a sampling of other time values and their equivalent time numbers:

3:00 AM	.125	One-eight of the day
6:00 AM	.25	One-fourth of the day
9:00 AM	.375	Three-eighths of the day
6:00 PM	.75	Three-fourths of the day
9:00 PM	.875	Seven-eighths of the day

To enter a time value in a cell, you type the value in a chronological format that 1-2-3 recognizes. Here are the four available formats, as shown in the Format selector list from the status bar:

The first two are AM/PM formats, and the second two are 24-hour international formats.

TIP

You can select a new international time format by choosing Tools ➤ User Setup, clicking the International button, and selecting a format in the Time list.

When you enter a value in any one of these four formats, 1-2-3 recognizes your entry as a time and stores the entry as a decimal time number. In the default Automatic format, the time format of your entry is applied to the cell.

In your first exercise with time values, you'll add yet another worksheet to the CONF.WK4 file—this time, the worksheet named C. You'll begin by entering one time value onto this worksheet, but then you'll use the sheet to build another document for Computer Conferences, Inc. Here are the beginning steps:

1. Select Discounts as the active sheet, and then click the New Sheet button. 1-2-3 adds sheet C to the file.

2. Select cell C:D8 for this first entry. (You'll see why shortly.) In the cell, enter the value **7:00 AM**. 1-2-3 automatically applies a time format to the cell.

3. As an experiment with the value you've entered, click the Format selector, the first panel on the status bar, and select General from the number format list.

In response, 1-2-3 displays the numeric equivalent of the time entry, 0.291667. This is the fraction of the day that has gone by at 7:00 AM.

4. To restore the entry to its original time format, click the first panel on the status bar and choose the time format represented as 11:59 AM.

In the next section you'll use this time entry as the starting point for an exercise in time arithmetic.

Performing Time Arithmetic

The conference organizers at Computing Conferences, Inc., are ready to begin planning the schedule for the one-day conference in St. Louis. During the course of the conference day there will be four major presentations, each lasting between one and two hours. In addition, there will be miscellaneous other activities, including an introduction, an hour of hands-on demonstrations, coffee breaks, and lunch. The planners therefore want to develop a worksheet that calculates the day's schedule, given the length of each event. They also want to be able to adjust the length of time allotted to a given activity, and immediately see the effect on the whole schedule.

You'll develop this schedule on worksheet C. Begin with the following formatting and data-entry tasks:

1. Select cell D8 and click the Copy Styles SmartIcon. Then drag the paint brush mouse pointer over the range C:D9..C:D18.

When you release the mouse button, 1-2-3 applies the time format to each cell in this range. (Because the range D9..D18 contains no data yet, no visible change takes place on the sheet.)

2. Press the Home key to select cell A1, and enter the following title into the cell:

Conference Schedule

3. Click the Discounts sheet tab to activate worksheet B. Select the range B:A4..B:B6 and press Ctrl+C to copy this selection to the Clipboard. Then click the C tab, select cell C:A3, and press

Ctrl+V to paste a copy of these entries to the new sheet.

4. Enter the following column headings:

CELL	ENTER
C:A7	**Event**
C:D7	**Start Time**
C:E7	**Minutes**

5. Select the range C:D7..C:E7 and click the Right SmartIcon to align the latter two column headings with the numeric entries that will eventually appear below them. Select the range C:A7..C:E7 and click the Bold SmartIcon.

6. Enter the following list of event descriptions into column A, from C:A8 to C:A18:

CELL	ENTER
C:A8	**Coffee and Pastries**
C:A9	**Introduction**
C:A10	**Managing a Video Database**
C:A11	**Coffee Break**
C:A12	**Managing a Customer Database**
C:A13	**Hands-on Demonstrations**
C:A14	**Lunch and Discussion**
C:A15	**Setting Up a Computer System**
C:A16	**Coffee Break**
C:A17	**Software Options**
C:A18	**No-Host Cocktail Hour**

7. In column E, from C:E8 to C:E18, enter values representing the planned length, in minutes, of each event:

CELL	ENTER
C:E8	**45**
C:E9	**30**
C:E10	**90**

C:E11	15
C:E12	120
C:E13	60
C:E14	60
C:E15	120
C:E16	30
C:E17	60
C:E18	60

8. Select cell C:D9 to prepare for the upcoming formula entry.

The result of your work appears in Figure 4.15.

FIGURE 4.15

Creating a Schedule worksheet

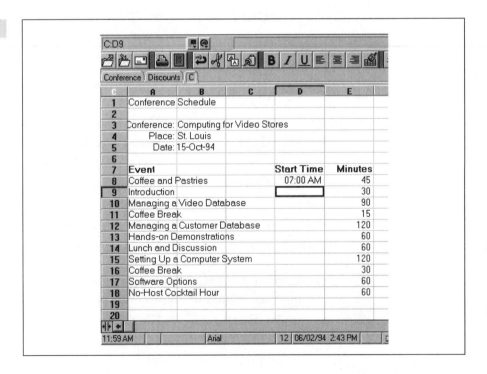

4

Formatting and Printing

TIP

In a worksheet that contains as much text as this one, you may want to check for spelling errors after you've completed the data entry. Choose Tools ➤ Spell Check and select the Current worksheet option on the resulting dialog box. Click OK, and 1-2-3 begins checking the spelling on the active sheet. For any word that 1-2-3 doesn't find in its dictionary, the Spell Check dialog box highlights the unknown word and provides possible alternatives. To correct the error, select the appropriate alternative and click Replace.

You now need to write a formula in D9 that calculates the starting time of the second event. The formula should be simple enough: Add the length in minutes of the first event (C:E8) to the starting time of the first event (C:D8). But there is one complication—the worksheet expresses these two values in incompatible terms. The starting time is stored as a decimal time number, and the length of the event is expressed in minutes. To add the two values you must first find a way to convert them into common terms.

In this worksheet, the best approach is to convert the minutes to a decimal time value. The following expression calculates the fraction of a 24-hour day represented by the minutes in cell C:E8:

    +C:E8/(60*24)

Multiplying 60 by 24 gives the number of minutes in a day. Dividing the value in cell E8 by this number results in the appropriate decimal time value. Given this expression, here is the formula that calculates the starting time of the second event:

    +C:D8+C:E8/(60*24)

In the following steps you'll use the pointing technique to enter this formula into cell D9. Then you'll copy the formula down the appropriate range in column D:

1. With the cell pointer positioned at D9, type **+** to start the formula entry.

2. Press ↑ once to point to the starting time in D8. Then type **+** again.

3. Press ↑ and → once each to point to the value in cell E8. Then complete the formula by typing **/(60*24)**. Press ↵ to confirm the formula entry. Cell D9 displays 07:45 AM as the formatted time value.

4. Press Ctrl+C to copy this formula to the Clipboard. Then select D10..D18 and press Ctrl+V to paste a copy of the formula to each cell in the range.

5. Double-click the C tab and type **Schedule** as the new name for this sheet. Press ↵ to confirm the new name.

Figure 4.16 shows the schedule worksheet. Examine the formulas that 1-2-3 has copied into cells D9 through D18. Do you see why relative references were appropriate for the addresses in this copy operation?

FIGURE 4.16

Entering and copying the formula to calculate the schedule

	A	B	C	D	E
	Conference	Discounts	Schedule		
1	Conference Schedule				
2					
3	Conference:	Computing for Video Stores			
4	Place:	St. Louis			
5	Date:	15-Oct-94			
6					
7	Event			Start Time	Minutes
8	Coffee and Pastries			07:00 AM	45
9	Introduction			07:45 AM	30
10	Managing a Video Database			08:15 AM	90
11	Coffee Break			09:45 AM	15
12	Managing a Customer Database			10:00 AM	120
13	Hands-on Demonstrations			12:00 PM	60
14	Lunch and Discussion			01:00 PM	60
15	Setting Up a Computer System			02:00 PM	120
16	Coffee Break			04:00 PM	30
17	Software Options			04:30 PM	60
18	No-Host Cocktail Hour			05:30 PM	60
19					
20					

Automatic | Arial | 12 | 06/02/94 2:57 PM

Now the conference planners want to adjust the schedule for the morning events. They want lunch to take place one-half hour earlier than its currently scheduled time at 1:00 PM. To accomplish this, they decide to reduce the time for the second presentation—"Managing a Customer Database," in row 12—by thirty minutes.

Enter a new value of 90 in cell C:E12, and watch what happens to the schedule. All the starting times from C:D13 down are adjusted for the half-hour change, as shown in Figure 4.17. The schedule worksheet is working according to design.

FIGURE 4.17

Changing the schedule

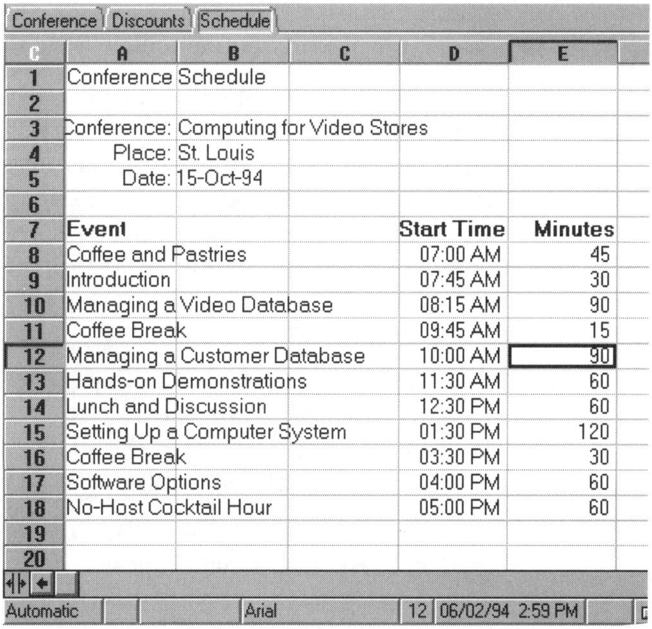

	A	B	C	D	E
1	Conference Schedule				
2					
3	Conference:	Computing for Video Stores			
4	Place:	St. Louis			
5	Date:	15-Oct-94			
6					
7	Event			Start Time	Minutes
8	Coffee and Pastries			07:00 AM	45
9	Introduction			07:45 AM	30
10	Managing a Video Database			08:15 AM	90
11	Coffee Break			09:45 AM	15
12	Managing a Customer Database			10:00 AM	90
13	Hands-on Demonstrations			11:30 AM	60
14	Lunch and Discussion			12:30 PM	60
15	Setting Up a Computer System			01:30 PM	120
16	Coffee Break			03:30 PM	30
17	Software Options			04:00 PM	60
18	No-Host Cocktail Hour			05:00 PM	60
19					
20					

Click the Save SmartIcon now to update the CONF.WK4 file to disk. In the next section you'll learn to protect the Conference worksheet from inadvertent revisions or deletions.

Protecting the Worksheet from Unwanted Revisions

The Conference worksheet is designed to be reused for planning other conferences. By entering new data values in the worksheet's "input" ranges, you can quickly produce financial projections for any conference in the future. When you create a tool like this one, you may find yourself distributing copies of the worksheet file to other people who need to perform similar tasks in 1-2-3. But other users may not be aware of your worksheet's carefully designed structure. In particular, a user may fail to distinguish between cells that contain simple data entries and cells that contain formulas. The structure of the worksheet can easily be ruined if a user inadvertently enters a new value in a formula cell.

To prevent this from happening, you can establish a protection scheme for the worksheet. The purpose of worksheet protection is to prohibit new entries in cells that contain formulas, allowing new entries only in appropriate "input" cells. Two commands are involved in establishing this protection scheme. First you use the Style ➤ Protection command to specify the ranges of cells that will *not* be protected—that is, the cells where you want to allow new entries. Then you use the File ➤ Protect command to *seal* the rest of the file.

In the following exercise you'll first designate the unprotected ranges and then you'll seal the worksheet:

1. Click the Conference tab to return to the first sheet in the file.

2. Select the range A:B4..A:B8. Then hold down the Ctrl key and select these additional ranges:

   - A:E8..A:F8
   - A:D13
   - A:E17..A:F20
   - A:D24..A:D26

1-2-3 highlights all five ranges as you select them. These are the five ranges containing "input" data that you may want to revise for a different conference projection. This multiple selection is known as a *collection*.

3. Choose the Style ➤ Protection command. The Protection dialog box appears:

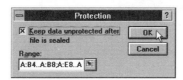

4. In the Protection dialog box, click the option labeled "Keep data unprotected after file is sealed." An *X* appears in the corresponding check box.

Notice that the Range box contains a reference to the collection of ranges you selected before choosing the command; in the notation for a collection, each range is separated from the next by a semicolon.

5. Click OK to confirm the unprotected ranges.

6. Back in the worksheet, press the Home key to move the cell pointer to A1. 1-2-3 highlights the unprotected ranges by displaying their contents in blue. These ranges are shown in bold in Figure 4.18.

7. Choose File ➤ Protect. The Protect dialog box appears:

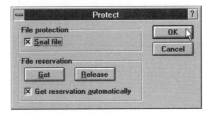

8. In the Protect dialog box, click the Seal file option to place an *X* in the corresponding check box. Then click OK. The Set Password dialog box appears on the screen, allowing you to establish an optional password protection for your worksheet:

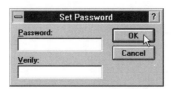

9. To protect the file without a password, leave the Password and Verify boxes empty and click OK.

Now the worksheet is protected from changes, except for the five ranges that you've designated as unprotected. For any cell you select on the worksheet, the status bar displays a *U* or a *Pr* to let you know whether the cell is protected or not. (This notation appears in the fourth panel from the right side of the status bar.)

You can now try entering a new value into one of the unprotected ranges. Select cell B8 and enter a new price of $225.00. When you do so, 1-2-3 accepts your new entry and instantly recalculates all the worksheet formulas that depend on this value, just as it did before you established protection. (Change the value in B8 back to $195.00 before you move on.)

FIGURE 4.18

Designating
unprotected ranges on
the worksheet

Conference	Discounts	Schedule				New Sheet
	A	B	C	D	E	F
1			Computing Conferences, Inc.			
2			Profit Projection for a One-Day Conference			
3						
4	Conference:	**Computing for Video Stores**				
5	Place:	**St. Louis**				
6	Date:	**15-Oct-94**			Expected Attendance	
7					Minimum	Maxim
8	Price:	**$195.00**			80	1
9						
10				Per Person	Min. Total	Max. Tc
11	Projected Revenues:					
12		Attendance			$15,600.00	$29,250.
13		Video Sales	**$35.00**		$1,400.00	$2,625.
14		Total Revenues			$17,000.00	$31,875.
15						
16	Projected Expenses – Fixed					
17		Conference Room			**$1,500.00**	**$2,000.0**
18		Video Production			**$1,000.00**	**$1,000.0**
19		Promotion			**$3,500.00**	**$3,500.0**
20		Travel			**$800.00**	**$800.0**

US Dollar | 2 | Arial | 12 | 06/02/94 3:46 PM | | | Ready

By contrast, 1-2-3 prevents changes in any protected cell. As an experiment, try entering a new value into any cell that's not displayed in blue. The following message pops up on the screen:

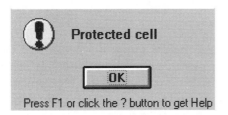

In summary, protection makes your worksheet a safer and more valuable tool for distribution to other users. By restricting new input to appropriate cells, a protection scheme insures the continued reliability of your formulas.

Deactivating protection mode For now, deactivate the protection mode so that you can perform some additional tasks on the Conference worksheet:

1. Choose File ➤ Protect.

2. In the Protect dialog box, uncheck the Seal file option and click OK.

3. Click OK on the Get Password dialog box.

When you complete these steps, notice that the unprotected ranges are still displayed in blue, even though protection is off. If you later decide to restore the global protection mode, these unprotected ranges will resume their role as the worksheet's input cells.

Creating a Finished Document

Now it's time to put the finishing touches on the Conference worksheet, in preparation for printing the document. In this section you'll examine 1-2-3's options for displaying—and ultimately printing—font sizes, type styles, borders, lines, and shadings on your worksheet. You apply these options by choosing commands from the Style menu, clicking SmartIcons, or making selections from the "live" status bar.

As you work with these effects, you may sometimes want to insert new blank rows into your worksheet to improve the overall visual impact. This is the case in the Conference worksheet. Use the Insert command in the Edit menu to insert an additional blank row at each of the following five locations (at some of these places there will now be two blank rows):

- Below row 2, which contains the worksheet's two-line title.
- Below row 9, which contains the attendance price and the minimum and maximum attendance estimates.
- Above row 16, which contains the Total Revenues.
- Above row 19, which contains the Projected Expenses—Fixed subtitle.
- Above row 33, the Projected Profit line.

When you complete these five row insertions, your worksheet appears as in Figure 4.19. Now you're ready to make some significant improvements in the appearance of the worksheet.

Font Sizes, Type Styles, Shadings, and Borders

Begin with the title lines displayed at the top of the worksheet. Keep in mind that these two labels are stored in cells B1 and B2. To place emphasis on the titles, you'll select a larger font size, display the text in combinations of bold

FIGURE 4.19

Inserting blank rows in the worksheet

	A	B	C	D	E	F
1			Computing Conferences, Inc.			
2			Profit Projection for a One-Day Conference			
3						
4						
5	Conference:	Computing for Video Stores				
6	Place:	St. Louis				
7	Date:	15-Oct-94			Expected Attendance	
8					Minimum	Maximum
9	Price:	$195.00			80	150
10						
11						
12				Per Person	Min.Total	Max.Total
13	Projected Revenues:					
14		Attendance			$15,600.00	$29,250.00
15		Video Sales		$35.00	$1,400.00	$2,625.00
16						
17		Total Revenues			$17,000.00	$31,875.00
18						
19						
20	Projected Expenses -- Fixed					
21		Conference Room			$1,500.00	$2,000.00
22		Video Production			$1,000.00	$1,000.00
23		Promotion			$3,500.00	$3,500.00
24		Travel			$800.00	$800.00
25		Total Fixed Expenses			$6,800.00	$7,300.00
26						
27	Projected Expenses -- Variable by Attendance					
28		Conference Materials		$8.25	$660.00	$1,237.50
29		Coffee and Pastries		$3.25	$260.00	$487.50
30		Box Lunch		$4.75	$380.00	$712.50
31		Total Variable Expenses			$1,300.00	$2,437.50
32						
33						
34	Projected Profit				$8,900.00	$22,137.50

and italics, apply a dark gray shading to the range and contrasting white to the text, and add a "designer" frame. Here are the steps:

1. Select B2 alone and click the Italics SmartIcon.

2. Select B1..B2 and click the Bold SmartIcon.

3. Without changing the selection, click the Point-size selector on the status bar (the fifth panel from the left) and select 18 from the resulting size list:

```
6
8
10
12
14
18
24
32
48
72
```

The type size increases accordingly, and the heights of rows 1 and 2 are automatically adjusted to accommodate the new size.

4. Select the range A:B1..A:E2 and then choose Style ➤ Lines & Color. The Lines & Color dialog box appears on the screen:

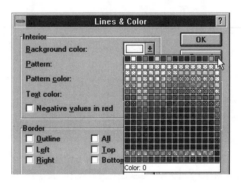

5. Click the down-arrow button at the right side of the Background color box. A color palette appears. Click the small gray box at the upper-right corner of the palette. This selection will become the background color of the range.

6. Now click the down-arrow button at the right side of the Text color box. On the resulting color palette, click the small white square located near the upper-left corner of the palette. This will become the color of the text.

7. Click the arrow button at the right side of the Designer frame box. In response, 1-2-3 displays a selection of predefined frames that you can display around the current range:

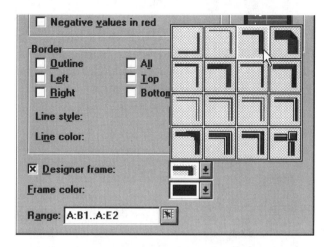

8. Click the third frame in the top row.

9. Click OK on the Lines & Color dialog box to confirm these changes.

10. Choose View ➤ Set View Preferences. On the resulting dialog box, click the Grid Lines option to remove the *X* from the corresponding check box. Then click OK. Once again the grid lines disappear from your worksheet.

Deselect the current range by moving the cell pointer to some other part of your worksheet. The titles appear as follows:

Formatting and Printing

4

TIP

You can change the font and size of a worksheet selection either by making selections from the Point-size and Font selectors on the status bar or by choosing the Style ➤ Font & Attributes command. The Font & Attributes dialog box has a list of all the fonts available in your installation of Windows, and also a group of options for applying bold, italics, underlining, and color to the values and text in a selected range.

TIP

As you've seen, 1-2-3 automatically increases the row height when you select a larger font than the current size. Alternatively, you can change the row height manually by choosing the Style ➤ Row Height command. The height of a row is measured in points, the same as the measurement for font sizes. You can also change the height of a row by dragging the row's lower border up or down with the mouse.

Continue your work on the Conference worksheet by copying the size, shading, and text color from the title lines to the Projected Profit line in row 34. Then practice using the Bold and Italics SmartIcons in the following exercise:

1. Select the range B1..E2.

2. Click the Copy Style SmartIcon.

3. Select the range A34..F34. (The mouse pointer appears as a small paintbrush.) When you release the mouse button, the styles are copied to the information in row 34.

4. Press Escape to toggle out of the copy style mode.

5. Select the range A:A5..A:A27 and click the Bold SmartIcon. 1-2-3 applies the boldface style to all the labels in the selected range. Repeat this step for the following cells and ranges: E7, D12..F12, B17..F17, B25..F25, B31..F31.

6. Select cell B5. Click the Bold SmartIcon and then the Italics SmartIcon. Repeat this combination for the following ranges: E8..F8, B14..B15, B21..B24, B28..B30.

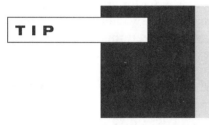

T I P   The Lines & Color dialog box contains a check box option labeled "Negative values in red." You can use this option to place emphasis on values that are less than zero on a worksheet that contains a range of positive and negative numbers.

Drawing Horizontal Lines

Next you'll use the Style ➤ Lines & Color command to draw horizontal lines between sections of the worksheet. The Border group in the Lines & Color dialog box contains a group of check boxes. To apply a line as a border on the worksheet, select the position where you want the line to appear within the current range selection. Optionally, select the line style and color from corresponding pull-down lists.

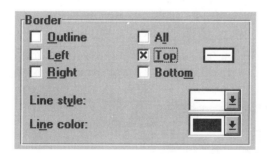

Here are the steps for drawing lines on the Conference worksheet:

1. Select the row range A:A11..A:F11.

2. Choose the Style ➤ Lines & Color command.

3. Click the Top option and then click OK.

Back on the worksheet, a horizontal line now separates the general conference information from the revenues section.

4. Select A:A19..A:F19.

5. Once again choose Style ➤ Lines & Color and click the Top option. After you confirm your selection by clicking OK, a second horizontal line appears on the worksheet, this time separating the revenue and expense sections.

As a final exercise with the tools of the Style menu, you'll next learn how to create a name—and a convenient selection method—for any frequently used style or combination of styles on your worksheet.

Defining Style Names

Using the Style ➤ Named Style command, you can create your own names for styles. The names you create are then available directly from the Style selector, the third panel of the "live" status bar. Each style name you add to the menu can represent a single style option or a combination of style effects. The Named Style dialog box has options for as many as sixteen style names. Here are the general steps for creating a new style name:

1. Apply one or more styles to a range on the worksheet.

2. Keep this range as the current selection, and choose Style ➤ Named Style. The Named Style dialog box appears:

3. In the Named Style dialog box, enter a name for the style you're defining. The name can contain up to 35 characters.

4. Click OK or press ↵.

When you click the Style selector on the status bar, the style name you've defined appears as one of the entries in the pop-up list. Style names are defined independently for each worksheet file. You can therefore define the style names that are most useful for a given worksheet. As a simple example of a style name, try the following exercise on the Conference worksheet:

1. Select the range A:B5..A:C9.

2. Choose Style ➤ Lines & Color. Click the arrow button next to the Background color box. On the resulting color palette, click the fifth small box in the last column of colors, a light gray shade option.

3. Click OK. 1-2-3 applies the light gray shading to the selected range.

4. Now select the range A:B5..A:B9 and click the Bold SmartIcon. (In this example, you'll define a named style to represent the light shading and the boldface text. The current selection represents both of these effects.)

5. Choose Style ➤ Named Style.

6. In the Style Name box, enter the name **LShade** and click OK to confirm this definition.

7. Now select A:E9..A:F9, another range to which you want to apply the style shading. Click the Style selector, the third panel in the status bar. A pop-up list shows the name of the style you've defined. Click this name. The light shading and bold text effects are applied to the range on the worksheet.

Now use this same technique to apply the LShade style to the other "input" areas on the worksheet—cell A:D15, and the ranges A:E21..A:F24 and A:D28..A:D30.

This completes your current work on the Conference worksheet. As a further exercise with the style options, you might want to try applying a variety of styles and alignments to the Discounts and Schedule worksheets (B and C). When you complete your work, click the Save SmartIcon to update the CONF.WK4 file.

In the final sections of this chapter you'll study the commands that deal with printing a worksheet.

Printing a Worksheet

All the special visual effects that you've created in this chapter can be printed on paper. But before you send your worksheet to the printer you'll want to take advantage of options that affect the layout and content of the printed page. Once you've made selections among these options, printing the worksheet is as simple as clicking the Print SmartIcon and selecting options from the resulting dialog box. Alternatively, you can view a preview of the printed page by clicking the Preview SmartIcon and clicking OK on the resulting Print Preview dialog box. When you take this intermediate step, 1-2-3 displays a preview like the one shown in Figure 4.20. On this screen you can examine the details of the document's layout without actually using paper.

In addition to the Print and Preview SmartIcons, there are four commands in the File menu—and one in the Style menu—that deal directly with printing. In the final exercises of this chapter you'll learn the significance of these tools:

- **File ➤ Print Preview.** This command displays a preview of the page or pages that will be printed from your worksheet. Like the Preview SmartIcon, this command begins by displaying a dialog

FIGURE 4.20

A preview of the printed page

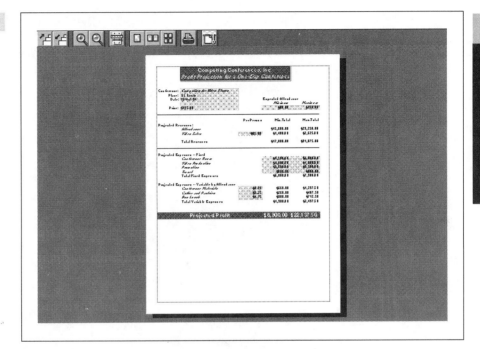

4

Formatting and Printing

box in which you specify the range you want to preview, along with other options:

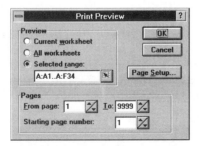

- **File ▶ Page Setup.** This command produces the dialog box shown in Figure 4.21. In this box you'll find a variety of important options that control the features of your printed worksheet.

- **File ▶ Print.** This command displays a dialog box in which you specify the print range, the pages, and the number of copies to print. Back on the worksheet itself, 1-2-3 encloses a print range within a border of light dashed lines:

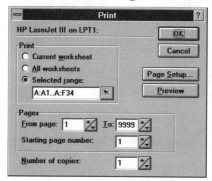

- **File ▶ Printer Setup.** This command identifies the printer or printers you have installed in Windows:

You can select the printer you want to use if two or more are shown in the Printers list box. If you have only one printer attached to your computer—and you've already successfully installed it for use in Windows—you will probably seldom use the File Printer Setup command.

- **Style ▶ Page Break.** This command allows you to specify exactly where the division will take place from one page to the next of your printed worksheet:

FIGURE 4.21

The Page Setup
dialog box

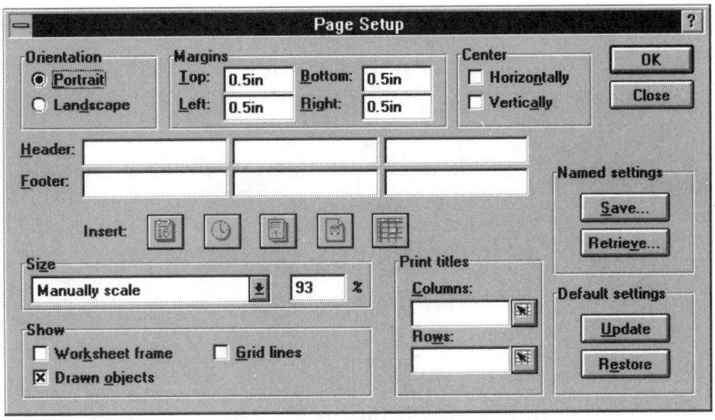

You can define row or column page breaks. This command is useful in printing a long single worksheet, or in printing two or more sheets stored in a single file.

For the most part, these commands are intuitive and easy to use, but the options of the Page Setup command require some explanation.

Using the Page Setup Command

The Page Setup dialog box (see Figure 4.21) includes tools for each of the following tasks:

- Selecting a horizontal or vertical orientation for the worksheet on the page.

- Changing the page margins.

- Selecting a centering option.

- Creating a header and/or a footer.

- Compressing the print size so the worksheet will fit on a page—or expanding the size so the worksheet will fill up a page.

- Specifying rows or columns of headings that will be printed on every page.

- Optionally printing the worksheet's frame, grid lines, and any graphic objects the sheet may contain.

You'll learn about each of these tasks in turn in the sections ahead.

Selecting an Orientation for the Printout

By default, 1-2-3 prints the rows of your worksheet one by one down the length of the page, in a mode called *Portrait orientation*. An example of this default orientation appears in the preview screen back in Figure 4.20. In a table that contains many columns, you might prefer to print the rows of the worksheet sideways, across the length of the paper; this option is called the *Landscape orientation*.

The Page Setup dialog box contains two option buttons, labeled Portrait and Landscape. These options control the orientation of your printout. Portrait is the default. Figure 4.22 shows a preview of the Conference worksheet under the Landscape option.

Specifying Margins and Choosing Centering Options

The Margins group in the Page Setup dialog box contains four text boxes, labeled Top, Bottom, Left, and Right. Into these boxes you enter specific numeric measurements for the four margins of the printed page. By default, 1-2-3 assumes your entries are in inches. For example, if you enter .75 into a box, 1-2-3 converts the entry into 0.75in.

Alternatively, you can use metric measurements, expressed in millimeters (mm) or centimeters (cm). To do so, include an abbreviation of mm or cm immediately after the number. 1-2-3 converts centimeter measurements into millimeters.

By checking one or both of the Center options (Horizontally and Vertically), you instruct 1-2-3 to center your worksheet lengthwise or widthwise on the page.

4

Formatting and Printing

FIGURE 4.22

FIGURE 4.22

The Landscape printing option. Compare this to Figure 4.20, which shows the worksheet in Portrait orientation.

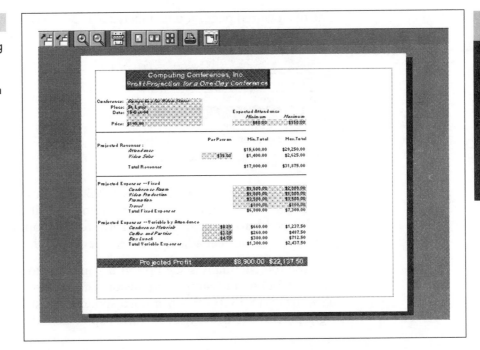

Creating a Header and Footer

A *header* is a line of text that 1-2-3 prints at the top of each page of the worksheet. A *footer* is a line of text printed at the bottom. You enter the text of these elements into the Header and Footer boxes on the Page Setup dialog box. Both the header and the footer are divided into three areas: left, center, and right. You can supply text for any or all of these areas. In addition, you can click the Insert buttons on the Page Setup dialog box to insert special information in a header or footer. From the left to right, the insert buttons are the date, the time, the page number, the file name, and the contents of a particular cell on your worksheet.

Compressing or Expanding the Printed Worksheet

The Size group in the Page Setup dialog box contains a drop-down list of special printing options. If the size of a worksheet doesn't quite match the size of a printed page, you can instruct 1-2-3 to compress the printout to create a single page of output or expand the printout to fill the page.

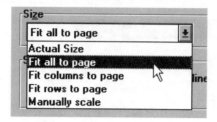

The Fit all to page option instructs 1-2-3 to contract or expand the worksheet data in two dimensions in an attempt to fit the page. By contrast, the Fit columns to page and Fit rows to page options allow individual horizontal or vertical adjustments in the size of the printed output.

Choose the Manually scale option if you want to supply a specific percentage for compression or expansion. In this case, you supply a percentage—from 15 to 1000—in a corresponding text box. Finding just the right percentage usually takes some experimentation.

Printing Headings on Every Page

When you print a long worksheet you might want to include column headings or row labels from your worksheet on each page of the printout. For example, imagine a worksheet that has five hundred rows of data, with column headings displayed in row 1. In the multiple-page printout of this worksheet you would want the column headings from row 1 to appear at the top of each page. Conversely, imagine a worksheet containing dozens of columns, with row labels in column A. You would want the row labels to be repeated on each page of the printed worksheet.

To accomplish these effects, you enter references into the Columns and Rows boxes in the Print titles group of the Page Setup dialog box. If you want to specify one row or one column to be printed on each page, you enter a reference to a single cell located in the row or column. For example, a reference to A1 could serve to identify column A in the Columns box or row 1 in the Rows box. Enter a range if you want to print headings from multiple rows or columns. For example, if the column headings in your worksheet are displayed in rows 1 and 2, enter the range A1..A2.

Printing Other Worksheet Elements

In some printouts you might want to include the column letters, row numbers, and grid lines in the worksheet. To do so, select check boxes displayed in the Show group of the Page Setup dialog box. The first of these check boxes, labeled Worksheet frame, refers to the column letters and row numbers. The second is labeled Grid lines.

The Drawn objects check box gives you the option of printing or omitting graphic objects that are part of your worksheet—that is, objects such as charts, buttons, and other graphics.

After entering new settings into the File Page Setup dialog box, you can click the Update button to make your settings the default. Or, click the Restore button to restore the current defaults back to the dialog box. You can also use the Save and Retrieve buttons to create or read page setup files containing specific layout settings. Lotus 1-2-3 saves such files with a default extension name of AL3.

Printing the Conference Worksheet

Figures 4.23 and 4.24 show the Conference, Discount, and Schedule sheets, printed together on two pages. These pages illustrate many of the options 1-2-3 offers you for controlling the layout of printed worksheets. In this chapter's final exercise, you'll follow through the steps of creating this printout yourself:

1. Choose the Range ➤ Name command and assign the name CON-FERENCE to the range A:A1..A:F34.

2. Click the Discounts sheet tab and select cell B:A1. Choose the Style ➤ Page Break command. Select the Row option and click OK.

3. Choose Range ➤ Name and assign the name DISCOUNT to the range B:A1..B:E17.

4. Click the Schedule sheet tab to activate the third sheet in the file. Choose Range ➤ Name command and assign the name SCHED-ULE to the range C:A1..C:E19. These three new range names—CONFERENCE, DISCOUNT, and SCHEDULE—will simplify the process of specifying a multiple print range, as you'll see in the next step.

FIGURE 4.23

Page 1 of the printed worksheet

08/17/94   Page 1

Computing Conferences, Inc.
Profit Projection for a One-Day Conference

Conference: *Computing for Video Stores*
Place: St. Louis
Date: 15-Oct-94

Expected Attendance

	Minimum	*Maximum*
Price: $195.00	80	150

Projected Revenues:	Per Person	Min.Total	Max.Total
Attendance		$15,600.00	$29,250.00
Video Sales	$35.00	$1,400.00	$2,625.00
Total Revenues		$17,000.00	$31,875.00
Projected Expenses -- Fixed			
Conference Room		$1,500.00	$2,000.00
Video Production		$1,000.00	$1,000.00
Promotion		$3,500.00	$3,500.00
Travel		$800.00	$800.00
Total Fixed Expenses		$6,800.00	$7,300.00
Projected Expenses -- Variable by Attendance			
Conference Materials	$8.25	$660.00	$1,237.50
Coffee and Pastries	$3.25	$260.00	$487.50
Box Lunch	$4.75	$380.00	$712.50
Total Variable Expenses		$1,300.00	$2,437.50

Projected Profit $8,900.00 $22,137.50

Computing Conferences, Inc.

FIGURE 4.24

Page 2 of the printed
worksheet

Discount Schedule for Advance Enrollment

Conference: Computing for Video Stores
     Place: St. Louis
      Date: 15-Oct-94

Price: $195.00

If paid by:	Discount	Price
17-Jul-94	20%	$156.00
31-Aug-94	10%	$175.50

Conference Schedule

Conference: Computing for Video Stores
     Place: St. Louis
      Date: 15-Oct-94

Event	Start Time	Minutes
Coffee and Pastries	07:00 AM	45
Introduction	07:45 AM	30
Managing a Video Database	08:15 AM	90
Coffee Break	09:45 AM	15
Managing a Customer Database	10:00 AM	90
Hands-on Demonstrations	11:30 AM	60
Lunch and Discussion	12:30 PM	60
Setting Up a Computer System	01:30 PM	120
Coffee Break	03:30 PM	30
Software Options	04:00 PM	60
No-Host Cocktail Hour	05:00 PM	60

Computing Conferences, Inc.

4

Formatting and Printing

5. Choose File ➤ Print. In the Selected Range text box, enter **CONFERENCE;DISCOUNT;SCHEDULE**, the multiple-range print area. Notice the use of the semicolon character to separate one range reference from the next in this collection.

6. Now click the Page Setup button on the Print dialog box. The Page Setup dialog box appears on the screen.

7. Activate the first Header text box and click the first of the Insert buttons to print the date in the left portion of the header line. 1-2-3 inserts @ into the text box to represent the date. Next activate the third Header text box and type the word **Page** followed by a space. Click the third Insert button to print the page number in the right portion of the header. 1-2-3 inserts # to represent the page number.

8. Activate the first Footer text box and click the last of the Insert buttons to print the contents of a specified cell on the worksheet. 1-2-3 inserts a backslash character (\) into the text box. Immediately following this character, type the reference **A:B1**. This notation arranges to print the company name—Computer Conferences, Inc.—at the left side of the footer.

9. Choose the Fit all to page option in the Size list.

10. Click OK to confirm the Page Setup options.

11. Back in the Print dialog box, click the Preview button. When the preview screen appears, examine the page layout you are about to print. Click the Next Page button to examine page 2.

12. Click the Close button to close the preview window. Then click the Print SmartIcon and click OK to print the worksheet. The results are shown in Figures 4.23 and 4.24.

Summary

In this chapter you've worked with commands and options that change the appearance of a worksheet. The Style ➤ Worksheet Defaults command allows you to establish default characteristics for an entire worksheet, including font, text size, the column width, alignment, number format, and colors. Alternatively, you can apply these properties selectively to individual cells or ranges on a worksheet, using commands from the Style menu: Font & Attributes, Column Width, Alignment, Number Format, Lines & Color. As always, 1-2-3 gives you a variety of ways to accomplish a task. Rather than choose commands from the Style menu, you can select options from the "live" status bar, click the corresponding SmartIcons, or choose commands from quick menus.

When you've defined the display properties of your worksheet, you can turn to the task of printing your work. The File menu contains four commands involved in printing. The Preview command allows you to view the layout of your worksheet on the screen before you actually send the document to the printer. The Page Setup command offers tools for creating headers and footers, setting margins, printing headings on every page, and compressing or expanding the worksheet to fit a page. In the Print dialog box you establish one or more print ranges. The Printer Setup command provides a list of Windows-installed printers.

CHAPTER

5

Worksheet Formulas and Functions

fast TRACK

WRITING formulas is the creative part of your work with the 1-2-3 spreadsheet. Without your precise and detailed instructions—which you express in formulas—a worksheet can do nothing. Formulas are responsible for establishing the relationships among data items, supplying the steps of operations, producing new values and labels, and defining the structure of your worksheet.

Depending upon the tasks you want the worksheet to accomplish, the formulas you write can be succinct and straightforward, or painstakingly complex. To simplify the task of writing formulas, Lotus 1-2-3 has a large library of functions that you can use within formulas—or, in many cases, as substitutes for formulas. A *function* is a predefined calculation or operation, represented by a specific name that denotes the function's role in the worksheet. Function names in 1-2-3 begin with the @ character.

N O T E

This chapter is a general introduction to the use of functions in several categories. For more complete coverage of the 1-2-3 function library, turn to Part Four of this book.

How Functions Work

Up to now you've seen a single function example—the @SUM function, which you entered into the Conference worksheet to find the total of a column of numbers. Like @SUM, many of the 1-2-3 functions are designed to replace formulas that you would otherwise have to write yourself. For instance, suppose you need to calculate the monthly payment for a fixed-rate bank loan, for which you know the principal, interest rate, and term in years. You've entered these three loan parameters into a column of your worksheet, and you've assigned the range names PRINCIPAL, RATE, and TERM to the three cells containing the data. Next you need to enter the formula for calculating the monthly payment on the loan.

Not many people can produce the formula for this loan calculation from memory. But you could look it up in a business mathematics book, and then carefully enter the formula into a cell of your worksheet. The entry would look something like this:

(PRINCIPAL*RATE/12)/(1–(1+RATE/12)^(–TERM*12))

Although it successfully calculates the monthly payment, this formula takes a lot of time and effort to produce. Fortunately, 1-2-3 offers a much simpler approach for this common calculation. The formula for finding a monthly loan payment is available as the function named @PMT. Using this function, you can calculate the loan payment without having to concern yourself with the details of the formula itself. Here is how you would enter the @PMT function:

@PMT(PRINCIPAL,RATE/12,TERM*12)

5

Formulas and Functions

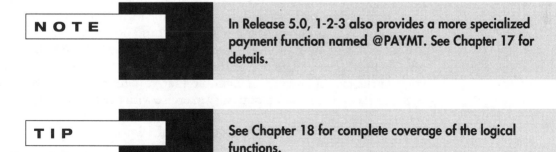

N O T E

In Release 5.0, 1-2-3 also provides a more specialized payment function named @PAYMT. See Chapter 17 for details.

T I P

See Chapter 18 for complete coverage of the logical functions.

Arguments The three loan parameters appear as the arguments of the @PMT function. An *argument* is a value you supply for a function to work with. In order to calculate the monthly payment amount, you express the rate and the term as monthly values; for this reason, two of the arguments you send to the @PMT function appear as calculated values (RATE/12 and TERM*12). As you can see, this use of the @PMT function is a lot simpler than the equivalent loan-payment formula.

Other functions are designed to perform specific data operations. The effect of these functions is to give you broader options and greater flexibility for the design of your worksheet. For example, you can use @HLOOKUP function to select values from a *look-up table*, a collection of numeric data items organized like an income tax table. Using this function, a formula can read appropriate data items from a two-dimensional data table that you've entered in a range of the worksheet.

In short, functions simplify your work and expand the range of tasks you can perform on a worksheet. In this chapter you'll see examples of @PMT and @HLOOKUP, along with many other functions in several categories.

Filling Ranges with Sample Data

As you proceed through this chapter, you'll find many individual exercises designed to help you understand specific formulas and functions. As a technique for supplying sample data in some of these exercises, you'll use an efficient new mouse action known as *drag-and-fill*. This action quickly produces a sequence of numbers or labels in a selected range on your worksheet, following an example that you enter into the beginning of the range. Here is an introductory exercise with the drag-and fill action:

1. On a blank worksheet, enter a value of **1** in cell A1.

2. While the cell pointer is still at A1, position the mouse pointer over the lower-right corner of the cell.

When you do so, two pairs of arrowheads—pointing down and to the right—are added to the mouse pointer icon:

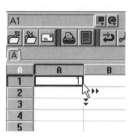

3. Hold down the left mouse button and drag the pointer down to cell A12.

4. Release the mouse button. When you do so, 1-2-3 fills the range A2..A12 with a column of numbers from 2 to 12.

5. Now select cell B1 and enter **January** into the cell. Using the same technique as before, drag the mouse pointer from B1 to B12, and then release the mouse button. 1-2-3 fills the range B2..B12 with month names from February to December.

6. Enter **Sunday** into cell B15, and **12** into B16. Then select the two-cell range B15..B16. Position the mouse pointer at the lower-right corner of the selection:

7. Drag the pointer from column B to column H and then release the mouse button.

1-2-3 fills row 15 with labels representing the days of the week, and row 16 with sequential digits from 12 to 18.

8. Enter a value of **5** in cell E1 and a value of **10** in E2. Then select the two-cell range E1..E2 and position the mouse pointer over the lower-right corner of the selection.

9. Drag the pointer down to E12, and then release the mouse button. Following the example of your initial two entries, 1-2-3 fills the range with a sequence of numbers in increments of 5.

10. Finally, enter **0** in F1 and **–0.75** in F2. Then select F1..F2 and use the drag-and-fill operation to fill the range F1..F12.

As you can see by studying the examples in Figure 5.1, the drag-and-fill operation is a simple but versatile way of entering an evenly incremented or decremented sequence of numbers—or a particular sequence of labels—into a range on your worksheet. You'll use this convenient tool in several exercises in this chapter.

FIGURE 5.1

Using drag-and-fill to create a sequence of numbers or labels

	A	B	C	D	E	F	G	H
1		1 January			5	0		
2		2 February			10	-0.75		
3		3 March			15	-1.5		
4		4 April			20	-2.25		
5		5 May			25	-3		
6		6 June			30	-3.75		
7		7 July			35	-4.5		
8		8 August			40	-5.25		
9		9 September			45	-6		
10		10 October			50	-6.75		
11		11 November			55	-7.5		
12		12 December			60	-8.25		
13								
14								
15		Sunday	Monday	Tuesday	Wednesday	Thursday	Friday	Saturday
16		12	13	14	15	16	17	18
17								
18								
19								
20								

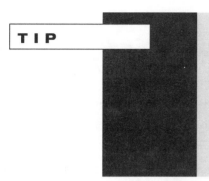

T I P

The Fill by Example command in the Range menu is an alternative tool for filling a range with a series of numbers or labels. To use this command, begin by entering the initial value or values into a worksheet and then select the entire range you want to fill. Choose Range ➤ Fill by Example to complete the operation. The Fill by Example command is also available in the quick menu that appears when you click a range with the right mouse button.

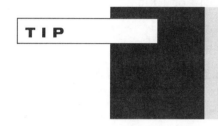

T I P

Yet another command you can use to fill a range with numeric values is Range ➤ Fill. In this command, you specify start and stop values and an increment for the sequence that 1-2-3 will enter into the selected range. You can also select special interval options for chronological series.

5

Formulas and Functions

Filling a range with labels Certain series of labels are defined as built-in *fill sequences* in 1-2-3. As you've seen, these include the days of the week and the names of the months. You can create your own custom fill sequences by adding them to a text file named FILLS.INI. Look for this file in the PROGRAMS subdirectory of the main 1-2-3 directory on your hard disk, and use any text editor (such as the Windows Notepad program) to add a new fill sequence to the file. Each sequence you add must follow a specific format, examples of which appear in the file. The first line in the sequence identifies the SET number in square brackets, and subsequent lines identify ITEM numbers and the actual labels in the sequence. For example, here's how you might create a sequence for the department names in a company:

    [SET 5]
    ITEM1=Editorial
    ITEM2=Technical
    ITEM3=Production
    ITEM4=Sales

ITEM5=Accounting

ITEM6=Support

Writing Formulas

As you've learned, formulas contain a variety of elements, including:

- Literal data values, such as 3.14 or 1000

- Operators, such as + or –

- Functions, such as @SUM or @PMT

- References to cell or range addresses, such as A1, $B:$C$5, or $B$3..$K$7; or range names that you've defined to represent particular cells or ranges on your worksheet.

Lotus 1-2-3 recognizes any one of several characters as the beginning of a formula entry. For example, the plus sign (+) often serves as the starting point of a formula that begins with a reference to a cell address, as you saw in Chapters 3 and 4. Following are the most common ways to begin formulas in 1-2-3.

Formulas that begin with numbers When the first element of a formula is a number, the formula can begin with a digit from 0 to 9, an optional plus sign (+), a minus sign (–), or a decimal point (.). For a positive numeric value, you can begin the formula with the first digit of the number, from 0 to 9. For example, the following formula multiplies a positive number by the value stored in cell A5:

    365*A5

You can begin this same formula with an optional plus sign, but 1-2-3 drops the + from the formula after you press ↵. When a formula begins with a negative number, you type a minus sign to start the formula; for example:

    −19*C2

If the first element is a decimal value, you can begin the formula with a decimal point, but 1-2-3 makes some changes in the format of your entry after you press ↵. For example, you can enter a formula as:

.123*B1

But once you complete the entry, the formula appears in the contents box as:

0.123*B1

If the decimal value is very small, 1-2-3 converts the number to scientific format. For example, consider this formula:

.0000123*B1

After you press ↵ to complete this entry, 1-2-3 changes the format of this number to:

1.23E–05*B1

Formulas that begin with an address reference A plus sign or a minus sign is required as the first character of a formula that begins with an address reference. For example, the following formula instructs 1-2-3 to multiply the value in cell E19 by 10:

+E19*10

This formula multiplies the result by –1:

–E19*10

After you type either the plus sign or the minus sign, you can type the address reference directly from the keyboard or you can use a pointing technique to enter the address. As you've learned, you can use either the mouse or the arrow keys on the keyboard to point to a cell or range while you're creating a formula (see page 130).

Formulas that begin with a function An initial @ character indicates that a formula begins with one of 1-2-3's built-in functions. A function can appear by itself as the complete entry in a cell, or a function name can be one of several elements in a formula. For example, the following function finds the sum of a range of values:

@SUM(C5..C10)

The following formula multiplies the sum by 25:

@SUM(C5..C10)*25

In both cases, the result of the function or the calculation appears in the cell where you enter the formula.

Formulas that begin with an open parenthesis Any formula can begin with an open parenthesis character. As you learned in Chapter 3, you can use parentheses to enclose operations in a formula when you want to override 1-2-3's default order of operations (see page 171). For example, the following formula adds two numbers together and then multiplies the sum by 5:

(A1+A2)*5

Here are two important facts to keep in mind as you write formulas: First, a formula entry shouldn't contain spaces. (The exception to this rule is for string values that appear within quotation marks; you'll learn about strings later in this chapter.) Usually 1-2-3 eliminates any spaces from a formula when you complete the entry. But to be safe you should learn to avoid pressing the spacebar while you're typing the elements of a formula.

Second, you can include a note or comment at the end of a formula to help you remember what the formula does. To place a note at the end of a formula, type a semicolon (;) immediately after the formula itself and then type your note; for example:

@PMT(PRINCIPAL,RATE/12,TERM*12); The monthly payment.

When you later examine the formula, your note appears along with the formula in the contents box on the edit line. This is an important feature, especially in a complicated worksheet that contains many formulas.

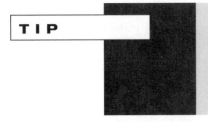

TIP Writing notes and comments is a simple way to document the structure of the worksheet, so that you can later review how you've organized your work. Ultimately this kind of documentation makes it easier to revise a worksheet if you ever want to change the way your formulas operate.

By the way, a formula entry—along with a note or comment—can be as long as 512 characters, although you're unlikely ever to reach this maximum, even if you write extensive comments along with your formulas.

Understanding the Categories of Formulas

A formula in 1-2-3 can perform several types of operations:

- Calculate a numeric value.

- Perform date or time arithmetic.

- Evaluate a logical condition—that is, an expression that is either true or false.

- Build a label or a text display.

You've already written formulas that perform some of these operations. In the upcoming sections you'll further examine each kind of formula.

Numeric Formulas

You've seen examples of the four most common numeric operations (addition, subtraction, multiplication, and division) and the operators that represent them: $-$, $\star$, and $/$. You've also seen the use of the plus and minus signs to represent positive and negative values or references.

NOTE Note the distinction between these two terms: an *operation* is a calculation that 1-2-3 performs; an *operator* is a character or symbol that represents the operation in a formula.

Lotus 1-2-3 has another numeric operation known as *exponentiation*. Given a base value x and an exponent y, this operation finds x to the power of y. In 1-2-3, exponentiation is represented by the caret symbol

5

Formulas and Functions

(^). For example, consider the following formula:

    +A1^3

If A1 contains a value of 5, this formula results in 125—or 5 to the power of 3. The exponent can also be fractional, in which case exponentiation produces a root value; for example:

    +A1^(1/4)

This formula finds the fourth root of the value in A1. To try this formula on your worksheet, enter a value of 2401 in cell A1, then enter +A1^(1/4) in cell A2. The result displayed in A2 is 7.

In the order of operations followed by 1-2-3, exponentiation has the highest precedence—that is, exponentiation is performed before any other numeric operation. Here is the complete list of numeric operations, in their order of precedence:

1. Exponentiation (^)

2. Positive and negative sign (+ and –)

3. Multiplication and division (* and /)

4. Addition and subtraction (+ and –)

As you know, parentheses override this order of precedence. For example, given the formula +A1^(1/4), 1-2-3 performs the division before the exponentiation.

In 1-2-3 the operations of date and time arithmetic are treated as numeric formulas, even though the results displayed on the worksheet appear to be very different from numbers. You began exploring the elements of date and time arithmetic in Chapter 4 (see pages 214 and 220). In the upcoming section of this chapter you'll see some further examples.

Date and Time Formulas

In the discount worksheet that you developed in Chapter 4, you subtracted 90 days and 45 days from a conference date to calculate two different payment due dates. Similarly, on the schedule worksheet you added the length in minutes of each conference activity to the starting time, to calculate the starting time for the next activity. Both of these operations involve adjusting individual chronological values (dates or times) by a fixed amount of elapsed time (days or minutes) to produce a new chronological value.

Another important operation finds the difference between two chronological values. Specifically, you can subtract one date from another in a worksheet:

    +DATE1–DATE2

This formula gives the number of days between the two dates. This result is a positive value if DATE1 is later on the calendar than DATE2, or a negative value if DATE1 is earlier on the calendar. You might want to find the difference between two dates in a variety of business contexts. For example, on a customer billing worksheet you might calculate the number of days a customer takes to pay your invoices—that is, the difference between the billing date and the payment date. On an employee worksheet, you might want to know the number of days that have elapsed since an employee's last evaluation, or the number of days since the employee was hired.

You can also subtract one time value from another:

    +TIME1–TIME2

This formula gives the elapsed time, expressed as a decimal fraction. You'll recall that a time number in 1-2-3 is a decimal that represents a portion of a 24-hour day (see page 218). Again, the result of the subtraction is positive if TIME1 is later than TIME2, or negative if TIME1 is earlier than TIME2. One common use for this operation is in determining the length of time spent on a given task or project.

The following exercise helps you experiment with these two important chronological operations:

1. On a blank worksheet, preselect the range A1..B5. Click the Format selector, the first panel on the status bar, and choose 31-Dec-93 from the resulting format list.

2. Enter **15-Apr-94** in cell A1 and **22-Apr-94** in cell A2. Select A1..A2, and use the drag-and-fill operation to fill the range

A1..A5 with a sequence of dates that are one week apart.

3. Enter today's date in cell B1. Use the 31-Dec-90 date format for the entry. Then select B1..B5, click the range with the right mouse button, and choose Copy Down from the resulting quick menu. This action copies today's date into each cell of the range.

4. Enter **+B1-A1** into cell C1. The result displayed in C1 is the number of days between the dates in A1 and B1. Use the Copy Down command to copy this formula down column C, to the range C1..C5.

The upper half of the worksheet in Figure 5.2 shows the result. Of course, the number of days displayed in column C on your own worksheet depends upon the date you enter in column B.

5. Preselect the range A8..B12 on the same worksheet. Click the Format selector on the status bar and choose the time format 11:59 AM from the resulting format list.

6. Enter **6:00 AM** in cell A8 and **9:00 AM** in A9. Then select A8..A9 and use the drag-and-fill operation to extend this sequence through the range A8..A12. As a result, time values from 6:00 AM to 6:00 PM appear in the selected range.

7. Enter **7:15 AM** in cell B8, and then use the Copy Down command to copy this time value down column B, to the range

FIGURE 5.2

Experimenting with date and time arithmetic

	A	B	C
1	15-Apr-94	25-Jul-94	101
2	22-Apr-94	25-Jul-94	94
3	29-Apr-94	25-Jul-94	87
4	06-May-94	25-Jul-94	80
5	13-May-94	25-Jul-94	73
6			
7			
8	06:00 AM	07:15 AM	-1.25
9	09:00 AM	07:15 AM	1.75
10	12:00 PM	07:15 AM	4.75
11	03:00 PM	07:15 AM	7.75
12	06:00 PM	07:15 AM	10.75
13			
14			

B8..B12.

8. Enter **(A8–B8)*24** into cell C8. The result displayed in C8 is the number of hours elapsed between the two time values in A8 and B8. (Do you see why the formula multiplies the difference by 24 in order to calculate the elapsed time in hours?) Copy this formula down column C, to the range C9..C12. The lower half of the worksheet in Figure 5.2 shows the result.

9. Close the worksheet without saving after you have completed the exercise.

Study Figure 5.2 carefully and make sure you understand the two operations represented in the worksheet. Later in this chapter you'll examine other chronological operations, represented by 1-2-3's built-in date and time functions.

Logical Formulas

The purpose of a *logical formula* is to determine whether a particular condition is true or false. A condition is typically expressed as a relationship between two or more data values on a worksheet. As the result of a logical formula, 1-2-3 generates a numeric value:

- A value of 1 represents true
- A value of 0 represents false

Relational operators To build logical formulas, you use 1-2-3's relational and logical operators. The six *relational operators* express relationships of equality or inequality between pairs of numbers. These operators are as follows:

OPERATOR	DESCRIPTION
=	is equal to
<>	is not equal to

OPERATOR	DESCRIPTION
<	is less than
>	is greater than
<=	is less than or equal to
>=	is greater than or equal to

Here is an example of a logical formula that compares the values stored in cells A1 and B1:

+A1<B1

This formula results in a value of 1 (true) if the number stored in A1 is less than the number stored in B1; or a value of 0 (false) if the number in A1 is greater than or equal to the number in B1.

Logical operators The three logical operators available in 1-2-3 are represented as #NOT#, #AND#, and #OR#. Note that these operators are always enclosed within a pair of number signs. The #AND# and #OR# operators are *binary*, meaning that they are each designed to work with two logical values. The #NOT# operator is *unary*: its role is to modify the result of a single logical value.

In the following descriptions, suppose that VAL1 and VAL2 are names of cells containing logical values of true or false:

- The expression #NOT#VAL1 results in the opposite value of VAL1. If VAL1 is true, #NOT#VAL1 is false; if VAL1 is false, #NOT# VAL1 is true. (Note that you can begin the entry of a logical formula with the # character if the formula begins with the #NOT# operator.)

- The expression +VAL1#AND#VAL2 is true if both VAL1 and VAL2 are true. If either VAL1 or VAL2 is false—or if both are false—the #AND# expression is also false.

- +VAL1#OR#VAL2 is true if either VAL1 or VAL2 is true, or if both are true. If both VAL1 and VAL2 are false, the #OR# expression is also false.

Here is an example of a logical formula that uses the #AND# operator:

+B1>A1#AND#B2>A2

This formula results in a value of 1 (true) if both of the relations are true—that is, if the value in B1 is greater than the value in A1 and the value in B2 is greater than the value in A2. If one or both of the two relations are false, the formula itself results in a value of 0 (false). You'll see additional examples in the upcoming exercise.

Logical formulas are sometimes useful as entries in a worksheet. In addition, logical expressions appear as arguments in a 1-2-3 function named @IF. As you'll learn later in this chapter, the @IF function chooses between two results, depending upon the true-or-false result of a logical expression.

Here's an exercise that demonstrates the results of logical formulas:

1. On a blank worksheet, enter the following six integers in the range A1..B3:

CELL	ENTER
A1	73
A2	53
A3	1
B1	0
B2	94
B3	32

2. In addition, enter the following labels in column A, from A5 through A10:

CELL	ENTER
A5	**A1 less than B1.**
A6	**A2 greater than or equal to B2.**

A7	**Opposite of B1.**
A8	**Opposite of A3.**
A9	**All values in B greater than values in A.**
A10	**Any value in B greater than value in A.**

3. Select the range A5..D10. Click the Bold SmartIcon to display the six labels in boldface. Then choose the Style ➤ Alignment, click the Right and Across Columns options, and click OK.

4. Enter the following logical formulas into column E, from E5 to E10:

CELL	ENTER
E5	**+A1<B1**
E6	**+A2>=B2**
E7	**#NOT#B1**
E8	**#NOT#A3**
E9	**+B1>A1#AND#B2>A2#AND#B3>A3**
E10	**+B1>A1#OR#B2>A2#OR#B3>A3**

Figure 5.3 shows the results. You can see that each of these six logical formulas has produced a value of 1 or 0, representing true or false. For comparison, Figure 5.4 shows the same worksheet with the range E5..E10 displayed in the Text format, so you can see the formulas themselves. Study each formula and make sure you understand why it produces the value it does. You'll learn more about logical values when you study 1-2-3's built-in logical functions later in this chapter.

All the formulas you've written up to now have resulted in numeric values. Even though the date, time, and logical formulas produce results that have special non-numeric meanings, the results are numeric nonetheless. In the next section, you'll learn that 1-2-3 also recognizes formulas that produce labels, or text values.

5

Formulas and Functions

FIGURE 5.3

Experimenting with
logical formulas

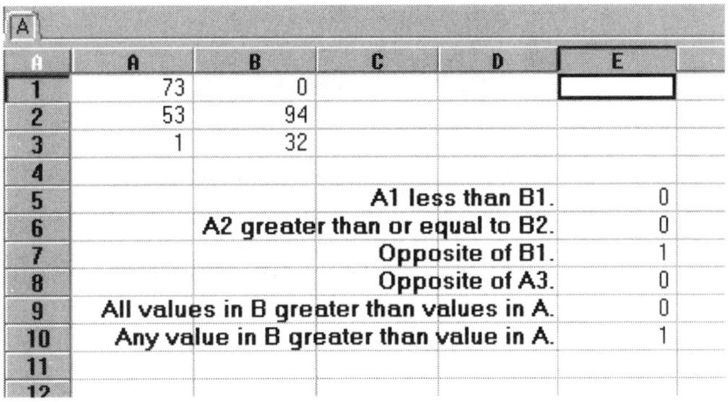

FIGURE 5.4

Viewing the formulas
in Text format
(compare this figure
with Figure 5.3)

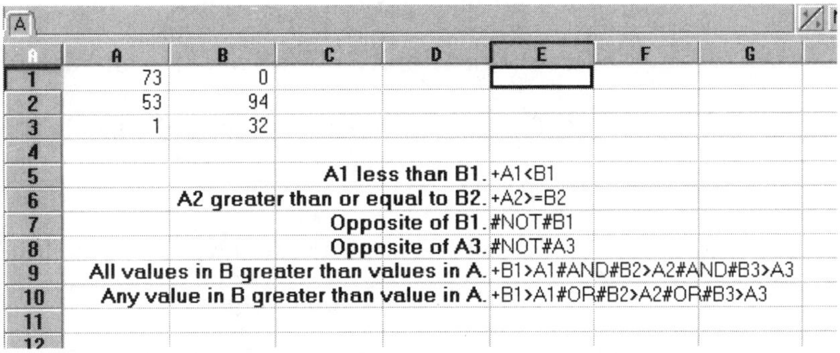

Text Formulas

A *text formula* combines two or more labels to produce a new text value.
Lotus 1-2-3 has one text operation, represented by the ampersand (&)
character. The & operator joins two text values. The 1-2-3 documentation
refers to & as the "text operator," but in other software packages you may
know of this operation as *concatenation*.

The text data items joined together in a text formula may include any of the following:

- References to cells that contain labels. As always, a cell reference can appear as an address or a name.

- *Literal strings*—that is, sequences of characters enclosed in double quotation marks (").

- Built-in 1-2-3 functions that produce text values.

Each data item in a text formula is joined to the previous item by the & operator. For example, the following formula joins labels stored in cells A1 and A2 with a literal string value:

> +A1&" and "&A2

Note that the formula begins with a plus sign, just like a numeric formula. Also notice the blank spaces enclosed within the quotation marks. This is one place where spaces are appropriate in a 1-2-3 formula.

Here is a brief exercise with a text formula:

1. On a blank worksheet, enter the labels from the first several lines of the Conference worksheet, as shown in rows 1 through 5 of Figure 5.5.

2. In cell A7, enter the following text formula:

> +B1&", invites you to attend '"&B4&"' in "&B5&"."

As usual, you can use the pointing technique to enter the cell references into the formula. Figure 5.5 shows the result of this formula—a sentence displayed across row 7.

3. Change the label in cell B4 to **Computing for Lawyers**. Then change the label in cell B5 to **New York**. After each one of these changes, 1-2-3 recalculates the value of the text formula in cell A7. The result is shown in Figure 5.6.

FIGURE 5.5

Experimenting with
concatenation

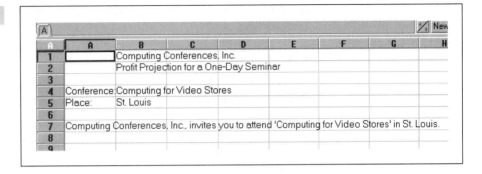

FIGURE 5.5

Experimenting with
concatenation

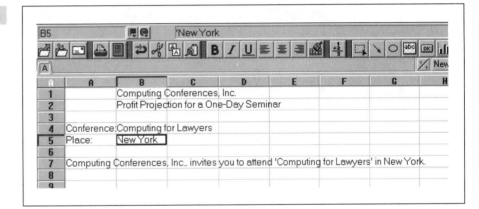

FIGURE 5.6

Changing the result of
the text formula

You'll learn much more about text formulas when you examine 1-2-3's
built-in text functions later in this chapter.

Finding Errors in Formulas

Occasionally 1-2-3 responds to a new formula entry by displaying ERR
in the formula's cell. As you can guess, the ERR message means that there
is an error in your formula. Because of the error, 1-2-3 can't calculate the
formula's result. Sometimes the error is in the formula itself, and sometimes
the problem is in the data that the formula reads from other cells. Either way,
the appearance of the ERR value in a cell means that you need to go back
and investigate the formula and perhaps other entries in your worksheet.

5

Formulas and Functions

A number of problems can cause the ERR message. Here are three of the most common:

- A reference to an undefined range name.
- An inappropriate mix of data types in a formula—for instance, a numeric data value in a text formula, or a text value in a numeric formula.
- An attempt to divide by zero in a numeric formula. (Division by zero is undefined in 1-2-3.)

In the following exercise, you'll simulate these three error conditions by entering formulas that are devised to produce intentional ERR values. Then you'll go through the steps to correct the errors by changing values on the worksheet:

1. On a blank worksheet, enter the following data values:

CELL	ENTER
A1	Lotus 1-2-3 for
A2	Windows
A3	3.1
A4	0

2. Select cell A1, choose Range ➤ Name, and enter **TITLE1** as the name for this cell. Click OK or press ↵ to confirm.

3. Enter the following text formula into cell A6:

+TITLE1&" "&TITLE2

Lotus 1-2-3 responds by displaying ERR in the cell. Can you identify the problem in the formula?

4. Enter **+A2&A3** into cell A7. The response is the same—another ERR message. Once again, examine the worksheet's data and try to find the error in the formula.

5. Finally, enter **365/A4** into cell A8. A third ERR message appears in column A:

A	A	B
1	Lotus 1-2-3 for	
2	Windows	
3	3.1	
4	0	
5		
6	ERR	
7	ERR	
8	ERR	
9		
10		

Here is what the worksheet's three formulas look like displayed in the Text format:

A	A	B
1	Lotus 1-2-3 for	
2	Windows	
3	3.1	
4	0	
5		
6	+TITLE1&" "&TITLE2	
7	+A2&A3	
8	365/A4	
9		
10		

6. Now begin correcting the conditions that produce the three ERR values. First, select cell A2 and choose Range ➤ Name. Enter **TITLE2** as the range name for the cell.

As soon as you complete this operation, 1-2-3 recalculates the formula in cell A6, which previously contained a reference to an undefined range name. Now the formula's result appears as a text value.

7. Select cell A3 and enter 3 as a label rather than a value: Begin the entry by pressing the spacebar; 1-2-3 switches into the Label mode. Next type **3.1** and press ⏎. Now 1-2-3 recalculates the text formula in cell A7, which previously contained an unusable reference to a numeric value.

5

Formulas and Functions

8. Finally, select cell A4 and enter a value of 5.

In response, 1-2-3 recalculates the numeric formula in cell A8. Because the denominator is no longer zero, 1-2-3 successfully calculates the numeric result of the formula.

Here are the results of all three formulas after you complete these corrections:

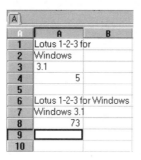

As you know from your experience with the Conference worksheet, formulas are often interconnected in a complex system of calculations. If 1-2-3 detects an error in one formula, all dependent formulas are also evaluated as ERR. As a result, a single error condition can produce ERR messages all over your worksheet. Conversely, a single correction can take away all of the ERR messages.

Using Functions

Lotus 1-2-3's function library is one of the application's most important features. The library includes groups of special-purpose functions designed for particular fields of work, such as accounting, engineering, and statistics. Other functions are designed for much more general use. Functions are among the tools you'll use the most in the 1-2-3 spreadsheet.

A library of over two hundred functions seems dauntingly hard to master. But as you work with 1-2-3 you'll gradually identify the dozen or so functions that are most useful to you in your own worksheets; these are the ones you'll become most adept at using. You can learn about other functions when occasions arise that call for their use.

N O T E   Part Four of this book explains all the 1-2-3 functions in detail.

Entering a Function into a Cell

1-2-3 offers you detailed and substantial help when you need to learn how to use a new function. Help comes in a variety of forms:

- **Function selector.** You can click the Function selector button on the edit line to see a list of commonly used functions (as you'll learn shortly, you can customize this list to match your own work patterns):

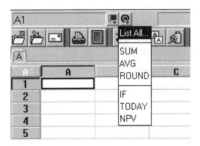

When you select a function name from the list, 1-2-3 enters the function into the current cell along with convenient placeholders for the arguments you need to supply. If the function you want to use is not in the list, choose the List All option to view the @Function List dialog box, which contains a complete list of all the 1-2-3 functions.

- **The @Function List dialog box.** Alternatively, you can type the @ character into a cell as the start of a function entry, and then press the F3 function key to view the @Function List dialog box:

When you select a name from the list, 1-2-3 copies the function to the edit line and supplies placeholders for arguments.

- **The Help Key.** Once a selected function name is displayed in a cell, you can place the flashing insertion point next to the name and press the F1 function key to go directly to the help topic for the function.

For example, imagine that you're building a worksheet like the one in Figure 5.7 to calculate the monthly payment on a bank loan. You're ready to enter the formula for calculating the payment in cell B4. You know that 1-2-3 has a function that will do the job, but you can't recall the name of the function or how it's used. Here are the steps you take to get help:

1. With B4 selected as the current cell, type the @ character to begin a function entry.

2. Press the F3 function key. In response, 1-2-3 displays the @Function List dialog box. Press P to scroll quickly down the alphabetically ordered list of function names. Press the down-arrow key several times until the PMT function is highlighted in the list, as shown in Figure 5.7.

3. Press ↵ to select this function. In response, 1-2-3 enters the function's name into the Edit box. Now use your mouse to move the flashing insertion point to a position just after the function name, and press the F1 function key to view the help topic for this function.

The Help window appears on the screen, as shown in Figure 5.8. This Help topic describes the PMT function in detail, giving you all the information you need to use the function successfully.

FIGURE 5.7

Using the @Function
List dialog box

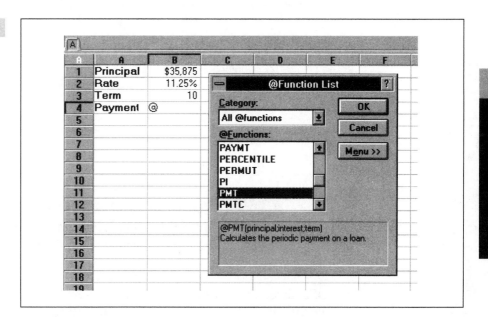

4. After you've read the information, press Esc to close the Help window and return to your work in 1-2-3. Then continue entering the function into the cell.

TIP

Notice that the Help topic in Figure 5.8 also describes the @PAYMT function, a new alternative to @PMT for more specialized payment calculations.

FIGURE 5.8

Getting help with
@functions

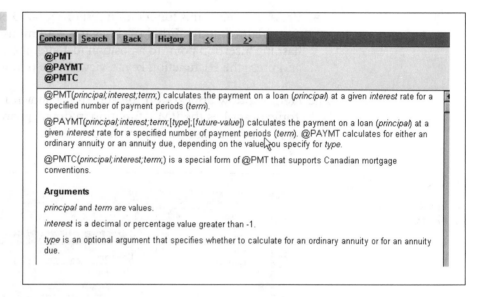

TIP

Notice that the Help topic in Figure 5.8 also describes the @PAYMT function, a new alternative to @PMT for more specialized payment calculations.

Of course, if you already know exactly how a function works, you can enter the function's name and arguments directly from the keyboard without using either of these help features. But even experienced spreadsheet users rely on the 1-2-3 Help system for reviewing the details of functions.

Customizing the Function Selector List

Because the function selector list initially contains only half-a-dozen function names, you'll probably want to add the functions that you use most frequently. Using the @Function List dialog box, changing the Function selector list is a simple task. For example, suppose you want to add the @PMT function to the list. Here are the steps:

1. Click the Function selector button on the edit line, and choose List All. The @Function List dialog box appears (see Figure 5.7).

2. Press **P** and then ↓ several times until the PMT function is highlighted in the @Functions box.

3. Click the Menu button. The dialog box expands to display the Current menu box, with a list of all the functions that are currently included in the Function selector list.

4. Scroll down to the end of the Current menu box, and highlight the last entry in the list.

5. Click the Add button, located just to the right of the @Functions box. In response, 1-2-3 adds the PMT function to the bottom of the Current menu list, as shown in Figure 5.9.

6. Click OK to close the dialog box.

FIGURE 5.9

Customizing the @Function selector list

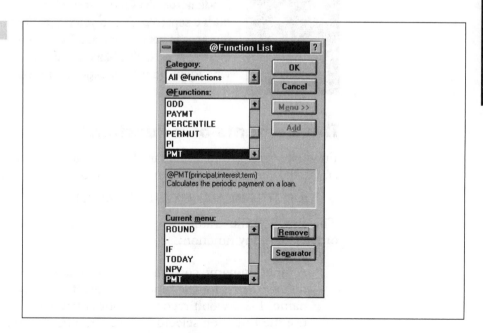

Now you can click the Function selector button to see the new entry in the list. Whenever you want to use the PMT function in a worksheet, you can select it instantly from this list:

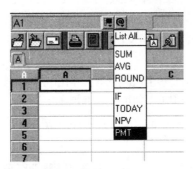

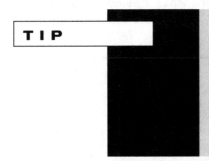

TIP

Notice two additional buttons on the expanded @Function List dialog box (see Figure 5.9). The Remove button deletes a function from the Current menu list. The Separator button adds a separator line so you can easily create groups of functions in your customized list. Before clicking either of these buttons, highlight the position in the Current menu list where you want the change to take place.

The Elements of a Function

Functions conform to a standard format, with only a few variations. To examine the elements of this format, take another look at the PMT function:

@PMT(PRINCIPAL,RATE/12,TERM*12)

This function illustrates the general features you need to understand in order to use any function:

- A function name consists of the @ character, followed by the predefined name for the function itself. If you misspell a function name, 1-2-3 won't recognize your entry. To avoid this problem, use the Function selector or press the F3 function key to view the @Function List dialog box.

- Immediately following the function name, an open parenthesis character marks the beginning of the argument list. A close parenthesis character goes at the end of the list.

- Between the parentheses you enter the function's arguments. Each argument is separated from the next with a comma, but no spaces. A given argument can be expressed in any form that produces the required type of data. For example, an argument can appear as a cell reference, a range name, an expression, or even as another function name.

- The correct number and type of arguments is defined for each function in the 1-2-3 library. A few functions take no argument. Do not enter the parentheses after the names of these functions. A few other functions have optional arguments, or varying lists of arguments.

You'll see many examples of this function format and its variations in upcoming exercises.

T I P

You can change the character used to separate the arguments of a function. Choose Tools ➤ User Setup, click the International button, and make a new selection in the Punctuation list.

5

Formulas and Functions

The Categories of Functions

The 1-2-3 documentation divides the function library into ten categories—statistical, financial, mathematical, engineering, calendar, logical, text, database, lookup, and information. There is nothing absolute about these categories. You are likely to find useful tools in unexpected places among them. You will also find yourself mixing functions from different categories to solve individual problems on a worksheet.

The following sections present a selective survey of some commonly used worksheet functions. You'll study additional functions in other chapters. Specifically, you'll look at database functions in Chapter 8, and at special macro functions in Part Three of this book. Part Four is a reference guide to the entire function library.

Statistical Functions

The *statistical functions* are tools for investigating groups of numbers. For example, you can use functions in this category to count the number of entries in a list; to find the sum, the average, the largest value, and the smallest value of the list; and to calculate the statistical values known as variance and standard deviation. In addition, there are many other statistical functions designed for specialized uses. Here are brief descriptions of ten commonly used functions in this category:

FUNCTION	DESCRIPTION
@COUNT	Counts the number of cells that contain entries in a range.
@SUM	Finds the total of a list of numbers.
@AVG	Calculates the average value of a list of numbers.
@MIN *and* @MAX	Find the smallest and largest numeric values in a list.
@VAR *and* @VARS	Represent two different ways of calculating the *variance*, a measure of how the numbers in a list diverge from the average. A large variance means great divergence, and a small variance means little divergence. The @VAR function performs the calculation known as the *population* variance, or the *n* method, a technique used to analyze a complete list of values from a given application. The @VARS function performs the sample variance, or the *n*−1 method, a technique designed for calculating the variance when the list is only a sample of all the values in an application. @VARS produces a larger variance than @VAR.

FUNCTION	DESCRIPTION
@STD *and* @STDS	Give the standard deviation, calculated as the square root of the variance. @STD supplies the standard deviation for a population—that is, the square root of @VAR. @STDS produces the result for a sample, the square root of @VARS.
@SUM PRODUCT	As its name indicates, performs two operations in one efficient step. First, the function multiplies corresponding values in a range, and then it finds the sum of all the multiplication products.

These functions accept lists of numeric arguments that can include ranges, individual cell references, literal numeric values, calculated values, and range names. The exception is @SUMPRODUCT, which accepts only ranges as arguments. Statistical functions can also operate on three-dimensional ranges—that is, ranges across multiple worksheets in a file.

NOTE   For a detailed look at statistical functions, see Chapter 19.

The worksheet in Figure 5.10 illustrates the statistical functions. The conference organizers at Computing Conferences, Inc., have compiled a list of conferences conducted in 1993, along with the number of people who attended each conference. As you can see, column A on the worksheet displays the city in which each conference was held, column B gives the date, and column C the number of participants. Columns D and E supply a variety of statistics about the conferences and the attendance records—including the number of conferences, the total attendance for all conferences, the average attendance, and the largest and smallest attendance records. In addition, the worksheet shows the variance and the standard deviation calculations, produced with both the n and n-1 methods. In Figure 5.11 you can see the functions that produce all these statistics. Notice that the column of attendance records, C6..C19, has the range name ATTENDANCE.

FIGURE 5.10

Using 1-2-3's statistical functions

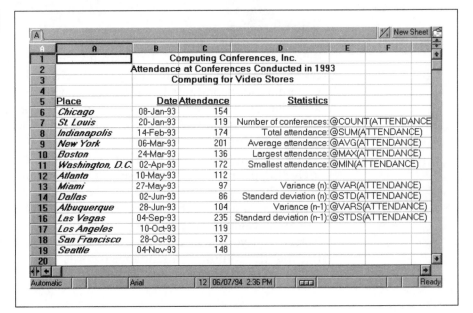

FIGURE 5.11

A text-format view of the statistical functions calculated in Figure 5.10

Place	Date	Attendance	Statistics		
Chicago	08-Jan-93	154			
St. Louis	20-Jan-93	119	Number of conferences:	@COUNT(ATTENDANCE	
Indianapolis	14-Feb-93	174	Total attendance:	@SUM(ATTENDANCE)	
New York	06-Mar-93	201	Average attendance:	@AVG(ATTENDANCE)	
Boston	24-Mar-93	136	Largest attendance:	@MAX(ATTENDANCE)	
Washington, D.C.	02-Apr-93	172	Smallest attendance:	@MIN(ATTENDANCE)	
Atlanta	10-May-93	112			
Miami	27-May-93	97	Variance (n):	@VAR(ATTENDANCE)	
Dallas	02-Jun-93	86	Standard deviation (n):	@STD(ATTENDANCE)	
Albuquerque	28-Jun-93	104	Variance (n-1):	@VARS(ATTENDANCE)	
Las Vegas	04-Sep-93	235	Standard deviation (n-1):	@STDS(ATTENDANCE)	
Los Angeles	10-Oct-93	119			
San Francisco	28-Oct-93	137			
Seattle	04-Nov-93	148			

Finally, Figure 5.12 provides an example of the @SUMPRODUCT function. Column D in this worksheet shows the individual attendance prices for each of the conferences held in 1993. The following @SUMPRODUCT function appears in cell F11:

```
@SUMPRODUCT(C6..C19, D6..D19)
```

The first range argument in this function represents the attendance records, and the second argument contains the prices. The function multiplies each attendance record by the corresponding price, and finds the sum of all the products. The result is displayed as $434,920.

FIGURE 5.12

Using the @SUMPRODUCT function to calculate total attendance revenues

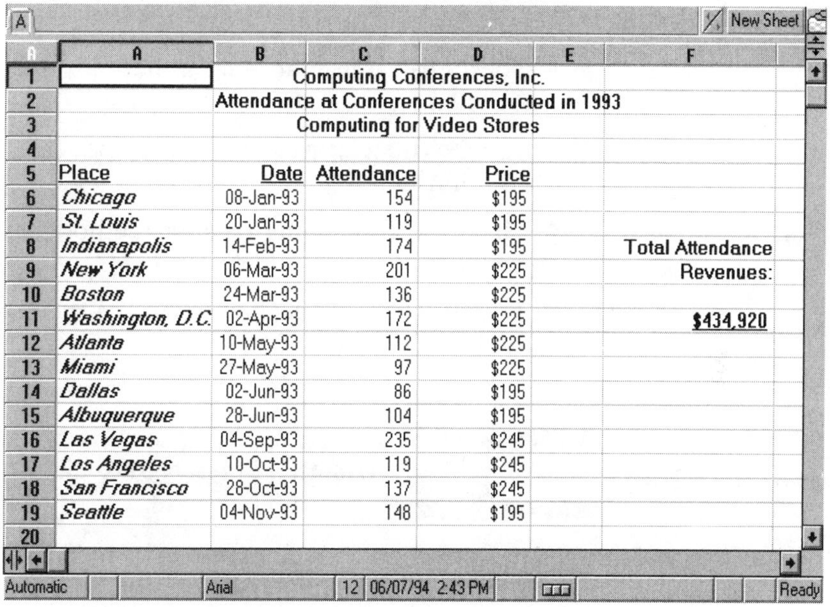

	A	B	C	D	E	F
1		Computing Conferences, Inc.				
2		Attendance at Conferences Conducted in 1993				
3		Computing for Video Stores				
4						
5	Place	Date	Attendance	Price		
6	*Chicago*	08-Jan-93	154	$195		
7	*St. Louis*	20-Jan-93	119	$195		
8	*Indianapolis*	14-Feb-93	174	$195		Total Attendance
9	*New York*	06-Mar-93	201	$225		Revenues:
10	*Boston*	24-Mar-93	136	$225		
11	*Washington, D.C.*	02-Apr-93	172	$225		$434,920
12	*Atlanta*	10-May-93	112	$225		
13	*Miami*	27-May-93	97	$225		
14	*Dallas*	02-Jun-93	86	$195		
15	*Albuquerque*	28-Jun-93	104	$195		
16	*Las Vegas*	04-Sep-93	235	$245		
17	*Los Angeles*	10-Oct-93	119	$245		
18	*San Francisco*	28-Oct-93	137	$245		
19	*Seattle*	04-Nov-93	148	$195		
20						

Financial Functions

The *financial functions* represent the formulas for calculations such as depreciation, loan payments, present value and future value, and investment analyses.

Depreciation Functions

Depreciation refers to any one of several standard methods for allocating the expense of a large purchase over the useful life of the asset. Because depreciation has an impact on taxes, businesses are always concerned with finding the most advantageous way to calculate this expense among the allowed methods.

Seven depreciation methods are available as functions in 1-2-3. The straight-line method, represented by the function named @SLN, is the simplest. It assigns equal portions of the asset's cost to each year of useful life. Other methods represent various approaches to *accelerated* depreciation—the process of assigning greater portions of the expense to the earlier years of useful life, and lesser portions to later years. These methods are:

- The sum-of-the-years'-digits method, calculated by the @SYD function

- The fixed-declining-balance method, calculated by the @DB function.

- The double-declining-balance method, calculated by the @DDB function

- The variable-rate declining balance method, calculated by the @VDB function

 **NOTE** Chapter 17 presents a detailed look at financial functions.

Arguments of the depreciation functions These functions have common arguments, which can be represented as cost, salvage, life, and period:

- *cost* is the original purchase price of the asset.

- *salvage* is the remaining value of the asset at the end of the useful life.

- *life* is the defined useful life of the asset, in years.

- *period* is the target year for which you want to calculate the depreciation.

The @SLN function takes only the first three arguments, because the result of straight-line depreciation is the same for each year of useful life:

@SLN(*cost,salvage,life*)

The @SYD,@DB, and @DDB functions calculate different amounts for each year of useful life. The target year therefore appears as the fourth argument, period:

@SYD(*cost,salvage,life,period*)
@DB(*cost,salvage,life,period*)
@DDB(*cost,salvage,life,period*)

The @VDB function is the most complex of all. It takes two period arguments, representing the start and the end of the target period; this allows you to calculate the depreciation expense for a portion of a year. In addition, @VDB takes two optional arguments, factor and switch:

@VDB(*cost,salvage,life,period1,period2,factor,switch*)

The *factor* argument is the percentage by which the remaining value of the asset is multiplied to calculate the accelerated depreciation for a given period. For example, you might enter a value of 150% or 175% for this argument. If you omit *factor*, the default is 200%; in this case, @VDB produces the same result as @DDB. In the *switch* argument you specify whether you want @VDB to switch to straight-line depreciation at the point when it is advantageous to do so. Supplying a switch value of 0 (or omitting the argument altogether) instructs 1-2-3 to make the switch; a value of 1 prevents the switch.

Figure 5.13 shows examples of four common depreciation methods, calculated for an asset with a four-year useful life. Here are the steps for producing this sample worksheet on your own computer:

1. Enter the following labels in cells A1 to A4:

CELL	ENTER
A1	**Asset**
A2	**Cost**
A3	**Life**
A4	**Salvage**

FIGURE 5.13

1-2-3's four
depreciation methods

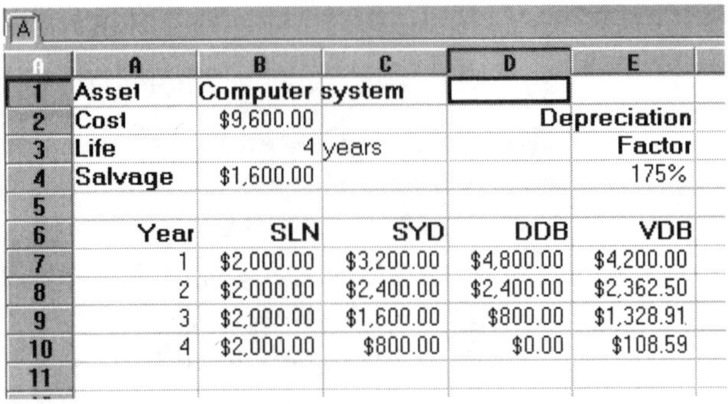

	A	B	C	D	E
1	Asset	Computer system			
2	Cost	$9,600.00			Depreciation
3	Life	4	years		Factor
4	Salvage	$1,600.00			175%
5					
6	Year	SLN	SYD	DDB	VDB
7	1	$2,000.00	$3,200.00	$4,800.00	$4,200.00
8	2	$2,000.00	$2,400.00	$2,400.00	$2,362.50
9	3	$2,000.00	$1,600.00	$800.00	$1,328.91
10	4	$2,000.00	$800.00	$0.00	$108.59
11					

2. Enter the following data items in cells B1 to B4:

CELL	ENTER
B1	**Computer system**
B2	**9600**
B3	**4**
B4	**1600**

3. Enter the label **years** in cell C3.

4. Enter the following labels in cells E2 and E3:

CELL	ENTER
E2	**Depreciation**
E3	**factor**

5. Enter the @VDB depreciation factor, **1.75**, in cell E4.

6. Enter the following column headings in cells A6 to E6:

CELL	ENTER
A6	**Year**
B6	**SLN**
C6	**SYD**
D6	**DDB**
E6	**VDB**

7. Enter the following year numbers in cells A7 to A10:

CELL	ENTER
A7	1
A8	2
A9	3
A10	4

8. Format all these entries as you see them displayed in Figure 5.13. Select the range B7..E10, click the Format selector in the status bar, and choose the US Dollar format.

9. Select the range A2..A4 and choose the Range ➤ Name command. Keep the default "to the right" option in the For cells dialog box, and click the Use Labels button. Then click OK. This action assigns the range names COST, LIFE, and SALVAGE to the appropriate cells in column B.

10. Select cell E3 and choose Range ➤ Name again. This time choose the Below option, click the Use Labels button, and click OK to confirm. This action assigns the name FACTOR to cell E4.

11. In cell B7, enter the formula for the straight-line depreciation method:

@SLN($COST,$SALVAGE,$LIFE)

Notice the absolute references to range names. This format is necessary for the upcoming copy operation.

10. In cell C7, enter the formula for the sum-of-the-years'-digits method:

@SYD($COST,$SALVAGE,$LIFE,A7)

11. In cell D7, enter the formula for the double-declining-balance method:

@DDB($COST,$SALVAGE,$LIFE,A7)

12. In cell E7, enter the formula for the variable-rate declining-balance method:

@VDB($COST,$SALVAGE,$LIFE,A7–1,A7,$FACTOR)

5

Formulas and Functions

13. Use the Copy Down command to copy the four depreciation formulas down their respective columns: Select the range B7..E7, and click the selection with the right mouse button. Then choose Copy Down from the resulting quick menu.

Try making changes in the basic data—the cost, the salvage value, and the depreciation factor—and watch as 1-2-3 recalculates the depreciation schedules. If you increase the useful life value, you also have to add a new row to the depreciation table for each year's increase.

Other Financial Functions

Here is a selection of other financial functions available in 1-2-3:

@PV	The present value function
@NPV	The net present value function
@FV	The future value function
@PMT	The payment function
@CTERM *and* @TERM	The investment term functions
@RATE	The interest rate function
@IRR	The internal rate of return function

Most of these functions take an interest rate as one of several arguments. You can supply this argument as a decimal value such as .085 or as a percentage such as 8.5%. Either way, 1-2-3 stores the argument in its decimal format. Of course, you can also provide the rate argument as a reference to a cell that contains the interest rate. If you enter 8.5% into a cell, 1-2-3 accepts the entry as 0.085 and applies the percentage format to the cell. Alternatively, you can enter the rate as 8.5 in a worksheet cell, and then divide the rate argument by 100 in the function itself:

RATE/100

If a financial function gives a value that you know is incorrect, you should double-check the interest rate argument. Make sure you have not inadvertently supplied a rate argument that is off by a factor of 100.

The @PV and @NPV functions The @PV function finds the present value of a series of future periodic income amounts, where each amount is the same. The present value calculation takes into account the time value of money at a given interest rate. @PV takes three arguments:

@PV(*payment,rate,term*)

The *payment* argument is the income amount that will be received at the end of each period in the term. The *rate* argument is the periodic rate of return. The periods of the *rate* and the *term* must be the same. For more about this function, see page 805.

The @NPV function finds the net present value of a series of future periodic cash flow amounts, positive or negative. @NPV takes two arguments, a rate and a range of cash flow amounts:

@NPV(*rate,cashflows*)

See page 794 for more about this function.

The worksheet in Figure 5.14 uses the @PV and @NPV functions to compare the following two five-year investments: Investment #1 provides five annual income amounts of $10,000 at the end of each year. Investment #2 provides an initial amount of $5,000 at the end of the first year, and then a final amount of $50,000 at the end of the fifth year. Using a rate of 8.5% for the comparison, which is the better investment?

FIGURE 5.14

Using @PV and @NPV to compare investments

	A	B	C	D	E
1	*Comparing Investments*				
2					
3	*Investment #1*			*Investment #2*	
4					
5	*Payment*	$10,000		Year	
6	*Years*	5		1	$5,000
7	*Rate*	8.5%		2	$0
8	*Present Value*	$39,406.42		3	$0
9				4	$0
10				5	$50,000
11					
12				Net Present	
13				Value	$37,860.57
14					

The @PV function in cell B8 gives the present value of the first investment:

   @PV(B5,B7,B6)

The @NPV function in cell E13 gives the present value of the second investment:

   @NPV(B5,E6..E10)

As you can see, the first investment has a greater present value, even though the net income of the second investment is $5,000 more than the first.

The @FV function The @FV function finds the future value of a series of equal periodic payments at a fixed periodic interest rate. @FV takes three arguments:

   @FV(*payment,rate,term*)

The future value is equal to the amount of the periodic payments, plus the accumulated interest over the specified term. For more about this function, see page 778.

Here's an illustration of the @FV function: The parents of a new baby girl have decided to deposit $1,500 in an account at the end of each year until their child is ready to go to college. How much will the account be worth at the end of 18 years, if the interest rate is 8%, compounded annually?

The @FV function in cell B7 is as follows:

   @FV(B3,B4,B5)

There will be $56,175.37 in the account at the end of the 18-year term:

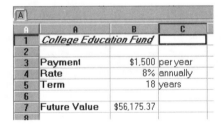

	A	B	C
1	*College Education Fund*		
2			
3	Payment	$1,500	per year
4	Rate	8%	annually
5	Term	18	years
6			
7	Future Value	$56,175.37	
8			

The @PMT function The @PMT function finds the fixed periodic payment amount required to pay back a loan. @PMT takes three arguments:

@PMT(*principal,rate,term*)

When you use @PMT to find the monthly payment for a bank loan, you must supply the monthly interest rate, and the term in months. For more about this function, see page 798.

In the following example, the principal of the loan is $35,825. The rate is 11.25% and the term is 10 years. The formula in cell B6 is @PMT(B3,B4/12,B5*12). Notice that the annual rate is divided by 12 to produce the monthly rate, and the term in years is multiplied by 12 to find the term in months. The monthly payment is $498.57:

	A	B	C
1	*Monthly Payment*		
2			
3	*Principal*	$35,825	
4	*Rate*	11.25%	
5	*Term*	10	years
6	Payment	$498.57	
7			

The @CTERM and @TERM functions The @CTERM function finds the number of compounding periods required to reach a specified future value from a one-time investment amount, given a fixed interest rate. This function takes three arguments:

@CTERM(*rate,futurevalue,presentvalue*)

For more about this function, see page 772.

The @TERM function finds the number of equal payments required to reach a specified future value, given a fixed interest rate. @TERM also takes three arguments, but in a different order:

@TERM(*payment,rate,futurevalue*)

Page 813 has more about this function.

5

Formulas and Functions

The following worksheet compares these two functions, analyzing two different scenarios for attaining a future value of $25,000. Under the first scenario, a one-time amount of $15,000 is deposited in an account at the beginning of the period. Under the second scenario, $1,000 is deposited in an account at the end of each year. In both cases, the accounts yield 8% interest annually. How long will it take each investment to reach the goal of $25,000?

	A	B	C	D	E	F
1	*Time Needed to Save $25,000*					
2						
3	*Single Deposit*			*Annual Deposits*		
4						
5	*Deposit*	$15,000		*Payment*	$1,000	annually
6	*Rate*	8%		*Rate*	8%	
7	*Goal*	$25,000		*Goal*	$25,000	
8	Term	7	years	Term	14	years
9						

The following @CTERM function is stored in cell B8:

    @CTERM(B6,B7,B5)

In this case, the required term is approximately 7 years. (The value in B8 has been rounded by formatting.) The following @TERM function is stored in cell E8:

    @TERM(E5,E6,E7)

Given annual deposits of $1000, the account balance would reach $25,000 in approximately 14 years.

The @RATE function The @RATE function calculates the interest rate corresponding to a fixed future return from a current investment amount. The function takes three arguments:

    @RATE(*futurevalue, presentvalue, term*)

For more about this function, see page 809.

Here is an illustration of the @RATE function: A friend asks to borrow $15,000 from you now, and promises to pay you $25,000 at the end of four years. What will be the annual interest rate that you will earn from the loan?

	A	B	C
1	*Calculating the Interest Rate*		
2			
3	*Present value*	$15,000	
4	*Future value*	$25,000	
5	*Term*	4	years
6	Rate	13.62%	
7			

The function @RATE(B4,B3,B5) is entered into cell B6. The resulting annual interest rate is 13.62%.

The @IRR function Finally, the @IRR function gives the internal rate of return from a series of positive and negative cash flow amounts. The internal rate of return is defined as the interest rate that gives a net present value of zero. @IRR takes two arguments, a rate and a range of cash flow amounts:

@IRR(*guess, cashflows*)

In the first argument you supply a reasonable guess for the internal rate of return. 1-2-3 uses this guess as a starting point for the iterative process that calculates the IRR. The second argument is a worksheet range that contains the positive and negative cash flow amounts. See page 785 for more about this function.

The following example uses @IRR to find the internal rate of return for a six-year investment project. In the first year, an output of $80,000 is required to start the investment. The five subsequent years produce various income amounts: $15,000 at the end of the second year, $20,000 at the end of the third and fourth years, and $25,000 at the end of the fifth and sixth years. What is the calculated IRR for this sequence of cash flow amounts?

	A	B	C	D
1	*Internal Rate of Return*			
2				
3	Year	Cash Flow		
4	1	($80,000)		
5	2	$15,000		
6	3	$20,000	IRR	NPV
7	4	$20,000	9.00%	($0.00)
8	5	$25,000		
9	6	$25,000		
10				

5

Formulas and Functions

The function @IRR(0.1,B4..B9) is stored in cell C7. The guess supplied as the first argument is 10%. The range of cash flow amounts is B4..B9. @IRR calculates the internal rate of return as 9%. To confirm that this figure matches the IRR definition, the formula @NPV(B11,B4..B9) appears in cell D7. Given the calculated IRR, the @NPV function gives an approximate result of zero.

Mathematical Functions

1-2-3 has a standard set of mathematical functions, including the trigonometric, logarithmic, and exponential functions. In addition, several of the mathematical functions have important roles in everyday business worksheets. For example, the @RAND function produces random numbers, which you can use to supply random data for testing worksheet formulas, or to rearrange data in a random order; and the @INT and @ROUND functions are useful for converting real numbers to integers, or for rounding numbers to a specified decimal place. In the sections ahead you'll see examples of these functions.

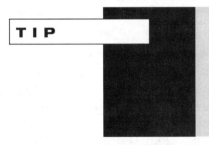

TIP

1-2-3 also has a set of specialized engineering functions, including Bessel, Beta, Gamma, and error functions. Read about these in Part Four of this book, or choose Help – Search and enter engineering functions as the search key. See Chapter 19 for an examination of all the mathematical functions.

Trigonometric Functions

Lotus 1-2-3 has a full set of trigonometric and inverse trigonometric functions. The trigonometric functions take arguments expressed in radians. The inverse functions produce radian values. A *radian* is a multiple of the value π, where the range 0 to $2^{\star}\pi$ is equivalent to 0 to 360 degrees.

Here are some sample radian equivalents:

RADIAN	EQUIVALENT IN DEGREES
0*π	0 degrees
π/4	45 degrees
π/2	90 degrees
π	180 degrees
3π*/2	270 degrees
2*π	360 degrees

To simplify the task of supplying arguments in radians, 1-2-3 has a built-in @PI function; this function gives the value of π, accurate to 17 digits:

3.14159265358979324

5

Formulas and Functions

T I P

1-2-3 also supplies the @DEGTORAD function for converting degrees to radians, and the @RADTODEG function for converting radians to degrees. See page 900 and 910 for details.

Figure 5.15 shows @SIN, @COS, and @TAN values for a range of radian arguments from –π/2 to +π/2. The sine and cosine values move through their familiar wave patterns in this range: sine goes from –1 to 0 to 1, and cosine goes from 0 to 1 to 0. The result of the tangent function approaches infinity for arguments approaching +π/2, and negative infinity for arguments approaching –π/2.

The following exercise guides you through the steps of producing the sine and cosine table on your own worksheet:

1. On a blank worksheet, enter **–0.5** in cell A4 and **–0.4375** in cell A5. Select A4..A5 and use the drag-and-fill technique to extend this sequence down to cell A20.

2. Click the Format selector in the status bar and choose the Fixed format. Then click the Decimal selector, the second panel, and

FIGURE 5.15

Examples of the trigonometric functions

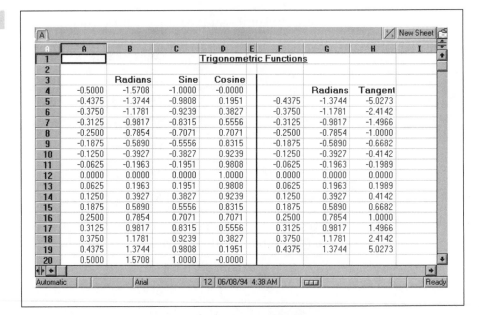

	A	B	C	D	E	F	G	H	I
1				Trigonometric Functions					
2									
3		Radians	Sine	Cosine					
4	-0.5000	-1.5708	-1.0000	-0.0000			Radians	Tangent	
5	-0.4375	-1.3744	-0.9808	0.1951		-0.4375	-1.3744	-5.0273	
6	-0.3750	-1.1781	-0.9239	0.3827		-0.3750	-1.1781	-2.4142	
7	-0.3125	-0.9817	-0.8315	0.5556		-0.3125	-0.9817	-1.4966	
8	-0.2500	-0.7854	-0.7071	0.7071		-0.2500	-0.7854	-1.0000	
9	-0.1875	-0.5890	-0.5556	0.8315		-0.1875	-0.5890	-0.6682	
10	-0.1250	-0.3927	-0.3827	0.9239		-0.1250	-0.3927	-0.4142	
11	-0.0625	-0.1963	-0.1951	0.9808		-0.0625	-0.1963	-0.1989	
12	0.0000	0.0000	0.0000	1.0000		0.0000	0.0000	0.0000	
13	0.0625	0.1963	0.1951	0.9808		0.0625	0.1963	0.1989	
14	0.1250	0.3927	0.3827	0.9239		0.1250	0.3927	0.4142	
15	0.1875	0.5890	0.5556	0.8315		0.1875	0.5890	0.6682	
16	0.2500	0.7854	0.7071	0.7071		0.2500	0.7854	1.0000	
17	0.3125	0.9817	0.8315	0.5556		0.3125	0.9817	1.4966	
18	0.3750	1.1781	0.9239	0.3827		0.3750	1.1781	2.4142	
19	0.4375	1.3744	0.9808	0.1951		0.4375	1.3744	5.0273	
20	0.5000	1.5708	1.0000	-0.0000					

choose 4 as the number of decimal places.

3. Enter the following in cells B4 to D4:

CELL	ENTER
B4	@PI★A4
C4	@SIN(B4)
D4	@COS(B4)

4. Select the range B4..D20. Click the selection with the right mouse button, and choose Copy Down from the resulting quick menu. Enter the column headings as you see them in Figure 5.15.

NOTE For complete information on @SIN, @COS, and @TAN, see page 918, 896, and 926, respectively.

Inverse trigonometric functions The *inverse* trigonometric functions take single numeric arguments and return angles in radians. For example,

Figure 5.16 shows the arcsine and arccosine values for a range of decimal arguments between –1 to 1. The arcsine value goes from –π/2 to π/2 for this range of arguments, and the arccosine value goes from π × 2 down to zero. Here are the functions entered into cells B4 and C4:

| B4 | @ASIN(A4) |
| C4 | @ACOS(A4) |

To produce the table, these functions were copied down columns B and C.

N O T E

For a complete examination of @ACOS, @ASIN, @ATAN, and @ATAN2, see page 890, 893, 894, and 895, respectively.

Figure 5.16 also shows examples of arctangent functions. As you can see, the arctangent approaches –π for large negative arguments, and +π for

FIGURE 5.16

Examples of inverse
trigonometric functions

	A	B	C	D	E	F	G	H	I	J	K
1			Inverse Trigonometric Functions								
2											
3	Argument	ASIN	ACOS		Argument	ATAN		x	y	ATAN2	
4	-1.0000	-1.5708	3.1416		-100000	-1.5708		-0.5	-1.0	-2.0344	
5	-0.8750	-1.0654	2.6362		-10000	-1.5707		-1.0	-1.0	-2.3562	
6	-0.7500	-0.8481	2.4189		-1000	-1.5698		-1.0	-0.5	-2.6779	
7	-0.6250	-0.6751	2.2459		-100	-1.5608		-1.0	0.0	3.1416	
8	-0.5000	-0.5236	2.0944		-10	-1.4711		-1.0	0.5	2.6779	
9	-0.3750	-0.3844	1.9552		-1	-0.7854		-1.0	1.0	2.3562	
10	-0.2500	-0.2527	1.8235		-0.1	-0.0997		-0.5	1.0	2.0344	
11	-0.1250	-0.1253	1.6961		0	0.0000		0.0	1.0	1.5708	
12	0.0000	0.0000	1.5708		0.1	0.0997		0.5	1.0	1.1071	
13	0.1250	0.1253	1.4455		1	0.7854		1.0	1.0	0.7854	
14	0.2500	0.2527	1.3181		10	1.4711		1.0	0.5	0.4636	
15	0.3750	0.3844	1.1864		100	1.5608		1.0	0.0	0.0000	
16	0.5000	0.5236	1.0472		1000	1.5698		1.0	-0.5	-0.4636	
17	0.6250	0.6751	0.8957		10000	1.5707		1.0	-1.0	-0.7854	
18	0.7500	0.8481	0.7227		100000	1.5708		0.5	-1.0	-1.1071	
19	0.8750	1.0654	0.5054					0.0	-1.0	-1.5708	
20	1.0000	1.5708	0.0000								

New Sheet

Automatic | Arial | 12 | 06/08/94 5:08 AM | | Ready

large positive arguments. Here is the formula stored in cell F4:

@ATAN(E4)

The @ATAN2 function supplies radian angles in a four-quadrant x-y coordinate system. This function takes two numeric arguments, forming a coordinate pair:

@ATAN2(*x, y*)

The result of @ATAN2 is the angle formed by two lines in the coordinate system: the x-axis extending horizontally to the right from the origin, and the line from (0,0) to (x,y). Figure 5.16 shows a range of examples. The formula in cell J4 is as follows:

@ATAN2(H4,I4)

TIP

In addition to the examples you've seen here, 1-2-3 also supplies secant, cosecant, and cotangent functions, along with the equivalent inverse trigonometric functions and hyperbolic functions. See Chapter 19.

Exponential and Logarithmic Functions

The exponential and logarithmic functions are @EXP and @LN, both based on the natural constant e; and @LOG, based on 10. The @EXP function calculates exponents of e, where the value of e is represented as:

2.71828182845904524

@EXP takes one numeric argument, *x*, and supplies the value of e to the *x* power. The @LN function finds the natural logarithm of its argument. @LN takes one argument, *x*, and supplies the power of e that produces *x*. The @LOG function gives the base-10 logarithm. @LOG takes one numeric argument, *x*, and returns the power of 10 that gives *x*. Figure 5.17 shows a range of examples for all three of these functions.

Finally, the @SQRT function gives the square root of its numeric argument. The argument must be greater than zero. The last column in

FIGURE 5.17

Examples of @EXP,
@LN, @LOG, and
@SQRT

	The Exponential, Logarithmic, and Square Root Functions							
	A	B	C D	E	F	G H	I	J
1		The Exponential, Logarithmic, and Square Root Functions						
2								
3	x	EXP(x)	x	LN(x)	LOG(x)	x	SQRT(x)	
4	-1.00	0.3679	0.50	-0.6931	-0.3010	0.25	0.5000	
5	-0.75	0.4724	1.00	0.0000	0.0000	0.50	0.7071	
6	-0.50	0.6065	1.50	0.4055	0.1761	0.75	0.8660	
7	-0.25	0.7788	2.00	0.6931	0.3010	1.00	1.0000	
8	0.00	1.0000	2.50	0.9163	0.3979	1.25	1.1180	
9	0.25	1.2840	3.00	1.0986	0.4771	1.50	1.2247	
10	0.50	1.6487	3.50	1.2528	0.5441	1.75	1.3229	
11	0.75	2.1170	4.00	1.3863	0.6021	2.00	1.4142	
12	1.00	2.7183	4.50	1.5041	0.6532	2.25	1.5000	
13	1.25	3.4903	5.00	1.6094	0.6990	2.50	1.5811	
14								

Figure 5.17 shows examples of @SQRT.

NOTE

@EXP, @LN, @LOG, and @SQRT are also discussed on page 901, 905, 906, and 921, respectively.

The @RAND Function

The @RAND function produces random numbers. The function takes no argument, and supplies a random decimal value between 0 and 1. If you want to generate random numbers in another range, you can multiply @RAND by the maximum value in the range. For example, the following formula produces random numbers between 0 and 100:

@RAND*100

To produce random integers, you can use 1-2-3's built-in @INT function with @RAND. @INT eliminates the decimal portion of a real number, and supplies the integer portion. For instance, the following formula gives random integers between 0 and 100:

@INT(@RAND*100)

This is an example of a formula in which one function appears as the argument of another function. You'll see other examples as you continue in this chapter. The @RAND and @INT functions are also discussed on page 909 and 903.

Figure 5.18 shows four columns of random numbers, generated using the @RAND and @INT functions. Column A contains random decimal values between 0 and 1; column B, random numbers from 0 to 100; column C, random integers from 0 to 10; and column D, random integers from 0 to 1000. To produce these numbers, the four formulas shown in row 3 were copied down their respective columns.

FIGURE 5.18

Examples of the @RAND function

A	A	B	C	D
1		The @RAND Function		
2				
3	@RAND	@RAND*100	@INT(@RAND*10)	@INT(@RAND*1000)
4	0.439488846082	40.97704335161	6	25
5	0.489036100213	1.167610567607	4	935
6	0.229736279338	24.03080976756	8	231
7	0.177646826104	85.81976335767	5	556
8	0.71020633155	72.76275231166	6	769
9	0.437814364879	23.57810205947	1	793
10	0.34603052649	77.16131344305	9	294
11	0.735058716841	50.19503741069	7	924
12	0.131853940027	27.99376138858	2	209
13	0.069170029866	91.14765789879	3	457
14	0.540691959923	18.68630494861	7	442
15				

@RAND and automatic recalculation The @RAND function is commonly used for producing random test data and for arranging records in random order. But before you use @RAND for these applications, you should consider the implications of 1-2-3's automatic recalculation mode. As you know, 1-2-3 recalculates formulas in a worksheet whenever a change occurs in the data that the formulas depend on. The @RAND function takes no argument and is therefore independent of any particular data value on the worksheet. However, whenever 1-2-3 recalculates any formula on the worksheet, it also recalculates all cells that contain

@RAND entries. For this reason, the random values on the worksheet appear to be unstable: They change whenever the worksheet is recalculated. This can be a problem if you are trying to perform a test with a fixed set of random numbers.

There are two different ways of solving this problem. One way is to switch 1-2-3 out of its automatic recalculation mode while you use the @RAND function, and the other way is to convert @RAND function entries into simple numeric values. You can switch out of automatic recalculation mode by choosing Tools ➤ User Setup, clicking the Recalculation button, and then selecting the Manual option in the resulting dialog box:

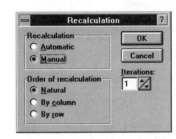

In the manual recalculation mode, 1-2-3 recalculates formulas on the worksheet only when you instruct it to do so: You force a recalculation by pressing the F9 function key. When formulas need to be recalculated— normally after a change in the worksheet's data—1-2-3 displays the word "Calc" in the second-to-last panel of the status bar. Ignore the Calc message if you are working with a particular set of random numbers that you want to keep. Press F9 only when you want to change the set of random numbers on your worksheet.

Try this exercise with the @RAND function in the manual recalculation mode:

1. On a blank worksheet, enter **@RAND** into cell A1. A random number between 0 and 1 appears in the cell.

2. Now select cell A2 and enter a value of **1**.

Even though this new entry has no relationship to the formula in cell A1—or to any other formula, since none other currently appears in the worksheet—1-2-3 recalculates the @RAND function anyway. A new random number appears in cell A1. This change could be disconcerting if you were using random numbers as test data on your worksheet. You'd prefer to have the opportunity to examine the results of one random scenario before suddenly jumping to a new one.

3. Now choose Tools ➤ User Setup and click the Recalculation button on the resulting dialog box. In the Recalculation dialog box, click the Manual option to switch into the manual recalculation mode. Click OK in both dialog boxes to confirm the change.

4. Now enter a value of **2** into cell A2.

In the manual mode, 1-2-3 does not automatically recalculate any formula on the worksheet. The random number displayed in cell A1 does not change.

Notice the word "Calc" at the right side of the status bar. This tells you that 1-2-3 has not recalculated the worksheet, because of the manual recalculation mode.

5. Press the F9 function key to force a recalculation. A new random number appears in cell A1, and the word "Calc" disappears from the status line.

6. Continue experimenting with this worksheet in the manual mode, if you wish. When you are finished, choose Tools ➤ User Setup again, click Recalculation, and switch 1-2-3 back into the Automatic mode. Then close this worksheet without saving.

By the way, the Recalculation settings apply to all worksheets that are open at the time you select a setting.

The second way to prevent 1-2-3 from recalculating random numbers is to convert a @RAND function entry into a simple numeric value entry. As a result of this conversion, a worksheet cell will contain a random number that was generated by @RAND, but the @RAND function itself will not be present in the cell. You can accomplish this conversion either before or after you complete the @RAND entry. To convert a function or formula to a value during the entry process, you simply press the F9 function key before pressing ↵. After a function or formula is already entered into a cell, you can make the same conversion by using the Edit ➤ Paste Special command.

You'll experiment with both of these techniques in the following exercise:

1. Select cell A1 on a blank worksheet, and type **@RAND** as a formula entry. Do not press ↵.

2. Press the F9 function key. In response, 1-2-3 converts the @RAND function into a random numeric value entry.

3. Now press ↵. The random number in A1 is now static, because the entry is a value rather than a formula.

4. Select cell A2 and type the **@RAND** function into the cell. Press ↵ to complete the entry. (Do not press F9 this time.)

5. Select A2..A10 and click the selection with the right mouse button. In the resulting quick menu, choose Copy Down. When you complete the copy operation, a different random number appears in each of the cells in the range.

6. With the range A2..A10 still selected, press Ctrl+C to copy the selection to the Clipboard. Then choose Edit ➤ Paste Special. In the resulting dialog box, select the option labeled Formulas as values:

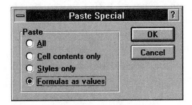

7. Click OK or press ↵ to confirm this option.

Back on your worksheet, the entries in the selected range are now numeric value entries, not functions. You can confirm this by selecting any cell in the range and examining the contents box. You'll see a long decimal number in the box, not a @RAND entry.

The Paste Formulas as Values SmartIcon 1-2-3 provides a SmartIcon that performs the formula-to-value conversion in two quick steps. You can find this tool by clicking the SmartIcons selector on the status bar and choosing the Editing SmartIcon set. The Paste Formulas as Values SmartIcon is located in the fourth group of SmartIcons in the set. To use this SmartIcon, select a range of formulas that you want to convert, press Ctrl+C to copy the range to the Clipboard, and then simply click the icon.

Now consider a situation in which you might use the @RAND function in a worksheet. Imagine that you have a group of employees whom you evaluate formally once a year. You hold individual evaluation meetings in September. To avoid conducting these meetings in the same alphabetical order each year, you want a way to rearrange the list of employees in random order.

The list of employee names appears in columns B and C in the worksheet shown in Figure 5.19. The list is currently in alphabetical order. Here are the steps you take to rearrange the list randomly:

1. Enter the formula @INT(@RAND*50) in cell A1. Select the range A1..A15, and click the selection with the right mouse button. Choose Copy Down from the resulting quick menu.

FIGURE 5.19

Using random numbers to rearrange a list of names

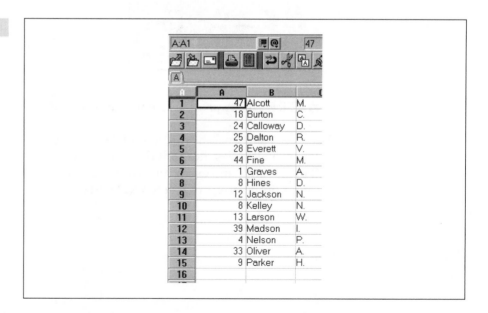

A random integer between 0 and 50 appears in each cell, as in Figure 5.19. (The random numbers on your worksheet will be different from the ones in this figure.)

2. Select the range A1..A15 and press Ctrl+C. Click the Paste Formulas as Values SmartIcon in the Editing SmartIcon set, or use the Edit ➤ Paste Special command to complete the same operation. Back on the worksheet, the random numbers in column A are now simple value entries rather than function entries.

3. Select the range A1..C15. Choose Range ➤ Sort. The Sort dialog appears on the screen:

Enter **A:A1** in the Sort by box, click Add Key, and then click OK.

Back on the worksheet, the list of employee names is now rearranged randomly according to the random numbers you entered into column A, as shown in Figure 5.20.

Once you've completed your employee evaluation, you can use the Range ➤ Sort command to realphabetize the list of employees. (You'll learn more about the Range ➤ Sort command in Chapter 7.)

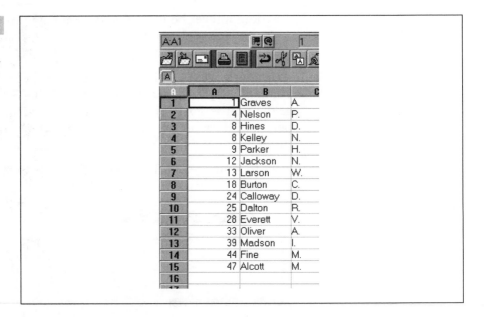

More Mathematical Functions

Among the remaining tools in this category are three miscellaneous but important functions named @ROUND, @MOD, and @ABS.

The @ROUND function The @ROUND function takes two numeric arguments. The first argument, x, is the number that you want to round, and the second, n, is an integer representing the decimal place at which you want the rounding to occur:

    @ROUND(x, n)

If n is positive, rounding takes place at the right side of the decimal point. For example, if you enter a value of **2** for n, the function rounds the value x to the nearest hundredth. If n is negative, rounding occurs at the left side of the decimal point. For example, if you enter –1 for n, the function rounds x to the nearest multiple of ten. Finally, a value of zero for n results in rounding to the nearest whole integer. See page 911 for more information on this function.

The worksheet in Figure 5.21 shows examples of the @ROUND function. Column A in this worksheet contains a series of random numbers between 0 and 100. In columns B through E, these numbers are rounded to the nearest thousandth, the nearest hundredth, the nearest integer, and the nearest multiple of ten, respectively. Here are the formulas in cells A4, B4, C4, D4, and E4:

A4	@RAND*100
B4	@ROUND(A4,3)
C4	@ROUND(A4,2)
D4	@ROUND(A4,0)
E4	@ROUND(A4,−1)

These formulas are copied down the worksheet, to the range A5..E13.

FIGURE 5.21

Experimenting with the @ROUND function

	A	B	C	D	E
1		The @ROUND Function			
2					
3	RAND*100	n=3	n=2	n=0	n=−1
4	65.21192	65.212	65.21	65	70
5	16.75987	16.76	16.76	17	20
6	83.15113	83.151	83.15	83	80
7	20.99883	20.999	21	21	20
8	27.32226	27.322	27.32	27	30
9	5.24926	5.249	5.25	5	10
10	24.36127	24.361	24.36	24	20
11	39.93576	39.936	39.94	40	40
12	0.26095	0.261	0.26	0	0
13	85.76428	85.764	85.76	86	90
14					

The @MOD function The @MOD function performs division between two integers, but unlike the division operator, @MOD supplies the remainder from the division, not the quotient. @MOD is known as the *modulus function*. It takes two arguments, the numerator and the denominator of the division operation:

@MOD(x, y)

If y divides evenly into x with no remainder, @MOD supplies a value of zero. Otherwise, @MOD returns the remainder from the division. For example, try entering @MOD(25,9) into a cell. The result is 7. The division of 9 into 25 gives a value of 2 with a remainder of 7.

@MOD is useful in a variety of applications. For example, suppose you have an alphabetized list of one hundred employees, with employee numbers that range from 1 to 100. For evaluation purposes, you want to divide this list randomly into five groups of 20 employees each. If the employee numbers are displayed in column A (from A1 to A100), you can copy the following formula down column B to assign each employee a group number from 1 to 5:

    @MOD(A1,5)+1

See page 906 for more information about this function.

The @ABS function Finally, the @ABS function gives the absolute value of a number. @ABS takes one numeric argument, x:

    @ABS(x)

Whether x is positive or negative, @ABS returns the unsigned (positive) equivalent of the argument.

Use this function when the sign of a numeric value is not relevant to your worksheet. When you subtract one number from another, the result may be positive or negative, depending upon which number is larger; applying @ABS to the subtraction guarantees a positive result. For example, the following worksheet displays the difference in days between two dates:

A	A	B
1	28-Nov-94	
2	08-Jun-94	
3	Difference in days:	
4		173
5		

Cell B4 contains a formula for finding the number of days between the two dates:

    @ABS(A2–A1)

This formula gives a positive number of days, regardless of which day is later in time. See page 890 for more information about this function.

Date and Time Functions

1-2-3 has a useful set of chronological functions for working with date and time values. You can use functions in this category to:

- Read the current date and time from the system calendar and clock
- Get information about existing date and time values
- Convert other types of data into date and time values
- Perform date arithmetic

Two important functions supply values representing the current date and time:

FUNCTION	USE
@TODAY	Returns a date number representing the current date. For example, @TODAY gives the integer value 34493 for the date 8-Jun-94. The @TODAY function takes no argument.
@NOW	Returns a combined date-and-time number representing both the current date and the current time. For example, @NOW supplies the combined value 34493.25 for the date 8-Jun-94 at 6:00 A.M. @NOW takes no argument.

5

Formulas and Functions

Several functions supply information about a date value or a time value. Among these are the following:

FUNCTION	USE
@DAY	Takes a date number as its argument—@DAY(*datenumber*)—and returns an integer from 1 to 31 representing the day of the month.
@WEEKDAY	Takes a date number argument—@WEEKDAY(*datenumber*)—and returns an integer from 0 to 6, representing a day from Monday to Sunday.
@MONTH	Takes a date number argument—@MONTH(*datenumber*)—and returns an integer from 1 to 12 representing the month.
@YEAR	Takes a date number argument—@YEAR(*datenumber*)—and returns an integer representing the year.
@DATEINFO	Takes two arguments, a date and an attribute number from 1 to 13—@DATEINFO(*datenumber, attribute*). As shown in Figure 5.22, this function returns a specific item of information about the date, depending upon the attribute number you select.
@HOUR	Takes a decimal time number as its argument—@HOUR(*timenumber*)—and returns an integer from 0 to 23 representing the hour.

The information
available from the
@DATEINFO function

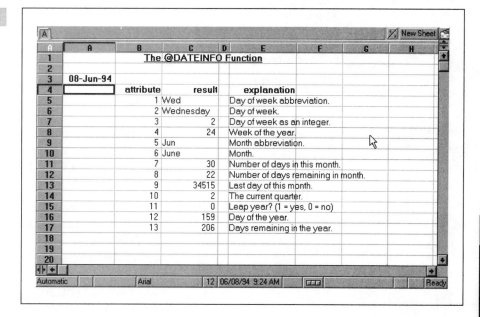

attribute	result	explanation
1	Wed	Day of week abbreviation.
2	Wednesday	Day of week.
3	2	Day of week as an integer.
4	24	Week of the year.
5	Jun	Month abbreviation.
6	June	Month.
7	30	Number of days in this month.
8	22	Number of days remaining in month.
9	34515	Last day of this month.
10	2	The current quarter.
11	0	Leap year? (1 = yes, 0 = no)
12	159	Day of the year.
13	206	Days remaining in the year.

(A3 = 08-Jun-94; The @DATEINFO Function)

FUNCTION   **USE**

@MINUTE   Takes a time number argument—
@MINUTE(*timenumber*)—and
returns an integer from 0 to 59
representing the minutes.

@SECOND   Takes a time number argument—
@SECOND(*timenumber*)—and
returns an integer from 0 to 59
representing the seconds.

These functions also accept combined date-and-time arguments, in the
form supplied by the @NOW function.

The following functions convert numeric values or strings into dates or strings:

FUNCTION	USE
@DATE	Takes three integer arguments representing the year, the month, and the day—@DATE(*year, month, day*). The function returns the corresponding date number. For example, @DATE(94,6,8) gives the date number 34493.
@DATEVALUE	Takes a string argument in a format that 1-2-3 can recognize as a date—@DATE(*string*). The function returns the corresponding date number. For example, @DATEVALUE("8-Jun-94") supplies the number 34493.
@DATESTRING	Converts a date value into a text date. For example, @DATESTRING(34493) returns 06/08/94 as a label.
@TIME	Takes three numeric arguments representing the hour, the minutes, and the seconds—@TIME(*hour, minutes, seconds*). The function returns the corresponding decimal time number. For example, @TIME(4,30,0) gives the value 0.1875.
@TIMEVALUE	Takes a string argument in a format that 1-2-3 can recognize as a time—@TIMEVALUE(*string*). The function returns the corresponding time number. For example, @TIMEVALUE("4:30 AM") gives the value 0.1875.

Finally, several functions perform special date arithmetic operations. Among them are these three:

FUNCTION	USE
@DATEDIF	Takes two dates and a format specifier as its arguments— @DATEDIF(*date1*, *date2*, *format*)—and returns the difference between the two dates in days, months, or years, depending on the *format* argument. Figure 5.23 provides a more thorough explanation of this function.

FIGURE 5.23

Using the @DATEDIF function

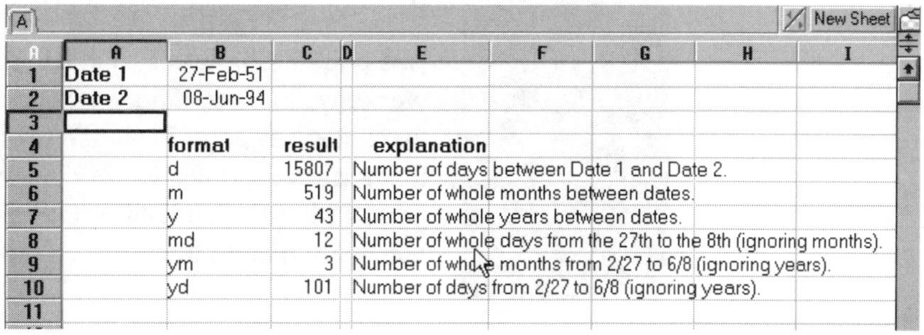

	A	B	C	D	E
1	Date 1	27-Feb-51			
2	Date 2	08-Jun-94			
3					
4		format	result		explanation
5		d	15807		Number of days between Date 1 and Date 2.
6		m	519		Number of whole months between dates.
7		y	43		Number of whole years between dates.
8		md	12		Number of whole days from the 27th to the 8th (ignoring months).
9		ym	3		Number of whole months from 2/27 to 6/8 (ignoring years).
10		yd	101		Number of days from 2/27 to 6/8 (ignoring years).
11					

FUNCTION	USE
@DAYS360	Takes two date numbers as arguments—@DAYS360(*date1*, *date2*). The function calculates the number of days between the two dates, using a standard algorithm based on a 360-day year.

FUNCTION	USE
@D360	Also takes two date numbers as arguments—@D360(*date1*, *date2*). This function calculates the number of days between the two dates, based on a year of twelve months with 30 days each.

NOTE Chapter 14 explains calendar functions in detail.

TIP Several other date functions perform calculations for specialized business uses: @DAYS uses one of four algorithms to find the number of days between two dates (see page 712). @NETWORKDAYS finds the number of workdays (not counting weekends and holidays) between two dates (see page 716). @WORKDAY finds a workday that is a specified number of days from a given date (see page 724). @NEXTMONTH finds the date that is a specified number of months from a given date (see page 718).

Working with Date and Time Functions

In upcoming exercises you'll see worksheet examples of date and time functions. To start, here's a simple experiment with the @NOW function and the six functions that supply information about date and time values—@DAY, @MONTH, @YEAR, @HOUR, @MINUTE, and @SECOND:

1. On a new blank worksheet, type the @NOW function into cell B1. (Recall that the function takes no argument.) To convert the function to a value, press the F9 key before you press ↵. A number representing the current date and time appears in B1. Choose Range

➤ Name and assign the name DATETIME to this cell.

2. In cells B2 through B7, enter the following six functions:

CELL	ENTER
B2	@DAY(DATETIME)
B3	@MONTH(DATETIME)
B4	@YEAR(DATETIME)
B5	@HOUR(DATETIME)
B6	@MINUTE(DATETIME)
B8	@SECOND(DATETIME)

These six functions give the components of the date and time value displayed in cell B1.

Here is an example of this experiment:

	A	B
1	Now	34493.43
2	Day	8
3	Month	6
4	Year	94
5	Hour	10
6	Minute	22
7	Second	15
8		

Of course, the date-and-time values shown here will be different from the ones on your own worksheet.

In Figure 5.24 you see a practical use of the @MONTH and @DAY functions, along with an example of the @TODAY function in a formula. The worksheet shows a list of employees. The employees' names are displayed in column A, and their birth dates are in column B. Column C contains a formula that calculates each employee's age. The formula (@TODAY–B4)/365 is entered in cell C4—for the first employee—and then copied down the column. (The Fixed format with no decimal places has been applied to the column of data.) Examine this formula carefully. The expression in parentheses finds an employee's age in days by subtracting the employee's birth date from today's date:

@TODAY–B4

Dividing this number of days by 365 gives the employee's age in years.

FIGURE 5.24

Using the @TODAY function to calculate employees' ages

	A	B	C	D	E
1		Employees' Birthdays			
2					
3	Name	Date of Birth	Age	Mo	Day
4	Graves, A.	23-Jun-35	59	6	23
5	Alcott, M.	05-Aug-39	55	8	5
6	Parker, H.	08-May-45	49	5	8
7	Dalton, R.	06-Jul-47	47	7	6
8	Hines, D.	27-Oct-51	43	10	27
9	Oliver, A.	03-Sep-54	40	9	3
10	Jackson, N.	19-Jun-59	35	6	19
11	Everett, V.	02-Dec-59	35	12	2
12	Larson, W.	07-Aug-65	29	8	7
13	Nelson, P.	02-Jan-67	27	1	2
14	Madson, I.	07-Apr-68	26	4	7
15	Burton, C.	05-Aug-69	25	8	5
16	Fine, M.	01-Feb-70	24	2	1
17	Kelley, N.	08-Nov-71	23	11	8
18	Calloway, D.	03-Mar-72	22	3	3
19					

NOTE

The @DATEDIF function is another way to carry out this calculation. You'll decide for yourself whether you prefer to use @DATEDIF or your own formulas for finding the difference between two dates. See page 706 for more information.)

Notice that this list is arranged by the employees' ages, in descending order—that is, from the oldest employee to the youngest, or from the earliest birth date to the most recent. Imagine the following situation: The company where these employees work has a policy of giving each employee an extra vacation day per year on the employee's birthday. To monitor these vacation days, the employees' manager would like to rearrange the employee list in order of calendar birthdays, from the first birthday in January to the last birthday in December. Accomplishing this calls for the use of the @MONTH and @DAY functions:

1. Enter the function **@MONTH(B4)** in cell D4, and the function **@DAY(B4)** in cell E4. Copy these two formulas down their respective columns, to the range D5..E18.

Together, these two functions give the month and day of each employee's birthday, as shown in Figure 5.24.

2. Select the range A4..E18 and choose Range ➤ Sort. Click Reset in the resulting dialog box to cancel any previous sorting instructions. Enter D4 in the Sort by box and click Add Key. Then enter E4 and click Add Key again. Then click OK or press ↵ to complete the operation.

As a result, 1-2-3 sorts the list by employees' birthdays, from January to December. As you can see in Figure 5.25, columns D and E show the month and the day of each birthday through the course of the calendar year. The manager can now use this worksheet to anticipate each employee's extra vacation day.

In some worksheet applications you might prefer to enter the day, month, and year components of dates in three separate columns, as shown in columns A, B, and C of the sheet on the following page.

	A	B	C	D
1	Day	Month	Year	Date
2	31	1	63	31-Jan-63
3	28	2	61	28-Feb-61
4	21	3	93	21-Mar-93
5	5	4	71	05-Apr-71
6	9	5	88	09-May-88
7	30	6	55	30-Jun-55
8	24	7	88	24-Jul-88
9	17	8	76	17-Aug-76

Some spreadsheet users find this arrangement more efficient for input purposes, especially when dates have to be read from hand-written forms

	A	B	C	D	E
1		Employees' Birthdays			
2					
3	Name	Date of Birth	Age	Mo	Day
4	Nelson, P.	02-Jan-67	27	1	2
5	Fine, M.	01-Feb-70	24	2	1
6	Calloway, D.	03-Mar-72	22	3	3
7	Madson, I.	07-Apr-68	26	4	7
8	Parker, H.	08-May-45	49	5	8
9	Jackson, N.	19-Jun-59	35	6	19
10	Graves, A.	23-Jun-35	59	6	23
11	Dalton, R.	06-Jul-47	47	7	6
12	Alcott, M.	05-Aug-39	55	8	5
13	Burton, C.	05-Aug-69	25	8	5
14	Larson, W.	07-Aug-65	29	8	7
15	Oliver, A.	03-Sep-54	40	9	3
16	Hines, D.	27-Oct-51	43	10	27
17	Kelley, N.	08-Nov-71	23	11	8
18	Everett, V.	02-Dec-59	35	12	2
19					

and entered manually into a worksheet. Given a list of dates in this three-column format, you can use 1-2-3's @DATE function to convert the date components into date numbers—so that you can ultimately perform date arithmetic operations on the worksheet. For example, the formula entered into cell D2 is @DATE(C2,B2,A2). After copying this formula down column D, you can click the Format selector, the first panel on the status bar, and select an appropriate date display format.

You may need to perform another kind of data conversion on a worksheet that contains date or time label entries. In particular, you might find yourself in this situation if you load data into a 1-2-3 worksheet from a different software environment. The following worksheet shows the date and time label formats that 1-2-3 can successfully convert into date and time numbers:

	A	B	C	D	E
1	Date String	Date Number		Time String	Time Number
2	1-Dec-94	34669		4:30:00 PM	0.6875
3	1-Dec	34669		4:30 PM	0.6875
4	Dec-94	34669		16:30:00	0.6875
5	12/1/94	34669		16:30	0.6875
6	12/1	34669			

Column A of this worksheet contains examples of five date formats 1-2-3 recognizes. The @DATEVALUE function converts these labels into date numbers. The formula @DATEVALUE(A5) has been entered into cell B5 and copied down column B. Column D of the same worksheet shows examples of four time formats that 1-2-3 recognizes. In this case, the @TIMEVALUE function converts these labels into decimal time numbers. The formula @TIMEVALUE(D5) in cell E5 has been copied down column E.

The @DAYS360 and @D360 functions are available for special financial contexts in which date arithmetic is based on a 360-day year. The worksheet in Figure 5.26 shows examples of these tools. Columns A and B in this worksheet show two lists of dates. Columns C, D, and E display the results of the three techniques for finding the difference in days between pairs of dates. Here are the three formulas in cells C4, D4, and E4:

C4	+B4–A4
D4	@DAYS360(A4,B4)
E4	@D360(A4,B4)

5

Formulas and Functions

	A	B	C	D	E
1			Difference between Two Dates		
2					
3	Date1	Date2	subtraction	DAYS360	D360
4	15-Jan-85	22-May-86	492	487	487
5	04-Sep-86	31-Aug-83	-1100	-1083	-1084
6	31-Oct-92	28-Feb-94	485	478	478
7	07-Jul-91	02-Nov-86	-1708	-1685	-1685
8	31-Oct-93	30-Oct-93	-1	0	0
9	11-Dec-85	27-Feb-82	-1383	-1364	-1364
10	18-Feb-89	06-Mar-87	-715	-702	-702
11	18-Feb-86	31-Aug-95	3481	3433	3432
12	30-Apr-95	30-Jun-93	-669	-660	-660
13	21-Jan-86	05-Jan-94	2906	2864	2864
14					

Of course, only the first of these formulas finds the exact number of days between two dates. The @DAYS360 and @D360 find approximations of the difference, for the convenience of particular financial applications. As you can see, the three formulas produce different results.

Logical Functions

1-2-3 has an interesting assortment of logical functions that supply information about a worksheet. Like logical formulas, these functions give values of 1 or 0, representing true or false. For example, the @ISNUMBER function takes a cell address as its argument, and returns a value of 1 (true) if the cell contains a value or 0 (false) if the cell is blank. You're more likely to use functions like this one in macros than in everyday worksheet applications.

TIP See Chapter 18 for complete coverage of the logical functions.

The @IF function But there is at least one tool in the logical function category that is very important in worksheets—the @IF function. This function evaluates a logical expression and chooses between one of two values, depending on whether the expression is true or false. The @IF function takes three arguments:

@IF(*expression,value1,value2*)

The first argument is the logical expression that @IF evaluates. You can use operators that you studied earlier in this chapter to build a logical expression for the @IF function—the relational operators, =, <>, <, >, <=, and >=; and the logical operators #NOT#, #AND#, and #OR# (see page 267).

The second and third arguments of the @IF function are the data items that the function chooses between. If the logical expression in the first argument is evaluated as true, @IF returns value1. If the logical expression is false, @IF gives value2. In other words, when you enter the @IF function into a worksheet cell, you can expect the function to display either value1 or value2 in the cell. (See page 854 for more detailed information.)

Try the following simple example:

1. Enter a value of **0** in cell A1 of a blank worksheet.

2. Enter the following formula in cell A2:

   @IF(A1=0,"zero","not zero")

   The word *zero* appears in cell A2.

3. Now select cell A1 again and enter a value of **10**. The display in cell A2 changes to *not zero*.

The @IF function evaluates the expression A1=0 to decide which label to display in cell A2.

The *value1* and *value2* arguments in the @IF function can be strings enclosed in quotes, as in the previous example, or they can appear as values or calculations. For a more interesting example of the @IF function, consider the following worksheet:

	A	B	
	Billing Date	**Due Date**	
1	Billing Date	Due Date	
2	14-Jan-94	14-Feb-94	
3	28-Jan-94	28-Feb-94	
4	05-Feb-94	07-Mar-94	
5	20-Feb-94	22-Mar-94	
6	14-Mar-94	13-Apr-94	
7			

5

Formulas and Functions

Imagine that the calculations on this worksheet are part of a billing application. Column A contains a list of dates on which a company has sent bills to its customers. Normally each invoice is payable in 30 days, as shown in column B. However, if a 30-day due date falls on a Sunday, the formula in column B adds an additional day, to produce a Monday due date. Here is the @IF function that performs this calculation in cell B2:

@IF(@WEEKDAY(A2+30)=6,A2+31,A2+30)

This formula is copied down column B, to the range B3..B6. The first argument in the @IF function is an expression that determines whether the 30-day due date falls on a Sunday:

@WEEKDAY(A2+30)=6

The argument of the @WEEKDAY function adds 30 to the date in column A. If this calculated date falls on a Sunday (with a @WEEKDAY result of 6) the @IF function chooses the *value1* argument, a 31-day due date:

A2+31

But if the @WEEKDAY function shows that the 30-day due date is not a Sunday, the *value2* argument is chosen:

A2+30

The use of the @IF function can become even more complex than this example. In some applications, you might write additional "nested" @IF functions in the positions of the *value1* and *value2* arguments of an initial @IF function. This can result in multifaceted decision-making processes for a worksheet.

Text Functions

A large library of text functions gives you the power to manipulate the contents of labels and strings in your worksheets. Like the logical functions, many of the text functions are more likely to be used in macros than in worksheets. Text-related tasks require careful attention to detail, and are more often the concern of programmers than everyday spreadsheet users. But some of the text functions prove to be useful worksheet tools, as you'll see in upcoming exercises.

The categories of text functions include the following:

- Substring functions, which find or extract sequences of characters from within existing labels

- Alphabetic case functions, which change letters to uppercase or lowercase

- Conversion functions, which produce text from numeric values, or numbers from text entries

- A miscellaneous variety of other text functions

NOTE   See Chapter 20 for a complete explanation of text functions.

Examples of all but a few of these functions appear in the worksheet you see in Figure 5.27. This worksheet is organized as follows: Cell A1 contains the label "Lotus 1-2-3 for windows." Each function example in the worksheet uses this label to illustrate a particular string operation. (Notice two odd details about the string in cell A1: There are two spaces between *for* and *windows*; and the word *windows* is not capitalized as it should be. Some functions in the worksheet illustrate ways to correct these details.) The results of the function examples appear in column B. In addition, column G shows complete text copies of the functions in column B.

Substring functions The first five examples in the worksheet show the substring functions:

FUNCTION	USE
@LEFT	Supplies a copy of a substring from the beginning of a string. @LEFT takes two arguments, a string and an integer: @LEFT(*string*, *n*). The function supplies the first *n* characters of string. For example, @LEFT(A1,5) displays the string "Lotus" in cell B3 of the worksheet in Figure 5.27.
@RIGHT	Supplies a copy of a substring from the end of a string. @RIGHT also takes two arguments: @RIGHT(*string*, *n*). The function supplies the last *n* characters of *string*. For example, @RIGHT(A1,7) displays the string "windows" in cell B4 of the worksheet in Figure 5.27.

FIGURE 5.27

Experiments with text functions

	A	B	C	D	E	F	G	H	I
1	Lotus 1-2-3 for windows								
2									
3	Left	Lotus					@LEFT(A1,5)		
4	Right	windows					@RIGHT(A1,7)		
5	Mid	1-2-3					@MID(A1,6,5)		
6	Find	6					@FIND("1-2-3",A1,0)		
7	Replace	Lotus 1-2-3 for Windows					@REPLACE(A1,16,10,"Windows")		
8									
9	Proper	Lotus 1-2-3 For Windows					@PROPER(A1)		
10	Upper	LOTUS 1-2-3 FOR WINDOWS					@UPPER(A1)		
11	Lower	lotus 1-2-3 for windows					@LOWER(A1)		
12									
13	Length	25					@LENGTH(A1)		
14	Exact	0					@EXACT(A1,B9)		
15	Repeat	Lotus 1-2-3 for windowsLotus 1-2-3 for windows					@REPEAT(A1,2)		
16									
17	Trim	Lotus 1-2-3 for windows					@TRIM(A1)		
18									
19	S	Lotus 1-2-3 for windows					@S(A1..A1)		
20	N	0					@N(A1..A1)		

Automatic | Arial | 12 06/08/94 1:39 PM | Ready

FUNCTION	USE
@MID	Supplies a copy of a substring from a position inside a string. @MID takes three arguments, a string and two integers: @MID(*string*, *pos*, *n*). The function copies *n* characters from *string*, starting from the position identified as *pos*. For example, @MID(A1,6,5) displays the string "1-2-3" in cell B5 of the Figure 5.27 worksheet. Note that the first character in a string has a *pos* value of 0; this value is sometimes called the *offset number*. The offset number for a character in a string is one less than the character's actual position in the string. For example, the seventh character in a string has a *pos* value of 6.
@FIND	Identifies the position of a substring inside a larger string. @FIND takes three arguments: @FIND(*substring*, *string*, *pos*). The function searches for *substring* inside *string*, starting the search at the *pos* character in *string*. If the search is successful, @FIND returns the offset number of the substring. For example, FIND("1-2-3",A1,0) searches for the string "1-2-3" in the label stored in cell A1. The search begins at the beginning of the label. It results in a value of 6, the offset where the substring is found.

FUNCTION	USE
@REPLACE	Writes a sequence of characters over existing characters in a string. @REPLACE takes four arguments: @REPLACE(*string*, *pos*, *n*, *substring*). The function replaces *n* characters of string, starting from *pos*. The substring argument supplies the replacement characters. For example, @REPLACE(A1,16,10,"Windows") replaces the final characters of the string.

Alphabetic case functions The next three examples in Figure 5.27 show the alphabetic case functions, @PROPER, @UPPER, and @LOWER. Each of these three functions takes a single string argument, and returns a copy of the same string with specified changes in the alphabetic case:

FUNCTION	USE
@PROPER	Capitalizes the first letter in each word of its string argument. An example appears in cell B9 in Figure 5.27.
@UPPER	Capitalizes all the letters in the string, as shown in cell B10.
@LOWER	Changes all the letters in the string to lowercase, as in cell B11.

Miscellaneous functions The remaining six functions illustrated in Figure 5.27—in cells B13 to B20—perform a variety of string operations:

FUNCTION	USE
@LENGTH	Supplies the length, in characters, of a string. @LENGTH takes one string argument. For example, @LENGTH(A1) displays 25 as the length of the string in Figure 5.27.
@EXACT	Compares two strings and determines whether or not they are the same. @EXACT returns a value of 1 (true) if its two string arguments are identical, or a value of 0 (false) if they are not. The comparison is case-sensitive For example, @EXACT(A1,B9) returns a value of 0.
@REPEAT	Generates a new string consisting of multiple copies of a string argument. The function takes two arguments: @REPEAT(*string, n*). The first argument is the string to be repeated, and the second argument is an integer that specifies the number of repetitions. For example, @REPEAT(A2,2) produces the display shown in cell B15.
@TRIM	Removes extraneous spaces from a string—that is, spaces at the beginning and the end of the string, and multiple consecutive spaces inside the string. For example, @TRIM(A1) in cell B17 removes the extra space between "for" and "windows."

5

Formulas and Functions

FUNCTION	USE
@S	Returns the label located in the first corner of a range. If this cell does not contain a label, @S returns an empty string. For example, the function @S(A1..A1) in B19 copies the label from cell A1.
@N	Returns the numeric value located in the first corner of a range. If this cell does not contain a value, @N returns a value of zero. For example, the function @N(A1..A1) in B20 returns a value of zero.

Among the remaining text functions, four perform conversions from one data type to another and give you access to the character code used in Lotus 1-2-3 for Windows:

FUNCTION	USE
@CHAR	Takes an integer as its argument, and supplies the corresponding character from the *Lotus Multibyte Character Set*. This character code, known by its abbreviation LMBCS, represents all the characters that can be produced and displayed from Lotus 1-2-3. Figure 5.28 shows an excerpt from the LMBCS code.
@CODE	Supplies the LMBCS code number of a given character. @CODE takes one string argument, and gives the code number of the first character in the string.

FIGURE 5.28

An excerpt from the LMBCS code

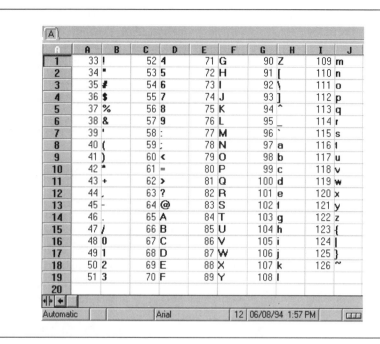

FUNCTION	USE
@STRING	Produces a string from a numeric value. @STRING takes two arguments: @STRING(*value*, *n*). The *value* argument is the number to be converted to a string, and the *n* argument specifies the number of decimal places that will be displayed in the result. For example, @STRING(123.456,1) produces the string "123.5" as its result.
@VALUE	Performs the opposite conversion, producing a number from a string of digits. The single argument of @VALUE must be a string that 1-2-3 can read as a number. For example, @VALUE("9876") produces the number 9876.

The worksheet in Figure 5.29 shows two short experiments with the @STRING and @VALUE functions. The @STRING function is important in situations where you need to incorporate a numeric value into a string. The & operation will not join a string and a number; before you can perform the concatenation, you must use @STRING to convert the number into a string. For example, cell A1 in the figure contains the calculated number of days between today's date and December 25; the following string formula combines this number with two strings to form the sentence displayed in cell A2:

+"There are "&@STRING(A1,0)&" shopping days 'til Christmas."

Conversely, you may sometimes need to convert a string of digits into a number so you can perform arithmetic operations on the value. The @VALUE function does this. For example, consider the sentence displayed in cell A4 of Figure 5.29: "We received 107 units @ $1.25 per unit." In order to perform arithmetic operations on the two numbers in this string, you have to extract the strings of digits and convert them into numeric values. The formulas in cells A11 and A12 illustrate the technique:

| A11 | @VALUE(@MID(A4,12,3)) |
| A12 | @VALUE(@MID(A4,25,4)) |

FIGURE 5.29

Experimenting with @STRING and @VALUE

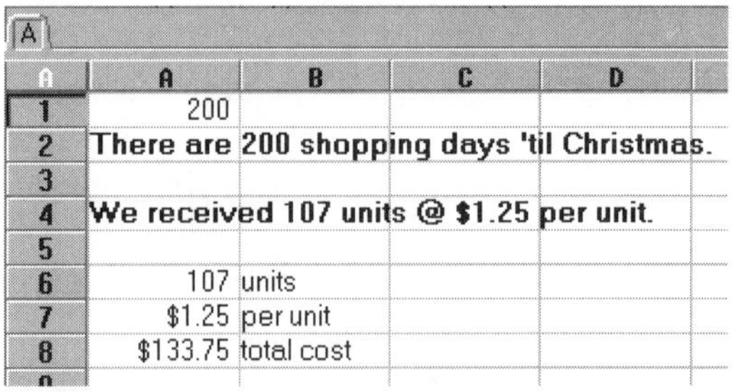

The argument in each of these @VALUE functions is a @MID function that extracts a string of digits from the sentence in cell A9. @VALUE then makes the conversion from string to number. After this conversion, the numbers can be formatted and used in numeric formulas; for example, cell A13 contains the formula +A11*A12.

Lookup Functions

The lookup functions make up an important category that includes tools such as @CHOOSE, @INDEX, @HLOOKUP, and @VLOOKUP. These functions allow you to select a data item from a table that you enter into a range of your worksheet—or, in the case of @CHOOSE, from a list that is contained within the arguments of the function itself. Using these functions requires some careful planning, because you have to begin by developing the list or table of data. But once you have organized your worksheet appropriately, these functions prove to be very powerful tools, as you'll see in this chapter's final exercises.

T I P

See Chapter 18 for complete coverage of the Lookup functions.

The @CHOOSE function @CHOOSE is the easiest function to use in this category. It takes one numeric argument, n, followed by a list of data values or references to cells:

@CHOOSE(n, *datalist*)

The purpose of n is to select one of the values in *datalist*. The elements of the list are separated by commas. The value of n must be within the range from 0 up to the number of entries in the list, minus 1. Using n as an offset number, @CHOOSE returns the nth value in the list. (See page 867 for more details concerning this function.)

For example, suppose you're using a worksheet to plan the visual elements of a graphic design. Each row of the worksheet describes the characteristics of one part of your design—position, shape, color, and so on. You've used numeric codes from 0 to 4 for five colors you're planning to use in the design—blue, green, red, yellow, and purple—and you've entered one of these codes into column B for each element of your design.

Now you want to translate these codes into the names of colors. To do so, you'll enter and copy this formula into C2 and copy the formula down column C:

@CHOOSE(B2,"blue","green","red","yellow","purple")

The @INDEX function By contrast, the @INDEX function selects a label or value from a table on your worksheet. @INDEX takes three required arguments and one optional argument. Here is its format with three arguments:

@INDEX(*range, column, row*)

The *range* argument is the location of the table where @INDEX reads a data item. The *column* and *row* arguments identify column and row offsets within range. The *column* argument ranges from 0 up to the number of columns in the table, minus 1. Likewise, the *row* argument ranges from 0 up to the number of rows in the table, minus 1. The fourth optional argument is an integer representing the worksheet that contains the lookup table:

@INDEX(*range, column, row, worksheet*)

This argument allows you to build the lookup table in a different worksheet location than the function itself.

For example, suppose you've entered the names of five colors (blue, green, red, yellow, purple) into the range F20..F24 of your graphic design worksheet. The following @INDEX function is an alternative approach for translating the color codes in column B into color names:

@INDEX($F$20..$F$24,0,B1)

This function uses each code number in column B as an index into the color table stored in F20..F24. (See page 871 for more details concerning this function.)

The @HLOOKUP and @VLOOKUP functions Finally, the @HLOOKUP and @VLOOKUP functions read values from specially organized lookup tables. The first row or column of a lookup table contains a range of reference values that are central to the process of searching for a target data item in the table.

NOTE

See pages 868 and 877 for more information about these functions.

For example, consider the Conference Room Price Table, shown in the lower part of the worksheet in Figure 5.30. The conference planners at Computing Conferences, Inc., use this table to determine the price of a downtown conference room for a one-day event. As you can see, the price of a conference room varies by the number of people attending and by the date of the event. To find the correct price for an expected attendance size, n, you begin by looking across the first row of the table, which contains a range of attendance figures from 1 to 300. Find the largest value in this row that is less than or equal to n. This value heads the column in which you will find the price for the conference room. Next look down the column to the row containing the date of the conference. The correct price is found in the cell at the intersection of the attendance column and date row.

5

Formulas and Functions

FIGURE 5.30

Using the @HLOOKUP function

	A	B	C	D	E	F	G	H	
1		Computing Conferences, Inc.							
2		Conference Room Expense							
3									
4	Conference:	Computing for Video Stores							
5	Place:	St. Louis							
6	Date:	15-Oct-94			Expected attendance:				
7					Min	Max			
8	Price:	$195			80	150			
9									
10									
11		Conference room cost			$1,750	$2,300			
12									
13									
14									
15	Conference Room Price Table								
16	Attendance	1	35	75	100	150	200	300	
17	1993 price	$400	$600	$1,500	$1,750	$2,000	$3,000	$3,500	
18	1994 price	$450	$700	$1,750	$1,900	$2,300	$3,400	$3,700	
19	1995 price	$500	$750	$1,900	$2,000	$2,500	$3,500	$3,850	
20									

Automatic   Arial   12 06/08/94 3:02 PM   Ready

The @HLOOKUP function The @HLOOKUP function automates this search. The function takes three arguments—a look-up value, a table range, and a row offset:

@HLOOKUP(*n*, *table*, *row*)

The first argument, *n*, is the value that the function looks for in the first row of the lookup table. The second argument, *table*, is the range of the lookup table itself, and the third argument, *row*, is the target row offset in the table.

In Figure 5.30, the @HLOOKUP function is used in cells E11 and F11 to find the conference room costs corresponding to the minimum and maximum attendance estimates. The table in the range B16..H19 is assigned the name ROOM. The two attendance estimates are in E8 and F8. Here is the function in cell E11:

@HLOOKUP(E8,$ROOM,2)

In this example, E8 is the attendance estimate that the function looks for in the first row of the ROOM range. A row offset of 2 gives the correct row for a 1994 conference date. In short, the @HLOOKUP function finds the conference room price corresponding to an estimated attendance of 80 people: In the first row of the look-up table, the largest value that is less than or equal to 80 is the attendance figure of 75 in cell D16. Searching down column D to the 1994 row, the function finds the correct price for the conference room, $1,750 in cell D18.

The @VLOOKUP function performs an equivalent data search, but in a vertically organized look-up table:

@VLOOKUP(*n*, *table*, *column*)

This function searches for *n* in the first column of table. The third argument, *column*, gives the column offset in the look-up table.

You can also enter labels rather than numbers in the first row or column of a look-up table. In this case, the first argument in the @HLOOKUP and @VLOOKUP functions is a string:

@HLOOKUP(*string*, *table*, *row*)
@VLOOKUP(*string*, *table*, *column*)

The @HLOOKUP function looks for a label that exactly matches *string* in the first row of the look-up table. Likewise, the @VLOOKUP function looks for a match for *string* in the first column of the table.

The @HLOOKUP and @VLOOKUP functions are versatile and powerful, especially in applications that require very large look-up tables. Of course, the classic example is an income tax table, in which the first column contains a range of income levels, and the first row contains taxpayer categories. The @VLOOKUP function is ideally suited to read tax amounts from such a table.

Summary

Each of the three major categories of formulas in 1-2-3—numeric, logical, and text—has its own set of operators:

- Numeric formulas use the familiar operators $*$, $/$, $+$, and $-$, along with the $\wedge$ operator for exponentiation.

- Logical formulas produce values of true or false, represented numerically by 1 and 0. There are two groups of logical operators: Relational operators determine equality or inequality; they are $=$, $<>$, $<$, $>$, $<=$, and $>=$. The three logical operators modify or combine logical expressions; they are #NOT#, #AND#, and #OR#.

- Finally, 1-2-3 has one text operator, &, which joins two labels or strings.

The 1-2-3 function library includes over two hundred tools that can be entered into cells by themselves or used in formulas. Here is a brief summary of the function categories presented in this chapter:

- The statistical functions include tools designed to calculate totals, averages, counts, maximum and minimum values, along with the more advanced statistical calculations known as variance and standard deviation.

- The financial functions include calculations for depreciation methods; present value and future value; payment, term, and rate values; and the internal rate of return.

- Mathematical functions include built-in formulas for trigonometric, logarithmic, and exponential values, plus an assortment of other important tools: a random number generator, integer and rounding functions, and the absolute value and modulus operations.

- The date and time functions include tools that supply the current date and time; functions that give information about date and time values; conversion functions; and date arithmetic functions.

- The most important logical function for spreadsheet use is @IF, which evaluates a logical expression and returns one of two values as its result.

- The text functions include tools that work with substrings, alphabetic case functions, and functions that convert between numeric and string values.

- The lookup functions include important tools that read values from tables and lists on the worksheet.

Charts,

Maps,

and

Graphics

fast TRACK

- **To create a chart from a table of worksheet data,** 346

    select an appropriate range of worksheet data, click the Chart SmartIcon, and drag the mouse pointer over the area where you want to display the chart.

- **To switch to a different chart type,** 359

    select the chart you want to change and choose Chart ➤ Type. In the Type dialog box, select a chart type and style, and click OK. (Alternatively, select a chart and click one of the available chart-type SmartIcons.)

- **To redefine data series by rows or by columns,** 359

    select the chart that you want to redefine, and choose Chart ➤ Ranges. In the Ranges dialog box, select an option from the Assign ranges list, and click OK.

- **To redraw a chart for new data in the underlying worksheet table,** 363

    simply enter the new data. 1-2-3 automatically redraws the chart to match the changes in the data.

- **To add a drawn object to a chart or a worksheet,** 363

    click the SmartIcon corresponding to the object you want to add—for example, the Text Block SmartIcon or the Arrow SmartIcon—and drag the mouse pointer through the area where you want to display the object.

To create a pie chart, 371

select a row or column of labels and a corresponding row or column of numeric data. (The two ranges need not be contiguous. To select noncontiguous ranges, hold down the Ctrl key while you drag the mouse over the second range.) Click the Chart SmartIcon and drag the mouse pointer to create the chart. Then click the Pie Chart SmartIcon to switch to the desired chart type.

To switch to a mixed chart format, 381

select the chart you want to modify, and choose the Chart ➤ Ranges command. In the Ranges dialog box, select a data series and then select a new chart type from the Mixed type list. (Optionally, select the Plot on 2nd Y-axis option.) Click OK to confirm these changes.

To create a map, 388

enter a list of state or country names (or map code abbreviations) into a worksheet range, along with a corresponding range of numeric data. Select the entire range of names and values, and choose Tools ➤ Map ➤ Insert Map Object. Move the mouse pointer to the worksheet position where you want to display the map and click the left mouse button.

To zoom in on a portion of a map, 388

double-click inside the map object to start the Lotus Map Viewer application. Hold down the Ctrl key and drag the mouse pointer around the map area that you want to zoom, and then release the mouse button. Choose File ➤ Exit and Return from the Map Viewer's menu bar to copy the revised map back to your 1-2-3 worksheet.

IN business, technology, and everyday life, charts have a universal appeal. People often prefer to look at pictorial representations of numbers rather than the numbers themselves. Grasping the sense of a table of numbers requires time, effort, and concentration—but a chart has an instant impact. When you look at a chart, you can answer many questions about the data, almost before you can even ask the questions: Which data item is the smallest and which is the largest? Is there a downward or upward trend over time? Are there any atypical values that don't conform to the trends of the other data? How significant is a given value in relation to the total? The answers to these and many other questions are visibly clear in a chart of numeric data.

Producing a chart in 1-2-3 is simple, yet you can create an extraordinary variety of visual effects. There are several major chart types to choose from. The most familiar are bar charts, line charts, area charts and pie charts; these are available in both two-dimensional and three-dimensional versions. In addition, you can create XY charts, mixed charts, HLCO (high-low-close-open) charts, and radar charts for special kinds of data.

A chart resides directly on a worksheet in 1-2-3—on the same sheet that displays the chart's underlying data, or on another sheet that you select. A chart is an *object* that can be moved and resized within the sheet that contains it. When you select a chart, 1-2-3 displays a new set of

SmartIcons, as you can see in Figure 6.1. 1-2-3 also replaces the Range menu with the Chart menu:

The SmartIcons and the commands of the Chart menu give you efficient and powerful ways to change the appearance of a chart.

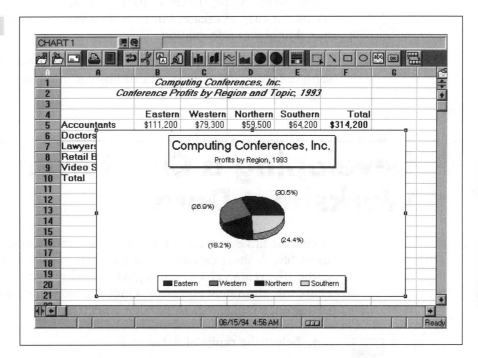

6

Charts, Maps, Graphs

As you'll learn in this chapter, you can also use a variety of simple mouse and keyboard actions to refine and clarify the message contained in a chart. For example, you can:

- Click any chart element with the right mouse button to view a quick menu of commands that apply to the selected object.
- Drag individual elements of a chart to new positions.
- Add *drawn objects* to a chart—special graphic objects such as arrows and text boxes, designed to highlight or emphasize specific elements of the chart.

Along with traditional charts, 1-2-3 now offers yet another dramatic way to present numeric data. When your data is geographically oriented—as in a table of state-by-state sales figures or a worksheet of international business activity—you can create a *map* to represent the information. In a map, 1-2-3 sets up a color code to represent numeric data, and assigns these colors appropriately to individual states or countries in the map. Maps are easy to create, but provide a very impressive medium for national or global information.

In this chapter you'll learn to create and refine all these visual representations of data—charts, drawn objects, and maps.

Developing a Chart from Worksheet Data

A chart is linked to data on a worksheet, and is saved as part of a worksheet file. A sheet can have multiple charts, each identified by a unique name. To create a chart, you begin by developing the table of data that the chart will ultimately represent. Once the worksheet is ready, you follow a pattern of simple steps to develop your chart:

1. Select the range of data.
2. Click the Chart SmartIcon.

3. Drag the mouse over the worksheet area where you want to display the chart. When you release the mouse button, the chart appears.

4. Change the chart's type, style, and appearance in any way that meets your requirements.

5. Optionally, print the chart—either by itself or with its underlying worksheet data.

In an initial series of exercises presented in this chapter, you'll create several different charts from one fairly simple worksheet example. The worksheet, shown in Figure 6.2, is a one-year profit summary from Computing Conferences, Inc. The worksheet's columns show the profits from each of the company's four regions—Eastern, Western, Northern, Southern. The rows represent the conference topics—that is, the various types of computer-training conferences that the company conducts in each region, including conferences designed for accountants, doctors, lawyers, retail businesses, and video stores.

FIGURE 6.2

The Conference profits worksheet

	A	B	C	D	E	F	G
1		Computing Conferences, Inc.					
2		Conference Profits by Region and Topic, 1993					
3							
4		Eastern	Western	Northern	Southern	Total	
5	Accountants	$111,200	$79,300	$59,500	$64,200	$314,200	
6	Doctors	$131,900	$116,900	$77,500	$96,700	$423,000	
7	Lawyers	$63,500	$81,500	$54,000	$88,400	$287,400	
8	Retail Business	$92,800	$88,600	$57,900	$78,400	$317,700	
9	Video Stores	$88,300	$63,200	$41,900	$61,900	$255,300	
10	Total	$487,700	$429,500	$290,800	$389,600	$1,597,600	
11							

To prepare for the exercises ahead, your first job is enter this table of data into your own worksheet. Here are the steps:

On a blank sheet, enter the following titles into cells A1 and A2:

CELL	ENTER
A1	**Computing Conferences, Inc.**
A2	**Conference Profits by Region and Topic, 1993**

2. Select the range A1..F2. To center the titles horizontally over this range, choose Style ➤ Alignment and click the Center and Across columns options. Click OK to confirm. Then click the Bold and Italics SmartIcons to set the display style for the titles.

3. Choose Style ➤ Worksheet Defaults. In the Number Format group, choose the Currency format. Enter a value of **0** in the Decimals box, and keep the default US Dollar option in the Currency box. Click OK to confirm.

4. Enter the following labels into cells A5 to A10:

CELL	ENTER
A5	**Accountants**
A6	**Doctors**
A7	**Lawyers**
A8	**Retail Business**
A9	**Video Stores**
A10	**Total**

5. Drag the border of column A to the right to increase the column width to 14.

6. Enter the following column headings in cells B4 to F4:

CELL	ENTER
B4	**Eastern**
C4	**Western**
D4	**Northern**
E4	**Southern**
F4	**Total**

7. Right-align each of these headings in its respective cell.

8. Enter the numeric profit values into the range B6..E10, as shown in Figure 6.2.

9. Select the range B5..F10 and click the Sum SmartIcon once. In response, 1-2-3 enters all the appropriate @SUM functions into column F and row 10.

10. Apply the boldface style to columns A and F and rows 4 and 10, as shown in Figure 6.2.

11. Select rows 1 through 10 and then click the Point-size selector, the fifth panel on the status bar. Choose a point size of 10 for this range of cells. By decreasing the size of the data table, you give yourself more room to display graphs below the numeric information. Also click the tab button at the far right side of the tab line, just above the worksheet. This action removes the tab line from view, giving you one more line of space for charting exercises.

12. Choose File ➤ Save As and save the worksheet as PROFITS.WK4.

The numeric data from which you'll create your first chart is located in the range B5..E9. The labels for this data are in column A and row 4. Before you create a chart from this worksheet, consider the two different ways in which 1-2-3 might translate this data into a chart.

Understanding Data Series

Suppose you're planning to create a vertical bar chart from the Profits worksheet. The height of each bar in the chart will represent the profit level from one conference topic in a particular region. Because the worksheet contains four columns by five rows of numbers, there will be twenty bars in a chart to represent all the data.

Within this context, there are two ways to organize the chart—by conference topic or by region. Grouping together all the bars for a given conference topic, 1-2-3 produces a chart that looks like this:

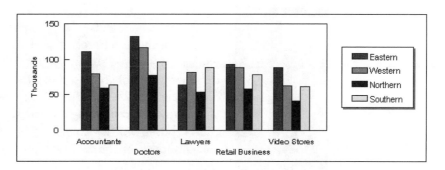

In this chart, each group of bars represents the four regional profit figures for one conference topic. The values displayed along the *y-axis* (the chart's vertical axis) show the profit levels. The labels along the *x-axis* (the horizontal axis) identify the conference topics, and the *legend* at the right side of the chart shows the color codes used to represent each region. This chart makes it easy to see which region has the highest profit for a particular type of conference. The regions make up the four distinctly colored *data series* in this chart.

By contrast, the following chart organizes the bars by region:

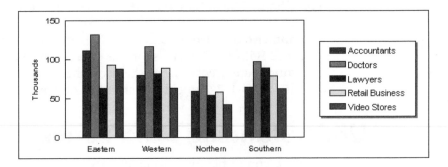

In this chart, each group of bars represents the five conference topics for a given region. The labels along the x-axis identify the regions, and the legend shows the color code for each conference topic. This chart clearly shows the most profitable and the least profitable conference topic in each region. The conference topics make up the five data series in this chart.

T I P

As you can see already, charts come with their own special vocabulary. Here's a quick review of the terms you've encountered so far: The *x-axis* is the horizontal axis along the bottom of a chart. The *y-axis* is the vertical axis at the left side of a chart. A *data series* is a distinct visual way of representing one range of data that the chart is based on. The *legend* is a box that identifies the colors, shades, or shapes that represent data series in the chart.

In short, 1-2-3 can create the data series for a chart from the rows or the columns of a worksheet table. Which of these two charts will 1-2-3 create initially? The answer depends on the number of rows and columns of numeric data in the table itself:

- If the number of rows is greater than the number of columns, the data series in the chart are based on columns of numeric data. This is the default in the Profits worksheet: There are five rows of conference topics and four columns of regional data. The initial chart is therefore based on regions.

- If the number of columns is greater than or equal to the number of rows, the data series are based on rows of data.

Look back at the Profits worksheet (see Figure 6.2) and the two column charts you can create from it; you'll quickly see the distinction between these two schemes. With this much background information, you're ready to create your first chart.

TIP

Whether 1-2-3 initially creates a chart by rows or by columns, you can easily switch between the two ways of organizing charts, using the Chart ➤ Ranges command. You'll learn how to make this switch later in this chapter (see page 359).

Creating the Profits Chart

In previous versions of 1-2-3, charting could turn into a long and complicated process. You began by developing a worksheet of data and creating an initial version of your chart. Then you went through many additional steps to add the finishing touches to the chart—the title and subtitle, the legend, and the axis labels.

The process is now considerably streamlined. By carefully selecting all the relevant information on the underlying worksheet, you can instantly create a chart that contains all the elements you want. Try it now:

1. Select the range A1..E9 on the Profits worksheet.

6

Charts, Maps, Graphs

This range includes the title, subtitle, row and column headings, and the actual numeric data. (It doesn't include the row and column of totals, which will not be part of this chart.)

2. Click the Chart SmartIcon, and then move the mouse pointer back into the worksheet area, to cell A11. The mouse pointer takes the shape of a chart icon:

9	Video Stores
10	Total
11	
12	
13	
14	

3. Hold down the left mouse button and drag the pointer from cell A11 down to cell H23. A dotted boundary marks the large rectangle where your chart will appear.

4. Release the mouse button. 1-2-3 immediately draws a chart based on the data in the Profits worksheet, as you can see in Figure 6.3.

Take a careful look at the chart you've created. In a process that Lotus calls "intelligent charting," 1-2-3 has made appropriate use of all the information you've selected on the Profits worksheet:

- The labels stored in cells A1 and A2 of the worksheet have become the chart's title and subtitle.

- The column headings in row 4 are displayed in the chart's legend, which identifies the colors that represent the four regions of data.

- The conference topics in column A appear along the x-axis to identify the five groups of bars in the chart.

All these elements have been included in your chart automatically, as a result of the worksheet range you selected before clicking the Chart SmartIcon. In a few seconds you've created a chart that is nearly ready to be used as a tool for presenting your data.

FIGURE 6.3

The first chart from the Profits worksheet

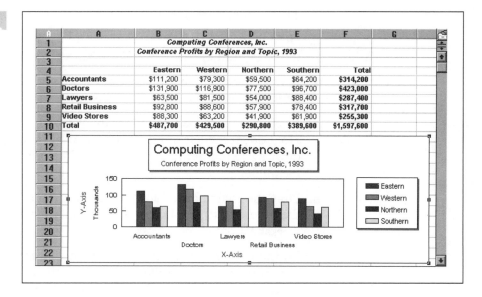

Moving and Resizing a Chart

1-2-3 gives you many interesting ways to refine and enhance charts. Notice the *selection handles*, the small black squares displayed around the perimeter of the chart box. These indicate that the chart object is selected and ready to be modified in any number of ways. For example, you can change the size and dimensions of the chart, and you can move it to a new location. In the following steps, you'll increase the height of the chart and then you'll move it further down the worksheet so that you can view the chart and data at the same time:

1. Position the mouse pointer over the selection handle located just above the chart title. When you do so, the pointer takes the shape of a cross with four arrowheads, pointing up, down, left, and right:

JU	$57,900
00	$41,900
00	**$290,800**

Conferences,

s by Region and Topic

This icon indicates that you can resize the chart.

2. Hold down the left mouse button and drag the chart's border up to the bottom of row 7 in the worksheet.

3. Release the mouse button. When you do so, 1-2-3 immediately redraws the chart within the new dimensions of the resized chart box.

4. Position the mouse pointer at any blank spot inside the chart box. Hold down the left mouse button and begin dragging the pointer down. The pointer takes the shape of a closed fist holding on to a rectangle.

5. Drag the chart border down to the bottom of row 10, and release the mouse button. The chart is now displayed just beneath the worksheet data.

6. Position the mouse pointer over the down-arrow button at the bottom of the vertical scroll bar, and click the left mouse button three times. This action scrolls the worksheet so that you can see the data and the chart, as in Figure 6.4.

The larger chart results in a clearer presentation, yet still gives you enough room to view the data along with the chart. Now you'll try changing the appearance and format of specific elements within the chart.

T I P

To *deselect* a chart object, click any cell in the worksheet that contains the chart. To select the chart again, click along the chart's border or at an empty area within the chart box.

Moving and resizing
the chart area

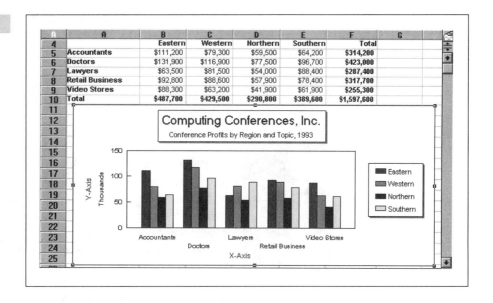

Changing the Elements of the Chart

Looking closely at the chart, you may find several items that you'd like to change. For example, 1-2-3 has supplied generic titles for the chart axes—currently these titles are displayed as *Y-Axis* and *X-Axis*. You may want to change these to titles that have meaning for your particular graph; alternatively, you have the option of deleting one or both of the titles to make more room for the data series themselves. In addition, it would be nice to apply a currency format to the numbers that appear along the vertical axis. And you may want to experiment with a new position for the legend.

To change the format or appearance of an item in a chart, you can pull down Chart menu and choose the appropriate command. For example:

- The Chart ➤ Headings command allows you to change the content and position of the chart's title and subtitle.

- Chart ➤ Legend is for changing the appearance and position of the legend.

6

Charts, Maps, Graphs

- Chart ➤ Axis ➤ X-Axis and Chart ➤ Axis ➤ Y-Axis control the format of use of the two axes, and the titles displayed along the axes.

Alternatively, you can use quick menus to make changes in chart items. To do so, you position the mouse pointer over an object in the chart, click the right mouse button, and select from the short list of relevant commands.

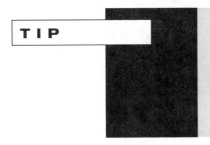

TIP

As you move the mouse pointer from one item to another in the chart, you'll see the pointer icon change to a variety of different shapes, representing the kinds of changes you can make on a given item. For example, when positioned over a text element, the mouse pointer takes the shape of a small white arrowhead with an *A* below it.

You'll use quick menus in the following exercise, as you go about changing the appearance of your chart:

1. Position the mouse pointer over the X-Axis title and click the right mouse button. In the resulting quick menu, choose the X-Axis command. 1-2-3 displays the X-Axis dialog box.

2. In the Axis title box, enter the new title as **Conference Topics**:

3. Click OK. The new title appears beneath the x-axis.

4. Now click the new x-axis title with the right mouse button, and this time choose the Font & Attributes command. In the resulting dialog box, click the Bold option and then click OK:

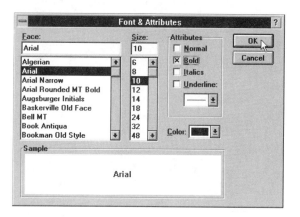

Notice that you can select a font, a point size, a set of style attributes, and a color for any text that appears in the chart.

5. Now click the Y-Axis title with the right mouse button, and this time choose the Clear command from the resulting quick menu. This action deletes the axis title from the chart area.

6. Move the mouse pointer to the vertical axis and click the right mouse button. Choose the Number Format command from the quick menu. In the resulting dialog box, choose the Currency option, and change the Decimal places setting to **0**:

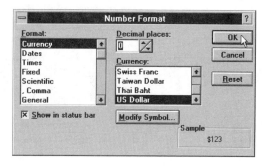

6

Charts, Maps, Graphs

Then click OK to confirm this change.

7. Finally, position the mouse pointer inside the legend box at the right side of the chart area, and click the right mouse button. Choose the Legend command from the quick menu. In the Legend dialog box, click the Below plot option and click OK:

As a result of this final step, 1-2-3 moves the legend to the bottom of the graph area, as shown in Figure 6.5. Suppose you're not satisfied with this

FIGURE 6.5

Moving the legend below the chart

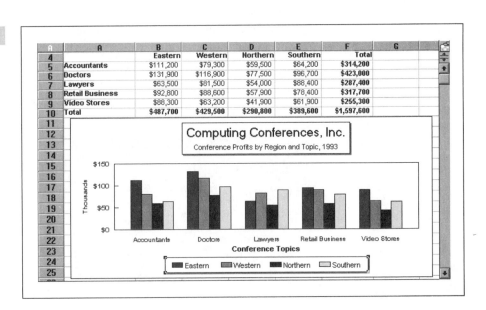

final change. Click the Undo SmartIcon now; the legend moves back to its original position.

Figure 6.6 shows the chart at this point in your work. In a very short time, you've made some small but important changes in several elements of the chart, including axis titles, axis labels, and the legend. You've seen that charting is a direct, efficient process in 1-2-3. Next you'll experiment with different ways of organizing and presenting your chart.

FIGURE 6.6

Making changes in the elements of a chart

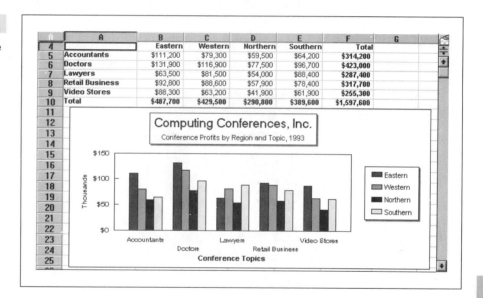

Changing the Data Series and the Chart Type

Now imagine that you want to transform this chart into a *stacked* bar chart, where the height of one bar represents the total profit for a given region, and the stacked components in a bar represent the profits from individual conference topics within a region. This change involves two main steps. First you'll switch from column-oriented to row-oriented data series. Then you'll make the change to a stacked bar chart. Along the way, you'll also experiment with the option of a three-dimensional chart. Although these steps will produce very dramatic revisions in the chart's appearance, you'll see that they are just as simple to carry out as the changes you've already made.

Once again you can choose the commands for these operations from quick menus or directly from the Chart menu. You'll try the latter approach in this exercise:

1. If the chart is not currently selected, click the mouse pointer along the border or at any empty position inside the chart box. 1-2-3 once again displays selection handles around the border of the chart object.

2. Choose Chart ➤ Ranges. In the Ranges dialog box, pull down the Assign ranges list and choose the "By row" option:

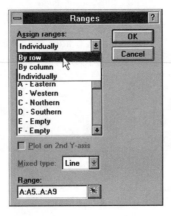

Click OK.

1-2-3 rearranges the chart into four groups of bars, as shown earlier in this chapter. Because the four region names are now displayed along the x-axis, you can see that the axis title "Conference Topics" is no longer appropriate.

3. Click the "Conference Topics" title with the right mouse button and choose the Clear command from the resulting quick menu. The axis title disappears from the chart.

4. Choose Chart ➤ Type. In the Type dialog box, click the 3D Bar option. Then click the stacked bar among the pictured chart types:

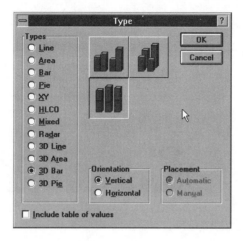

Click OK.

5. Finally, add horizontal grid lines to the chart to make the stacked bars easier to read: Choose Chart ➤ Grids and then choose the Both option in the Y-axis list box. Click OK to confirm:

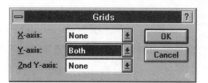

Figure 6.7 shows the result of your work in this exercise. You've achieved the effect that you wanted: Each stacked bar represents one of the four regions, and each portion of a given bar represents one of the conference topics. This presentation makes it easy to compare the profits of the four regions and the profits from specific conference topics within a region.

6

Charts, Maps, Graphs

FIGURE 6.7

Creating a stacked bar
chart

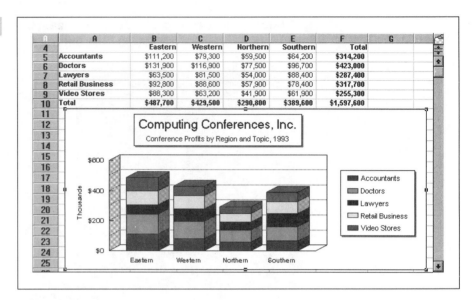

TIP

Interestingly, the Type dialog box gives you a simple way to view a data table along with the chart. With the chart selected, choose Chart ➤ Type, and click the "Include table of values" option. An *X* appears inside the check box. Then click OK or press ↵. Beneath each bar, 1-2-3 displays the data values that the bar represents. You can click the Undo SmartIcon to restore the chart to its previous appearance.

TIP

The Chart ➤ Type command also gives you options for changing a default vertical bar chart to a horizontal chart. Choose Chart ➤ Type and click the Horizontal option in the Orientation group. Then click OK. In the resulting chart, the bars extend from the left side of the chart to the right instead of from bottom to top. Click the Undo SmartIcon to switch back to a vertical chart. The Horizontal option is available for all chart types except pie charts and radar charts.

Performing What-If Experiments with a Chart

What happens now if you make a change in the original data on the worksheet to which the charts are linked? For example, imagine this situation: After creating these charts, one of the managers at Computing Conferences, Inc., discovers a clerical error. The profit amount for video store training conferences in the Southern region has been underreported by $100,000. Instead of the current $61,900, the figure in cell E9 should be $161,900. What will the chart look like when this figure is corrected?

To find out, follow these steps:

1. Double-click cell E9 to switch into the Edit mode.

2. Press the Home key to move the flashing insertion point to the beginning of the entry in the cell.

3. Type **1** from the keyboard, and press ↵ to enter the corrected profit value, $161,900.

As shown in Figure 6.8, 1-2-3 has redrawn the chart in response to the correction on the worksheet. Now the Southern region has the highest profits of the four regions.

To focus attention on a particular value in the chart, you can add a block of text and an arrow that points from the text to the appropriate item in the chart. These are examples of *drawn objects*, which you can place anywhere on a chart or worksheet. In the next section you'll try your hand at adding such objects to the stacked bar chart.

Adding Drawn Objects to a Chart

Drawn objects can be displayed in any size and at any position in a chart; you may need to experiment for a while before you're satisfied with the results of your work in the upcoming exercise. You'll begin by adding a

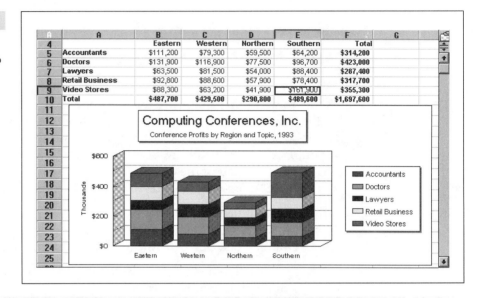

	A	B	C	D	E	F	G
4		Eastern	Western	Northern	Southern	Total	
5	Accountants	$111,200	$79,300	$59,500	$64,200	$314,200	
6	Doctors	$131,900	$116,900	$77,500	$96,700	$423,000	
7	Lawyers	$63,500	$81,500	$54,000	$88,400	$287,400	
8	Retail Business	$92,800	$88,600	$57,900	$78,400	$317,700	
9	Video Stores	$88,300	$63,200	$41,900	$161,900	$355,300	
10	Total	$487,700	$429,500	$290,800	$489,600	$1,697,600	

block of text to the chart, and then you'll draw an arrow from the rectangle to the chart. The purpose of these additions is to draw attention to the unusually high profits for the Video conferences in the Southern region:

1. Click the Text Block SmartIcon. (This icon is available on both the default worksheet SmartIcon palette and on the palette that appears when a chart is selected.)

2. Drag the mouse pointer to form a rectangle in the blank space at the upper-right corner of the chart box. Release the mouse button, and a flashing insertion point appears inside the box you've created.

3. Type **Congratulations** and press ↵. Then type **Video Group!**. Click in a blank part of the chart box to deselect the text box you've created.

4. Now click the Arrow SmartIcon.

5. Drag the mouse pointer from the text box down to the top stack of the bar representing profits in the Southern region. Release the mouse button to complete the arrow drawing, then click elsewhere in the graph to deselect the object.

Figure 6.9 shows how these two drawn objects look inside the chart. As you can see, objects are a good way to point out extraordinary data values in a chart or a worksheet.

This is the end of your work with the Profits worksheet and chart. Click the Save SmartIcon to save the worksheet file to disk. If you like, you can try printing the worksheet with its chart. Click the Print SmartIcon and select a print range that includes both the data and the chart.

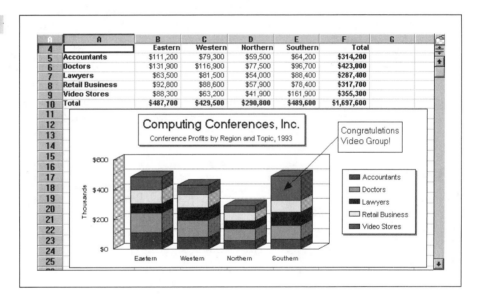

Working with Other Chart Types

To complete your introduction to charts, you'll now take a look at the other chart types available in 1-2-3, including line charts, area charts, pie charts, XY charts, mixed charts, HLCO charts, and radar charts. Along the way, you'll also learn how to set the *preferred* chart type.

Creating Line Charts and Area Charts

Line and *area charts* are useful for illustrating the upward or downward trends in data over time. Both chart types are available in two-dimensional and three-dimensional formats, and in unstacked and stacked versions. In an *unstacked* chart, each point on a line represents an actual value from the corresponding data range. In a stacked chart, the values of each data range are added to the accumulated values of previous data ranges, so that the top line of the chart represents the totals of all the data ranges.

For example, the worksheet at the top of Figure 6.10 shows a table of yearly regional profit figures over a five-year period. Below the data table you see a line chart created from this profit table. Each line in the chart represents regional profit variations. Notice that some of the lines cross each other one or more times; this is typical of an unstacked line chart.

FIGURE 6.10

An unstacked line chart of regional profits over a five-year period

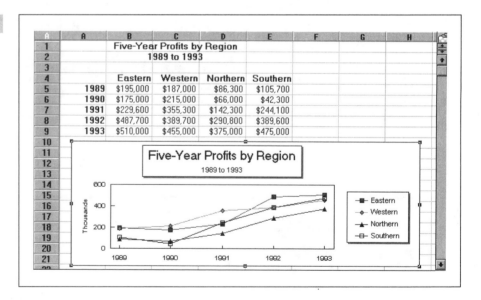

By contrast, Figure 6.11 shows the stacked version of the same chart, and Figure 6.12 shows a stacked area chart. In both of these stacked charts, the upward trend of the top line shows how combined profits for the four regions have grown over the five-year period.

A stacked line chart, showing combined profit growth over the period

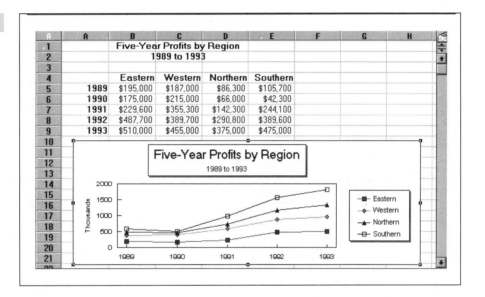

A stacked area chart of the same regional profit data

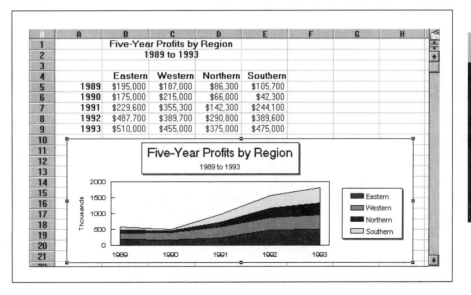

Charts, Maps, Graphs

6

You'll create these three charts in the upcoming exercise. Start your work by creating the data table that the charts will be based on:

1. Enter the data table from Figure 6.10 onto a blank worksheet. Enter the title and subtitle into cells A1 and A2, and then center them horizontally over the range A1..E2.

2. Type the profit figures into the range B5..E9, and format them as currency values, with no digits after the decimal point.

3. In the range A5..A9, enter the five years (1989 to 1993) as labels rather than values. Type the first year as "**1989** (using the double quotation mark to right-justify the label in its cell), and then use a drag-and-fill action to enter the remaining four dates.

> **WARNING**
>
> If you were to enter 1989, 1990, 1991, 1992, and 1993 as numeric values rather than labels, 1-2-3 would attempt to plot them as a data series in the chart itself. To make 1-2-3 recognize these years as labels for the x-axis, you have to enter them into column A as labels.

Here are the steps for creating the three versions of the line chart:

1. Select the range A1..E9.

2. Click the Chart SmartIcon.

3. Drag the mouse pointer from A10 down to H22. 1-2-3 creates a bar chart from the data.

4. Click the Y-Axis title to select it, and then press the Delete key to remove it from the chart. Then select the X-Axis title and delete it as well.

 5. Click the Line Chart SmartIcon. (This icon is displayed in the middle of the icon palette when you select a chart in 1-2-3.) The chart now looks like the one in Figure 6.10.

6. Choose Chart ➤ Type. The Type dialog box appears:

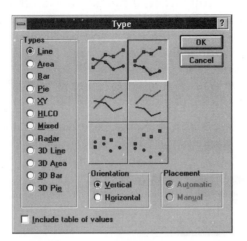

This dialog box shows the six different line chart formats that are available in 1-2-3. The column of pictures on the left shows the three unstacked line charts, and the column on the right shows the stacked line charts.

7. Click the first option in the right-hand column of pictures, and then click OK. Back on your worksheet, the chart now looks like the one in Figure 6.11.

8. Finally, click the Area Chart SmartIcon. This action transforms the example into the stacked area chart you see in Figure 6.12.

A stacked area chart is the same as a stacked line chart, except that the areas beneath the lines are filled in with shades or colors. In this area chart (see Figure 6.12), the area between the x-axis and the top line of the chart represents the total profit for all four regions in a given year.

Assigning a Name to a Chart

Next you'll add a second graph to this same worksheet. But before you do, there are a few additional tasks to take care of. You may have already noticed that 1-2-3 assigns a default name to each new chart you create on a worksheet. For example, when you select the area chart you've just created, the name CHART1 appears in the Selection indicator, the first panel of the edit line. You can give the chart a more descriptive name by choosing the Chart ➤ Name command. In the steps ahead, you'll change the name of the current chart and you'll move it to a new location on the worksheet; you'll also save your work to disk:

1. If you don't see selection handles around the border of the chart box, click along the border of the box to select the object.

2. Choose Chart ➤ Name. The Name dialog shows the chart's current name as CHART1:

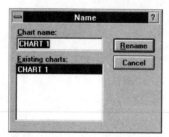

3. Enter **fiveyears** into the Chart name text box.

4. Click the Rename button, or press ↵. The Edit line now shows the chart's name as FIVEYEARS.

5. Now use the mouse to drag the chart down the worksheet to a location just below row 26. Press the Home key to return the cell pointer to A1. The chart is no longer in view, but it's still stored on your worksheet.

6. Choose File ➤ Save As and enter **profits5** into the File name text box.

7. Click OK or press ↵. 1-2-3 saves your worksheet as PROFITS5.WK4.

Now you're ready to add another chart to the Profits5 worksheet. In the next exercise you'll learn how to create a pie chart.

TIP

In a worksheet that contains two or more charts, you can use the Edit ➤ Go To command to view a list of all the current chart names and to select any chart in the list. Begin by selecting a chart. Then choose Edit ➤ Go To or press F5. Highlight the name of a chart in the list and click OK. 1-2-3 selects and displays the chart you've chosen.

Creating Pie Charts

A *pie chart* depicts one range of numeric data. The wedges (or "slices") of the pie show how each individual data value relates to the total, and how each value compares in importance with all the other values. Pie charts are available in two-dimensional and three-dimensional formats. You saw a three-dimensional pie chart back in Figure 6.1.

In its simplest format, a pie chart uses only two columns of data—a row or column of labels for the legend, and another row or column containing the numeric data depicted in the chart. For example, Figure 6.13 shows a pie chart created from the total annual profits in the four regions of the Profit5 worksheet. Each wedge of the chart represents one of the four regions, as identified in the legend. The label displayed alongside each wedge shows the dollar profit represented by the wedge, and the percentage of the total; for example:

$1,602,000 (29.6%)

Here are the steps for creating this pie chart on your own Profits5 worksheet:

1. Scroll the sheet vertically so that row 4 is at the top of the worksheet window. Then select the range B10..E10 and click the Sum SmartIcon. In response, 1-2-3 enters the total regional profit figures at the bottom of the table.

2. While the totals are still selected, click the Format selector, the first panel on the status bar and choose the US Dollar format. Then click the Decimal selector, the second panel on the status bar, and choose 0 as the number of digits after the decimal point.

FIGURE 6.13

A pie chart representing total regional profits over a five-year period

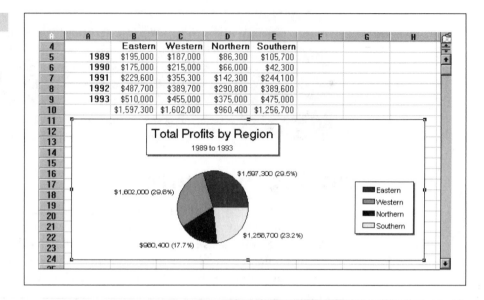

3. Without deselecting the row of totals, hold down the Ctrl key and use your mouse to select the range B4..E4. Now the selection consists of two noncontiguous rows of data:

A	A	B	C	D	E
4		**Eastern**	**Western**	**Northern**	**Southern**
5	**1989**	$195,000	$187,000	$86,300	$105,700
6	**1990**	$175,000	$215,000	$66,000	$42,300
7	**1991**	$229,600	$355,300	$142,300	$244,100
8	**1992**	$487,700	$389,700	$290,800	$389,600
9	**1993**	$510,000	$455,000	$375,000	$475,000
10		$1,597,300	$1,602,000	$960,400	$1,256,700
11					

As you'll recall, this kind of selection is known as a *collection* in 1-2-3 (see page 226). This particular collection contains the data you need to create a pie chart—a row of labels and a row of numeric data.

4. Click the Chart SmartIcon, and then drag the mouse from cell A11 down to cell H24. When you release the mouse button, 1-2-3 initially creates a bar chart:

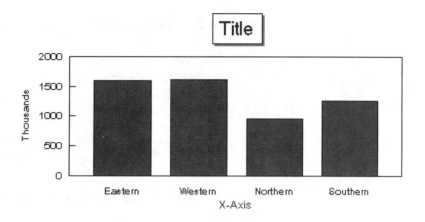

5. While the chart is still selected, click the Pie Chart SmartIcon. In response, 1-2-3 creates a pie chart:

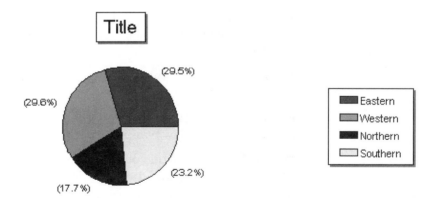

Now you need to supply a title for the chart and revise the labels that appear next to each wedge.

6. Click the chart's title with the right mouse button, and choose the Headings command from the resulting quick menu. The Headings dialog box appears on the screen:

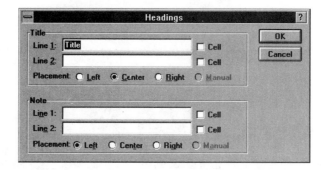

7. In the Title group, enter **Total Profits by Region** into the Line 1 text box.

8. Click the Cell option next to the Line 2 box, placing an *X* in the corresponding check box. This option tells 1-2-3 that you want to take the chart's subtitle from a label stored in a cell on the worksheet.

9. Click the range selector button at the right side of the Line 2 text box. The Headings dialog box temporarily disappears from the screen.

10. Select cell A2 on the worksheet. This cell contains the text for your chart's subtitle.

11. Back on the Headings dialog box, click OK to confirm the title changes. The new two-line title appears at the top of the chart box.

12. Finally, click any one of the four wedge labels with the right mouse button, and choose the Data Labels command from the

resulting quick menu. The Data Labels dialog box appears:

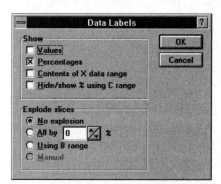

13. Click the Values option, placing an *X* in the corresponding check box, and then click OK. Back on the chart, the wedge labels now display both dollar amounts and percentages.

Your chart and worksheet now look the same as Figure 6.13. Click the Save button to save your work to disk.

TIP

Notice that the Headings dialog box contains two groups of Line 1 and Line 2 text boxes—one group labeled Title, and the other labeled Note. If you want to display footnotes at the bottom of your chart, enter labels into the two Note boxes. The Headings dialog box also gives you options for controlling the horizontal placement of titles and footnotes. By default, the titles are centered horizontally and the footnotes are displayed at the lower-left corner of the chart box.

6

Charts, Maps, Graphs

A Three-Dimensional Pie Chart

You can quickly switch to a three-dimensional pie chart by clicking the 3D Pie Chart SmartIcon. Here's what your chart will look like:

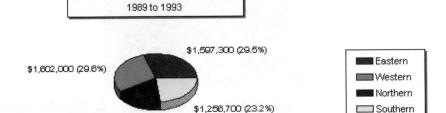

After examining this new chart, click the Pie Chart SmartIcon to switch back to a two-dimensional chart.

Exploding a Wedge on a Pie Chart

Sometimes you may want to place special emphasis on a particular wedge of a pie chart. For example, you may want to highlight the largest or smallest wedge, or the wedge that is the most important to a particular audience. One way to do this is to *explode* the wedge—that is, to separate it slightly from the circumference of the rest of the pie.

You can use your mouse to drag a wedge slightly away from its original position in the chart. For example, suppose you want to explode the wedge representing the Northern region in the Profits pie chart. Here are the steps:

1. Position the mouse pointer over the wedge.

2. Hold down the left mouse button and drag the wedge slightly away from the center of the pie chart. A dotted border represents

the new position of the wedge:

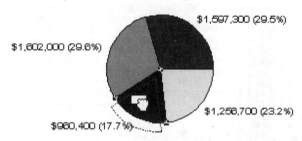

3. Release the mouse button. 1-2-3 redraws the pie chart with the exploded wedge in its new position:

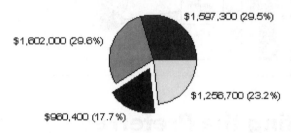

As a finishing touch, you might consider adding some drawn objects to the chart—for example, a text block and an arrow to further identify the exploded wedge (see page 363 for instructions). Figure 6.14 shows what your chart might look like after these additions.

TIP

You can explode all the wedges of a pie chart by the same amount. Choose Chart ➤ Data Labels and click the All by option in the Explode slices group. Then enter the percentage by which you want to explode the wedges. Try out different percentages until you find the visual effect you're looking for.

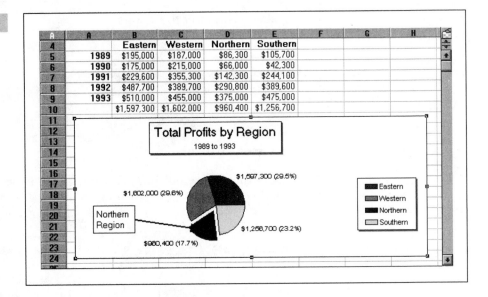

Setting the Preferred Chart Type

You've now seen examples of all the most commonly used chart types, including bar, line, area, and pie charts. As you know, 1-2-3 initially uses the bar chart as the default for all new charts you create. In other words, the bar chart is the *preferred* type when you first start creating charts in 1-2-3. Given a chart in the preferred type, you can switch to a new type by clicking the appropriate chart SmartIcon or by choosing the Chart ➤ Type command. Conversely, you can switch any chart back to the preferred type by selecting the chart and choosing Chart ➤ Use Preferred.

But what if you want to create several charts in a type that's not the preferred setting? For example, suppose you're planning a series of pie charts to represent various data ranges in a profit worksheet. You face the inconvenience of starting each new chart as a bar chart and then switching to the pie chart type.

For situations like this, 1-2-3 gives you the option of changing the preferred setting to any of the available chart types. The steps are easy:

1. Create a chart and assign it the type that you want to establish as the new preferred type.

2. Make sure the chart is selected.

3. Choose Chart ➤ Set Preferred.

After these steps, the new preferred chart type is automatically applied to all new charts you create with the Chart SmartIcon. The new preferred setting remains in effect until you change it again.

Next you'll take a look at several of the more complex chart types available in 1-2-3, including XY, mixed, and radar charts.

Creating XY Charts

An *XY chart* contains points that are plotted in a true x-y coordinate system, where one range of numeric values is shown as a function of another. The first data range supplies the x-coordinate of each plotted point in the chart and a second data range supplies the y-coordinate.

For example, Computing Conferences, Inc., has developed the worksheet in Figure 6.15 to search for a correlation between conference attendance and advertising. Column C shows the amounts spent on advertising for a series of conferences, and column D shows the attendance levels for the same conferences. An XY chart created from this information appears in Figure 6.16. Each point on the chart represents an advertising amount and the attendance level as an (x, y) ordered pair of values in the coordinate system. The chart seems to suggest a positive correlation—attendance goes up as more money is spent on advertising.

If you want to try developing this chart on your own computer, begin by creating the worksheet in Figure 6.15. Then follow these steps:

1. Select the range C5..D19, which contains the two columns of numeric data—the advertising expenditures and the corresponding attendance levels.

FIGURE 6.15

A worksheet containing attendance and advertising data

	A	B	C	D
1	Computing Conferences, Inc.			
2	Attendance and Advertising			
3	*Computing for Video Stores*			
4				
5	Place	Date	Advertising	Attendance
6	Chicago	09-Jan-93	$5,000	154
7	St. Louis	21-Jan-93	$3,500	119
8	Indianapolis	15-Feb-93	$6,000	174
9	New York	07-Mar-93	$6,000	201
10	Boston	25-Mar-93	$3,500	136
11	Washington, D.C.	03-Apr-93	$5,000	172
12	Atlanta	11-May-93	$3,500	112
13	Miami	28-May-93	$1,000	97
14	Dallas	03-Jun-93	$1,000	86
15	Albuquerque	29-Jun-93	$1,000	104
16	Las Vegas	05-Sep-93	$7,500	235
17	Los Angeles	11-Oct-93	$1,500	119
18	San Francisco	29-Oct-93	$2,500	137
19	Seattle	05-Nov-93	$3,500	148
20				

FIGURE 6.16

An XY chart correlating conference attendance with advertising dollars (the data comes from the worksheet in Figure 6.15)

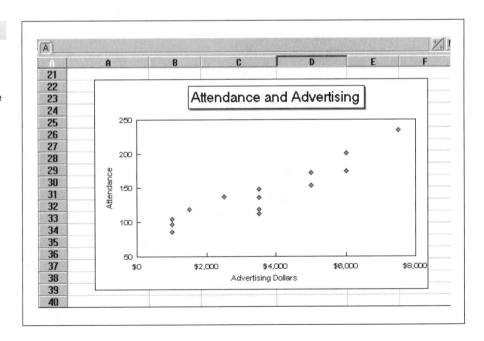

2. Click the Chart SmartIcon and drag the mouse pointer through the range A22..F39. When you release the mouse button, 1-2-3 creates a chart in the preferred format.

3. Choose Chart ➤ Type, and click XY option in the Types group. The Type dialog box displays pictures of the six different XY chart styles:

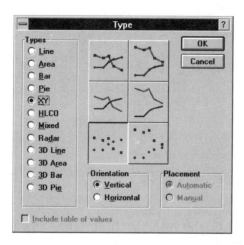

4. Click the third picture in the first column of styles, and then click OK. 1-2-3 creates the XY chart shown in Figure 6.16.

5. Select the legend and press the Delete key to remove it from the chart. Then use the techniques you've learned to change the chart's title and axis labels.

Creating Mixed Charts

A *mixed chart* superimposes a line chart over a bar chart. The two chart types represent different sets of data, and can be scaled independently. For example, Figure 6.17 shows a mixed chart created from the attendance-and-advertising worksheet shown in Figure 6.15.

Here are the steps for creating this mixed chart from the worksheet data in Figure 6.15:

1. Select the range A5..A19 in the worksheet. Then hold down the Ctrl key and select C5..D19.

6

Charts, Maps, Graphs

FIGURE 6.17

A mixed chart showing advertising expenditures as a bar chart, and attendance as a line chart

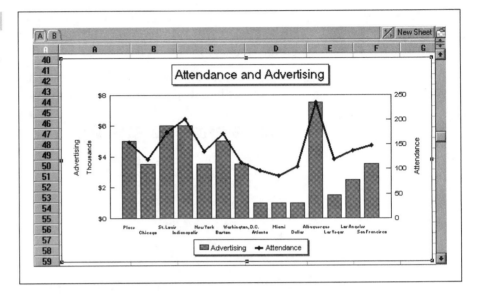

The first of these ranges contains the labels you'll see along the x-axis of the chart, and the second contains the two columns of numeric data that will be represented in the chart.

2. Scroll down to a blank worksheet range beneath the XY chart.

3. Click the Chart SmartIcon, and then drag the mouse pointer to define a rectangular area for the new chart. 1-2-3 initially creates a chart in the preferred format.

4. Choose the Chart ➤ Ranges command.

5. In the Ranges dialog box, choose the third entry in the Series box, B - Attendance. Then click the Plot on 2nd Y-axis option, placing an X in the corresponding check box, and choose the Line option from the Mixed type list.

Here's what the Ranges dialog box looks like when you complete these selections:

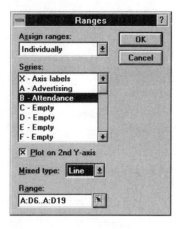

6. Click OK. 1-2-3 creates a mixed chart similar to the one in Figure 6.17.

7. Click the legend with the right mouse button, and choose the Legend command from the resulting quick menu. The Legend dialog box appears:

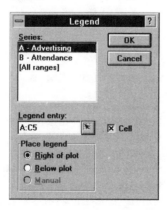

8. Click the Below plot option in the Place legend group, and then click OK.

6

Charts, Maps, Graphs

In response, 1-2-3 moves the legend to a position beneath the chart, leaving a greater amount of horizontal space for the chart and the labels along the x-axis.

9. Now use the techniques you've learned to revise the titles and the axis labels, as shown in Figure 6.17.

The resulting mixed chart contains two y-axes, one on the left and one on the right. The y-axis on the left contains a scale of values for the bar chart representing advertising expenditures. The y-axis on the right is the scale for the line chart, which represents attendance.

Creating HLCO Charts

A *high-low-close-open chart* is also known as a "stock market chart." This chart type displays vertical lines representing pairs of high and low values. In addition, special markings along each vertical line represent opening and closing values. The HLCO chart is a special form of the mixed chart type; it uses as many as six data ranges that supply several kinds of data:

- A range of labels that will appear along the x-axis.

- Two numeric ranges representing high and low values, respectively.

- Two numeric ranges representing closing and opening values, respectively.

- An additional numeric range that becomes a bar chart, located beneath the high-low lines.

- A numeric range that supplies average readings. This data series becomes a line chart that runs through the high-low lines.

All of these ranges have typical uses for reporting stock market data: The high-low lines represent stock prices, as do the opening and closing values; the bar chart beneath the lines represents trading volume; and the horizontal line chart represents stock averages.

But you may find other uses for the HLCO chart. For example, consider the weather worksheet shown in Figure 6.18. This worksheet contains data ranges displaying daily high and low temperatures; morning and evening readings; daily rainfall; and average temperatures. Using these six columns as the data ranges, 1-2-3 creates the HLCO chart shown in Figure 6.19.

If you want to try creating this HLCO chart, open a new worksheet and enter the table of weather data into a range at the top of the sheet, as shown in Figure 6.18. Then follow these steps:

1. Select the range A4..G11.

FIGURE 6.18

Weather Data

One Week of February Weather
San Francisco

	High	Low	06:00 AM	06:00 PM	Rainfall (in)	Avg. Temp.
Mon	53	32	43	50	0.75	41
Tue	76	35	51	62	1.25	49
Wed	71	38	59	67	1.25	54
Thu	55	30	39	50	2.00	40
Fri	50	28	39	50	1.25	38
Sat	59	29	43	55	2.25	43
Sun	68	37	49	60	2.00	49

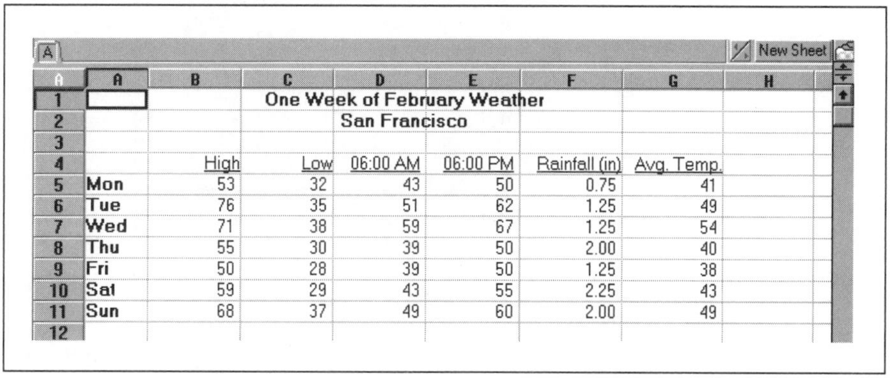

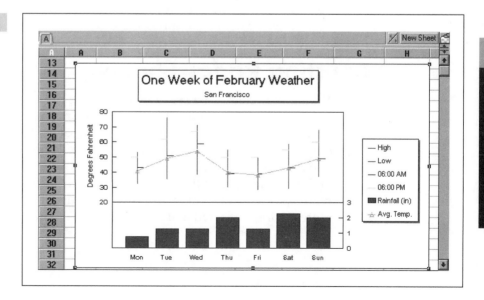

FIGURE 6.19

An HLCO chart from the weather data in Figure 6.18

2. Click the Chart SmartIcon, and then drag the mouse pointer to define a chart box beneath the data table. When you release the mouse button, 1-2-3 draws a chart in the current preferred format.

3. Choose Chart ➤ Type, and click the HLCO option in the Type group. The Type dialog box offers two styles of HLCO charts:

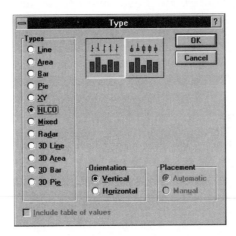

4. Select the first of the two types, and click OK. 1-2-3 draws an HLCO chart like the one shown in Figure 6.19.

5. Use the techniques you've learned to modify the titles and axis labels of the chart appropriately.

Creating Radar Charts

Yet another chart type available in 1-2-3 is the *radar chart*. Radar charts plot numeric data around a central point, and are useful for showing data projections against actual amounts for a particular time period. For example, Figure 6.20 shows a table of projected and actual sales figures over a four-quarter period. The accompanying radar chart plots the two sets of figures along lines that represent the four quarters. By connecting the points plotted along these lines, the chart displays two four-sided figures representing projected and actual sales.

FIGURE 6.20

A radar chart comparing sales projections with actual sales data

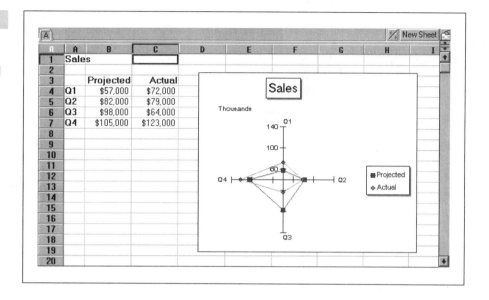

Maps

In addition to the standard chart types, 1-2-3 now provides a dramatic new way to illustrate geographic data. Using 1-2-3's mapping feature, you can portray geographic information related to business, industry, natural resources, economics, politics, populations and cultures, languages, history, health statistics, religions, or any other relevant topic. For example, you might use a map to depict business activity in any region of the globe—from states across the U.S. to countries around the world. Like the other chart types you've examined in this chapter, maps are easy to create from any appropriate range of worksheet data.

Figure 6.21 shows a map of business activity by Computing Conferences, Inc., in eleven Western states. Specifically, it shows the number of technical conferences that the company conducted in each state during 1993. As you can see in the map's legend, 1-2-3 organizes the numeric data into six *bins* (0 to 12, 13 to 24, 25 to 36, and so on) and assigns a unique color code to each bin. Thanks to this coding, you can instantly gauge the level of business activity in any state pictured in the map.

FIGURE 6.21

A map showing business activity in Western states

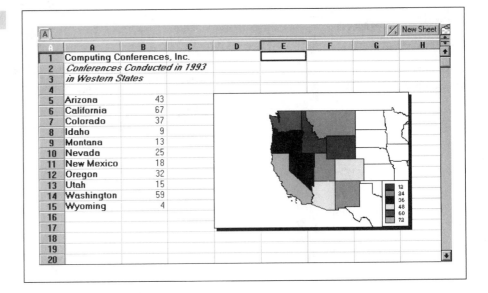

Mapping is nearly automatic in 1-2-3. When you select a range of data for a map, 1-2-3 examines the names of states or countries that you supply in the range and determines which map to add to your worksheet. Once the map object is displayed, you can use a companion program called the Lotus Map Viewer to revise the map in some important and versatile ways.

TIP

If you prefer, you can use abbreviated *map codes* instead of the full names of states or countries in the worksheet for a map. For example, use AZ, CA, and CO for Arizona, California, and Colorado. To see lists of the map codes that 1-2-3 recognizes, choose Help ➤ Search and enter Map Codes as the search key.

Creating a Map

In the following exercise you'll see how easy it is to create a map, as you go through the steps to duplicate the one shown in Figure 6.21. Begin your work by opening a new worksheet and creating the data table in the range A1..Bl5. Then proceed as follows:

1. Select the range A5..B15.

2. Choose Tools ➤ Map. On the resulting cascade menu, choose the first command, Insert Map Object.

3. Position the mouse pointer over your worksheet, a couple columns to the right of the data table. The mouse pointer takes the shape of a globe icon:

4			
5	Arizona	43	
6	California	67	
7	Colorado	37	
8	Idaho	9	
9	Montana	13	
10	Nevada	25	
11	New Mexic	18	
12	Oregon	32	
13	Utah	15	
14	Washingto	59	
15	Wyoming	· 4	
16			

4. Click the left mouse button. After a few seconds, 1-2-3 displays the initial version of the map on your worksheet:

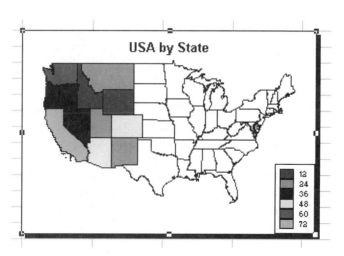

5. Position the mouse pointer anywhere inside the map object, and double-click the left mouse button.

This action starts the Lotus Map Viewer program, and copies your map into the program's work area, as shown in Figure 6.22.

6. Click the map's title ("USA by State") with the right mouse button, and choose the Clear command from the resulting quick menu. This action deletes the title from the map object.

7. Position the mouse pointer above and to the left of the map area (just off the northwest corner of Washington state) and hold down the Ctrl key. Then hold down the left mouse button and drag the mouse down and to the right until you see a dotted border around the eleven western states that are the subject of this map:

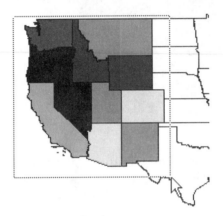

8. Release the mouse button, and the Map Viewer program performs a Zoom operation, increasing the size of the map area that you've marked off.

9. Choose File ➤ Exit and Return from the Map Viewer menu bar. Lotus copies the revised map back to your worksheet, which now looks like Figure 6.21.

Using the Zoom feature in the Lotus Map Viewer, you can create maps of any selected geographical region in the country or the world. Figure 6.23 shows another example, a population map of West Africa. Given the list of

FIGURE 6.22

Switching to the Lotus
Map Viewer
application

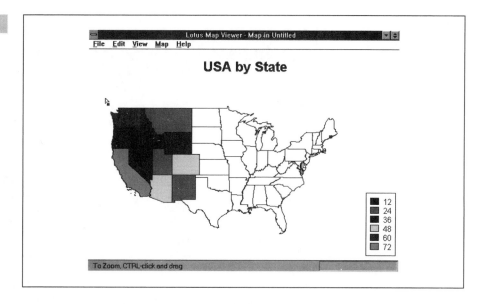

countries and population figures in the range A3..B17, Lotus initially creates a map of the world:

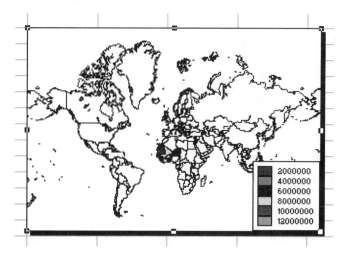

By switching to the Lotus Map Viewer application, you can increase the size of the focus area in West Africa, producing the map in Figure 6.23.

6

Charts, Maps, Graphs

FIGURE 6.23

A population map of
West Africa

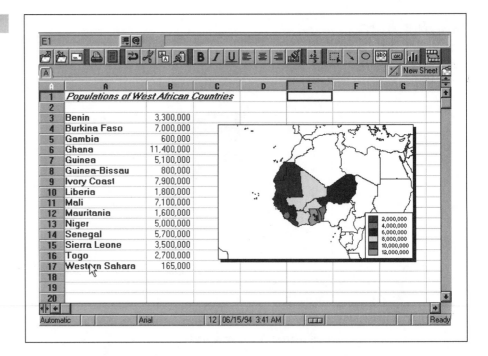

| TIP | In addition to United States and world maps, Lotus provides maps of Canadian provinces, Mexico, Australia, Japan, Taiwan, and the European Economic Community. |

Summary

A chart resides on a worksheet in 1-2-3, and is saved as part of the work-sheet file. You can produce a chart from a range that includes labels, numeric values, and titles. After selecting an appropriate range, you simply click the Chart SmartIcon and then drag the mouse through the area where you want to create the chart. 1-2-3 determines how to use the information in the worksheet and can automatically include titles, axis labels, data series, and a legend in the resulting chart.

When a chart object is selected, 1-2-3 replaces the Range menu with the Chart menu and displays a distinct SmartIcon palette, offering tools for modifying, refining, and enhancing the elements of a chart. In particular, the Chart ➤ Type command provides a variety of chart types, including bar, line, area, pie, XY, mixed, HLCO, and radar charts.

1-2-3 defines the data series for a chart depending on the row-and-column arrangement of the underlying data table. But once a chart is created, you can choose the Chart ➤ Ranges command to redefine the data series for the chart by row or by column. The choice between row and column data series often determines the focus and emphasis of the chart itself.

Drawn objects such as text blocks and arrows can be useful additions to a chart. A block of text with an arrow is a way of focusing attention on a particular element of the chart itself. To add one of these objects to a chart or a worksheet, simply click the appropriate SmartIcon and then drag the mouse pointer over the area where you want to display the object.

Each of the chart types available in 1-2-3 is suited to a particular variety of data. For example, line and area charts typically depict data values that change over time. Pie charts show the importance of individual data items in relation to the total of all the data. In an XY chart, sets of paired data values are plotted as points against an x-y coordinate system. A mixed chart shows a combination of bar and line charts. The HLCO chart displays high and low values as vertical lines, with closing and opening points marked along the length of each line. Finally, a radar chart plots points around a center point and can prove useful for comparing projected and actual data sets.

Maps are a dramatic new form of charting now available in 1-2-3. In a map, you can depict geographic data related to business, economics, politics, populations, or any other topic. 1-2-3 creates maps automatically from worksheet data that include a range of geographic names.

Database

Essentials

f a s t TRACK

To create a query table,   433

> choose Tools ➤ Database ➤ New Query and specify a data-
> base range. Click the Choose Fields button in the New Query
> dialog box if you want to develop a list of fields for the query
> table. (By default, a query table includes all the fields from the
> original database.) Click the Set Criteria button if you want
> to create selection criteria for selecting the records for the
> query. (By default, a query table includes all the records from
> the original database.) Specify the location where you want to
> display the new query. Then Click OK to complete the query
> operation.

**To revise database records that match
the stated criteria,**   443

> Create a query table that contains the records you want to re-
> vise. Choose the Query ➤ Set Options command and click
> the option labeled "Allow updates to database table." (An X
> appears in the corresponding check box.) Click OK both in
> the Set Options dialog box and in the warning box that 1-2-3
> displays next. Make any changes you want in the records of
> the query table. Then choose Query ➤ Update Database Ta-
> ble to copy the changes to the original database table.

To combine information from multiple databases,   445

> create a query that selects records from the first database, and
> then choose Query ➤ Join. Confirm the join definition that
> 1-2-3 displays in the Join dialog box (or develop a different
> definition), and click OK. Then select fields from both tables
> in the Choose Fields dialog box, and click OK.

A DATABASE is a collection of information, systematically organized to provide convenient access to individual records. Business databases are created for a great variety of subjects, including inventory, product lines, sales transactions, business assets, employee directories, client lists, regional offices, sales people, and so on.

The 1-2-3 database component is ideal for managing such information at your own desk. The commands on the Tools ➤ Database submenu, shown in Figure 7.1, help you perform important database tasks such as:

- Finding information that meets specific conditions (Tools ➤ Database ➤ Find Records)

- Deleting information that you no longer need to keep (Tools ➤ Database ➤ Delete Records)

FIGURE 7.1

The Tools ➤ Database commands

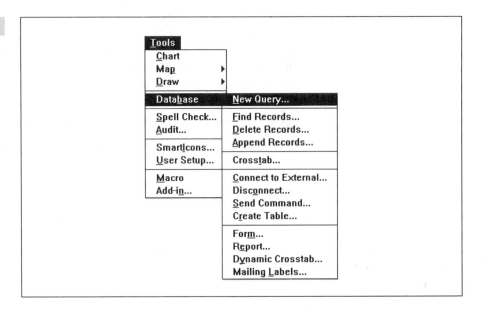

7

- Creating a *query table*, a selection of data that 1-2-3 copies to a new worksheet location (Tools ➤ Database ➤ New Query)

A query table is, in turn, a special type of object that significantly expands the scope of database operations. When you create a query table, 1-2-3 provides a whole new set of commands and features for managing information. These include tools for:

- Updating a database from revisions you make in a query table (Query ➤ Update Database Table)

- Combining information from two or more related database tables (Query ➤ Join)

In this chapter you'll learn how to organize a 1-2-3 database and you'll master the basic operations available for database tables and query tables.

Defining a Database

A database is an arrangement of *records* and *fields*:

- **Records.** A record contains all the information describing a single item or person in the database—for example, a product, a transaction, a property, an employee, a client, a regional office, or a salesperson.

- **Fields.** A field is one category of information for each record in the database—for example, the product name, the transaction date, the property value, the employee's salary, the client's business address, the office manager, or the sales region.

In 1-2-3 you store a database in the rows and columns of a worksheet:

- Records are stored in consecutive rows of the worksheet. All the information for a given record is displayed in one row.

- Fields appear side-by-side in adjacent columns of the worksheet. Each entry in a given column belongs to the same field and the same data type. At the top of each field column, just above the first record in the database, is a *field name*, a label that identifies the field.

In short, a database table is a collection of records organized into distinct fields of information and stored in a worksheet. Every database table begins with a row of field names. For successful *query* operations, a consistent data type within each field is an essential part of database design.

The best way to clarify these terms and concepts is to consider an example. In the exercises of this chapter you'll once again look into the business files of Computing Conferences, Inc., this time to examine the company's database of conference instructors. This database contains information about computer specialists around the country whom the company engages to present specific topics at training conferences.

Figure 7.2 shows the beginning of the database, displayed inside a worksheet window. Each record in the database is stored in a row of the worksheet and contains all the information about one instructor. The first record is in row 4. There are eleven fields, displayed across the worksheet in columns A through K. The field names are in row 3. As you can see, a complete record consists of one entry for each of the eleven fields. Here

FIGURE 7.2

The beginning of the instructor database, displayed in a worksheet window

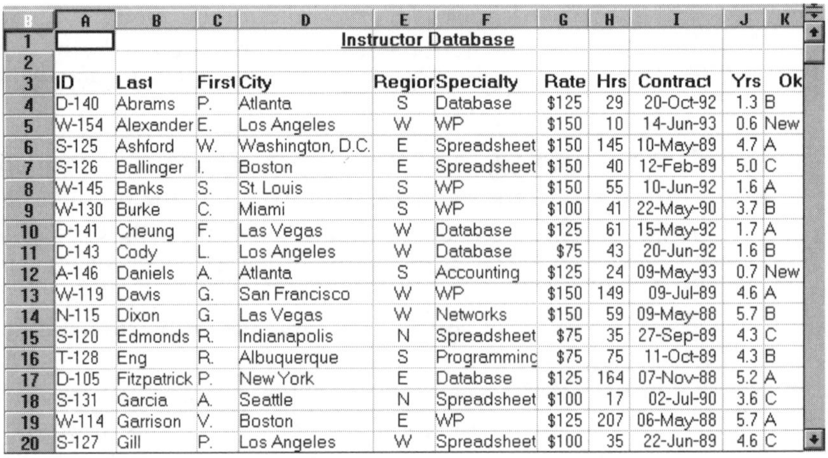

	A	B	C	D	E	F	G	H	I	J	K
1					Instructor Database						
2											
3	ID	Last	First	City	Region	Specialty	Rate	Hrs	Contract	Yrs	Ok
4	D-140	Abrams	P.	Atlanta	S	Database	$125	29	20-Oct-92	1.3	B
5	W-154	Alexander	E.	Los Angeles	W	WP	$150	10	14-Jun-93	0.6	New
6	S-125	Ashford	W.	Washington, D.C.	E	Spreadsheet	$150	145	10-May-89	4.7	A
7	S-126	Ballinger	I.	Boston	E	Spreadsheet	$150	40	12-Feb-89	5.0	C
8	W-145	Banks	S.	St. Louis	S	WP	$150	55	10-Jun-92	1.6	A
9	W-130	Burke	C.	Miami	S	WP	$100	41	22-May-90	3.7	B
10	D-141	Cheung	F.	Las Vegas	W	Database	$125	61	15-May-92	1.7	A
11	D-143	Cody	L.	Los Angeles	W	Database	$75	43	20-Jun-92	1.6	B
12	A-146	Daniels	A.	Atlanta	S	Accounting	$125	24	09-May-93	0.7	New
13	W-119	Davis	G.	San Francisco	W	WP	$150	149	09-Jul-89	4.6	A
14	N-115	Dixon	G.	Las Vegas	W	Networks	$150	59	09-May-88	5.7	B
15	S-120	Edmonds	R.	Indianapolis	N	Spreadsheet	$75	35	27-Sep-89	4.3	C
16	T-128	Eng	R.	Albuquerque	S	Programming	$75	75	11-Oct-89	4.3	B
17	D-105	Fitzpatrick	P.	New York	E	Database	$125	164	07-Nov-88	5.2	A
18	S-131	Garcia	A.	Seattle	N	Spreadsheet	$100	17	02-Jul-90	3.6	C
19	W-114	Garrison	V.	Boston	E	WP	$125	207	06-May-88	5.7	A
20	S-127	Gill	P.	Los Angeles	W	Spreadsheet	$100	35	22-Jun-89	4.6	C

are descriptions of the fields:

FIELD NAME	DESCRIPTION
ID	An identification number.
Last	The instructor's last name.
First	The initial of the instructor's first name.
City	The city where the instructor is based.
Region	A single letter—N, S, E, or W—designating one of the company's four regions. This is the instructor's home region.
Specialty	The instructor's primary area of expertise. The entry in this field is one of the following six categories: Spreadsheet, Database, WP (for word processing), Accounting, Networks, or Programming.
Rate	The instructor's current hourly rate for conference presentations, an amount that varies from one instructor to the next. As you can see, the numeric entries in this field range from $75 to $150.
Hrs	The total number of conference hours the instructor has worked for the company.
Contract	The date of the instructor's first work contract with the company.
Yrs	The number of years since the instructor's first job.
Ok	A rating of A, B, or C, indicating the instructor's level of experience. If the instructor has worked for Computing Conferences, Inc. for less than a year, the entry in this field is New.

As you'll see in this chapter, field names play an important role in database operations. Each field has a unique name. For convenience, you should try to write field names that are clear, concise, and easy to remember.

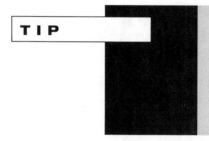

TIP Field names need not be restricted to a single word. For example, you could write Last Name, First Name, Home Region, Hourly Rate, and Years of Work as field names in the Instructor database. But it's often more convenient to write short, one-word field names, because in the long run they're easier for you to use in database operations.

Figure 7.3 shows the complete database table, describing all the instructors who work for Computing Conferences, Inc., in the four regions. There are over fifty records. In this particular listing, the records are arranged in alphabetical order by the instructors' names. Notice that the entries in a given field column all belong to the same data type, and are formatted consistently. The first six fields are labels. The next four are numeric fields—the hourly rate, formatted as a dollar amount; the hours, an integer; the first contract date, a date number formatted in a date display format; and the years, formatted as a numeric value with one decimal place. The last field, Ok, is a label.

Creating a Database

For the exercises of this chapter, you'll need a copy of the Instructor database table in your own worksheet; but to avoid spending too much time creating this example, you can enter a shortened form of the database. The short version, shown in Figure 7.4, contains a selection of 17 record entries in rows 4 through 20.

To create the shortened database, start with a new blank worksheet and follow these steps:

1. Click the New Sheet button to insert worksheet B into the window. You'll enter the instructor database into worksheet B, saving worksheet A for a later exercise.

FIGURE 7.3

The complete instructor
database table

Database Essentials

<u>Instructor Database</u>

ID	Last	First	City	Region	Specialty	Rate	Hrs	Contract	Yrs	Ok
D-140	Abrams	P.	Atlanta	S	Database	$125	29	20-Oct-92	1.3	B
W-154	Alexander	E.	Los Angeles	W	WP	$150	10	14-Jun-93	0.6	New
S-125	Ashford	W.	Washington, D.C	E	Spreadsheet	$150	145	10-May-89	4.7	A
S-126	Ballinger	I.	Boston	E	Spreadsheet	$150	40	12-Feb-89	5.0	C
W-145	Banks	S.	St. Louis	S	WP	$150	55	10-Jun-92	1.6	A
W-130	Burke	C.	Miami	S	WP	$100	41	22-May-90	3.7	B
D-141	Cheung	F.	Las Vegas	W	Database	$125	61	15-May-92	1.7	A
D-143	Cody	L.	Los Angeles	W	Database	$75	43	20-Jun-92	1.6	B
A-146	Daniels	A.	Atlanta	S	Accounting	$125	24	09-May-93	0.7	New
W-119	Davis	G.	San Francisco	W	WP	$150	149	09-Jul-89	4.6	A
N-115	Dixon	G.	Las Vegas	W	Networks	$150	59	09-May-88	5.7	B
S-120	Edmonds	R.	Indianapolis	N	Spreadsheet	$75	35	27-Sep-89	4.3	C
T-128	Eng	R.	Albuquerque	S	Programming	$75	75	11-Oct-89	4.3	B
D-105	Fitzpatrick	P.	New York	E	Database	$125	164	07-Nov-88	5.2	A
S-131	Garcia	A.	Seattle	N	Spreadsheet	$100	17	02-Jul-90	3.6	C
W-114	Garrison	V.	Boston	E	WP	$125	207	06-May-88	5.7	A
S-127	Gill	P.	Los Angeles	W	Spreadsheet	$100	35	22-Jun-89	4.6	C
S-156	Hale	S.	San Francisco	W	Spreadsheet	$75	28	09-Jun-93	0.6	New
S-149	Harris	P.	Dallas	S	Spreadsheet	$150	17	12-Feb-93	1.0	New
D-109	Hayes	S.	San Francisco	W	Database	$75	95	07-Feb-88	6.0	B
T-138	Hermann	J.	Los Angeles	W	Programming	$125	74	24-May-91	2.7	B
S-132	Jones	L.	Atlanta	S	Spreadsheet	$125	5	10-Feb-90	4.0	C
W-116	Jordan	E.	Dallas	S	WP	$100	17	06-Oct-88	5.3	C
W-117	Kim	E.	Washington, D.C	E	WP	$100	137	11-Oct-88	5.3	B
N-144	King	T.	New York	E	Networks	$75	13	06-Jan-92	2.1	C
D-136	Koenig	O.	Albuquerque	S	Database	$125	20	02-Jun-91	2.7	C
S-111	Kwan	O.	New York	E	Spreadsheet	$100	71	21-Jun-88	5.6	B
D-123	Lambert	S.	Dallas	S	Database	$150	145	26-Jun-89	4.6	A
D-134	Lee	H.	Seattle	N	Database	$150	21	17-Dec-90	3.1	C
W-150	Leung	M.	Chicago	N	WP	$100	16	26-Mar-93	0.9	New
W-112	Manning	P.	Atlanta	S	WP	$75	71	09-Nov-88	5.2	B
W-107	Martinez	G.	Las Vegas	W	WP	$150	178	15-Mar-88	5.9	A
N-129	McKay	J.	Washington, D.C	E	Networks	$150	35	09-May-89	4.7	C
W-124	Meyer	J.	New York	E	WP	$150	85	05-May-89	4.7	B
A-135	Meyer	L.	New York	E	Accounting	$100	57	17-Aug-90	3.5	B
T-148	Miranda	O.	Las Vegas	W	Programming	$75	9	04-Jan-93	1.1	C
S-153	Nichols	B.	Albuquerque	S	Spreadsheet	$150	19	28-Feb-93	0.9	New
N-118	O'Neil	P.	Atlanta	S	Networks	$75	5	01-May-89	4.8	C
A-103	Perez	D.	Las Vegas	W	Accounting	$100	5	11-Jul-88	5.6	C
W-113	Porter	D.	Seattle	N	WP	$125	59	02-Aug-88	5.5	B
D-139	Porter	M.	Washington, D.C	E	Database	$150	26	28-Mar-91	2.8	B
T-133	Ramirez	F.	Boston	E	Programming	$150	73	08-Feb-90	4.0	B
S-155	Roberts	P.	Chicago	N	Spreadsheet	$100	10	21-Aug-93	0.4	New
D-137	Sanchez	W.	Indianapolis	N	Database	$100	47	16-Apr-91	2.8	B
N-101	Schwartz	B.	Boston	E	Networks	$150	178	02-Mar-88	5.9	A
W-151	Schwartz	P.	Indianapolis	N	WP	$150	23	10-May-93	0.7	New
D-104	Taylor	F.	Boston	E	Database	$100	17	24-Oct-88	5.3	C
D-142	Thomas	T.	St. Louis	S	Database	$150	35	23-Dec-92	1.1	A
S-108	Tong	C.	St. Louis	S	Spreadsheet	$150	35	12-Nov-88	5.2	C
N-152	Tong	P.	San Francisco	W	Networks	$150	23	13-May-93	0.7	New
N-110	Tong	W.	Los Angeles	W	Networks	$150	83	09-May-88	5.7	B
S-122	Vasquez	T.	Las Vegas	W	Spreadsheet	$75	5	27-Apr-89	4.8	C
T-102	Vaughn	A.	Washington, D.C	E	Programming	$75	53	11-Sep-88	5.4	B
T-147	Webb	F.	New York	E	Programming	$125	32	27-Jan-93	1.0	A
D-106	Weinberg	P.	Miami	S	Database	$75	59	18-Jan-88	6.0	B
D-121	Williams	C.	Chicago	N	Database	$150	30	02-Oct-89	4.3	C

FIGURE 7.4

The short version of the instructor database table

	A	B	C	D	E	F	G	H	I	J	K
1						Instructor Database					
2											
3	ID	Last	First	City	Region	Specialty	Rate	Hrs	Contract	Yrs	Ok
4	S-149	Harris	P.	Dallas	S	Spreadsheet	150	17	12-Feb-93		
5	A-146	Daniels	A.	Atlanta	S	Accounting	125	24	09-May-93		
6	A-103	Perez	D.	Las Vegas	W	Accounting	100	5	11-Jul-88		
7	W-113	Porter	D.	Seattle	N	WP	125	59	02-Aug-88		
8	N-101	Schwartz	B.	Boston	E	Networks	150	178	02-Mar-88		
9	S-155	Roberts	P.	Chicago	N	Spreadsheet	100	10	21-Aug-93		
10	S-125	Ashford	W.	Washington, D.C.	E	Spreadsheet	150	145	10-May-89		
11	D-106	Weinberg	P.	Miami	S	Database	75	59	18-Jan-88		
12	W-119	Davis	G.	San Francisco	W	WP	150	149	09-Jul-89		
13	W-124	Meyer	J.	New York	E	WP	150	85	05-May-89		
14	W-145	Banks	S.	St. Louis	S	WP	150	55	10-Jun-92		
15	D-137	Sanchez	W.	Indianapolis	N	Database	100	47	16-Apr-91		
16	D-139	Porter	M.	Washington, D.C.	E	Database	150	26	28-Mar-91		
17	T-133	Ramirez	F.	Boston	E	Programming	150	73	08-Feb-90		
18	D-143	Cody	L.	Los Angeles	W	Database	75	43	20-Jun-92		
19	S-127	Gill	P.	Los Angeles	W	Spreadsheet	100	35	22-Jun-89		
20	T-128	Eng	R.	Albuquerque	S	Programming	75	75	11-Oct-89		

2. Use your mouse to adjust columns A through K to the following widths: A, **6**; B, **8**; C, **4**; D, **13**; E, **6**; F, **10**; G, **5**; H, **4**; I, **9**; J, **4**; K, **4**.

N O T E

Recall that the column width is displayed in the first panel of the edit line whenever you use the mouse to drag the border.

3. Enter the title **Instructor Database** into cell A1, and use the Style ➤ Alignment command to center the title horizontally over columns A through K. Click the Bold and Underline SmartIcons to apply these styles to the title.

4. Enter the field names shown in Figure 7.4 into row 3, cells A3 through K3. Then select the range A3..K3 and click the bold icon.

5. Enter the first six fields of information into columns A, B, C, D, E, and F. Copy each entry exactly as you see it in Figure 7.4. Center the entries of the Region field in column E.

6. Enter the numeric data of the next two fields, Rate and Hrs, into columns G and H.

7. Enter the dates into column I just as they appear in Figure 7.4. As you know, 1-2-3 converts these entries into date numbers, which you can use in date arithmetic operations.

8. Choose the File Save As command, and save this file as INSTRUCT.WK4.

The Yrs and Ok fields, in columns J and K, remain blank in Figure 7.4. Yrs and Ok are calculated fields in the instructor database.

Creating Calculated Fields

You can write a formula to calculate the data for any field in a database table. To create a calculated field, you enter the formula as the field entry for the first record in the database, then you copy the formula down the field column—just as you would do in an ordinary worksheet application. Formulas for calculated fields often contain references to values in other fields of the database table. As you would expect, 1-2-3 recalculates a field formula whenever you make a change in the data that the formula uses.

The Yrs field in the Instructor database table shows the number of years an instructor has worked with Computing Conferences, Inc. This number would normally be calculated as the difference between today's date and the date in the Contract field, as in the following formula:

(@TODAY–I4)/365

This formula finds the difference, in days, between today's date (@TO-DAY) and the first contract date (I4); then the result is divided by 365 to calculate the difference in years. The advantage of this formula in a database is that 1-2-3 can recalculate the Yrs field each time the value of @TODAY changes—that is, every day. This means that the values in the Yrs field are always up to date.

But for the exercises in this chapter, you'll replace this formula with one that supplies a fixed date instead of @TODAY:

(@DATE(94,1,31)–I4)/365

By making this small adjustment, you'll be able to duplicate each database example exactly as it appears in this chapter.

T I P

The @DATEDIF function is an alternate tool for finding the difference in years between two dates. See page 706 for details.

The value in the Ok field for a given instructor is based on the instructor's experience level—specifically, the average number of conference hours the instructor has worked per year since the initial contract:

- An instructor who has worked an average of 30 hours or more per year receives an Ok rating of A.

- An instructor who has worked fewer than 30 hours but at least 9 hours per year receives a rating of B.

- An instructor who has worked fewer than 9 hours per year receives a rating of C.

- An instructor who has worked for less than a year receives a "New" entry in this field instead of an A, B, or C rating.

Here are the steps for entering these two formulas into the first record of the database table, and copying them down their respective field columns:

1. Enter the following formula into cell J4, to calculate the number of years since the initial contract:

   (@DATE(94,1,31)–I4)/365

2. Enter this formula carefully into cell K4:

   @IF(J4<1,"New",@IF(H4/J4>=30,"A",@IF(H4/J4<9,"C","B")))

This formula uses a sequence of nested @IF functions to select a label of New, A, B, or C for the Ok field. (You may want to turn briefly back to page 324 to review the structure and use of 1-2-3's built-in @IF function.) The outermost @IF function enters a label of New if the value of the Yrs field is less than 1. Otherwise, the middle @IF function enters A if the average yearly work hour amount (H4/J4) is greater than or equal to 30. Finally, if neither of these first two conditions is true, the innermost @IF function chooses between label C or B, depending upon whether the average work hour figure is less than or greater than 9.

3. To copy these two formulas down columns J and K, respectively, select the range J4..K20, click the selection with the right mouse button, and choose the Copy Down command from the resulting quick menu.
4. Preselect the range J4..J20 and click the Format selector on the status bar. Choose Fixed from the format list. Then click the Decimal selector, the second panel of the status bar and choose 1 as the number of digits after the decimal point. When you complete this step, the two calculated fields, Yrs and Ok, appear as shown in Figure 7.5.
5. Click the Save SmartIcon to update the file on disk.

FIGURE 7.5

Entering calculated fields—columns J and K—in the database table

D	A	B	C	D	E	F	G	H	I	J	K
1						Instructor Database					
2											
3	ID	Last	First	City	Region	Specialty	Rate	Hrs	Contract	Yrs	Ok
4	S-149	Harris	P.	Dallas	S	Spreadsheet	150	17	12-Feb-93	1.0	New
5	A-146	Daniels	A.	Atlanta	S	Accounting	125	24	09-May-93	0.7	New
6	A-103	Perez	D.	Las Vegas	W	Accounting	100	5	11-Jul-88	5.6	C
7	W-113	Porter	D.	Seattle	N	WP	125	59	02-Aug-88	5.5	B
8	N-101	Schwartz	B.	Boston	E	Networks	150	178	02-Mar-88	5.9	A
9	S-155	Roberts	P.	Chicago	N	Spreadsheet	100	10	21-Aug-93	0.4	New
10	S-125	Ashford	W.	Washington, D.C.	E	Spreadsheet	150	145	10-May-89	4.7	A
11	D-106	Weinberg	P.	Miami	S	Database	75	59	18-Jan-88	6.0	B
12	W-119	Davis	G.	San Francisco	W	WP	150	149	09-Jul-89	4.6	A
13	W-124	Meyer	J.	New York	E	WP	150	85	05-May-89	4.7	B
14	W-145	Banks	S.	St. Louis	S	WP	150	55	10-Jun-92	1.6	A
15	D-137	Sanchez	W.	Indianapolis	N	Database	100	47	16-Apr-91	2.8	B
16	D-139	Porter	M.	Washington, D.C.	E	Database	150	26	28-Mar-91	2.8	B
17	T-133	Ramirez	F.	Boston	E	Programminc	150	73	08-Feb-90	4.0	B
18	D-143	Cody	L.	Los Angeles	W	Database	75	43	20-Jun-92	1.6	B
19	S-127	Gill	P.	Los Angeles	W	Spreadsheet	100	35	22-Jun-89	4.6	C
20	T-128	Eng	R.	Albuquerque	S	Programminc	75	75	11-Oct-89	4.3	B

Creating Multiple Tables in a Database

In 1-2-3 a database may consist of a single table or a collection of two or more tables. Given a database containing multiple tables, you can use a *join* operation to match records from related tables and build new combinations of data.

Anticipating this option, you'll now enter a second database table in worksheet A, which you've left empty up to now. This new table, shown in Figure 7.6, contains information about the regional offices of Computing Conferences, Inc. The Office database table has only four records, one for each of the four regional offices. There are seven fields in the database:

FIELD NAME	DESCRIPTION
Region	Contains an entry of N, S, E, or W.
Address	The street address.
City	The city name.
State	The state.
Zip	The zip code
Phone	The phone number.
Manager	The name of the regional manager in charge of operations at each office.

	A	B	C	D	E	F	G
1	Regional Offices						
2							
3	Region	Address	City	State	Zip	Phone	Manager
4	E	222 Allen Street	New York	NY	10103	(212) 555-4678	Campbell, R.
5	N	Mills Tower, Suite 992	Chicago	IL	60605	(312) 555-8803	Logan, C.
6	S	11 Maple Street	Dallas	TX	75210	(214) 555-6754	Harvey, J.
7	W	432 Market Avenue	Los Angeles	CA	90028	(213) 555-9974	Garcia, M.
8							

Notice that this new table has the Region field in common with the Instructor table. This field allows you to correlate records in the two tables. For example, imagine the steps you might take to find the name of the regional manager who supervises a particular instructor. You would begin by searching for the instructor's name in the instructor table. After locating the correct record, you would make note of the instructor's region. Then you would switch over to the office database, look up the office record corresponding to the same region, and find the manager's name in the Manager field.

Later in this chapter you'll learn how 1-2-3 automates this sequence of steps in a query operation that joins data from multiple database tables. For now, take the following steps to enter the Office database table into worksheet A:

1. Click the A tab to activate the first sheet in the file.

2. Use your mouse to adjust the widths of columns A through G: A, **7**; B, **17**; C, **11**; D, **5**; E, **7**; F, **12**; G, **12**.

3. Enter the title **Regional Offices** into cell A1. Click the Bold and Underline SmartIcons to apply these two styles to the title.

4. Enter the seven field names into row 3, as shown in Figure 7.6. Then select the range A3..G3 and click the Bold SmartIcon.

5. Select the range E4..F7, where you'll be entering zip codes and telephone numbers. Click the Format selector, the first panel on the status bar, and choose the Label format for this range.

Recall that the Label format gives you a convenient way to enter labels into a worksheet, even when an entry looks like a numeric value. Zip and Phone are label fields.

6. Enter the four regional office records into rows 4 through 7 of the worksheet.

7. Use the Center SmartIcon to center the Region and Zip field values in their respective columns.

TIP

Thanks to the Label format that you applied to the range E4..F7, you don't have to worry about starting zip codes and phone numbers with special label prefixes. As for the addresses in column B, 1-2-3 automatically recognizes each field item as a label once you complete the entry—even though an address may begin with a digit.

Defining Range Names for Database Tables

Now this file consists of two database tables—the Office table in sheet A, and the Instructor table in sheet B. Creating range names will simplify your work in upcoming exercises with these two tables. (See page 134 if you need to review range names.) In the following steps, you'll assign two range names to each table; in addition, you'll assign meaningful names to the two sheet tabs.

1. On worksheet A, select the range A3..G7, which contains the entire Office table, including the field names. Choose Range ➤ Name and assign the name OFFICEDB (for "Office database") to this range:

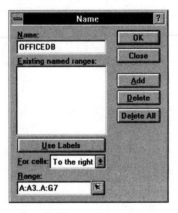

2. Now select the range A:A4..A:G7. This range contains the four regional office records, without the field names. Choose Range ➤ Name and enter OFFICERECS ("Office records") as the name for this range.

3. Double-click the A tab on the tab line just above the worksheet area. Type **Offices** as the new name for this sheet, and press ↵.

4. Click the B tab to activate the second sheet. Select the range B:A3..B:K20. This range contains the entire Instructor database table, including the field names. Choose Range ➤ Name and

assign the name INSTRUCTDB ("Instructors database") to this range.

5. Next select the range B:A4..BK20. This range contains the instructor records, without the field names. Choose Range ➤ Name and enter INSTRUCTRECS ("Instructor records") as the name for this range.

6. Double-click the B tab and type **Instructors** as the new name for this sheet. Press ↵ to confirm the name change.

7. Click the Save SmartIcon to update the database file to disk.

A list of range names from the Navigator button To confirm that you've defined these four range names correctly, click the Navigator button on the edit line. You'll see the names in the resulting drop-down list:

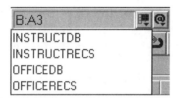

Notice that all four names are available regardless of which sheet is currently active. As always, the Navigator button is a convenient tool for jumping from one named range to another in a worksheet file. You'll use the OFFICEDB and INSTRUCTDB range names in query operations that require references to the entire database tables, including field names. By contrast, the OFFICERECS and INSTRUCTRECS names will prove convenient in procedures for sorting the database records.

Sorting a Database

Once you create a database, you may want to *sort* the records, rearranging them in a new order. You accomplish this operation by choosing the Range ➤ Sort command.

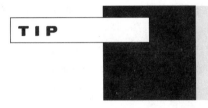

TIP

As you learned in Chapter 5, Range ➤ Sort is not exclusively for use in databases (see page 308). You can use this command to sort the data in any range of rows, whether or not they form a database.

You can probably imagine several useful new arrangements for the records in the Instructor database. For example, you might decide to sort the database in alphabetical order by instructors' ID numbers; in numerical order by their hourly rates; or in chronological order by their first contract dates. In each of these examples, the specified field—ID, Rate, or Contract—is called the *key* to the sort.

Given a sorting key and a database range to be sorted, the Data Sort command can arrange the records in *ascending* or *descending* order. The difference between these two sorting directions depends on the type of data stored in the key field and on the standard sort order that is currently in effect. Here is how 1-2-3 sorts data by default:

- **Labels.** If the key field contains labels, an ascending sort arranges the records in alphabetical order, from A to Z. If two labels are identical except for alphabetic case, lowercase letters are placed before uppercase letters. Labels that begin with digits are placed *before* labels that begin with letters. A descending sort produces the reverse order, from Z to A, followed by labels that begin with digits.

- **Numeric values.** If the key field contains numeric values, an ascending sort arranges the records from the smallest value to the largest; and a descending sort arranges the records from the largest to the smallest.

- **Date numbers.** If the key contains dates that have been entered as 1-2-3 date numbers, an ascending sort arranges the database from the earliest to the latest date; and a descending sort arranges the records from the latest to the earliest date.

N O T E   Blank cells are arranged first in an ascending sort, and last in a descending sort.

Using the Sort Command

When you choose Range ➤ Sort, the Sort dialog box appears on the screen:

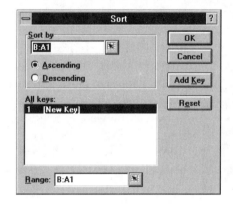

For a simple sort, you need to specify three items of information:

- In the Range box (at the bottom of the Sort dialog box) you enter the range of records that you want to sort.

- In the Sort by box you enter a reference to a cell inside the selected key field.

- You make a choice between the Ascending and Descending options.

WARNING

As a general rule, you shouldn't include the row of field names in the range to be sorted. If you do, the field names may leave their correct position at the top of the database and end up somewhere within the range of records. Actually, 1-2-3 makes an attempt to determine whether the top row of a sort range is a row of field names. For example, when you sort the Instructors table by a numeric key, 1-2-3 recognizes the field names and avoids sorting them into the table, even if you inadvertently include the top row in the sort range. 1-2-3 can do this because all the field names are labels, and the data records themselves contain combinations of numbers, dates, and labels. But in the Offices table all the field columns consist of labels; 1-2-3 therefore has no way of determining whether the top row contains field names. If you were to select the entire table as the sort range, the field names would be sorted into the data records. In this event, click the Undo SmartIcon immediately after the sort to revert to the previous order.

In the following exercise you'll sort the Instructor database in ascending chronological order by contract dates:

1. Select the Instructors sheet if it is not already active, and choose Range ➤ Sort. If any key definitions are listed in the All keys box (from a previous sort operation), click the Reset button to remove them.

2. Activate the Range box by pressing Alt+R or by clicking inside the text box.

3. Press the F3 function key. In response, 1-2-3 displays the Range Names dialog box on the screen, with a list of all the range names

7

Database Essentials

you've defined up to now for your database worksheet:

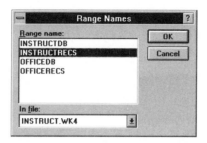

Click the name INSTRUCTRECS. This name represents the range of records without the row of field names. Click OK. The Range Names box disappears and 1-2-3 enters the name into the Range box.

4. Click the range selector button at the right side of the Sort by box. The Sort dialog box temporarily disappears from the screen.

5. Click cell I4 in the Instructors table.

This cell contains the contract date for the first record in the database. In response to your mouse click, 1-2-3 enters a reference to this cell into the Sort by box. This reference is sufficient to select the Contract field as the key to the sort.

6. Click the Ascending option if it's not already selected. At this point in your work, the Sort dialog box appears as follows:

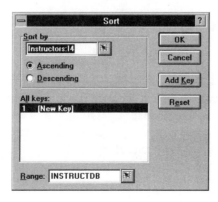

7. Click the Add Key button. 1-2-3 transfers the key definition to the All keys box.

8. Click OK or press ↵ to complete the sort operation. Then press Home to move the cell pointer to A1.

The sorted database appears in Figure 7.7. As you can see in column I, 1-2-3 has rearranged the instructor records in order of contract dates, from the earliest to the most recent.

FIGURE 7.7

The Instructor database sorted chronologically by contract date

	A	B	C	D	Region	Specialty	Rate	Hrs	Contract	Yrs	Ok
1					Instructor Database						
2											
3	ID	Last	First	City	Region	Specialty	Rate	Hrs	Contract	Yrs	Ok
4	D-106	Weinberg	P.	Miami	S	Database	75	59	18-Jan-88	6.0	B
5	N-101	Schwartz	B.	Boston	E	Networks	150	178	02-Mar-88	5.9	A
6	A-103	Perez	D.	Las Vegas	W	Accounting	100	5	11-Jul-88	5.6	C
7	W-113	Porter	D.	Seattle	N	WP	125	59	02-Aug-88	5.5	B
8	W-124	Meyer	J.	New York	E	WP	150	85	05-May-89	4.7	B
9	S-125	Ashford	W.	Washington, D.C.	E	Spreadsheet	150	145	10-May-89	4.7	A
10	S-127	Gill	P.	Los Angeles	W	Spreadsheet	100	35	22-Jun-89	4.6	C
11	W-119	Davis	G.	San Francisco	W	WP	150	149	09-Jul-89	4.6	A
12	T-128	Eng	R.	Albuquerque	S	Programming	75	75	11-Oct-89	4.3	B
13	T-133	Ramirez	F.	Boston	E	Programming	150	73	08-Feb-90	4.0	B
14	D-139	Porter	M.	Washington, D.C.	E	Database	150	26	28-Mar-91	2.8	B
15	D-137	Sanchez	W.	Indianapolis	N	Database	100	47	16-Apr-91	2.8	B
16	W-145	Banks	S.	St. Louis	S	WP	150	55	10-Jun-92	1.6	A
17	D-143	Cody	L.	Los Angeles	W	Database	75	43	20-Jun-92	1.6	B
18	S-149	Harris	P.	Dallas	S	Spreadsheet	150	17	12-Feb-93	1.0	New
19	A-146	Daniels	A.	Atlanta	S	Accounting	125	24	09-May-93	0.7	New
20	S-155	Roberts	P.	Chicago	N	Spreadsheet	100	10	21-Aug-93	0.4	New

Sorting by More than One Key Field

Sometimes a single key is not enough to produce a complete or useful sort. When two or more records have the same entry in the *primary* key field, you need to choose a *secondary* key to decide the order of these matching records. One simple example of this occurs in the Instructor database: There are two instructors with the last name of Porter. When you sort the records alphabetically by instructors' names, you need to select the Last field as the first, or primary, key, and the First field as the second key, to make sure that these two names appear in the correct order. Try this second sorting exercise now:

1. Choose Range ➤ Sort. In the Sort dialog box, you'll notice that the Range text box still contains a correct reference to the range of database records.

2. Click the Reset button to delete the reference to the sort key you used in the previous exercise.

3. Click the range selector button at the right side of the Sort by box. The Sort dialog box disappears temporarily.

4. Click cell B4, the first entry in the Last field. The Sort dialog box reappears, with a reference to B4 in the Sort by box. Make sure that the Ascending option is selected.

5. Click the Add Key button. The reference to B4 as an Ascending sort key becomes the first entry in the All keys box. The Sort by box is empty now, ready for you to define the next key to the sort.

6. Repeat steps 3, 4, and 5, this time specifying cell C4—the first entry in the First field—as the second key to the sort. When you complete these steps, the Sort dialog box appears as follows:

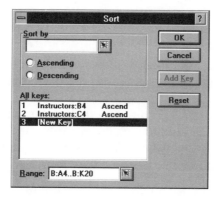

7. Click OK or press ↵ to complete the sort.

The resulting sort is shown in Figure 7.8. The records are now arranged by the Last and First fields. In particular, notice in rows 14 and 15 that the two Porters are in the correct order: first comes D. Porter of Seattle, then M. Porter of Washington, D.C.

FIGURE 7.8

Sorting the database by two keys. Notice that the two instructors named Porter are sorted in the correct order.

	ID	Last	First	City	Region	Specialty	Rate	Hrs	Contract	Yrs	Ok
1				Instructor Database							
2											
3	ID	Last	First	City	Region	Specialty	Rate	Hrs	Contract	Yrs	Ok
4	S-125	Ashford	W.	Washington, D.C.	E	Spreadsheet	150	145	10-May-89	4.7	A
5	W-145	Banks	S.	St. Louis	S	WP	150	55	10-Jun-92	1.6	A
6	D-143	Cody	L.	Los Angeles	W	Database	75	43	20-Jun-92	1.6	B
7	A-146	Daniels	A.	Atlanta	S	Accounting	125	24	09-May-93	0.7	New
8	W-119	Davis	G.	San Francisco	W	WP	150	149	09-Jul-89	4.6	A
9	T-128	Eng	R.	Albuquerque	S	Programming	75	75	11-Oct-89	4.3	B
10	S-127	Gill	P.	Los Angeles	W	Spreadsheet	100	35	22-Jun-89	4.6	C
11	S-149	Harris	P.	Dallas	S	Spreadsheet	150	17	12-Feb-93	1.0	New
12	W-124	Meyer	J.	New York	E	WP	150	85	05-May-89	4.7	B
13	A-103	Perez	D.	Las Vegas	W	Accounting	100	5	11-Jul-88	5.6	C
14	W-113	Porter	D.	Seattle	N	WP	125	59	02-Aug-88	5.5	B
15	D-139	Porter	M.	Washington, D.C.	E	Database	150	26	28-Mar-91	2.8	B
16	T-133	Ramirez	F.	Boston	E	Programming	150	73	08-Feb-90	4.0	B
17	S-155	Roberts	P.	Chicago	N	Spreadsheet	100	10	21-Aug-93	0.4	New
18	D-137	Sanchez	W.	Indianapolis	N	Database	100	47	16-Apr-91	2.8	B
19	N-101	Schwartz	B.	Boston	E	Networks	150	178	02-Mar-88	5.9	A
20	D-106	Weinberg	P.	Miami	S	Database	75	59	18-Jan-88	6.0	B

Multiple Sort Keys

The Data Sort command allows you to select more than just two key fields. For example, imagine that you have sorted the database by the Region field as the primary key and the City field as the secondary key, as shown in Figure 7.9. Examining the result of this sort, you realize that you would like to be able to sort the records within each city in alphabetical order by the Specialty field. In other words, your goal is three sorting keys: First the Region field, then the City field, and finally the Specialty field.

To sort by more than two keys, you simply continue developing a list of keys in the All keys box, as in the previous exercise. For example, here are

FIGURE 7.9

The Region field as the primary key and the City field as the secondary key. Notice that the Specialty field is not yet in alphabetical order within a given city; this field is therefore a candidate to become a third key to the sort.

Offices | Instructors | New Sheet

	A	B	C	D	E	F	G	H	I	J	K
1				Instructor Database							
2											
3	ID	Last	First	City	Region	Specialty	Rate	Hrs	Contract	Yrs	Ok
4	T-133	Ramirez	F.	Boston	E	Programminc	150	73	08-Feb-90	4.0	B
5	N-101	Schwartz	B.	Boston	E	Networks	150	178	02-Mar-88	5.9	A
6	W-124	Meyer	J.	New York	E	WP	150	85	05-May-89	4.7	B
7	S-125	Ashford	W.	Washington, D.C.	E	Spreadsheet	150	145	10-May-89	4.7	A
8	D-139	Porter	M.	Washington, D.C.	E	Database	150	26	28-Mar-91	2.8	B
9	S-155	Roberts	P.	Chicago	N	Spreadsheet	100	10	21-Aug-93	0.4	New
10	D-137	Sanchez	W.	Indianapolis	N	Database	100	47	16-Apr-91	2.8	B
11	W-113	Porter	D.	Seattle	N	WP	125	59	02-Aug-88	5.5	B
12	T-128	Eng	R.	Albuquerque	S	Programminc	75	75	11-Oct-89	4.3	B
13	A-146	Daniels	A.	Atlanta	S	Accounting	125	24	09-May-93	0.7	New
14	S-149	Harris	P.	Dallas	S	Spreadsheet	150	17	12-Feb-93	1.0	New
15	D-106	Weinberg	P.	Miami	S	Database	75	59	18-Jan-88	6.0	B
16	W-145	Banks	S.	St. Louis	S	WP	150	55	10-Jun-92	1.6	A
17	A-103	Perez	D.	Las Vegas	W	Accounting	100	5	11-Jul-88	5.6	C
18	S-127	Gill	P.	Los Angeles	W	Spreadsheet	100	35	22-Jun-89	4.6	C
19	D-143	Cody	L.	Los Angeles	W	Database	75	43	20-Jun-92	1.6	B
20	W-119	Davis	G.	San Francisco	W	WP	150	149	09-Jul-89	4.6	A

the steps for achieving the three-key sort by the Region, City, and Specialty fields:

1. Choose Range ➤ Sort. In the Sort dialog box, the Range box still contains a correct reference to the range of records in the Instructors table.
2. Click the Reset button to delete references to sort keys you defined in the previous sorting exercise.
3. Click the range selector button at the right side of the Sort by box. The Sort dialog box disappears temporarily.
4. Click cell E4, the first entry in the Region field. The Sort dialog box reappears. Make sure the Ascending option is selected.
5. Click the Add Key button. A reference to cell E4 as an ascending sort key appears in the All keys list.
6. Repeat steps 3, 4, and 5 twice—first to define cell D4 (the first entry in the City field) as the second key to the sort, and then to define F4 (the first entry in the Specialty field) as the third key. When you

finish these steps, the Sort dialog box appears as follows:

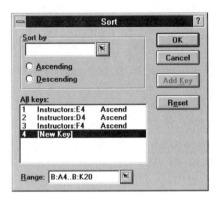

7. Click OK to complete the sort operation.

The sorted database appears in Figure 7.10. You can see that the database has indeed been sorted by three keys: First the records are arranged by region. Then, within each region, they are arranged by city. And where there are duplicate city entries—specifically, Boston, Washington D.C., and Los Angeles—the records are arranged by the instructors' specialties.

FIGURE 7.10

Sorting the database by three key fields—Region, City, and Specialty

ID	Last	First	City	Region	Specialty	Rate	Hrs	Contract	Yrs	Ok
N-101	Schwartz	B.	Boston	E	Networks	150	178	02-Mar-88	5.9	A
T-133	Ramirez	F.	Boston	E	Programming	150	73	08-Feb-90	4.0	B
W-124	Meyer	J.	New York	E	WP	150	85	05-May-89	4.7	B
D-139	Porter	M.	Washington, D.C.	E	Database	150	26	28-Mar-91	2.8	B
S-125	Ashford	W.	Washington, D.C.	E	Spreadsheet	150	145	10-May-89	4.7	A
S-155	Roberts	P.	Chicago	N	Spreadsheet	100	10	21-Aug-93	0.4	New
D-137	Sanchez	W.	Indianapolis	N	Database	100	47	16-Apr-91	2.8	B
W-113	Porter	D.	Seattle	N	WP	125	59	02-Aug-88	5.5	B
T-128	Eng	R.	Albuquerque	S	Programming	75	75	11-Oct-89	4.3	B
A-146	Daniels	A.	Atlanta	S	Accounting	125	24	09-May-93	0.7	New
S-149	Harris	P.	Dallas	S	Spreadsheet	150	17	12-Feb-93	1.0	New
D-106	Weinberg	P.	Miami	S	Database	75	59	18-Jan-88	6.0	B
W-145	Banks	S.	St. Louis	S	WP	150	55	10-Jun-92	1.6	A
A-103	Perez	D.	Las Vegas	W	Accounting	100	5	11-Jul-88	5.6	C
D-143	Cody	L.	Los Angeles	W	Database	75	43	20-Jun-92	1.6	B
S-127	Gill	P.	Los Angeles	W	Spreadsheet	100	35	22-Jun-89	4.6	C
W-119	Davis	G.	San Francisco	W	WP	150	149	09-Jul-89	4.6	A

As you've seen, 1-2-3 retains your previous sorting instructions each time you choose Data ➤ Sort. If you want to start over again with a new set of sort keys, you simply click the Reset button on the Sort dialog box. To prepare for upcoming exercises, take a minute now to sort the database once again by instructors' names:

1. Choose Range ➤ Sort and click the Reset button on the Sort dialog box.

2. Define B4 as the first sort key and C4 as the second. Then click OK or press ↵.

3. Click the Save SmartIcon to update the INSTRUCT.WK4 worksheet on disk.

Changing 1-2-3's Default Sort Order

The *sort order* refers to 1-2-3's default technique for sorting a database when a key field contains some label entries that begin with digits and others that begin with letters of the alphabet. You can see an example of this situation by looking back at the Office database table in Figure 7.6 (see page 408). The Address field contains three labels that begin with digits, and one that begins with a letter. If you sort this table by the Address field, what will be the resulting order?

By default, 1-2-3 uses the *numbers first* sort order. To demonstrate that this is so, try the following brief exercise:

1. Click the Offices tab to activate the first worksheet in the file.

2. Choose Range ➤ Sort, and click the Reset button to clear the previous sort keys.

3. Select the Range box, press F3, and double-click the OFFICERECS entry in the Range Names dialog box. 1-2-3 copies this name into the Range text box.

4. Click the range selector button at the right side of the Sort by box. The Sort dialog box disappears temporarily.

5. Click cell B4 in the Offices table. When the Sort dialog box returns, you'll see a reference to Offices:B4 in the Sort by box. Click the Ascending option if it's not already selected. The Sort dialog box now looks like this:

6. Click the Add Key button to move the key reference to the All keys box.

7. Click OK or press ↵ to complete the sort.

Figure 7.11 shows the Office database, sorted by the Address field. You can see the result of 1-2-3's default sort order: The addresses that begin with digits come first, followed by the address that begins with a letter.

Except for the purposes of this experimental exercise, it is a little unlikely that you would actually want to sort the office database by the Address field, because the four addresses in the table are all in different cities. But a sort by addresses may be realistic in a database containing many addresses in the same city.

FIGURE 7.11

A demonstration of the *numbers-first* sort order

	A	B	C	D	E	F	G
1	Regional Offices						
2							
3	Region	Address	City	State	Zip	Phone	Manager
4	S	11 Maple Street	Dallas	TX	75210	(214) 555-6754	Harvey, J.
5	E	222 Allen Street	New York	NY	10103	(212) 555-4678	Campbell, R.
6	W	432 Market Avenue	Los Angeles	CA	90028	(213) 555-9974	Garcia, M.
7	N	Mills Tower, Suite 992	Chicago	IL	60605	(312) 555-8803	Logan, C.
8							

Offices | Instructors   New Sheet

In some specific cases you may want to change 1-2-3's default sort order. To do so, you run a special application that comes with 1-2-3, a program named Country Sorting. You'll find the icon for this application in the same program group where the 1-2-3 icon is displayed:

Country Sorting

Double-click the icon to start the program. In the resulting dialog box, you can select from a list of 1-2-3's sort orders, including US Numbers First, US Numbers Last, US ASCII, and options that conform to sort standards used in other countries:

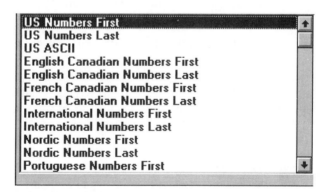

Performing Query Operations

When you need to find, delete, copy, or revise selected database records, you choose commands from the Tools ➤ Database menu. In general, an operation that selects records by condition is known as a *query*, and the conditions themselves are called *criteria*. The expressions for criteria can be simple or complex. For example, in the instructor database you might want to look for any of the following combinations of records:

- Instructors in the Southern region
- Instructors in the Southern region who specialize in spreadsheets or databases
- A Los Angeles instructor who specializes in spreadsheets
- Cities where programming or networking experts are available
- Western region instructors whose hourly rate is less than or equal to $100 per hour
- Spreadsheet experts who have an A rating in the Ok field
- Southern or eastern database experts who have an A or B rating and work for less than $100 per hour
- Eastern region instructors who have worked at least four years for Computing Conferences, Inc., and have an A or B rating

To simplify the process of developing criteria for queries like these, 1-2-3 provides a special dialog box in which the relationships between criteria are represented graphically. Using the tools of this dialog box, you'll be able to build efficient and reliable criteria.

NOTE In older versions of 1-2-3 (before Release 4.0 for Windows), selection criteria were stored directly on a worksheet, in a *criteria range.* The use of a dialog box for building criteria expressions is a much simpler and more elegant approach, as you'll see shortly.

In the sections ahead you'll first look at two operations that 1-2-3 performs directly on a database table:

- **Tools ➤ Database ➤ Find Records.** This command locates and highlights records that match the criteria you express.
- **Tools ➤ Database ➤ Delete Records.** This command removes records that match your criteria.

As you work through examples of these two operations, you'll learn how to express criteria in 1-2-3, and you'll begin to see the advantages of building criteria in a dialog box.

Then you'll turn your attention to the subject of *query tables*. A query table is a copy of a database, or a copy of selected fields and records from a database. In 1-2-3, a query table is a distinct object that you can move, copy, reformat, redefine, or delete as a unit. You create a query by choosing the Tools ➤ Database ➤ New Query command. When a query table is selected, 1-2-3 replaces the Range menu with the Query menu and displays a new set of SmartIcons that apply specifically to queries.

In the final sections of this chapter, you'll begin examining the general characteristics of query tables and you'll work through exercises that illustrate two important commands from the Query menu:

- **Query ➤ Update Database Table.** This command allows you to update the contents of a database from revisions you've made in a query table.

- **Query ➤ Join.** This command combines fields from two or more related database tables.

NOTE Chapter 8 covers additional query operations, including the use of a query table to work with data from an external database.

Finding Records in a Database

As your first database experiment with the Tools ➤ Database ➤ Find Records command, suppose you want to locate all the instructor records in the Southern region. In this case, you can expect the criterion to be expressed as a simple equality:

Region=S

Any record in which this condition is true will be selected; other records will remain unselected.

Here are the steps for carrying out this first exercise:

1. With the Instructors sheet active, choose Tools ➤ Database and then choose the Find Records command from the resulting cascade menu. The Find Records dialog box appears:

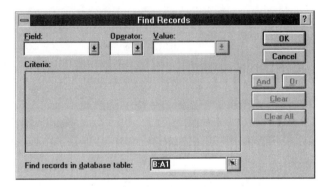

This dialog box contains a variety of boxes and controls for defining selection criteria. The text box at the bottom labeled "Find records in database table" has the initial focus.

2. Press the F3 function key. A second dialog box named Database Names pops up onto the screen. The first item in the Database name list is INSTRUCTDB, the name you've assigned to the Instructors database:

3. Click OK to close the Database Names dialog box and copy the database name to the "Field records in database table" box. In the

background of the dialog box, 1-2-3 highlights the entire database table.

4. Pull down the Field list at the upper-left corner of the Find Records dialog box. The list contains the names of all the fields in the selected database.

5. To begin creating a selection criterion, choose the Region field from the list:

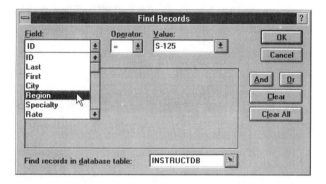

6. Pull down the Value list, and choose S as the value that you'll be searching for in the Region field.

(Notice that the Operator box displays an equal sign by default. Keep this operator as it is.) The Criteria box now displays the single criterion that you set out to build for this Find operation:

7. Click OK.

In response, 1-2-3 highlights all the records in the database that match the criterion. As you can see in Figure 7.12, five instructor records are highlighted for the Southern region.

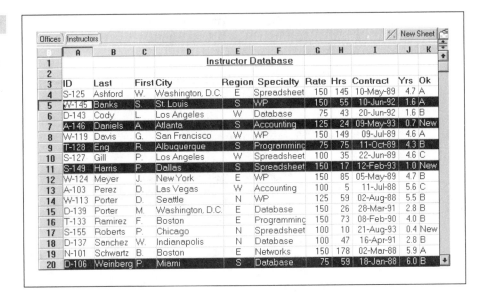

	ID	Last	First	City	Region	Specialty	Rate	Hrs	Contract	Yrs	Ok
4	S-125	Ashford	W.	Washington, D.C.	E	Spreadsheet	150	145	10-May-89	4.7	A
5	W-145	Banks	S.	St. Louis	S	WP	150	55	10-Jun-92	1.6	A
6	D-143	Cody	L.	Los Angeles	W	Database	75	43	20-Jun-92	1.6	B
7	A-146	Daniels	A.	Atlanta	S	Accounting	125	24	09-May-93	0.7	New
8	W-119	Davis	G.	San Francisco	W	WP	150	149	09-Jul-89	4.6	A
9	T-128	Eng	R.	Albuquerque	S	Programming	75	75	11-Oct-89	4.3	B
10	S-127	Gill	P.	Los Angeles	W	Spreadsheet	100	35	22-Jun-89	4.6	C
11	S-149	Harris	P.	Dallas	S	Spreadsheet	150	17	12-Feb-93	1.0	New
12	W-124	Meyer	J.	New York	E	WP	150	85	05-May-89	4.7	B
13	A-103	Perez	D.	Las Vegas	W	Accounting	100	5	11-Jul-88	5.6	C
14	W-113	Porter	D.	Seattle	N	WP	125	59	02-Aug-88	5.5	B
15	D-139	Porter	M.	Washington, D.C.	E	Database	150	26	28-Mar-91	2.8	B
16	T-133	Ramirez	F.	Boston	E	Programming	150	73	08-Feb-90	4.0	B
17	S-155	Roberts	P.	Chicago	N	Spreadsheet	100	10	21-Aug-93	0.4	New
18	D-137	Sanchez	W.	Indianapolis	N	Database	100	47	16-Apr-91	2.8	B
19	N-101	Schwartz	B.	Boston	E	Networks	150	178	02-Mar-88	5.9	A
20	D-106	Weinberg	P.	Miami	S	Database	75	59	18-Jan-88	6.0	B

When you've finished examining the record selection, press the Home key to move the cell pointer to A1. This action also deselects all the records.

TIP

Immediately after a Find Records operation, you can use the keyboard to move the cell pointer within the selected records: Press Ctrl+↵ to move from the beginning of one selected record to the next. (Press Ctrl+Shift+↵ repeatedly to move backward through the selected records.) Within a selected record, press ↵ to move from one field to the next. If your goal after a Find operation is to make revisions in the content of the selected records, these key combinations can help you move quickly to the records and fields that you want to revise.

Finding Records that Match Multiple Criteria

Now imagine that you want to find a subset of the previous selection. Specifically, suppose you want to see all the Southern instructors who have Ok ratings of A or B. You might express this criterion as:

Region = S and (Ok = A or Ok = B)

In other words, a record must have a value of S in the Region field *and* a value of either A or B in the Ok field. As you build this combination of criteria in the Find Records dialog box, you click the And and Or buttons to combine criteria appropriately.

Begin this operation by repeating steps 1 to 6 of the previous exercise. As a result, the Criteria box in the Find Records dialog box contains the expression *Region=S*. Now continue as follows to add the other criteria:

1. Click the And button.

In the Criteria box, 1-2-3 adds *and* along with a new expression just beneath *Region=S*. The new criterion is displayed in bold to indicate that it's selected for change.

2. Pull down the field list and click the Ok field. The new criterion now appears as *Ok=A*, which is just the expression you want.

3. Click the Or button.

A third expression now appears in the Criteria box, just to the right of the previous one. Again the latest expression is displayed in bold.

4. Pull down the Value list and click the B entry. The new expression now appears as *Ok=B*. Here's what the Find Records dialog box looks like now:

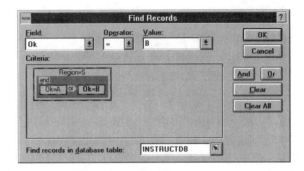

Notice that *Region=S* is connected to the other two expressions by an *and* condition, and the other two expressions are connected by *or*. This combination will produce the selection you want.

5. Click OK to complete the Find operation.

As shown in Figure 7.13, three records match the criteria. All three records are in the Southern region, and each has an entry of either A or B in the Ok field.

	ID	Last	First	City	Region	Specialty	Rate	Hrs	Contract	Yrs	Ok
				Instructor Database							
4	S-125	Ashford	W.	Washington, D.C.	E	Spreadsheet	150	145	10-May-89	4.7	A
5	W-145	Banks	S.	St. Louis	S	WP	150	55	10-Jun-92	1.6	A
6	D-143	Cody	L.	Los Angeles	W	Database	75	43	20-Jun-92	1.6	B
7	A-146	Daniels	A.	Atlanta	S	Accounting	125	24	09-May-93	0.7	New
8	W-119	Davis	G.	San Francisco	W	WP	150	149	09-Jul-89	4.6	A
9	T-128	Eng	R.	Albuquerque	S	Programming	75	75	11-Oct-89	4.3	B
10	S-127	Gill	P.	Los Angeles	W	Spreadsheet	100	35	22-Jun-89	4.6	C
11	S-149	Harris	P.	Dallas	S	Spreadsheet	150	17	12-Feb-93	1.0	New
12	W-124	Meyer	J.	New York	E	WP	150	85	05-May-89	4.7	B
13	A-103	Perez	D.	Las Vegas	W	Accounting	100	5	11-Jul-88	5.6	C
14	W-113	Porter	D.	Seattle	N	WP	125	59	02-Aug-88	5.5	B
15	D-139	Porter	M.	Washington, D.C.	E	Database	150	26	28-Mar-91	2.8	B
16	T-133	Ramirez	F.	Boston	E	Programming	150	73	08-Feb-90	4.0	B
17	S-155	Roberts	P.	Chicago	N	Spreadsheet	100	10	21-Aug-93	0.4	New
18	D-137	Sanchez	W.	Indianapolis	N	Database	100	47	16-Apr-91	2.8	B
19	N-101	Schwartz	B.	Boston	E	Networks	150	178	02-Mar-88	5.9	A
20	D-106	Weinberg	P.	Miami	S	Database	75	59	18-Jan-88	6.0	B

TIP

As you begin building complex expressions in the Criteria box, you may sometimes want to change the relationships between criteria. To do so, you can use your mouse to drag an expression to a new location. For example, in the exercise above, you could drag the expression *Ok=A* to a position outside of the group of criteria in which it's located. Doing so results in a new *or* relationship and an entirely new meaning for the query. A good way to learn how to revise criteria is to experiment with mouse actions inside the Criteria box and then study the resulting queries.

Deleting Records from a Database

The Tools ➤ Database ➤ Delete Records command removes selected records from a database. Like delete operations in any software environment, this command requires some care. Accidental or incorrect use of the Delete Records command can result in large losses of data. For this reason, you should take one or more of the following precautions when you use this command:

- Save your database just before you perform the Delete command. If Delete produces unexpected results, you can close the current worksheet window without saving it, and then reopen the original version from disk.

- Perform a Find operation before Delete. The Find command allows you to examine the records that will be removed from your database if you go through with the Delete operation.

- Click the Undo SmartIcon immediately after a Delete operation if you decide you want to bring back the deleted records. You lose this option as soon as you perform some other command; for this reason, you should examine your database carefully just after the Delete command.

As an experiment with the Delete Records command, imagine that you've decided to drop instructors who have Ok ratings of C. Here are the steps for accomplishing this:

1. Press Home to move the cell pointer to A1.

2. Choose Tools ➤ Database, and then click the Delete Records command from the resulting cascade menu. The Delete Records dialog box looks much like the Find Records dialog box.

3. Press F3 to view the Database Names box. With INSTRUCTDB highlighted in the database list, click OK.

4. Pull down the Field list and choose Ok from the bottom of the list.

5. Pull down the Value list and choose C. The Delete Records dialog box now looks like this:

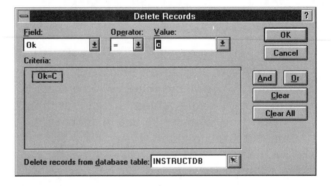

With this criterion, the command will delete all records that contain an entry of C in the Ok field.

6. Click the OK button to carry out the Delete operation.

7. Examine the database, as shown in Figure 7.14.

You can see that the table has two fewer records than it had before. There is now no record with an entry of C in the Ok field.

8. Now click the Undo SmartIcon to restore the original database. The two deleted records reappear.

FIGURE 7.14

Deleting records from a database

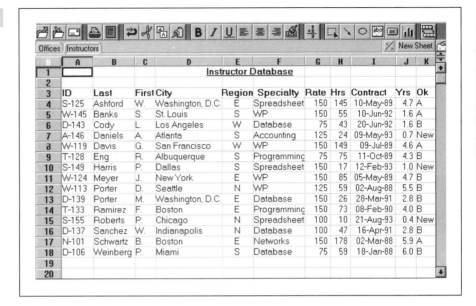

7

Database Essentials

	A	B	C	D	E	F	G	H	I	J	K
1					Instructor Database						
2											
3	ID	Last	First	City	Region	Specialty	Rate	Hrs	Contract	Yrs	Ok
4	S-125	Ashford	W.	Washington, D.C.	E	Spreadsheet	150	145	10-May-89	4.7	A
5	W-145	Banks	S.	St. Louis	S	WP	150	55	10-Jun-92	1.6	A
6	D-143	Cody	L.	Los Angeles	W	Database	75	43	20-Jun-92	1.6	B
7	A-146	Daniels	A.	Atlanta	S	Accounting	125	24	09-May-93	0.7	New
8	W-119	Davis	G.	San Francisco	W	WP	150	149	09-Jul-89	4.6	A
9	T-128	Eng	R.	Albuquerque	S	Programming	75	75	11-Oct-89	4.3	B
10	S-149	Harris	P.	Dallas	S	Spreadsheet	150	17	12-Feb-93	1.0	New
11	W-124	Meyer	J.	New York	E	WP	150	85	05-May-89	4.7	B
12	W-113	Porter	D.	Seattle	N	WP	125	59	02-Aug-88	5.5	B
13	D-139	Porter	M.	Washington, D.C.	E	Database	150	26	28-Mar-91	2.8	B
14	T-133	Ramirez	F.	Boston	E	Programming	150	73	08-Feb-90	4.0	B
15	S-155	Roberts	P.	Chicago	N	Spreadsheet	100	10	21-Aug-93	0.4	New
16	D-137	Sanchez	W.	Indianapolis	N	Database	100	47	16-Apr-91	2.8	B
17	N-101	Schwartz	B.	Boston	E	Networks	150	178	02-Mar-88	5.9	A
18	D-106	Weinberg	P.	Miami	S	Database	75	59	18-Jan-88	6.0	B
19											
20											

If for some reason the Undo SmartIcon didn't work, close your worksheet without saving it. Then reopen INSTRUCT.WK4 from disk.

As you've seen, the Find Records and Delete Records commands work directly on the database itself. Next you'll learn how to perform another kind of query operation that results in a separate query table.

Using the New Query Command

Unlike the Find Records command, which merely highlights selected records, the New Query command actually makes a copy of records that meet the selection criteria and displays those records in a query table. To create a query table you supply the following information:

- The name or range of the database from which you want to create the query table

- The names of the fields that you want to include in the query

- The criteria for selecting records for the query
- The worksheet location where you want to display the query table

Actually, selecting fields and building criteria are both optional parts of the process. If you don't select a subset of fields, 1-2-3 includes *all* fields from the database in the query table. If you don't create any criteria, 1-2-3 includes *all* records from the database in the query table.

Several important database operations are available only from a query table. For example, you can use a query table to make revisions in selected database records, and then update the database itself when you're ready to do so. You can also perform a *join* operation, combining information from two or more database tables. Another advantage of a query table is that its selection criteria are saved as part of the table; you can view and modify these criteria at any time. These and other operations are represented by commands in the Query menu, which replaces the Range menu when a query table is selected.

Creating a Query

In the following exercise you'll begin by creating a query table for a selection of records that you've worked with before—the southern instructors who have Ok ratings of A or B. As you can see back in Figure 7.13 (see page 430), the Find Records operation highlighted three records that match these criteria. The New Query command will make a copy of these rec-ords in a new worksheet location:

1. Click the Instructors tab, if necessary, to activate the second sheet in the file.

2. Click the New Sheet button to create sheet C.

3. Double-click the C tab and enter **Selection** as the name for this new sheet. As always, this new sheet name is a convenience, not a requirement; you can save a query on a sheet of any name.

4. Choose Tools ➤ Database ➤ New Query. The New Query dialog box appears on the screen:

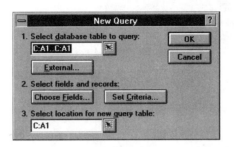

5. Press F3 to view the Database Names dialog box. Select IN-STRUCTDB as the database, and click OK. Back on the New Query dialog box, this name appears in the text box labeled "Select database table to query."

6. Click the Choose Fields button. The Choose fields dialog box appears:

This dialog box supplies a list of all the fields in the database table, and allows you to select the fields that you want to include in the query.

7. Click the Clear button once to remove the ID field from the Selected fields list. Then highlight the Hrs field and click Clear again. Repeat this step to remove the Contract and Yrs fields as well. The dialog box now appears as follows:

8. Click the OK button on the Choose Fields dialog box. Then, back at the New Query dialog box, click the Set Criteria button. The Set Criteria dialog box appears on the screen.

9. Follow the steps you've performed before to create multiple criteria: Choose Region from the Field list and S from the Value list, then click the And button. Choose Ok from the Field list, then click the Or button. Finally, choose B from the Value list. The three criteria you've built are displayed as follows:

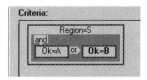

10. Click OK on the Set Criteria dialog box. Back in the New Query dialog box, make sure the reference C:A1 is displayed in the text box labeled "Select location for new query table." Then click OK. 1-2-3 builds the query table and displays it on the sheet you've named Selection.

11. Notice that a new set of SmartIcons appears for the selected query table. Click the Size Columns SmartIcon to adjust the column widths for the new query table. When you do so, the table appears as follows:

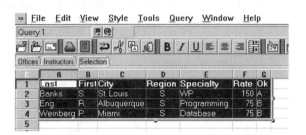

Working with a Query Table

As you can see, 1-2-3 has copied a selection of records and fields to the query table from the database table, following the instructions you provided in the New Query dialog box. Notice that the query table has a border with selection handles. As this border suggests, the query table is an object that you can move from one place to another in your worksheet. 1-2-3 provides special mouse techniques for working with the table:

• To select the entire table, click anywhere along the query's border.

• To move the query table, drag the border to the new location.

• To change the number of fields displayed in the query table, select the table and drag the handle located along the right-hand border. Drag to the right to display fields that you didn't include in the query, or drag to the left to eliminate fields from the display.

• To select an entire field column in the table, click a field name.

NOTE

With one exception, the operations you perform on a query table have no effect on the original database table. The exception is the Query ➤ Update Database Table command, which you'll learn about later in this chapter (see page 443).

Commands on the Query Menu

When you select a query table or any field or cell within the table, 1-2-3 replaces the Range menu with the Query menu. The menu looks like this:

All the commands in this menu apply specifically to the selected query, or in some cases to the database table from which the query was created. Here are descriptions of the Query menu commands:

COMMAND	DESCRIPTION
Set Criteria	Allows you to view and modify the selection criteria that define the contents of the query.
Choose Fields	Provides a list of the fields in the query table, and gives you simple ways to modify the list.
Sort	Displays the Sort dialog box for changing the order of records within the query table.
Aggregate	Provides a special tool for performing arithmetic operations on categories of records within the query. You'll explore this command in Chapter 8 (see page 470).

COMMAND	DESCRIPTION
Show Field As	Allows you to change the name displayed for a particular field. This command is useful when you join two tables in one query, as you'll learn later in this chapter.
Name	Lets you change the name assigned to a query object. By default, 1-2-3 assigns names like Query 1, Query 2, Query 3, and so on to query tables you create.
Set Options	Displays a short list of query properties that you can activate or disable. (One of these properties allows you to use a query for updating the original database, as you'll see shortly.)
Show SQL	Displays the SQL equivalent of the selection criteria you've built for your query.
Set Database Table	Allows you to change the database on which the query is based.
Join	Adds fields to the query from a related database table.
Update Database Table	Transfers changes from the query table to the original database table.
Refresh Now	Updates the query table after you make changes in the criteria, field list, or database table. (Updating is automatic by default; you need to use the Refresh Now command only if you turn off the Auto Refresh option in the Set Options command.)

You'll learn more about the commands in the Query menu as you continue through the exercises of this chapter and the next.

Modifying a Query

In the next two exercises you'll experiment with the Query ➤ Set Criteria and Query ➤ Choose Fields commands to change the contents of the query you've created. You'll discover that you can completely change the criteria for the query to generate a new selection of records. In addition, you can easily revise the list of fields included in the query.

To start, suppose you want to see records of all the instructors who have worked more than 100 hours for Computing Conferences, Inc. Follow these steps to revise your query accordingly:

1. Select the query table, and choose Query ➤ Set Criteria. The Set Criteria dialog box appears on the screen.

2. Click the Clear button three times to remove the three expressions currently displayed in the Criteria box.

3. Pull down the Fields list and choose the Hrs field.

4. Pull down the Operator list and choose >, the *greater than* symbol.

5. Press Tab to select the Value box, and enter **100** into the box directly from the keyboard. Make sure the Limit records box is unchecked. Here's what the Set Criteria dialog box looks like at this point in your work:

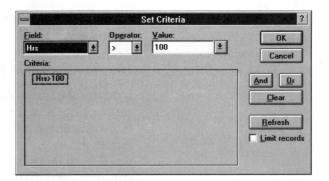

6. Click OK to confirm the new query.

7

On the worksheet, 1-2-3 displays a new selection of records; but the Hrs field by which the records are selected is not displayed. You'll correct this omission next.

7. Pull down the Query menu and click the Choose Fields command. In the Choose Fields dialog box, click the Add button. The Add Fields dialog box lists all the database fields that are not currently included in the query:

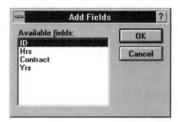

8. Select Hrs and click OK. Back on the Choose Fields dialog box, Hrs now appears at the top of the field list. Click the down-arrow button (displayed at the lower-left corner of the dialog box) six times to move the Hrs field down to the second-to-last position in the list.

9. Click OK. Then click the Size Columns SmartIcon.

The new query displays the three instructors who have worked more than 100 hours for the company:

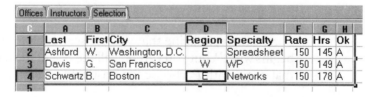

	A	B	C	D	E	F	G	H
1	Last	First	City	Region	Specialty	Rate	Hrs	Ok
2	Ashford	W.	Washington, D.C.	E	Spreadsheet	150	145	A
3	Davis	G.	San Francisco	W	WP	150	149	A
4	Schwartz	B.	Boston	E	Networks	150	178	A
5								

Now try creating a criterion based on the date field named Contract:

1. Choose Query ➤ Set Criteria, and create the following expression:

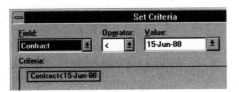

2. Enter the date **15-Jun-88** into the Value box directly from the keyboard, and click OK.

3. Pull down the Query menu and click the Choose Fields command. Add the Contract field to the query table. As a result, your table shows the two instructors who have worked longest for the company:

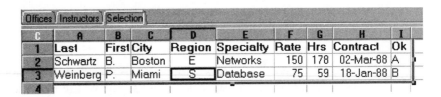

C	A	B	C	D	E	F	G	H	I
1	Last	First	City	Region	Specialty	Rate	Hrs	Contract	Ok
2	Schwartz	B.	Boston	E	Networks	150	178	02-Mar-88	A
3	Weinberg	P.	Miami	S	Database	75	59	18-Jan-88	B
4									

Using Wildcards in Label Criteria

Label criteria can appear in a variety of forms. You can use *wildcard characters* to search for labels that contain certain combinations of characters. The wildcard characters are the question mark and the asterisk:

? Represents any single character in a label.

* Represents an unspecified number of characters.

For example, imagine that you are searching for an instructor whose name begins with *P*, but you can't recall the rest of the name. To find all the names that begin with *P*, choose the Last field and enter **P*** into Value box:

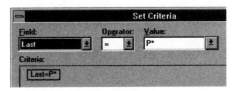

1-2-3 finds the three instructors whose names begin with *P*:

C	A	B	C	D	E	F	G	H	I
1	Last	First	City	Region	Specialty	Rate	Hrs	Contract	Ok
2	Perez	D.	Las Vegas	W	Accounting	100	5	11-Jul-88	C
3	Porter	D.	Seattle	N	WP	125	59	02-Aug-88	B
4	Porter	M.	Washington, D.C.	E	Database	150	26	28-Mar-9	B
5									

Tabs: Offices | Instructors | Selection

Using a Query to Update the Original Database

The Query ➤ Update Database Table command gives you a convenient way to revise selected records in your database from changes you make in a query table. This is, of course, a procedure that you would not want to perform inadvertently, because it can result in major changes in the content of your database. Accordingly, 1-2-3 imposes special safeguards on the process. Here are the general steps for updating a database from a query:

1. Create a query table that contains the records you want to modify.

2. Make any changes you want in the content of these selected records.

3. Choose Query ➤ Set Options and activate the Allow Updates option.

4. Choose Query ➤ Update Database Table to transfer the changes from the query table to the original database.

Here is a situation for testing this procedure. The Western region has just completed a series of training conferences focusing on spreadsheets and word processing. The regional instructors specializing in these fields each worked for ten hours at the conferences. Your job is to locate the records for these instructors and increase the entries in their Hrs fields. Proceed as follows:

1. Select the query table and choose Query ➤ Set Criteria. Use the techniques you've learned to create criteria that will select Western region instructors specializing in spreadsheets and word

processing. Here's what the criteria will look like in the Set Criteria dialog box:

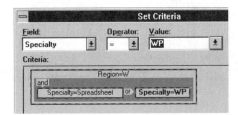

2. Click OK. The resulting query table contains two records:

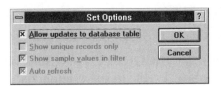

3. Choose Query ➤ Set Options. In the Set Options dialog box, click the check box labeled "Allow updates to database table." When you do so, the other options in the dialog box are dimmed:

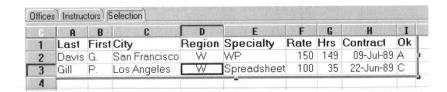

As you'll find out shortly, 1-2-3 prohibits other query operations while the Allow updates option is enabled.

4. Click OK on the Set Options dialog box. 1-2-3 immediately displays the following warning message on the screen:

5. Click OK to continue with the update operation.

6. Now select the Hrs entry for the instructor named Davis, and enter a new value of **159**. Likewise, select the Hrs entry for Gill and enter a new value of **45**. In both cases, these values are ten hours greater than the previous entries. Select the query table when you've finished the new entries.

7. Pull down the Query menu. Notice that only two commands are available at this point—Set Options and Update Database Table:

```
┌─────────────────────────┐
│ Query                   │
├─────────────────────────┤
│ Set Criteria...         │
│ Choose Fields...        │
│ Sort...                 │
│ Aggregate...            │
│ Show Field As...        │
├─────────────────────────┤
│ Name...                 │
├─────────────────────────┤
│ Set Options...          │
│ Show SQL...             │
├─────────────────────────┤
│ Set Database Table...   │
│ Join...                 │
├─────────────────────────┤
│ Update Database Table   │
│ Refresh Now             │
└─────────────────────────┘
```

8. Choose the Update Database Table command.

In response, 1-2-3 copies the revised records to the database table and then automatically disables the Allow updates option. You can perform only one update at a time.

Now click the Instructors tab to see what's happened to the original database table. The records for Davis and Gill have been updated from the changes you made in the query table, as shown in Figure 7.15 (the two records have been highlighted for clarity).

Joining Two Database Tables

Another important query operation is represented by the Query ➤ Join command. You can use this command to combine information from related database tables. For example, the INSTRUCT.WK4 file contains two database tables—the Offices database on the first sheet and the

FIGURE 7.15

Updating a database from changes in a query table

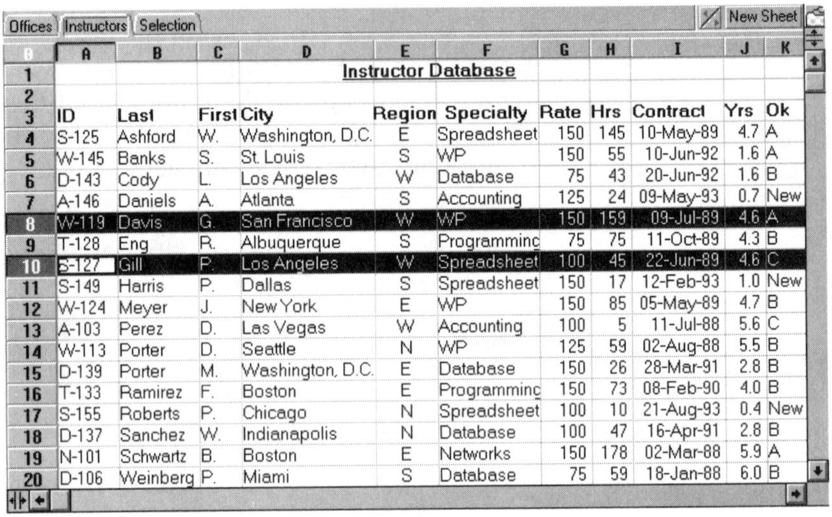

	A	B	C	D	E	F	G	H	I	J	K
	Offices	Instructors	Selection						New Sheet		
1					Instructor Database						
2											
3	ID	Last	First	City	Region	Specialty	Rate	Hrs	Contract	Yrs	Ok
4	S-125	Ashford	W.	Washington, D.C.	E	Spreadsheet	150	145	10-May-89	4.7	A
5	W-145	Banks	S.	St. Louis	S	WP	150	55	10-Jun-92	1.6	A
6	D-143	Cody	L.	Los Angeles	W	Database	75	43	20-Jun-92	1.6	B
7	A-146	Daniels	A.	Atlanta	S	Accounting	125	24	09-May-93	0.7	New
8	W-119	Davis	G.	San Francisco	W	WP	150	159	09-Jul-89	4.6	A
9	T-128	Eng	R.	Albuquerque	S	Programming	75	75	11-Oct-89	4.3	B
10	S-127	Gill	P.	Los Angeles	W	Spreadsheet	100	45	22-Jun-89	4.6	C
11	S-149	Harris	P.	Dallas	S	Spreadsheet	150	17	12-Feb-93	1.0	New
12	W-124	Meyer	J.	New York	E	WP	150	85	05-May-89	4.7	B
13	A-103	Perez	D.	Las Vegas	W	Accounting	100	5	11-Jul-88	5.6	C
14	W-113	Porter	D.	Seattle	N	WP	125	59	02-Aug-88	5.5	B
15	D-139	Porter	M.	Washington, D.C.	E	Database	150	26	28-Mar-91	2.8	B
16	T-133	Ramirez	F.	Boston	E	Programming	150	73	08-Feb-90	4.0	B
17	S-155	Roberts	P.	Chicago	N	Spreadsheet	100	10	21-Aug-93	0.4	New
18	D-137	Sanchez	W.	Indianapolis	N	Database	100	47	16-Apr-91	2.8	B
19	N-101	Schwartz	B.	Boston	E	Networks	150	178	02-Mar-88	5.9	A
20	D-106	Weinberg	P.	Miami	S	Database	75	59	18-Jan-88	6.0	B

Instructors database on the second sheet. As discussed earlier in this chapter, these two tables are related by their Region fields. To locate the regional office for a given instructor, you could manually search through the two tables for the information you need. But the Query ➤ Join command simplifies and automates this process by creating a table in which information from the two databases is combined. In the join operation, 1-2-3 uses the Region field to correlate information from the two tables.

To see exactly how this works, suppose you want to create a table that includes instructor records along with the names of the corresponding regional managers and the phone numbers of regional offices. In the upcoming exercise, you'll begin by revising the existing query so that it shows fields from *all* the records in the Instructors database table. Then you'll use the Join command to add information from the Offices database table:

1. Select the query table in the third sheet and choose Query ➤ Set Criteria. In the Set Criteria dialog box, click the Clear button three times to delete the criteria you created for the previous exercise, then click OK. The query table now shows all the records

from the Instructors database, in alphabetical order by instructors' names.

2. Choose Query ➤ Choose Fields. In the Choose Fields dialog box, use the Clear command to remove the Hrs, Contract, and Ok fields from the list. Then click OK. Back in the query table, click the Size Columns SmartIcon to adjust the column widths appropriately. The query table appears as shown in Figure 7.16.

3. Choose Query ➤ Join.

In the Join dialog box, shown in Figure 7.17, 1-2-3 has foreseen the join you want to create, and has correctly established the join definition. As you can infer from the various notations in the Join dialog box, the Instructors database table will be joined with the Offices database table by their common Region field.

4. Click OK.

FIGURE 7.16

Creating a query table that contains all the records from the original database

	A	B	C	D	E	F	G	H	I	J
1	Last	First	City	Region	Specialty	Rate				
2	Ashford	W.	Washington, D.C.	E	Spreadsheet	150				
3	Banks	S.	St. Louis	S	WP	150				
4	Cody	L.	Los Angeles	W	Database	75				
5	Daniels	A.	Atlanta	S	Accounting	125				
6	Davis	G.	San Francisco	W	WP	150				
7	Eng	R.	Albuquerque	S	Programming	75				
8	Gill	P.	Los Angeles	W	Spreadsheet	100				
9	Harris	P.	Dallas	S	Spreadsheet	150				
10	Meyer	J.	New York	E	WP	150				
11	Perez	D.	Las Vegas	W	Accounting	100				
12	Porter	D.	Seattle	N	WP	125				
13	Porter	M.	Washington, D.C.	E	Database	150				
14	Ramirez	F.	Boston	E	Programming	150				
15	Roberts	P.	Chicago	N	Spreadsheet	100				
16	Sanchez	W.	Indianapolis	N	Database	100				
17	Schwartz	B.	Boston	E	Networks	150				
18	Weinberg	P.	Miami	S	Database	75				
19										
20										

Offices / Instructors / Selection   New Sheet

FIGURE 7.17

The Join dialog box 1-2-3 has correctly determined the join operation that you want to carry out.

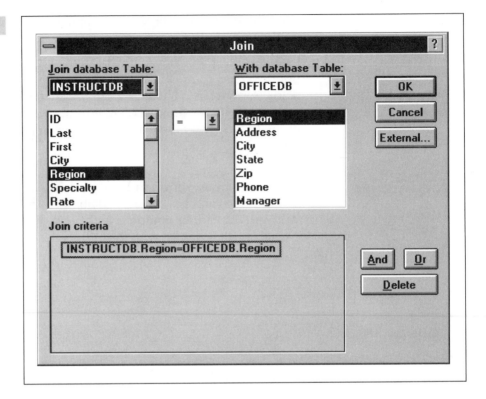

The Choose Fields dialog box appears, giving you the opportunity to select fields from both database tables for the resulting query:

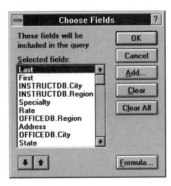

Notice the special *DATABASE.Field* notation that 1-2-3 uses to identify fields that have common names in the two database tables. For example, the Region field from the Instructors database is named IN-STRUCTDB.Region. The same field from the Offices database is named OFFICEDB.Region:

5. Use the Clear button to remove five field names from the Selected fields list: OFFICEDB.Region, Address, OFFICEDB.City, State, and Zip. The names that remain include the six fields from the Instructors database, along with the Phone and Manager fields from the Offices database.

6. Click OK to complete the Join operation.

1-2-3 adds the two fields from the Offices database to the query table. The process results in two side effects that you'll now want to correct: Two of the field names are now displayed in the long *DATABASE.Field* format; and the query table has been sorted by the Region Field.

7. Click the INSTRUCTDB.City field name, and then click the Rename field SmartIcon. (Alternatively, choose the Query ➤ Show Field As command.) In the Show Field As dialog box, enter **City** in the Show As text box:

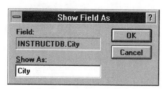

8. Click the INSTRUCTDB.Region field, choose Query ➤ Show Field As, then click the Rename Field SmartIcon again. Enter **Region** in the Show As box, and click OK.

9. Select the query table and choose Query ➤ Sort. In the Sort dialog box, define the Last and First fields as the two keys to the sort, as you learned to do earlier in this chapter (see page 413):

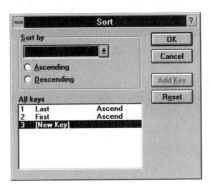

10. Click OK to complete the sort operation. Then click the Size Columns SmartIcon to adjust the column widths within the query table.

The result of your work appears in Figure 7.18. The joined query now shows the office phone number and the manager's name for each of the instructors in the database.

FIGURE 7.18

The result of the join operation. Each record now contains information from both the Instructors database table and the Offices database table.

	A	B	C	D	E	F	G	H	I
	Offices	Instructors	Selection					New Sheet	
1	Last	First	City	Region	Specialty	Rate	Phone	Manager	
2	Ashford	W.	Washington, D.C.	E	Spreadsheet	150	(212) 555-4678	Campbell, R.	
3	Banks	S.	St. Louis	S	WP	150	(214) 555-6754	Harvey, J.	
4	Cody	L.	Los Angeles	W	Database	75	(213) 555-9974	Garcia, M.	
5	Daniels	A.	Atlanta	S	Accounting	125	(214) 555-6754	Harvey, J.	
6	Davis	G.	San Francisco	W	WP	150	(213) 555-9974	Garcia, M.	
7	Eng	R.	Albuquerque	S	Programming	75	(214) 555-6754	Harvey, J.	
8	Gill	P.	Los Angeles	W	Spreadsheet	100	(213) 555-9974	Garcia, M.	
9	Harris	P.	Dallas	S	Spreadsheet	150	(214) 555-6754	Harvey, J.	
10	Meyer	J.	New York	E	WP	150	(212) 555-4678	Campbell, R.	
11	Perez	D.	Las Vegas	W	Accounting	100	(213) 555-9974	Garcia, M.	
12	Porter	D.	Seattle	N	WP	125	(312) 555-8803	Logan, C.	
13	Porter	M.	Washington, D.C.	E	Database	150	(212) 555-4678	Campbell, R.	
14	Ramirez	F.	Boston	E	Programming	150	(212) 555-4678	Campbell, R.	
15	Roberts	P.	Chicago	N	Spreadsheet	100	(312) 555-8803	Logan, C.	
16	Sanchez	W.	Indianapolis	N	Database	100	(312) 555-8803	Logan, C.	
17	Schwartz	B.	Boston	E	Networks	150	(212) 555-4678	Campbell, R.	
18	Weinberg	P.	Miami	S	Database	75	(214) 555-6754	Harvey, J.	
19									
20									

Summary

A 1-2-3 database table is a collection of records that you enter into consecutive rows of a worksheet. Each database table begins with a row of field names. The entries within a field all belong to the same data type.

You use the Range ➤ Sort command to rearrange the records of a database table in alphabetical, numeric, or chronological order. The Sort dialog box allows you to define multiple sorting keys, with options for ascending or descending sorts.

The commands of the Tools ➤ Database submenu are central to the 1-2-3 database component. You use these commands to perform a variety of query operations. For example, the Find Records command highlights records that match specific criteria, and the Delete Records command removes matching records from the database.

The Tools ➤ Database ➤ New Query command creates a new type of object known as a query table. When a query table is selected, 1-2-3 makes available a number of additional database operations in the Query menu. For example, you can use the commands in this menu to modify the definition of the query itself, to update the original database from changes you make in the records of the query table, and to perform a *join* operation to combine information from two or more database tables.

CHAPTER 8

Database Calculations and Operations

fast TRACK

- **To use statistical database functions such as @DSUM or @DAVG,** 458

  supply three arguments: the database range (or a query name enclosed in quotes), the target field name enclosed in quotes, and a *criteria expression* for selecting records from the range. 1-2-3 applies the function to the records that meet the criteria.

- **To read field entries from an individual record,** 463

  use the @DGET function with a criterion that uniquely identifies the target record.

- **To create a computed column in a query table,** 466

  select the query, pull down the Query menu, and click the Choose Fields command. Click the Formula button on the Choose Fields dialog box. In the Formula dialog box, enter a formula and a field name for the computed column.

- **To create an aggregate column in a query table,** 470

  select the query and use the Choose Fields command to display an appropriate selection of fields in the query table. In the table, select the numeric field that will be the subject of the aggregate operation. Then choose Query ➤ Aggregate. In the Aggregate dialog box, select the operation you want to perform (Sum, Avg, Count, Min, or Max) and click OK.

**To create a crosstab table from a database
or a query,**   **473**

choose Tools ➤ Database ➤ Crosstab. In the Crosstab dialog
box, enter the range name of the database from which you
want to create a crosstab table, and click Continue. In the
Crosstab Heading Options dialog box, select fields for the table's row and column headings and click Continue. In the
Crosstab Data Options dialog box, select the field that will be
the subject of the crosstab table, and select a calculation
(Sum, Average, Count, Minimum, or Maximum). Click Continue to complete the process. 1-2-3 creates a new sheet for
the crosstab table.

**To establish a connection to an external
database,**   **477**

activate the worksheet on which you want to establish the connection, and choose Tools ➤ Database ➤ Connect to External. 1-2-3 supplies a sequence of four dialog boxes to guide
you through the process of creating the connection. First select the DataLens driver appropriate to the database you want
to connect. Then select the directory where the database is located, and the name of the database itself. Finally, enter a
name that will represent the database on the worksheet while
the connection is active.

**To create a query table from an external
database,**   **482**

choose Tools ➤ Database ➤ New Query and enter the name
you've assigned to the connected database. (If the database
isn't connected yet, you can click the External button on the
New Query dialog box to establish the connection.) Then proceed with the process of creating a new query, just as you
would for a 1-2-3 database.

N ADDITION to the operations you learned about in Chapter 7, Lotus 1-2-3 has several other important features to help you get information from a database or a query table. Using a variety of built-in functions and menu commands, you can:

- Calculate statistical values and other numeric data from selected groups of records.

- Create *aggregate* columns in a query table, summarizing numeric data by categories.

- Create *crosstabs* to display totals, averages, or other values in a two-dimensional table format.

- Perform queries on an *external database*, a file developed in some other database-management environment.

To explore these operations in this chapter, you'll continue working with the Instructor database for Computing Conferences, Inc. Open the IN-STRUCT.WK4 file from disk now and briefly review its current contents: The sheets labeled Offices and Instructors contain the office and instructor database tables, respectively; and the sheet named Selection contains a query table combining information from the two database tables. You've defined some important range names, including OFFICEDB for the office database table, and INSTRUCTDB for the Instructor database table. In upcoming exercises you'll reuse the database and query tables.

Performing Calculations on Database Records

Given a database table containing one or more numeric fields, you can perform a variety of numeric and statistical calculations on selected records. For example, suppose you're focusing on one of the four regions in the Instructor database and you want to find answers to questions like these:

- What's the average number of hours an instructor has worked in this region?

- How much has each instructor in the region earned from working at conferences?

- What is the average hourly rate for instructors in the region? What are the highest and lowest rates?

There are several general approaches to answering questions like these. First, 1-2-3 has a useful group of statistical functions that operate on database records. You use these tools to perform statistical calculations selectively, on records that meet specific criteria. In addition, you can use the Tools ➤ Database ➤ Crosstab and Query ➤ Aggregate commands to create tables of statistics from your database. You'll study these tools and techniques in the upcoming sections.

NOTE See Chapter 15 for a reference guide to the database functions.

8

Database Operations

Understanding the Database Functions

Lotus 1-2-3 supplies a group of functions for calculating statistical values on records in a database. Given a selection of records that you specify by criteria, here is what these functions do:

Function	Use
@DSUM	Finds the total of the numeric entries in a field.
@DCOUNT	Counts nonblank entries in a field.
@DPURE-COUNT	Finds the number of numeric values in a field.
@DAVG	Computes the average of values in a field.
@DMAX	Finds the largest value in a field.
@DMIN	Finds the smallest value in a field.
@DVAR *and* @DVARS	Compute the variance, using the population method and the sample method, respectively.
@DSTD *and* @DSTDS	Compute the standard deviation using the population method and the sample method, respectively.

These database functions represent the same statistical formulas as the equivalent worksheet functions, @SUM, @COUNT, @AVG, and so on. The difference is that the database functions perform their calculations on a *selection* of records in a database or query table. You define this selection by writing criteria formulas designed to select the records you want to work with.

Using the Database Functions

In general, the statistical database functions take three arguments:

- **Database.** The first argument is the *input range*—that is, the range or name of the database itself. Alternatively, this argument can be the name of a query table in quotes.

- **Field.** The second argument identifies the field on which the calculation will be performed. This argument typically appears as a field name in quotes, but you can also supply this value as an *offset number* from 0 to *n*-1, where *n* is the number of fields in the database.

- **Criteria.** The third argument expresses the criteria for selecting records from the database.

For example, consider the following @DSUM function:

    @DSUM(INSTRUCTDB,"Hrs",REGION="S")

This function selects all the records in the Instructor database that match the criterion REGION="S"—that is, all the instructors in the southern region. Then, within this selection of records, the function finds the sum of all the entries in the Hrs field.

The following worksheet shows the result of a similar @DSUM function, along with five other database functions—@DCOUNT, @DAVG, @DMIN, @DMAX, and @DSTD:

	A	B	C	D	E	F	G
1	Conference Hours in Region:			S			
2							
3	Number of instructors		5		Lowest instructor hours		17
4	Average instructor hours		46.00		Highest instructor hours		75
5	Total instructor hours		230		Standard deviation		21.98
6							

The calculations focus on the work hours recorded for the instructors in the Southern region. As you can see, this worksheet shows the number of instructors in the region (5), the average number of conference hours worked by these instructors (46), the total hours they've worked (230), the smallest number of hours worked by an individual instructor (17), the largest number of hours worked (75), and the standard deviation calculated for this set of data (displayed as 21.98). The six database functions that produce these calculations all use the value in cell D1 to range to select records. Notice that this cell currently contains the label S; the cell's range name is REGIONCHOICE.

To create this example for yourself in the upcoming exercise, you'll begin by adding a fourth sheet to the INSTRUCT.WK4 file. Here are the steps:

1. Click the tab labeled Selection to activate the third sheet in the file, and then click the New Sheet button. 1-2-3 adds sheet D to the file.

2. Double-click the D tab and enter **Hours** as the new name for the sheet. Press ↵ to confirm.

3. Enter the title **Conference Hours in Region:** in cell D:A1, and click the Bold SmartIcon to apply the bold style to the cell. Then enter the value **S** in cell D:D1.

4. Choose Range ➤ Name and enter **REGIONCHOICE** as the range name of cell D:D1. Press ↵ to confirm.

5. Enter the following three labels into the range D:A3..D:A5:

Cell	Enter
D:A3	**Number of instructors**
D:A4	**Average instructor hours**
D:A5	**Total instructor hours**

6. Enter these three labels in the range D:E3..D:E5:

Cell	Enter
D:E3	**Lowest instructor hours**
D:E4	**Highest instructor hours**
D:E5	**Standard deviation**

7. Enter these six functions into the worksheet, the first three in the range D:C3..D:C5, and the remaining three in the range D:G3..D:G5:

Cell	Enter
D:C3	**@DCOUNT(INSTRUCTDB,"Hrs", REGION=REGIONCHOICE)**
D:C4	**@DAVG(INSTRUCTDB,"Hrs", REGION=REGIONCHOICE)**
D:C5	**@DSUM(INSTRUCTDB,"Hrs", REGION=REGIONCHOICE)**
D:G3	**@DMIN(INSTRUCTDB,"Hrs", REGION=REGIONCHOICE)**
D:G4	**@DMAX(INSTRUCTDB,"Hrs", REGION=REGIONCHOICE)**
D:G5	**@DSTD(INSTRUCTDB,"Hrs", REGION=REGIONCHOICE)**

8. With the cell pointer at D:G5, click the Format selector, the first panel of the status bar, and choose the Fixed format. Apply the same format to cell D:C4.

9. Click the Save SmartIcon to save your work to disk.

Notice the criterion you've used in each of the six database functions you've entered into this worksheet:

REGION=REGIONCHOICE

Because cell D1 is named REGIONCHOICE and contains the label S, this expression is equivalent to:

REGION="S"

In other words, this criterion selects all the database records in the Southern region.

8

Database Operations

In a sense, the database functions perform individual queries. They use a criteria expression to select records from the database, and they read data from a specific field. Because the criterion in this particular example depends on the value stored in the cell named REGIONCHOICE, 1-2-3 automatically recalculates the six functions if you change the value in the cell. To see how this recalculation works, select cell D:D1 and enter the new label E. Then examine the result. The Hours worksheet now contains statistical data about the instructors in the Eastern region:

Offices	Instructors	Selection	Hours			
D	**A**	**B**	**C**	**D**	**E**	**F**	**G**
1	Conference Hours in Region:			E			
2							
3	Number of instructors		5		Lowest instructor hours		26
4	Average instructor hours	101.40			Highest instructor hours		178
5	Total instructor hours		507		Standard deviation		53.91
6							

Now try entering labels representing the remaining two regions, N and W, into cell D1. With each change, 1-2-3 recalculates all six formulas on the sheet.

Criteria ranges in previous releases of 1-2-3 The use of criteria expressions in the third argument of the database functions is a feature that was introduced in Release 4.0 of 1-2-3 for Windows. Previously, you had to create a separate *criteria range* on a worksheet in order to use these functions. A criteria range consists of a row of field names followed by one or more rows of entries that 1-2-3 can read as criteria for selecting records from the target database. In older versions of 1-2-3, the third argument of a database function was always a reference to a criteria range. Release 5 of 1-2-3 still *allows* this usage; if you use old worksheets that are organized in this way, the database functions will still work. But you'll generally find the use of criteria expressions is much more convenient in the database functions. Oddly enough, the @DPURECOUNT function is a holdout—it *still* requires a criteria range, not a criteria expression, as its third argument.

T I P

In functions like @DCOUNT, @DAVG, @DSUM, @DMIN, @DMAX, and @DSTD, you can omit the third argument altogether. If you do so, the functions perform their statistical calculations on *all* the records of the target database. (The @DPURECOUNT function is an exception; it *always* requires a criteria range as its third argument.) Another interesting variation in these func-tions is that you can include more than one database reference as the first argument; but in this case, the third argument is no longer optional.

Two additional tools available in 1-2-3's collection of database functions are @DGET and @DQUERY. The @DQUERY function is for use on external databases, a subject you'll study in the final sections of this chapter (see page 482). @DGET reads and returns individual field entries from a database; this function is useful when you need to build a worksheet that lists values from a single record.

The @DGET Function

The @DGET function takes the same three arguments as other database functions you've examined—a database range, a field name, and a criteria expression. For a successful use of the @DGET function, however, the expressions in the criteria range must select a *single* record from the database. @DGET returns a label or a value from a specified field in this selected record. If two or more records match the criteria, @DGET returns an ERR value.

The following simple worksheet shows some examples of the @DGET function:

Cell D:D7 is named INSTRUCTNAME, and contains the name of one of the instructors in the database. The cells D:D8, D:D9, and D:D10 contain @DGET functions that use this cell in criteria expressions to select a single record from the database. For example, this is the function that finds the instructor's home city in cell D:D8:

> @DGET(INSTRUCTDB,"City",LAST=INSTRUCTNAME)

This function's first argument is a reference to the database itself, and the second argument identifies the City field as the target for the data query. The third argument is the criteria expression LAST=INSTRUCTNAME. In other words, the function finds the City entry for the record containing a Last field that matches the value in the cell named INSTRUCTNAME. As you can see, the result of the function is Los Angeles, the home city of the instructor named Cody.

Here are the steps for setting up this example on the fourth sheet of INSTRUCT.WK4:

1. Scroll down the Hours sheet by several rows, so that row 6 is displayed at the top of the worksheet window. Enter the labels:

Cell	Enter
D:C7	**Name:**
D:C8	**City:**
D:C9	**Specialty:**
D:C10	**Rate:**

2. Select this range of cells and click the Bold SmartIcon.

3. Enter the label **Cody** in cell D:D7. Then choose Range ➤ Name and enter **INSTRUCTNAME** as the range name for cell D7.

4. Enter the following three @DGET functions in cells D:D8, D:D9, and D:D10:

Cell	Enter
D:D8	**@DGET(INSTRUCTDB,"City", LAST=INSTRUCTNAME)**
D:D9	**@DGET(INSTRUCTDB,"Specialty", LAST=INSTRUCTNAME)**

Cell	Enter
D:D10	**@DGET(INSTRUCTDB,"Rate", LAST=INSTRUCTNAME)**

5. Use the Format selector on the status bar to apply the US Dollar format to cell D:D10. Then select 0 from the Decimal selector on the status bar, and click the Left SmartIcon to left-justify the value in its cell.

6. Click the Save SmartIcon to save your work to disk.

Now try selecting a new record from the database. Enter the new name **Daniels** in cell D:D7. 1-2-3 immediately recalculates the @DGET functions to display entries from the record for the instructor named Daniels:

D	A	B	C	D
6				
7			Name:	Daniels
8			City:	Atlanta
9			Specialty:	Accounting
10			Rate:	$125
11				

Offices | Instructors | Selection | Hours

Finally, try one more experiment with this worksheet. Enter the name **Porter** in cell D:D7. As you may recall, the database contains two instructors named Porter. Because the criteria expression now selects more than one record, the three @DGET functions all return values of ERR:

D	A	B	C	D
6				
7			Name:	Porter
8			City:	ERR
9			Specialty:	ERR
10			Rate:	ERR
11				

Offices | Instructors | Selection | Hours

8

Database Operations

Whenever you use the @DGET function you have to keep in mind this unique characteristic: The function operates successfully only on a single selected record. For more about his function, see page 736.

The database functions are not the only tools available for producing calculations from a database table. For some applications you may prefer to use special menu commands to create tables of calculations. In the upcoming sections you'll learn to work with computed and aggregate fields in a query table, and you'll find out how to create a crosstab table from a database.

Creating Computed Columns in a Query Table

Return now to the third sheet in the INSTRUCT.WK4 file to reexamine the query you created in Chapter 7. Click the Selection tab to view the sheet. The query currently displays eight fields of data—six from the Instructors database table, and two from the Offices table. Here are the first several rows of the query:

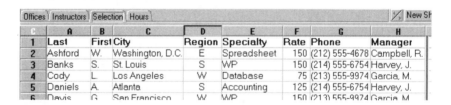

As you'll recall, you can change the assortment of fields by selecting the query and choosing the Query ➤ Choose Fields command. The Choose Fields dialog box allows you to add or remove fields from the query table or to rearrange the order of the fields.

In addition, you can use the Choose Fields command to create *computed columns* in a query table. You might want to take advantage of this feature to perform calculations based on existing numeric fields in the query. For example, suppose you want to see the total amount that individual instructors have earned from Computer Conferences, Inc.—that is, the product of the hourly rate and the total hours worked by each instructor.

You can easily add a column to the query to supply this calculation. In the following steps you'll begin by adding the Hrs field to the query, and then you'll write a formula for the new computed field:

1. Click the border of the query table to select the query. The Query menu appears on the menu bar.

2. Pull down the Query menu and click the Choose Fields command. The Choose Fields dialog box lists the fields that are currently displayed in the query table:

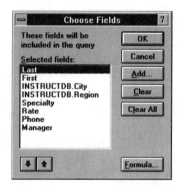

3. Select the Phone field and click the Clear button to remove this field from the list.

4. Click the Add button. In the Add Fields dialog box, select the Hrs field and then click OK to add this field to the query table:

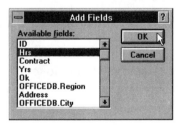

5. Highlight the Hrs field in the Selected fields list, and click the Formula button at the lower-right corner of the Choose Fields dialog box. The Formula dialog box appears on the screen as follows:

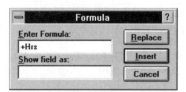

Notice that the expression +Hrs appears as the beginning of a formula in the Enter Formula text box.

6. Complete the formula by adding ***Rate** to the Enter Formula text box.

7. Press Tab to select the Show field as box, and enter **Total Paid**. This label will appear in the query as the field name of the calculated column. The Formula dialog box now appears as follows:

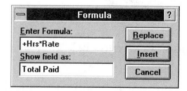

8. Press ↵ to enter this formula as a field into the query table.

Back in the Choose Fields dialog box, the formula appears between the Rate and Hrs fields.

9. Select the formula and click the down-arrow button at the lower-left corner of the dialog box to move the calculated field down the list by one position:

10. Click OK on the Choose Fields dialog box. The new calculated column now appears as the eighth field in the query table.

11. Click the Size Columns SmartIcon to adjust the table's column widths appropriately.

12. Click the Total Paid field name to select the column. Then click the Format selector on the status bar and choose the US Dollar format. Click the Decimal selector and choose 0. Deselect the Total Paid column by clicking elsewhere in the query.

The result of your work appears in Figure 8.1. The Total Paid field now displays the calculation you're interested in—the total earnings of each instructor in the database.

You can now use the Query ➤ Set Criteria command to focus on a selection of records in the query table. For example, choose the command and create a criterion that selects all the instructors in the Southern region:

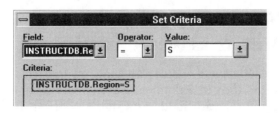

8

Database Operations

When you click OK, 1-2-3 reduces the selection of records in the query table accordingly:

	A	B	C	D	E	F	G	H	I
	Last	First	City	Region	Specialty	Rate	Hrs	Total Paid	Manager
2	Banks	S.	St. Louis	S	WP	150	55	$8,250	Harvey, J.
3	Daniels	A.	Atlanta	S	Accounting	125	24	$3,000	Harvey, J.
4	Eng	R.	Albuquerque	S	Programming	75	75	$5,625	Harvey, J.
5	Harris	P.	Dallas	S	Spreadsheet	150	17	$2,550	Harvey, J.
6	Weinberg	P.	Miami	S	Database	75	59	$4,425	Harvey, J.

FIGURE 8.1

A computed column in the query table. The Total Paid field shows the product of the Hrs and Rate fields.

	A	B	C	D	E	F	G	H	I
1	Last	First	City	Region	Specialty	Rate	Hrs	Total Paid	Manager
2	Ashford	W.	Washington, D.C.	E	Spreadsheet	150	145	$21,750	Campbell, R.
3	Banks	S.	St. Louis	S	WP	150	55	$8,250	Harvey, J.
4	Cody	L.	Los Angeles	W	Database	75	43	$3,225	Garcia, M.
5	Daniels	A.	Atlanta	S	Accounting	125	24	$3,000	Harvey, J.
6	Davis	G.	San Francisco	W	WP	150	159	$23,850	Garcia, M.
7	Eng	R.	Albuquerque	S	Programming	75	75	$5,625	Harvey, J.
8	Gill	P.	Los Angeles	W	Spreadsheet	100	45	$4,500	Garcia, M.
9	Harris	P.	Dallas	S	Spreadsheet	150	17	$2,550	Harvey, J.
10	Meyer	J.	New York	E	WP	150	85	$12,750	Campbell, R.
11	Perez	D.	Las Vegas	W	Accounting	100	5	$500	Garcia, M.
12	Porter	D.	Seattle	N	WP	125	59	$7,375	Logan, C.
13	Porter	M.	Washington, D.C.	E	Database	150	26	$3,900	Campbell, R.
14	Ramirez	F.	Boston	E	Programming	150	73	$10,950	Campbell, R.
15	Roberts	P.	Chicago	N	Spreadsheet	100	10	$1,000	Logan, C.
16	Sanchez	W.	Indianapolis	N	Database	100	47	$4,700	Logan, C.
17	Schwartz	B.	Boston	E	Networks	150	178	$26,700	Campbell, R.
18	Weinberg	P.	Miami	S	Database	75	59	$4,425	Harvey, J.

Creating an Aggregate Column in a Query Table

An *aggregate column* displays a statistic that describes or summarizes groups of records in a database. You create an aggregate query table by selecting the relevant fields and then choosing the Query ➤ Aggregate command. 1-2-3 calculates a statistic—the sum, the average, the count, or the largest or smallest value—for a specified groups of records.

For example, suppose you want to create a table showing the average hourly rates charged by instructors in each of the four regions. An easy way to produce this table is to create an aggregate column in a query. In the following exercise you'll create a new query in the INSTRUCT.WK4 worksheet to experiment with aggregate columns:

1. Click the Hours tab to activate the fourth sheet in the file. Then click the New Sheet button to add sheet E to the file.

2. Double-click the E tab and enter **Aggregate** as the new name for the sheet. Press ↵ to confirm.

3. Choose Tools ➤ Database ➤ New Query. The New Query dialog box appears on the screen.

4. Press F3 to view the Database Names dialog box. Select IN-STRUCTDB in the name list and click OK.

5. Click the Choose Fields button. In the Choose Fields dialog box, clear all the field names except Region and Rate. Then click OK.

6. Click OK on the New Query dialog box. A two-column query table appears on the active sheet.

7. Click the Rate field name at the top of the query table's second column. This action highlights the entire field, as shown in Figure 8.2.

8. Choose Query ➤ Aggregate. (Note that this command is available only when you select a single field within a query table.)

9. In the Compute group of the Aggregate dialog box, click the Avg option:

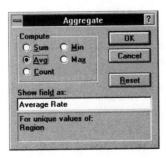

Notice how 1-2-3 describes the Aggregate table that you're about to create: The table will show the selected field as the average rate for unique values of the Region field.

10. Click OK on the Aggregate dialog box. Then click the Format selector on the status bar and choose the US Dollar format for the Average Rate column. Click elsewhere on the sheet to deselect the column.

The Aggregate Rate column appears as follows:

As you can see, the table displays the average hourly rates for each of the four regions. As a result of the Aggregate operation, the table contains exactly one record for each region.

Continue experimenting with this table. Try replacing the first column in the table with the Specialty field: Select the query and choose Query ➤ Choose Fields. Clear the Region field and add the Specialty field in its place. Click OK. After some additional formatting, the query table looks like this:

	A	B	
1	Specialty	Average Rate	
2	Accounting	$112.50	
3	Database	$100.00	
4	Networks	$150.00	
5	Programming	$112.50	
6	Spreadsheet	$125.00	
7	WP	$143.75	
8			

Offices | Instructors | Selection | Hours | Aggregate

This new aggregate shows the average rate in each specialty area. As you can see, creating an aggregate column in a query is an efficient way to generate statistical information about specific groups of records in a database.

Using the Crosstab Command

The Tools ➤ Database ➤ Crosstab command is another important feature that 1-2-3 provides for calculating statistics from a database. Using this command, you can quickly create a two-dimensional table of database calculations (sum, average, count, maximum, or minimum), where the row and column headings are entries from two fields and the numeric entries in the body of the table are calculated from a third field.

For example, suppose you want to build a table that shows the average hourly rate for instructors by specialty and region. The specialty areas will appear as row headings in the first column of the table, and the regions will appear as column headings in the first row. To create this kind of table manually from a large database table could require a considerable amount of time and effort; but using the Crosstab command, you can complete the task in minutes. Here are the steps:

1. Click the Instructors tab to view the database table that will be the subject of this operation.

2. Choose Tools ➤ Database ➤ Crosstab. The Crosstab dialog box appears on the screen. It contains one text box, in which you enter the range or name of the target database.

3. Press F3 and choose INSTRUCTDB from the Range Names dialog box. Click OK, and 1-2-3 copies the database name to the Crosstab dialog box:

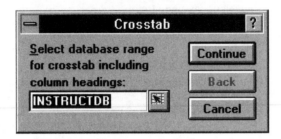

4. Click Continue.

The next dialog box to appear is named Crosstab Heading Options. You use this box to specify the row and column headings for your crosstab table.

5. Pull down the Row headings list and choose the Specialty field. Then pull down the Column headings list and choose the Region field. At this point the Crosstab Heading Options dialog box looks like this:

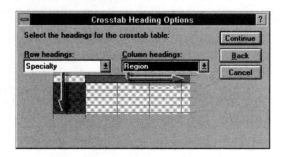

6. Click Continue.

The next dialog box is called Crosstab Data Options. You use this box to choose the field that will be summarized in the crosstab table and the statistical operation for the calculations.

7. Click the Rate field in the Summarize field list. Then select the Average option in the Calculate group. The dialog box appears as follows:

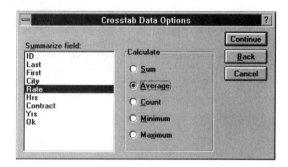

8. Click Continue.

At this point, 1-2-3 adds a new sheet to your worksheet file and builds the crosstab table according to your instructions.

Spend a few moments formatting the new table. Adjust column widths as necessary, and apply the US Dollar format to the numeric values. Double-click the C tab and enter Crosstab as the new name for the sheet. Here's the result of your work:

	A	B	C	D	E	F
1						
2						
3	Crosstab Table For Average Rate by Specialty and Region					
4		E	N	S	W	
5	Accounting			$125	$100	
6	Database	$150	$100	$75	$75	
7	Networks	$150				
8	Programming	$150		$75		
9	Spreadsheet	$150	$100	$150	$100	
10	WP	$150	$125	$150	$150	
11						

Tabs: Offices | Instructors | Crosstab | Selection | Hours | Aggregate

8

Database Operations

As you can see, 1-2-3 has calculated the average hourly rate for each specialty in each region. Blank cells indicate that a particular specialty area is not available in a given region.

In this exercise you've created a crosstab from a very small number of records. But 1-2-3 performs this operation just as efficiently on a large database. For example, here is the same crosstab table, created for the complete version of the Instructor database (shown back in Figure 7.3 on page 403):

	A	B	C	D	E	F
1						
2						
3	Crosstab Table For Average Rate by Specialty and Region					
4		E	N	S	W	
5	Accounting	$100		$125	$100	
6	Database	$125	$133	$125	$92	
7	Networks	$125		$75	$150	
8	Programming	$117		$75	$100	
9	Spreadsheet	$133	$92	$144	$83	
10	WP	$125	$125	$106	$150	
11						

In the complete database, regions may have multiple instructors for a given specialty; accumulating the data is therefore a larger task. But 1-2-3 still builds the crosstab table quickly and efficiently.

Working with External Databases

Finally, you can use 1-2-3 to gain access to *external* databases created in other database-management programs. To work with an external database, you begin by establishing a connection between the file on disk and the current worksheet. At the time you create this connection, you also define the equivalent of a 1-2-3 range name for the external database. This name represents the database as long as the connection is active. Using this name, you can perform a variety of operations on the external database file, as though it were stored in the open worksheet file. For example, you can use the 1-2-3 database functions to perform statistical calculations on selected records of the external database; and you can create query tables, copying records from the external database to a worksheet.

DataLens drivers The software that makes this kind of connection possible is called a *DataLens driver*. You can copy DataLens drivers to your disk at the time you install 1-2-3. The appropriate driver must be available on your hard disk if you want to use 1-2-3 to access an external database.

In the final sections of this chapter, you'll look at a few examples of external database queries. For these exercises, imagine that the original instructor database from Computing Conferences, Inc., is a dBASE IV database file stored on disk as INSTRUCT.DBF in a directory named C:\DBASE. In the upcoming sections you'll learn how to connect a file like this one to a 1-2-3 worksheet, and how to perform a variety of queries on the database.

Connecting to an External Database

To establish a connection with an external database, you have to supply four items of information:

- The name of the appropriate DataLens driver.
- The directory location of the database file.
- The database file name—that is, the external table.
- The 1-2-3 range name that you'll use to represent the external database table once the connection is made.

The starting point for your work with an external database is the Tools ➤ Database ➤ Connect to External command. When you choose this command, 1-2-3 supplies a sequence of dialog boxes—all titled "Connect to External"—to guide you through the process of making the connection.

As an illustration of the Connect to External command, the following steps show you how you would establish a connection to a dBASE file named C:\DBASE\INSTRUCT.DBF. You can use these same steps on an external database file of your own by substituting the appropriate driver, directory, file, and range name:

1. Open the 1-2-3 worksheet file to which you want to connect the database. (Even if the worksheet file was formerly connected to an external database, you must reestablish the connection every time you reopen the file.)

2. Choose Tools ➤ Database ➤ Connect to External.

The first dialog box contains a list of the DataLens drivers that are installed in your system:

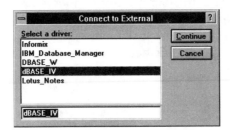

3. For this example, select the dBASE_IV option in the Select a driver list, and click Continue.

The next dialog box shows a list of directories where the database might be found:

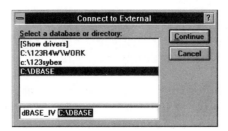

If one of these is the correct directory, you can select it in the list. Otherwise, you can enter the full directory into the text box, just after the notation dBASE IV.

4. In this example, select C:\DBASE and click Continue.

The next dialog box shows a list of all the database files found in the directory:

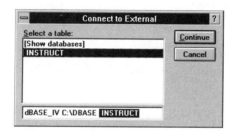

5. Select the INSTRUCT database and click Continue.

Finally, the fourth Connect to External dialog box gives you the opportunity to create a name that will represent the external database:

6. In this case, enter **dbaseinst** as the name, and click OK:

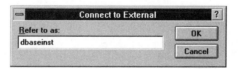

After these steps are complete, the name DBASEINST represents the external dBASE file in database operations that you perform on the active worksheet. For example, this name can appear as the first argument in a database function, as you'll learn in the next section of this chapter.

Using Database Functions with an External Database

To use database functions on an external table, you supply the three arguments just as you would for any other database table:

- **Database.** The first argument is the name you've assigned to the external database.

- **Field.** The second argument is a field name from the external database, enclosed in quotes.

- **Criteria.** The third argument is a criteria expression for selecting records from the external database.

For example, the following worksheet makes use of six database functions—@DCOUNT, @DAVG, @DSUM, @DMIN, @DMAX, and @DSTD—to get information from the connected external database:

A	A	B	C	D
1	External Database:	INSTRUCT.DBF		
2			(DBASE IV)	
3	Region:	S		
4				
5	*Statistical Database Functions:*			
6				
7	Number of Instructors		16	
8	Average instructor hours		40.75	
9	Total instructor hours		652	
10	Lowest instructor hours		5	
11	Highest instructor hours		145	
12	Standard deviation		34.06	

Figure 8.3 displays the functions in the text format. As you can see, each function uses the external database name DBASEINST as the input range, the field name "Hrs" as the target field, and the expression REGION=$REGIONCHOICE as the criterion for selecting records. Cell B3 on the worksheet is named REGIONCHOICE, and currently contains the label S. As a result, each function calculates a statistic from records in the Southern region. For example, the following function finds

FIGURE 8.3

Using database functions with the external database. Here the functions are displayed in text format so you can see exactly how they're written.

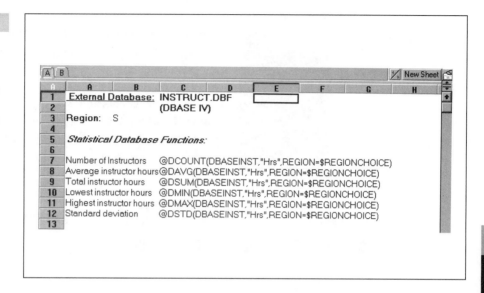

the sum of all the hours worked by instructors in this region:

@DSUM(DBASEINST,"Hrs",REGION=$REGIONCHOICE)

If you revise the criterion for selecting data, 1-2-3 reads a new selection of records from the external file and recalculates the database functions accordingly. For example, in the following sheet a new criterion, N, has been entered into the REGIONCHOICE cell at B3:

	A	B	C	D
1	External Database:		INSTRUCT.DBF	
2			(DBASE IV)	
3	Region:	N		
4				
5	Statistical Database Functions:			
6				
7	Number of Instructors		9	
8	Average instructor hours		28.67	
9	Total instructor hours		258	
10	Lowest instructor hours		10	
11	Highest instructor hours		59	
12	Standard deviation		15.03	
13				

The new results are the statistics for the Northern region.

N O T E   If you close this worksheet, 1-2-3 disconnects the external database. When you later reopen the worksheet, the database functions return values of ERR, because the range name DBASEINST is no longer defined. To reestablish the connection with the external database, choose the Connect to External command again. When you complete the connection, 1-2-3 correctly recalculates the database functions.

Creating a Query Table from an External Database

To extract records from an external database, you use the Tools ➤ Database ➤ New Query command. Once again, you begin the procedure by establishing the connection with the external database. Except for this initial task, the general steps for creating a query table from a connected external database are the same as for a 1-2-3 database:

1. Choose Tools ➤ Database ➤ New Query. The New Query dialog box appears.

2. Press F3 to view the Database Names dialog box. In the list you'll see the name you've assigned to the external database that is connected to the active worksheet:

Select this name from the list and click OK.

3. Click the Choose Fields button, and select the fields that you want to extract from the external database.

4. Click the Set Criteria button and build the criteria you want to use to select records from the external database.

5. Indicate the cell or range where you want to display the new query table.

6. Click OK to complete the operation.

TIP

If you haven't yet connected the external database at the time you choose the Tools ➤ Database ➤ New Query command, you can do so by clicking the External button on the New Query dialog box. In response, 1-2-3 displays the first of the four Connect to External dialog boxes.

8

Database Operations

Suppose you want to create a query table containing a selection of fields and records from the external INSTRUCT.DBF database. You begin by connecting to the database, choosing the New Query command, and entering DBASEINST as the name of the external database. You click the Choose Fields button and select ID, FIRST, and CITY as the fields you want to see. Then you click the Set Criteria button and build the following set of criteria:

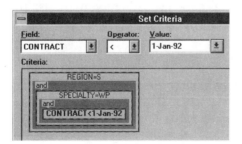

These criteria are designed to find the Southern region instructors who specialize in word processing and began working for the company before

1/1/92. When you click OK on the New Query dialog box, 1-2-3 creates the following query table from the external database:

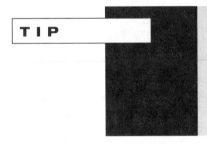

	A	B	C	D
1	External Database:		INSTRUCT.DBF	
2			(DBASE IV)	
3				
4				
5	ID	LAST	CITY	
6	W-130	Burke	Miami	
7	W-116	Jordan	Dallas	
8	W-112	Manning	Atlanta	
9				

Three records have been found that match your criteria.

TIP

You can use the @DQUERY function with some external databases to send application-specific commands to the database. @DQUERY takes a string argument representing the name of an external function, followed by any arguments required by the external function itself: @DQUERY("*FunctionName*",*ArgumentList*)

Disconnecting an External Database

The Tools ➤ Database ➤ Disconnect command terminates the connection to an external database. When you choose this command, the Disconnect dialog box appears on the screen:

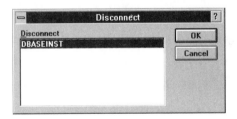

To disconnect, you simply choose the name you've assigned to the connected database and click OK. After you disconnect, any database functions that refer to the external database return values of ERR.

Summary

To calculate statistics from a database, you use database functions such as @DSUM, @DAVG, @DCOUNT, @DMIN, and @DMAX. These functions calculate totals, averages, or other statistical values from numeric field entries in selected database records. Each of the statistical database functions takes three arguments: a database range or name, a field name or offset number, and a criteria expression.

There are several other good ways to perform calculations from the information stored in a database. In a query table, you can create a computed column that displays the result of a formula for each record in the query; to do so, you click the Formula button on the New Query dialog box. Also in a query table, an aggregate column uses a statistical calculation to summarize the information stored in categories of records. You create an aggregate column by selecting a query, making an appropriate field selection, and choosing the Query ➤ Aggregate command. Finally, the Tools ➤ Database ➤ Crosstab command creates a two-dimensional table of statistics based on varying entries in two fields.

An external database is a file that originates from a database-management program other than 1-2-3. To establish a connection between an external database and a 1-2-3 worksheet, you use the Tools ➤ Database ➤ Connect to External command. As long as the connection is active, you can apply 1-2-3 database functions to the external database, and you can use the Tools ➤ Database ➤ New Query command to create query tables from the external database.

Macros

fast TRACK

● **To run a macro that has an ordinary range name,**   **500**

choose the Tools ➤ Macro ➤ Run command, or press Alt+F3. Select the name of the macro you want to run.

● **To call one macro as a subroutine from within another macro,**   **502**

enter the macro's range name within braces, in the format {\N} or {Name}.

● **To record a keystroke macro from actions you perform in 1-2-3,**   **507**

choose Tools ➤ Macro ➤ Record, and then use the keyboard and/or the mouse to perform the actions you want to record. (Choose Tools ➤ Macro ➤ Stop Recording when you've finished.) Then choose the Tools ➤ Macro ➤ Show Transcript command to view the Transcript window. Use a copy-and-paste operation to copy some or all of the window's contents to the worksheet where you're developing a macro.

● **To create an autoexecute macro,**   **518**

assign the macro the special name \0 (backslash, zero).

● **To create a macro library that is automatically opened when you start 1-2-3,**   **525**

save the file as AUTO123.WK4 in the default directory.

MACROS are tools you create to streamline your activities in 1-2-3. You can design macros to perform any variety of tasks, from simple keystoke repetitions and menu commands to sophisticated programming procedures. While it's possible to work effectively in 1-2-3 without macros, many users employ macros as an integral part of their daily operations. As you begin experimenting with a variety of macro tools, you'll be able to choose the ones that seem useful to you.

At the simplest level, a macro is a record of a particular sequence of commonly used keystrokes. When you run the macro, 1-2-3 repeats the keystrokes as though you had typed them directly from the keyboard. For example, you might write a macro to enter your company's name and address into consecutive cells of a worksheet column.

In addition to ordinary keystrokes, 1-2-3 provides two important kinds of instructions that you can include in the macros you write:

- *Macro key names* represent operations you perform from the keyboard, such as pressing arrow keys or function keys.

- *Macro commands* represent specific tasks, such as menu commands or other special procedures.

The macro key names and commands make up a versatile programming language that operates within the 1-2-3 environment.

In this chapter you'll create and run several small macros, and you'll begin learning to use the tools available for developing them.

NOTE If you want to learn more about macros, Chapter 12 is an introduction to the concepts and techniques of macro programming. Chapter 21 is a complete reference guide to the macro commands.

Creating Keystroke Macros

Macros are created and saved in 1-2-3 worksheet files. A worksheet can contain any number of macros, and all are available for use as soon as you open the worksheet that contains them. Conveniently, you can store a collection of your favorite general-purpose macros in a single worksheet. Opening this one worksheet then gives you access to the entire collection.

A worksheet that contains a collection of macros is sometimes known as a *macro library*. Because 1-2-3 allows you to open multiple worksheet files concurrently, your macro library can be open at the same time that you are working on one or more other open worksheets. Typically, a keystroke macro is designed to accomplish its task on the worksheet that's active at the time you run the macro.

Entering Macro Instructions

You enter the instructions of a macro into consecutive cells of a worksheet column. Here are the two basic steps for creating a macro:

1. Enter the macro instructions into a column of contiguous cells.

2. Assign a name to the first cell of the macro column.

9

Macros

The range name is the key to running a macro. For convenience, 1-2-3 allows you to create a special kind of macro name consisting of two characters, a backslash followed by a letter from A to Z. For example, \D, \N, and \H are all macro names. When you assign a name like this to a macro, you can then run the macro by pressing the Ctrl key along with the designated letter key. For example, you press Ctrl+N to run the macro named \N.

NOTE

Macro names have precedence over 1-2-3's built-in keyboard shortcuts. For example, Ctrl+B is normally the shortcut for applying the bold style to a cell or range. But if you open a worksheet that contains a macro named \B, the Ctrl+B keystroke sequence instead runs the macro. The Bold shortcut is therefore unavailable until you close the macro sheet again. Avoid using macro names that will override your favorite keyboard shortcuts.

In the following brief exercise, you'll create your first macro and assign it a name. Then you'll try running it. The macro performs the simple job of entering a company's name into a selected cell on a worksheet:

1. Select cell B2 on a new blank worksheet. Enter the following label into the cell:

Computing Conferences, Inc.~

The last character of this entry is a *tilde*. In a macro, a tilde represents ↵, the Enter key.

2. With the cell pointer still at B2, choose Range ➤ Name. Enter \N as the two-character range name. Click OK to confirm.

3. Choose File ➤ Save As and save the worksheet file as COM-PANY.WK4. Here's what your macro looks like:

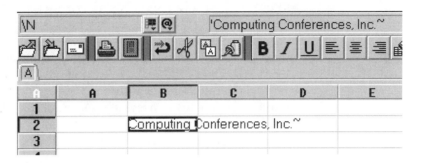

4. Choose File ➤ New to open another worksheet.

5. With the cell pointer positioned at cell A1 of the new worksheet, press Ctrl+N. The macro you've created enters the company name as a label in the current cell.

6. Now select a new cell, say D8, and press Ctrl+N again. The macro repeats its task by entering company name again as a label in the selected cell:

In this first exercise you've created a simple example of a keystroke macro. Except for the final tilde character, the entire example consists of characters that are entered into the current cell when you run the macro. The tilde character represents the action of completing the entry. It is the equivalent of pressing ↵ when you finish typing a label onto the edit line.

9

Macros

Using Macro Key Names

Other keys and commands in a macro are represented by names enclosed within braces ({}). The macro key names are generally easy to recognize and remember, because many of them match the names that appear directly on your keyboard. For example, the macro key names {Home}, {End}, {PgUp}, {PgDn}, {Ins}, and {Del} correspond to the keys located on the number pad at the side of your keyboard. Other readily identifiable macro key names include {Backspace}, {Esc}, and {Tab}. In addition, four of the most commonly used macro key names represent the arrow keys on your keyboard: {Up}, {Down}, {Right} and {Left}.

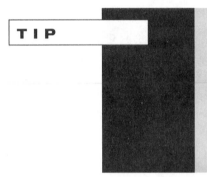

TIP

Some variations are allowed in the representation of keys in a 1-2-3 macro. For instance, you can enter the macro key names in any combination of uppercase or lowercase letters: {Down}, {DOWN}, and {down} all represent the ↓ key. In addition, some of the keys have abbreviated forms. For example, you can use {Ins} for {Insert}; {Del} for {Delete}; {BS} for {Backspace}; and {U}, {D}, {R} and {L} for the four arrow keys.

Function keys in macros The function keys F1 to F9 are represented by the tasks they perform in 1-2-3:

MACRO KEY NAME	FUNCTION KEY	USE IN MACROS
{Help}	F1	The command to open the 1-2-3 Help system.
{Edit}	F2	The command to edit the contents of the current cell.
{Name}	F3	The command to request a list of range names in Edit, Point, or Value modes.

MACRO KEY NAME	FUNCTION KEY	USE IN MACROS
{Anchor}	F4	In the Ready mode, this is the command for preselecting a range on the worksheet.
{Abs}	F4	In the Edit, Point, or Value modes, the command for creating an absolute, relative, or mixed reference.
{Goto}	F5	The command that displays the Go To dialog box.
{Window}	F6	The command for moving the cell pointer between panes.
{Query}	F7	The command to refresh a query.
{Table}	F8	A command for repeating an opera-tion on a What-if table. (You'll learn about this feature in Chapter 10.)
{Calc}	F9	The command to recalculate the active worksheet.

Other macro key names represent key combinations. For example, the Ctrl+→ and Ctrl+← combinations are represented by the names {BigRight} and {BigLeft}, respectively.

TIP

For a complete list of macro key names, type { into a worksheet cell and then press F3. The Macro Keywords dialog box appears on the screen. In the Category list, choose Keystroke Equivalents to see all the key names.

9

Macros

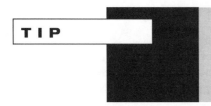

T I P

With some of the key names, 1-2-3 allows you to include an integer to represent repetitions of the keystroke. For example, the instruction {Down 3} (or simply {D 3}) is equivalent to {Down}{Down}{Down}.

Organizing Macros on a Worksheet

Because macros can become complex and difficult to read, it's a good idea to make room for brief comments and explanations on the sheets where you enter your macros. One common way to organize macros is in the following three-column format:

- In column A, enter the name you plan to assign to each macro in the cell just to the left of the macro's first line. (As you'll see shortly, this arrangement allows you to assign names to your macros quickly and efficiently.)

- In column B, enter the macro instructions themselves. Each entry in a macro is a label, consisting of keystrokes, macro key names, and macro commands. While a macro is running, 1-2-3 reads down the column from one instruction to the next. A blank cell, or a cell with a numeric value rather than a label, marks the end of a macro.

- In column C, enter brief comments that explain the lines and instructions of the macro. Lotus 1-2-3 does not read these comments as part of your macro; rather, the third column is for your own benefit, or for any other person who is trying to understand what your macro does. In short macros, you can write a single comment to describe the macro; in longer and more complex macros, you may want to write individual comments for each row of instructions.

In addition, each macro presented in this book begins with a title, displayed in boldface type and located just above the first line of macro instructions. This title is inside the macro column, but is not part of the macro. The first named cell of the macro is the line immediately beneath the title.

WARNING
Be careful not to include blank cells or numeric entries inside the contiguous range of a macro. 1-2-3 reads a blank or a nonlabel entry as a marker for the end of a macro.

The following sheet illustrates this three-column macro format:

A	B	C
1	Company Name	Enter the company name
2	\N Computing Conferences, Inc.~	
3		
4	Address of Western Office	Enter the address
5	\W 432 Market Avenue{D}	of the Western regional office
6	Los Angeles, CA 90028~	

The first macro is the one you've entered into your own worksheet, but it now includes the following new elements:

- A title in cell B1
- The macro's assigned name in cell A2
- A brief comment in cell C1

A second macro, entitled Address of Western Office, is located beneath the first one. Notice that a blank cell separates the two macros. This second macro performs another simple data-entry task: It displays a two-line address in consecutive cells of a worksheet column.

Activate your own copy of the COMPANY.WK4 worksheet now, so you can complete the first macro and enter the second one.

9

Macros

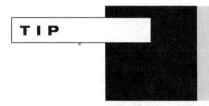

TIP   With multiple worksheet files open at once, you can press Ctrl+F6 to switch from one worksheet to the next. Alternatively, pull down the Window menu and choose the name of the open file you want to activate.

Here are some tips to guide you as you enter the macros into the worksheet:

- Begin by adjusting the widths of the three columns appropriately. One convenient arrangement is to assign a width of 3 to column A, and a width of 34 to both columns B and C. This allows as much space as possible for the columns containing the macro instructions and the comments.

- When you enter the macro range names into column A, begin each entry with a double quotation mark (") to right-justify the label in its cell. (Without a quotation mark, 1-2-3 reads the backslash character as a label prefix, resulting in a repeating character.) Make sure you enter these names in their correct cells, just to the left of the first line of instructions in each macro—not next to the boldfaced title.

- Don't enter any extraneous spaces or other characters in the macro instructions. For example, notice that there is no space between the end of the address and the {D} instruction in cell B5. When you run a macro, 1-2-3 assumes that every letter, character, and space in the macro is significant.

Assigning Names to Macros

When you finish entering the macros, your next task is to apply the range names displayed in column A to the adjacent cells in column B. (Actually, you've already named the first macro, but for the purpose of the upcoming exercise you'll proceed as though you hadn't done so yet.) Here are the steps:

1. Select the range A2..A5.

2. Choose the Range ➤ Name command.

3. Make sure the setting in the For cells box is "To the right."

4. Click the Use Labels button. Both of the selected macro names appear in the Existing named ranges list:

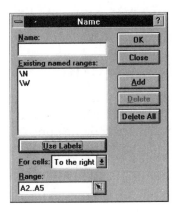

5. Click OK. Then click the Save SmartIcon to update COM-PANY.WK4 on disk.

As a result of the Use Labels button, the name \N is assigned (or *re-*assigned in this case) to the first cell of the Company Name macro, and \W is assigned to the first cell of the Address of Western Office macro.

Now you can try running the macros. Activate the other open worksheet, on which you've already been experimenting with the first macro. Select cell A3 and press Ctrl+N to make sure the first macro still works properly. Then select cell A4 and press Ctrl+W to run the second macro. Press Home and examine the result:

Notice that the second macro enters two labels into consecutive cells of the column. The {D} instruction performs two tasks in the first line of this macro: First, it completes the entry of the street address; and second, it moves the cell pointer down by one row for the city, state, and zip code entry. (You can use the ↓ key for this same purpose when you are entering a sequence of data values into a column.)

Using the Run Command

The Tools ➤ Macro ➤ Run command provides a list of the macros currently available in all open worksheets—and allows you to select a macro to run. For a macro that has a name consisting of a backslash character and a letter, the use of the Run command is normally unnecessary; it's easier to press the Ctrl+*letter* keyboard sequence to run the macro. But 1-2-3 also allows you to assign any ordinary range name to a macro. If the name is not a backslash with a letter, you have to use the Run command to run the macro.

While the worksheet on which you've been testing the macros is still active, try the following exercise with the Run command:

1. Pull down the Tools menu and choose the Macro command. A cascade menu appears:

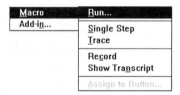

2. Choose Run, the first command on the menu. The Macro Run
dialog box appears:

3. Click the down-arrow button at the right side of the In file box.

The resulting drop-down list displays the name of the worksheet file that's
currently serving as your macro library, COMPANY.WK4:

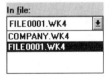

4. Select this file name in the list box. When you do so, 1-2-3 displays a list of all the macros stored in the file:

You can now run any macro in the list by selecting the macro's name and
clicking OK.

5. Select the \W macro and click OK. Back on the worksheet, the macro once again enters the two lines of the address. After you've examined the results, close this worksheet without saving it; the macro library worksheet, COMPANY.WK4, remains open.

Now you've seen two ways to run a macro. If the macro has a name consisting of a backslash and a letter, press the designated Ctrl+*letter* key combination. Alternatively, choose the Tools ➤ Macro ➤ Run command to run any macro, regardless of its range name. By the way, the keyboard shortcut for the Run command is Alt+F3.

Interestingly enough, you can also run one macro from within another macro. In programming terms, this is known as *calling a macro as a subroutine*.

Using Macros as Subroutines

When one macro calls another, 1-2-3 performs all the instructions of the called macro and then returns control to the original macro. To write a call instruction you simply enclose the range name of the macro within braces. For example, the instruction {\N} calls the macro named \N.

A call instruction works successfully regardless of the format of the macro name. For instance, suppose you assign the range name SCHEDULE to a macro you have written; the instruction {Schedule} represents a call to this macro. (Alphabetic case is not significant in a call instruction.) Organizing a macro into small subroutines is an effective way to avoid entering duplicate instructions for the same task in a long macro.

Figure 9.1 displays a third macro in the COMPANY.WK4 worksheet. This new macro contains three lines of instructions:

- The first line, in cell B9, calls the macro named \N, and then moves the cell pointer down by one row:

  {N}{D}

- The second line enters a label into the current cell and then moves the cell pointer down again:

  Western Region{D}

FIGURE 9.1

Calling macros as
subroutines

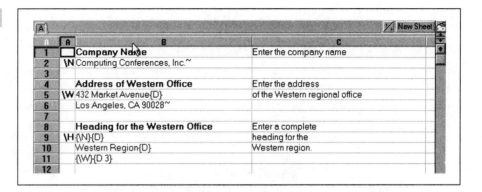

- The third line calls the macro named \W, and moves the cell pointer down by three rows:

  {\W}{D 3}

Enter this macro into your own copy of the COMPANY.WK4 worksheet. Also enter the macro name, **\H**, in column A, and the comment in column C. Select cell A9, choose the Range ➤ Name command, and click the Use Labels button to designate \H as the name of the macro. Click the Save SmartIcon to update COMPANY.WK4 on disk.

Now choose the File ➤ New command to open a new blank worksheet, and press **Ctrl+H** to run the new macro. The result is a four-line heading that contains the company name, the region name, and the regional office address:

A	A	B	C
1	Computing Conferences, Inc.		
2	Western Region		
3	432 Market Avenue		
4	Los Angeles, CA 90028		
5			
6			
7			
8			

As you can see, the output from the \H macro includes labels produced by calls to the \N and \W macros.

9

Macros

Organizing the Instructions of a Macro

Take a moment to reexamine this third macro before you move on. The instructions of the macro are divided into three parts, which you entered into three consecutive cells of column B. But this division is arbitrary. Lotus 1-2-3 would run the macro in exactly the same way if you divided its instructions into only two parts:

```
{\N}{D}Western Region
{D}{\W}{D 3}
```

or even if you entered the entire macro into a single cell:

```
{\N}{D}Western Region{D}{\W}{D 3}
```

The purpose of dividing the instructions into smaller sections is to make the macro easy for people to read. For 1-2-3, this division is irrelevant, as long as you follow the few simple rules you've learned for entering a macro:

- Enclose macro key names within braces.

- Don't enter any extraneous spaces or characters in the macro instructions.

- Use a blank cell to mark the end of the macro.

In preparation for this chapter's next exercises, you can now close both the COMPANY.WK4 file and the worksheet you've used to test the third macro. In the new Untitled worksheet that 1-2-3 opens you'll develop a second library of macros.

Writing Macros as Menu Shortcuts

You can create a useful variety of menu-shortcut macros—that is, macros that choose commands from the 1-2-3 menu system. Like a SmartIcon, a menu-shortcut macro streamlines the multi-step process of pulling down a menu, choosing a command, and selecting options from a dialog box. Instead of going through these steps, you can simply press the Ctrl+*letter* keyboard combination that runs your macro.

A macro that chooses a command from a pull-down menu consists of the following information, enclosed in a pair of braces:

- The macro command that represents the menu choice. This kind of command typically consists of two or more menu keywords separated by hyphens.

- The arguments that the command requires. Each argument is separated from the next by a semicolon or a comma. (Extra semicolons or commas represent optional arguments that have been omitted.)

For example, consider the following macro instruction:

{Range-Name-Label-Create "Right"}

The {Range-Name-Label-Create} command is equivalent to choosing the Range ➤ Name menu command and clicking the Use Labels button. This macro command takes an argument that indicates the direction in which the labels will be created—equivalent to pulling down the For cells list and selecting one of the options. In this macro command, the argument "Right" is the same as choosing the "To the right" option in the For cells list. (Actually, the {Range-Name-Label-Create} macro command takes a second argument, indicating the range over which the names will be created. The second argument is omitted in this example.)

As you'll see shortly, this macro command is an ideal tool to use while you are developing other macros in the three-column macro library format. To assign a name to a macro, you move the cell pointer to the cell in the first column that contains the name, and run this macro.

Here is another example of a menu-shortcut macro, also useful in the development of other macros:

{Column-Width 3,A1}

The {Column-Width} macro command is equivalent to choosing Style ➤ Column Width. The macro command takes two arguments—the new width you want to assign, and a range that indicates the target column or columns. This particular example assigns a new width of 3 to column A in the active worksheet.

Figure 9.2 shows versions of these two menu-shortcut macros in a worksheet. In the following exercise you'll enter them into a worksheet of your own, as the first two tools of a new macro library that you'll save on disk as MACROLIB.WK4:

1. Enter the macro names **\R** in cell A2 and **\M** in cell A5. Click the Bold SmartIcon for each cell. Then enter the titles and the macro instructions themselves in column B, exactly as you see them in Figure 9.2.

2. Select cell A2 and choose Range ➤ Name. Click the Use Labels button and then click OK to assign the name \R to the macro. The Right Label macro is now ready to use.

3. Select cell A5, and press Ctrl+R to run the Right Label macro. As a result, 1-2-3 assigns the name \M to the Macro Sheet macro. To confirm that this has actually happened, press Alt+F3 to choose the Tools Macro Run command; examine the list of defined macro names in the current worksheet. As you can see, the two macro names have both been defined successfully:

(Press Escape to close the Macro Run dialog box.)

4. Press Ctrl+M to run the second macro. This assigns appropriate column widths for the sheet.

FIGURE 9.2

Two menu-shortcut
macros

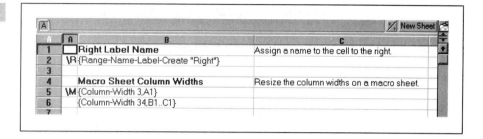

	A	B	C
1	☐	Right Label Name	Assign a name to the cell to the right.
2		\R{Range-Name-Label-Create "Right"}	
3			
4		Macro Sheet Column Widths	Resize the column widths on a macro sheet.
5		\M{Column-Width 3,A1}	
6		{Column-Width 34,B1..C1}	
7			

5. Enter the comments in column C as you see them in Figure 9.2.

6. Choose File ➤ Save As and save this worksheet on disk as MACROLIB.WK4.

Using the Transcript Window to Develop Macros

You've now created two separate sheets of macros—COMPANY.WK4 and MACROLIB.WK4—by entering instructions directly from the keyboard. After this much experience, you may be happy to learn that 1-2-3 offers an alternate approach that often simplifies the process of planning and writing macros. The central tool in this method is called the Transcript window.

When you choose Tools ➤ Macro ➤ Record, 1-2-3 starts recording your subsequent actions in the Transcript window. The recordings are stored as macro instructions, using the key names and commands you've begun to learn about in this chapter. Once you've recorded a particular sequence of actions, you can copy the contents of the Transcript window to a worksheet, and use the copy to create a new macro.

To view the Transcript window, you choose the Tools ➤ Macro ➤ Show Transcript command. When the window is active, the Transcript menu replaces Range on the 1-2-3 menu bar, and a new set of SmartIcons appears above the worksheet. Using the SmartIcons and the commands from the Transcript menu, you can perform several important operations

9

Macros

with the Transcript window. Specifically, you can:

- Clear the entire current recording from the window, so you can start afresh with a new recording.

- Rerun a selection of keystrokes in the current recording to examine the actions they represent.

- Copy a selection of entries from the current recording to the Clipboard. Then you can paste this selection to a worksheet to create a new macro.

NOTE A macro you create by copying a selection from the Transcript window may not always be identical to an equivalent macro you would write yourself. There are almost always several different ways to structure a macro for a particular task, and the Transcript window has its own way of recording events.

The following exercise serves as a brief introduction to the Transcript window. In the course of this exercise, you'll create a new macro that converts formulas to values in a selected range, and then you'll copy this macro to your MACROLIB file. Close MACROLIB.WK4 for the moment; when you do so, 1-2-3 creates a new Untitled file for you to work with. Proceed with these steps:

1. In cell A1 of the new worksheet, enter the formula **@INT(@RAND*100)**. The result is a random integer between 0 and 100.

2. Select the range A1..A10, click the selection with the right mouse button, and choose the Copy Down command. Then press Home

to select A1. Ten random integers now appear in the range:

A	A
1	46
2	63
3	2
4	1
5	75
6	7
7	88
8	77
9	6
10	98
11	

Note that the integers on your sheet will not be the same as shown above—and the values will be recalculated as a result of some actions during the upcoming exercise. You'll use this range of formulas to test the macro you're about to develop.

3. Choose Tools ➤ Macro ➤ Show Transcript.

The empty Transcript window appears over your worksheet. (If it happens not to be empty, select its contents with the mouse, and press the Delete key.)

4. Choose Window ➤ Tile. 1-2-3 resizes the two open windows and displays them side-by-side, as shown in Figure 9.3.

5. With the cell pointer still positioned at cell A1 in the Untitled worksheet, choose Tools ➤ Macro ➤ Record.

The notation "Rec" appears in the fourth panel from the right side of the status bar to indicate that you have begun recording.

6. Choose Edit ➤ Copy (or click the Copy SmartIcon) to copy the contents of cell A1 to the Clipboard. An equivalent macro command appears in the Transcript window.

FIGURE 9.3

The Transcript window. By arranging the Transcript window next to a worksheet, you can view the recording that 1-2-3 creates as you perform actions in the worksheet.

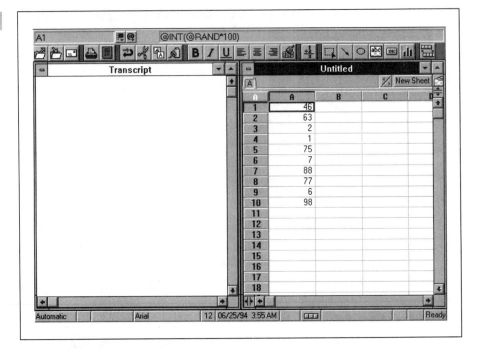

7. Choose Edit ➤ Paste Special. In the Paste Special dialog box, choose the Formulas as values option, and click OK:

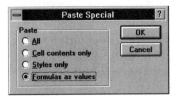

Two things happen when you complete this operation. First, the contents of cell A1 are transformed to the current value displayed in the cell (and the formula is lost, as you can see on the edit line). Also, a second new macro instruction appears in the Transcript window:

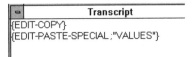

8. Choose Tools ➤ Macro ➤ Stop Recording. No further macro instructions will appear in the Transcript window during the remainder of this exercise.

9. Press ↓ to select cell A2.

10. Use your mouse to highlight the two instructions in the Transcript window; then choose Transcript ➤ Playback.

Back in the Untitled worksheet, 1-2-3 performs the Copy and Paste Special operations on cell A2. The formula in the cell is duly converted to a value, as you can see on the edit line. The macro you've recorded works correctly.

11. Highlight the two instructions in the Transcript window once again, and then choose Edit ➤ Copy or click the Copy SmartIcon. Then choose Tools ➤ Macro ➤ Hide Transcript to close the Transcript window.

12. Pull down the File menu and reopen the MACROLIB.WK4 file by choosing its name near the bottom of the menu list.

13. Select cell B9 in the sheet of macros, and press Ctrl+V to paste the two macro instructions into the sheet. Then add a macro name in cell A9, a title in B8, and a comment in column C, as shown below:

8	Convert Formulas to Values	Convert any formulas
9	\F {EDIT-COPY}	to their current values
10	{EDIT-PASTE-SPECIAL ;"VALUES"}	in the selected range.
11		

14. Select cell A9 and press Ctrl+R to assign the name \F to your new macro. Click the Save SmartIcon to update the MACROLIB.WK4 file on disk.

15. Finally press Ctrl+F6 to activate the Untitled worksheet. Select the range A3..A10 and press Ctrl+F to run the Convert macro. All the formulas in the range are converted to their current values. (You can now close this Untitled file without saving it.)

In short, the Transcript window is an excellent source of ready-made macro instructions, recorded from your own actions in 1-2-3 worksheets.

9

Macros

Of course, you're free to edit and modify any recording that you paste from the Transcript window. You can also combine recorded passages from the window with macro instructions that you write yourself; this is a common way to build a large macro project.

Creating a New SmartIcon for a Macro

Another significant step you can take in customizing 1-2-3 is to create a new SmartIcon to represent a macro you've written yourself. Any macro that you use during most sessions with 1-2-3 is a good candidate for a SmartIcon. So is a macro that performs a task you find inconvenient to perform or difficult to remember.

For example, in the upcoming exercise you'll create a new SmartIcon to represent the Convert macro you just developed. Actually, the Editing SmartIcon set already has a tool that's similar to the one you'll create:

The Paste Formulas SmartIcon converts formulas to their current values, but only after you select a range and copy the contents to the Clipboard.

In this exercise, you'll create a Convert Formulas SmartIcon that performs both steps of the operation—copying the current selection to the Clipboard and then pasting the current values back to the selection. When you're done, here's what your SmartIcon will look like in the default

SmartIcon set:

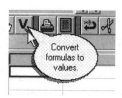

You'll be able to click this new icon to convert any formula or range of formulas into their current calculated values.

Developing an icon for a macro is a detailed process, but not really very difficult. The Tools ➤ SmartIcons command provides all the resources you need to complete the task. Using this command, you can

- Design a graphic to be displayed on the new SmartIcon.
- Attach a macro to the SmartIcon.
- Write a brief description that will appear in a bubble when the SmartIcon is selected.

Here are the steps for creating the Convert Formulas SmartIcon as a new tool in the default set:

1. Make sure the Default Sheet SmartIcon set is displayed at the top of the screen. If it isn't, click the SmartIcons selector on the status bar and choose the Default Sheet option.

2. In the MACROLIB.WK4 worksheet, select the range B9..B10, which contains the two instructions of the Convert macro. Press Ctrl+C to copy these instructions to the Clipboard.

3. Choose Tools ➤ SmartIcons. In the SmartIcons dialog box, click the Edit Icon button. A large dialog box named Edit Icon appears on the screen.

9

Macros

4. Click the New Icon button. In the Save as a New Icon dialog box, enter **VAL** as the file name for your new SmartIcon, and click OK:

The Edit Icon dialog box now displays a large blank icon in which you can create a new graphic.

5. Click the Paste Macro button. The instructions of the Convert macro (which you copied to the Clipboard back in step 2) appears in the text box labeled "Enter macro here."

6. Enter the following text into the Description text box: **Convert formulas to values.**

7. Use your mouse to draw a bold **V** in the large empty SmartIcon box, as shown in Figure 9.4.

This step takes a little practice and experimentation, but you'll quickly catch on to the technique of building a graphic pixel-by-pixel. Notice the color palette just beneath the SmartIcon box; you can make selections

Creating a new SmartIcon. In the Edit Icon dialog box you can create the graphic for a SmartIcon, attach a macro, and write a description.

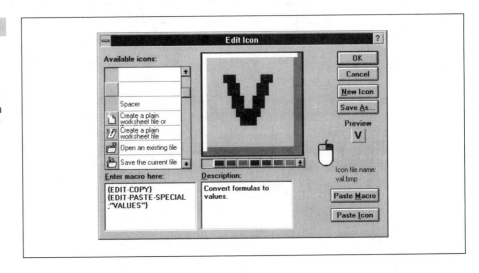

from this palette to add color to your graphic. (Feel free to draw a fancier graphic for this SmartIcon if you're so inclined.)

8. Click OK when you've completed the definition of the new SmartIcon. The SmartIcons dialog box remains on the screen.

9. Use the steps you learned back in Chapter 2 to replace the Mail SmartIcon with your new Convert Formulas SmartIcon (see page 90): Drag the Mail SmartIcon out of the Default Sheet set. Then find your new Convert Formulas SmartIcon at the bottom of the Available Icons list and drag it to its new position in the Default Sheet set.

10. Click OK to complete the operation. The Convert Formulas SmartIcon now appears in the icon palette at the top of the screen.

Now try experimenting with the tool you've created. On a blank sheet, enter some new formulas using the @RAND function. Then select the range of formulas and click the Convert Formulas SmartIcon. In response, 1-2-3 runs your macro and converts the formulas to their current values.

Restore the original Mail SmartIcon to its original place in the Default Sheet set if you wish. Choose Tools ➤ SmartIcons, drag the Convert Formulas SmartIcon out of the Default Sheet set, and drag the Mail SmartIcon back in.

Creating a Macro Button on a Worksheet

You can also create a *macro button* directly on a worksheet to represent a macro that's available only when the worksheet is open:

1. Click the Draw Macro SmartIcon and click the mouse at the worksheet location where you want to place the button. The

MACROS

Assign to Button dialog box appears on the screen:

2. In the "Enter macro here" box you can enter or paste the instructions of a macro.

3. In the Button text box, enter the text that will be displayed on the face of the button itself. Then click OK.

The button appears on the active worksheet. When you position the mouse pointer over the button, the pointer takes the shape of a hand with an index finger that seems poised to click the button; for example:

To run the macro, you simply click the button.

TIP

A macro button is a good tool to represent macros you develop for use only on a specific worksheet. For instance, suppose you've created some macros that perform operations on a database worksheet. You might add one or more macro buttons to the sheet to give the user an easy way to run your macros.

Writing Macro Programs

As you examine advanced macro programs, you'll begin learning about 1-2-3's significant vocabulary of macro commands. As you've seen, some commands are designed to perform menu operations. Others represent programming tasks such as decision making, repetition, and interaction with the user during the program run. Most macro commands require arguments, which you supply inside the braces after the command itself. Depending upon the requirement of a particular macro command, arguments may appear as values or labels; arithmetic, string, or logical expressions; functions; cell or range references; or range names.

One interesting example of a macro command is {GetLabel}. This command is a central element in an *interactive macro*, a program that pauses one or more times during the run to get input from the user at the keyboard. The {GetLabel} command displays a dialog box on the screen, asking the user for a particular item of information. After the user types the information and presses ↵, {GetLabel} copies the input as a label to a specified worksheet cell.

The {Get-Label} command takes six arguments, but several of them are optional:

> {Get-Label *prompt;range;default;title;x;y* }

9

Macros

Here are descriptions of the arguments:

ARGUMENT	DESCRIPTION
prompt	The input prompt that {Get-Label} displays in the dialog box.
range	A reference to the worksheet location where {Get-Label} will copy the input.
default	The text value that initially appears in the dialog box.
title	The text that appears in the title bar.
x and *y*	The horizontal and vertical coordinates where the dialog box will appear on the screen.

All of these arguments are optional except for *range*. Notice that there is one space between the command itself and the first argument, but no spaces between arguments. The entire command, with its arguments and braces, must appear in a single cell of the macro column. You can't break up a macro command into multiple cells.

You'll see examples of {Get-Label} in the sample macro presented in the next section of this chapter.

Creating an Interactive Macro

The Send Memo macro, shown in Figure 9.5, is a useful office tool for writing quick memos to business associates and co-workers. The program asks you to enter three strings of information from the keyboard, one at a time:

- The name of the person who is to receive the memo
- The name of the sender
- The text of the message itself

Given this information, the macro organizes the memo neatly on a worksheet, along with entries for the current date and time. It then defines the memo as a print range and displays the Print dialog box. When the macro

FIGURE 9.5

The Send Memo macro. This macro is an interactive program that automates the process of writing and printing business memos.

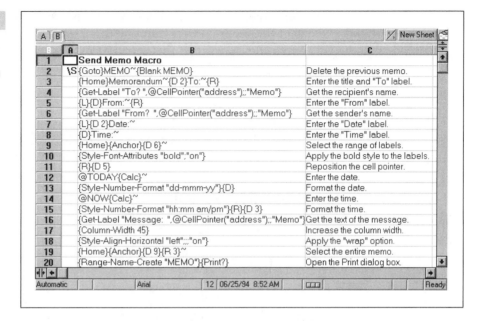

	B	C
1	Send Memo Macro	
2	\S{Goto}MEMO~{Blank MEMO}	Delete the previous memo.
3	{Home}Memorandum~{D 2}To:~{R}	Enter the title and "To" label.
4	{Get-Label "To? ",@CellPointer("address");;"Memo"}	Get the recipient's name.
5	{L}{D}From:~{R}	Enter the "From" label.
6	{Get-Label "From? ",@CellPointer("address");;"Memo"}	Get the sender's name.
7	{L}{D 2}Date:~	Enter the "Date" label.
8	{D}Time:~	Enter the "Time" label.
9	{Home}{Anchor}{D 6}~	Select the range of labels.
10	{Style-Font-Attributes "bold";"on"}	Apply the bold style to the labels.
11	{R}{D 5}	Reposition the cell pointer.
12	@TODAY{Calc}~	Enter the date.
13	{Style-Number-Format "dd-mmm-yy"}{D}	Format the date.
14	@NOW{Calc}~	Enter the time.
15	{Style-Number-Format "hh:mm am/pm"}{R}{D 3}	Format the time.
16	{Get-Label "Message: ",@CellPointer("address");;"Memo"}	Get the text of the message.
17	{Column-Width 45}	Increase the column width.
18	{Style-Align-Horizontal "left";;;"on"}	Apply the "wrap" option.
19	{Home}{Anchor}{D 9}{R 3}~	Select the entire memo.
20	{Range-Name-Create "MEMO"}{Print?}	Open the Print dialog box.

Automatic | Arial | 12 | 06/25/94 8:52 AM | | Ready

run is over, you can click the Preview button to view a preview of the memo, or click OK to print it.

The Send Memo macro is designed to be saved on disk as a self-contained program file. The file contains two sheets: Sheet A is reserved for the text of the memo created during a program run, and sheet B contains the macro itself. The contents of worksheet A change each time you run the macro. Follow these steps to create your own copy of this macro:

1. On a blank worksheet, use the Range ➤ Name command to assign the name **MEMO** to cell A:A1.

2. Click the New Sheet button to add sheet B to the window. Carefully enter the three columns of the Send Memo macro into worksheet B (copy the macro from Figure 9.5).

3. Select cell B:A2, where the macro name \S is displayed. Choose the Range ➤ Name command and click the Use Labels button to assign this name to B:B2, the first cell of the macro.

9

Macros

4. Select cell B:B2, and choose the Range ➤ Name command. Assign the second range name \0 (backslash, zero) to the cell. You'll learn the purpose of this second range name later in this chapter.

5. Save the file as MEMO.WK4.

Now you can try running the macro. Press Ctrl+S to start. The macro moves to worksheet A and displays the first input box on the screen, displaying "To?" as a one-word prompt. At this point you enter the name of the person to whom you're sending a memo:

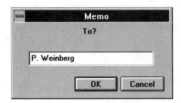

When you press ↵, the macro enters the name onto the memo worksheet. Then another dialog box appears with a new prompt, "From?" Here you enter the sender's name:

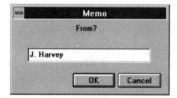

The macro does some more work on the memo worksheet, and then displays a third dialog box with the prompt "Message:". To complete your memo, you enter the text of your message in the text box. The message can be as long as 511 characters, or approximately one hundred words.

When you press ↵ at the end of the message text, the Memo macro enters and formats the message text. Then the Print dialog box appears on the screen, indicating the worksheet range that will be printed:

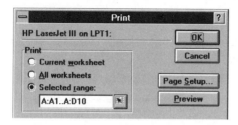

This is the end of the macro run. Figure 9.6 shows an example of the memo worksheet that the macro creates. As you can see, the memo's heading includes the names of the recipient and the sender, and the date and time when the memo was written. To view a preview of the memo, click the Preview button in the Print dialog box. An example of the Print Preview window appears in Figure 9.7.

Examining the Memo Macro

Although this macro is longer than the macros you created earlier in this chapter, it is really not much more complicated. Its major new element is

FIGURE 9.6

A memo created by
the Send Memo macro

	A	B	C	D
1	Memorandum			
2				
3	To:	P. Weinberg		
4	From:	J. Harvey		
5				
6	Date:	25-Jun-94		
7	Time:	09:02 AM		
8				
9				
10			Please examine the enclosed schedule for our upcoming conference on Computers for Lawyers. You will be teaching two seminars for intermediate spreadsheet users, and one general introduction to database management. I'm allowing extra time for you to prepare the spreadsheet course, because this isn't your usual topic. I know you'll do a fine job. Thanks. J.H.	
11				

9

Macros

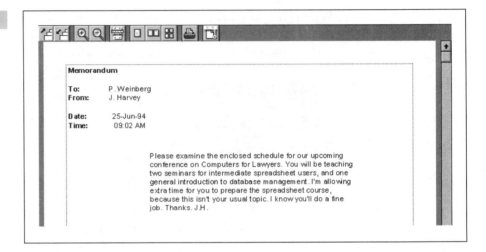

the {GetLabel} command. Here are brief line-by-line explanations of the program instructions, identified by their cell locations in worksheet B, shown back in Figure 9.5 (see page 519):

CELL	INSTRUCTION
B2	First a {Goto} instruction moves the cell pointer to the beginning of the MEMO range. This instruction is included in case worksheet B is active at the time the macro run begins. Then a macro command named {Blank} erases the former contents of the memo worksheet, stored in the range MEMO:

{Blank MEMO}

(As you'll see later, an instruction at the end of the macro reassigns the range name MEMO to the entire text of the current memo.)

CELL	INSTRUCTION
B3	The labels Memorandum and To: are entered into their respective cells in the memo worksheet.

CELL	INSTRUCTION
B4	A {Get-Label} instruction elicits the name of the person who is to receive the memo. Notice the format of the command:

{Get-Label "To? ",@CELLPOINTER
("address");;"Memo"}

The first augment, "To? ", is the prompt displayed in the input box. The second argument is a call to the special function @CELLPOINTER. Given an argument of "address", this function supplies a reference to the address of the current cell. The final argument supplies a title for the dialog box. (Notice the extra semicolon, representing an omitted argument.) Once the input is complete, the {Get-Label} command copies the input to the current location of the cell pointer.

B5	The label From: is entered onto the worksheet macro.
B6	Another {Get-Label} command elicits the name of the person who is writing the memo.
B7	The label Date: is entered onto the memo worksheet.
B8	The label Time: is entered.
B9	The macro selects all the labels in column A.
B10	The boldface style is applied to the range of labels, using the {Style-Font-Attributes} command.
B11	The cell pointer is moved down and to the right, to the location for today's date.
B12	The value of the @TODAY function is entered into the current cell:

@@TODAY{Calc}~

This instruction is equivalent to pressing the F9 function key while @TODAY is still displayed on the Edit line.

CELL	INSTRUCTION
B13	The {Style-Number-Format} command applies a date format to the date entry, and then the cell pointer is moved down by one position.
B14	The value of the @NOW function is entered into the current cell.
B15	The {Style-Number-Format} command applies a time format to the time entry. Then the cell pointer is repositioned for the message text.
B16	A third {Get-Label} command elicits the text of the message and then enters the entire long label into the current cell.
B17	The width of column C is increased to 45.
B18	The {Style-Align-Horizontal} command "wraps" the text of the memo within the cell that contains it.
B19	The entire range of the memo is selected.
B20	The program assigns the name MEMO to the range, and then uses the {Print?} command to display the Print dialog box.

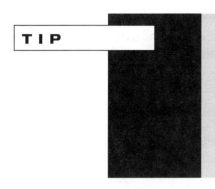

T I P

There are a couple of easy ways to get help with macro commands. When you've entered the name of a command into a cell (and before you press ⏎), press F1 to go directly to the Help topic devoted to the command. For a complete reference to all the macro commands available in 1-2-3, choose Help ➤ Contents, click the Macros button, and then select Macro Command Categories.

Creating an Autoexecute Macro

You'll recall that you assigned two different range names to the first cell in the Send Memo macro: \S and \0. You've seen the purpose of the first of these names; you can press Ctrl+S to run the macro.

The second name has a different purpose. Assigning \0 to a macro in a worksheet file creates an *autoexecute macro*. When you open a file from disk, 1-2-3 looks to see if the range name \0 exists anywhere in the worksheet. If it does, the macro with this name is automatically run as the first event on the newly opened worksheet.

You can see how this works with the MEMO.WK4 file. Close the file now without saving the current changes. Then pull down the File menu and select the file's name to reopen the worksheet. As soon as you do so, 1-2-3 runs the Send Memo macro. As you've seen, the macro begins by clearing the previous memo from worksheet A and displaying a dialog box on the screen to elicit the first input label.

9

Macros

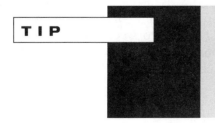

T I P

To open a file like MEMO.WK4 without performing the autoexecute macro that it contains, choose Tools ➤ User Setup and remove the *X* from the Run autoexecute macros option. When you next open the file, the macro will *not* be performed automatically.

Another way to automate macros is to create a macro file named AUTO123.WK4 in the *default* directory. The default directory is defined at the bottom of the User Setup dialog box:

Worksheet directory:

```
C:\123R5W\WORK
```

(Choose Tools ➤ User Setup to view or change the name of the default directory.) If a worksheet file named AUTO123.WK4 exists in this directory, 1-2-3 automatically opens the file at the beginning of each session. Furthermore, if the file contains an autoexecute macro named \0, the macro is run as the first action in the new session.

Summary

A macro is a program that records and performs a particular operation in the 1-2-3 environment. Macros can include literal keystrokes, specific menu commands, or detailed sequences of programmed activities. Lotus 1-2-3 has two categories of special reserved words that you can use in macros: macro key names and macro commands. The macro key names represent nonprinting keyboard operations, such as {Right}, {Alt}, {Home}, and {Anchor}. The tilde character (~) represents ↵. Macro commands perform specific programming activities; for example {Get-Label} elicits input from the user during a macro performance. (You'll learn more about macro commands in Chapter 12.)

You enter the instructions of a macro as labels in consecutive cells of a worksheet column. Assign a range name to the first cell of every macro, using the Range ➤ Name command. It is also a good idea to document a macro inside the worksheet: Include a column of range names at the left side of the macro, and a column of explanatory comments at the right. A worksheet that contains a collection of macros is sometimes known as a macro library. When you open such a worksheet, all the macros in the library are available for use.

There are two ways to run a macro, depending upon the macro's range name. For convenience, you can assign a special two-character range name consisting of the backslash character followed by a letter from A to Z; this name allows you to run the macro directly from the keyboard. For example, you press Ctrl+M to run a macro named \M. Alternatively, if a macro has an ordinary range name (not the backslash and a letter) you must use the Tools Macro Run command to run it.

Macros can be automated, and integrated into the 1-2-3 environment. A macro with the name \0 (backslash, zero) is an autoexecute macro; 1-2-3 starts a run of this macro as soon as you open the worksheet that contains it. A macro library stored in the default 1-2-3 directory with the file name AUTO123.WK4 is automatically opened at the beginning of each session with 1-2-3. In addition, you can use the Tools ➤ SmartIcons command to assign a macro to a new SmartIcon you create, and then to add the SmartIcon to the palette.

The Transcript window can help you develop certain kinds of macros. When you choose Tools ➤ Macro ➤ Record, this window records your activities in macro format. To view the Transcript window, choose the Tools ➤ Macro ➤ Show Transcript command. Then use a copy-and-paste operation to copy a selection of instructions from the Transcript window to a macro worksheet.

9

Macros

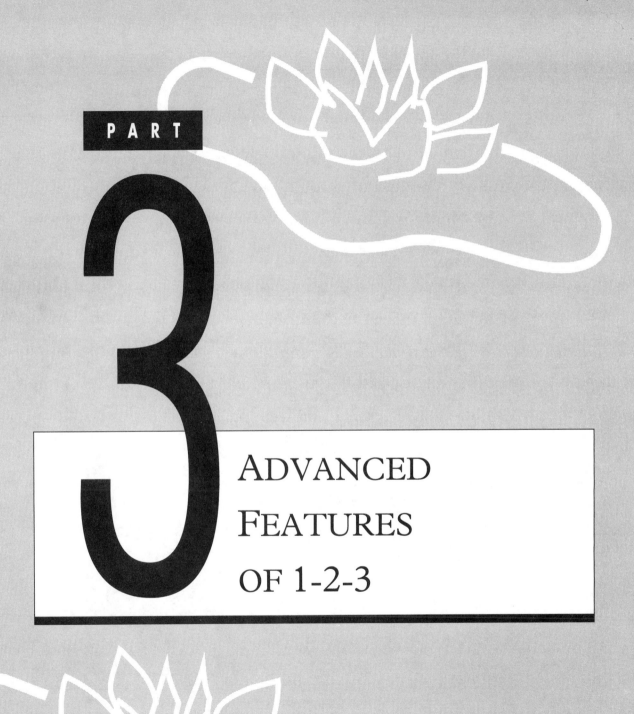

3

ADVANCED
FEATURES
OF 1-2-3

CHAPTER 10

Advanced Worksheet Tools

fast TRACK

- **To build a worksheet based on a SmartMaster,**   **537**

  choose File ➤ New and select a SmartMaster from the New File dialog box. (In the Tools ➤ User Setup dialog box, make sure the "Skip New File dialog box" option is unchecked, and the "Run autoexecute macros" option is checked before you choose File ➤ New.)

- **To save versions and scenarios of a worksheet,**   **543**

  open the worksheet for which you want to create versions. Choose Range ➤ Version and click Create to define a new version. For each new version, you can change values directly on the worksheet while the Version Manager dialog box is open. After creating a set of versions, click the To Index button. In the Version Manager Index box, select the versions that you want to include in the scenario, and click the Scenario button.

- **To create a one-variable what-if table,**   **563**

  enter a column of input values at the left side of the table range, and enter one or more formulas at the top of each column in the table range. Create an *input cell* where 1-2-3 will substitute the input values one at a time to develop the what-if table. Select the table range, and choose Range ➤ Analyze ➤ What-if Table. Select 1 from the Number of variables list and enter a reference to the input cell in the Input cell 1 box.

- **To recalculate a defined what-if table,**   **566**

  press the F8 function key.

● **To create a two-variable what-if table,**   567

  enter a column of values at the left side of the table range for a first input cell, and a row of values at the top of the table range a the second input cell. Enter the target formula into the upper-left corner of the table range. Select the table range, and choose Range ➤ Analyze ➤ What-if Table. Select 2 from the Number of variables list, and enter references into the Input cell 1 and Input cell 2 boxes.

● **To analyze a complex data problem on a worksheet,**   572

  create a range of logical formulas to represent the constraints. Then choose the Range ➤ Analyze ➤ Solver command. Specify the adjustable cells, the constraint cells, and the optimum formula cell, and click OK.

● **To find the input value that yields a target result from a worksheet formula,**   577

  choose the Range ➤ Analyze ➤ Backsolver command. Specify the formula location, the target result, and the adjustable cell, and click OK.

● **To count the number of values that belong to specified numeric categories,**   579

  create a bin range that defines the categories. Then select the values range, and choose Range ➤ Analyze ➤ Distribution. Enter a reference to the bin range and click OK.

● **To analyze the mathematical correlation between two or more columns of values,**   581

  choose Range ➤ Analyze ➤ Regression. Enter the X-range, Y-range, and output range and click OK.

-2-3 furnishes several powerful tools designed to help you create, organize, and analyze worksheets:

- *SmartMasters* are professional-quality templates you can use as the basis for a variety of practical business worksheets.

- The *Version Manager* gives you simple and convenient ways to store and compare different versions of data in a single worksheet.

- The commands of the Tools ➤ Analysis menu perform advanced analytical calculations on the numeric information in a sheet.

This chapter presents these important features as independent topics that you can read in any order you want. Along the way, you'll also find information about other relevant commands in the File, Tools, and Range menus.

Preparing a Sample Worksheet

In some of this chapter's exercises, you'll work with an abbreviated form of the Conference worksheet that you first developed in Chapters 3 and 4. Figure 10.1 shows this new version of the worksheet. You can create it by reentering all the data and formulas into a new worksheet; if you choose this approach, Figure 10.2 shows the formulas you should enter into column H. Save this new file as CONF2.WK4.

Alternatively, you can copy a range of data from the original CONF.WK4 file and then reformat and reorganize the worksheet to match Figure 10.1. The File ➤ Open command contains a Combine button that simplifies this task. This operation copies data to the current worksheet

FIGURE 10.1

The shortened version of the Conference worksheet

	A	B	C	D	E	F	G	H
1	Computing for Video Stores				Projected Revenues			
2	Place	St. Louis			Attendance			$12,675.00
3	Date	15-Oct-94			Video Sales		$35.00	$1,137.50
4	Attendance	65			**Total Revenues**			**$13,812.50**
5	Price	$195.00						
6					Projected Expenses — Fixed			
7					Conference Room			$1,500.00
8					Video Production			$1,000.00
9					Promotion			$3,500.00
10					Travel			$800.00
11					**Total Fixed Expenses**			**$6,800.00**
12								
13					Projected Expenses — Variable by Attendance			
14					Conference Materials		$8.25	$536.25
15					Coffee and Pastries		$3.25	$211.25
16					Box Lunch		$4.75	$308.75
17					**Total Variable Expenses**			**$1,056.25**
18								
19					Projected Profit			$5,956.25
20								

FIGURE 10.2

The formulas in column H of the CONF2.Wk4 file

	B	C	D	E	F	G	H	I
1	r Video Stores			Projected Revenues:				
2	St. Louis			Attendance			+$B$5*B4	
3	15-Oct-94			Video Sales		$35.00	+G3*B4/2	
4	65			**Total Revenues**			@SUM(H2..H3)	
5	$195.00							
6				Projected Expenses — Fixed				
7				Conference Room			$1,500.00	
8				Video Production			$1,000.00	
9				Promotion			$3,500.00	
10				Travel			$800.00	
11				**Total Fixed Expenses**			@SUM(H7..H10)	
12								
13				Projected Expenses — Variable by Attendance				
14				Conference Materials		$8.25	+$G14*B$4	
15				Coffee and Pastries		$3.25	+$G15*B$4	
16				Box Lunch		$4.75	+$G16*B$4	
17				**Total Variable Expenses**			@SUM(H14..H16)	
18								
19				Projected Profit			+H4-(H11+H17)	
20								

from a file stored on disk. Here's an outline of this approach:

1. If necessary, choose the File ➤ New command to open a new blank worksheet.

2. Choose File ➤ Open. Use the Drives and Directories boxes to find the directory location of the original CONF.WK4 file, and select the file in the File name box. Then click the Combine button at the right side of the Open File dialog box:

3. The Combine 1-2-3 File dialog box appears. Click the Range option and enter **A5..F34** as the range from which to copy data:

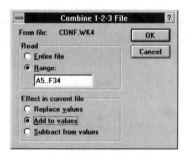

4. Click OK to complete the operation. In response, 1-2-3 copies the data from CONF.WK4 to your current worksheet.

5. Delete the final column of data and the extra blank rows from the worksheet. Enter the label **Attendance** in cell A4. Then move ranges of data to their new positions on the worksheet, as shown in Figure 10.1.

As you do so, 1-2-3 automatically makes the appropriate adjustments in the worksheet's formulas. (In the end, the formulas in column H should be the same as shown in Figure 10.1.)

6. Confirm that these adjustments have been made correctly by entering a new attendance projection of **65** in cell B4; in response,

1-2-3 recalculates the worksheet formulas that depend on this value, including the bottom-line profit.

7. To complete your work, apply the appropriate formats and styles to the worksheet. Then choose the File Save As command and save the file on disk as CONF2.WK4.

Close the CONF2 file for now. You'll open it again when you need it for specific exercises in this chapter.

Using SmartMasters to Streamline Your Work

Much of the work that people do in spreadsheets falls into certain generic categories. Budgets, expense reports, invoices, purchase orders, time sheets, financial statements, loan amortizations, sales records—these worksheets are reinvented time and time again by business people everywhere.

In Release 5.0, Lotus supplies standard forms of these worksheets in a library of *templates* known as *SmartMasters*. Each SmartMaster creates a professionally designed worksheet, complete with formulas, instructions, sample data, macros, and one-click techniques for accomplishing major tasks.

When you open a new worksheet based on a SmartMaster, 1-2-3 copies all the information from the SmartMaster to your new worksheet. You can then begin entering data and completing operations on the worksheet. When you're done, you save the worksheet under a file name of your choice. The original SmartMaster template is left intact for future reuse.

Setting Up for SmartMasters

You select a SmartMaster by choosing the File ➤ New command. But first you have to make sure that some important options are set correctly in the User Setup dialog box. Choose Tools ➤ User Setup and examine the beginning of the Options list:

The option labeled "Skip New File dialog box" must be *un*checked to provide access to the New File dialog box. If this option is checked, click it once to remove the *X* from the check box.

At some point during your work in the previous chapters, you may have activated the Skip New File dialog box option. When this option is checked, the File ➤ New command instantly opens a new blank worksheet without displaying a dialog box. Up to now, this is exactly what you've wanted to happen. But to see a list of SmartMasters when you choose File ➤ New, you now need to uncheck Skip New File option.

Further down the User Setup dialog box comes another option that is important to your work with SmartMasters:

☒ Run autoexecute macros

SmartMasters contain macros that run in the background to simplify your work. These include *autoexecute* macros designed to run as soon as a worksheet is opened. In order for these macros to operate properly, the User Setup option labeled "Run autoexecute macros" must be on. If it isn't, click the option to place an *X* in the corresponding check box.

NOTE

As you'll recall from Chapter 9 (see page 525), an autoexecute macro is assigned the special name \0 (backslash, zero). Whenever you open a worksheet, 1-2-3 looks for a macro that has this name. If it exists, 1-2-3 runs it automatically at the outset.

10

Worksheet Tools

Once these two options are set correctly, you're ready to start using SmartMasters.

Creating a Worksheet Based on a SmartMaster

Now when you choose File ➤ New, the New File dialog box appears, as shown in Figure 10.3. The list of SmartMasters is the central feature of this dialog box. You can browse through the list for a preview of what each of these tools does. When you highlight a name in the list, the Comments box gives a brief description of the SmartMaster you've selected. For example, Figure 10.3 shows the description of the SmartMaster named "Amortize a Loan."

FIGURE 10.3

The New File dialog box. This dialog box lists the names of 1-2-3 SmartMasters.

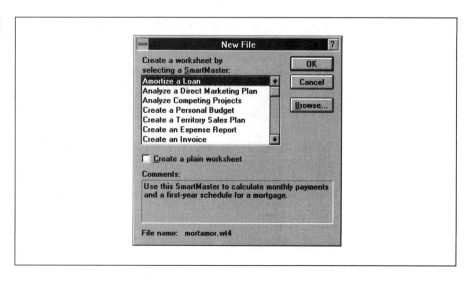

Here are the general steps for creating a new worksheet based on a Smart-Master:

1. Choose File ➤ New.

2. In the New File dialog box, scroll down the list of SmartMasters until you see the one you want. Click its name to select it.

3. Click OK. 1-2-3 opens a new worksheet and copies data, formats, formulas, and macros from the template to the worksheet.

A Table of Contents, describing the various features that the SmartMaster offers, appears as the first sheet of the file. For example, Figure 10.4 shows the Table of Contents for the Mortgage Amortization SmartMaster.

FIGURE 10.4

The Table of Contents for the Mortgage Amortization SmartMaster. Click a button to go to the feature you want to use.

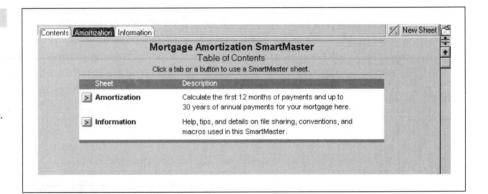

4. Click the button representing the feature you want to go to, and then begin entering your own data into the sheet that the Smart-Master provides.

For example, Figure 10.5 shows the Mortgage Amortization worksheet. The input area—where you enter the information about a particular mortgage—is near the upper-right corner of the sheet. As you enter data, the SmartMaster builds the Payments table shown in the lower part of the sheet.

FIGURE 10.5

A sheet produced by the Mortgage Amortization SmartMaster. To create a payment table for a particular mortgage, you simply begin entering data in the input area near the upper-right corner of the sheet.

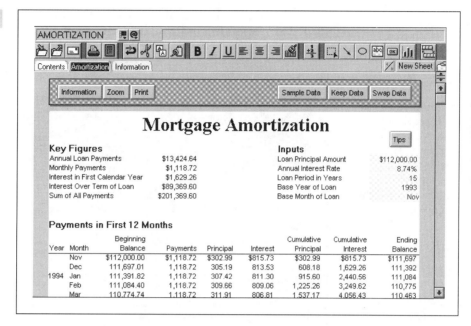

5. Click the Information button to get help with your work, or click other buttons at the top of the sheet to perform specific operations on your data.

6. When you've completed the worksheet, choose File ➤ Save and enter a new name for your file.

Although each SmartMaster has its own organization and purpose, the worksheet files produced by SmartMasters all have similar features. Figure 10.6 shows another example, a sheet from the Expense Report Smart-Master. Notice that the file consists of three tabbed sheets, labeled Contents, Expense Report, and Information. Buttons at the top of the sheet provide shortcuts for moving around the file and for accomplishing specific tasks related to expense data.

Finally, each SmartMaster comes with extensive information about usage and features. To view the index for a given SmartMaster, click the Information button in the table of contents, or click the Information tab from anyplace in the file. Figure 10.7 shows the Information Index for the Expense Report SmartMaster. As you can see, there are buttons labeled

Overview, Steps, Tips, and so on; clicking one of these buttons leads you to the corresponding information section.

FIGURE 10.6

FIGURE 10.6

A sheet produced by the Expense Report SmartMaster. The file contains three sheets, and several buttons that you can click to run the macros in the SmartMaster.

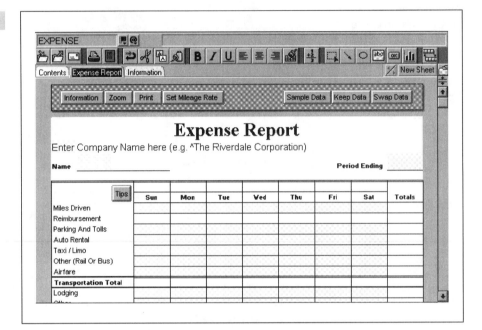

FIGURE 10.7

The Information Index for the Expense Report SmartMaster. Click any button to go to a particular information section.

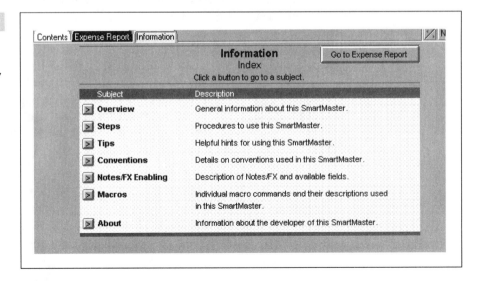

TIP   If you wish, you can even take a look at the macros included in a SmartMaster. Click the Macros button in the Information Index. When you do so, a previously hidden Macros sheet appears. Scroll through the sheet to see the macros that operate behind the scenes in the SmartMaster. Click Hide Macros to return to the Index.

TIP   To create a new blank worksheet—not based on a SmartMaster—choose File ➤ New and select the option labeled "Create a plain worksheet." Then click OK. If you're not planning to work with SmartMasters for a while, choose Tools ➤ User Setup and check the "Skip New File dialog box" option again.

Understanding the Version Manager

The Version Manager allows you to save many different versions and combinations of data within a single worksheet file. Using the Version Manager, you can quickly switch to a different data set—or to a combination of several data sets—and view the new calculations that result on your worksheet. Although the Version Manager offers a wide variety of features, its basic operations are easy to use on any worksheet you've developed. Whenever you find yourself changing the data on a worksheet frequently over time—and wishing you could keep records of previous data sets—the Version Manager is the tool you need.

A first look at the Version Manager   The Version Manager actually consists of two main windows, titled Version Manager and Version Manager

Index. To begin exploring the features of these windows, try this exercise:

1. Open any worksheet on which you might want to develop multiple versions of data. (You'll work with the CONF2.WK4 worksheet in the *next* exercise; open it now if you wish.) The Version Manager is most effective on a worksheet that contains a combination of data and formulas.

2. Choose Range ➤ Version. The Version Manager window appears over the top of your worksheet:

Once you begin creating versions, this window gives you direct access to any set of data you've saved. The Version Manager is conveniently sized so that you can keep it on the screen while you're viewing and changing the data on your worksheet.

3. Click the To Index button at the lower-right corner of the Version Manager window. When you do so, the Version Manager Index window appears on the screen:

This window gives you an overview of all the versions you've saved on the current worksheet. It also allows you to combine several versions together in a group called a *scenario*.

4. Click the To Manager button in the lower-right corner of the Version Manager Index window.

The Version Manager window returns to the screen. You can switch between these two windows at any time while you are developing versions and scenarios on a worksheet.

5. Click the Close button to close the Version Manager.

The versions and scenarios you create with the Version Manager are retained as part of your worksheet when you save the file to disk. To work with them again, you simply reopen the worksheet and choose Range ➤ Version.

TIP

The Version Manager and Version Manager Index windows can be resized, maximized, minimized, or restored to their original dimensions. You'll probably find that the Version Manager window is easiest to work with in its original size— large enough to display all its major features, but small enough to stay out of your way as your work with data on worksheets. By contrast, the Version Manager Index window is often most convenient in its maximized form, especially after you've developed a long list of versions and scenarios. The Index window gives you an overview of all the data sets you've saved on the worksheet.

TIP

The Version Manager stays in the foreground—that is, in front of your worksheet—until you close it. But you can activate your worksheet and make changes in your data even while the Version Manager window is displayed. To switch from the Version Manager window to the worksheet, press Alt+F6 or simply click a cell on the worksheet. Likewise, press Alt+F6 to switch back to the Version Manager window, or simply click one of its controls with the mouse.

Using the Version Manager

The best way to learn to use the Version Manager is to begin experimenting with it on a worksheet you've already developed. The shortened Conference worksheet is an ideal example. Imagine that the managers at Computing Conference, Inc., are experimenting with various pricing levels and attendance estimates in an attempt to predict the profitability of a given conference. Specifically, they want to study the result of varying three values on the CONF2 worksheet: the per-person price of the conference, the attendance estimate, and the unit price of the conference video. The managers want to try several different versions of the data, as illustrated in the following table:

	Minimum	Medium	Maximum
Attendance	65	95	135
Price	$195	$225	$245
Video	$35	$40	$50

Although this table contains only nine data values, the numbers can be combined in many different ways on the Conference worksheet. For example, you might want to examine the result of combining all the minimum or all the maximum values, or you might want to see what happens to the profit when you combine the minimum price with the maximum attendance. The Version Manager puts all these possibilities at your fingertips.

Open CONF2.WK4 now if you haven't already. In the following exercise, you'll set up these versions on the Conference worksheet and you'll learn how to use the Version Manager and Version Manager Index windows to experiment with the results:

1. Select cell B4, the location of the attendance estimate.

The value stored in this cell is currently 65. The cell is unnamed at the moment. The Version Manager will assign it a range name when you create your first version.

2. Choose Range ➤ Version. The Version Manager window appears on the screen. Initially no versions are defined for the worksheet; the Named range and With version(s) boxes are empty.

3. Click the Create button at the lower-left corner of the Version Manager window. The Create Version dialog box appears on the screen:

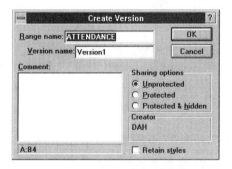

1-2-3 suggests ATTENDANCE as the range name for B4, copying the label from cell A4.

4. Press Tab to select the Version name box and enter **Minimum** as the name of the version. Then press Tab again to select the Comment text box, and enter **Lowest likely attendance.**

5. Click OK to create the version. The Version Manager window now shows the cell's range name and the name of the version you've created:

6. Press Alt+F6 to activate the worksheet, where B4 is still the current cell. Enter a new value of **95** into the cell. Then press Alt+F6 again to activate the Version Manager.

7. Repeat steps 3, 4, and 5 to create a new version, this time entering **Medium** as the version name and **Middle-range attendance estimate.** as the comment. Click OK on the Create Version dialog box to complete the definition.

8. Create a third version by entering **135** into cell B4 and clicking the Create button. Enter **Maximum** as the new version name and **Highest possible attendance.** as the comment. Then click OK.

You've now created three versions for the Attendance cell.

9. Click the down-arrow button at the right side of the With version(s) box, and 1-2-3 shows you a list of all three version names:

T I P

For a useful guide to the buttons and other controls displayed in the Version Manager window, click the ? button at the upper-right corner of the window. The Range Version Manager help topic contains a "live" picture of the Version Manager window. Click any control in this picture and a pop-up box provides a brief description of the control. A similar help feature is available for the Version Manager Index window. When you've learned all you need to know, press Escape to close the Help window and return to your worksheet.

Choosing a Version

To switch data on the worksheet—that is, to view the effect of any one of these versions on the bottom-line profit—you simply select one of the names in the With version(s) list. For example, click the Medium version. When you do so, 1-2-3 enters the medium attendance estimate into cell B4 and instantly recalculates all the formulas that depend on that value. As you can see in Figure 10.8, the entire worksheet shows the result of the change.

FIGURE 10.8

Viewing the result of a newly selected version. When you select a new version name in the Version Manager window, the worksheet instantly shows you the result of the change.

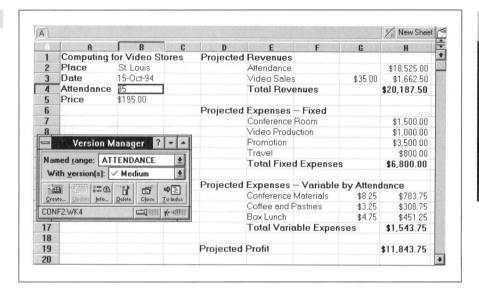

Next you'll define versions for the conference price and the video price. In each case, you'll begin by creating a version name for the current value displayed on the worksheet, and then you'll create two additional versions for new values that you enter. Follow the same steps you used to create three versions of the attendance estimate.

Conference price versions When you create the first version for the conference price in cell B5, 1-2-3 suggests PRICE as the range name for the cell. Here are the values, version names, and comments to enter for this cell:

Value	Version Name	Comment
$195	Minimum	1993 pricing.
$225	Medium	1994 pricing.
$245	Maximum	1995 pricing.

Video price versions The per-unit video price is displayed in cell G4. When you define the first version for this cell, enter VIDEO as the range name. Then enter the following values, version names, and comments for the cell:

Value	Version Name	Comment
$35	Minimum	1993 pricing
$40	Medium	1994 pricing
$50	Maximum	1995 pricing

Now you've defined nine different versions of the Conference worksheet. Viewing any one of these versions on the worksheet is a two-step process:

1. Click the down-arrow button at the right side of the Named range box, and choose the name of the cell in which you want to see a new version:

2. Click the down-arrow button next to the With version(s) box and choose the version you want to see.

Spend some time now experimenting with this process. Each time you choose a new version, 1-2-3 recalculates all the formulas that depend on the new data value, and displays the new results.

TIP

In this example, each version represents a value for a single cell of the Conference worksheet. By contrast, you can define version names for ranges of cells. The range for a version may include values, formats, and even formulas. When you select the version in the Version Manager window, 1-2-3 restores the contents of the entire range.

The Version Manager Index Window

Now click the To Index button at the lower-right corner of the Version Manager window. Click the maximize button at the upper-right corner of the Version Manager Index window. As you can see in Figure 10.9, this window displays an outline of all the versions you've created. The information about a given version includes the range name, the version name, the name of the person who created the version, the date the version was created, and the comment for the version. Check marks in the list indicate which versions are currently active on your worksheet.

FIGURE 10.9

The Version Manager Index, with a list of all the versions you've created in the Conference worksheet

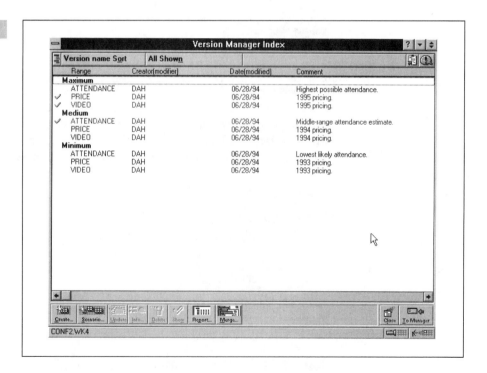

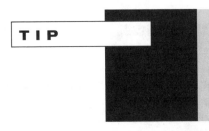

You can use the Version Manager Index window to select any combination of versions to view on your worksheet. To change the current version, double-click any version name in the Index list. Then switch to your worksheet to view the result.

Views of the index The Sort button, located near the upper-left corner of the Index window, allows you to change the order in which versions are listed. (The button is initially labeled "Version name Sort," but the label changes each time you select a different sort option.) When you click this button, a list of options appears:

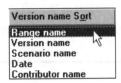

Select any of these options to change the view of the Index list. For example, select the Range name option, and 1-2-3 reorganizes the index by range names rather than by version names, as shown here:

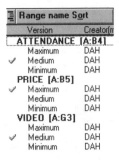

Buttons in the Version Manager Index window At the bottom of the Version Manager Index window you can see a variety of important tools, including the Scenario and Report buttons:

- The Scenario button opens the Create Scenario dialog box, where you can combine two or more versions and define them as a scenario.

- The Report button opens the Version Report dialog box, which you use to create a report from versions defined on your worksheet.

You'll round out your introduction to the Version Manager by looking briefly at each of these features.

Creating Scenarios

A *scenario* gives you a quick way to switch to several different versions in one step. In a scenario you combine a group of versions to produce a particular result on your worksheet. When you choose the scenario, all the versions are selected at once.

Suppose the managers at Computing Conferences, Inc., would like to compare two combinations of data, which they refer to as the Highest Price and Medium Price scenarios:

- In the Highest Price scenario, they'll apply the maximum conference price per person; as a result of the high price, they anticipate only medium attendance at the event.

- In the Medium Price scenario, they'll use the middle conference price; as a result, they expect the maximum attendance.

They'll use the medium video price for both of these scenarios. Their question is clear: Which of these strategies results in the highest profit?

With the Version Manager Index window still displayed on the screen, follow these steps to create these two scenarios:

1. Begin by selecting the three version names for the first scenario: Hold down the Ctrl key and click the medium attendance, the maximum price, and the medium video version names in the

Index list. 1-2-3 highlights all three versions in the list:

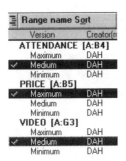

2. Click the Scenario button at the bottom of the Index window.

The Create Scenario dialog box appears on the screen. The Selected versions list, at the lower-left corner of the dialog box, shows the names of the three versions you've selected.

3. Enter **Highest Price** as the name for the scenario you're about to create. Then enter **Expect only medium attendance.** into the Comment box. At this point, the Create Scenario dialog box appears as follows:

4. Click OK. The scenario you've defined is now listed in the Index window.

5. Click the Sort button at the upper-left corner of the window, and choose the Range name option to return to the list of ranges and versions.

6. Select the three version names for the second scenario: Hold down the Ctrl key and click the maximum attendance, the medium price, and the medium video versions.

7. Click the Scenario button again. The Create Scenario dialog box reappears.

8. In the Create Scenario dialog box, enter **Medium Price** as the scenario name and **Expect maximum attendance.** as the comment.

9. Click OK to complete the scenario. The Index window now lists the elements of both scenarios you've created:

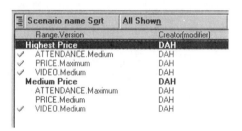

10. Click the Outline button located just to the left of the Sort button. (The Outline button collapses or expands the outline displayed in the Index list.) Now only the two scenario names are displayed, not the versions they represent.

11. Click the Restore button at the upper-right corner of the Index window. The window now appears as follows:

Move the window toward the left side of the screen so that you can see most of the information on your worksheet. You can now switch quickly between these two scenarios by simply double-clicking a scenario name in the Version Manager Index list. For example, double-click the Medium Price scenario, and then take a look at the Projected Profit figure at the lower-right corner of the worksheet, as shown in Figure 10.10. This scenario results in a much higher profit calculation than the Highest Price scenario.

FIGURE 10.10

Changing the scenario. Here the Medium Price scenario results in a higher profit calculation than the Highest Price scenario.

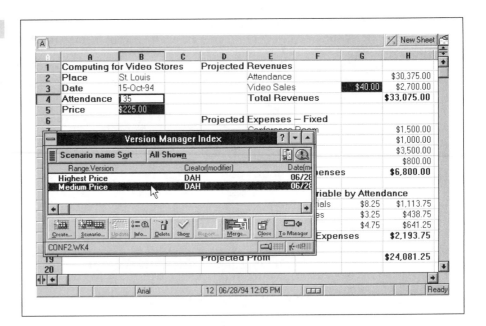

Creating a Report from the Version Manager

Finally, the Report button on the Version Manager Index window allows you to create a summary of the results from several versions. 1-2-3 creates a new worksheet for each report you create from the Version Manager. You can then reformat, save, and print the report.

For example, suppose you want to compare profit calculations for the three versions of attendance data, while holding the conference price and the video price constant at their medium levels. Here are the steps for producing a report for this comparison:

1. Maximize the Version Manager Index window.

2. Click the Sort button and choose the Range name option.

3. Click the Outline button to expand the view of range names and versions. Make sure the Medium versions are checked for both the PRICE and VIDEO ranges. (If they aren't, double-click the appropriate version names with the mouse.)

4. Click the Report button at the bottom of the window. The Version Report dialog box appears on the screen.

5. Pull down the list labeled "Report on named range" and choose the ATTENDANCE range.

6. In the Versions list, click each of the three version names in turn. 1-2-3 highlights all three of them, as you can see in Figure 10.11.

7. Enter **H19** in the range box labeled "Include results for formulas from this range."

8. In the Include group, keep the Version data option checked, but uncheck the Audit information option. The Version Report dialog box now appears as shown in Figure 10.11.

9. Click OK. 1-2-3 creates a new worksheet file named RE-PORT01.WK4, and creates the report in the worksheet.

10. Reformat the numeric values and adjust the column widths to produce a readable report, as shown below:

	A	B	C	D
2	Named range	ATTENDANCE (A:B4)		
3				
4	Version name	Maximum	Medium	Minimum
5	Version cells			
6				
7	A:B4	135	95	65
8				
9	Formula results			
10				
11	A:H19	$24,081.25	$14,931.25	$8,068.75
12				

FIGURE 10.11

The Version Report
dialog box

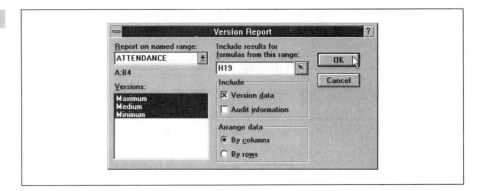

This report compares the profit calculations resulting from each of the three attendance versions. When you've finished looking at it, you can save it to disk or close it without saving. Then activate the CONF2.WK4 file, choose File ➤ Save As, and save your work as VERSIONS.WK4. (This step leaves the original CONF2.WK4 file intact and unrevised for upcoming exercises.)

In summary, the Version Manager is an excellent tool to use whenever you need to save and investigate different sets of data in a single worksheet.

The Audit Command

To understand fully the result of a version or scenario, you may sometimes need to review the inner organization of your worksheet. Specifically, you may want a quick way to review the locations of formulas and to find out how formulas interact on the sheet. The Tools ➤ Audit command proves useful in this context. You can use this command to find:

- All cells that contain formulas.

- All values that are part of the result of a selected formula. These are known as *precedent cells*.

- All formulas that are directly or indirectly dependent on the value in a selected cell. These are known as *dependent formulas*.

These operations are represented by the first three options in the Audit dialog box:

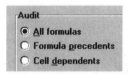

To see how this command works, try the following exercise on the Conference worksheet:

1. Choose Tools ➤ Audit and select the All formulas option. Then click OK. In response, 1-2-3 highlights all the cells that contain formulas:

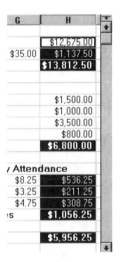

2. Select cell H19, the location of the profit projection. Then choose Tools ➤ Audit, select the Formula precedents option, and click OK. 1-2-3 highlights all the values that play a part in the profit calculation.

3. Select cell B4, the location of the attendance estimate. Then choose Tools ➤ Audit, select the Cell dependents option, and click OK. 1-2-3 highlights all the cells containing formulas that are dependent on the attendance value.

Use the Audit command whenever you need a quick review of the formulas behind your worksheet.

The Tools of the Range ➤ Analyze Menu

The seven commands in the Range ➤ Analyze menu provide a variety of mathematical techniques for analyzing data in a worksheet:

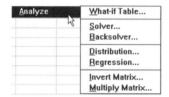

Here are brief summaries of these commands:

COMMAND	DESCRIPTION
What-if Table	Calculates worksheet formulas multiple times while varying the data in one, two, or three input cells.
Solver	Produces worksheet scenarios from a system of variables, formulas, and constraints that you specify.
Backsolver	Finds the numeric input value that produces a desired result in a selected worksheet formula.
Distribution	Counts the number of entries that belong to specified numeric categories.

COMMAND	DESCRIPTION
Regression	Examines the correlation between sets of numeric data, in a series of calculations known as *regression analysis*.
Invert Matrix	Produces the inverse of a square matrix.
Multiply Matrix	Performs matrix multiplication between two matrices. You can use the two matrix operations together to find solutions for simultaneous equations.

In the upcoming sections you'll see examples of each of these commands.

Using the What-if Table Command

The What-if Table command is a tool for exploring multiple what-if scenarios on a worksheet. For example, consider the shortened Conference worksheet that you developed at the beginning of this chapter (see Figure 10.1 on page 535). Most of the formulas on this worksheet depend directly or indirectly on the values entered for the attendance level and the per-person attendance price. These two key values appear in cells B4 and B5, respectively:

A	A	B	C
1	Computing for Video Stores		
2	Place	St. Louis	
3	Date	15-Oct-94	
4	Attendance	65	
5	Price	$195.00	
6			

By changing the values in one or both of these cells, you can explore *individual* changes in the bottom-line profit (cell H19) under different projections for attendance and price.

But in some applications you may want to build an entire *table* of what-if projections. For example, in the conference worksheet you might want to examine a table of profit calculations for a range of attendance and price levels:

B	A	B	C	D	E
1	Profits				
2			Price		
3			$145.00	$170.00	$195.00
4	Attendance	65	$2,706.25	$4,331.25	$5,956.25
5		75	$4,168.75	$6,043.75	$7,918.75
6		85	$5,631.25	$7,756.25	$9,881.25
7		95	$7,093.75	$9,468.75	$11,843.75
8		105	$8,556.25	$11,181.25	$13,806.25
9		115	$10,018.75	$12,893.75	$15,768.75
10		125	$11,481.25	$14,606.25	$17,731.25

This is an example of a *two-variable* table; each profit calculation is the result of a change in both the attendance projection and the price. To create this table manually you would have to enter many different values into cells B4 and B5, and then copy each of the resulting profit calculations to your table from cell H19. Fortunately, this is exactly the kind of task that the What-if Table command is designed to automate.

Choose the Range ➤ Analyze ➤ What-if Table command now. In the What-if Table dialog box, click the down-arrow button located just to the right of the box labeled "Number of variables." This command allows you to build tables with one, two, or three variables:

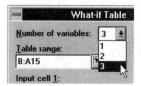

Click Cancel to close the dialog box. In upcoming sections you'll learn to create all three types of what-if tables.

Creating a One-Variable What-if Table

To create a one-variable what-if table you begin by preparing three ranges of information:

- A column of input values that 1-2-3 can insert one at a time into the worksheet calculations.

- The input location where these values will be substituted one at a time.

- The formula that 1-2-3 will recalculate after each new input entry.

For example, Figure 10.12 shows a range of attendance projections in A10..A18. The goal of the upcoming operation is to display the profit amounts corresponding to each of these attendance values. To produce this information, 1-2-3 needs to insert each of the attendance figures into the input cell, B4, and then recalculate the formula that gives the profit. Accordingly, cell B9 contains a copy of the profit formula: +H4–(H11+H17), or the total revenues minus the sum of the fixed and variable expenses.

FIGURE 10.12

Preparing for a one-variable what-if table. The text format has been applied to the formula in cell B9 so you can see exactly how the table is created.

	A	B	C	D	E	F	G	H
1	Computing for Video Stores			Projected Revenues				
2	Place	St. Louis			Attendance			$12,675.00
3	Date	15-Oct-94			Video Sales		$35.00	$1,137.50
4	Attendance	65			Total Revenues			$13,812.50
5	Price	$195.00						
6					Projected Expenses – Fixed			
7					Conference Room			$1,500.00
8	Attendance	Profit			Video Production			$1,000.00
9		+H4-(H11+H17)			Promotion			$3,500.00
10	45				Travel			$800.00
11	55				Total Fixed Expenses			$6,800.00
12	65							
13	75				Projected Expenses – Variable by Attendance			
14	85				Conference Materials		$8.25	$536.25
15	95				Coffee and Pastries		$3.25	$211.25
16	105				Box Lunch		$4.75	$308.75
17	115				Total Variable Expenses			$1,056.25
18	125							
19					Projected Profit			$5,956.25
20								

You can use the What-if Table command successfully after you've entered the column of input values and the target formula. Here are the steps for producing the table:

1. Enter **45** into cell B10 and **55** in cell B11. Then select B10..B11 and use the drag-and-fill mouse technique to extend this series of values down to cell A18, as shown in Figure 10.12.

2. Enter the formula **+H4–(H11+H17)** into cell B9. Click the Format selector, the first panel of the status bar, and select the Text format for this cell so you can see the formula itself.

3. Enter the labels **Attendance** and **Profit** into cells A8 and B8, respectively. Right-justify the label in B8, and apply the Bold style to cells A8, B8, and B9. Apply the US Currency style to the range B10..B18.

4. Select the range A9..B18.

5. Choose Range ➤ Analyze ➤ What-if Table.

The What-if Table dialog box appears. Notice that the Table range box contains a reference to the range you've selected; this is where 1-2-3 will build the what-if table.

6. Pull down the Number of variables list and choose 1.

7. Enter a reference to cell **B4** in the Input cell 1 box. The dialog box now appears as follows:

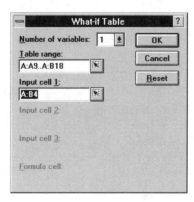

8. Click OK to confirm. Back on the worksheet, move the cell pointer to A7, out of the way of the what-if table.

9. Choose the File Save As command and save this worksheet as WHATIF.WK4. (The original file, named CONF2.WK4, remains unchanged on disk for upcoming exercises.)

As a result of these steps, 1-2-3 fills in the what-if table with a range of profit calculations in B10..B18:

A	B	C
1 Computing for Video Stores		
2 Place	St. Louis	
3 Date	15-Oct-94	
4 Attendance	65	
5 Price	$195.00	
6		
7		
8 Attendance	Profit	
9	+H4-(H11+H17)	
10	45	$2,031.25
11	55	$3,993.75
12	65	$5,956.25
13	75	$7,918.75
14	85	$9,881.25
15	95	$11,843.75
16	105	$13,806.25
17	115	$15,768.75
18	125	$17,731.25
19		

Each of these figures represents the value that would appear in cell H19 of the worksheet if you were to enter the corresponding attendance value into cell B4. The What-if Table command has generated the entire column of figures in a single operation.

This command also allows you to create one-variable what-if tables for more than one formula at a time. For example, suppose you want to add a column to display the expenses corresponding to each of the projected attendance levels:

1. Enter the formula **@SUM(H14..H16)** into cell C9 to accomplish this.

2. Select the range A9..C18, and choose Range ➤ Analyze ➤ What-if Table again. Specify **B4** as the input cell, and click OK.

The results of this second formula appear in the range C10..C18:

	Attendance	Profit	Variable Expenses	
6				Prc
7				
8	Attendance	Profit	Variable Expenses	
9		+H4-(H11+H17)	@SUM(H14..H16)	
10	45	$2,031.25	$731.25	
11	55	$3,993.75	$893.75	
12	65	$5,956.25	$1,056.25	
13	75	$7,918.75	$1,218.75	Prc
14	85	$9,881.25	$1,381.25	
15	95	$11,843.75	$1,543.75	
16	105	$13,806.25	$1,706.25	
17	115	$15,768.75	$1,868.75	
18	125	$17,731.25	$2,031.25	
19				Pro

Using the F8 Function Key to Recalculate a What-if Table

The entries that 1-2-3 places in the what-if table are values, not formulas; they are therefore not subject to automatic recalculation when you make changes on the worksheet. However, 1-2-3 gives you a convenient way to repeat the last What-if Table operation: Simply press the F8 function key. For example, suppose you make some changes in the column of input values in A10..A18. After you revise the entries in this range, pressing F8 produces a new version of the what-if table.

Try this exercise with the F8 key:

1. Use the drag-and-fill operation to enter a new range of attendance projections into A10..A18—values from **60** to **220** in step increments of **20**.

2. Press the F8 function key.

The new what-if table appears as follows:

	Attendance	Profit	Variable Expenses	
6				Prc
7			Variable	
8	Attendance	Profit	Expenses	
9		+H4-(H11+H17)	@SUM(H14..H16)	
10	60	$4,975.00	$975.00	
11	80	$8,900.00	$1,300.00	
12	100	$12,825.00	$1,625.00	
13	120	$16,750.00	$1,950.00	Prc
14	140	$20,675.00	$2,275.00	
15	160	$24,600.00	$2,600.00	
16	180	$28,525.00	$2,925.00	
17	200	$32,450.00	$3,250.00	
18	220	$36,375.00	$3,575.00	
19				Pro

Creating a Two-Variable Table

To prepare a two-variable table, you begin by entering a column of values for the first input cell, and a row of values for the second input cell. For example, suppose you want to generate a profit table for a range of attendance projections and a range of prices. To do so, you enter the attendance values down a column, just as you did for the one-variable table. Then you enter the range of prices across a row at the top of the table range. In the upper-left corner cell of the table range you enter the formula that 1-2-3 will use for calculating the what-if table.

In the following exercise, you'll generate a two-variable what-if table in worksheet B of the WHATIF.WK4 file:

1. Click the New Sheet button to add worksheet B to the file.

2. In cell B:A2, enter the formula **+A:H4-(A:H11+A:H17)**. Apply the text format and the bold style to this cell, and widen column A so that the entire formula is displayed within the width of the column.

3. Enter the **Prices** as a right-aligned label in B:B1. Then enter **Attendance** into cell B:A1. Apply the bold style to both labels.

4. Use the drag-and-fill operation to enter a column of attendance projections into the range B:A3..B:A12—values from **45** to **135** in increment steps of **10**.

5. Use drag-and-fill again to enter a row of prices in the range B:C2..B:F2—values from **145** to **220** in increments of **25**.

6. Select the range B:B2..B:E12 and apply the US Dollar format.

7. Select the range B:A2..B:E12, and choose Range ➤ Analyze ➤ What-if Table. Notice that the range you've selected appears in the Table range box.

8. Pull down the Number of variables list and choose 2.

9. Enter **A:B4** as the reference to Input cell 1, and **A:B5** as the reference for Input cell 2, as shown here:

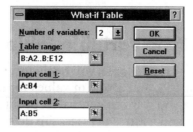

10. Click OK to confirm.

Here is the resulting what-if table:

B	A	B	C	D	E
1	Attendance	Prices			
2	+A:H4-(A:H11+A:H17)	$145.00	$170.00	$195.00	$220.00
3	45	($218.75)	$906.25	$2,031.25	3156.25
4	55	$1,243.75	$2,618.75	$3,993.75	5368.75
5	65	$2,706.25	$4,331.25	$5,956.25	7581.25
6	75	$4,168.75	$6,043.75	$7,918.75	9793.75
7	85	$5,631.25	$7,756.25	$9,881.25	12006.25
8	95	$7,093.75	$9,468.75	$11,843.75	14218.75
9	105	$8,556.25	$11,181.25	$13,806.25	16431.25
10	115	$10,018.75	$12,893.75	$15,768.75	18643.75
11	125	$11,481.25	$14,606.25	$17,731.25	$20,856.25
12	135	$12,943.75	$16,318.75	$19,693.75	$23,068.75
13					

As you can see, 1-2-3 has calculated forty different what-if scenarios in the conference worksheet. The profit figures resulting from these scenarios are displayed in the range B:B3..B:E12.

Creating a Three-Variable Table

A three-variable what-if table is organized over a three-dimensional worksheet range. Each worksheet in the range contains a column of entries for the first input cell and a row of entries for the second input cell, just as in a two-variable table. But instead of entering a formula in the upper-left corner of the table, you enter a value for the third input cell. Each worksheet in the three-dimensional range displays a different value in this cell. You then specify the formula for the what-if table in the What-if Table dialog box rather than in the table range itself.

For example, worksheets C, D, and E in Figure 10.13 are prepared for a three-variable what-if table. The purpose of this example is to generate profit scenarios by varying the values in three input cells: the attendance estimate (A:B4), the per-person admission price (A:B5), and the cost of renting a conference room (A:H7). The range B3..B7 on each of the three worksheets displays a column of attendance projections, and the range C2..G2 displays a row of conference prices. In cell B2, each worksheet contains a different dollar amount for the conference room rental.

FIGURE 10.13

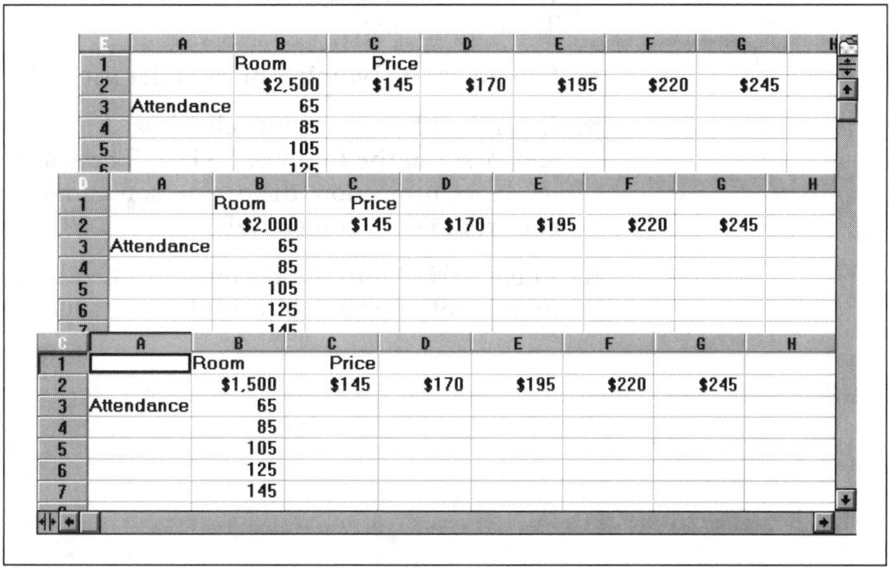

Preparing for a three-variable what-if table. Cell B2 represents the third variable; it contains a different dollar amount on each of the sheets.

Here are the steps for creating this three-variable what-if table in your own copy of the WHATIF.WK4 worksheet:

1. With the cell pointer located in worksheet B, click the New Sheet button three times to add sheets C, D, and E to the file.

2. Choose View ➤ Split, select the Perspective option, and click OK to view the three new sheets all at once.

3. Enter the labels and values into worksheet C, and format them as they appear in Figure 10.13. Then use copy-and-paste operations to copy the contents of worksheet C to worksheets D and E. Enter a new value of **$2,000.00** into cell D:B2 and a new value of **$2,500.00** into cell E:B2.

4. Select the three-dimensional range C:B2..E:G7. To do so, begin by selecting the two-dimensional range C:B2..C:G7 on worksheet C; then hold down the Shift and Ctrl keys while you press the PgUp key twice. When you release all the keys, the selection appears as in Figure 10.14.

5. Choose Range ➤ Analyze ➤ What-if Table. Notice that a reference to the three-dimensional range you've selected appears in the Table range box.

6. Pull down the Number of variables list and choose 3.

7. Enter **A:B4** in the Input cell 1 box, **A:B5** in the Input cell 2 box, and **A:H7** in the Input cell 3 box. These are references to the attendance projection, the per-person admission price, and conference room cost, respectively.

8. Enter **A:H19** into the Formula cell text box; this is a reference to the profit formula in worksheet A. When you finish all these

entries, the What-if Table dialog box appears as follows:

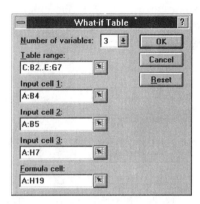

9. Click OK to confirm the entries in the dialog box. Back in the worksheet, select the three-dimensional range C:C3..E:G7 and apply the US Dollar format. Then press the Home key to position the cell pointer at C:A1.

10. Click the Save SmartIcon to update the WHATIF.WK4 file on disk.

FIGURE 10.14

A three-dimensional range for the what-if table. You can select this range by selecting B2..G7 on sheet C and then pressing Shift+Ctrl+PgUp twice.

E	A	B	C	D	E	F	G	H
1		Room	Price					
2		$2,500	$145	$170	$195	$220	$245	
3	Attendance	65						
4		85						
5		105						
6		125						

D	A	B	C	D	E	F	G	H
1		Room	Price					
2		$2,000	$145	$170	$195	$220	$245	
3	Attendance	65						
4		85						
5		105						
6		125						
7		145						

C	A	B	C	D	E	F	G	H
1		Room	Price					
2		$1,500	$145	$170	$195	$220	$245	
3	Attendance	65						
4		85						
5		105						
6		125						
7		145						

ADVANCED WORKSHEET TOOLS

Figure 10.15 shows the what-if table that 1-2-3 creates in response to these steps. In this example, 1-2-3 has calculated 75 different scenarios of the conference worksheet and has copied the profit figure from each scenario to the what-if table.

FIGURE 10.15

A three-variable what-if table

	A	B	C	D	E	F	G	H
1		Room	Price					
2		$2,500	$145	$170	$195	$220	$245	
3	Attendance	65	$1,706.25	$3,331.25	$4,956.25	$6,581.25	$8,206.25	
4		85	$4,631.25	$6,756.25	$8,881.25	$11,006.25	$13,131.25	
5		105	$7,556.25	$10,181.25	$12,806.25	$15,431.25	$18,056.25	
6		125	$10,481.25	$13,606.25	$16,731.25	$19,856.25	$22,981.25	

	A	B	C	D	E	F	G	H
1		Room	Price					
2		$2,000	$145	$170	$195	$220	$245	
3	Attendance	65	$2,206.25	$3,831.25	$5,456.25	$7,081.25	$8,706.25	
4		85	$5,131.25	$7,256.25	$9,381.25	$11,506.25	$13,631.25	
5		105	$8,056.25	$10,681.25	$13,306.25	$15,931.25	$18,556.25	
6		125	$10,981.25	$14,106.25	$17,231.25	$20,356.25	$23,481.25	
7		145	$13,906.25	$17,531.25	$21,156.25	$24,781.25	$28,406.25	

	A	B	C	D	E	F	G	H
1		Room	Price					
2		$1,500	$145	$170	$195	$220	$245	
3	Attendance	65	$2,706.25	$4,331.25	$5,956.25	$7,581.25	$9,206.25	
4		85	$5,631.25	$7,756.25	$9,881.25	$12,006.25	$14,131.25	
5		105	$8,556.25	$11,181.25	$13,806.25	$16,431.25	$19,056.25	
6		125	$11,481.25	$14,606.25	$17,731.25	$20,856.25	$23,981.25	
7		145	$14,406.25	$18,031.25	$21,656.25	$25,281.25	$28,906.25	

Using the Solver

The Solver command is designed to calculate meaningful variations in a worksheet, in response to specific patterns that you define. You typically use this command on worksheets that contain interrelated formulas of some complexity. To set up a successful problem for the Solver, you need to identify the following elements in your worksheet:

- **Adjustable cells.** Cells containing numeric values that you want the Solver to modify are called the *adjustable cells*.

- **Constraint cells.** A range of cells containing logical formulas are known as the *constraint cells*. You write these formulas to impose limits on the changes that the Solver can make in the adjustable values.

- **Optimal cell.** A formula for which you want to find the optimum result within the constraints defined on your worksheet is known as the *optimal cell.*

For example, consider Figure 10.16, a worksheet from one of the regional offices of Computing Conferences, Inc. To conduct its computer-training conferences, this office uses instructors who are full-time employees of the company, along with other instructors who work for the company on a short-term contractual basis. This worksheet analyzes the costs related to these two groups of workers. The goal of applying the Solver to this worksheet is to determine the most cost effective mix of employee and contract instructors.

At the present time, the regional office has four employee instructors along with a group of six contract instructors. Here is how the information about these two groups is organized:

- The top section of the worksheet shows the costs related to the four employees: Their individual salaries, benefits, and support costs appear in E3..E5, and the totals for the four employees are calculated in F3..F5. In addition, cell B4 displays the current number of employee instructors, 4.

FIGURE 10.16

Analyzing the mix of instructors. In preparation for the Solver, this sheet has two adjustable cells (B4 and B12), three constraint cells (E18..E20), and an optimal cell (F15).

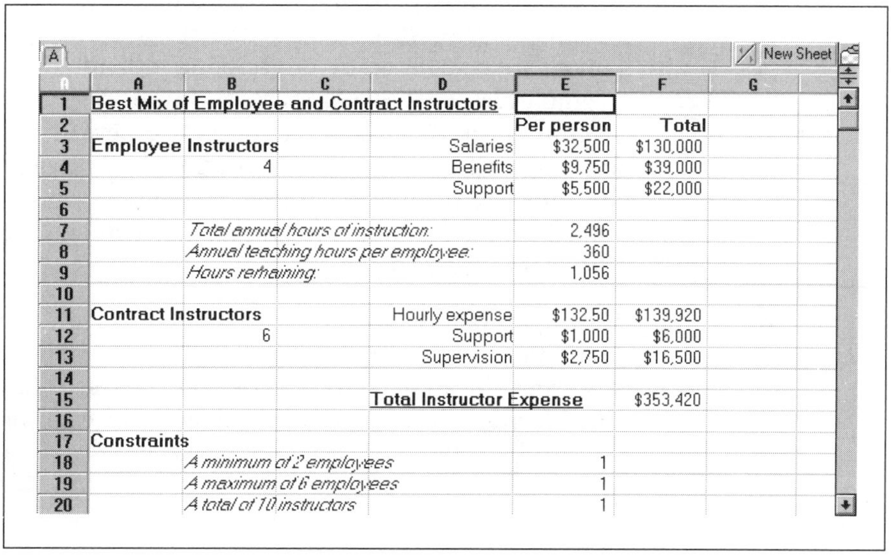

	A	B	C	D	E	F	G
1	Best Mix of Employee and Contract Instructors						
2					Per person	Total	
3	Employee Instructors			Salaries	$32,500	$130,000	
4		4		Benefits	$9,750	$39,000	
5				Support	$5,500	$22,000	
6							
7		*Total annual hours of instruction:*			2,496		
8		*Annual teaching hours per employee:*			360		
9		*Hours remaining:*			1,056		
10							
11	Contract Instructors			Hourly expense	$132.50	$139,920	
12		6		Support	$1,000	$6,000	
13				Supervision	$2,750	$16,500	
14							
15				Total Instructor Expense		$353,420	
16							
17	Constraints						
18		*A minimum of 2 employees*			1		
19		*A maximum of 6 employees*			1		
20		*A total of 10 instructors*			1		

- Rows 7, 8, and 9 display information about the number of hours of instruction: the total number of instruction hours planned for a given year (E7); the number of hours assigned per year to each individual employee (E8); and a calculation of the number of remaining hours that must be assigned to contract instructors (E9).

- The next section down the worksheet shows information about the contract instructors. Cell B12 shows the current number of contract instructors, 6. The average hourly rate paid to these instructors appears in cell E11, and the corresponding total cost of this hourly instruction for the year is in F11. Rows 12 and 13 show the support and supervision costs related to these contract instructors.

- The total costs for both groups of instructors is calculated in cell F15.

- Finally, rows 18, 19, and 20 describe the constraints that will apply to the Solver's calculations on this worksheet: There should be a minimum of two employee instructors, and a maximum of six. The combined number of employee and contract instructors is fixed at ten. The logical formulas expressing these constraints are in the range E18..E20; as you can see, all three formulas yield values of true for the current data.

Figure 10.17 displays the formulas that calculate the data and the constraints on this worksheet. In the range F3..F5, the total employee expenses are calculated by multiplying individual expenses by the number of employees. Cell E9 computes the number of instruction hours assigned to contract instructors—the difference between the total annual hours, and the total hours taught by employees. The range F11..F13 calculates the expenses related to contract instructors, and the @SUM function in cell F15 finds the total costs for all instructors. Finally, the constraint formulas appear in E18..E20.

When you choose Range ➤ Analyze ➤ Solver, a dialog box titled Solver Definition appears on the screen. In this dialog box you identify the worksheet locations of the adjustable values, the constraints, and the optimal formula in your Solver problem. For example, here are the correct

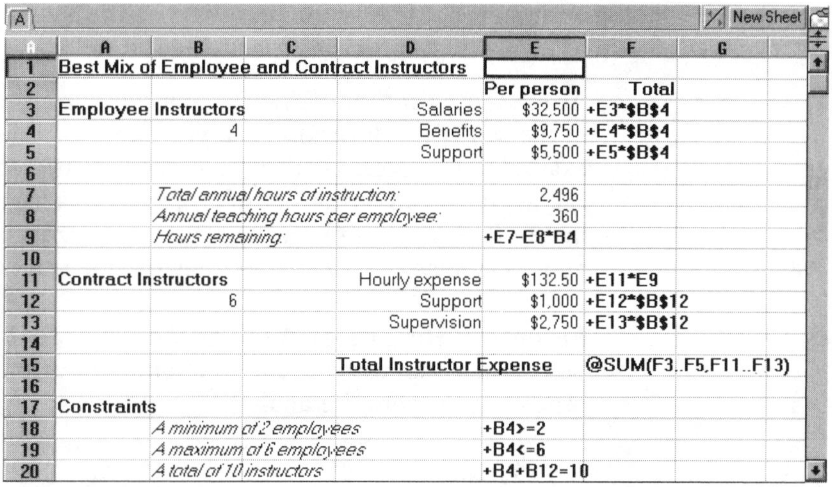

FIGURE 10.17

Formaulas behind the instructor-mix worksheet. The constraint cells are entered as logical expressions resulting in values of *true*.

	A	B	C	D	E	F	G
1	Best Mix of Employee and Contract Instructors						
2					Per person	Total	
3	Employee Instructors			Salaries	$32,500	+E3*$B$4	
4		4		Benefits	$9,750	+E4*$B$4	
5				Support	$5,500	+E5*$B$4	
6							
7		Total annual hours of instruction:			2,496		
8		Annual teaching hours per employee:			360		
9		Hours remaining:			+E7-E8*B4		
10							
11	Contract Instructors			Hourly expense	$132.50	+E11*E9	
12		6		Support	$1,000	+E12*$B$12	
13				Supervision	$2,750	+E13*$B$12	
14							
15				Total Instructor Expense		@SUM(F3..F5,F11..F13)	
16							
17	Constraints						
18		A minimum of 2 employees			+B4>=2		
19		A maximum of 6 employees			+B4<=6		
20		A total of 10 instructors			+B4+B12=10		

references and ranges for the instructor-mix worksheet:

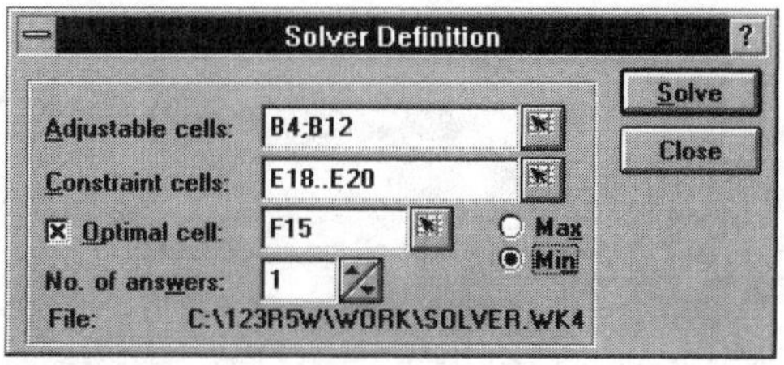

The adjustable cells are B4 (the number of employee instructors) and B12 (the number of contract instructors). The constraint cells are in the range E18..E20. The optimal cell is F15—the location of the formula that calculates the total cost of instructors. The Solver can find the minimum or maximum value for the optimal formula. In this example, the option button labeled Min has been selected, because the goal of this analysis is to find the instructor mix that results in the lowest cost.

Once you've defined a problem by making the appropriate entries in the Solver Definition dialog box, you are ready to begin the analysis. To do so, you click the Solve button. When 1-2-3 completes the analysis, a new dialog box named Solver Answer takes the place of the Solver Definition box. The Solver finds two answers in this example—one of which is the optimal result; consequently you see the message "Optimal answer (#1 of 2)" in the Solver Answer dialog box.

At the same time, you'll notice that the Solver has actually made changes in the worksheet locations that you designated as the adjustable cells. For example, in Figure 10.18 the Solver has entered a new value of 6 in cell B4, as the optimal number of employee instructors; and a new value of 4 in cell B12 as the optimal number of contract instructors. The total expense associated with this optimal instructor mix is $346,020, in cell F15.

Buttons in the Solver Answer dialog box The Solver Answer dialog box contains an assortment of command buttons you can use to examine other results from the analysis:

BUTTON	USE
Next	Displays the next-best answer the Solver has found for your problem.

FIGURE 10.18

The optimal answer from the Solver analysis. The Solver has replaced the values in the adjustable cells (B4 and B12) and recalculated the optimal cell (F15) accordingly.

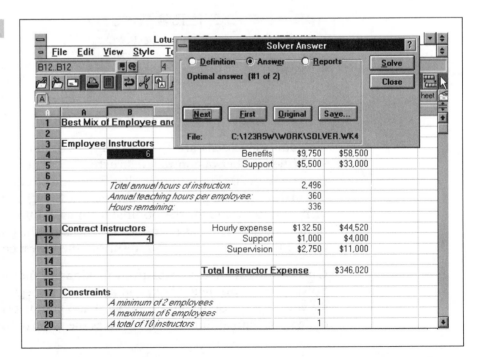

10

Worksheet Tools

BUTTON	USE
First	Goes back to the optimal answer.
Original	Displays the data values as they were displayed before the Solver analysis.
Reports	Displays the Solver Reports dialog box. This dialog box offers a number of special-purpose reports from the analysis:

You request a report by selecting a report type from the dialog box and clicking Table or Cell. If you select Table, 1-2-3 creates a new worksheet file for the report. If you select the Cell option, the report appears in a dialog box on the screen.

Using the Backsolver Command

The Backsolver is a simple but valuable tool to use when you want to work backward through a worksheet scenario—specifically when you have determined a bottom-line figure as your projection or goal, and you want to discover the input value necessary to achieve this goal. For example, suppose you want to find the attendance level necessary to yield a total profit of $10,000 on the CONF2.WK4 worksheet. One way to find the correct attendance value would be to experiment with new entries in cell B4 until you find the value that gives a profit of $10,000. But this trial-and-error approach could be time-consuming.

The 1-2-3 Backsolver performs this task for you much more efficiently. To use this command successfully, you supply three items of information:

- A worksheet cell that contains the target formula for the Backsolver operation.

- The projected value that you want this formula to yield.

- The cell containing the input value that 1-2-3 will adjust in order to achieve the specified result from the target formula.

In the following exercise you'll experiment with the Backsolver on the CONF2.WK4 worksheet:

1. Reopen the CONF2.WK4 worksheet from disk.

2. Choose Range ➤ Analyze ➤ Backsolver.

3. In the Make cell box, enter a reference to **H19**, the cell that contains the profit formula.

4. Enter **10000** in the Equal to value text box; this is the value that you want the profit formula to yield.

5. In the By changing cell text box, enter a reference to cell **B4**, which contains the current attendance projection; this is the cell that you want 1-2-3 to adjust, in order to achieve the desired profit projection. The Backsolver dialog box now appears as follows:

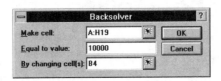

6. Click OK to perform the Backsolver operation.

When you complete this operation, the worksheet looks like Figure 10.19. As you can see, an attendance level of about 86 people is necessary to achieve a profit of $10,000. To avoid changing the original CONF2.WK4 file, save this version of the worksheet under a new name, or close it without saving.

	A	B	C	D	E	F	G	H
1	Computing for Video Stores			Projected Revenues				
2	Place	St. Louis			Attendance			$16,692.99
3	Date	15-Oct-94			Video Sales		$35.00	$1,498.09
4	Attendance	86			Total Revenues			$18,191.08
5	Price	$195.00						
6					Projected Expenses — Fixed			
7					Conference Room			$1,500.00
8					Video Production			$1,000.00
9					Promotion			$3,500.00
10					Travel			$800.00
11					Total Fixed Expenses			$6,800.00
12								
13					Projected Expenses — Variable by Attendance			
14					Conference Materials		$8.25	$706.24
15					Coffee and Pastries		$3.25	$278.22
16					Box Lunch		$4.75	$406.62
17					Total Variable Expenses			$1,391.08
18								
19					Projected Profit			$10,000.00
20								

Using the Distribution Command

The Distribution command counts the number of entries that fall within specified numeric categories. To prepare for this command, you begin by entering a series of numbers into a column of the worksheet. These numbers, known as the *bin range*, express the numeric intervals into which you want to distribute a range of values. Then you select the *values range*—that is, the worksheet range that is the subject of the frequency distribution. Given these two ranges, the Data Distribution command creates a new column of numbers representing the frequency count.

For example, Figure 10.20 shows a use of this command on the Yrs field in the Instructor database. (This database was discussed in Chapter 7, starting on page 399.) Four fields have been copied to this worksheet from the database. As you'll recall, Yrs is a calculated field that shows the number of years each instructor has worked for Computing Conferences, Inc. The purpose of this particular worksheet is to count the number of instructors whose length of employment falls within each of several categories: one year or less, one to two years, two to three years, and so on. The bin range representing these categories appears in F7..F12.

FIGURE 10.20

Using the Data
Distribution command.
The bin range is
F7..F12. The values
range is D4..D20.

	A	B	C	D	E	F	G
1	Instructor Database						
2							
3	ID	Last	First	Yrs		Frequency Distribution	
4	S-125	Ashford	W.	4.7			
5	W-145	Banks	S.	1.6		Years as	Number of
6	D-143	Cody	L.	1.6		Instructor	Instructors
7	A-146	Daniels	A.	0.7		1	3
8	W-119	Davis	G.	4.6		2	2
9	T-128	Eng	R.	4.3		3	2
10	S-127	Gill	P.	4.6		4	1
11	S-149	Harris	P.	1.0		5	5
12	W-124	Meyer	J.	4.7		6	3
13	A-103	Perez	D.	5.6			1
14	W-113	Porter	D.	5.5			
15	D-139	Porter	M.	2.8			
16	T-133	Ramirez	F.	4.0			
17	S-155	Roberts	P.	0.4			
18	D-137	Sanchez	W.	2.8			
19	N-101	Schwartz	B.	5.9			
20	D-106	Weinberg	P.	6.1			

Once you have established the bin range, using the Data Distribution command is simple. Here are the steps to produce the frequency distribution shown in G7..G13:

1. Select the values range, in this case the data in the Yrs field, D4..D20.

2. Choose Range ➤ Analyze ➤ Distribution. The range you've selected appears in the Range of values text box.

3. Enter **F7..F12** in the Bin range text box, as shown here:

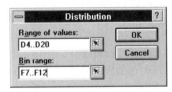

4. Click OK to complete the operation.

The command instantly enters the frequency distribution into the column located immediately to the right of the bin range. In Figure 10.20, you can see that there are three instructors who have worked for one year or less; two who have worked between one and two years; and so on. In addition, you'll notice that the frequency distribution range contains one more entry than the bin range. The final entry shows the number value-range entries found to be greater than the last entry in the bin range. In this example, there is one instructor who has worked for more than six years.

Using the Regression Command

Regression analysis is an attempt to discover the strength of the mathematical correlation between two or more sets of data. For example, column B of the following worksheet shows the amount that Computing Conferences, Inc. has spent on advertising for several recent computer-training conferences; and column C shows the attendance at those same conferences:

	A	B	C
1	Computing Conferences, Inc.		
2	Attendance and Advertising		
3	*Computing for Video Stores*		
4			
5	Date	Advertising	Attendance
6	09-Jan-93	$5,000	154
7	21-Jan-93	$3,500	119
8	15-Feb-93	$6,000	174
9	07-Mar-93	$6,000	201
10	25-Mar-93	$3,500	136
11	03-Apr-93	$5,000	172
12	11-May-93	$3,500	112
13	28-May-93	$1,000	97
14	03-Jun-93	$1,000	86
15	29-Jun-93	$1,000	104
16	05-Sep-93	$7,500	235
17	11-Oct-93	$1,500	119
18	29-Oct-93	$2,500	137
19	05-Nov-93	$3,500	148

The general question posed by this worksheet is clear: Does attendance go up when the company spends more money on advertising? In other words, is there a correlation between advertising and attendance? In an analysis of this particular example, attendance is referred to as the *dependent variable*, because the goal of the analysis will be to discover the extent to which advertising affects attendance. Accordingly, advertising is called the *independent variable*.

You might recall working with this same data in Chapter 6 while you were studying the variety of 1-2-3 chart types. Specifically, Figure 6.16 displays an XY chart in which advertising dollars are plotted against attendance in an x-y coordinate system (see page 380). This graph seems to show a relationship between the two data sets. In effect, an XY chart is a pictorial form of regression analysis. Suppose you were to draw a straight diagonal line somewhere through the middle of the plotted points in Figure 6.16; you might then formulate an approximate equation describing the relationship between advertising and attendance.

The general equation for a straight line is:

$$y = mx + b$$

where

- y is the dependent variable,

- x is the independent variable,

- m is the slope of the straight line that represents the relationship, and

- b is the y-intercept, or the value of y when x is zero.

To the extent that the equation you develop is a reliable description of the relationship between the two variables, you can use this equation to make predictions about the dependent variable.

The Range ➤ Analyze ➤ Regression command performs this same kind of analysis, but produces specific mathematical results rather than graphic approximations. Regression allows you to select a range containing one or more independent variables (known as the *X-range*) and one dependent variable (known as the *Y-range*). In addition, you specify an output range on your worksheet, where the command can display the results of its analysis.

Here is the Regression dialog box, filled in with appropriate ranges for an analysis of the advertising and attendance worksheet:

The X-range text box contains a reference to the range of advertising data in column B; and the Y-range text box contains a reference to the range of attendance data in column C. Cell E5 is specified as the upper-left corner of the output range. In addition, the Y-intercept box presents two option buttons, giving you a choice between calculating the actual *y*-intercept (the Compute option) or hypothesizing a value of zero for the *y*-intercept (the Set to zero option). For the advertising and attendance data, you want 1-2-3 to calculate the actual y-intercept; in theory, this value represents the expected attendance level when no money is spent on advertising.

In Figure 10.21 you see the results of the regression analysis. At the top of the output table, the Constant value (displayed as 74.83875 in cell H6) is the *y*-intercept. Near the bottom of the table, the X Coefficient(s) value (displayed as 0.018738 in cell G12) is the slope of the line that theoretically describes the relationship between the two variables. Rounding these two values, you can formulate the following equation for the line:

$$y = 0.019x + 75$$

or

$$\text{attendance} = 0.019 * \text{advertising} + 75$$

You can substitute actual advertising amounts into this equation to calculate the corresponding attendance projection. For example, according to this equation, attendance should be at a level of 75 people when no money is spent on advertising, and approximately 150 people when $4,000 is spent.

FIGURE 10.21

The output from the Regression command

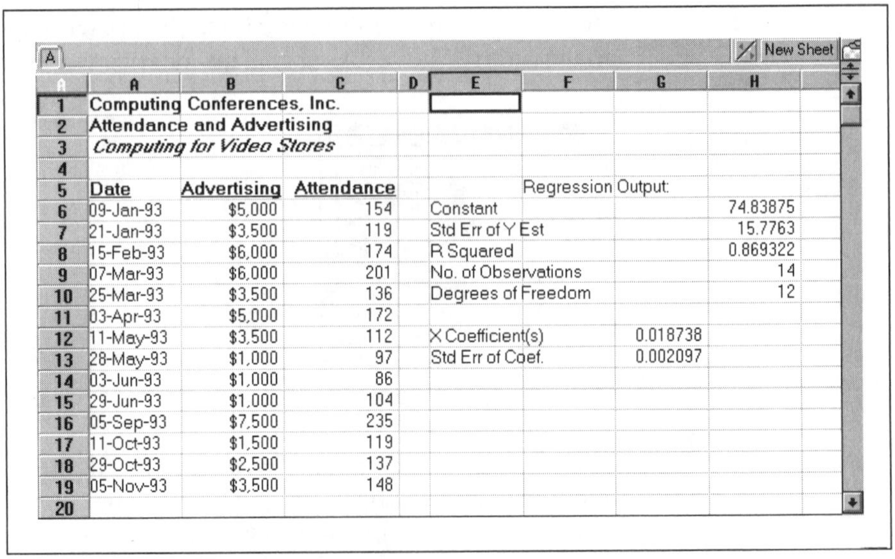

	A	B	C	D	E	F	G	H
1	Computing Conferences, Inc.							
2	Attendance and Advertising							
3	*Computing for Video Stores*							
4								
5	Date	Advertising	Attendance			Regression Output:		
6	09-Jan-93	$5,000	154		Constant			74.83875
7	21-Jan-93	$3,500	119		Std Err of Y Est			15.7763
8	15-Feb-93	$6,000	174		R Squared			0.869322
9	07-Mar-93	$6,000	201		No. of Observations			14
10	25-Mar-93	$3,500	136		Degrees of Freedom			12
11	03-Apr-93	$5,000	172					
12	11-May-93	$3,500	112		X Coefficient(s)		0.018738	
13	28-May-93	$1,000	97		Std Err of Coef.		0.002097	
14	03-Jun-93	$1,000	86					
15	29-Jun-93	$1,000	104					
16	05-Sep-93	$7,500	235					
17	11-Oct-93	$1,500	119					
18	29-Oct-93	$2,500	137					
19	05-Nov-93	$3,500	148					
20								

Other Values in the Regression Output Table

The Regression command also displays output values that tell you the extent to which you can rely on this particular regression analysis as a tool for predicting the behavior of the dependent variable:

- **R Squared.** The R Squared value is a general measurement of the reliability of the analysis. For a strong correlation between the dependent and independent variables, the R Squared value is close to 1; for a weak correlation, the value is close to zero.

- **Std Err of Y Est.** The value labeled Std Err of Y Est (standard error of the y estimate) indicates the range of accuracy for calculated values of y. In Figure 10.21, the Std Err of Y Est value is approximately 16. This implies that any attendance value you calculate from the equation is accurate within a range of plus-or-minus 16.

- **Std Err of Coef.** The value labeled Std Err of Coef. (standard error of the x coefficient) indicates the reliability of the slope calculation. The smaller this value is in relation to the X Coefficient(s), the better the reliability.

Using the Matrix Commands

A group of numbers arranged in rows and columns is called a *matrix*. In mathematics, a matrix is represented as a rectangular array of numbers enclosed in parentheses. In a worksheet, a matrix is an ordinary table of numbers in a range where you can successfully use 1-2-3's matrix commands.

The Range ➤ Analyze menu contains two matrix commands, named Invert Matrix and Multiply Matrix. You can use these commands to solve simultaneous equations in business, financial, or technical applications. A set of simultaneous equations has a common group of unknown values, known as variables. In typical examples, each equation has the same number of variables, and the number of equations is equal to the number of unknowns. For instance, in a set of four simultaneous equations, each equation has the same four variables. To solve these equations, you must find a set of four numeric values that satisfy all four equations.

Consider the example shown in Figure 10.22. The central office of Computing Conferences, Inc., has incurred expenses for curriculum development in each of four topic areas: computer training courses for accountants, doctors, lawyers, and video store owners. These expenses

FIGURE 10.22

Setting up the curriculum expense worksheet. The goal is to find the percentage of each region's profits to charge for curriculum development.

	A	B	C	D	E	F	G
1	Distributing the Cost of Curriculum Development						
2						Cost of	
3		Profits by Region				Curriculum	
4	Topic	Eastern	Western	Northern	Southern	Development	
5	Accountants	$111,200	$79,300	$59,500	$64,200	$8,058.76	
6	Doctors	$131,900	$116,900	$77,500	$96,700	$10,852.33	
7	Lawyers	$63,500	$81,500	$54,000	$88,400	$7,376.34	
8	Video Stores	$88,300	$63,200	$41,900	$161,900	$9,619.99	
9							
10							
11							
12							
13							
14							
15							
16	Region	% of Profit					
17	Eastern						
18	Western						
19	Northern						
20	Southern						

will be shared among the company's four regions in relation to each region's profits. The table of numbers in the range B5..E8 represents the profits earned from regional conferences in the four topic areas. Column F shows the expenses for curriculum development. The problem of this worksheet is to find the fixed percentage of each region's profits to charge for curriculum costs.

This problem can be expressed as a group of four simultaneous equations with four unknowns. In this case, the unknowns are the percentages to charge the four regions—that is, the fixed amount by which each region's profit figures should be multiplied to find the correct share of the curriculum expense. In the following equations, these unknowns are represented as E, W, N, and S:

$$111200*E + 79300*W + 59500*N + 64200*S = 8058.76$$
$$131900*E + 116900*W + 77500*N + 96700*S = 10852.33$$
$$63500*E + 81500*W + 54000*N + 88400*S = 7376.34$$
$$88300*E + 63200*W + 41900*N + 161900*S = 9619.99$$

Accordingly, the goal of the worksheet in Figure 10.22 is to find values for E, W, N, and S that satisfy all four equations.

To prepare for the upcoming exercise, enter the values and labels of the curriculum expense worksheet onto a new blank worksheet of your own, and format the data as shown in Figure 10.22. Save the worksheet as CURREXP.WK4.

Understanding Matrix Arithmetic

Before you start using the Matrix commands, you may find it helpful to review briefly the mathematical background of matrices. The worksheet in Figure 10.23 displays a group of matrices generated from the curriculum expense problem:

- **Coefficient matrix.** In the range A2..D5, the coefficient matrix is the table of regional profits, the numbers by which the four variables are multiplied in the simultaneous equations.

- **Constant matrix.** The constant matrix, shown in the range F2..F5, is the column of values from the right side of each equation, the expense amounts for curriculum development.

FIGURE 10.23

Matrices and matrix
arithmetic

	A	B	C	D	E	F	G
1	Coefficient Matrix					Constant Matrix	
2	111200	79300	59500	64200		8058.76	
3	131900	116900	77500	96700		10852.33	
4	63500	81500	54000	88400		7376.34	
5	88300	63200	41900	161900		9619.99	
6							
7	Inverse Matrix						
8	-1.4E-07	0.000019	-3.2E-05	6.1E-06			
9	-9.6E-05	0.000099	-3.5E-05	-2.1E-06			
10	0.000145	-0.00016	0.0001	-1.7E-05			
11	2.1E-08	-7.9E-06	4.9E-06	8.2E-06			
12							
13	Identity Matrix					Solution Matrix	
14	1	-0	0	0		0.028618	
15	-0	1	-0	0		0.024705	
16	-0	-0	1	0		0.016878	
17	-0	-0	0	1		0.029799	
18							
19							
20							

Here is a summary of the two operations you can perform on matrices using the Matrix commands:

- The Range ➤ Analyze ➤ Invert Matrix command can be performed on a square matrix—that is, any matrix that contains an equal number of rows and columns. The result of this operation is a second matrix that has the same dimensions as the first. For example, the inverse of the coefficient matrix appears in the range A8..D11 in Figure 10.23.

- The Range ➤ Analyze ➤ Matrix Multiply operation is performed between two matrices and results in a third matrix. The number of columns in the first matrix must be the same as the number of rows in the second matrix. In this operation, 1-2-3 multiplies values in each row of the first matrix by the corresponding values in each column of the second matrix; the sums of these products become the elements of the third matrix. If the first matrix in the operation has $r1$ rows and $c1$ columns, and the second matrix has $r2$ rows and $c2$ columns, the resulting matrix will have $r1$ rows and $c2$ columns.

By definition, the result of multiplying a matrix by its own inverse matrix is the identity matrix. As you can see in the range A14..D17 of Figure 10.23, an identity matrix consists of values of 0 and 1, where the values of 1 are arranged in a diagonal from the upper-left to the lower-right corners of the matrix. (Due to the limits of precision in the matrix operations, the values displayed as zero are actually very small positive or negative numbers.)

The identity matrix suggests an approach to solving the simultaneous equations. If the four equations can be rearranged so that one variable in each equation has a coefficient of 1 and the remaining variables have coefficients of 0, the resulting constants on the right sides of the equations are the solutions to the problem. Keep in mind that the identity matrix is the result of multiplying the coefficient matrix by its own inverse. This implies the basic rule that you use to solve simultaneous equations: The one-column solution matrix is found by multiplying the inverse of the coefficient matrix by the constant matrix, the column of values from the right sides of the original equations.

For example, consider the solution matrix displayed in the range F14..F17 in Figure 10.23. This column of values is the result of using the Multiply Matrix command to multiply the inverse matrix in the range A8..D11 by the constant matrix in F2..F5. Each element in the solution matrix is the value for one of the four variables, E, W, N, or S.

Solving the Simultaneous Equations

Returning now to the original curriculum expense worksheet, CURREXP.WK4 (see Figure 10.22), here are the steps for finding the correct percentage for each region:

1. Select the range of profit figures, in B5..E8.

2. Choose Range ➤ Analyze ➤ Invert Matrix. In the resulting dialog box, the selected range is displayed in the From text box.

3. In the To: box, enter a reference to cell B11, as shown here:

This is the upper-left corner of the range where 1-2-3 will generate the inverse matrix.

4. Click OK, and the inverse matrix appears on the worksheet, as shown in Figure 10.24.

5. Now select the inverse matrix, in the range B11..E14.

6. Choose Range ➤ Analyze ➤ Multiply Matrix. In the resulting dialog box, the selected range (of the inverse matrix) appears in the First matrix text box.

7. Enter the range of the constant matrix, F5..F8, in the Second matrix text box. Then enter B17 in the Resulting matrix text box:

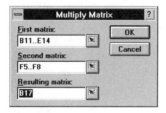

Click OK to complete the operation.

8. Select the range of the solution matrix, B17..B20. Click the Format selector, the first panel of the status bar, and select the Percent format. Your worksheet now appears as shown in Figure 10.25.

9. Click the Save SmartIcon to save your work to disk.

In effect, you have now solved the four simultaneous equations. The values in the range B17..B20 show the percentage to take from each region's profits to cover the shared expense of curriculum development.

FIGURE 10.24

Generating the inverse matrix

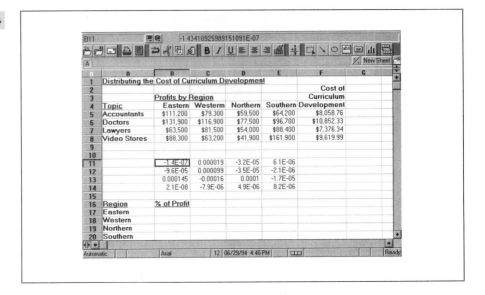

FIGURE 10.25

Producing the solution matrix. The values in the range B17..B20 represent the percentages of profit to charge for curriculum development.

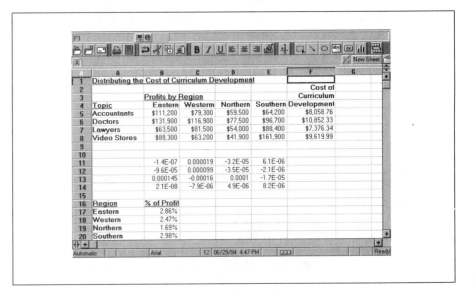

Now suppose you want to produce a table that shows the actual curriculum expense amount to be charged against the earnings for each conference topic in each region. For this table, you need to display the four percentages across a row, rather than down a column as they currently appear. The Range ➤ Transpose command is a convenient tool for accomplishing this task.

Using the Transpose Command

The Range ➤ Transpose command copies the row entries of a source range to the columns of a destination range, or, conversely, the column entries of a source to the rows of a destination. If the source range contains formulas, the Transpose command replaces those formulas with their current values in the destination range. (The original formulas in the source range are not affected.) This command also copies formats and display styles from the source to the destination range.

To produce the detailed table of curriculum expenses, you want to copy the percentages currently displayed in the column range B17..B20 to the row range B10..E10. (Note that these entries are simple values, not formulas.) Because you have no further use for the inverse matrix in the curriculum expense worksheet, you'll begin this next exercise by deleting the matrix:

1. Select the range B11..E14. Press the Delete key on your keyboard to erase the entries in this entire range.

2. Select the range of labels in A5..A8 and press Ctrl+C. Then select cell A11 and press Ctrl+V to copy these labels to the range A11..A14.

3. Select the range of percentages in B17..B20 and choose Range ➤ Transpose. The selected range appears in the From text box. Enter B10 into the To text box, as shown here:

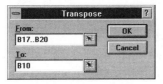

Click OK to complete the operation. The column of percentages has now been transposed to a row.

4. Enter the formula **+B5*B$10** into cell B11.

5. Select the range B11..B14. Click the range with the right mouse button and choose Copy Down from the resulting quick menu.

6. Select the range B11..E14. Click the range with the right mouse button and choose Copy Right from the quick menu.

7. Select the range F11..F14 and click the Sum SmartIcon to enter @SUM formulas into column F.

8. Apply the US Dollar format to the values in B11..E14. Then move the cell pointer to F1, out of the way of any data. Your worksheet now appears as shown in Figure 10.26.

9. Click the Save SmartIcon to save your work to disk.

Notice that the expense totals you've produced in the range F11..F14 are the same as the original curriculum costs that you entered into F5..F8. These matching values confirm your solution for the simultaneous equations.

FIGURE 10.26

Producing the curriculum expense table. The column of percentages has been transposed into a row in B10..E10.

	A	B	C	D	E	F	G
1	Distributing the Cost of Curriculum Development						
2						Cost of	
3		Profits by Region				Curriculum	
4	Topic	Eastern	Western	Northern	Southern	Development	
5	Accountants	$111,200	$79,300	$59,500	$64,200	$8,058.76	
6	Doctors	$131,900	$116,900	$77,500	$96,700	$10,852.33	
7	Lawyers	$63,500	$81,500	$54,000	$88,400	$7,376.34	
8	Video Stores	$88,300	$63,200	$41,900	$161,900	$9,619.99	
9							
10		2.86%	2.47%	1.69%	2.98%		
11	Accountants	$3,182.33	$1,959.10	$1,004.22	$1,913.11	$8,058.76	
12	Doctors	$3,774.73	$2,888.00	$1,308.02	$2,881.58	$10,852.33	
13	Lawyers	$1,817.25	$2,013.45	$911.39	$2,634.25	$7,376.34	
14	Video Stores	$2,526.98	$1,561.35	$707.17	$4,824.49	$9,619.99	
15							
16	Region	% of Profit					
17	Eastern	2.86%					
18	Western	2.47%					
19	Northern	1.69%					
20	Southern	2.98%					

Summary

Beyond basic spreadsheet operations, 1-2-3 provides a selection of tools that help you develop, organize, and analyze information on a worksheet. For example, SmartMasters are templates you can use to create professionally-designed worksheets for specific business purposes. The Version Manager is a major feature that allows you to save multiple versions of data for a worksheet, and to organize your versions into scenarios.

The Range ➤ Analyze menu contains a variety of commands and groups of commands that perform advanced mathematical calculations in appropriately organized worksheets. The What-if Table command produces one-, two-, and three-variable what-if tables representing multiple worksheet scenarios. In complex systems of worksheet formulas, the Solver command can find data solutions that fit within specifically formulated constraints. The Backsolver command finds the input value that produces a specified bottom-line result from a formula on your worksheet. The Distribution command counts the worksheet entries that fit into numerical categories in a bin range. The Regression command analyzes the correlation between a dependent variable and one or more independent variables. The Invert Matrix and Multiply Matrix commands are tools to use for solving simultaneous equations, represented as matrix tables in a worksheet.

CHAPTER 11

Links between Files

fast TRACK

● **To create a link between the current worksheet
and a second worksheet,** 601

enter a formula that has a file reference to the second worksheet. The complete notation for a file reference contains the drive name, directory path, file name, and extension of the second worksheet, all enclosed in pairs of angle brackets, (<<>>). The file reference is followed by an ordinary range reference, in the form <<file>>range. The purpose of the link is to copy data from the second worksheet to the current worksheet, and to update the current worksheet whenever the data changes on the second worksheet. In this context, the current worksheet is called the destination file, and the second worksheet is called the source file.

● **To use the Range Names list box to create a
reference to an open file,** 603

begin the formula entry with an appropriate operator, then press the F3 function key to view the Range Names list box. Select the name of a file from the In file list to view the range names defined in the file. Select the name that you want to include in the reference. In response, 1-2-3 enters a complete file reference and range name into the formula.

● **To create a link to a disk file that is not
currently open,** 607

type the complete file reference and range reference directly from the keyboard. No pointing technique is available.

● **To update a destination file if the linked source
file is not currently open,** 608

open the destination file from disk, and choose the Edit ➤ Links command.

To create a table of information about the source files linked to the current file,   **608**

> select the upper-left corner cell of a blank range on the current worksheet and choose the Tools ➤ Audit command. In the resulting dialog box, select the File links and Report at range options, and click OK.

To create a worksheet that displays the sum of data contained in other worksheets,   **611**

> choose the File ➤ Open command, select the name of a source file, and click the Combine button. In the Combine 1-2-3 File dialog box, choose the Add to values option, and click OK. Repeat these steps for each file that you want to add to the current worksheet. This command does not establish links.

To create a link in which a 1-2-3 worksheet is the server,   **613**

> select a range of data in the worksheet and press Ctrl+C. Then move to the second application and select the location where you want to transfer the data. In the second application, choose File ➤ Paste Link.

To create a link in which a 1-2-3 worksheet is the client,   **614**

> move to the source application and select the data that is to be transferred to the 1-2-3 worksheet. In the source application, press Ctrl+C. Move to the 1-2-3 window and choose Edit ➤ Paste Link.

BUSINESS worksheets are often organized into multiple files on disk. Consider the following typical examples:

- Accounting figures and calculations for a given year can be stored in twelve monthly worksheet files.

- Business information for a particular company might initially be accumulated in individual regional files.

- Financial worksheets can appear in separate files for revenues, expenses, deprecations, deductions, and so on.

- Inventory data might be separated into files for individual product categories or inventory locations.

Because you can open multiple worksheet files into the 1-2-3 environment, you may often be able to view all the parts of these applications on the screen at once. Furthermore, 1-2-3 has a very important feature that allows you to integrate and coordinate the parts of a multifile application: You can establish *links* between worksheets, resulting in automatic exchange of information between the corresponding worksheet files.

Worksheet links are expressed as special formulas that include file references along with the familiar forms of range references. In response to such a formula, 1-2-3 transfers data to the current worksheet from the worksheet named in the file reference. The worksheet that contains a link formula is the *destination file*, and the worksheet that is named in the file reference is the *source file*.

In an application consisting of multiple files, you can use links to create a master worksheet file that consolidates information from several other files. For example, each of the sample worksheets described in the following list represents an overview of data stored in a group of files:

- A year-end file that displays totals from twelve monthly files

- A corporate file that brings together data from all regions

- A profit worksheet that calculates the bottom line from data stored in various financial files

- A master inventory worksheet that consolidates information about several categories of products, or summarizes the status of several inventory locations.

To develop these worksheets, you write formulas to link the individual source files with the current destination worksheet. If you later make changes in the data stored in one of the source files, 1-2-3 can automatically update the destination file by transferring the new data to the cell that contains the link formula. In this chapter you'll learn to write formulas to integrate the parts of a multifile worksheet application.

Analogous features in the Windows environment are known as *Dynamic Data Exchange* (DDE) and *Object Linking* and *Embedding* (OLE). With programs that support these protocols, you can establish links between documents that you create in different Windows applications. A 1-2-3 worksheet can be the server (the application that supplies data) or the client (the application that requests data). DDE and OLE links are introduced as the final topics of this chapter.

11

Links between Files

Creating Regional Worksheets

In this chapter's exercises, you'll be working with a group of files from the four regions of Computing Conferences, Inc. Suppose that the company's central office has asked each of the regional managers to prepare a monthly business summary worksheet. As you can see in Figure 11.1, each of these sample worksheets contains five items of information about a given region's business activities for the month of February 1994:

- The number of computer-training conferences conducted in the region.

- The total number of people who attended these conferences.

FIGURE 11.1

Monthly business
summaries from the
four regions

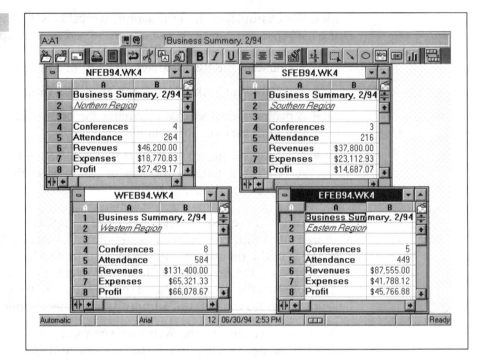

- The dollar revenues from the conferences.

- The total expenses associated with conducting the conferences.

- The total profit for the month.

The sample files in Figure 11.1 have been sized and positioned so that the contents of all four files can be seen at once. To prepare for your work in this chapter, begin by creating copies of these four files on your own computer. Here is an outline of the steps for creating each file; you'll perform these steps four times to develop the set of four files:

1. If necessary, use the File ➤ New command to open a new worksheet window. Click the Tab button, just to the right of the New Sheet button; this hides the tab line and brings an extra row of cells into view in the worksheet.

2. Enter the appropriate labels into column A of the new worksheet, and apply the boldface, italic, and underlining styles shown in Figure 11.1.

3. Select the range A4..A8 and choose the Range ➤ Name command. Make sure that the For cells box displays the "To the right" option, and click the Use Labels button. Then click OK.

4. Enter the first four numeric data items into column B: the number of conferences, the attendance, the revenue amount, and the expenses.

5. Enter the formula **+REVENUES–EXPENSES** into cell B8. This calculates the region's total profit for the month.

6. Apply the US Dollar format to the range B6..B8. Increase the widths of columns A and B so that the labels and values in the range A4..B8 can be viewed within their respective cells.

7. Choose File ➤ Save As and save each file under its appropriate name: **NFEB94.WK4**, **SFEB94.WK4**, **WFEB94.WK4**, and **EFEB94.WK4**, for the Northern, Southern, Western, and Eastern regions, respectively. Save the files in the root directory of your hard disk.

8. Resize and reposition each worksheet window so that you can view all four files at once, in an arrangement similar to what you see in Figure 11.1.

With these sample files displayed on your screen, you are ready to begin experimenting with 1-2-3 worksheet links.

Creating Links between Worksheets

A reference to a cell or range on another worksheet consists of two parts: a file reference and a range reference. If the source file is currently open, an adequate file reference is simply the name of the file, enclosed within two pairs of angle brackets:

<<file>>

The range appears immediately after the file reference:

<<file>>range

For example, the following formula copies the entry from cell A:A1 in an open file named SUMMARY:

+<<SUMMARY>>A:A1

When you enter this formula into a cell in the current worksheet, the contents of cell A1 in the SUMMARY worksheet appears in the destination cell. 1-2-3 automatically expands the cell reference to a range reference, as follows:

+<<SUMMARY>>A:A1..A:A1

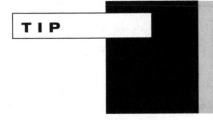

T I P

In the special case of an unsaved worksheet named Untitled, a file reference appears as two pairs of angle brackets with no name between them. For example, a reference to cell A1 in the Untitled worksheet is +<<>>A:A1..A:A1.

If the source worksheet is saved on disk but not currently open, the file reference must include a complete path name and file name, including the extension. For example, the following formula copies an entry from cell A1 of SUMMARY.WK4, a file that is stored in the root directory of disk C:

+<<C:\SUMMARY.WK4>>A:A1..A:A1

To enter a reference to a file that is not open, you type the complete reference directly from the keyboard. But if the source file is open, you can use pointing techniques to create the reference. If you've arranged your worksheets so that the source and destination files are both in view, you can easily use your mouse to create the reference: Begin your formula with an operator (+, for example) and then click the mouse at the target location of the source worksheet. In response, 1-2-3 enters a complete file reference and range reference into the current cell in the destination worksheet.

If the target cell has a range name in the source file, you can use the F3 function key to select a range name while you're building a formula. This is probably the clearest and simplest way to establish a link between two open files. Because you've taken the trouble to define range names in the regional business summary files currently displayed on your screen, you can use this technique in the upcoming exercise.

Building a Totals Worksheet from the Four Source Worksheets

Your goal in this exercise is to create a new worksheet file that displays the total of the numeric figures in these four regional files. Here are the steps:

1. Select the range A1..A8 in any one of the four files, and then press Ctrl+C.

2. Click the minimize icon button on each of the four worksheets in turn to reduce the files to icons in the 1-2-3 window.

3. Choose the File ➤ New command to create a new worksheet file. With the cell pointer at A:A1, press Ctrl+V to paste the labels into column A of the new worksheet. Enter the new label **Totals for Four Regions** in cell A2.

4. Resize the new worksheet to approximately the same dimensions as the other four worksheets, and move the worksheet to a position near the center of the screen. Increase the widths columns of A and B to 12.

5. Choose File Save As, and save the file to the root directory of your hard disk as TOTFEB94.WK4. Then select cell B4.

6. Type the + key and press the F3 function key to view the Range Names list. Click the down-arrow button at the right side of the In file box.

The resulting drop-down list contains the names of the five open worksheet files:

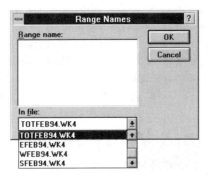

(Although only four of the names are in view at once, the list is scrollable. Use the list's vertical scroll bar to view the fifth file name.)

7. Select EFEB94.WK4 in the list. When you do so, the Range Names list box displays a list of the names defined in this file:

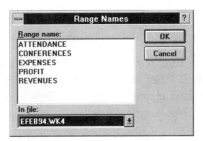

8. Select the range name CONFERENCES and click OK. A complete reference to the cell appears as follows in the contents box on the edit line:

+<<C:\EFEB94.WK4>>CONFERENCES

9. Now repeat steps 6, 7, and 8 three times, each time selecting a different file reference from the Range Names list box: first <<NFEB94.WK4>>, then <<SFEB94.WK4>>, and finally <<WFEB94.WK4>>. (Don't forget to type + between each reference.)

As you complete these steps, 1-2-3 builds the following formula:

+<<C:\EFEB94.WK4>>CONFERENCES
+<<C:\NFEB94.WK4>>CONFERENCES
+<<C:\SFEB94.WK4>>CONFERENCES
+<<C:\WFEB94.WK4>>CONFERENCES

This formula finds the sum of the values stored in the cells named CONFERENCES in the four source worksheets.

10. Press ↵ to complete the formula entry.

When you do so, the TOTFEB94.WK4 worksheet appears as shown in Figure 11.2. As you can see, a total of 20 conferences were conducted in the four regions during the month of February 1994.

11

Links between Files

FIGURE 11.2

Entering a formula that finds the sum of the Conferences entries in the four regional worksheets

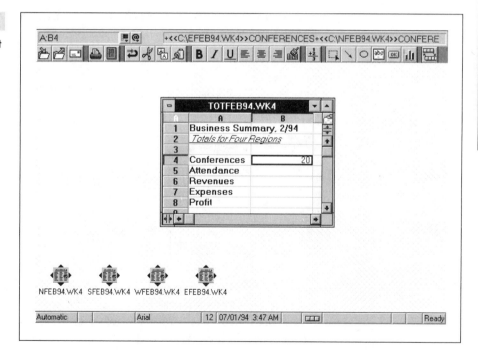

11. Select the range B4..B8 on the TOTFEB94 worksheet. Click the selection with the right mouse button, and choose Copy Down from the resulting quick menu.

In response, 1-2-3 copies the formula from cell B4 down to the cells in the range B5..B8. Because the original formula contains relative references to cells in the source worksheets, the references in the new copied formulas are automatically adjusted according to their positions in the column. For example, here is the formula that 1-2-3 copies into cell B8 to calculate the total profit from the four regional files:

```
+<<C:\EFEB94.WK4>>PROFIT
+<<C:\NFEB94.WK4>>PROFIT
+<<C:\SFEB94.WK4>>PROFIT
+<<C:\WFEB94.WK4>>PROFIT
```

12. Apply the Comma format (with no decimal places) to cell B5 and the US Dollar format to the range B6..B8.

13. Click the Save SmartIcon to save your work to disk.

When you complete these steps, the TOTFEB94.WK4 worksheet appears as follows:

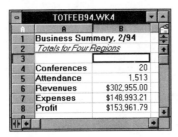

A quick look back at the worksheets in Figure 11.1 (see page 600) confirms that 1-2-3 has successfully found the totals of the data in the four source worksheets: the total number of conferences in the four regions, the total attendance, the total revenues, expenses, and profit.

Revising a Source Worksheet

Now if you revise the data in any one of the source worksheets, 1-2-3 automatically updates the corresponding formulas in TOTFEB94.WK4. For example, suppose you reach this point in your work only to discover that one of the conferences conducted in the Southern region was inadvertently omitted from SFEB94.WK4. Here is the corrected worksheet:

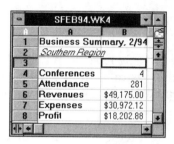

As you can see, the entries in cells B4, B5, B6, and B7 have been changed, and 1-2-3 has recalculated the formula in cell B8. Make these changes now in your own copy of SFEB94.WK4:

1. Double-click the icon representing SFEB94.WK4 to view the open file once again on the screen.

2. Make the four new entries in the range B4..B7:

B4	4
B5	281
B6	$49,175.00
B7	$30,972.12

   Notice that the value in B8 is recalculated.

3. Click the Save SmartIcon to save the new version of the file to disk. Then click the Minimize button on the SFEB94.WK4 window to reduce the file once again to an icon.

11

Links between Files

Now look at what has happened to TOTFEB94.WK4:

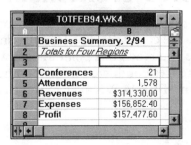

All the values in the range B4..B8 have been revised to reflect the changes in the source file. This demonstrates the advantage of linked worksheets: The destination file is updated when you revise the data in one or more source files.

To prepare for the next exercise, save the current version of TOT-FEB94.WK4 and then close the file. Also close all the source files except the worksheet for the Northern region, NFEB94.WK4.

Updating Files

Sometimes you might find yourself making revisions on a source worksheet at a time when the linked destination worksheet is not currently open in the 1-2-3 window. Conversely, you might later open the destination file when the source files are not open. The destination file can still be updated to reflect new data in the source, but the updating is not automatic. To ensure that the destination file accurately reflects the data in the source files, you use the Links command in the Edit menu.

In the following exercise, you'll make a single revision in the data contained in NFEB94.WK4, and then you'll close the file. When you reopen the TOTFEB94.WK4 file, you'll have the opportunity to experiment with the Edit ➤ Links command. You'll also learn how to produce a report of the formulas that link the worksheet to other files:

1. Double-click the icon representing NFEB94.WK4 to view the open worksheet file.

2. Enter the new value **56200** in cell B6.

The entry is displayed in the currency format, as $56,200.00. In addition, 1-2-3 recalculates the profit formula in cell B8:

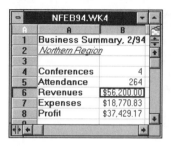

3. Click the Save SmartIcon to update this file to disk, then close the file.

4. Open TOTFEB94.WK4 from disk.

The file's contents are still the same as before. The worksheet has not yet been updated to reflect the latest changes you made in NFEB94.WK4.

5. Choose Edit ➤ Links. The Links dialog box appears.

6. Pull down the Link type list and choose the File Links option. When you do so, the dialog box displays a list of all the source files that are linked to TOTFEB94.WK4:

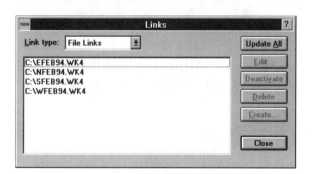

7. Click the Update All button, and then click Close to close the Links dialog box.

When you look again at the TOTFEB94 worksheet, you'll see that 1-2-3 has successfully updated the data from worksheet files on disk:

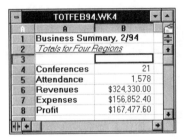

8. Now maximize the worksheet and select cell A11.

9. Choose Tools ➤ Audit. In the Audit dialog box, select the File links option in the Audit group. Then click the Report at range option in the lower-left corner:

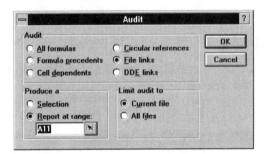

10. Click OK. 1-2-3 produces a list of all the formulas that link this file to other worksheet files on disk:

The formulas are, of course, very long; you'll have to scroll your worksheet to view them to their ends. But you can see that this report is a useful way to review the formula links on a worksheet.

11. Click the Save SmartIcon to save the new version of this file to disk. Then close the file.

Now you've seen the full significance of the linked worksheet file, TOT-FEB94.WK4. It consolidates the data from the four regional source files and can be updated whenever the data in one of these source files changes. Another way to create a totals worksheet that is similar in appearance to this file is with the Combine button on the File ➤ Open dialog box.

Combining Files

You can use the Combine button to read data from a worksheet file on disk and incorporate the data into the current worksheet. This operation does not create a link between the current file and the file on disk; it merely transfers data statically and enters the data onto the current worksheet. You used this command in Chapter 10, when you copied part of the CONF.WK4 worksheet to a new file (see page 534).

The Combine operation can also add data to values contained in specified cells of the current worksheet. This process requires some careful planning to make sure the data values from disk are added to the correct locations on the current worksheet. But the Add option is useful when you want to create a totals worksheet without establishing links between source and destination worksheets.

Here is a brief exercise with this command:

1. With the cell pointer located at A1 on a new Untitled worksheet, choose File ➤ Open. In the Open File dialog box, select the root directory of your hard disk so you can see a list of the files you've been working with in this chapter:

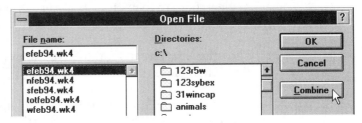

2. Select EFEB94.WK4 in the list, and then click the Combine button. The Combine 1-2-3 File dialog box appears.

3. Keep the Entire file option selected, and click the Add to values option:

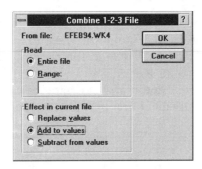

(Alternatively, you can retain the default Replace values option for this very first Combine operation, because the Untitled worksheet does not yet contain any values. But for the next three files you must select the Add option.)

4. Click OK. 1-2-3 copies the contents of the EFEB94 file to the Untitled worksheet.

5. Repeat steps 1 through 4 for the remaining three source files: NFEB94.WK4, SFEB94.WK4, and WFEB94.WK4. Each operation adds the data from one of these files to the current worksheet.

When you complete these steps, the data displayed in the worksheet is the same as in the TOTFEB94 file. But notice the important difference: The

TOTFEB94 worksheet contains formulas that link it to the source worksheets; but this new Untitled worksheet contains only data, with no formulas and no links. (You can now close this worksheet without saving it.)

Creating Links between Documents in Different Applications

In the Windows environment you can easily *copy* data values from 1-2-3 worksheets to documents you create in other applications. The Clipboard is the key to this procedure:

1. Select a range of data in a 1-2-3 worksheet.

2. Choose the Edit ➤ Copy command or press Ctrl+C. This copies the data to the Clipboard.

3. Activate the other Windows application, and move to the location where you want to copy the data.

4. Choose the Edit ➤ Paste command or press Ctrl+V. This command pastes the data from the Clipboard to the selected location in the second application.

The Edit ➤ Paste simply makes a copy of the data itself in the new location.

A more powerful command, available in 1-2-3 and in many other Windows applications, is Edit ➤ Paste Link. This command uses Dynamic Data Exchange (DDE) or Object Linking and Embedding (OLE) to establish a link between documents created in two different applications. In a DDE or OLE link, the source document is known as the *server* and the destination document is known as the *client*. While a link is active, data changes that take place in the server can automatically be sent to the client.

Transferring Data from a Worksheet to Another Document

For example, Figure 11.3 shows the 1-2-3 application window alongside Microsoft Write, a simple word-processing program that comes with Windows 3.1. The two application windows have been resized so that each takes up about half the screen. In the 1-2-3 window you can see the TOTFEB94.WK4 worksheet. In the Write document window you see the beginning of a memo directed to the regional managers of Computing Conferences, Inc.

Imagine that you are writing this memo, and you have reached the point where you want to insert the data from the TOTFEB94.WK4 worksheet into the word processed document. Because you are anticipating possible

FIGURE 11.3

Working with two applications in Windows

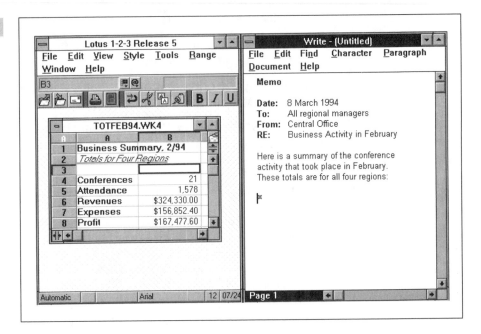

changes in the worksheet data, you want to establish a link between the worksheet and the document. Here are the steps you take:

1. Activate the worksheet window, and select the range A4..B8.

2. Pull down the Edit menu in 1-2-3 and choose the Copy command, or simply press Ctrl+C.

3. Activate the Write document window and move the cursor to the end of the memo text.

4. Pull down the Edit menu in the Write window and choose the Paste Link command. As you can see in Figure 11.4, the data from the 1-2-3 worksheet appears as a table at the bottom of the Word document.

Now imagine that your phone rings just as you are completing your work on the memo. It is Mary Garcia, the manager of the Western region. She's calling to let you know that she inadvertently omitted a $7,000 expense item for advertising in her February worksheet. No problem, you tell her;

11

Links between Files

FIGURE 11.4

The result of the link

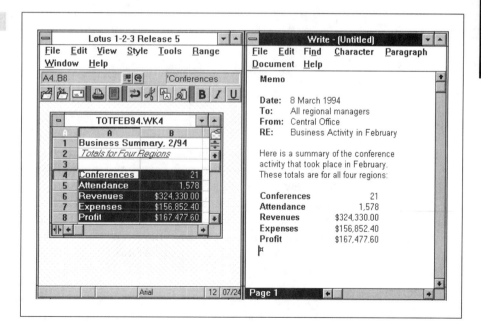

you can fix the error right away. You continue your work as follows:

5. Open the WFEB94.WK4 worksheet in the 1-2-3 window, and select cell B7. As you can see in Figure 11.5, the current expense amount displayed in the cell is $65,321.33.

6. Enter the revised figure into the cell, $72,321.33.

FIGURE 11.5

Revising the data in the server document

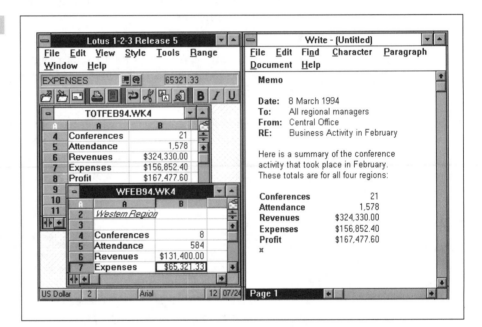

When you do so, several changes take place on the screen almost at once. First, a new profit figure is calculated in cell B8 of WFEB94.WK4. Then the new expense and profit figures are passed to the TOTFEB94.WK4 worksheet, which is linked to WFEB94.WK4 through formulas. And finally, the newly revised data is automatically sent to the memo document in Write, thanks to the link between the document and the TOTFEB94.WK4 worksheet. The Windows desktop now appears as shown in Figure 11.6.

7. Save the revised worksheets in the 1-2-3 window. Then save and print the memo document in the Write window.

FIGURE 11.6

The revised data is sent automatically to the client document.

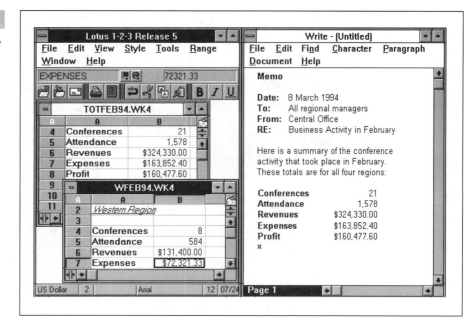

Transferring Data from Another Document to a 1-2-3 Worksheet

In the previous example, the 1-2-3 worksheet was the server, the source of the data in the link. A worksheet can also be the client. The steps for establishing the link are the essentially the same, but reversed:

1. In the other application, select the data that you want to transfer to the 1-2-3 worksheet, and then choose Edit ➤ Copy to copy the data to the Clipboard.

2. Activate 1-2-3, and open the worksheet that is to be the client in the link.

3. Pull down the Edit menu in the 1-2-3 window and choose the Paste Link command.

As a result of these steps, the data is copied from the source document, and a link is established in which the 1-2-3 worksheet is the client.

NOTE The Paste Link command is available only when the Clipboard contains data from an application that can act as the server in a DDE/OLE link; otherwise, Paste Link appears dimmed in the Edit menu.

When 1-2-3 is the client, you can use the Edit ➤ Links command to examine and modify the characteristics of the link. For example, Figure 11.7 shows the Links dialog box with a description of an active link between a Microsoft Excel worksheet and the current 1-2-3 worksheet. The link has the default name LINK1. The Information frame describes the characteristics of the link. The server is defined by three elements:

- **Application.** The *application* is the name of the Windows program that is supplying the data.

FIGURE 11.7

The Links dialog box

Links		?
Link type: DDE/OLE Links ▼		Update
LINK1	Information	Edit...
	Application: Excel	Deactivate
	Topic: C:\EXCEL\[DEBT.XLS]S	
	Item: R2C1:R14C6	Delete
	Format: Text	
	Update mode: Automatic	Create...
	Link status: Active	
	Range: A:A1..A:F13	Close

- **Topic.** The *topic* is the name of the document or worksheet that is the actual source of the data.

- **Item.** The *item* identifies the exact location of the target data in the source document or worksheet.

You can use the command buttons on the right side of the Links dialog box to perform specific actions related to this link, or to modify the characteristics of the link. For example, the Deactivate button switches the link into an inactive mode while retaining the link definition. In contrast, the Delete button removes the link between the two Windows documents and deletes the link definition altogether.

The Update button in the Edit Link Options dialog box forces an update on a link that is in the manual update mode. You might sometimes prefer to work in this mode if you need to make many changes in the source document before updating the destination worksheet in 1-2-3.

To switch a link to the manual update mode, follow these steps:

1. Choose Edit ➤ Links. In the resulting dialog box, select the name of the link that you want to change.

2. Click the Edit button.

The Edit Link dialog box appears on the screen. As in the example shown in Figure 11.8, this dialog box contains text boxes and option buttons representing the link characteristics that you can modify.

3. Click the Manual button in the Update mode frame and click OK in the Edit Link dialog box. Then click Close in the Edit Link Options dialog box.

Now the destination worksheet is no longer updated automatically in response to changes in the source document.

4. To force an update of the destination worksheet, choose the Edit ➤ Links command, select the name of the target link, and click the Update button.

11

Links between Files

FIGURE 11.8

The Edit Link
dialog box

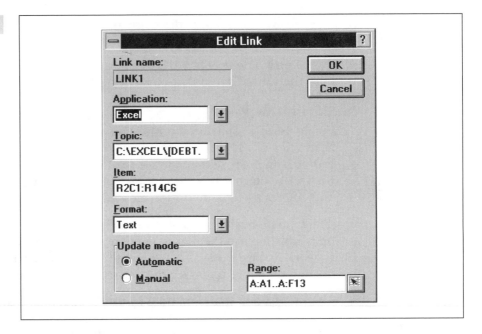

TIP

An *embedded object* is an item that is created in one application and displayed in another. For example, you can add an embedded Microsoft Word object to a 1-2-3 worksheet. One way to do so is to copy part of a Word document to the Clipboard, and then use 1-2-3's Edit ➤ Paste Special command to paste the selection as an embedded object. Another way is to choose 1-2-3's Edit ➤ Insert Object command and select the application you want to use to created the embedded object. An embedded object can be moved and resized within the worksheet that contains it. You can double-click the object to activate the server application.

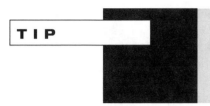

TIP

The 1-2-3 macro language contains two dozen commands designed to perform DDE and OLE operations. You can use these commands to automate a link between applications in Windows. See Chapter 21 for details.

Summary

The purpose of establishing a link between two files is to exchange data between the files and to ensure that the destination file will be updated when there is a change in the source file.

A link between two worksheets is expressed as a formula that includes both a file reference and a range reference. The worksheet containing the formula is the destination file, and the worksheet named in the file reference is the source file. If the source and destination worksheets are both open, 1-2-3 automatically updates the destination file to reflect changes in the source file. However, if you open the destination file at a time when the source file is closed, you must choose the Edit ➤ Links command to update the destination file.

Thanks to the Windows data-exchange protocols known as DDE and OLE, you can also establish links between documents that are created in different Windows applications. To create such a link, you choose the Edit ➤ Copy command to copy data from the source document to the Clipboard. Then you move to the destination document and choose the Edit ➤ Paste Link command from the main menu of the second application. For example, you can create a link between a source worksheet and a destination document in

11

Links between Files

a word-processing program. While the link is active, the word processed document is updated whenever you make changes in the worksheet data. When a 1-2-3 worksheet is the client in a link, you can use the Edit ➤ Links command to view or modify the characteristics of the link.

Macro

Programming

fast TRACK

To create a conditional branch in a macro,   651

use an {If} instruction to express the condition of the branch. The {If} command takes a single argument, a logical expression. Immediately following the {If} instruction, in the same cell of the macro worksheet, write a {Branch} command that identifies the destination of the branch. {Branch} also takes a single argument, a reference to the macro location that receives control of the program if the branch is performed.

To locate a logical error in a macro,   652

choose the Tools ➤ Macro command and activate both the Single Step and Trace options. Then run the macro and examine the contents of the Macro Trace window as you move step-by-step through the program performance.

To create a custom dialog box for a 1-2-3 macro,   658

start the Lotus Dialog Editor and choose File ➤ New to start a new dialog box design. Select options from the Control menu to add objects to the new dialog box. When your design is complete, select the box and press Ctrl+C to copy the definition to the Clipboard. Then return to 1-2-3 and open the worksheet where you want to store the definition table for the custom dialog box. Select a cell and press Ctrl+V. Lotus creates a definition table corresponding to the design you created in the Dialog Editor. Write a macro that uses the {Dialog} command to display the custom dialog box on the screen.

A **PROGRAMMING** language is a collection of tools designed to help you plan and perform tasks on your computer. Accordingly, a *program* is a sequence of steps, expressed in the commands and keywords of a particular language. In the process of writing a program, regardless of the language, you typically focus on several essential categories of activity:

- **Data Operations.** Programs perform operations on specific types of data values, including numbers, strings, and logical values.

- **Input and Output.** Programs typically read input from a variety of sources and write output to a variety of destinations. For example, an *interactive* program reads the user's input from the keyboard and displays output on the screen. Disk files can be both the source of input and the destination of output.

- **Decisions.** A decision statement results in a choice between different options for the program's next action. Decisions are based on expressed conditions.

- **Repetition.** A *loop* repeats the performance of a command or group of commands a specified number of times.

- **Flow of control.** A *call* to a subroutine changes the sequential line-by-line flow of control in a program. A subroutine performs a particular task and then returns control of the program to the location of the original call. By contrast, a *branch* command simply sends control of the program to a new location, with no expectation of a return.

The 1-2-3 macro language includes commands for carrying out these and other programming activities within the context of worksheets, charts, and databases. The language contains hundreds of commands, each represented by a unique keyword. As you first learned in Chapter 9, macro commands appear within braces({}). Most macro commands require specific arguments, which may include numeric values, strings, logical expressions, or range references. Each argument is separated from the next by a comma or a semicolon.

For example, in Chapter 9 you worked with a command named {Get-Label} (see page 517). This command displays a dialog box on the screen and waits for the user to enter a string from the keyboard. When the user completes the entry and clicks OK, the {Get-Label} command copies the input to a specified cell location as a label entry. Accordingly, the first two arguments of the {Get-Label} command are a string representing the input prompt, and a cell reference representing the eventual destination of the input:

> {Get-Label *prompt,reference*}

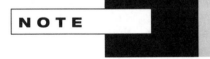

N O T E — See Chapter 21 for a discussion of all the macro commands.

Exploring the macro commands 1-2-3 provides a quick technique for viewing a list of the macro commands and opening a Help topic for a selected command. Follow these steps:

1. Type an opening brace character, {, into a worksheet cell.

2. While you are still in the Label mode, press the F3 function key. The Macro Keywords dialog box appears:

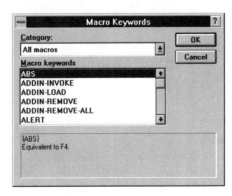

12

Macro Programming

MACRO PROGRAMMING

The Macro keywords list initially contains the names of all the macro commands and keynames available in the language. When you select an item in this list, the framed area at the bottom of the Macro Keywords dialog box provides a brief explanation of the command you've selected.

3. Optionally, click the down-arrow button at the right side of the Category box. The resulting drop-down list shows the categories into which Lotus divides the macro commands:

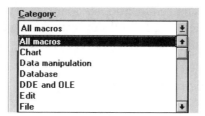

If you select an item from this list, 1-2-3 limits the Macro keywords list to the commands belonging to the category you've selected. This step may make it easier for you to find a command that you're looking for.

4. Scroll down the Macro keywords list to the command you want to learn about, and click the command's name with the mouse. Read about the command at the bottom of the dialog box.

5. Press the F1 function key. In response, 1-2-3 opens the Help topic for the command you've selected. For example, here is the Help topic that covers {Get-Label} and several related commands:

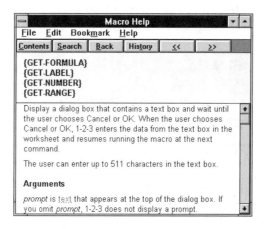

6. Press Escape to close the Help window when you've finished reading the information it contains. The Macro Keywords dialog box is still open on the screen.

7. Optionally, click OK to enter the selected command into the current cell of your worksheet. Still in the Label mode, 1-2-3 presents a template for the command with placeholders for each of the command's arguments. To complete the entry, you enter the actual arguments and press ↵.

TIP

Another way to find information about macros and macro programming is to choose Help ➤ Contents and click the Macros button. Then select an item from the list of macro topics that appears on the screen.

Macro programming is a broad and detailed subject; in fact, you'll find entire books devoted to the techniques of writing macros. This chapter is a short introduction to macros and the basic concepts of macro programming. In the course of this introduction you'll see examples of some commonly used macro commands. You'll also work with two complete examples of macro programs:

- The Schedule macro, which creates worksheets for keeping track of business appointments. You'll see three versions of this programming exercise, each illustrating different macro commands.

- The Mailing List macro, which reads an address database and creates a text file of address labels from the database. This particular example is designed to work with the Instructor database from Computing Conferences, Inc.; but you can revise the program to create labels from any other address database that you use.

These examples illustrate general categories of programming tasks: data operations, input and output, decisions, loops, subroutine calls, and branches of control.

12

Macro Programming

Writing Programs that Interact with the User

The Schedule macro creates worksheets in which you can record daily business activities. For example, the following schedule worksheet displays hourly time slots from 6:00 A.M. to 6:00 P.M. for a particular date:

A	A	B
1	Daily Business Schedule	
2		
3	09-Jul-94	
4		
5	06:00 AM	
6	07:00 AM	
7	08:00 AM	
8	09:00 AM	
9	10:00 AM	
10	11:00 AM	
11	12:00 PM	
12	01:00 PM	
13	02:00 PM	
14	03:00 PM	
15	04:00 PM	
16	05:00 PM	
17	06:00 PM	

To create it, the macro program begins by choosing the File ➤ New command to open a new blank worksheet, and then it proceeds to elicit your instructions for the contents of the worksheet. Specifically, the program offers these variations:

- You can create a schedule worksheet for today, tomorrow, or the next day; or, in the second version of the Schedule macro, you can enter a date directly from the keyboard.

- You can choose between one-hour, half-hour, or quarter-hour increments for the worksheet.

To elicit your instructions, the program displays dialog boxes on the screen for the choice of dates and time increments. The first of these dialog boxes contains a group of option buttons representing the date options:

To make a selection, you can click an option or press the underlined shortcut key. Then you click OK to continue the program. If you choose the fourth option, Another date (it is available in the second version of the program), another dialog box elicits a date entry from you:

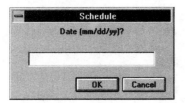

When you type a date and click OK, the program enters the date onto the Schedule worksheet.

The next dialog box contains option buttons representing three available time increments for your schedule worksheet:

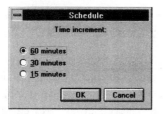

Again, you click a button or press the underlined digit to make a selection on this dialog box, and then you click OK.

Figures 12.1 and 12.2 show two additional examples of the program's output. The first of these worksheets displays time slots in half-hour increments, and the second in quarter-hour increments. After creating a schedule worksheet, the program moves the cell pointer to the first time slot, 6:00 A.M. Then the program run is complete, and you can begin entering your appointments and activities onto the worksheet.

FIGURE 12.1

A schedule worksheet with half-hour increments

	A	B	C
1	Daily Business Schedule		
2			
3	10-Jul-94		
4			
5	06:00 AM		
6	06:30 AM		
7	07:00 AM		
8	07:30 AM		
9	08:00 AM		
10	08:30 AM		
11	09:00 AM		
12	09:30 AM		
13	10:00 AM		
14	10:30 AM		
15	11:00 AM		
16	11:30 AM		
17	12:00 PM		
18	12:30 PM		
19	01:00 PM		
20	01:30 PM		

Automatic   Arial

Creating the Schedule Macro

The first version of the Schedule macro appears in columns A through F of a worksheet that you'll create on disk as C:\S1.WK4. The first two columns of the worksheet are shown in Figure 12.3. In Figure 12.4, the width of column B has been decreased so you can see the comments in column C. The first cell in the macro, at B3, is named \S. You therefore begin a run of the program by pressing Ctrl+S. This main part of the program consists of eleven lines of macro instructions. Here is a general

FIGURE 12.2

A schedule worksheet with quarter-hour increments

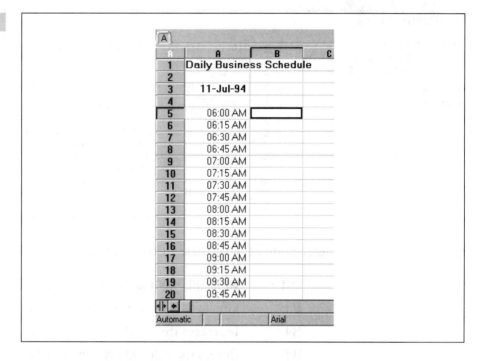

FIGURE 12.3

The first two columns of the Schedule macro (Version 1). Columns C through F are shown in Figures 12.4 and 12.5.

	A	B
1	Schedule Macro (C:\S1.WK4)	
2	Action	
3	\S {File-New}	
4	{Column-Width 11}	
5	Daily Business Schedule~	
6	{Style-Font-Attributes "bold","on"}	
7	{Down 2}	
8	{Choose-One <<C:\S1.WK4>>DCh,<<C:\S1.WK4>>Action,"Date choice:","Schedule"}	
9	{Style-Number-Format "dd-mmm-yy"}	
10	{Style-Font-Attributes "bold","on"}	
11	{Down 2}6:00 AM~{Down}	
12	{Choose-One <<C:\S1.WK4>>TCh,<<C:\S1.WK4>>Action,"Time increment:","Schedule"}	
13	{Right}{Up}{Quit}	

12

Macro Programming

	A	B	C
1	Schedule Macro (C:\S1.WK4)		
2	Action		
3	\S {File-New}		Create a new worksheet.
4	{Column-Width 11}		Widen column A.
5	Daily Business Schedule~		Enter the title.
6	{Style-Font-Attributes "bold","on"}		Boldface the title.
7	{Down 2}		Move down two cells.
8	{Choose-One <<C:\S1.WK4>>DCh,<<C:		Display the date choices.
9	{Style-Number-Format "dd-mmm-yy"}		Format the date entry.
10	{Style-Font-Attributes "bold","on"}		Boldface the date.
11	{Down 2}6:00 AM~{Down}		Enter the first time.
12	{Choose-One <<C:\S1.WK4>>TCh,<<C:		Display the time choices.
13	{Right}{Up}{Quit}		Position the pointer.

description of what these instructions do:

CELL	WHAT THE PROGRAM DOES
B3	Creates a new worksheet.
B4	Increases the width of column A to 11.
B5	Enters the title "Daily Business Schedule" into cell A1.
B6	Displays the title in boldface type.
B7	Moves the cell pointer down to A3.
B8	Uses the {Choose-One} command to display the first dialog box on the screen, and to enter the date you choose onto the worksheet. You'll learn about the {Choose-One} command later in this chapter.
B9	Formats the new entry as a date.
B10	Applies the boldface style to the date.
B11	Moves down by two cells and enters 6:00 A.M. as the first time entry.

CELL	WHAT THE PROGRAM DOES
B12	Uses the {Choose-One} instruction to display the second dialog box on the screen. A second time value is entered onto the worksheet, corresponding to the time increment you choose. As you'll see shortly, another part of the program performs a fill-by-example operation to enter a range of time values into column A.
B13	Positions the cell pointer just to the right of the first time entry and then stops the program.

As you can see, the {Choose-One} command is responsible for displaying the program's two dialog boxes on the screen, each presenting you with a group of option buttons. For successful use of this command, a macro must contain a specially organized definition table that describes the option button choices. In the S1.WK4 worksheet, two such tables appear in columns D, E, and F, as shown in Figure 12.5:

- The definition table for the date options is in the range D2..F4. The name DCH (for "Date Choices") has been assigned to this range.

- The definition table for the time options is in D7..F10. The name TCH (for "Time Choices") has been assigned to the range.

The {Choose-One} commands in the main part of the program use these tables to create dialog boxes and to determine the resulting actions.

12

Macro Programming

FIGURE 12.5

The definition tables in columns D, E, and F of the Schedule macro (Version 1). These tables define the option buttons that will appear in the dialog boxes created by the {Choose-One} command.

A	D	E	F
1	Date choice		
2	&Today	To&morrow	&Day after tomorrow
3	1	0	0
4	@TODAY{Calc}~	@TODAY+1{Calc}~	@TODAY+2{Calc}~
5			
6	Time choice		
7	&60 minutes	&30 minutes	&15 minutes
8	1	0	0
9	7:00 AM~	6:30 AM~	6:15 AM~
10	{Fill-By-Example A5..A17}	{Fill-By-Example A5..A29}	{Fill-By-Example A5..A53}
11			

Before you examine the precise structure of these definition tables, take the time to produce your own copy of the Schedule macro. Open a new blank worksheet for the macro, and carefully enter the range names, macro instructions, and comments into columns A through F of the worksheet, as shown in Figures 12.3, 12.4, and 12.5. Once you've finished typing the contents of the macro, here are the steps for completing your work:

1. Use the Range ➤ Name command to assign the labels displayed in cells A2 and A3 to the adjacent cells in column B. Cell B2, named Action, is reserved for special use by the {Choose-One} commands, as you'll learn shortly.

2. Select the range of the first definition table, D2..F4, and use the Range ➤ Name command to assign it the name DCH.

3. Select the range of the second definition table, D7..F10, and use Range ➤ Name to assign it the name TCH.

4. Save the worksheet in the root directory of drive C, as C:\S1.WK4. (Later you'll be saving the two other versions of the program as C:\S2.WK4 and C:\S3.WK4.) If you decide to save the worksheet in a different directory, or under a different file name, you must revise the file references in cells B8 and B12 accordingly.

When you finish your work, try running the macro a few times, pressing Ctrl+S to start each performance. Depending upon your selections in the two dialog boxes, the macro produces Schedule worksheets like the ones in Figures 12.1 and 12.2.

Using the {Choose-One} Command

As this program illustrates, a dialog box with a group of option buttons is a clear and efficient way to elicit instructions from the user during a macro run. The {Choose-One} command displays such a dialog box on the screen and waits for the user to choose one of the options. In the Schedule macro the command requires four arguments, starting with a reference to the definition table that describes the option buttons:

{Choose-One *choicesRange,resultRange,prompt,title*}

Here are brief descriptions of these four arguments:

ARGUMENT	DESCRIPTION
choicesRange	The entire range of the definition table.
resultRange	A cell where the {Choose-One} command can enter a result value. Specifically, {Choose-One} enters a value of 1 in this cell if the user clicks the OK button on the dialog box, or a value of 0 if the user clicks the Cancel button.
prompt	The text that appears near the top of the dialog box, above the option buttons.
title	The text that appears on the title bar of the dialog box.

In addition to these four arguments, you can supply *x* and *y* arguments to specify the position where the dialog box will appear on the screen. If you omit these final two arguments, 1-2-3 displays the dialog box in the center of the screen.

For example, the first {Choose-One} command in the Schedule macro displays the dialog box for the date options:

{Choose-One <<C:\S1.WK4>>DCh,<<C:\S1.WK4>>
Action,"Date choice:","Schedule"}

The *choicesRange* is the range named DCH on the S1.WK4 worksheet, and the *resultRange* is the cell named ACTION. The *prompt* is "Date choice:" and the *title* is "Schedule." The program's second {Choose-One} command displays the dialog box for the time options:

{Choose-One <<C:\S1.WK4>>TCh,<<C:\S1.WK4>>
Action,"Time increment:","Schedule"}

Here the *choicesRange* is TCH and the *resultRange* is ACTION. The *prompt* is "Time increment" and the *title* is "Schedule."

12

Macro Programming

NOTE See page 1231 for further information about {Choose-One}.

Reference Formats in Macros

Notice that these commands use a file reference and a range reference in the form <<*file*>>*range* to identify the *choicesRange* and *resultRange* arguments. Normally {Choose-One} would look for these two ranges on the *current* worksheet file—that is, the file that contains the cell pointer at the time the macro is running. This creates an interesting problem for the Schedule macro, because S1.WK4 is not the current worksheet during most of the program run.

By default, 1-2-3 follows two rules for evaluating references that appear as arguments in macro commands:

- In commands that send control of the program to a new location in the macro sheet—specifically, subroutine calls and branches of control—1-2-3 evaluates range arguments as references to the macro worksheet itself. (You'll learn more about calls and branches later in this chapter.)

- In other macro commands, 1-2-3 evaluates range arguments as references to the worksheet that is current at the time the macro is running.

To override these default rules for references in macro commands, you must include a file reference, in the form <<*file*>>*range*. As you've seen, this is how the references appear in both of the {Choose-One} commands in the Schedule program.

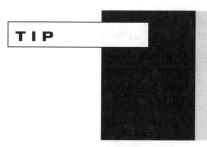

TIP

Because of the distinct rules for evaluating references in macro commands, reference arguments are a common source of errors in programs. If 1-2-3 interrupts a macro and displays an *Invalid range* error message, check to see if a reference in the current instruction should include a file reference.

Definition Tables for the {Choose-One} Command

A definition table for the {Choose-One} command is a range of columns in which you describe the option buttons that will appear in the resulting dialog box. Each column in the range defines one option:

- The first cell in the column supplies the caption for the option button. You can use an ampersand (&) in this entry to identify the character that will be underlined in the caption.

- The second cell in the column is a value of 1 or 0. A 1 means that the option is *on* and a 0 means it is *off*. In a given table, only one option may have a value of 1. (A third possible value, NA, produces a dimmed option.)

- The third cell—and, optionally, subsequent cells down the column—provide the macro instructions that 1-2-3 performs if the user chooses this option and clicks OK on the dialog box.

A dialog box produced by {Choose-One} can contain up to eight option buttons. In other words, 1-2-3 recognizes as many as eight columns of individual option definitions in the range. In the Schedule macro, each of the two dialog boxes has three option buttons, defined in columns D, E, and F of the S1.WK4 worksheet. (Look back at Figure 12.5 on page 635 to review these tables.)

12

Macro Programming

Choosing a Date for the Schedule worksheet For example, here is the complete definition for the first option in the date dialog box:

	D
2	&Today
3	1
4	@TODAY{Calc}~
5	

As you can see, the first cell defines the caption for the option: &Today. Thanks to the ampersand, the *T* in "Today" is underlined in the dialog box, and the user can simply press T to select it. The second cell contains a value of 1, meaning that this option will be *on*. The third cell contains a macro instruction, @TODAY{Calc}~, which enters the date number for today's date into the current cell.

The second column of the definition table for the date dialog box contains the macro instruction @TODAY+1{Calc}~ in cell E4; this action corresponds to the Tomorrow option in the dialog box. The third column contains the instruction @TODAY+2{Calc}~ (in cell F4), corresponding to the Day after tomorrow option.

When the user chooses an option in the dialog box, {Choose-One} performs the macro instructions in the corresponding column of the definition table. Then the program returns to the location of the {Choose-One} command and continues with the next instruction.

In summary, each of the instructions in the definition table for the date dialog box enters a date in cell A3 of the Schedule worksheet. When control of the program subsequently returns to the main part of the macro, the instructions in cell B9 and B10 of the macro worksheet format this entry as a date and apply the boldface style.

Choosing a Time increment for the Schedule worksheet The instructions in the definition table for the time dialog box also perform data entries. Specifically, each column contains instructions for the following actions:

1. Enter a second time value in column A. This second entry serves as a pattern that represents the increment between one time value and the next.

2. Perform the equivalent of a drag-and-fill operation to fill the appropriate range of cells with time entries.

For example, the following column defines the first option in the time dialog box:

The caption for the option button is 60 minutes, as specified in the first cell of this column. The second cell contains a value of 1, indicating that this option is *on*. Finally, the third and fourth cells contain the macro instructions that will be performed if the user chooses this option. First, 7:00 AM is entered as the second time value in the column. Then a macro command named {Fill-By-Example} fills the appropriate range with time entries. This command takes one argument, the range that is to be filled with values:

    {Fill-By-Example A5..A17}

As a result, the Schedule worksheet displays a column of time entries that are one hour apart. Similar instructions for the other two options produce columns of entries that are a half-hour or a quarter-hour apart. (Look back at Figure 12.5 on page 635 to review these instructions.)

TIP

The {Fill} command is available for filling a range of cells with a specific series of values. This command takes five arguments, which correspond to the information you supply when you choose the Range ➤ Fill command: {FILL *range;start;step;stop;units*}. All five arguments are optional. See page 1176 for all the details.

12

Macro Programming

Working with Loops, Decisions, and Branches of Control

The second version of the schedule macro differs from the first in several details. First, the date dialog box now has a fourth option labeled *Another date*:

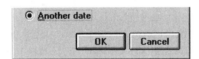

As you saw at the beginning of this chapter, this option allows you to enter a date of your choice to be displayed at the top of the Schedule worksheet.

In addition to this change, the second version of the macro employs a new technique for entering the range of time values into the schedule worksheet. Specifically, this version illustrates the use of a macro command named {For} to create a loop in the program. The {For} loop produces the time entries on the schedule worksheet one by one, in a repetitive process defined by a start value, a stop value, and a step value.

The main part of the new program appears in Figure 12.6, and the definition tables are shown in Figures 12.7 and 12.8. To create this macro, you can start with your copy of the first version, S1.WK4. Here are the steps for making the appropriate revisions:

1. Close any Schedule worksheets you created from the previous version of the program, and select S1.WK4.

2. Choose Edit ➤ Find & Replace.

This command performs search-and-replace operations, which can prove particularly useful for making global changes on a macro worksheet. In this case, you'll use it to change all the S1.WK4 references to S2.WK4.

FIGURE 12.6

The second version of the Schedule macro. This version illustrates the {For} command.

	A	B
1	Schedule Macro (C:\S2.WK4)	
2	Action	
3	\S	{File-New}
4		{Column-Width 11}
5		Daily Business Schedule~
6		{Style-Font-Attributes "bold","on"}
7		{Down 2}
8		{Choose-One <<C:\S2.WK4>>DCh,<<C:\S2.WK4>>Action,"Date choice:","Schedule"}
9		{Style-Number-Format "dd-mmm-yy"}
10		{Style-Font-Attributes "bold","on"}
11		{Down 2}
12		{Choose-One <<C:\S2.WK4>>TCh,<<C:\S2.WK4>>Action,"Time increment:","Schedule"}
13		{For <<C:\S2.WK4>>Time,0.25,0.76,<<C:\S2.WK4>>Incr,Entry}
14		{Style-Number-Format "hh:mm am/pm",,,A5..A53}
15		{Home}{Down 4}{Right}{Quit}
16		
17	Incr	
18	Time	
19		
20	Entry	{Let @CELLPOINTER("coord"),<<C:\S2.WK4>>Time}{Down}

FIGURE 12.7

The first three columns of the option definition tables in S2.WK4

	D	E	F
1	Date choice		
2	&Today	To&morrow	&Day after tomorrow
3	1	0	0
4	@TODAY{Calc}~	@TODAY+1{Calc}~	@TODAY+2{Calc}~
5			
6	Time choice		
7	&60 minutes	&30 minutes	&15 minutes
8	1	0	0
9	{Let <<C:\S2.WK4>>Incr,1/24}	{Let <<C:\S2.WK4>>Incr,1/48}	{Let <<C:\S2.WK4>>Incr,1/96}
10			

12

Macro Programming

FIGURE 12.8

The final column of the first definition table in S2.WK4

	G
1	
2	&Another date
3	0
4	{Get-Number "Date (mm/dd/yy)?",A3,,"Schedule"}
5	

3. Enter **S1.WK4** into the Search for text box. Select the Replace with option in the Action frame, and enter **S2.WK4** in the corresponding text box.

At this point the Edit Find dialog box appears like this:

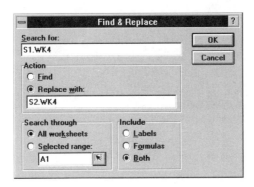

4. Click OK to begin the search-and-replace operation. Then click Replace All on the Replace dialog box that appears next on the screen:

In response, 1-2-3 changes all the file references in the macro worksheet. Press Home to move the cell pointer back to the beginning of the macro.

5. Enter new instructions in cells B11, B13, B14, B15, and B20, as shown in Figure 12.6.

6. Enter the new labels in the range A17..A20, also shown in Figure 12.6. Use the Range ➤ Name command to assign the labels in column A as the range names for the adjacent cells in column B.

7. In the definition table for the time dialog box, delete the instructions in the range E9..F10 and replace them with the new {Let} commands shown in row 9 of Figure 12.7.

8. Enter the new option definition in column G, as shown in Figure 12.8.

9. Select the range D2..G4, and use the Range ➤ Name command to assign the name DCH to this selection. This action expands the definition table by one column.

10. Choose the File Save As command and save the new version of the macro as C:\S2.WK4. (The former version remains unchanged on disk, saved as C:\S1.WK4.)

As an additional exercise, you may also want to add new comments to column C as you become more familiar with this program.

Now try running this new version of the macro two or three times. Press Ctrl+S to start each performance. (In one run, try choosing the Another date option in the date dialog box and enter the date you want to appear on the Schedule worksheet.) Just as in the first version, the program follows you instructions to produce a range of time entries in column A of the Schedule worksheet. But now the entries are produced by a {For} loop rather than the {Fill-By-Example} command.

Using the {For} Command

The {For} command is 1-2-3's main tool for creating loops in a macro. {For} makes repeated calls to a subroutine while incrementing or decrementing the value stored in a designated counter cell. The command requires five arguments:

{For *counterCell,startValue,stopValue,stepValue,subroutine*}

Here are descriptions of these arguments:

ARGUMENT	DESCRIPTION
counterCell	A reference to the cell that {For} uses as a numeric counter to control the looping process.

ARGUMENT	DESCRIPTION
startValue	The first value that the loop enters into *counterCell*.
stopValue	The value that signals the end of the looping.
stepValue	The increment or decrement amount by which the value in *counterCell* is changed for each iteration of the loop.
subroutine	A reference to the subroutine that the loop calls repeatedly.

The action of the {For} loop depends directly on the numbers you supply as the start, stop, and step values. If the step value is greater than zero and the start value is less than or equal to the stop value, the subroutine is called once for each increment from start to stop. More specifically, here is how the loop proceeds:

- The start value is copied to the counter cell.

- If the value in the counter cell is less than or equal to the stop value, a call is made to the subroutine. When control returns from the subroutine, 1-2-3 increases the number in the counter cell by the step amount, and then repeats this entire step.

- At the point when the value in the counter cell is greater than the stop value, the action of the {For} command is ended, and the macro continues with the next instruction.

By contrast, if the step value is negative and the start value is greater than or equal to the stop value, the subroutine is called once for each decrement from start down to stop:

- The start value is copied to the counter cell.

- If the value in the counter cell is greater than or equal to the stop value, a call is made to the subroutine. When control returns from the subroutine, 1-2-3 decreases the number in the counter cell by the negative step amount, and then repeats this entire step.

- At the point when the value in the counter cell is less than the stop value, the action of the {For} command is terminated, and the macro continues with the next instruction.

In the second version of the schedule macro (see Figure 12.6), the {For} loop is responsible for producing time entries from 6:00 A.M. to 6:00 P.M. in the time increment you choose from the time dialog box:

{For <<C:\S2.WK4>>Time,0.25,0.76,<<C:\S2.WK4>> Incr,Entry}

Here are descriptions of the arguments that appear in this instruction:

- The cell named TIME serves as the counter cell in this {For} command. Because TIME is on the macro worksheet, a file reference is required to identify the cell: <<C:\S2.WK4>>Time.

- The start value for the loop is 0.25, the decimal value that represents 6:00 A.M.

- The stop value is 0.76, just slightly later than 6:00 P.M. (There is a slight accumulation of error in the time calculations that the loop performs; for this reason, the looping sometimes stops before 6:00 P.M. if 0.75 is used as the stop value.)

- The step value is the current value in the macro worksheet's INCR cell. The instruction selected from the time definition table (Figure 12.7) places one of three values in the INCR cell: 1/24, representing a one-hour increment; 1/48, representing a half-hour increment; or 1/96, representing a quarter-hour increment.

- The subroutine call appears as Entry. Because the cell named EN-TRY is on the macro worksheet itself, this call does not require a file reference.

NOTE   See page 1152 for further information about {For}.

12

Macro Programming

Using the {Let} Command

The {Let} command simply enters a label or a value into a specified cell location:

> {Let *reference,entry*}

The destination cell is identified by the first argument, *reference*, and the label or value to be entered into the cell is identified by the second argument, *entry*. For example, the following instruction stores a value in the INCR cell:

> {Let <<C:\S2.WK4>>Incr,1/24}

As you can see in Figure 12.7 (see page 643), there are three instructions like this one in the last row of the definition table for the time dialog box. Each one defines a different increment amount for use in the {For} loop.

The Entry subroutine, in cell B20 of the macro worksheet (see Figure 12.6 on page 643), uses a {Let} instruction to copy the time value from the TIME cell to the current cell in the Schedule worksheet:

> {Let @CELLPOINTER("coord"),<<C:\S2.WK4>>Time}

With a string argument of *coord*, the @CELLPOINTER function returns the complete address of the current cell—that is, the current location of the cell pointer in the schedule worksheet. After copying a time value to this current cell, the Entry subroutine uses a {Down} instruction to move the cell pointer down to the next cell in column A of the schedule worksheet. Then control of the program automatically goes back to the {For} command.

In the third version of the Schedule macro you'll explore the use of two additional macro commands, {If} and {Branch}.

NOTE   See page 1081 for more information about {Let}.

Using the {If} and {Branch} Commands

The {If} command expresses a decision in a macro, and the {Branch} command sends control of the program to a new location in the macro worksheet. You can use these two commands together to create a repetition loop in a macro. For example, the third version of the Schedule program illustrates these commands as a substitute for the {For} instruction.

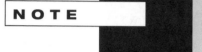

N O T E   In some programming contexts, {If} and {Branch} are the only appropriate tools for creating particular kinds of loops, as you'll see in the Mailing List macro presented later in this chapter.

The new instructions for the third version of the Schedule macro appear in Figure 12.9. Once again you can start with the previous version, S2.WK4, to create this new file. Here are the steps:

1. Close any schedule worksheets you created with the previous version of the program. Select S2.WK4.

2. Use the Edit ➤ Find & Replace to change all occurrences of S2.WK4 to S3.WK4. (Except for this change, the definition tables in columns D through G of the third version of the program are identical to the second version.)

3. Delete the {For} command from cell B13. Then select the range A14..B20 and use the drag-and-drop technique to move the selection down by three rows. The range A13..B16 is now blank.

4. Enter the four new macro instructions into B13..B16, as shown in Figure 12.9. Enter the **Loop** label into cell A14, and use the Range ➤ Name command to assign this label as a range name to cell B14.

5. Choose the File Save As command and save the file as **C:\S3.WK4**.

12

Macro Programming

FIGURE 12.9

The third version of the schedule macro. This version illustrates the {If} and {Branch} commands as a way of creating a loop in a macro program.

	A	B
1	Schedule Macro (C:\S3.WK4)	
2	Action	
3	\S	{File-New}
4		{Column-Width 11}
5		Daily Business Schedule~
6		{Style-Font-Attributes "bold","on"}
7		{Down 2}
8		{Choose-One <<C:\S3.WK4>>DCh,<<C:\S3.WK4>>Action,"Date choice:","Schedule"}
9		{Style-Number-Format "dd-mmm-yy"}
10		{Style-Font-Attributes "bold","on"}
11		{Down 2}
12		{Choose-One <<C:\S3.WK4>>TCh,<<C:\S3.WK4>>Action,"Time increment:","Schedule"}
13		{Let <<C:\S3.WK4>>Time,0.25}
14	Loop	{Entry}
15		{Let <<C:\S3.WK4>>Time,<<C:\S3.WK4>>Time+<<C:\S3.WK4>>Incr}
16		{If <<C:\S3.WK4>>Time<0.76}{Branch Loop}
17		{Style-Number-Format "hh:mm am/pm",,,A5..A53}
18		{Home}{Down 4}{Right}{Quit}
19		

Again, you may want to enter your own new comments into column C when you become more familiar with this program.

Try running the program. It works the same as the second version. The difference is in the logical structure of the new version: A sequence of {Let}, {If}, and {Branch} instructions have replaced the second version's {For} command.

The {If} Command

The {If} command takes a single argument, a logical expression that results in a value of true or false. This expression represents a decision that the macro makes during a performance. In the same cell as the {If} command, you always include a second macro command:

{If condition}command

The result of {If} is as follows:

- If condition is evaluated as true, 1-2-3 performs the command located in the same cell as the {If} instruction.

- If condition is false, 1-2-3 skips the command, and instead continues at the next cell in the column of macro instructions.

N O T E The {If} command is also discussed on page 1154.

The {Branch} Command

Often the command located after {If} is a {Branch} command. {Branch} sends control of the program to a new location in the current macro. This instruction takes a single reference argument:

{Branch *reference*}

As usual, the reference argument can appear as a cell address or a range name. As long as the reference identifies a cell location in the macro worksheet, you do not need to use a file reference.

For example, consider the {If} and {Branch} statements in cell B16 of the new Schedule macro (Figure 12.9):

{If <<C:\S3.WK4>>Time<0.76}{Branch Loop}

If the value in the cell named TIME is less than 0.76, the {Branch} instruction is performed, resulting in a jump back to the instruction stored at LOOP. Alternatively, if the value in TIME is 0.76 or greater, 1-2-3 skips the {Branch} instruction and instead moves on to the next line in the macro.

To put these two commands in context, here are brief descriptions of the instructions you've entered into this new macro in the range B13..B16:

CELL	WHAT THE PROGRAM DOES
B13	A {Let} command stores an initial value of 0.25 (representing 6:00 A.M.) in the TIME cell.
B14	The program makes a first call to the Entry subroutine. As a result, the current value of the TIME cell is copied to the current cell in the Schedule worksheet.
B15	A {Let} command replaces the current value of the TIME cell with an incremented value.

12

Macro Programming

CELL	WHAT THE PROGRAM DOES
B16	An {If} command examines the current value of the TIME cell, and determines whether the value is less than 0.76. If this condition is true, the subsequent {Branch} statement sends control of the program back to the statement named LOOP in cell B14.

The loop represented by the statements in cells B14, B15, and B16 continues until the TIME cell contains a value that is greater than or equal to 0.76.

N O T E   See page 1150 for more advice about the {Branch} command.

Debugging a Macro

The logical structure in a sequence of {If} and {Branch} statements presents many opportunities for error. Problems can result from a mistaken data entry, a faulty calculation, an incorrectly expressed condition, a misnamed cell, or any number of other common errors. In some cases, an error may actually cause an interruption in your program. When this happens, 1-2-3 stops the macro at a particular instruction and displays an error message that identifies the problem. At other times, however, a macro completes its performance from beginning to end without interruption, but fails to produce the results that you planned. When this happens, you may need to examine the macro's actions step-by-step during a performance in an effort to identify the instruction that is causing the trouble.

To help you in this effort, the Tools ➤ Macro submenu has two special commands named Single Step and Trace. These commands represent features that you can turn on or off in advance of a given macro run. Both are off by default. In most debugging procedures you use these two options together. Here is what the two commands look like after they've both been selected:

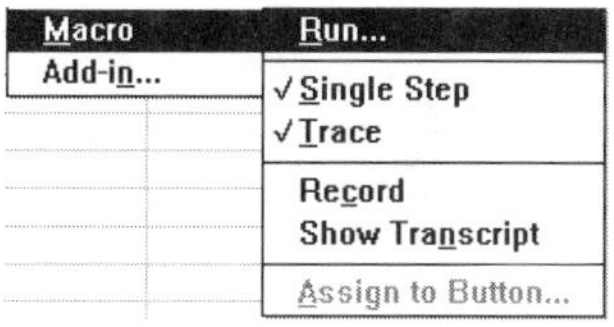
Macro
Add-in...
Run...
√Single Step
√Trace
Record
Show Transcript
Assign to Button...

When you activate these options, 1-2-3 modifies the action of the subsequent macro performance:

- **Single Step option.** If the Single Step option is active, 1-2-3 performs a macro in steps consisting of one instruction at a time. To proceed from one instruction to the next during the macro run, you press any key at the keyboard. (You can toggle in and out of the Step mode by pressing Alt+F2 at the keyboard.)
- **Trace option.** If the Trace option is active, 1-2-3 displays a special Macro Trace window on the screen. This window displays the cell location and the contents of each macro instruction that 1-2-3 is about to perform. Here's how Macro Trace window first appears on the screen, before you start a macro's performance:

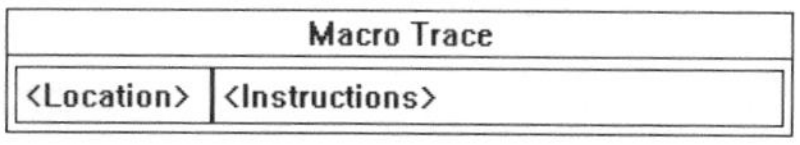
Macro Trace
<Location>
<Instructions>

As an exercise with these two commands, imagine that you've made the following error in the third version of the schedule macro: Rather than assigning the name LOOP to represent the instruction in cell B14, you've inadvertently assigned the range name to cell B15. If you want to experiment with the Single Step and Trace options, you can actually create this error now in your copy of the program: Reassign the LOOP range name to cell B15. When you next run the macro, the performance proceeds without interruption from beginning to end; 1-2-3 supplies no error message. But the output of the macro is incorrect. The program then enters 6:00 AM in column A of the schedule worksheet, but makes no further entries:

A	A	B
1	Daily Business Schedule	
2		
3	09-Jul-94	
4		
5	06:00 AM	
6		
7		

As you think about this problem, your initial guess may be that you've made a mistake in the {If} command that controls the looping (in cell B16). But a close look at this instruction fails to reveal the problem; the {If} condition appears to be written correctly.

This is an opportunity to take advantage of the Single Step and Trace options. Here's how to proceed:

1. Choose Tools ➤ Macro ➤ Single Step. The word *Step* appears on the status bar to indicate that this option is on.

2. Choose Tools ➤ Macro ➤ Trace to turn on the second of the two debugging options.

3. Press Ctrl+S to run the Schedule macro again. Press the spacebar (or any other key) multiple times to step through the initial instructions of the program. Select options from both of the program's dialog boxes when they appear on the screen.

4. Pause when the Macro Trace window first displays the instructions from cell B16:

This is where you initially guessed the error was taking place. Press the spacebar several more times.

As you do so, you discover that the loop is moving repeatedly between cells B15 and B16, without ever performing the subroutine call in cell B14. As you examine this action, you realize that the problem is not in the {If} instruction, but rather in the {Branch} command. {Branch Loop} is sending control of the program up to cell B15 rather than B14. This is a clear indication of the problem.

5. When the performance is complete, select the S3.WK4 worksheet. Click the Navigator button and choose LOOP in the drop-down list of the range names. When you do so, the cell pointer moves to cell B15, not B14.

6. Use the Range ➤ Name to reassign the name LOOP to the correct cell, B14.

7. Choose Tools ➤ Macro twice and deactivate both the Single Step and Trace options.

8. Press Ctrl+S to try running the program again. This time, the program runs as expected.

As you can see, the Single Step and Trace options are simple features, but they can prove very helpful in the process of finding a logical error in a macro.

Other Commands for Interactive Macros

In the three versions of the Schedule macro, you've learned how to use the {Choose-One} command to display dialog boxes on the screen. In addition, you've seen examples of the {Get-Label} command (in Chapter 9) to elicit a text entry from the keyboard, also by displaying a dialog box. These are only two of several macro tools designed to help you design an *interactive* program—that is, a program that displays options on the screen and elicits choices from a user who is sitting at the keyboard. The following list is a sampling of other such commands:

MACRO COMMAND	DESCRIPTION
{Choose-Item}	Displays a dialog box containing a scrollable list of items. The user selects any item in the list and then clicks OK to confirm the selection.
{Choose-Many}	Displays a dialog box containing a group of check boxes. The user activates any number of options in the group.
{Get-Number}	Displays a dialog box with a text box in which the user can enter a numeric value.
{Get-Formula}	Displays a dialog box in which the user can enter a formula.
{Get-Range}	Displays a dialog box in which the user can enter or point to a range reference.

MACRO COMMAND	DESCRIPTION
{Menu-Create}	Replaces the default 1-2-3 menu bar with a custom menu.
{Menu-Reset}	Restores the default 1-2-3 menu bar.
{Dialog?}	Displays a selected dialog box from one of 1-2-3's menu commands.
{Dialog}	Displays a custom dialog box.

Like the {Choose-One} command, several of these tools require you to create definition tables to describe the elements of the dialog box or menu that will appear on the screen during a macro run. Specifically, {Choose-Item}, {Choose-Many}, {Menu-Create}, and {Dialog} all require definition tables.

To investigate these commands in detail, open the Macro Keywords dialog box as follows:

1. Type { into any cell, and press F3. The Macro Keywords dialog box appears.

2. Pull down the Category list and choose the User environment option.

3. Scroll through the Macro keywords list and select the command that you want to learn about.

4. Press F1 to open the Help topic for the command you've selected.

TIP

Another way to learn about these and other "user environment" commands is to open the file named UIMACROS.WK4 from the \Sample subdirectory in the 1-2-3 directory. This worksheet—which is copied onto your hard disk when you install 1-2-3—contains explanations and examples of the interactive commands. They are also discussed in Chapter 21.

12

Macro Programming

Using the Lotus Dialog Editor

Of all these macro commands, {Dialog} is the ultimate tool for creating customized dialog boxes. You can use {Dialog} to produce a dialog box containing a specific assortment of controls for a particular application. For example, suppose you want to restructure the Schedule macro so that it displays a single dialog box presenting all the program's options at once. You would use {Dialog} to display these options on the screen.

The {Dialog} command takes only one argument:

{Dialog *dialogTable*}

The *dialogTable* argument is the range of a definition table you create to describe the elements of the custom dialog box. The rows of this definition table define each object in the dialog box. Fortunately, Lotus provides a software tool you can use to develop a custom dialog box *visually* and then translate your design automatically into a correctly structured definition table. The tool is a separate application called the *Lotus Dialog Editor.* You'll find the icon for this application in the 1-2-3 program group (in the Windows Program Manager):

Here are the general steps for using the Dialog Editor to produce a custom dialog box for a 1-2-3 macro:

1. Start the application by double-clicking the Lotus Dialog Editor icon in the 1-2-3 program group.

2. Choose File ➤ New to start a new design. In the New dialog box, enter a name and a title for the custom dialog box you plan to create.

3. Click OK, and then click the mouse at any position in the Dialog Editor's work area. A frame for your new dialog box appears on the screen.

4. Select this frame by clicking inside it. Optionally, use your mouse to resize the frame to the dimensions you want for your custom dialog box.

5. Pull down the Control menu to view the list of controls you can place inside a custom dialog box:

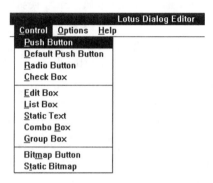

6. Select any one of these controls and then click inside the frame to place an object in your dialog box. Repeat this step for each item you want to include in the box. (You can use your mouse to move controls to any position within the frame.)

For example, here is how you might design a dialog box for the Schedule macro:

7. To define groups of items, choose Edit ➤ Order Items. The resulting Order Groups dialog box lists all the controls you've placed in the current frame. Select the first item in a sequence of objects

12

Macro Programming

that you want to define as a group, and click the Add Group button. Repeat this step for any other groups you want to define, and then click OK. (The Schedule dialog box contains two groups of option buttons, one for the Date options and another for the Time Increment options.)

8. Select the entire frame again, and press Ctrl+C to copy your dialog box definition to the Clipboard.

9. Return to 1-2-3 and open the worksheet in which you want to create a definition table for the dialog box.

10. Select the upper-left corner of the range where you want to store the table, and press Ctrl+V. Lotus automatically translates your custom dialog box design into a definition table.

11. Select the entire table plus two blank columns at the right side of the table (eleven columns in all). Then use the Range ➤ Name command to assign a range name to the selection.

12. In a sequence of macro instructions on the same worksheet, include a {Dialog *dialogTable*} command, where *dialogTable* is the range name you've assigned to the definition table. When you run the macro, this {Dialog} command will display your custom dialog box on the screen.

For example, here's how your Schedule dialog box might appear when you run the macro:

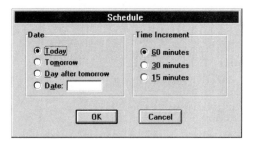

After the {Dialog} command, your macro can read the results—that is, the selections the user has made on your custom dialog box—directly from the eleventh column of the definition table.

T I P

{Dialog} is a powerful and versatile command, but it requires some elaborate planning. Before you decide to create a custom dialog box, consider using a combination of other commands that present ready-made dialog boxes on the screen—for example, {Choose-One}, {Choose-Item}, {Choose-Many}, {Get-Label}, and so on.

Creating a Database Macro

There are many useful ways to apply macro programming to a 1-2-3 database. For example, you might write macros for any of the following purposes:

- To simplify the process of entering records into a database.
- To automate queries on the database.
- To perform difficult database calculations.
- To produce special reports or lists from a database, in formats that can't otherwise be produced from 1-2-3.

In the final programming exercise of this chapter, you'll work with a macro that creates a file of mailing labels from the Instructor database. Figure 12.10 shows a sample of this program's output. The program writes this list to disk as a text file, which can be easily printed out onto gummed mailing labels.

You'll create the mailing list macro in the same worksheet file as the Instructor database itself, which you've saved in the file INSTRUCT.WK4. Open this file now and review the sheets that it currently contains. The first sheet, labeled Offices, is a database table showing the four regional

12

Macro Programming

FIGURE 12.10

A sample of the output from the mailing list macro. The program saves these address labels in a text file on disk.

```
W. Ashford
Computing Conferences, Inc.
222 Allen Street
New York, NY 10103


S. Banks
Computing Conferences, Inc.
11 Maple Street
Dallas, TX 75210


L. Cody
Computing Conferences, Inc.
432 Market Avenue
Los Angeles, CA 90028


A. Daniels
Computing Conferences, Inc.
11 Maple Street
Dallas, TX 75210


G. Davis
Computing Conferences, Inc.
432 Market Avenue
Los Angeles, CA 90028
```

office addresses for Computing Conferences, Inc. The second sheet, labeled Instructors, contains the table of instructor records. You've added several other sheets to the file to experiment with a variety of database tools. In the upcoming exercise, you'll create two more sheets for the purposes of the Mailing List macro:

- On a sheet named Addresses you'll create a new query containing the name and address of each instructor, as shown in Figure 12.11.

- On a sheet named Mailing List you'll enter the instructions of the macro itself, shown in Figure 12.12.

Here are the instructions for creating the new query and the Mailing List macro:

1. Select the last sheet in the INSTRUCT.WK4 file and click the New Sheet button to add another sheet.

FIGURE 12.11

A query containing instructors' names and office addresses. This query combines information from the Offices and Instructors database tables.

	A	B	C	D	E	F
	Offices	Instructors	Crosstab	Selection	Hours	Aggregate	Addresses	Mailing List
1	First	Last	Address	OFFICEDB.City	State	Zip
2	W.	Ashford	222 Allen Street	New York	NY	10103
3	S.	Banks	11 Maple Street	Dallas	TX	75210
4	L.	Cody	432 Market Avenue	Los Angeles	CA	90028
5	A.	Daniels	11 Maple Street	Dallas	TX	75210
6	G.	Davis	432 Market Avenue	Los Angeles	CA	90028
7	R.	Eng	11 Maple Street	Dallas	TX	75210
8	P.	Gill	432 Market Avenue	Los Angeles	CA	90028
9	P.	Harris	11 Maple Street	Dallas	TX	75210
10	J.	Meyer	222 Allen Street	New York	NY	10103
11	D.	Perez	432 Market Avenue	Los Angeles	CA	90028
12	M.	Porter	222 Allen Street	New York	NY	10103
13	D.	Porter	Mills Tower, Suite 992	Chicago	IL	60605
14	F.	Ramirez	222 Allen Street	New York	NY	10103
15	P.	Roberts	Mills Tower, Suite 992	Chicago	IL	60605
16	W.	Sanchez	Mills Tower, Suite 992	Chicago	IL	60605
17	B.	Schwartz	222 Allen Street	New York	NY	10103
18	P.	Weinberg	11 Maple Street	Dallas	TX	75210
19						
20						

Automatic   Arial   12   07/10/94 2:43 AM

FIGURE 12.12

The Mailing List macro. This program creates the mailing labels shown back in Figure 12.10.

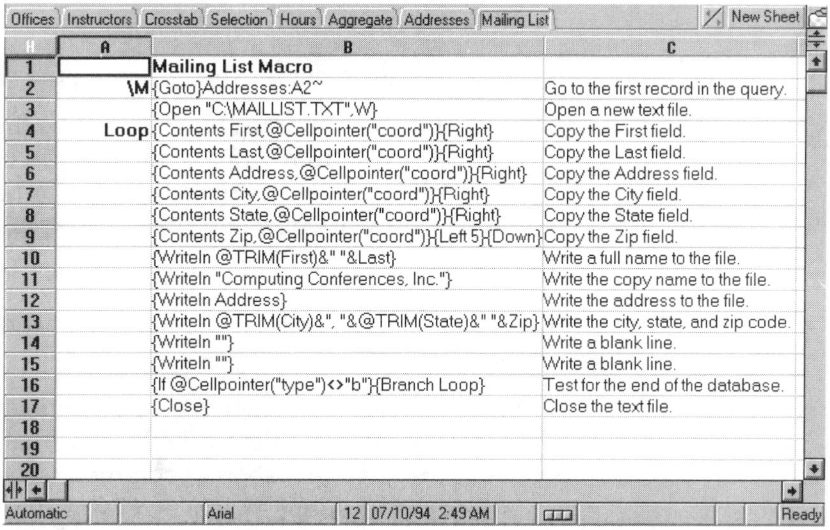

	A	B	C
	Offices	Instructors	Crosstab	Selection	Hours	Aggregate	Addresses	Mailing List	New Sheet
1		Mailing List Macro	
2	\M	{Goto}Addresses:A2~	Go to the first record in the query.
3		{Open "C:\MAILLIST.TXT",W}	Open a new text file.
4	Loop	{Contents First,@Cellpointer("coord")}{Right}	Copy the First field.
5		{Contents Last,@Cellpointer("coord")}{Right}	Copy the Last field.
6		{Contents Address,@Cellpointer("coord")}{Right}	Copy the Address field.
7		{Contents City,@Cellpointer("coord")}{Right}	Copy the City field.
8		{Contents State,@Cellpointer("coord")}{Right}	Copy the State field.
9		{Contents Zip,@Cellpointer("coord")}{Left 5}{Down}	Copy the Zip field.
10		{Writeln @TRIM(First)&" "&Last}	Write a full name to the file.
11		{Writeln "Computing Conferences, Inc."}	Write the copy name to the file.
12		{Writeln Address}	Write the address to the file.
13		{Writeln @TRIM(City)&", "&@TRIM(State)&" "&Zip}	Write the city, state, and zip code.
14		{Writeln ""}	Write a blank line.
15		{Writeln ""}	Write a blank line.
16		{If @Cellpointer("type")<>"b"}{Branch Loop}	Test for the end of the database.
17		{Close}	Close the text file.
18			
19			
20			

Automatic   Arial   12   07/10/94 2:49 AM   Ready

12

Macro Programming

2. Double-click the tab of the new sheet and type **Addresses**. Press ↵ to enter this name as the tab label.

3. Choose Tools ➤ Database ➤ New Query. The New Query dialog box appears.

4. Press F3 to view the list of database names. Select INSTRUCT-DB and click OK. This name appears in the text box labeled "Select database table to query."

5. Click the Choose Fields button. In the Choose Fields dialog box, click the Clear button multiple times to delete all the fields except Last and First from the Selected fields list. Then select the First field and click the up-arrow button at the bottom of the dialog box to switch the order of the two fields.

6. Click OK on the Choose Fields and New Query dialog boxes. The resulting query contains the first and last names of all the instructors.

7. While the query is still selected, choose Query ➤ Join. In the Join dialog box, 1-2-3 automatically determines the correct expression for joining the Offices and Instructors databases by their common Region fields. Click OK to confirm. The Choose Fields dialog box appears.

8. Use the Clear button to remove the OFFICEDB.Region, Phone, and Manager fields from the list. Six fields remain: First, Last, Address, OFFICEDB.City, State, and Zip.

9. Click OK to create the query joining the two database tables.

10. Click the Size Columns SmartIcon and then use the Query ➤ Sort command to rearrange the query in alphabetical order by instructors' last names. Click elsewhere on the sheet to deselect the query. Your work now appears as shown back in Figure 12.11.

11. Click the New Sheet button to add yet another sheet to the file.

12. Double-click the tab for the new sheet and enter **Mailing List** as the name.

13. Enter the labels, instructions, and comments of the mailing list macro, as shown in Figure 12.12. Use the Range ➤ Name command to assign the labels in column A as range names to the adjacent cells in column B.

14. In column D of the Mailing List sheet, enter the following six labels in these cells:

D1	**First**
D2	**Last**
D3	**Address**
D4	**City**
D5	**State**
D6	**Zip**

15. Select the range D1..D6, and click the Bold and Right Smart-Icons. Then use the Range ➤ Name command to assign these six labels as range names to the adjacent cells in column E.

The macro will use this range to make a temporary copy of each record it reads from the query. For example, here's what the range will look like at the end of a program run:

H	D	E	F
1	First	P.	
2	Last	Weinberg	
3	Address	11 Maple Street	
4	City	Dallas	
5	State	TX	
6	Zip	75210	
7			

16. Click the Save SmartIcon to update the INSTRUCT.WK4 file on disk.

Now you're ready to run the macro. Press Ctrl+M to begin. The macro creates a new text file named MAILLIST.TXT in the root directory of drive C. Next, the macro moves record-by-record through the query in the Addresses sheet, copying the fields in each record to its own temporary storage place in the range D1..D6. After reading each record, the program formats the field entries as a mailing label, and writes lines of text to the MAILLIST.TXT file. When all the addresses have been written, the program closes the file and the performance is complete.

To view the program's output, start up the Windows Notepad application. Pull down Notepad's File menu and choose the Open command. Select the MAILLIST.TXT file from the root directory of drive C. When the Notepad opens the file, you'll see the list of mailing labels as shown back in Figure 12.10 (see page 662).

Return to 1-2-3 now, and look again at the macro instructions you've entered into the Mailing List sheet. The program illustrates several new macro commands.

The {Contents} command The {Contents} command copies data from one cell to another in a worksheet. This command requires two references as arguments:

    {Contents *reference1,reference2*}

The command copies the contents of *reference2* to *reference1*. For example, here is how the mailing list program copies the first name field of each record to the cell named FIRST in worksheet E:

    {Contents First,@CELLPOINTER("coord")}

Notice that the mailing list program does not need to use file references in the {Contents} commands, because the macro is stored in the same file as the database.

Using Text File Commands in a Macro

The {Open}, {Writeln}, and {Close} commands are responsible for creating the text file on disk. The {Open} command takes two arguments: a string representing the file name, and a single letter code representing the operation for which the file will be opened:

    {Open *file,code*}

The code argument can be R, W, M, or A, for reading, writing, modifying, or appending data. In the mailing list program, the MAILLIST.TXT file is opened for writing:

{Open "C:\MAILLIST.TXT",W}

Once a file is open in this mode, the {WRITELN} command sends a line of text to the open file. This command takes a single string argument:

{WRITELN *string*}

The Mailing List program provides string arguments in a variety of formats for the {Writeln} command. For example, the argument in the program's first {Writeln} command is a concatenation of three strings and includes a call to the @TRIM function to eliminate spaces from the end of the first string:

{Writeln @TRIM(First)&" "&Last}

After the last line of text is written to the file, a {Close} command completes the write operation and closes the file. This command takes no arguments.

Here is a summary of the instructions in the mailing list program:

CELL(S)	WHAT THE PROGRAM DOES
B2	The macro selects the first cell in the first record of the query you've created in the Addresses sheet.
B3	The {Open} command creates the file MAILLIST.TXT on disk. (If a previous version of the file already exists, it is overwritten.)
B4..B9	A series of {Contents} commands copies each field from the current record in the query to the cells named FIRST, LAST, ADDRESS, CITY, STATE, and ZIP in the macro sheet. At the end of this sequence, the cell pointer is moved to the beginning of the next record in the query.

CELL(S)	WHAT THE PROGRAM DOES
B10..B15	A sequence of {Writeln} commands formats the record as a mailing label and writes each line of the label to the open text file.
B16	An {If} instruction examines the contents of the current cell in the Addresses worksheet.. If the cell is not empty, a {Branch} instruction sends control back up to the cell named LOOP, and the program once again begins reading a new record from the database. But if the cell is empty—that is, if the program has reached the end of the database—the {Branch} instruction is skipped.
B17	A {Close} instruction closes the text file.

This macro is easy to adapt for use in an address database that you use in your own work. After each {Contents} command, the program uses {Right}, {Left}, and {Down} instructions to move the cell pointer to a new field or record in the query. Then a subsequent {Contents} command uses the @CELLPOINTER function to identify the address of the current cell. To revise this program, you simply need to make sure that the movement of the cell pointer matches the structure of your own database. And, of course, you should revise the {Writeln} command in E:B11, which currently writes the name Computing Conferences, Inc., as the second line of each mailing label.

NOTE See page 1216 for further information about the {Writeln} command.

Summary

The 1-2-3 macro language provides commands for major categories of programming activity. In this chapter you've seen a selection of these macro commands:

- Data operations. The {Let} and {Contents} commands store data values in cells and copy values from one cell to another.

- Input and output. In an interactive program, commands such as {Get-Label} and {Choose-One} display dialog boxes on the screen, and accept the user's input and instructions from the keyboard. In a data file program, the {Open}, {Writeln}, and {Close} commands together create a file on disk and write lines of text as output to the file.

- Decisions. The {If} statement makes a decision that results in a choice between alternative courses of action during the macro performance.

- Loops. The {For} command is the main tool for creating loops in a macro. But when the loop cannot be based on specific start, stop, and step values, you can instead use the {If} and {Branch} commands to form a loop.

- Subroutines and flow of control. A subroutine call consists of a reference to the first cell in the subroutine, enclosed in braces. A {Branch} statement sends control of the program to a specified location without anticipating a return.

This is just a small sampling of the many tools available in the 1-2-3 macro language. To explore the language further, study the wealth of information available on macro programming and on individual macro commands in the 1-2-3 Help window, or turn to Chapter 21.

12

Macro Programming

PART

4

FUNCTIONS AND
MACRO LANGUAGE
REFERENCE

CHAPTER 13

An Overview of 1-2-3's Functions

AS DISCUSSED in Chapter 5, 1-2-3 Release 5 comes with a function library that contains well over two hundred functions. This library includes groups of special-purpose functions designed for particular fields of work, such as accounting, engineering, and statistics, while other functions are designed for much more general use and can be valuable to almost any user of 1-2-3. The program also comes with many built-in macro commands. These are explained in chapter 21.

Few users could hope to swiftly master such a cornucopia of functions—but, fortunately, very few users need to do so. Most users quickly identify the fistful of functions most useful to them or to their business and become adept in using them. 1-2-3 provides a number of tools to help you enter and use functions.

Part Four of this book is set up to help you find out immediately about the functions you need and how to use them. This part looks in detail at each of 1-2-3's functions, discussing its syntax and purpose, and illustrating its use. For convenience and wieldiness, the functions are divided by group into chapters, as shown in the following list:

FUNCTION CATEGORY	CHAPTER
Calendar functions	14
Database functions	15
Engineering functions	16
Financial functions	17
Information functions	18
Logical functions	18
Lookup functions	18
Mathematical functions	19

FUNCTION CATEGORY	CHAPTER
Statistical functions	19
Text functions	20

The next section of this chapter, "Using Functions," provides a quick recapitulation of how to enter and use functions. For a more detailed discussion of this topic, see Chapter 5.

The final section of this chapter, "1-2-3 Functions Quick Reference," provides an alphabetical list of 1-2-3's functions, together with a brief description of what each does and the page on which you can find a more detailed discussion.

Using Functions

This section of the chapter provides a quick summary of how to enter functions in cells and how to use functions.

Entering Functions into Cells

As discussed in Chapter 5, 1-2-3 offers several ways of entering a function into a cell:

- Type in the function and its arguments. This is the swiftest and easiest way of entering functions into worksheets and is best suited for those functions with fewer arguments. For example, if your worksheet contains a range named SQUIRRELS, you can find out the average of the values in the range (excluding any labels) by entering the following function statement into a cell:

  @PUREAVG(SQUIRRELS)

- Click the Function selector button on the edit line to see a list of commonly used functions. When you select a function name from the list, 1-2-3 enters the function into the current cell along with

13

Functions Overview

- Click the Function selector button on the edit line to see a list of commonly used functions. When you select a function name from the list, 1-2-3 enters the function into the current cell along with convenient placeholders for the arguments you need to supply. If the function you want to use is not in the list, choose the List All option to display the @Function List dialog box with the complete list of all the 1-2-3 functions.

TIP   As discussed in Chapter 5, you can customize the list of functions in the Function selector by choosing the List All option from the Function selector drop-down list and choosing the Menu>> button in the @Function List dialog box, then using the Add and Remove buttons in the expanded @Function List dialog box.

- Display the @Function List dialog box by typing @ into a cell and pressing the F3 function key, then choose a function from the @Function List dialog box. 1-2-3 copies the function to the edit line and supplies placeholders for arguments.

Getting Help with Functions

The easiest way to get help with functions is to enter the function into a cell using any of the methods described in the previous section, then press the F1 function key. 1-2-3 will take you directly to the help topic for that function.

When you've finished with the help topic, press Esc or double-click the control-menu box in the Help window to close Help and return to your worksheet.

The Elements of a Function

1-2-3's functions conform to a standard format, as you can see by looking at the following example:

@DATEDIF(*start-date,end-date,format*)

- A function name consists of the @ character, followed by the pre-defined name for the function itself—in this case, **DATEDIF**.

- Immediately following the function name, an open parenthesis character marks the beginning of the argument list. A close parenthesis character goes at the end of the list.

- Between the parentheses you enter the function's arguments. Each argument is separated from the next with an argument separator (such as a comma or a semicolon), but no spaces. Each argument can be expressed in any form that produces the required type of data. For example, an argument can appear as a cell reference, a range name, an expression, or even as another function name. For example, the *start-date* argument for the @DATEDIF function could be a cell reference such as A1, an expression that produced a date number, or another date function.

- The correct number and type of arguments is defined for each function in the 1-2-3 library. For example, the @DATEDIF function shown here requires three arguments—*start-date*, *end-date*, and *format*—and will not run without them. A few functions (for example, @ERR and @NA) take no arguments and therefore need no parentheses. Many other functions have optional arguments in addition to their required arguments. While you need not include any of the optional arguments when you enter such a function, if you do use any of the optional arguments, you must use all the optional arguments that precede it so that 1-2-3 can correctly identify all the arguments you enter.

1-2-3 Functions Quick Reference

This section of the chapter provides an alphabetical list of 1-2-3's functions, together with a brief description of what each does and the page on which you can find a more detailed discussion.

TABLE 13.1: 1-2-3 Functions Quick Reference

FUNCTION	RETURNS	SEE PAGE
@@	The contents of the cell specified by means of a reference through the contents of another cell	866
@ABS	The absolute value of *number*, where *number* is any number	890
@ACCRUED	The accrued interest for a security of a given value	769
@ACOS	The angle that is the arc cosine of *number*, where *number* is a value between −1 and 1	890
@ACOSH	The arc hyperbolic cosine of the given angle	891
@ACOT	The arc cotangent of the given angle	891
@ACOTH	The arc hyperbolic cotangent of the given angle	891
@ACSC	The arc cosecant of the given angle	892
@ACSCH	The arc hyperbolic cosecant of the given angle	892
@ASEC	The arc secant of the given angle	892
@ASECH	The arc hyperbolic secant of the given angle	893
@ASIN	The arc sine of the given angle	893
@ASINH	The arc hyperbolic sine of the given angle	894
@ATAN	The arc tangent of the given angle	894
@ATAN2	The arc tangent of the given angle determined by the x and y coordinates using the tangent y/x (*n1/n*)	895
@ATANH	The arc hyperbolic tangent of the given angle	896

TABLE 13.1: 1-2-3 Functions Quick Reference (continued)

FUNCTION	RETURNS	SEE PAGE
@AVEDEV	The average of the absolute deviations of the values in the given list	933
@AVG	The average of the values contained in the given list	934
@BESSELI	The modified Bessel integer function $In(x)$	752
@BESSELJ	The Bessel integer function $Jn(x)$	753
@BESSELK	The modified Bessel integer function $Kn(x)$	754
@BESSELY	The Bessel integer function $Yn(x)$	754
@BETA	The Beta integer function	755
@BETAI	The incomplete Beta integer function	755
@BINOMIAL	The binomial probability mass function or the cumulative binomial distribution	935
@CELL	Information about the upper-left cell in a reference; for example, the cell's contents, color, or file name	825
@CELLPOINTER	Information about the current cell's formatting, location, or contents	829
@CHAR	The character of the Lotus Multibyte Character Set (LMBCS) that corresponds to the number code specified	999
@CHIDIST	The one-tailed probability of the chi-square distribution	937

TABLE 13.1: 1-2-3 Functions Quick Reference (continued)

FUNCTION	RETURNS	SEE PAGE
@CHITEST	The independence on the data in a given range or the goodness of fit for the data in two given ranges	938
@CHOOSE	A value or label from a list or range of values	867
@CLEAN	The specified text string with all nonprinting characters removed from it	1000
@CODE	The code for the Lotus Multibyte Character Set (LMBCS) code that corresponds to the first character in a text string	1000
@COLS	The number of columns in a range	829
@COMBIN	The binomial coefficient for two specified values	940
@COORD	A cell reference from given values for *worksheet*, *column*, and *row*	830
@CORREL	The correlation coefficient of the values for two given ranges	940
@COS	The cosine of the given angle	896
@COSH	The hyperbolic cosine of the given angle	897
@COT	The cotangent of the given angle	898
@COTH	The hyperbolic cotangent of the given angle	898
@COUNT	The number of nonblank cells in the given list	941
@COV	Either the population or the sample covariance of the values in two given ranges	942

TABLE 13.1: 1-2-3 Functions Quick Reference (continued)

FUNCTION	RETURNS	SEE PAGE
@CRITBINOMIAL	The largest integer for which the cumulative binomial distribution is less than or equal to alpha	943
@CSC	The cosecant (the reciprocal of the sine) of the given angle	899
@CSCH	The hyperbolic cosecant (the reciprocal of the hyperbolic sine) of the given angle	899
@CTERM	The number of compounding periods required for a one-time investment earning a fixed periodic interest rate to reach a specified future value	772
@D360	The number of days between two date numbers	703
@DATE	A date number from three integer arguments representing the year, the month, and the day	705
@DATEDIF	The number of days, months, or years between two date numbers	706
@DATEINFO	Various kinds of information about a date number	708
@DATESTRING	Text that resembles its equivalent date	709
@DATEVALUE	A date number from a text string	710
@DAVG	The average of selected values in a database range	734
@DAY	An integer from 1 to 31, representing the day of the month	712
@DAYS	The number of days between two date numbers using a user-specified *basis* for day-count	712

TABLE 13.1: 1-2-3 Functions Quick Reference (continued)

FUNCTION	RETURNS	SEE PAGE
@DAYS360	The number of days between two dates based on a 360-day year (12 months of 30 days each)	713
@DB	The depreciation value of an asset, calculated using the declining-balance method	773
@DCOUNT	The number of selected values in a database range	735
@DDB	The depreciation value of an asset, calculated using the double-declining-balance method	774
@DDELINK	Establishes a DDE link in the current cell to another Windows application or another 1-2-3 file	831
@DECIMAL	A signed decimal value from a hexadecimal string	756
@DEGTORAD	The value in radians of the angle given in degrees	900
@DEVSQ	The sum of squared deviations of the values in the given list from their mean (average)	944
@DGET	The field item from a single database record selected by the expressions in the criteria range	736
@DMAX	The largest value among selected entries in a database range	738
@DMIN	The smallest value among selected entries in a database range	738

TABLE 13.1: 1-2-3 Functions Quick Reference (continued)

FUNCTION	RETURNS	SEE PAGE
@DPURECOUNT	The number of a cells in a database that contain a value in the specified field that match specified criteria	740
@DQUERY	Calls a function defined in an external database	742
@DSTD	The population standard deviation of selected values in a database range	743
@DSTDS	The sample standard deviation of selected values in a database range	743
@DSUM	The sum of selected values in a database range	745
@DURATION	The annual duration for a security that pays periodic interest	777
@DVAR	The population variance of selected values in a database range	746
@DVARS	The sample variance of selected values in a database range	747
@ERF	The error function	757
@ERFC	The complementary error function	758
@ERFD	The derivative of the error function	759
@ERR	The value ERR (for forcing an error condition in formulas when a certain result would be undesirable)	835

TABLE 13.1: 1-2-3 Functions Quick Reference (continued)

FUNCTION	RETURNS	SEE PAGE
@EVEN	The nearest even integer to the number; positive values are rounded up and negative values are rounded down	900
@EXACT	1 (TRUE) if the two specified sets of characters match exactly; 0 (FALSE) if the two sets do not match exactly	1001
@EXP	The value of the constant e (approximately 2.718282, the base of the natural logarithm) raised to the specified power	901
@EXP2	The value of the constant e (approximately 2.718282, the base of the natural logarithm) raised to the power (*numeric-value^2*)	902
@FACT	The factorial of the given number (the product of all positive integers from 1 to the number)	902
@FACTLN	The natural logarithm of the factorial of a number	903
@FALSE	The logical value 0 (FALSE), the opposite of the logical value 1 (TRUE)	853
@FDIST	The F-distribution of probability for the two given ranges (for determining the degree to which two samples vary)	945
@FIND	The position in a given text string at which 1-2-3 finds the first occurrence of the specified search text, the search beginning at the given position	1002

TABLE 13.1: 1-2-3 Functions Quick Reference (continued)

FUNCTION	RETURNS	SEE PAGE
@**FTEST**	The associated probability of an F probability test for the two given ranges (to test if two samples have different variances)	946
@**FV**	The future value of a series of equal periodic payment amounts over term periods at a fixed periodic interest rate	778
@**FVAL**	The future value of an item based on the present value	779
@**GAMMA**	The Gamma function	759
@**GAMMAI**	The incomplete Gamma function	760
@**GAMMALN**	The natural logarithm of the Gamma function	761
@**GEOMEAN**	The geometric mean of the values in the given list	947
@**GRANDTOTAL**	The sum of all the cells in the given list that contain the function @SUBTOTAL	948
@**HARMEAN**	The harmonic mean of the values in the given list	948
@**HEX**	A hexadecimal string from a signed decimal value	761
@**HLOOKUP**	The contents of the cell indicated by a specified key in a specified row of a horizontal lookup table	868
@**HOUR**	An integer from 0 to 23, representing the hour	714

TABLE 13.1: 1-2-3 Functions Quick Reference (continued)

FUNCTION	RETURNS	SEE PAGE
@IF	The result given for *true* if the given condition evaluates as TRUE (not equaling zero) or the result given for *false* if condition evaluates as FALSE (equaling zero)	854
@INDEX	The contents of the cell located at the intersection of a specified column, row, and worksheet of a range	871
@INFO	System information for the current 1-2-3 session, such as the current directory path or the current operating system	835
@INT	The integer value of the given number, disregarding any fractional portion	903
@IPAYMT	The cumulative interest on a loan	781
@IRATE	A value equivalent to the periodic interest rate of an investment	783
@IRR	The internal rate of return from a series of positive and negative cash-flow amounts	785
@ISAAF	1 (TRUE) if the given name is that of a defined add-in function for 1-2-3; 0 (FALSE) if it is not	856
@ISAPP	1 (TRUE) if the given name is that of a defined add-in application for 1-2-3; 0 (FALSE) if it is not	857
@ISEMPTY	1 (TRUE) if the specified location is a blank cell; 0 (FALSE) if it is not blank	857

TABLE 13.1: 1-2-3 Functions Quick Reference (continued)

FUNCTION	RETURNS	SEE PAGE
@ISERR	1 (TRUE) if the given value is the value ERR and 0 (FALSE) if *value* is not the value ERR	858
@ISFILE	1 (TRUE) if the specified file-name exists and 0 (FALSE) if it does not exist	859
@ISMACRO	1 (TRUE) if the specified name is a defined add-in macro command and 0 (FALSE) if it is not	860
@ISNA	1 (TRUE) if the specified value is the value NA and 0 (FALSE) if *value* is not the value NA	860
@ISNUMBER	1 (TRUE) if the specified value contains a value, NA, ERR, or a blank cell; 0 (FALSE) if the specified value is text or a cell containing a label or a formula that results in a label	860
@ISRANGE	1 (TRUE) if the specified range is a defined range name or valid range address; 0 (FALSE) if it is not	861
@ISSTRING	1 (TRUE) if the specified value is text or a cell that contains a label or a formula that results in a label; 0 (FALSE) if the specified value is a value, ERR, NA, or a blank cell	862

TABLE 13.1: 1-2-3 Functions Quick Reference (continued)

FUNCTION	RETURNS	SEE PAGE
@KURTOSIS	The kurtosis of the values in the given range—the concentration of a distribution around the mean of a range of values	950
@LARGE	The nth largest value in the given range	904
@LEFT	The specified number of the first (leftmost) characters in a given text string	1003
@LENGTH	The number of characters in a string	1005
@LN	The natural logarithm of the given value	905
@LOG	The common or base-10 logarithm (base 10) of the given value	906
@LOWER	The given string with all letters converted to lowercase	1006
@MATCH	The offset position in a range of the cell containing specified contents	873
@MAX	The largest value in the given list	950
@MAXLOOKUP	An absolute reference to the cell containing the largest value in a list of ranges	875
@MDURATION	The modified annual duration for a security that pays periodic interest	788
@MEDIAN	The median value in the given list	952

TABLE 13.1: 1-2-3 Functions Quick Reference (continued)

FUNCTION	RETURNS	SEE PAGE
@MID	The specified number of characters from a text string, beginning with the character at the offset specified	1008
@MIN	The smallest value in the given list	952
@MINLOOKUP	An absolute reference to the cell containing the smallest value in a list of ranges	875
@MINUTE	An integer from 0 to 59, representing the minutes	715
@MIRR	The modified internal rate of return for a series of positive and negative cash-flow amounts	790
@MOD	The *modulus* (remainder) after the given number is divided by the given divisor	906
@MONTH	An integer from 1 to 12, representing the month	715
@N	The entry in the first cell of a specified range as a value	876
@NA	The value NA ("not available") indicating that no value is available; for use as a placeholder for key cells that need to be filled for a formula to be valid	839
@NETWORKDAYS	The number of working days (days excluding weekends and holidays) between two date numbers	716

TABLE 13.1: 1-2-3 Functions Quick Reference (continued)

FUNCTION	RETURNS	SEE PAGE
@NEXTMONTH	The date number for the date that falls a specified number of months before or after a given date	718
@NORMAL	The normal distribution function for the specific mean (average) and standard deviation	954
@NOW	A date number and time number representing the current date and the current time	720
@NPER	The number of periods required to reach a specified future value at a given interest rate	792
@NPV	The net present value of a series of positive or negative future periodic cash-flow amounts	794
@ODD	The given value rounded away from 0 to the nearest odd integer; positive values are rounded up and negative values are rounded down	908
@PAYMT	The payments necessary to reach a specified principal over a given term at a fixed interest rate	797
@PERCENTILE	The xth sample percentile among the values in the given range	956
@PERMUT	The number of permutations (ordered sequences) of objects that can be selected from a given number of objects	955
@PI	The value of the mathematical constant	908
@PMT	The periodic payment required to pay back a loan over a given term at a fixed interest rate	798

TABLE 13.1: 1-2-3 Functions Quick Reference (continued)

FUNCTION	RETURNS	SEE PAGE
@PMTC	The periodic payment required to pay back a loan over a given term at a fixed interest rate (@PMTC is a version of @PMT adjusted for Canadian mortgage conventions)	800
@POISSON	The Poisson distribution (for predicting the number of events that will occur over a specific period of time)	957
@PPAYMT	The principal value of payments made on a loan	801
@PRANK	The percentile of the given value among the values in the given range	959
@PRICE	The price per $100 of value for investments that pay a periodic interest	803
@PRODUCT	The product of the values in the given list	960
@PROPER	The given string with all the letters converted to initial capital style (i.e., the first letter of each word in uppercase and the remaining letters all lowercase)	1010
@PUREAVG	The average of the values contained in the given list, ignoring cells in the range that contain labels	961
@PURECOUNT	The number of nonblank cells in the given list, ignoring cells in the range that contain labels	961

TABLE 13.1: 1-2-3 Functions Quick Reference (continued)

FUNCTION	RETURNS	SEE PAGE
@PUREMAX	The largest value	962
@PUREMIN	The smallest value in the given list, ignoring cells that contain labels	963
@PURESTD	The population standard deviation of the values in the given list, ignoring cells that contain labels	963
@PURESTDS	The sample standard deviation of the values in the given list, ignoring cells that contain labels	966
@PUREVAR	The population variance in the given list, ignoring cells that contain labels	968
@PUREVARS	The sample population variance in the given list, ignoring cells that contain labels	970
@PV	The present value of a series of equal future cash-flow amounts	805
@PVAL	The present value of an investment	807
@QUOTIENT	The integer result of the given number divided by the given divisor	909
@RADTODEG	The value in degrees of a value given in radians	910
@RAND	A random value between 0 and 1 calculated to seventeen decimal places	909
@RANGENAME	The name of the range in which a given cell is located	841
@RANK	The rank of the given value relative to other values in the range	971

TABLE 13.1:   1-2-3 Functions Quick Reference (continued)

FUNCTION	RETURNS	SEE PAGE
@RATE	The interest rate that will produce a fixed future return from an initial investment over a specified term	809
@REFCONVERT	The corresponding numbers (1–256) for the 1-2-3 column or worksheet letters (A–IV) to numbers from 1 through 256, and the corresponding column or worksheet letters for the numbers 1–256	841
@REGRESSION	The statistic specified from a multiple linear regression	973
@REPEAT	The specified string repeated the specified number of times	1012
@REPLACE	The specified text string with the given replacement text added or appended	1013
@RIGHT	The specified number of characters last (rightmost) in a text string	1015
@ROUND	The given number rounded to the nearest specified multiple of the power of 10	911
@ROUNDDOWN	The given value rounded down to the nearest multiple of the specified power	912
@ROUNDM	The given value rounded to the nearest specified multiple	914
@ROUNDUP	The given value rounded up to the nearest multiple of the specified power	915

TABLE 13.1: 1-2-3 Functions Quick Reference (continued)

FUNCTION	RETURNS	SEE PAGE
@ROWS	The number of rows in a given range	842
@S	The entry in the first cell of a given range as a label. If the entry is a value, @S returns a blank cell	1017
@SCENARIOINFO	Information about a scenario— for example, the user who last modified a scenario or the latest comment attached to a scenario	842
@SCENARIO-LAST	The name of the scenario that was last displayed in a file during the current 1-2-3 session	844
@SEC	The secant (the reciprocal of the cosine) of the given angle	917
@SECH	The hyperbolic secant (the reciprocal of the hyperbolic cosine) of the given angle	918
@SECOND	An integer from 0 to 59, representing the seconds	721
@SEMEAN	The standard error of the sample mean (or average) for the values in the given range	920
@SERIESSUM	The sum of a power series	762
@SETSTRING	A label the specified number of characters long consisting of the specified text string and enough blank spaces to align the text string with the chosen alignment	1018
@SHEETS	The number of worksheets in a given range	845
@SIGN	The sign of the given number	918
@SIN	The sine of the given angle	918

TABLE 13.1: Table 13.1: 1-2-3 Functions Quick Reference (continued)

FUNCTION	RETURNS	SEE PAGE
@SINH	The hyperbolic sine of the given angle	919
@SKEWNESS	The skewness of the values in the given range—the symmetry of a distribution around its mean (average)	975
@SLN	The depreciation of an asset, using the straight-line method	809
@SMALL	The nth smallest value in the given range	920
@SOLVER	A value that gives information about the status of Solver	845
@SQRT	The positive square root of the given value	921
@SQRTPI	The square root of the given value multiplied by ~PI	921
@STD	The population standard deviation of the values in the given list	976
@STDS	The sample standard deviation of the values in the given list	978
@STRING	The specified value converted to a label using the format specified	1020
@SUBTOTAL	The total of the values in a list. @SUBTOTAL also indicates to @GRANDTOTAL which subtotals to include in the grand total	922
@SUM	The sum of the values in the given list	923

TABLE 13.1: 1-2-3 Functions Quick Reference (continued)

FUNCTION	RETURNS	SEE PAGE
@SUMNEGATIVE	The sum of the negative values in the given list	980
@SUMPOSITIVE	The sum of the positive values in the given list	980
@SUMPRODUCT	The sum of the products of values in corresponding cells in multiple ranges	924
@SUMSQ	The sum of the squares of the values in the given list	925
@SUMXMY2	The sum of the squared differences after the values in one range have been subtracted from the corresponding cells in another range	925
@SYD	The depreciation of an asset, using the sum-of-the-years'-digits method	811
@TAN	The tangent of the given angle	926
@TANH	The hyperbolic tangent of the given angle	927
@TDIST	The Student's t-distribution (the distribution of the ratio of a standardized normal distribution to the square root of the quotient of a chi-square distribution by the number of its degrees of freedom)	982
@TERM	The number of equal payment amounts required to reach a specified future value at a fixed interest rate	813
@TIME	A decimal time number from three numeric arguments representing the hour, the minutes, and the seconds	721

TABLE 13.1: 1-2-3 Functions Quick Reference (continued)

FUNCTION	RETURNS	SEE PAGE
@TIMEVALUE	A decimal time number from a string argument entered in one of four forms that 1-2-3 recognizes	722
@TODAY	A date number representing the current date	723
@TRIM	The specified text string with all leading, trailing, and consecutive space characters stripped from it	1021
@TRUE	The logical value 1 (TRUE)	863
@TRUNC	The given value truncated to the number of decimal places specified	927
@TTEST	The associated probability of a Student's t-test on the data in two given ranges (to establish whether two samples are likely to have come from the same two underlying populations)	984
@UPPER	The specified string with all its letters converted to uppercase	1021
@VALUE	The value corresponding to a number entered as a text string in one of the four formats 1-2-3 recognizes	1023
@VAR	The population variance in the given list of values	986
@VARS	The sample population variance in the given list of values	988
@VDB	The depreciation of an asset, using the variable-declining-balance method	815

TABLE 13.1: 1-2-3 Functions Quick Reference (continued)

FUNCTION	RETURNS	SEE PAGE
@VERSION-CURRENT	The name of the current version in a range	848
@VERSIONDATA	The contents of a specified cell in a version	848
@VERSIONINFO	Information about a version—for example, the name of the user who created it or who last modified it	850
@VLOOKUP	The contents of the cell indicated by a given key in a specified column of a vertical lookup table	877
@WEEKDAY	An integer from 0 through 6, representing the day of the week (0 = Monday, 6 = Sunday)	724
@WEIGHTAVG	The weighted average of values in a data range	990
@WORKDAY	The date number for the date that falls a specified number of working days before or after a given date	724
@XINDEX	The contents of the cell located at the intersection of a specified column_heading, row_heading, and worksheet_heading of a range	879
@YEAR	An integer representing the year	726
@YIELD	The yield on an interest-bearing security	818
@ZTEST	The associated probability of a z-test on one or two populations (for judging the likelihood that a particular observation is drawn from a particular population)	992

14

Calendar

Functions

Reference

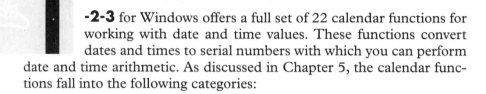

-2-3 for Windows offers a full set of 22 calendar functions for working with date and time values. These functions convert dates and times to serial numbers with which you can perform date and time arithmetic. As discussed in Chapter 5, the calendar functions fall into the following categories:

- Functions that supply the current date and time
- Functions that give information about existing time and date values
- Functions that convert other types of data into date and time values
- Functions that perform date arithmetic

The next section gives a quick overview of the calendar functions. In the section after that, you will find detailed descriptions of the calendar functions.

NOTE   See "Date and Time Functions" in Chapter 5 (starting on page 312) for a general explanation of how to use calendar functions.

Overview of the Calendar Functions

For quick reference, Table 14.1 lists the 22 calendar functions in their four categories, with page numbers indicating their detailed discussions in the next section of this chapter, "Descriptions of the Calendar Functions."

TABLE 14.1: Calendar Functions Quick Reference

FUNCTION	RETURNS	SEE PAGE
CURRENT DATE AND TIME CALCULATIONS		
@NOW	A date number and time number representing the current date and the current time	720
@TODAY	A date number representing the current date	723
INFORMATION ABOUT DATE AND TIME VALUES		
@DATEINFO	Various kinds of information about a date number	708
@DAY	An integer from 1 to 31, representing the day of the month	712
@HOUR	An integer from 0 to 23, representing the hour	714
@MINUTE	An integer from 0 to 59, representing the minutes	715
@MONTH	An integer from 1 to 12, representing the month	715
@SECOND	An integer from 0 to 59, representing the seconds	721
@WEEKDAY	An integer from 0 through 6, representing the day of the week (0 = Monday, 6 = Sunday)	724
@YEAR	An integer representing the year	726
CONVERSION OF DATA INTO DATE AND TIME VALUES		
@DATE	A date number from three integer arguments representing the year, the month, and the day	705
@DATESTRING	Text that resembles its equivalent date	709
@DATEVALUE	A date number from a text string	710

14

Calendar Functions

CALENDAR FUNCTIONS REFERENCE

TABLE 14.1: Calendar Functions Quick Reference (continued)

FUNCTION	RETURNS	SEE PAGE
@TIME	A decimal time number from three numeric arguments representing the hour, the minutes, and the seconds	721
@TIMEVALUE	A decimal time number from a string argument entered in one of four forms that 1-2-3 recognizes	722
DATE ARITHMETIC		
@D360	The number of days between two date numbers	703
@DATEDIF	The number of days, months, or years between two date numbers	706
@DAYS	The number of days between two date numbers using a user-specified *basis* for day-count	712
@DAYS360	The number of days between two dates based on a 360-day year (12 months of 30 days each)	713
@NETWORKDAYS	The number of working days (days excluding weekends and holidays) between two date numbers	716
@NEXTMONTH	The date number for the date that falls a specified number of months before or after a given date	718
@WORKDAY	The date number for the date that falls a specified number of working days before or after a given date	724

NOTE

The @DATESTRING, @NETWORKDAYS, and @NEXTMONTH functions are new in Release 5 of 1-2-3.

Descriptions of the Calendar Functions

This section contains detailed descriptions of each calendar @ function.

@D360(*start-date,end-date*)

The @D360 function returns the number of days between two dates, *start-date* and *end-date*, which are both date numbers based on a 360-day year (12 months of 30 days apiece, as per the 1990 modifications to the Securities Industry Association's 1986 edition of Standard Security Calculation Methods).

For example, to calculate the number of days between January 1, 1995 (date number 34700), and May 27, 1995 (date number 34846), you could use:

```
@D360(34700,34846)
```

The answer returned is 146 days. Note that this total includes the start date and the end date.

WARNING

@D360 and @DAYS360 may return different answers for the same data when either *start-date* or *end-date* is the last day of the month.

Figure 14.1 illustrates the different values produced by @D360, @DAYS360, and @DAYS. The cells contain the following function statements:

CELL	STATEMENT
C6	@D360(A6,B6)
D6	@DAYS360(A6,B6)
E6	@DAYS(A6,B6)
F6	@DAYS(A6,B6,1)
G6	@DAYS(A6,B6,2)
H6	@DAYS(A6,B6,3)

Note the different values produced by the four permutations of @DAYS.

See Also @DATE, @DATEDIF, @DAYS

FIGURE 14.1

@D360, @DAYS360, and @DAYS produce different results

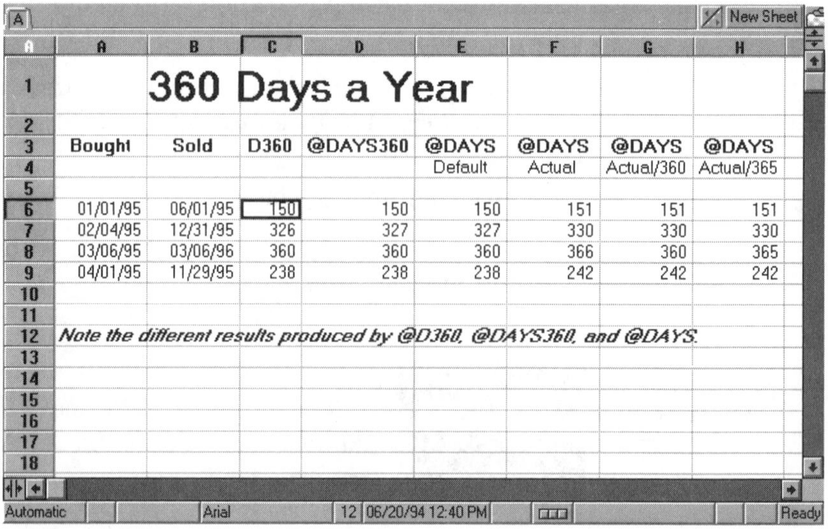

360 Days a Year

	Bought	Sold	D360	@DAYS360	@DAYS	@DAYS	@DAYS	@DAYS
					Default	Actual	Actual/360	Actual/365
	01/01/95	06/01/95	150	150	150	151	151	151
	02/04/95	12/31/95	326	327	327	330	330	330
	03/06/95	03/06/96	360	360	360	366	360	365
	04/01/95	11/29/95	238	238	238	242	242	242

Note the different results produced by @D360, @DAYS360, and @DAYS.

@DATE(*year,month,day*)

The @DATE function returns the date number for the *year*, *month*, and *day* entered. Turning a date into a date number that 1-2-3 can use is usually the first step in using dates in arithmetic operations, and you'll probably find yourself using the @DATE function frequently.

The arguments for @DATE are as follows:

ARGUMENT	DESCRIPTION
year	An integer from 0 through 199. Zero represents 1900, 199 represents 2099, 95 represents 1995, and so on.
month	An integer from 1 through 12. One represents January, 12 represents December.
day	An integer from 1 through 31 (or 28, 29, or 30, depending on the number of days in the month). If you try to enter a date that doesn't exist—for example, February 30—1-2-3 will return an error.

Consider the following example of the @DATE function:

@DATE(95,6,3)

This returns 34853, the date number for June 3, 1995. To make the results of @DATE appear in a date format (such as 03-Jun-95), format the cell by using the Format selector in the status bar or the Number Format dialog box.

You can use @DATE with algebraic symbols for calculations. For example, to find the date five days before May 9, 1987, you could use

@DATE(87,5,9)-5

which returns 31901, the date number for May 4, 1987. You might be tempted to use @DATE to calculate the date a bill is due or overdue, but you'd do better to use the @WORKDAY function instead, which you can set up to exclude weekends and holidays from the calculation.

14

Calendar Functions

WARNING

How well does 1-2-3 handle February 29 on leap years? Perfectly, apart from February 29, 1900, a day that 1-2-3 assigns but which did not take place, as 1900 was not a leap year. So if you're using dates between January 1, 1900 and March 1, 1900, you'll need to subtract 1 from any results to get the correct date. Otherwise, don't worry.

See Also @DATEVALUE, @NOW, @TIME

@DATEDIF(*start-date,end-date, format*)

The @DATEDIF function returns the number of years, months, or days between two date numbers, where *start-date* and *end-date* are date numbers and *format* is a text code that specifies the format in which to calculate and return the result. Following are the *format* text codes:

FORMAT	RETURNS THE NUMBER OF
y	years
m	months
d	days
md	days, ignoring months and years
ym	months, ignoring years
yd	days, ignoring years

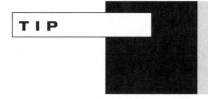

TIP

Use the @DATE function together with @DATEDIF to keep your worksheets neat: Use @DATEDIF(@DATE(64,11,28),@DATE(100,1,1),"y") rather than @DATEDIF(23709,36526).

For example, you could use @DATEDIF to calculate the length of time between November 28, 1964 and January 1, 2000 in several different ways. This returns 35, the number of years between November 28, 1964 and January 1, 2000:

> @DATEDIF(@DATE(64,11,28),@DATE(100,1,1),"y")

This returns 421, the number of months between November 28, 1964 and January 1, 2000:

> @DATEDIF(@DATE(64,11,28),@DATE(100,1,1),"m")

This returns 12817, the number of days between November 28, 1964 and January 1, 2000:

> @DATEDIF(@DATE(64,11,28),@DATE(100,1,1),"d")

This returns 4, the number of days (ignoring months and years) between November 28, 1964 and January 1, 2000:

> @DATEDIF(@DATE(64,11,28),@DATE(100,1,1),"md")

This returns 1, the number of months (ignoring years) between November 28, 1964 and January 1, 2000:

> @DATEDIF(@DATE(64,11,28),@DATE(100,1,1),"ym")

This returns 34, the number of days (ignoring years) between November 28, 1964 and January 1, 2000:

> @DATEDIF(@DATE(64,11,28),@DATE(100,1,1),"yd")

Figure 14.2 illustrates the use of @DATEDIF in a human-resources worksheet. Cell F5 contains the function statement

> @DATEDIF(D5,@TODAY,"y")

to calculate the difference between the employee's date of birth and the present date and return the result—the employee's age—in years; this formula is copied down the column to produce the ages of the other employees. Similarly, cell G5 calculates the employee's length of service in years by using

> @DATEDIF(E5,@TODAY,"y")

to calculate the difference in years between the employee's date of hire and the present date.

14

Calendar Functions

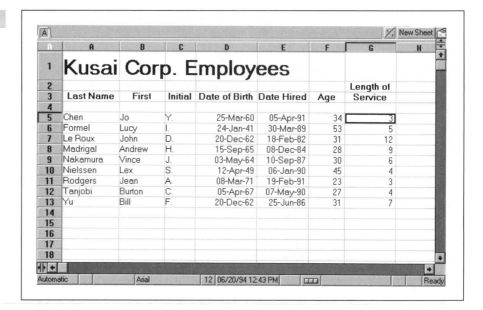

See Also @D360, @DAYS, @DAYS360

@DATEINFO(*date,attribute*)

The @DATEINFO function returns information about *date*, where *date* is a date number and *attribute* is one of the following:

ATTRIBUTE	RETURNS
1	The day of the week as a label in short format (Mon)
2	The day of the week as a label in long format (Monday)
3	The day of the week as an integer from 0 (Monday) through 6 (Sunday)
4	The week of the year as an integer from 1 to 53

ATTRIBUTE	RETURNS
5	The month of the year as a label in short format (Jan)
6	The month of the year as a label in long format (January)
7	The number of days in the month specified by *date*
8	The number of days left in the month specified by *date*
9	The last day of the month specified by *date*
10	The Quarter *date* is in, as an integer from 1 (Q1) through 4 (Q4)
11	One if the year specified by *date* is a leap year; 0 if the year is not a leap year
12	The day of the year specified by *date*, as a number from 1 to 366
13	The number of days left in the year specified by *date*, as a number

14

Calendar Functions

For example, to find the date of the last day of the month in which date number 23699 fell, you could use

@DAY(@DATEINFO(23699,9))

and get the result 30, the date of the last day of November 1964.

@DATESTRING(*date-number*)

The @DATESTRING function returns from *date-number* a label that resembles its equivalent date (using the default International Date format), where *date-number* is a date number. For example,

@DATESTRING(34819)

returns 04/30/95 if the default International Date format is *mm/dd/yy*.

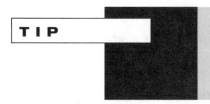

TIP

To change the default International Date format, choose Tools ➤ User Setup ➤ International and choose a format from the Format drop-down list in the International dialog box.

See Also @DATE, @DATEVALUE

@DATEVALUE(*text*)

The @DATEVALUE function returns the date number for the date specified in *text*, where *text* is a date expressed as text within double quotation marks (" "), a formula that results in text, the address or name of a cell that contains a label, or a formula that results in a label.

If you use text, it must be in one of the five 1-2-3 date formats:

DATE FORMAT	EXAMPLE
Day-Month-Year	27-May-63
Day-Month	27-May
Month-Year	May-63
Long International Date	5/27/63
Short International Date	5/27

Note that in the Day-Month and Short International Date formats, the year is not specified.

For example, the following statement returns **23158**:

@DATEVALUE("5/27/63")

(Note that the double quotation marks [" "] are necessary to stop 1-2-3 from dividing the values 5, 27, and 63.) To return an actual date from an

@DATEVALUE calculation (rather than returning a date number), format the appropriate cell with one of the date formats by using the Format selector in the status bar.

Why would you use @DATEVALUE rather than @DATE? You may find @DATEVALUE especially valuable with data imported from another application that uses a format unsuitable for @DATE. For example, a word-processing application might not support the date format 95,3,15 that @DATE needs. Figure 14.3 shows the use of @DATEVALUE to convert date strings to date serial numbers. Cell A5 contains the function statement

@DATEVALUE(B5)

to return the date number for the text string in cell B5.

See Also @DATE

14

Calendar Functions

FIGURE 14.3

Using @DATEVALUE to convert date strings to date serial numbers

Date Value	Date	# Herons	Comments	Category
34805	04/16/95	1	Fleeting sighting down river	C
34806	04/17/95	1	Older bird	B
34807	04/18/95	1	Younger bird, damaged right wing	B
34808	04/19/95	1	Poor sighting on far bank	D
34809	04/20/95	2	Flew abreast past viewing platform!	A
34810	04/21/95	1	? Seen in the distance at twilight	D
34811	04/22/95	1	Flew repeatedly over river	A
34812	04/23/95	3	Trio at dawn and dusk	A
34813	04/24/95	1	Damaged right wing; younger bird again	B
34814	04/25/95	2	?Same bird twice	D
34815	04/26/95	2	Perched and preening	A

Blue Heron Sightings

@DAY(*date-number*)

The @DAY function returns the day of the month represented by *date-number*, a value from 1 (January 1, 1900) through 73050 (December 31, 2099). @DAY returns a value from 1 through 31 representing the day of the month. For example, date number 34666 is November 28, 1994, so

@DAY(34666)

returns 28. Alternatively, you can combine @DAY with other date functions:

@DAY(@DATE(94,11,28))

This statement also returns 28. You can use @DAY with cell addresses. You can also use @DAY(@NOW) to return the current day of the month. For example, if run on December 31, 1994,

@DAY(@NOW)

would return 31.

N O T E   You may find @DAY most useful for supplying the day argument for use with other 1-2-3 date @functions.

See Also @MONTH, @WEEKDAY, @YEAR

@DAYS(*start-date,end-date,* [*basis*])

The @DAYS function returns the number of days between two dates using a user-specified *basis* for day-count. *start-date* and *end-date* are both date numbers; @DAYS will return a positive result if *start-date* is before *end-date*, a negative result if *start-date* is after *end-date*, or 0 if *start-date* and *end-date* are the same. *basis* is the type of day-count basis:

BASIS	MEANING
0	30/360

BASIS	MEANING
1	Actual/actual
2	Actual/360
3	Actual/365

TIP

As with the @DAY function, you will probably find @DAYS most useful in conjunction with other date functions, such as @DATE, as illustrated below.

For example, if you were born on June 3, 1936 and wanted to calculate how many days you'd lived by your sixtieth birthday (June 3, 1996), you could use the following statement:

@DAYS(@DATE(36,6,3),@DATE(96,6,3),1)

which returns 21549. This uses an actual day count, denoted by *basis* being 1.

If you wanted to calculate the number of days between two dates based on a 360-day year consisting of twelve months of thirty days each, you could use

@DAYS(@DATE(94,11,28),@DATE(95,5,27))

See Figure 14.1 on page 704 for an illustration of the @DAYS function.

See Also @D360, @DATEDIF, @DAYS360

@DAYS360(*start-date,end-date*)

The @DAYS360 function returns the number of days between two dates, *start-date* and *end-date*, based on a 360-day year (12 months of 30 days each). *start-date* and *end-date* are date numbers. @DAYS360 calculates a result according to the standards of the U.S. securities industry, conforming to the 1990 modifications of the Securities Industry Association's 1986 edition of Standard Security Calculation Methods.

Note that @AND360 and @DAYS360 will typically return different results when either *start-date* or *end-date* is the last day of a month because of their different calculation methods.

For example, the following statement calculates the number of days between the Fourth of July 1994 and Christmas Day 1994 (the result is 171 days):

@DAYS360(34519,34693)

Usually, you will find it more convenient to combine @DAYS360 with other date @functions:

@DAYS(@DATE(94,7,4), @DATE(94,12,25))

which of course gives the same result. See Figure 14.1 on page 704 for an illustration of the @DAYS function.

See Also @DATEDIF, @DAYS

@HOUR(*time-number*)

The @HOUR function returns an integer value from 0 (midnight) through 23 (11 P.M.) the hour corresponding to *time-number*. *time-number* is a value between 0.0000000 (which represents midnight) and 0.999994 (which represents 11:59:59 P.M.; [0.999995 and above return 0, midnight, again]).

For example, this statement returns 12 (noon):

@HOUR(0.5)

Consider using @HOUR with other time @functions that supply a time number. For example, this function statement returns 17, the seventeenth hour of the day:

@HOUR(@TIMEVALUE("5:15pm"))

T I P

Since @HOUR returns only an hour value, it is most useful for projects that require times calculated in hours without minutes. For example, a law firm might use @HOUR to calculate billable hours to clients (and it might be tempted to use it in conjunction with @ROUNDUP rather than @ROUNDDOWN). Other uses include calculating hourly wages and the like.

See Also @MINUTE, @SECOND

@MINUTE(*time-number*)

The @MINUTE function returns an integer between 0 and 50 for the minute corresponding to *time-number*. *time-number* is a value between 0.0000000 (which represents midnight) and 0.999994 (which represents 11:59:59 P.M.; [0.999995 and above return 0, midnight, again]).

For example, this statement returns 55, the fifty-fifth minute of the hour:

    @MINUTE(0.58)

Consider using @MINUTE with other time @functions that supply a time number. For example, this function statement returns 15, the fifteenth minute of the hour:

    @MINUTE(@TIMEVALUE("5:15pm"))

See Also @HOUR, @SECOND

@MONTH(*date-number*)

@MONTH returns the month of the year from *date-number* as a value from 1 (January) through 12 (December). *date-number* is a value from 1 (January 1, 1900) through 73050 (December 31, 2099).

For example, as 34700 is the date number for January 1, 1995, the following statement returns 1, representing January, the first month of the year:

    @MONTH(34700)

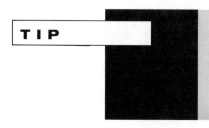

TIP

You'll usually find it easier to use another date function to provide *date-number* than entering *date-number* directly. For example, use @MONTH in combination with @DATE or another date function—@MONTH(@DATE(95,1,1)) or the like.

To return the current month, use @MONTH in combination with @NOW:

@MONTH(@NOW)

This statement would return 7 if the current month were July.

See Also @DAY, @YEAR

@NETWORKDAYS(*start-date, enddate,[holidays-range], [weekends]*)

The @NETWORKDAYS function returns the number of working days between *start-date* and *end-date*. The number of working days is considered to be the number of days excluding weekends and holidays.

The arguments for @NETWORKDAYS are as follows:

ARGUMENT	DESCRIPTION
start-date	A date entered as a date number (e.g., 34666 for November 28, 1994). *start-date* counts as a day in the @NETWORKDAYS calculation.
end-date	A date entered as a date number (e.g., 35031 for November 28, 1995). *end-date* counts as a day in the @NETWORKDAYS calculation.

ARGUMENT	DESCRIPTION
holidays-range	The name or address of a range containing date numbers that specify holidays to exclude from the calculation of working days. *holidays-range* is an optional argument and can contain date numbers, formulas that produce date numbers, and range addresses or range names containing date numbers.
weekends	An optional argument to specify which days of the week are considered weekend days, entered as text, where the days are represented as listed below. The default setting is "56" to indicate that Saturday and Sunday are considered weekend days.

0 = Monday
1 = Tuesday
2 = Wednesday
3 = Thursday
4 = Friday
5 = Saturday
6 = Sunday
7 = no holidays

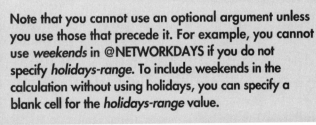

WARNING Note that you cannot use an optional argument unless you use those that precede it. For example, you cannot use *weekends* in @NETWORKDAYS if you do not specify *holidays-range*. To include weekends in the calculation without using holidays, you can specify a blank cell for the *holidays-range* value.

For example, suppose you need to calculate the number of working days in December 1995. Your company generously gives December 24, 25, 26, and 31 as holidays, so you enter these in a range that you call HOLIDAYS (well, why not?). Everyone in the company works a five-day week, with Friday and Saturday off, which gives "45" as the *weekends* argument. So the calculation looks like this:

@NETWORKDAYS(@DATE(95,12,1),@DATE(95,12,31),
HOLIDAYS,"45").

which gives 21, the number of working days excluding holidays and the specified weekend days.

See Also @D360, @DAYS, @DAYS360, @NEXTMONTH

@NEXTMONTH(*start-date, months, [day-of-month],[basis]*)

The @NEXTMONTH function returns the date number for the date that falls a specified number of months before or after *start-date*.

The arguments for the @NEXTMONTH function are as follows:

ARGUMENT	DESCRIPTION
start-date	A date entered as a date number.
months	An integer indicating the number of months before or after *start-date* that you want to calculate. A positive integer indicates months after *start-date*; a negative integer indicates months before *start-date*.
day-of-month	A value (0, 1, or 2) specifying the day of the month you want the result of @NEXTMONTH to fall on, as follows:

ARGUMENT	DESCRIPTION
	0 Returns the date that falls on the same day of the month as *start-date* (the default setting if you omit the *day-of-month* argument). If the new month does not have the relevant day of the month (for example, if *start-date* is 31 and the new month is February, April, June, September, or November, none of which has a thirty-first day), @NEXTMONTH will return the date for the last day of the month (i.e., February 28 or 29, April 30, and so on). 1 Returns the date that is the first day of the month. 2 Returns the date that is the last day of the month.
basis	A value (0, 1, 2, or 3) to specify the day-count basis to use for the calculation. *basis* is an optional argument and the values are as follows:
	0 specifies a 30/360 day count.
	1 specifies an actual/actual day count. This is the default if you omit the *basis* argument.
	2 specifies an actual/360 day count.
	3 specifies an actual/365 day count.

14

Calendar Functions

WARNING   Note that you cannot use an optional argument unless you use those that precede it. For example, you cannot use the optional argument *basis* in @NEXTMONTH if you do not specify *day-of-month*.

For example, to work out the date of the last day of the month that's six months after July 4, 1995, you would use this statement:

@NEXTMONTH(@DATE(95,7,4),2)

This returns 35095, the date number for ... wait, for what? It would be clearer to combine @NEXTMONTH with the @DATESTRING function:

@DATESTRING(@NEXTMONTH(@DATE(95,7,4),2))

This returns 01/31/96, which is indeed the date value 35095.

See Also @D360, @DAYS360, @NETWORKDAYS, @WORKDAY

@NOW

The @NOW function returns the date number as determined by your computer's built-in clock. The date number includes a time number: The date number is the integer portion and the time number is the decimal portion. For example, if today's date is November 11, 1994 and the time is 11:00 A.M., then the @NOW function returns 34649.4583, of which 34649 represents November 11, 1994, and .4583 represents 11:00 A.M. For a more user-friendly display, choose a date or time format in the Format Number dialog box (Style ➤ Format Number). In a date-formatted cell, @NOW will display only the date; in a time-formatted cell, @NOW will display only the time.

T I P

If you find yourself getting improbable values from function statements using @NOW, check your recalculation settings in the Recalculation dialog box and check your computer's clock setting.

Note that @NOW function statements will be recalculated every time you recalculate your worksheet, either automatically (if you choose Automatic in the Recalculation dialog box that you reach via Tools ➤ User Setup ➤ Recalculation ➤ Automatic) or manually (by pressing F9 or by clicking the Recalculate SmartIcon).

Two frequent uses of @NOW are to time-stamp worksheets or to calculate elapsed time.

See Also @TODAY

@SECOND(*time-number*)

The @SECOND function returns an integer between 0 and 59 for the seconds corresponding to *time-number*. *time-number* is a value between 0.0000000 (which represents midnight) and 0.999994 (which represents 11:59:59 PM; [0.999995 and above return 0, midnight, again]).

For example, this statement returns 17, the seventeenth second of the minute:

    @SECOND(@TIMEVALUE("10:15:17PM"))

See Also @HOUR, @MINUTE

@TIME(*hour,minutes,seconds*)

The @TIME function returns the time number for the specified hour, minutes, and seconds.

The arguments for the @TIME function are as follows:

ARGUMENT	DESCRIPTION
hour	An integer from 0 (midnight) through 23 (11:00 P.M.)
minutes	An integer from 0 through 59
seconds	An integer from 0 through 59

For example, this statement returns 0.55, the time for 13:12:00:

    @TIME(13,12,00)

Format the relevant cell to display a time number by using the Format selector in the status bar or by choosing Style ➤ Number Format and choosing a format from the Number Format dialog box.

Perhaps more useful than a single time on its own is the use of @TIME to calculate the amount of time elapsed. For example, if a temporary worker in your office worked from 7:45 A.M. to 1:15 P.M., you could calculate his or her pay (at a meager $13.40 per hour, including an exorbitant agency fee) by subtracting the start time from the end time and multiplying the result by the hourly pay rate, as follows:

@TIME(13,15,0)-@TIME(7,45,0)*13.4*24

This produces $73.70.

See Also @TIMEVALUE

@TIMEVALUE(*text*)

The @TIMEVALUE function returns the time number for *text*. *text* can be a time entered as text within double quotation marks (" "), a formula resulting in text, or the address of a cell containing a label or a formula resulting in a label. Text for *text* must conform to one of 1-2-3's four time formats:

22:15:17 PM
22:15 PM
22:15:17
22:15

For example, this statement returns 0.604167, the time value for 2:30 P.M:

@TIMEVALUE("14:30")

Similarly, if the cell named APPOINTMENT contains the label 15:45, this statement returns 0.65625, the time value for 3:45 P.M

:

@TIMEVALUE(APPOINTMENT)

To make the time value appear in a time format, choose a suitable format by using the Format selector in the status bar.

TIP

@TIMEVALUE may appear to have little advantage over @TIME—or indeed may appear completely pointless—until you find yourself stuck with times entered as labels in a worksheet or imported in label format from another program, such as a word-processing application or presentation. For most conventional purposes, you'll probably find it easiest to enter times in the 22,15,17 format that @TIME uses.

See Also @TIME

@TODAY

The @TODAY function calculates the date number as determined by your computer's built-in clock, without a time value. It is equivalent to @INT(@NOW). Not surprisingly, @TODAY has no arguments.

TIP

If you find yourself getting improbable values from @TODAY function statements, check to see if anyone's been messing with the clock on your computer.

Note that @TODAY function statements will be recalculated every time you recalculate your worksheet, either automatically (choose Automatic in the Recalculation dialog box that you reach via Tools ➤ User Setup ➤ Recalculation ➤ Automatic) or manually (by pressing F9 or by clicking the Recalculate SmartIcon).

For example, on New Year's Day, 1996, this statement will return 35065:

    @TODAY

To display the date in a user-friendly format, format the cell for Date by using the Format selector in the status bar, or use the @DATESTRING function in combination with @TODAY:

    @DATESTRING(@TODAY)

See Also @NOW, @TIME

@WEEKDAY(*date-number*)

The @WEEKDAY function returns the day of the week from *date-number* as an integer from 0 (Monday) through 6 (Sunday). *date-number* is a value from 1 (January 1, 1900) through 73050 (December 31, 2099).

For example, this statement returns 3, indicating that April 19, 2001, is a Thursday:

    @WEEKDAY(37000)

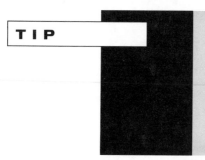

T I P

Usually you'll find the @WEEKDAY function more useful in combination with other date functions that supply a date number. For example, if you are planning the mother of all parties and want to know what day of the week December 31, 1999, will fall on, use @WEEKDAY(@DATE(99,12,31)) to find the answer— Friday (how appropriate!).

See Also @MONTH, @YEAR

@WORKDAY(*start-date,days,* [*holidays-range*],[*weekends*])

The @WORKDAY function returns the date number for the date that falls a specified number of working days before or after *start-date*. You can instruct @WORKDAY to ignore weekends and various holidays.

The arguments for @WORKDAY are as follows:

ARGUMENT	DESCRIPTION
start-date	A date entered as a date number (e.g., 34666 for November 28, 1994). *start-date* counts as a day in the @WORKDAYS calculation.
end-date	A date entered as a date number (e.g., 35031 for November 28, 1995). *end-date* counts as a day in the @WORKDAYS calculation.
holidays-range	The name or address of a range containing date numbers that specify holidays to exclude from the calculation of working days. *holidays-range* is an optional argument and can contain date numbers, formulas that produce date numbers, and range addresses or range names containing date numbers.
weekends	An optional argument to specify which days of the week are considered weekend days, entered as text, where the days are represented as listed below. The default setting is "56" to indicate that Saturday and Sunday are considered weekend days. 0 = Monday 1 = Tuesday 2 = Wednesday 3 = Thursday 4 = Friday 5 = Saturday 6 = Sunday 7 = no holidays

14

Calendar Functions

WARNING Note that you cannot use an optional argument unless you use those that precede it. For example, you cannot use *weekends* in @WORKDAY if you do not specify *holidays-range*. To include weekends in the calculation without using holidays, you can specify a blank cell for the *holidays-range* value.

For example, say you want to calculate ten working days as a payment period for the invoices you are sending out on February 28, 1995. You have a company holiday (Founder's Day) on March 3, which you enter in a range named HOLIDAYS; and the problem is further complicated by the company's working Tuesday to Friday, with Sunday and Monday off, which gives you a weekends value of "06". Use this function statement:

@WORKDAY(@DATE(95,2,28),10,HOLIDAYS,"06")

It returns 34772, the date number for March 14, 1995. To better see the due date for the invoices, weave the @DATESTRING function into the statement:

@DATESTRING(@WORKDAY(@DATE(95,2,28),10,HOLIDAYS,"06"))

This statement returns 03/14/95.

See Also @D360, @DAYS360

@YEAR(*date-number*)

The @YEAR function returns the year from *date-number* as an integer from 0 (representing 1900) to 199 (representing 2099). *date-number* is an integer, or the address or name of a cell that contains an integer, from 1 (January 1, 1900) through 73050 (December 31, 2099).

For example, if you knew the date number for November 28, 1994 was 34666, you could use

@YEAR(34666)

to return the year for that date, 94. Usually, though, it would be more useful to use @YEAR in combination with @DATE to produce the date number and then extract the year from it:

@YEAR(@DATE(94,11,28))

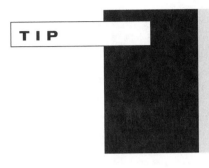

T I P

To return the year as a conventional and user-friendly four-digit number rather than as a two-digit number, simply add 1900 to the result of @YEAR. For example, use @YEAR(@DATE(94,11,28))+1900 to return 1994 rather than 94. To return the present year, use @YEAR with @NOW—@YEAR(@NOW) or @YEAR(@NOW)+1900.

See Also @DAY, @MONTH

14

Calendar Functions

Database

Functions

Reference

The twelve database functions perform statistical calculations and queries on database tables, scanning the specified database tables and selecting the records that match the specified criteria before performing the calculations on them.

Most of the database functions are database variations of other 1-2-3 functions. The main difference between similarly named database functions (such as @DAVG and @DMIN) and statistical functions (such as @AVG and @MIN) is that the database functions operate on selected field entries in a database table rather than simply operating on lists.

TIP

Note that functions that refer to external database tables are recalculated each time any value in the worksheet changes—unlike functions that refer to database tables in a single worksheet file, which are recalculated only when a value changes on which the function depends.

This chapter is divided into three sections. The first section, "Overview of the Database Functions," provides a reference table of the database functions. The second section, "Arguments for the Database Functions," lists the arguments for the database functions, since nearly all of them take exactly the same arguments. The third section, "Descriptions of the Database Functions," discusses each database function in detail and gives examples.

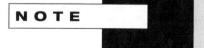

NOTE

Chapters 7 and 8 explain how to work with databases in 1-2-3.

This chapter uses a sample file of Frequently Accessed Newsgroups on the Internet to illustrate the various database functions. The worksheet includes:

- The location of each newsgroup in the Location column
- The name of the newsgroup in the Newsgroup column
- The date of the first access to the newsgroup in the First Access column
- The date of the last (i.e., the latest) access to the newsgroup in the Last Access column
- The total number of accesses to the newsgroup in the Total column
- Other information as necessary to illustrate the database functions

Overview of the Database Functions

For quick reference, Table 15.1 lists the database functions, with page numbers indicating where to find their detailed discussion.

TABLE 15.1: Database Functions Quick Reference

FUNCTION	RETURNS	SEE PAGE
@DAVG	The average of selected values in a database range	734
@DCOUNT	The number of selected values in a database range	735

TABLE 15.1: Database Functions Quick Reference (continued)

FUNCTION	RETURNS	SEE PAGE
@DGET	The field item from a single database record selected by the expressions in the criteria range	736
@DMAX	The largest value among selected entries in a database range	738
@DMIN	The smallest value among selected entries in a database range	738
@DPURECOUNT	The number of a cells in a database that contain a value in the specified field that match specified criteria	740
@DQUERY	Calls a function defined in an external database	742
@DSTD	The population standard deviation of selected values in a database range	743
@DSTDS	The sample standard deviation of selected values in a database range	743
@DSUM	The sum of selected values in a database range	745
@DVAR	The population variance of selected values in a database range	746
@DVARS	The sample variance of selected values in a database range	747

Arguments for the Database Functions

All the 1-2-3 database functions except the @DQUERY function take the same arguments. Table 15.2 summarizes those arguments to avoid numbing repetition through the rest of this chapter.

TABLE 15.2: Arguments for the Database Functions

ARGUMENT	DESCRIPTION
input	The name or address of a range containing a database table, the name of an external table, or the name of a query table enclosed in double quotation marks (″ ″).
field	The name of the field, enclosed in double quotation marks (″ ″), on which you want the function to operate. Note that if *input* is from an external table, *field* must be from that table too. If you are using more than one *input* argument and *field* appears in more than one input table (in other words, it is not unique), you need to specify *field* as the name of the table, followed by a period and the field name. For example, if the tables DESKTOPS and LAPTOPS both contained a PROCESSOR field, you would specify "LAPTOPS.PROCESSOR" to indicate the PROCESSOR field in the LAPTOPS table.
criteria	A criteria formula or the name or address of a range that contains a criteria formula. If you use only one table for *input*, you can omit *criteria*.

15

Database Functions

Descriptions of the Database Functions

This section contains detailed descriptions of each database @function. For details of the arguments for the database @functions, see Table 15.2 in the previous section.

@DAVG(*input,field,*[*criteria*])

The @DAVG function calculates the average of the values in a field of a database table that meet specified *criteria*. The arguments for the @DAVG function are discussed in Table 15.2 in the previous section.

For example, column G in Figure 15.1 shows the use of @DAVG to produce averages from a database table. Cell G6 contains the function statement

@DAVG(A3..E18,"total",LOCATION="alt")

FIGURE 15.1

Using the @DVAG function to produce averages for a database table

	A	B	C	D	E	F	G
1		**Frequently Accessed Newsgroups**					
2							
3	Location	Newsgroup	First Access	Last Access	Total		Average Accesses
4	Alt	Anonymous	19-Nov-93	09-Sep-94	22		
5	Alt	Asian Movies	05-Jan-94	06-Jun-94	56		Alt
6	Alt	Backrubs	09-Sep-94	09-Sep-94	1		27
7	Alt	Baldspot	05-Feb-94	12-Apr-94	4		Biz
8	Biz	Control	04-Nov-93	09-Jan-94	2		3
9	Misc	Entrepreneurs	14-Nov-93	11-Jul-94	11		Misc
10	Alt	Fashion	28-Apr-94	03-Jul-94	93		9
11	Alt	Feminism	08-Apr-94	13-Jun-94	2		Rec
12	Rec	Great Outdoors	27-Jan-94	03-Apr-94	3		6
13	Alt	Human Brain	15-Mar-93	20-May-93	12		All
14	Rec	Motorcycles	31-Dec-93	07-Mar-94	15		16
15	Rec	Pyrotechnics	01-Feb-94	01-Feb-94	1		
16	Misc	Rural	01-Apr-94	09-Oct-94	14		
17	Biz	Stolen	05-Nov-93	10-Jan-94	3		
18	Misc	Writing	25-Dec-94	11-Oct-94	2		
19							

Fixed   0   Arial   12   06/20/94 7:45 AM   Ready

to find the average number of accesses to the newsgroups in the Location "Alt": 27. Similarly, cells G8, G10, and G12 contain the following function statements, respectively:

```
@DAVG(A3..E18,"total",LOCATION="biz")
@DAVG(A3..E18,"total",LOCATION="misc")
@DAVG(A3..E18,"total",LOCATION="rec")
```

These statements find the average number of accesses to the newsgroups in the Locations "Biz," "Misc," and "Rec," respectively. Cell G14 contains a function statement to produce the average number of accesses for all newsgroups:

```
@DAVG(A3..E18,"total")
```

See Also   @AVG, @PUREAVG

@DCOUNT(*input,field,*[*criteria*])

The @DCOUNT function returns the number of nonblank cells in a *field* of a database *input* table that meet specified *criteria*. The arguments for the @DCOUNT function are discussed in Table 15.2 on page 733.

For example, Figure 15.2 shows a database of Frequently Accessed Newsgroups. Cell G5 contains a statement that returns 15, the count of newsgroups accessed:

```
@DCOUNT(A2..E17,"Newsgroup")
```

Cell G7 contains a statement that returns 7, the count of Alt newsgroups within the Location list:

```
@DCOUNT(A2..E17,"Location",LOCATION="Alt")
```

Cell G9 contains a statement that returns 3, the count of Misc newsgroups within the Location list:

```
@DCOUNT(A2..E17,"Location",LOCATION="Misc")
```

Cell G11 contains a statement that returns 3, the count of Rec newsgroups within the Location list:

```
@DCOUNT(A2..E17,"Location",LOCATION="Rec")
```

FIGURE 15.2

Using the @DCOUNT function to return the number of nonblank fields that meet specific criteria

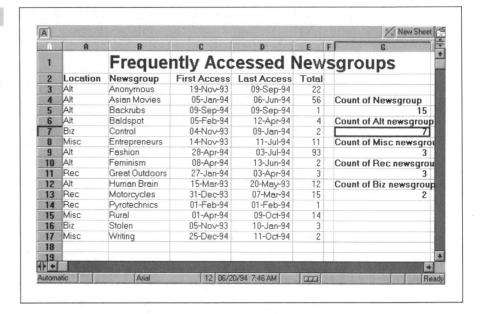

And cell G13 contains a statement that returns 2, the count of Biz newsgroups within the Location list:

@DCOUNT(A2..E17,"Location",LOCATION="Biz")

See Also @COUNT, @DPURECOUNT, @PURECOUNT

@DGET(*input,field,*[*criteria*])

The @DGET function retrieves a value or label from a *field* of a database table that meets specified *criteria*. Use @DGET to retrieve a single value that meets particular *criteria*. You can use the result of @DGET in a macro or in a function. The arguments for @DGET are discussed in Table 15.2 on page 733.

WARNING Be careful when specifying criteria for @DGET, because @DGET will return ERR if more than one entry meets the given criteria.

For example, Figure 15.3 uses @DGET as follows to retrieve information about the Baldspot newsgroup in the Frequently Accessed Newsgroups database. The function statement in cell G6 returns Alt, the Location of the Baldspot newsgroup:

@DGET(A3..E18,"Location",NEWSGROUP="Baldspot")

The function statement in cell G9 returns 05-Feb-94, the First Access date for Baldspot (the cell is formatted to present a date format rather than a date number):

@DGET(A3..E18,"First Access",NEWSGROUP="Baldspot")

Cell G12 contains this function statement:

@DGET(A3..E18,"Last Access",NEWSGROUP="Baldspot")

15

Database Functions

FIGURE 15.3

Using the @DGET function to retrieve single values from a database

	A	B	C	D	E	F	G
2							
3	Location	Newsgroup	First Access	Last Access	Total		BALDSPOT
4	Alt	Anonymous	19-Nov-93	09-Sep-94	22		
5	Alt	Asian Movies	05-Jan-94	06-Jun-94	56		Location of Newsgroup
6	Alt	Backrubs	09-Sep-94	09-Sep-94	1		Alt
7	Alt	Baldspot	05-Feb-94	12-Apr-94	4		
8	Biz	Control	04-Nov-93	09-Jan-94	2		First Access
9	Misc	Entrepreneurs	14-Nov-93	11-Jul-94	11		05-Feb-94
10	Alt	Fashion	28-Apr-94	03-Jul-94	93		
11	Alt	Feminism	08-Apr-94	13-Jun-94	2		Last Access
12	Rec	Great Outdoors	27-Jan-94	03-Apr-94	3		12-Apr-94
13	Alt	Human Brain	15-Mar-93	20-May-93	12		
14	Rec	Motorcycles	31-Dec-93	07-Mar-94	15		Total Accesses
15	Rec	Pyrotechnics	01-Feb-94	01-Feb-94	1		4
16	Misc	Rural	01-Apr-94	09-Oct-94	14		
17	Biz	Stolen	05-Nov-93	10-Jan-94	3		
18	Misc	Writing	25-Dec-94	11-Oct-94	2		
19							
20							
21							

It returns 12-Apr-94, the Last Access date for the newsgroup. Finally, cell G15 contains a statement that returns 4, the Total number of accesses for the newsgroup:

@DGET(A3..E18,"Total",NEWSGROUP="Baldspot")

For more about this function, see page 463.

See Also @CHOOSE, @HLOOKUP, @INDEX, @VLOOKUP, @XINDEX

@DMAX(*input,field,[criteria]*)

The @DMAX function retrieves the largest value in a *field* of a database table that meets the specified *criteria*. The arguments for the @DMAX function are discussed in Table 15.2 on page 733.

While an obvious use for @DMAX would be to retrieve the highest sales figure from a range, you can also use @DMAX to retrieve the most recent date or time from a list of dates or times.

For example, in Figure 15.4, cell G6 contains a function statement that retrieves the latest Last Access date for the database:

@DMAX(A3..E18,"Last Access")

Cell G8 retrieves the latest Last Access date to an Alt newsgroup in the database:

@DMAX(A3..E18,"Last Access",LOCATION="ALT")

And cell G10 retrieves the most accessed Rec newsgroup in the database:

@DMAX(A3..E18,"Total",LOCATION="REC")

See Also @MAX, @PUREMAX

@DMIN(*input,field,[criteria]*)

The @DMIN function retrieves the smallest value in a *field* of a database table that meets specified *criteria*. The arguments for the @DMIN function are discussed in Table 15.2 on page 733.

FIGURE 15.4

Using the @DMAX function to retrieve values from a database

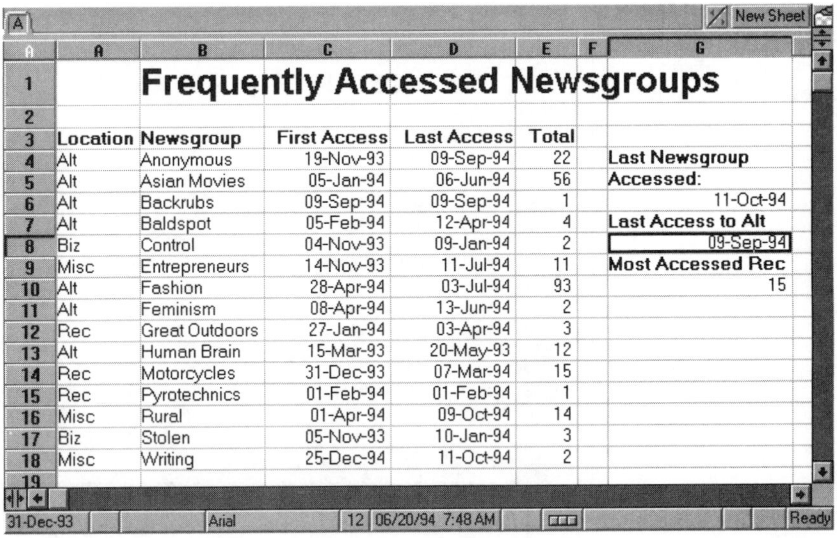

	A	B	C	D	E	F	G
1		Frequently Accessed Newsgroups					
2							
3	Location	Newsgroup	First Access	Last Access	Total		
4	Alt	Anonymous	19-Nov-93	09-Sep-94	22		Last Newsgroup
5	Alt	Asian Movies	05-Jan-94	06-Jun-94	56		Accessed:
6	Alt	Backrubs	09-Sep-94	09-Sep-94	1		11-Oct-94
7	Alt	Baldspot	05-Feb-94	12-Apr-94	4		Last Access to Alt
8	Biz	Control	04-Nov-93	09-Jan-94	2		09-Sep-94
9	Misc	Entrepreneurs	14-Nov-93	11-Jul-94	11		Most Accessed Rec
10	Alt	Fashion	28-Apr-94	03-Jul-94	93		15
11	Alt	Feminism	08-Apr-94	13-Jun-94	2		
12	Rec	Great Outdoors	27-Jan-94	03-Apr-94	3		
13	Alt	Human Brain	15-Mar-93	20-May-93	12		
14	Rec	Motorcycles	31-Dec-93	07-Mar-94	15		
15	Rec	Pyrotechnics	01-Feb-94	01-Feb-94	1		
16	Misc	Rural	01-Apr-94	09-Oct-94	14		
17	Biz	Stolen	05-Nov-93	10-Jan-94	3		
18	Misc	Writing	25-Dec-94	11-Oct-94	2		
19							

You can use @DMIN not only to retrieve, say, the lowest sales figure from a range, but also to retrieve the earliest date or time from a list of dates or times.

For example, in Figure 15.5, cell G6 contains a function statement that retrieves the earliest First Access date for the database:

@DMIN(A3..E18,"First Access")

Cell G8 retrieves the latest First Access date to a Rec newsgroup in the database:

@DMIN(A3..E18,"First Access",LOCATION="Rec")

And cell G10 retrieves the number of accesses to the least accessed Biz newsgroup in the database:

@DMIN(A3..E18,"Total",LOCATION="Biz")

See Also @MIN, @PUREMIN

Using the @DMIN
function to retrieve
values from a database

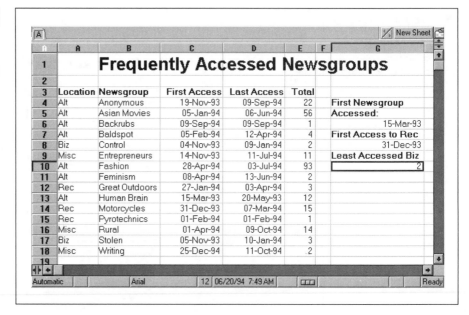

@DPURECOUNT
(*input,field,[criteria]*)

The @DPURECOUNT function returns the number of cells that contain values in a *field* of a database table that meet specified *criteria*. The arguments for @DPURECOUNT are discussed in Table 15.2 on page 733. Note, however, that unlike the other database functions, @DPURECOUNT requires *criteria* every time. @DPURECOUNT's *criteria* must satisfy the following rules:

- *criteria* must be the name or address of a range containing two or more rows. This range *must not* be a 3-D range.

- *criteria*'s first row must list some or all of the field names from a database table.

- *criteria*'s second (and subsequent) rows must contain the criteria: values, labels, formulas, functions, or logical expressions.

For example, Figure 15.6 shows a query table with *criteria* set as follows:

- *Field* was set to Location
- *Operator* was set to =
- *Value* was set to Biz

Cell F13 contains this function statement to return the number of Biz newsgroups included in the database:

@DPURECOUNT(A3..E18,"Total",A20..E22)

The result is 2.

See Also @COUNT, @DCOUNT, @PURECOUNT

15

Database Functions

FIGURE 15.6

Using the @DPURECOUNT function to return the number of nonblank cells that meet specific criteria

	A	B	C	D	E	F
3	Location	Newsgroup	First Access	Last Access	Total	
4	Alt	Anonymous	19-Nov-93	09-Sep-94	22	
5	Alt	Asian Movies	05-Jan-94	06-Jun-94	56	
6	Alt	Backrubs	09-Sep-94	09-Sep-94	1	
7	Alt	Baldspot	05-Feb-94	12-Apr-94	4	
8	Biz	Control	04-Nov-93	09-Jan-94	2	
9	Misc	Entrepreneurs	14-Nov-93	11-Jul-94	11	
10	Alt	Fashion	28-Apr-94	03-Jul-94	93	
11	Alt	Feminism	08-Apr-94	13-Jun-94	2	
12	Rec	Great Outdoors	27-Jan-94	03-Apr-94	3	**Number of Biz newsgroups**
13	Alt	Human Brain	15-Mar-93	20-May-93	12	2
14	Rec	Motorcycles	31-Dec-93	07-Mar-94	15	
15	Rec	Pyrotechnics	01-Feb-94	01-Feb-94	1	
16	Misc	Rural	01-Apr-94	09-Oct-94	14	
17	Biz	Stolen	05-Nov-93	10-Jan-94	3	
18	Misc	Writing	25-Dec-94	11-Oct-94	2	
19						
20	Location	Newsgroup	First Access	Last Access	Total	
21	Biz	Control	04-Nov-93	09-Jan-94	2	
22	Biz	Stolen	05-Nov-93	10-Jan-94	3	

Automatic   Arial   12 | 06/20/94 7:50 AM   Ready

@DQUERY(*function,* [*ext-arguments*])

The @DQUERY function sends a command to an external database. *function* is the name of the external database command to be executed and *ext-arguments* (an optional argument) lists the arguments needed by the external command, separated by valid argument separators.

WARNING While you can use @DQUERY with other database @functions to select records from an external database table, @DQUERY will not work with an input range that contains more than one table.

To use @DQUERY, you need to establish the name of the external table by using Tools ➤ Database ➤ Connect to External. In the Connect to External dialog box, select a DataLens driver from the list. You'll then be able to connect to an external database table and work with it as if it were a 1-2-3 database table. See page 477 for detailed instructions.

WARNING Before attempting to connect to an external database, make sure the driver for the external database supports @DQUERY.

For example, suppose you want to send a command to an external database-management program that has a function called CENTOFAR that converts degrees Centigrade to degrees Fahrenheit and requires one argument (for the degrees Centigrade). You might use

    +TEMP=@DQUERY("CENTOFAR",20)

in a criteria range of a 1-2-3 database function to retrieve entries from the TEMP field of an external table that matches the temperature in Fahrenheit that equals 20 degrees Centigrade.

@DSTD(*input,field,[criteria]*)

The @DSTD function returns the population standard deviation of the values in a *field* of a database *input* table that meet specified *criteria*. The population standard deviation assumes that the values selected represent the entire population; if the values do not represent the whole population, the standard deviation will return a biased result. (For sample standard deviation, use @DSTDS rather than @DSTD.) The arguments for @DSTD are discussed in Table 15.2 on page 733.

N O T E Standard deviation is the square root of the variance of all individual values from the mean.

For example, Figure 15.7 shows a Frequently Accessed Newsgroups database with costs included. In cell D19, this function statement returns the standard deviation of the Cost field:

    @DSTD(A3..F18,"Cost")

The result is $38.74. The function statement in cell D20 returns $29.05, the standard deviation of the Cost field for Cost greater than $50:

    @DSTD(A3..F18,"Cost",Cost>50)

See Also @DSTDS, @PURESTD, @PURESTDS, @STD, @STDS, @DVAR

@DSTDS(*input,field,[criteria]*)

The @DSTDS function calculates the sample standard deviation of sample values in a field of a database table that meet specified criteria. The arguments for @DSTDS are discussed in Table 15.2 on page 733.

FIGURE 15.7

Using the @DSTD function to return the population standard deviation

	A	B	C	D	E	F
3	Location	Newsgroup	First Access	Last Access	Total	Cost
4	Alt	Anonymous	19-Nov-93	09-Sep-94	22	$34.54
5	Alt	Asian Movies	05-Jan-94	06-Jun-94	56	$87.92
6	Alt	Backrubs	09-Sep-94	09-Sep-94	1	$1.57
7	Alt	Baldspot	05-Feb-94	12-Apr-94	4	$6.28
8	Biz	Control	04-Nov-93	09-Jan-94	2	$3.14
9	Misc	Entrepreneurs	14-Nov-93	11-Jul-94	11	$17.27
10	Alt	Fashion	28-Apr-94	03-Jul-94	93	$146.01
11	Alt	Feminism	08-Apr-94	13-Jun-94	2	$3.14
12	Rec	Great Outdoors	27-Jan-94	03-Apr-94	3	$4.71
13	Alt	Human Brain	15-Mar-93	20-May-93	12	$18.84
14	Rec	Motorcycles	31-Dec-93	07-Mar-94	15	$23.55
15	Rec	Pyrotechnics	01-Feb-94	01-Feb-94	1	$1.57
16	Misc	Rural	01-Apr-94	09-Oct-94	14	$21.98
17	Biz	Stolen	05-Nov-93	10-Jan-94	3	$4.71
18	Misc	Writing	25-Dec-94	11-Oct-94	2	$3.14
19		DSTD of Cost	$38.74			
20		DSTD of Cost >50	$29.05			
21		DSTDS of Cost	$40.10			
22		DSTDS of Cost>50	$41.08			

US Dollar 2   Arial   12 06/20/94 7:51 AM   Ready

TIP

Use @DSTDS to return an unbiased standard deviance for sample values that do not represent the whole population. If your values represent the whole population, use @DSTD instead of @DSTDS.

For example, Figure 15.7 shows the Frequently Accessed Newsgroups database with costs included. The function statement in cell D21 returns the standard deviation of sample values for the Cost field:

    @DSTDS(A3..F18,"Cost")

The result is $40.10. In cell D22, the function statement returns $41.08, the standard deviation of sample values of the Cost field for Cost greater than $50:

    @DSTDS(A3..F18,"Cost",Cost>50)

See Also   @DVAR, @PURESTD, @PURESTDS, @STD, @STDS

@DSUM(*input,field,*[*criteria*])

The @DSUM function returns the sum of the values in a *field* of a database *input* table that meet specified *criteria*. The arguments for @DSUM are discussed in Table 15.2 on page 733.

For example, in Figure 15.8, cell C19 contains the following function statement:

@DSUM(A3..F18,"Cost")

It returns the sum of the values in the Cost field of the Frequently Accessed Newsgroups database: $378.37. The function statement in cell C20 returns $298.30, the sum of the values in the Cost field for Alt newsgroups:

@DSUM(A3..F18,"Cost",Location="Alt")

See Also @SUM

FIGURE 15.8

Using the @DSUM function

	A	B	C	D	E	F
3	Location	Newsgroup	First Access	Last Access	Total	Cost
4	Alt	Anonymous	19-Nov-93	09-Sep-94	22	$34.54
5	Alt	Asian Movies	05-Jan-94	06-Jun-94	56	$87.92
6	Alt	Backrubs	09-Sep-94	09-Sep-94	1	$1.57
7	Alt	Baldspot	05-Feb-94	12-Apr-94	4	$6.28
8	Biz	Control	04-Nov-93	09-Jan-94	2	$3.14
9	Misc	Entrepreneurs	14-Nov-93	11-Jul-94	11	$17.27
10	Alt	Fashion	28-Apr-94	03-Jul-94	93	$146.01
11	Alt	Feminism	08-Apr-94	13-Jun-94	2	$3.14
12	Rec	Great Outdoors	27-Jan-94	03-Apr-94	3	$4.71
13	Alt	Human Brain	15-Mar-93	20-May-93	12	$18.84
14	Rec	Motorcycles	31-Dec-93	07-Mar-94	15	$23.55
15	Rec	Pyrotechnics	01-Feb-94	01-Feb-94	1	$1.57
16	Misc	Rural	01-Apr-94	09-Oct-94	14	$21.98
17	Biz	Stolen	05-Nov-93	10-Jan-94	3	$4.71
18	Misc	Writing	25-Dec-94	11-Oct-94	2	$3.14
19		Sum of Cost	$378.37			
20		Sum of Alt	$298.30			
21		Sum of Biz	$7.85			
22		Sum of Rec	$29.83			

US Dollar | 2 | Arial | 12 | 06/20/94 7:52 AM | | Ready

@DVAR(*input,field,[criteria]*)

The @DVAR function returns the population variance of the values in a *field* of a database *input* table that meet specified *criteria*. The arguments for @DVARS are discussed in Table 15.2 on page 733.

The population variance assumes that the values selected represent the entire population; if the values do not represent the whole population, the population variance will return a biased result, and you should use the sample variance instead (the @DVARS function).

NOTE

Variance—the square of standard deviation—measures the degree to which individual values in a list vary from the average of all the values in the list. A lower variance indicates a more reliable average or mean, since the individual values vary from it less. If all the values in a list are equal, @DVAR will return a variance of 0. Note that to obtain true results in several analysis-of-variance (ANOVA) statistical tests, you need to have variance—i.e., you cannot use a variance of 0.

For example, Figure 15.9 calculates the population variance for the Frequently Accessed Newsgroups database. Cell C19 contains a function statement to calculate the population variance of the Total field of the database:

@DVAR(A3..F18,"Total")

The result is 608.73. Cell C20 calculates the population variance of the Total field over 10:

@DVAR(A3..F18,"Total",Total>10)

The result is 835.84.

See Also   @DSTD, @DSTDS, @DVARS, @PUREVAR, @VAR

Calculating population
variance and sample
variance with the
@DVAR and @DVARS
functions

	A	B	C	D	E	F
3	Location	Newsgroup	First Access	Last Access	Total	Cost
4	Alt	Anonymous	19-Nov-93	09-Sep-94	22	$34.54
5	Alt	Asian Movies	05-Jan-94	06-Jun-94	56	$87.92
6	Alt	Backrubs	09-Sep-94	09-Sep-94	1	$1.57
7	Alt	Baldspot	05-Feb-94	12-Apr-94	4	$6.28
8	Biz	Control	04-Nov-93	09-Jan-94	2	$3.14
9	Misc	Entrepreneurs	14-Nov-93	11-Jul-94	11	$17.27
10	Alt	Fashion	28-Apr-94	03-Jul-94	93	$146.01
11	Alt	Feminism	08-Apr-94	13-Jun-94	2	$3.14
12	Rec	Great Outdoors	27-Jan-94	03-Apr-94	3	$4.71
13	Alt	Human Brain	15-Mar-93	20-May-93	12	$18.84
14	Rec	Motorcycles	31-Dec-93	07-Mar-94	15	$23.55
15	Rec	Pyrotechnics	01-Feb-94	01-Feb-94	1	$1.57
16	Misc	Rural	01-Apr-94	09-Oct-94	14	$21.98
17	Biz	Stolen	05-Nov-93	10-Jan-94	3	$4.71
18	Misc	Writing	25-Dec-94	11-Oct-94	2	$3.14
19		DVAR of Total	608.73			
20		DVAR of Total >10	835.84			
21		DVARS of Total	652.21			
22		DVARS of Total >10	975.14			

New Sheet

Fixed 2 Arial 12 06/20/94 7:52 AM Ready

15

Database Functions

@DVARS(*input,field,*[*criteria*])

The @DVARS function returns the sample variance of the values in a *field*
of a database *input* table that meet specified *criteria*. The arguments for
@DVARS are discussed in Table 15.2 on page 733.

The sample variance assumes that the values selected represent only a
sample of the entire population; if the values represent the whole population,
you should use the population variance instead (the @DVAR function).

For example, Figure 15.9 calculates the sample variance for the Frequently Accessed Newsgroups database. Cell C21 contains a statement
to calculate the sample variance of the Total field of the database:

    @DVARS(A3..F18,"Total")

The result is 652.21. Cell C22 calculates the sample variance of the Total field over 10:

@DVARS(A3..F18,"Total",Total>10)

The result is 975.14.

See Also @DSTD, @DVAR, @PUREVAR, @VAR

CHAPTER 16

Engineering

Functions

Reference

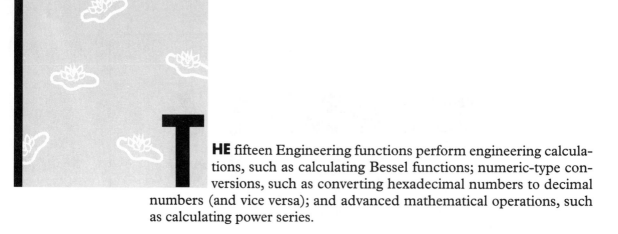

HE fifteen Engineering functions perform engineering calculations, such as calculating Bessel functions; numeric-type conversions, such as converting hexadecimal numbers to decimal numbers (and vice versa); and advanced mathematical operations, such as calculating power series.

Overview of the Engineering Functions

For quick reference, the fifteen engineering functions are listed here in Table 16.1 with page numbers indicating their detailed discussions in the next section, "Descriptions of the Engineering Functions."

TABLE 16.1: Engineering Functions Quick Reference

FUNCTION	RETURNS	SEE PAGE
@BESSELI	The modified Bessel integer function $\mathrm{I}n(x)$	752
@BESSELJ	The Bessel integer function $\mathrm{J}n(x)$	753
@BESSELK	The modified Bessel integer function $\mathrm{K}n(x)$	754
@BESSELY	The Bessel integer function $\mathrm{Y}n(x)$	754
@BETA	The Beta integer function	755

TABLE 16.1: Engineering Functions Quick Reference (continued)

FUNCTION	RETURNS	SEE PAGE
@BETAI	The incomplete Beta integer function	755
@DECIMAL	A signed decimal value from a hexadecimal string	756
@ERF	The error function	757
@ERFC	The complementary error function	758
@ERFD	The derivative of the error function	759
@GAMMA	The Gamma function	759
@GAMMAI	The incomplete Gamma function	760
@GAMMALN	The natural logarithm of the Gamma function	760
@HEX	A hexadecimal string from a signed decimal value	761
@SERIESSUM	The sum of a power series	761

A quick look through their names and definitions reveals the engineering functions to be specialized beyond the needs of the average user, though they can prove invaluable to engineers. Before you skip this section completely, though, note that the engineering functions include @HEX and @DECIMAL, functions which may prove of use to the non-engineer. These two functions allow you to convert hexadecimal numbers (which are used by computer programmers *inter alia*) to decimal numbers and vice versa. If you need to tinker with memory addresses in your PC, @HEX and @DECIMAL can come in handy.

The @HEX function converts normal decimal numbers (in base 10) to hexadecimal numbers. For example, to discover the hexadecimal equivalent of 180, you could use

@HEX(180)

which returns B4. The @DECIMAL function converts hexadecimal numbers into normal decimal numbers (in base 10) and is essentially the opposite of the @HEX function. For example, to find the decimal equivalent of the hexadecimal number FFFF0000, you could use

@DECIMAL("FFFF0000")

which returns −65,536.

Descriptions of the Engineering Functions

This section contains detailed descriptions of each engineering function.

@BESSELI(*numeric_value,order*)

The @BESSELI function calculates the modified Bessel function of integer order Iorder(*numeric_value*), in which *numeric_value* is the value at which to evaluate the function and is any value, and *order* is the order of the function and can be any positive integer including 0. For example, this function statement returns 0.504724:

@BESSELI(4,5)

See Figure 16.1 for an illustration of the Bessel functions; note the very different results produced from the same *order* and *numeric_value*.

NOTE Bessel functions are primarily used for problems involving cylindrical symmetry, in connection with wave propagation, fluid motion, elasticity, and diffusion. 1-2-3's Bessel functions approximate their functions to within $\pm 5*10^{-8}$.

FIGURE 16.1

Using the @BESSEL functions

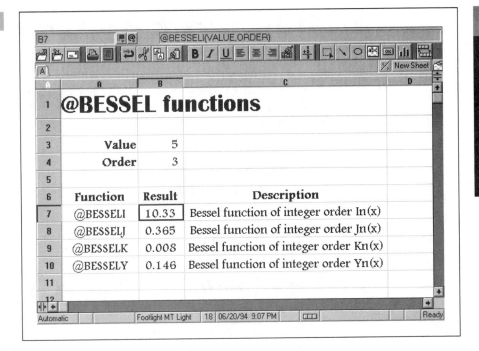

See Also @BESSELJ, @BESSELK, @BESSELY

@BESSELJ(*numeric_value,order*)

The @BESSELJ function calculates the Bessel function of integer order J *order*(*numeric_value*), in which *numeric_value* is the value at which to evaluate the function and is any value, and *order* is the order of the function and can be any positive integer. For example, this function statement returns −0.06604:

@BESSELJ(4,1)

The @BESSELJ function approximates to within ±5*10^−8. See Figure 16.1 for an illustration of the Bessel functions; note the very different results produced from the same *order* and *numeric_value*.

See Also @BESSELI, @BESSELK, @BESSELY

@BESSELK(*numeric_value,order*)

The @BESSELK function calculates the modified Bessel function of integer order K *order*(*numeric_value*), in which *numeric_value* is the value at which to evaluate the function and is any value, and *order* is the order of the function and can be any positive integer including 0. For example, this function statement returns 0.25376:

@BESSELK(2;2)

The @BESSELK function approximates to within ±5*10^–8. See Figure 16.1 on page 753 for an illustration of the Bessel functions; note the very different results produced from the same *order* and *numeric_value*.

See Also @BESSELI, @BESSELJ, @BESSELY

@BESSELY(*numeric_value,order*)

The @BESSELY function calculates the Bessel function of integer order Y*order*(*numeric_value*), in which *numeric_value* is the value at which to evaluate the function and is any value, and *order* is the order of the function and can be any positive integer. For example, this function statement returns –46.914:

@BESSELY(2,6)

NOTE

The Bessel function of integer order Yn(x) is also called the *Neumann function*. It approximates to within ±5*10^–8. See Figure 16.1 on page 753 for an illustration of the Bessel functions; note the very different results produced from the same *order* and *numeric_value*.

See Also @BESSELI, @BESSELJ, @BESSELK

16

@BETA(*numeric_value1, numeric_value2*)

The @BETA function calculates the Beta function, where *numeric_value1* and *numeric_value2* are any values. For example, this function statement produces a result of 2.846527:

@BETA(1.5,0.3)

N O T E　　@BETA produces a result accurate to within at least six significant digits.

See Also　@BETAI, @GAMMA

@BETAI(*numeric_value1, numeric_value2,numeric_value3*)

The @BETAI function calculates the incomplete Beta function, where *numeric_value1* and *numeric_value2* are any values, and *numeric_value3* is any value from 0 to 1. For example, this function statement produces a result of 0.984375:

@BETAI(2,4,0.75)

N O T E　　Like @BETA, @BETAI produces a result accurate to within at least six significant digits.

See Also　@BETA, @GAMMA

@DECIMAL(*hexadecimal*)

The @DECIMAL function converts a hexadecimal value to its signed decimal equivalent, where *hexadecimal* is a value from 00000000 through FFFFFFFF.

hexadecimal should be entered as text, within double quotation marks (" "); can be up to eight characters long; and can contain only numbers from 0 through 9 and letters from A through F (entered as uppercase or lowercase—@DECIMAL is not case-sensitive, so ffff0000 is the same value as FFFF0000).

For example, this function statement returns 123:

> @DECIMAL("7B")

But this one returns ERR because it lacks the double quotation marks (" "):

> @DECIMAL(7B)

Be careful to include the double quotation marks when using the @DECIMAL function—it's very easy to forget them, particularly as @HEX, the sister function of @DECIMAL, does not need them. Figure 16.2 shows a worksheet with a chart that uses the @DECIMAL function to convert hexadecimal values to decimal values.

N O T E

Hexadecimal values 00000000–7FFFFFFF represent 0 and all positive decimal values; hexadecimal values 80000000–FFFFFFFF represent negative decimal values.

See Also @HEX

FIGURE 16.2

Using the @DECIMAL
function to create a
chart showing the
decimal equivalents of
hexadecimal values.
Note that @DECIMAL
needs the *hexadecimal*
argument to be
entered in double
quotation marks (" ").

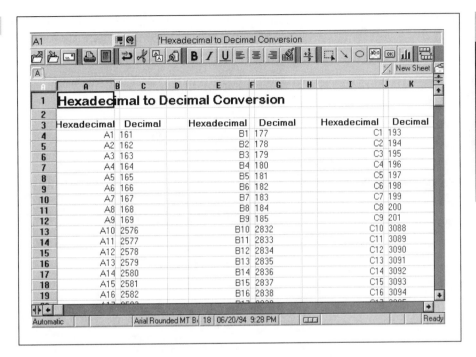

@ERF(*lower-limit,[upper-limit]*)

The @ERF function is an approximation function that returns the error
function integrated between *lower-limit* and *upper-limit*:

- *lower-limit* is any value representing the lower boundary for inte-
  grating @ERF

- *upper-limit* is any value specifying the upper boundary for integrat-
  ing @ERF.

You can omit *upper-limit*, in which case @ERF integrates between 0 and
lower-limit.

For example, this function statement returns 0.00466

    @ERF(2,3)

Note that omitting the second argument—the *upper-limit* argument—produces substantially different results:

> @ERF(2)

This function statement returns 0.995322. Figure 16.3 illustrates the use of 1-2-3's error functions.

See Also @ERFC, @ERFD

FIGURE 16.3

Using 1-2-3's error functions

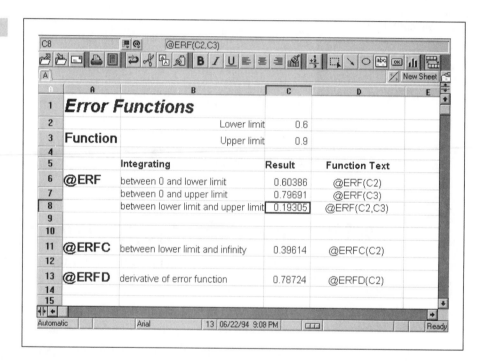

@ERFC(*numeric_value*)

The @ERFC function calculates the complementary error function, integrated between *numeric_value* and infinity. *numeric_value* can be any value. For example, this function statement returns 0.05624:

> @ERFC(1.35)

To return the error function of the absolute value of a cell, use @ERFC in combination with @ABS:

@ERFC(@ABS(Z255))

Figure 16.3 illustrates the use of 1-2-3's error functions.

See Also @ERF, @ERFD

@ERFD(*numeric_value*)

The @ERFD function calculates the derivative of the error function using the formula $(2/@SQRT(@PI))\star@EXP(-x\textasciicircum 2)$. *numeric_value* can be a value from approximately −106.560 to approximately 106.560; if *numeric_value* is smaller than −106.560 or larger than 106.560, the @ERFD calculation is too large for 1-2-3 to store, and you'll see ERR.

WARNING

If *numeric_value* is outside the range −15.102 to 15.102 (i.e., between −106.560 and −15.102 or between 15.102 and 106.560), 1-2-3 will be able to calculate the result of @ERFD but it will not be able to display it. You'll see a series of asterisks in the cell instead.

For example, this function statement returns 0.000139, the derivative of the error function of 3:

@ERFD(3)

Figure 16.3 on page 758 illustrates the use of 1-2-3's error functions.

See Also @ERF

@GAMMA(*numeric_value*)

The @GAMMA function calculates the Gamma distribution function to within six significant figures, where *numeric_value* is any value except 0 and negative integers. For example, this function statement returns 6:

@GAMMA(4)

See Also @BETA, @BETAI, @GAMMAI, @GAMMALN

@GAMMAI (*numeric_value1, numeric_value2,[complement]*)

The @GAMMAI function returns the incomplete gamma function to within six significant figures. The arguments for @GAMMAI are as follows:

ARGUMENT	DESCRIPTION
numeric_value1	A positive value
numeric_value2	A positive value or 0
complement	(optional) 0 or 1 to specify how 1-2-3 calculates the @GAMMAI function:
	0 = P(*numeric_value1,numeric_value*). This is the default if you omit the *complement* argument.
	1 = Q(*numeric_value1, numeric_value*). This equals 1– P(*numeric_value1,numeric_value*).

For example, this function statement returns 0.714943:

@GAMMA(5,6)

This one returns 0.285057:

@GAMMAI(5,6,1)

See Also @GAMMA, @GAMMALN

@GAMMALN(*numeric_value*)

The @GAMMALN function calculates the natural logarithm of the gamma function, where *numeric_value* is a value greater than 0. For example, this function statement returns 39.33988:

    @GAMMALN(20)

See Also @GAMMA, @GAMMAI

@HEX(*number*)

The @HEX function converts a decimal number to its hexadecimal equivalent. *number* can be any value between –2,147,483,648 and 2,147,483,647. If *number* is not an integer, 1-2-3 will truncate it to an integer. For example, this function statement returns E4, the hexadecimal equivalent of 228:

    @HEX(228)

This one returns FFFFFFFC, the hexadecimal equivalent of –4:

    @HEX(–4)

Figure 16.4 shows a worksheet with a chart that uses the @HEX function to convert decimal values to hexadecimal values.

N O T E   Hexadecimal values 00000000–7FFFFFFF represent 0 and all positive decimal values; hexadecimal values 80000000–FFFFFFFF represent negative decimal values.

See Also @DECIMAL

FIGURE 16.4

Using the @HEX function to create a chart showing the hexadecimal equivalents of decimal values

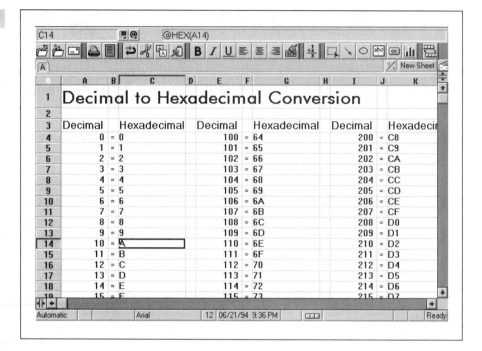

@SERIESSUM(*value,power, increment,coefficients*)

The @SERIESSUM function calculates the sum of a power series. The arguments for the @SERIESSUM function are as follows:

ARGUMENT	DESCRIPTION
value	A value indicating the input value for the power series.
power	A value indicating the initial power to which to raise *value*.
increment	A value indicating the increment by which to increase *value* for each term in the series.

ARGUMENT	DESCRIPTION
coefficients	The address or name of a range containing the coefficients by which @SERIESSUM multiplies each successive power of *value*. The number of cells that *coefficients* contains determines the number of terms in the series. If *coefficients* is a range consisting of six cells, there will be six terms in the power series.

For example, say you have a range named POWER that consists of five cells, which contain the values 1, 2, 3, 4, and 5. With an input *value* of 3, a *power* of 4, and an increment of 2, this function statement returns 2914623:

@SERIESSUM(3,4,2,POWER)

Figure 16.5 illustrates this function statement.

FIGURE 16.5

Using the @SERIESSUM function to return the sum of a power series

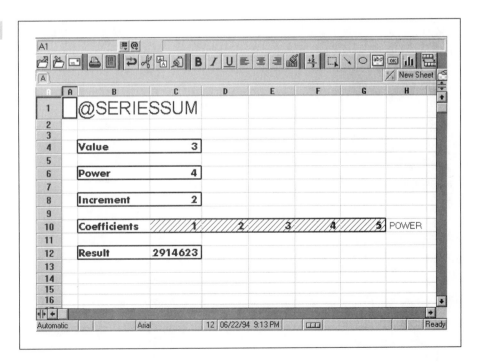

CHAPTER 17

Financial

Functions

Reference

THE financial functions include functions to calculate discounted cash flow (for example, @IRR and @NPV), loan amortization (@NPER), depreciation (@DB and @SYD), investment analysis (@RATE), and annuities (@FV).

Overview of the Financial Functions

For quick reference, the financial functions are listed here in Table 17.1 in their five categories, with page numbers indicating their detailed discussions in the next section, "Descriptions of the Financial Functions."

TABLE 17.1: Financial Functions Quick Reference

FUNCTION	RETURNS	SEE PAGE
@FV	The future value of a series of equal periodic payment amounts over term periods at a fixed periodic interest rate	778
@FVAL	The future value of an item based on the present value	779
@IPAYMT	The cumulative interest on a loan	781
@IRATE	A value equivalent to the periodic interest rate of an investment	783
@NPER	The number of periods required to reach a specified future value at a given interest rate	792

TABLE 17.1: Financial Functions Quick Reference (continued)

FUNCTION	RETURNS	SEE PAGE
@PAYMT	The payments necessary to reach a specified principal over a given term at a fixed interest rate.	797
@PMT	The periodic payment required to pay back a loan over a given term at a fixed interest rate	798
@PMTC	The periodic payment required to pay back a loan over a given term at a fixed interest rate (@PMTC is a version of @PMT adjusted for Canadian mortgage conventions)	800
@PPAYMT	The principal value of payments made on a loan	801
@PV	The present value of a series of equal future cash-flow amounts	805
@PVAL	The present value of an investment	807
@TERM	The number of equal payment amounts required to reach a specified future value at a fixed interest rate	813
BONDS		
@ACCRUED	The accrued interest for a security of a given value	769
@DURATION	The annual duration for a security that pays periodic interest	777
@MDURATION	The modified annual duration for a security that pays periodic interest	788
@PRICE	The price per $100 of value for investments that pay a periodic interest	803
@YIELD	The yield on an interest-bearing security	818

17

Financial Functions

FINANCIAL FUNCTIONS REFERENCE

TABLE 17.1: Financial Functions Quick Reference

FUNCTION	RETURNS	SEE PAGE
CAPITAL-BUDGETING TOOLS		
@IRR	The internal rate of return from a series of positive and negative cash-flow amounts	785
<64>MIRR	The modified internal rate of return for a series of positive and negative cash-flow amounts	790
<64>NPV	The net present value of a series of positive or negative future periodic cash-flow amounts	794
DEPRECIATION		
@DB	The depreciation value of an asset, calculated using the declining-balance method	773
@DDB	The depreciation value of an asset, calculated using the double-declining-balance method	774
@SLN	The depreciation of an asset, using the straight-line method	809
@SYD	The depreciation of an asset, using the sum-of-the-years'-digits method	811
@VDB	The depreciation of an asset, using the variable-declining-balance method	815
ANNUITIES		
@CTERM	The number of compounding periods required for a one-time investment earning a fixed periodic interest rate to reach a specified future value	772
@RATE	The interest rate that will produce a fixed future return from an initial investment over a specified term	809

Descriptions of the Financial Functions

This section contains detailed descriptions of 1-2-3's financial functions.

NOTE

Chapter 5 explains the financial functions as well. See page 287 for further discussion.

@ACCRUED(*settlement,issue, first-interest,coupon,*[*par*], [*frequency*],[*basis*])

The @ACCRUED function returns the accrued interest for securities with periodic interest payments. @ACCRUED works for short, standard, and long coupon periods.

The arguments for the @ACCRUED function are as follows:

ARGUMENT	DESCRIPTION
settlement	A date number indicating the security's settlement date. Note that *settlement* must be greater than *issue* for 1-2-3 to produce a valid result; if it is less, @ACCRUED will return ERR.
issue	A date number indicating the security's issue date or dated date.

ARGUMENT	DESCRIPTION
first-interest	A date number indicating the security's first interest date. Note that *first-interest* must be greater than *issue* for 1-2-3 to produce a valid result; if it is less, @ACCRUED will return ERR.
coupon	Zero or a positive value, indicating the security's annual coupon rate.
par	A value indicating the security's par value. The par value is the amount of principal paid at maturity; the default setting if you omit the *par* argument is 100.
frequency	1, 2, 4, or 12, specifying the number of coupon payments per year as follows:

1   Annual

2   Semiannual (this is the default if *frequency* is omitted)

4   Quarterly

12   Monthly

basis	An optional value specifying the type of day-count to use, as follows:

0   30/360 (this is the default if you omit *basis*)

1   Actual/actual

2   Actual/360

3   Actual/365

WARNING

Note that you cannot use an optional argument unless you use those that precede it. For example, you cannot use *basis* in @ACCRUED if you do not specify *frequency*, and you cannot use *frequency* if you do not specify *par*.

For example, Figure 17.1 illustrates a bond with a settlement date of November 28, 1996; an issue date of April 1, 1995; a first-interest date of June 1, 1995; a coupon rate of 8.125 percent; a par of 100; a quarterly frequency; and a 30/360 day-count basis. To work out the result, you could enter this formula:

@ACCRUED(@DATE(96,11,28),@DATE(95,4,1),@DATE(95,6,1), 0.08125,100,4,0)

It results in 1.96354. But you would probably find it much easier to enter the values into a range of cells (here these values are entered into cells B3..B9) and set up a function statement to provide a result for whatever values you enter in those cells. In Figure 17.1, cell B11 contains the function statement

@ACCRUED(B3,B4,B5,B6,B7,B8,B9)

It produces the same result, 1.96354, but is much easier to work with and more flexible. Creating this type of spreadsheet can help you greatly with projects requiring swift what-if analyses.

17

Financial Functions

FIGURE 17.1

Using the @ACCRUED function to return the accrued interest for securities with periodic interest payments

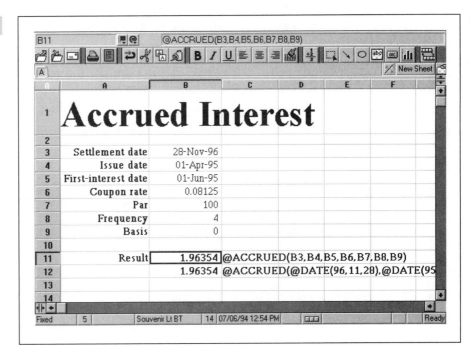

See Also @PRICE, @YIELD

@CTERM(*interest,future-value, present-value*)

The @CTERM function returns the number of compounding periods required for an investment of the amount *present-value* to grow to the amount *future-value* while earning a fixed rate of *interest* per compounding period.

present-value and *future-value* are any values. Both must be either positive or negative. *interest* can be any value greater than −1 except 0.

For example, suppose the high-risk bonds in which you just invested a $25,000 windfall have just hit a good streak, returning 22 percent annually (a rate of 0.22). If this rate holds (fat chance), how long will it take you to double your windfall? You could use this function statement to find out:

    @CTERM(.22,50000,25000)

The answer is 3.49 years. Not bad at all.

To run @CTERM calculations using interest compounded monthly or daily instead of yearly, divide both the interest rate and the result by 12 or 360, respectively, as in these examples:

    @CTERM(.22/12,50000,25000)/12
    @CTERM(.22/360,50000,25000)/12

NOTE See page 295 for more worksheet examples of using @CTERM.

See Also @NPER, @TERM

@DB(*cost,salvage,life,period*)

The @DB function returns the depreciation allowance of an asset using the fixed-declining-balance method. This method slows the rate of depreciation in comparison to the double-declining-balance method, so more depreciation expense occurs (and can be written off) in later periods. Depreciation stops when the asset's book value (its total cost minus its total depreciation) reaches the salvage value.

The arguments for the @DB function are as follows:

ARGUMENT	DESCRIPTION
cost	The amount originally paid for the asset, entered as any positive value or 0. (Note that if cost is given as 0, @DB will give a result of 0.)
salvage	The estimated value of the asset at the end of its useful life, entered as any positive value or 0. @DB will return a negative value if *salvage* is greater than *cost*.
life	The number of periods the asset takes to depreciate from its *cost* value to its *salvage* value. *life* is any value greater than or equal to 1 and less than or equal to *period*.
period	The time for which you want to find the depreciation allowance, entered as a value greater than or equal to 1.

NOTE The *life* and *period* arguments must be expressed in the same units (usually years) for the @DB function to produce a usable result.

For example, the new 100-MHz Pentium screamer on which you're running 1-2-3 cost you $3,000 a few days ago. Its useful life is five years, after which it will have a salvage value of $600. To calculate the depreciation expense for the third year, you could use this function statement:

@DB(3000,600,5,3)

The expense would be $433.72. Figure 17.2 illustrates the depreciation on the Pentium computer for its five-year life span.

See Also @DDB, @SLN, @SYD, @VDB

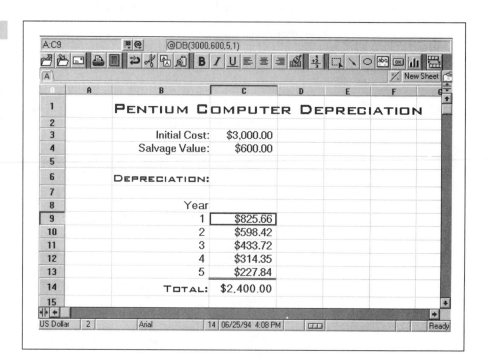

FIGURE 17.2

Using the @DB function to calculate depreciation on a computer system

@DDB(*cost,salvage,life,period*)

The @DDB function returns the depreciation allowance of an asset using the double-declining-balance method. (Chapter 5 offers worksheet examples using the depreciation functions. See page 288.)

TIP

The difference between the fixed-declining-balance method (calculated by the function @DB) is that the double-declining-balance method accelerates the rate of depreciation so that more depreciation expense occurs (and can be written off) in earlier periods than in later ones. As with the fixed-declining-balance method, in the double-declining-balance method, depreciation stops when the book value of the asset (the asset's total cost minus its total depreciation over all prior periods) reaches the salvage value.

The arguments for the @DDB function are as follows:

17

Financial Functions

ARGUMENT	DESCRIPTION
cost	The amount originally paid for the asset, entered as any positive value or 0. (Note that if cost is given as 0, @DB will give a result of 0.)
salvage	The estimated value of the asset at the end of its useful life, entered as any positive value or 0. @DB will return a negative value if *salvage* is greater than *cost*. (Note that *salvage* can be the same as *cost*, though not greater.)
life	The number of periods the asset takes to depreciate from its *cost* value to its *salvage* value. *life* is any value greater than or equal to 2 and less than or equal to *period*.
period	The time for which you want to find the depreciation allowance, entered as a value greater than or equal to 1.

NOTE

The *life* and *period* arguments must be expressed in the same units (usually years) for the @DB function to produce a usable result. Note also that you may want to use @VDB rather than @DDB to accurately depreciate an asset that has a relatively low salvage value.

For example, that new $3,000, 100-MHz Pentium thunderbolt you just depreciated in the @DB section produces very different figures when depreciated with the double-declining-balance method. Using the format

@DDB(3000,600,5,4)

you would establish the third-year depreciation for the Pentium to be $432.00, as shown in Figure 17.3.

See Also @DB, @SLN, @SYD, @VDB

FIGURE 17.3

Depreciation using the @DDB function produces very different results from depreciation using the @DB function.

	Year	
		PENTIUM COMPUTER DEPRECIATION
	Initial Cost:	$3,000.00
	Salvage Value:	$600.00
	DEPRECIATION:	
	Year	
	1	$1,200.00
	2	$720.00
	3	$432.00
	4	$48.00
	5	$0.00
	TOTAL:	$2,400.00

@DURATION(*settlement, maturity,coupon,yield, [frequency],[basis]*)

The @DURATION function returns the annual duration for a security that pays periodic interest. (*Duration* is the weighted average term to maturity of the cash flows of a security.)

The arguments for @DURATION are as follows:

ARGUMENT	DESCRIPTION
settlement	A date number representing the security's settlement date.
maturity	A date number representing the security's maturity date. *maturity* must be greater than settlement; otherwise @DURATION will return ERR.
coupon	Any positive value (or 0) representing the security's annual coupon rate.
yield	Any positive value (or 0) representing the annual yield.
frequency	An optional value specifying the number of coupon payments per year, as follows:

1   Annual

2   Semiannual (this is the default if *frequency* is omitted)

4   Quarterly

12   Monthly

basis	An optional value specifying the type of day-count to use, as follows:

0   30/360 (this is the default if you omit *basis*)

1   Actual/actual

ARGUMENT	DESCRIPTION
2	Actual/360
3	Actual/365

WARNING You cannot use an optional argument unless you use those that precede it. For example, you cannot use *basis* in @DURATION if you do not specify *frequency*.

For example, say you have a security with a February 1, 1995 settlement date and a July 1, 1999 maturity date. The quarterly coupon rate is 2.85 percent, and the annual yield is 6.5 percent. The bond uses an actual/365 day-count basis. You could determine the security's annual duration by using this function statement:

@DURATION(@DATE(95,2,1),@DATE(99,7,1),0.0285,0.065,4,3)

It returns 4.127.

TIP To work out the modified annual duration for a security, use @MDURATION instead of @DURATION.

See Also @ACCRUED, @MDURATION, @PRICE, @YIELD

@FV(*payments,interest,term*)

The @FV function returns the future value of an investment, based on a series of equal payments, earning a constant rate of *interest*, over the number of *payment* periods in *term*. *payments* and *term* can be any values; *interest* is a value greater than −1. (See page 294 in Chapter 5 for more examples of using the @FV function.)

T I P

The @FV function is included in this release of 1-2-3 for backward compatibility with previous releases. This release also contains @FVAL, a significantly improved version of @FV that adds an optional *type* argument to specify whether the investment is an ordinary annuity or an annuity due. See the next section, "@FVAL," for de-tails. If you don't need the extra options that @FVAL includes, however, @FV still works perfectly well and is easier to type—so there's really no reason to stop using it.

For example, you reckon to add $5,000 to your 401K plan, where it should earn 13 percent interest every year for the next ten years. To calculate how much it will be worth at the end of that time, you could use this function statement:

@FV(5000,0.13,10)

It returns a paltry $92,098.75. Twenty years—@FV(5000,0.13,20)—produces a much more promising $404,734.14. Ah well, investing always was a long-term game....

See Also @FVAL, @NPV, @PV, @PVAL

@FVAL(*payments,interest,term,* [*type*],[*present-value*])

@FVAL is an improved version of the @FV function and calculates the future value of an investment with a specified present-value over a specified term, based on periodic, constant payments, and earning a periodic interest rate. By specifying a value for *type*, you can have @FVAL calculate for either an ordinary annuity or an annuity due.

17

Financial Functions

The arguments for @FVAL are similar to those for @FV:

ARGUMENT	DESCRIPTION
payments	A value indicating the fixed, periodic payment. Note that *payments* cannot change during the life of the annuity.
interest	A value greater than –1 indicating the constant interest rate per period.
term	A positive value indicating the total number of period payments. Note that *term* cannot be negative.
type	Zero or 1. *type* is an optional argument used to specify whether 1-2-3 calculates for an ordinary annuity or for an annuity due:
	0 Indicates an ordinary annuity, in which the payments are due at the end of a period. This is the default if you omit the argument *type*.
	1 Indicates an annuity due, in which the payments are due at the beginning of a period.
present-value	Any value representing the present value of the series of future payments. If you omit *present-value*, 1-2-3 uses the default value of 0. Note that, since *present-value* and *type* are both optional arguments, to use *present-value* you need to specify *type*.

WARNING

Be careful when using @FVAL to use the same period for calculating *interest* as you used for *term*. When calculating a monthly payment, for instance, you will need to enter *interest* and *term* in monthly units—perhaps by multiplying the number of years in term by 12 and dividing the interest rate by 12.

To illustrate the difference between @FVAL and @FV, let's take the example used for @FV again: You plan to deposit $5,000 a year for the next ten years to your 401K plan, where it should earn 13 percent interest. To calculate how much it will be worth at the end of that, based on payments at the end of each year, you could use this function:

@FVAL(5000,0.13,10)

It returns $92,098.75, the same as for @FV(5000,0.13,10). But if you make the payments at the beginning of each year, it returns $104,071.58:

@FVAL(5000,0.13,10,1)

See Also @FV, @NPV, @PV, @PVAL

@IPAYMT(*principal,interest, term,start-period,*[*end-period*], [*type*],[*future-value*])

The @IPAYMT function returns the cumulative interest payment of the periodic payment on a loan (*principal*), based on periodic, constant payments at a given interest rate over *term*. By contrast, the @PPAYMT function (see page 801) returns the principal payment on a loan (*principal*), based on periodic, constant payments at a given interest rate over *term*.

The arguments for @IPAYMT are as follows:

ARGUMENT	DESCRIPTION
principal	A value representing the amount borrowed.
term	Any value except zero, indicating the number of periods in the loan. Be sure to use the same units for *term* as you use for *interest*.
interest	A decimal or percentage value greater than −1, representing the fixed periodic interest rate for the loan. Use the same units for *interest* as you use for *term*.

17

Financial Functions

ARGUMENT	DESCRIPTION
start-period	A value greater than or equal to 1 (but not greater than *term*) representing the point in *term* at which the calculation of interest is to start.
end-period	A value greater than or equal to 1 (but not greater than *term*) representing the point in *term* at which the calculation of interest is to stop. The default setting for *end-period* (if you omit the argument) is the same as *start-period*.
type	Zero or 1. *type* is an optional argument used to specify whether 1-2-3 calculates for an ordinary annuity or for an annuity due:
	0 Indicates an ordinary annuity, in which the payments are due at the end of a period. This is the default if you omit the argument *type*.
	1 Indicates an annuity due, in which the payments are due at the beginning of a period.
future-value	Any value representing the future value of the series of payments. Note that this is an optional argument; if you do not specify *future-value*, 1-2-3 will use the default value of 0.

WARNING
You cannot use an optional argument unless you use those that precede it. For example, you cannot use *type* in @IPAYMT if you do not specify *end-period*.

For example, suppose you were thinking of borrowing $25,000 for two years to buy a shiny new sport-utility vehicle with big tires. The best rate of interest you can get is 7.2 percent; how much money will you pay in interest in the first year? You would use this function statement to find out:

@IPAYMT(25000,0.072,3,1)

The answer is $1,800.

T I P

To calculate the principal payment on a loan (rather than the interest payment), use the @PPAYMT function instead of the @IPAYMT function.

See Also @PMT, @PPAYMT

@IRATE(*term,payment,present-value,[type],[future-value], [guess]*)

The @IRATE function returns the necessary periodic interest rate to produce *future-value* from an annuity of *present-value* over the number of compounding periods in *term*.

The arguments for the @IRATE function are as follows:

ARGUMENT	DESCRIPTION
term	Any positive integer representing the number of periodic payments.
payment	A value expressing the amount of the periodic payments
present-value	A value representing the current value of the investment.

ARGUMENT	DESCRIPTION
type	Zero or 1. *type* is an optional argument used to specify whether 1-2-3 calculates for an ordinary annuity or for an annuity due: 0 Indicates an ordinary annuity, in which the payments are due at the end of a period. This is the default if you omit the argument *type*. 1 Indicates an annuity due, in which the payments are due at the beginning of a period.
future-value	Any value representing the future value of the series of payments. Note that this is an optional argument; if you do not specify *future-value*, 1-2-3 will use the default value of 0.
guess	A value from 0 through 1 representing your estimate of the interest rate. This is an optional argument; 1-2-3 uses the default setting of 0.1 (10 percent) if you omit the *guess* argument.

WARNING

Note that you cannot use an optional argument unless you use those that precede it. For example, you cannot use *guess* in @IRATE if you do not specify *future-value*.

For example, if you want to buy a new house for $200,000 and can afford payments of $1500 for twenty years, you can figure out the interest rate needed by using this function statement:

@IRATE(20*12,1500,200000,0,0)

It produces 0.005479—an interest rate of 0.05479 percent compounded monthly.

You can also use @IRATE with the *guess* argument, by starting with a *guess* value that seems reasonable. Note that there may be more than one possible solution, so keep trying values for *guess* if you get results less than 0 or greater than 1.

TIP

@IRATE will return ERR if it cannot approximate the result to within 0.0000001 after thirty calculation iterations. If you find this happening with a number of your entries for *guess*, try using the @NPV function (see page 794) to establish a better value for *guess*. If you find @NPV returns a positive value, adjust your value for *guess* upwards; if @NPV returns a negative value, adjust your value for *guess* downwards. (When your *guess* is accurate, @NPV will return 0.)

See Also @FV, @FVAL, @NPV, @PV, @PVAL, @RATE

@IRR(*guess,range*)

The @IRR function calculates the internal rate of return on an investment—the interest rate received for an investment consisting of payments (negative value) that occur at regular periods. You can use @IRR to calculate the profitability of an investment by discounting the investment's cash benefits over time to zero, including the initial cash cost of the investment.

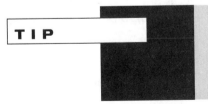

TIP

Typical uses for the internal rate of return are to rank different projects—for example, real-estate investments or joint ventures—by profitability, and to make capital-asset budget decisions.

The internal rate of return tries to produce a single number summarizing the merits of a project, a single number not dependent on the interest rate (hence the appellation *internal*—the number depends solely on the cash flows of the project). The general rule of investment is to accept a project whose internal rate of return is greater than the discount rate, and to reject a project whose internal rate of return is less than the discount rate.

The arguments for the @IRR function are as follows:

ARGUMENT	DESCRIPTION
guess	A decimal or percentage value between 0 and 1 (e.g., 0.15 for 15 percent) representing your estimate of the internal rate of return.
range	The address or name of a range that contains the cash flows. Negative numbers represent cash outflows and positive numbers represent cash inflows. The first cash-flow amount in the range is usually a negative number (i.e., a cash outflow) representing the investment.

TIP For many calculations, you can leave *guess* at 0 (the default setting), but *guess* is more important when working with very large cash flows.

WARNING When using the @IRR function, beware that 1-2-3 includes any blank cells or labels contained in *range* in the calculation. It assigns the value 0 to blank cells and labels.

To assess an investment, you can combine @IRR with other financial functions (such as @NPV).

TIP

@IRR will return ERR if it cannot approximate the result to within 0.0000001 after thirty calculation iterations. If you find this happening with a number of your entries for *guess,* try using the @NPV function (see page 794) to establish a better value for *guess.* If you find @NPV returns a positive value, adjust your value for *guess* upwards; if @NPV returns a negative value, adjust your value for *guess* downwards. (When your *guess* is accurate, @NPV will return 0.)

For example, Figure 17.4 illustrates a project that involves an initial outlay of $100,000 and promises to bring in cash flows as shown in cells D5..D14. You could calculate the internal rate of return with the function statement that appears in cell C16:

> @IRR(0,C4..C14)

17

Financial Functions

FIGURE 17.4

Using @IRR to assess the profitability of an investment

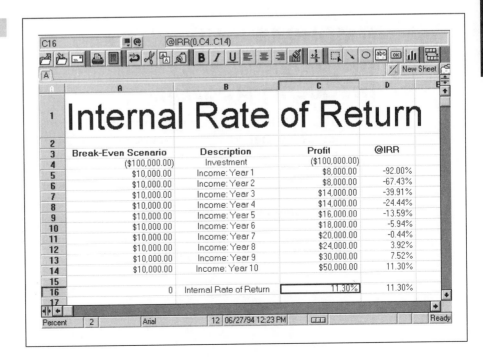

This produces 11.30%. For comparison, cell A16 contains the function statement to calculate the internal rate of return for the break-even scenario:

@IRR(A4..A14)

It of course returns 0. (Cells D5 through D14 contain @IRR function statements to illustrate how the rate changes.)

Alternatively, you could enter the cash-flow values in a range called CASHFLOW and the *guess* value in a cell named GUESS, and use a function statement such as

@IRR(GUESS,CASHFLOW)

N O T E — For more examples of using this function, see page 297.

See Also @FV, @FVAL, @MIRR, @NPV, @PV, @PVAL, @RATE

@MDURATION(*settlement, maturity,coupon,yield, [frequency],[basis]*)

The @MDURATION function returns the modified annual duration for a security that pays periodic interest. (*Duration* is the weighted average term to maturity of the cash flows of a security.)

The arguments for @MDURATION are as follows:

ARGUMENT	DESCRIPTION
settlement	A date number representing the security's settlement date.

ARGUMENT	DESCRIPTION
maturity	A date number representing the security's maturity date. *maturity* must be greater than settlement; otherwise @MDURATION will return ERR.
coupon	Any positive value (or 0) representing the security's annual coupon rate.
yield	Any positive value (or 0) representing the annual yield.
frequency	1, 2, 4, or 12: an optional value specifying the number of coupon payments per year as follows:

1   Annual

2   Semiannual (this is the default if *frequency* is omitted)

4   Quarterly

12   Monthly

basis	An optional value specifying the type of day-count to use, as follows:

0   30/360 (this is the default if you omit *basis*)

1   Actual/actual

2   Actual/360

3   Actual/365

WARNING

Note that you cannot use an optional argument unless you use those that precede it. For example, you cannot use *basis* in @MDURATION if you do not specify *frequency*.

17

Financial Functions

For example, say you have a security with a February 1, 1995 settlement date and a July 1, 1999 maturity date. The quarterly coupon rate is 2.85 percent, and the annual yield is 6.5 percent. The bond uses an actual/365 day-count basis. You could determine the security's modified annual duration by using this function statement:

@MDURATION(@DATE(95,2,1),@DATE(99,7,1),0.0285,0.065,4,3)

It returns 4.06066—substantially different from the 4.126652 that the @DURATION function produces for the same data.

TIP To work out the (unmodified) annual duration for a security, use @DURATION instead of @MDURATION. @DURATION is covered on page 777.

See Also @ACCRUED, @DURATION, @PRICE, @YIELD

@MIRR(*range,finance-rate, reinvest-rate*)

The @MIRR function calculates the modified internal rate of return on an investment—the interest rate received for an investment consisting of payments (negative value) that occur at regular periods.

The arguments for @MIRR are as follows:

ARGUMENT	DESCRIPTION
range	The address or name of a range that contains the cash flows. Negative numbers represent cash outflows and positive numbers represent cash inflows. The first cash-flow amount in the range is usually a negative number (i.e., a cash outflow) representing the investment.
finance-rate	A value indicating the interest rate paid on the money used in cash flows.

ARGUMENT	DESCRIPTION
reinvest-rate	A value indicating the interest rate you receive on cash flows that you reinvest.
type	An optional argument specifying when the cash flow occurs, as follows:

0   Indicates a cash flow at the beginning of the period. This is the default if you omit the *type* argument.

1   Indicates a cash flow at the end of the period.

17

Financial Functions

WARNING

Note that any blank cells or labels within the *range* argument are included in the @MIRR calculation. They receive a value of 0.

You can combine the @MIRR function with other financial functions (for example, @NPV) to assess the profitability of an investment.

As an illustration of using the @MIRR function, assume you own a record store, Protozoa Records, that you purchased at the end of 1987 for $250,000. As shown in Figure 17.5, you've made a steady profit, though your expenses have been growing steadily too. Your profit or loss is stored in the range PROFIT OR LOSS in the worksheet, currently cells D4..D12. Your finance rate is stored in the range named FINANCE RATE, and your reinvestment rate in the range named REINVEST-MENT.

Cell D14 contains the function statement to work out the modified internal rate of return on your investment in Protozoa Records:

    @MIRR(PROFIT OR LOSS,FINANCE RATE,REINVESTMENT)

It returns 0.16136106, or 16.14 percent. Were you able to reinvest your profits at the end of the year rather than at the beginning, you could make rather more money:

    @MIRR(PROFIT OR LOSS,FINANCE RATE,REINVESTMENT,1)

FIGURE 17.5

Using the @MIRR
function to calculate
the modified internal
rate of return on an
investment

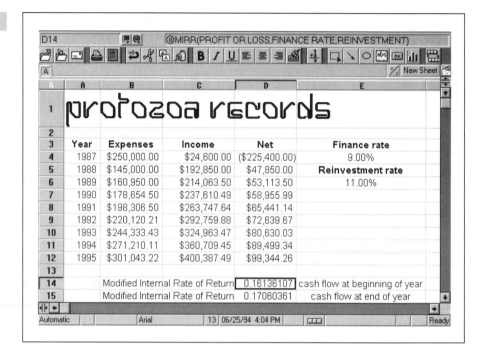

FIGURE 17.5

Using the @MIRR function to calculate the modified internal rate of return on an investment

This function statement returns 0.170603609, or 17.06 percent.

See Also @IRR

@NPER(*payments,interest,future-value,[type],[present-value]*)

The @NPER function returns the number of periods required for a series of equal payments with a specified *present-value* to accumulate a *future-value* at a periodic rate of *interest*.

NOTE

The @NPER function is an enhanced version of the @TERM function (see page 813). Unlike @TERM, you can specify a present value, and you can also specify a value for the *type* argument to make @NPER calculate for either an ordinary annuity or an annuity due.

The arguments for the @NPER function are as follows:

ARGUMENT	DESCRIPTION
payments	Any value except 0, indicating the value of the equal investments.
interest	Any value greater than −1, indicating the periodic interest rate.
future-value	A value indicating the amount you want to accumulate.
type	Zero or 1. *type* is an optional argument used to specify whether 1-2-3 calculates for an ordinary annuity or for an annuity due:
	0 Indicates an ordinary annuity, in which the payments are due at the end of a period. This is the default if you omit the argument *type*.
	1 Indicates an annuity due, in which the payments are due at the beginning of a period.
present-value	Any value, indicating the present value of the series of future payments. *present-value* is an optional argument; if you omit *present-value*, 1-2-3 uses the value of 0.

WARNING Note that you cannot use an optional argument unless you use those that precede it. For example, you cannot use *present-value* in @NPER if you do not specify *type*.

As an example of @NPER, assume that you have the princely sum of $1,776 in your savings account, where it earns a steady 8.25 percent interest. Being patriotic, you plan to deposit the same amount into the account at the end of each year. How long will it take you to reach your target of $17,760 for your sabbatical walk from Alaska to Tierra del Fuego? To find out, you use this function statement:

    @NPER(1776,0.0825,17760,0,1776)

It returns 6.56 years. Bear in mind that the fractional part of the result means that you'll get the sabbatical funds only at the end of the sixth year.

You can use @NPER just as you would use @TERM—for example, to calculate the number of periods necessary to pay back a loan. For the loan of $25,000 you foolishly took out from a Vegas shark at a happy 25 percent interest, you might use the following function statement to find out how long it will take you to regain your feet if you can pay off $7,500 a year:

    @NPER(7500,0.25,–25000)

The answer is 8.03 years. Note that this function statement returns a negative value because the loan amount is entered as a negative value, –25000. Either ignore the negative—the number of years for the repayment is unfortunately always going to be positive—or add the @ABS function to the function statement to return a positive result:

    @ABS(@NPER(7500,0.25,-25000))

See Also @CTERM, @TERM

@NPV(*interest,range,*[*type*])

The @NPV function calculates the net present value of a series of future estimated cash-flow values indicated by *range* discounted at a fixed periodic rate of *interest*.

TIP

The net present value of an investment is today's value of a series of future payments (negative cash flows) and income (positive cash flows). You can use @NPV either to evaluate an investment or to compare one investment with others by calculating the initial investment necessary to achieve a certain cash outflow at a certain rate.

The arguments for the @NPV function are as follows:

ARGUMENT	DESCRIPTION
interest	A value greater than −1 indicating the constant interest rate per period.
range	The range containing the cash flows, entered either as a range name or a range address. Note that *range* cannot be more than a single row or a single column—if it is, @NPV will return ERR.
type	Zero or 1. *type* is an optional argument used to specify whether 1-2-3 calculates for an ordinary annuity or for an annuity due:

0 Indicates an ordinary annuity, in which the payments are due at the end of a period. This is the default if you omit the argument *type*.

1 Indicates an annuity due, in which the payments are due at the beginning of a period.

Figure 17.6 illustrates the use of @NPV to estimate the value of an investment discounted to today's dollars. The range named CASH (cells C3..C11) contains an initial investment of $66,000 and cash returns for the years 1995–2000 of $2,800.00, $5,320.00, $10,108.00, $19,205.20, $36,489.88, and $69,330.77, respectively. Cell C13 contains the function statement

@NPV(0.1,CASH)

17

Financial Functions

It calculates the net present value of the investments at a 10 percent discount rate; the result is $7,202.56. If payments are made at the beginning of each period rather than at the end, the result is different:

@NPV(0.1,CASH,1)

This statement produces $7,922.82.

NOTE   For more about @NPV, see page 293.

See Also @FV, @PV

FIGURE 17.6

Using the @NPV function to calculate the net present value of an asset

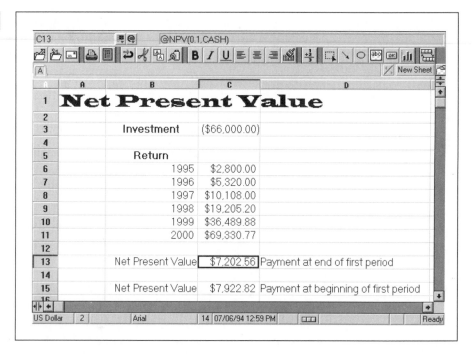

@PAYMT(*principal,interest,term,* [*type*],[*future-value*])

The @PAYMT function calculates the payment on a loan (principal) at a given rate of *interest* for a specified number of payment periods indicated by *term*.

NOTE   The @PAYMT function is similar to the @PMT function but can calculate for either an ordinary annuity or an annuity due, depending on the *type* specified.

The arguments for the @PAYMT function are as follows:

ARGUMENT	DESCRIPTION
principal	A value indicating the amount borrowed.
interest	A decimal or percentage value greater than −1, indicating the interest rate of the loan. Note that the period used to calculate *interest* must be the same as the period used for *term*. If necessary, divide the annual interest rate by 12 to get the monthly interest and multiply the term by 12.
term	A value indicating the number of periods of the loan.
type	Zero or 1. *type* is an optional argument used to specify whether 1-2-3 calculates for an ordinary annuity or for an annuity due:
	0 Indicates an ordinary annuity, in which the payments are due at the end of a period. This is the default if you omit the argument *type*.

17

Financial Functions

ARGUMENT	DESCRIPTION
	1 Indicates an annuity due, in which the payments are due at the beginning of a period.
future-value	A value indicating the future value of the series of payments. *future-value* is an optional argument; if you do not specify *future-value*, 1-2-3 uses the default value of 0.

WARNING

Note that you cannot use an optional argument unless you use those that precede it. For example, you cannot use *future-value* in @PAYMT if you do not specify *type*.

For example, say you're thinking of buying a hundred-CD changer for $799. If you want to finance it for a year at 7.75 percent interest, you could use @PAYMT to work out the payments you'd need to make on the first day of each month to pay it off:

@PAYMT(799,0.0775/12,1*12)

This returns a monthly payment of $69.41.

See Also @IPAYMT, @PMT, @PMTC, @PPAYMT, @TERM

@PMT(*principal,interest,term*)

The @PMT function calculates the payment on a loan (*principal*) at a given rate of *interest* for a specified number of payment periods indicated by *term*.

TIP

The @PMT function is included in 1-2-3 Release 5 for backward compatibility with older versions of 1-2-3. @PMT assumes that the investment being calculated is an ordinary annuity. Generally speaking, @PMT has been largely superseded by the @PAYMT function (discussed earlier in this chapter), which allows you to calculate for either an ordinary annuity or an annuity due. However, if you don't need the extra amenities that @PAYMT offers, @PMT remains a valid and viable function—and in fact is rather easier to use than @PAYMT, if only through being shorter to type.

17

Financial Functions

The arguments for the @PMT function are as follows:

ARGUMENT	DESCRIPTION
principal	A value indicating the amount borrowed.
interest	A decimal or percentage value greater than −1, indicating the interest rate of the loan. Note that the period used to calculate *interest* must be the same as the period used for *term*. If necessary, divide the annual interest rate by 12 to get the monthly interest and multiply the term by 12.
term	A value indicating the number of periods of the loan.

For example, suppose you're considering taking out a loan of $100,000 to expand your business of teaching sign language to primates. You'll be able to finance the loan for six years at 3.85 percent interest, and you'll be making payments on the last day of each month. To work out how much those payments will be, use this function statement:

```
@PMT(100000,0.0385/12,6*12)
```

It returns $1557.69. Note that to calculate for payments at the beginning of each month rather than at the end of each month, you'd need to use the @PAYMT function rather than the @PMT function.

N O T E   Chapter 5 also discusses the @PMT function. See page 295.

See Also   @IPAYMT, @PAYMT, @PMTC, @PPAYMT, @TERM

@PMTC(*principal,interest,term*)

The @PMTC function calculates the payment on a loan (*principal*) at a given rate of *interest* for a specified number of payment periods indicated by *term*. @PMTC is a variant of @PMT adapted to support Canadian mortgage conventions.

The arguments for the @PMTC function are as follows:

ARGUMENT	DESCRIPTION
principal	A value indicating the amount borrowed.
interest	A decimal or percentage value greater than −1, indicating the interest rate of the loan. Note that the period used to calculate *interest* must be the same as the period used for *term*. If necessary, divide the annual interest rate by 12 to get the monthly interest and multiply the term by 12.
term	A value indicating the number of periods of the loan.

As an illustration of @PMTC, consider the following example. You're considering taking out a mortgage of $200,000 to buy a house in either the U.S. or Canada. Either way, you'll be using U.S. dollars and suffering 9 percent interest for ten years. To find out how much you'd be paying on the loan each year in Canada, you could use the following function statement:

@PMTC(200000,0.09,10)

This returns $20,818.86, a fairly painful blow to the third button of the financial waistcoat—but not nearly as bad as you'd be paying in the U.S.:

@PMT(200000,0.09,10)

This returns $31,164.02. Time to emigrate and telecommute.

See Also @IPAYMT, @PAYMT, @PMT, @PPAYMT, @TERM

@PPAYMT(*principal,interest, term,start-period,[end-period], [type],[future-value]*)

The @PPAYMT function returns the principal payment on a loan (*principal*), based on periodic, constant payments at a given *interest* rate over *term*. The arguments for @PPAYMT are as follows:

ARGUMENT	DESCRIPTION
principal	A value representing the amount borrowed.
term	Any value except 0, indicating the number of periods in the loan. Be sure to use the same units for *term* as you use for *interest*.
interest	A decimal or percentage value greater than −1, representing the fixed periodic interest rate for the loan. Use the same units for *interest* as you use for *term*.
start-period	A value greater than or equal to 1 (but not greater than *term*) representing the point in *term* at which the calculation of interest is to start.
end-period	A value greater than or equal to 1 (but not greater than *term*) representing the point in *term* at which the calculation of interest is to stop. The default setting for *end-period* (if you omit the argument) is the same as *start-period*.

17

Financial Functions

ARGUMENT	DESCRIPTION
type	Zero or 1. *type* is an optional argument used to specify whether 1-2-3 calculates for an ordinary annuity or for an annuity due:
	0 Indicates an ordinary annuity, in which the payments are due at the end of a period. This is the default if you omit the argument *type*.
	1 Indicates an annuity due, in which the payments are due at the beginning of a period.
future-value	Any value representing the future value of the series of payments. Note that this is an optional argument; if you do not specify *future-value*, 1-2-3 will use the default value of 0.

WARNING Note that you cannot use an optional argument unless you use those that precede it. For example, you cannot use *type* in @PPAYMT if you do not specify *end-period*.

For example, suppose you were thinking of borrowing $25,000 for two years at 7.2 percent interest to buy a shiny new Monster Truck with jacked-up suspension and gigantic tires. How much money would you pay against the principal of the loan in the first year? To find out, you could use this function statement:

@PPAYMT(25000,0.072,3,1)

The answer is $7,761.

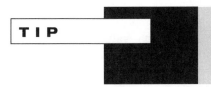

T I P   To calculate the interest payment on a loan (rather than the principal payment), use the @IPAYMT function (see page 781) instead of the @PPAYMT function.

See Also @IPAYMT, @PMT

@PRICE (*settlement,maturity, coupon,yield,*[*redemption*], [*frequency*],[*basis*])

The @PRICE function returns the price per $100 face value for securities that pay periodic interest. The arguments for the @PRICE function are as follows:

ARGUMENT	DESCRIPTION
settlement	A date number representing the security's settlement date.
maturity	A date number representing the security's maturity date. *maturity* must be greater than *settlement*; otherwise @PRICE will return ERR.
coupon	Any positive value (or 0) representing the security's annual coupon rate.
yield	Any positive value (or 0) representing the annual yield.
redemption	Any positive value (or 0) representing the security's redemption value per $100 face value. The default value for *redemption* is 100.

17

Financial Functions

ARGUMENT	DESCRIPTION
frequency	1, 2, 4, or 12: an optional value specifying the number of coupon payments per year as follows:

1   Annual

2   Semiannual (this is the default if *frequency* is omitted)

4   Quarterly

12   Monthly

basis	An optional value specifying the type of day-count to use, as follows:

0   30/360 (this is the default if you omit *basis*)

1   Actual/actual

2   Actual/360

3   Actual/365

WARNING

Note that you cannot use an optional argument unless you use those that precede it. For example, you cannot use *basis* in @PRICE if you do not specify *frequency*, and you cannot use *frequency* if you do not specify *redemption*.

For example, say you needed to establish the price of a bond that has the following terms:

- A settlement date of April 1, 1994
- A maturity date of January 1, 2001
- A quarterly coupon rate of 4.5 percent
- An annual yield of 5.7 percent

- A redemption value of $120
- A quarterly frequency
- A 30/360 day-count basis

To establish the price of the bond, you could use this function statement:

@PRICE(@DATE(94,4,1),@DATE(101,1,1),0.045,0.057,120,4,0)

It returns $106.96.

See Also @ACCRUED, @DURATION, @MDURATION, @YIELD

@PV(*payments,interest,term*)

The @PV function calculates the present value of an investment with a specified *future-value*, based on a series of equal cash flows, discounted at a periodic interest rate over the number of periods in *term*.

T I P

The @PV function is included in 1-2-3 Release 5 for compatibility with earlier versions of 1-2-3. It has been largely superseded by the @PVAL function, which allows you to specify a future value for the investment and to calculate either an ordinary annuity or an annuity due, depending on the value you specify for *type*. However, if you don't need the future value and annuity options that @PVAL offers, @PV remains a valid and viable function—there's no reason to stop using it if it fulfills your needs.

The arguments for the @PV function are as follows:

ARGUMENT	DESCRIPTION
payments	A value indicating the amount borrowed.

ARGUMENT	DESCRIPTION
interest	A value greater than −1 indicating the constant interest rate per period. Note that the period used to calculate *interest* must be the same as the period used for *term*. If necessary, divide the annual interest rate by 12 to get the monthly interest and multiply the term by 12.
term	A positive value indicating the total number of period payments. Note that *term* cannot be negative.

The main use of the @PV function is to compare one investment with another. For example, say your spouse's devoted filling in of the ceaseless mailings from Publishers Clearing House has finally paid off, and you've hit a jackpot worth either $666,000 in one lump sum or $30,000 a year for the next twenty-five years of your natural term. To find out which is the better deal, check your interest rate (7 percent annually in this example), and then use this function statement:

@PV(30000,0.07,25)

It tells you that the twenty-five payments of $30,000 are worth only $349,706.50 in today's dollars.

Rather more practically, you could use @PV in conjunction with @PMT to work out how large a loan you can afford from the size of the monthly payment you can scrape together. And vice versa, of course—you could use @PMT to find out how painful your monthly payment will be for a loan of a given size.

N O T E   See page 293 for further practical examples of using @PV.

See Also @FV @FVAL, @NPV, @PMT, @PAYMT, @PMTC

@PVAL(*payments,interest,term,* [*type*],[*future-value*])

The @PVAL function calculates the present value of an investment with a specified *future-value*, based on a series of equal cash flows, discounted at a periodic interest rate over the number of periods in *term*.

TIP

The @PVAL function is an enhanced version of the @PV function. @PVAL allows you to specify a future value for the investment; it is also able to calculate either an ordinary annuity or an annuity due, depending on the value you specify for *type*.

17

Financial Functions

The arguments for the @PVAL function are as follows:

ARGUMENT	DESCRIPTION
payments	A value indicating the amount borrowed.
interest	A value greater than −1 indicating the constant interest rate per period. Note that the period used to calculate *interest* must be the same as the period used for *term*. If necessary, divide the annual interest rate by 12 to get the monthly interest and multiply the term by 12.
term	A positive value indicating the total number of period payments. Note that *term* cannot be negative.

ARGUMENT	DESCRIPTION
type	Zero or 1. *type* is an optional argument used to specify whether 1-2-3 calculates for an ordinary annuity or for an annuity due:
	0 Indicates an ordinary annuity, in which the payments are due at the end of a period. This is the default if you omit the argument *type*.
	1 Indicates an annuity due, in which the payments are due at the beginning of a period.
future-value	Any value representing the present value of the series of future payments. If you omit *future-value*,

WARNING Note that you cannot use an optional argument unless you use those that precede it. For example, you cannot use *future-value* in @PVAL if you do not specify *type*.

For example, the new workstation you're considering buying for running your company's Internet node costs $28,000 on the hoof, but you have the option of paying $1,400 a month at the beginning of each month for two years at 8 percent interest. Would the never-never be a better option for you? To calculate the total cost, use this function statement:

@PVAL(1400,0.08/12,2*12,1)

It returns $31,161.13—not the greatest of deals for you. Paying at the end of each month would serve you a little better:

@PVAL(1400,0.08/12,2*12,0)

This function statement returns $30,954.76.

See Also   @FV, @FVAL, @NPV, @PAYMT @PMT, @PMTC

@RATE(*future-value,present-value,term*)

The @RATE function calculates the periodic interest rate necessary for an investment of value *present-value* (present-value) to increase to a future value of *future-value* over the number of compounding periods in *term*. The arguments for the @RATE function are all values.

The @RATE function is a valuable instrument for examining investment opportunities. You could use it for anything from analyzing stocks professionally to choosing a better savings account.

For example, if you have $33,000 to invest and want to have $50,000 in three years, you could use the @RATE function as follows to find out what interest rate you need:

@RATE(50000,33000,3)

This returns 0.148556—a rate of nearly 15 percent. This is going to be a high-risk investment. To discover the monthly interest rate, you could use

@RATE(50000,33000,3*12)

which returns 0.011609, or 1.2 percent.

NOTE For another example of how the @RATE function works, see page 296.

See Also @IRATE

@SLN(*cost,salvage,life*)

The @SLN function calculates the straight-line depreciation allowance of an asset for one period. The asset has an initial value of *cost*, an expected useful *life* (the number of years over which the asset is to be depreciated), and a final value of *salvage*.

17

Financial Functions

TIP

Straight-line depreciation divides the depreciable cost equally into each period of the useful life of the asset. The depreciable cost is the actual cost of the item minus the salvage value of the item. Compare @SLN to 1-2-3's other depreciation functions: @DB, which uses the declining balance method; @DDB, which uses the double-declining balance method; and @SYD, which uses the sum-of-the-years'-digits method.

The arguments for the @SLN function are as follows:

ARGUMENT	DESCRIPTION
cost	Any value indicating the amount paid for the asset
salvage	Any value indicating the value of the asset at the end of its expected useful life
life	Any value greater than or equal to 1 indicating the number of periods the asset takes to depreciate to its salvage value
period	Any value greater than or equal to 1 indicating the time for which you want to find the depreciation allowance

For example, to calculate straight-line yearly depreciation on a color laser printer that cost $6,000, will have a useful life of seven years, and will be worth all of $500 after that, you could use this function statement:

@SLN(6000,500,7)

It returns $785.71, the yearly depreciation on the printer.

NOTE

See page 288 for more examples of using @SLN.

See Also @DB, @DDB, @SYD @VDB

@SYD(*cost,salvage,life,period*)

The @SYD function calculates the sum-of-the-years'-digits depreciation allowance of an asset that has an initial value of *cost*, an expected useful *life*, and a final value of *salvage*, over a specified *period*.

The arguments for the @SYD function are as follows:

ARGUMENT	DESCRIPTION
cost	Any value indicating the amount paid for the asset
salvage	Any value indicating the value of the asset at the end of its expected useful life
life	Any value greater than or equal to 1 indicating the number of periods the asset takes to depreciate to its salvage value
period	Any value greater than or equal to 1 indicating the time for which you want to find the depreciation allowance

17

Financial Functions

T I P

What's the difference between the @DB, @SYD, and @DDB functions? Compared to @DB, which calculates the fixed-declining balance method to calculate depreciation, @SYD (which uses the sum-of-the-years'-digits method to calculate depreciation) speeds the rate of depreciation so that more depreciation expense occurs in earlier periods than in later ones. @DDB, which uses the double-declining balance method to calculate depreciation, causes even more depreciation expense to occur in earlier periods than does @SYD. @SYD calculates the depreciable cost as the actual cost minus the salvage value. @SYD is particularly useful for occasions requiring a higher depreciation expense early in the life of an asset, such as in preparing tax returns.

For example, you could calculate the sum-of-the-years'-depreciation on your new Pentium computer system as illustrated in Figure 17.7.

You reckon the computer will have a useful life of five years; you paid $3,000 for it just a few days ago; and the salvage value is unlikely to be more than $600. To calculate the sum-of-the-years'-digits depreciation for the first year, use this function statement:

@SYD(3000,600,5,1)

It returns $800.00. (Cells C10, C11, C12, and C13 contain the same function statement except for the *period* argument, which is changed to 2, 3, 4, and 5, respectively.)

N O T E For more about the @SYD function, see page 288.

See Also @DB, @DDB, @SLN, @VDB

FIGURE 17.7

Using the @SYD function to calculate the sum-of-the-years'-digits depreciation

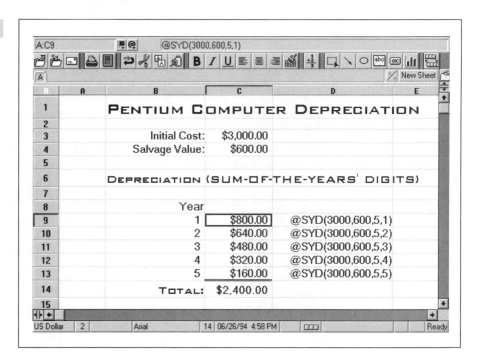

@TERM(*payments,interest, future-value*)

The @TERM function returns the number of periods required for a series of equal *payments* to increase to a *future-value* at a periodic rate of *interest*. The arguments for the @TERM function are as follows:

ARGUMENT	DESCRIPTION
payments	Any value except 0 indicating the fixed, periodic payments. Note that *payments* cannot change during the life of the annuity.
interest	A value greater than –1 indicating the constant interest rate per period.
future-value	Any value indicating the amount you want to accumulate.
type	Zero or 1. *type* is an optional argument used to specify whether 1-2-3 calculates for an ordinary annuity or for an annuity due:
	0 Indicates an ordinary annuity, in which the payments are due at the end of a period. This is the default if you omit the argument *type*.
	1 Indicates an annuity due, in which the payments are due at the beginning of a period.
present-value	Any value indicating the present value of the series of future payments. *present-value* is an optional argument; if you omit it, 1-2-3 uses the default value of 0.

17

Financial Functions

WARNING Note that you cannot use an optional argument unless you use those that precede it. For example, you cannot use *present-value* in @TERM if you do not specify *type*.

As an example of @TERM, assume that you're just firing up a 401K account and will be able to put $2,400 into it each year, where it will earn a steady 10.5 percent interest. Once your 401K reaches $250,000, you swear to yourself, you'll throw your job in and buy a salmon farm in Alaska. To calculate how far away your earthly paradise is, use this function statement:

@TERM(2400,0.105,250000)

It returns 24.84 years—rather a long way in the future. Suppose you reduce your target to $200,000:

@TERM(2400,0.105,200000)

Now the time is reduced only as far as 22.81 years. (This is a nice illustration of the benefits of starting your 401K plan as early as possible: With the same saving schedule, it will take you 20 years to reach $150,000, 31 years to reach $500,000, and only 38 years to reach $1 million.)

You can use @TERM to calculate the number of periods necessary to pay back a loan. As a domestic example, you could work out how long it would take your son to repay the $2,000 damage he did to your Porsche with the $240 a month he makes from his McJob, at the generous 3.5 percent interest rate you and he negotiated:

@TERM(240,0.035/12,2000)

This returns –8.25 months. Note that this function statement returns a negative value because the loan amount is entered as a negative value, –2000. Either ignore the negative—you know that the number of months for the repayment is going to be positive—or add the @ABS function to the function statement to return a positive result:

@ABS(@TERM(240,0.035/12,2000))

NOTE Chapter 5 also discusses the @TERM function. See page 295.

See Also @CTERM

@VDB(*cost,salvage,life, start-period,end-period, [depreciation-factor],[switch]*)

The @VDB function calculates the depreciation allowance of an asset for a period you specify with *start-period* and *end-period*, using the variable-rate declining balance method. The asset has an initial value of *cost*, an expected useful *life*, and a final *salvage* value.

The arguments for the @VDB function are as follows:

ARGUMENT	DESCRIPTION
cost	Any value indicating the amount paid for the asset. *cost* must be greater than *salvage*.
salvage	Any value indicating the value of the asset at the end of its expected useful life.
life	Any value greater than 0 indicating the number of periods the asset takes to depreciate to its salvage value.
start-period	Any value greater than or equal to 0 but less than or equal to *life*, indicating the point in the asset's life at which to begin calculating depreciation. *start-period* corresponds to the asset's life, relative to the fiscal period. Note that if both *start-period* and *end-period* have fractional parts, 1-2-3 uses the fractional part of *start-period*.

17

Financial Functions

ARGUMENT	DESCRIPTION
end-period	Any value greater than *start-period* indicating the point in the asset's life at which to stop calculating depreciation. *end-period* corresponds to the asset's life, relative to the fiscal period. Note that if both *start-period* and *end-period* have fractional parts, 1-2-3 uses the fractional part of *start-period*.
depreciation-factor	A value greater than or equal to 0 indicating the percentage of straight-line depreciation you want to use as the depreciation rate. *depreciation-factor* is an optional argument; if you omit it, @VDB will use the default value of 200 percent, the double-declining balance rate. Common rates for *depreciation-factor* are 1.25, 1.50, 1.75, and 2.
switch	Zero or 1, an optional argument used to prevent @VDB from switching to straight-line depreciation for the remaining useful life of the asset. Under normal circumstances in this type of calculation, declining-balance switches to straight-line depreciation when it is greater than declining-balance.
	0 If switch = 0, @VDB automatically switches to straight-line depreciation when straight-line is greater than declining-balance. This is the default setting if you omit the *switch* argument.
	1 If switch = 1. @VDB does not switch to straight-line depreceiation, no matter what the relative values of straight-line depreciation and eclining-balance depreciation.

WARNING

Note that you cannot use an optional argument unless you use those that precede it. For example, you cannot use *switch* in @VDB if you do not specify *depreciation-factor*.

For example, let's consider the Pentium computer system we looked at earlier in this chapter—a machine with an initial cost of $3,000, a salvage value of $600, and a life of six years. Figure 17.8 shows a worksheet that calculates depreciation for the first month, the first year, the second year, and the second year with a depreciation factor of 1.75.

Cell B8 contains this function statement to calculate the depreciation for the first month:

@VDB(3000,600,6*12,0,1)

Note the use of 6*12 in this cell for *life* to provide the number of months, which means that the 0 for *start-period* and the 1 for *end-period* also refer

17

Financial Functions

FIGURE 17.8

Using the @VDB function

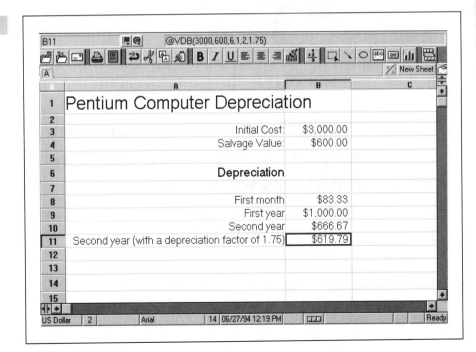

to months.

By contrast, cell B9 contains this function statement to calculate the depreciation for the first year:

@VDB(3000,600,6,0,1)

Since *life* is the number of years, the 0 for *start-period* and the 1 for *end-period* also refer to years.

Similarly, cell B10 contains this function statement to calculate the depreciation for the second year:

@VDB(3000,600,6,1,2)

By contrast, cell B11 calculates the depreciation for the second year with a depreciation fact of 1.75:

@VDB(3000,600,6,1,2,1.75)

This produces a substantially different result—$619.79 rather than $666.67.

N O T E   See page 288 for more about the @VDB function.

See Also @DDB, @SLN, @SYD

@YIELD(*settlement,maturity, coupon,price,*[*redemption*], [*frequency*],[*basis*])

The @YIELD function calculates the yield for securities that pay periodic interest. The arguments for the @YIELD function are as follows:

ARGUMENT	DESCRIPTION
settlement	A date number representing the security's settlement date.

ARGUMENT	DESCRIPTION
maturity	A date number representing the security's maturity date. 1-2-3 will produce ERR for @YIELD if maturity is less than or equal to settlement.
coupon	Any positive value (or 0) representing the security's annual coupon rate.
price	Any positive value representing the security's price per $100 face value.
redemption	Any positive value (or 0) representing an optional argument that specifies the security's redemption value per $100 face value. This is an optional argument with a default of 100 if omitted.
frequency	1, 2, 4, or 12, to specify the number of coupon payments per year. This is an optional argument; the values have the following meanings:

    1 Annual

    2 Semiannual (this is the default value if you omit the *frequency* argument)

    4 Quarterly

    12 Monthly

| *basis* | 0, 1, 2, or 3, to specify the type of day-count basis to use. This is an optional argument; the values have the following meanings: |

    0 30/360 (this is the default value if you omit the *basis* argument)

    1 Actual/actual

    2 Actual/360

    3 Actual/365

17

Financial Functions

WARNING Note that you cannot use an optional argument unless you use those that precede it. For example, you cannot use *basis* in @YIELD if you do not specify *frequency* and redemption.

For example, suppose you had a bond with the following details: a settlement date of January 1, 1990; a maturity date of January 1, 2000; a coupon rate of 6 percent; a price of $93.00; a redemption value of $100; a semiannual frequency; and an actual/actual day-count basis. You could calculate its yield with this function statement:

@YIELD(@DATE(90,1,1),@DATE(100,1,1),0.06,93,100,2,1)

It returns 0.069844.

See Also @ACCRUED, @DURATION, @MDURATION, @PRICE

18

Information, Logical, and Lookup Functions Reference

THIS chapter examines three groups of 1-2-3's functions: the information functions, the logical functions, and the lookup functions.

The information functions fall into two general categories:

- Functions returning information about cells or ranges, the PC's operating system, or 1-2-3's tools

- Functions marking where information is missing from the worksheet or is incorrect

The logical functions calculate the results of logical formulas. Examples of the logical functions include @TRUE and @FALSE, which check to see whether a condition returns the value of TRUE (1) or FALSE (1), respectively; @ISNUMBER, which checks to see if the contents of a cell (or a part of the contents) are a number; and @ISSTRING, which checks to see if the contents of a cell (or a part of the contents) is a string; and @ISEMPTY, which checks to see if a cell is empty.

The lookup functions find the contents of a cell. Examples of the lookup functions include @HLOOKUP and @VLOOKUP, which look up specified entries in a horizontal lookup table and a vertical lookup table, respectively; @MAXLOOKUP and @MINLOOKUP, which return an absolute reference (including the file name) to the cell that contains the largest value in a list of ranges and the smallest value in a list of ranges, respectively; and @MATCH, which returns the location of a cell whose contents match those specified.

Overview of the Information Functions

For quick reference, the information functions are listed here in Table 18.1, with page numbers indicating their detailed discussions in the next section of this chapter, "Descriptions of the Information Functions."

TABLE 18.1: Information Functions Quick Reference

FUNCTION	RETURNS	SEE PAGE
@CELL	Information about the upper-left cell in a reference; for example, the cell's contents, color, or file name.	825
@CELL-POINTER	Information about the current cell's formatting, location, or contents.	829
@COLS	The number of columns in a range.	829
@COORD	A cell reference from given values for *worksheet*, *column*, and *row*.	830
@DDELINK	Establishes a DDE link in the current cell to another Windows application or another 1-2-3 file.	831
@ERR	The value ERR (for forcing an error condition in formulas when a certain result would be undesirable).	835
@INFO	System information for the current 1-2-3 session, such as the current directory path or the current operating system.	835
@NA	The value NA ("not available") indicating that no value is available; for use as a placeholder for key cells that need to be filled for a formula to be valid.	839

18

Info, Lookup Functions

TABLE 18.1: Information Functions Quick Reference (continued)

FUNCTION	RETURNS	SEE PAGE
@RANGENAME	The name of the range in which a given cell is located.	841
@REFCONVERT	The corresponding numbers (1–256) for the 1-2-3 column or worksheet letters (A–IV) to numbers from 1 through 256, and the corresponding column or worksheet letters for the numbers 1–256.	841
@ROWS	The number of rows in a given range.	842
@SCENARIO-INFO	Information about a scenario—for example, the user who last modified a scenario or the latest comment attached to a scenario.	842
@SCENARIO-LAST	The name of the scenario that was last displayed in a file during the current 1-2-3 session.	844
@SHEETS	The number of worksheets in a given range.	845
@SOLVER	A value that gives information about the status of Solver.	845
@VERSION-CURRENT	The name of the current version in a range.	848
@VERSION-DATA	The contents of a specified cell in a version.	848
@VERSIONINFO	Information about a version—for example, the name of the user who created it or who last modified it.	850

Descriptions of the Information Functions

This section contains detailed descriptions of the information functions.

@CELL(*attribute,location*)

The @CELL function returns information about the upper-left cell in a reference, where *location* is the address or name of a range and *attribute* is one of the items shown in the list below.

NOTE For information about the current cell, use @CELL-POINTER instead of @CELL.

NOTE *attribute* must be enclosed in double quotation marks (" ") and can also be the address or name of a cell containing one of the items listed below.

ATTRIBUTE	RETURNS THIS INFORMATION
address	The abbreviated absolute address—column letter and row number.
col	The column letter in the reference, expressed as a value from 1 through 256. Column A returns 1, column Z returns 26, column AA returns 27, etc.
color	One if the cell is formatted in color for negative numbers, 0 if the cell is not.

18

Info, Lookup Functions

ATTRIBUTE	RETURNS THIS INFORMATION
contents	The contents of the cell (the upper-left cell in the reference).
coord	The full form of the absolute cell address—worksheet letter, column letter, and row number. Unlike "col", "coord" returns letters as letters rather than as numeric equivalents.
filename	The file name (including the full path) of the file that contains the cell referred to.
format	The cell format as follows:
	Currency returns C0 to C15 for 0 to 15 decimal places.
	Fixed returns F0 to F15 for 0 to 15 decimal places.
	General
	Percent returns P0 to P15 for 0 to 15 decimal places.
	Scientific returns S0 to S15 for 0 to 15 decimal places.
	Comma returns ,0 to ,15 for 0 to 15 decimal places.
	± returns +.
	Date format 11-Nov-94 returns D1.
	Date format 11-Nov returns D2.
	Date format Nov-94 returns D3.
	Date format 12/11/94 returns D4.
	Date format 12/11 returns D5.
	Time format 10:15:00 AM returns D6.
	Time format 10:15 AM returns D7.
	Time format 22:15:00 returns D8.

ATTRIBUTE	RETURNS THIS INFORMATION
	Time format 15:30 returns D9.
	Text returns T.
	Hidden returns H.
	Label returns L.
	Automatic returns A.
	Color for negative numbers returns - - (two hyphens).
	Parentheses returns 1 if the cell has parentheses and 0 if it does not.
prefix	The label prefix character, as follows:
	A left-aligned label returns '.
	A right-aligned label returns ".
	A centered label returns ^.
	A repeating label returns \.
	A nonprinting label returns |.
	A blank cell or a cell containing a value returns a blank (an empty cell).
protect	1 if the cell is protected and 0 if it is not protected.
row	The row number of the cell referred to, returned as a value from 1 through 8192.
sheet	The letter of the worksheet containing the cell referred to, returned as a value from 1 through 256—1 for worksheet A, 27 for worksheet AA, and so on.
sheetname	The name of the worksheet containing the cell referred to. If the worksheet is not named, the worksheet letter is returned instead.

18

Info, Lookup Functions

ATTRIBUTE	RETURNS THIS INFORMATION
type	The type of data the cell contains, as follows:
	A blank cell returns b.
	A cell containing a numeric value, a numeric formula, or a text formula returns v.
	A cell containing a label returns 1.
width	The column width as a number of characters (e.g., 25).

WARNING To make sure your results are up to date, always recalculate your work before using @CELL—this function does not automatically recalculate for you.

One use of @CELL well worth knowing is how to use it in conjunction with @IF and @ERR to ensure that you get the correct type of user input in a particular cell. For example, say you have a campaign spreadsheet with a cell called CONTRIBUTION. You could check that the user enters a value in CONTRIBUTION (and return that value) by using the following function statement:

@IF(@CELL("type",CONTRIBUTION)="v",CONTRIBUTION,@ERR)

If the user does anything in CONTRIBUTION that would throw the spreadsheet a curveball, such as entering text or meanly leaving the cell blank, the cell will display ERR.

You can also use @CELL to direct the execution of macros by assigning different subroutines based on what the user enters in a cell. If you build an automated application, you can use @CELL to change cell attributes, again based on what the user enters into cells.

See Also @CELLPOINTER

@CELLPOINTER(*attribute*)

The @CELLPOINTER function returns information about the current cell's formatting, location, or contents. See the list in the entry for @CELL for the list of attributes for @CELLPOINTER.

WARNING   To make sure your results are up to date, always recalculate your work before using @CELLPOINTER—this function does not automatically recalculate for you.

You can use @CELLPOINTER to determine which cell the cell pointer is currently in or to evaluate a formula based on the contents of the current cell. Once you have established what's in the cell, you can direct the macro accordingly.

For example, you could use the following function statement to test for a blank cell in a list of items and stop the macro if it encounters one:

    {IF @CELLPOINTER("type")="b"}{QUIT}

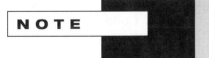

NOTE   See page 523 for an example of how @CELLPOINTER can be used in macro programming.

See Also @@, @CELL

@COLS(*range*)

The @COLS function returns the number of columns in *range*, where *range* is the address or name of a range. For example, if you had a range named PENGUINS SEEN to which you added a new column each day with total numbers of penguins sighted that day, you could use @COLS to find out the number of columns in PENGUINS SEEN in order to print the appropriate range. You would use the following function statement:

@COLS(PENGUINS SEEN)

TIP Consider using @COLS when using a {FOR} statement in a macro to determine on how many columns the macro should repeat the series of actions.

See Also @REFCONVERT, @ROWS, @SHEETS

@COORD(*worksheet,column, row,absolute*)

The @COORD function returns a cell reference from the values for *worksheet*, *column*, and *row*. The arguments for the @COORD function are as follows:

ARGUMENT	DESCRIPTION
worksheet	Any integer from 1 to 256, corresponding to the worksheet letter: 1 represents worksheet A, 2 represents worksheet B, and so on.
column	Any integer from 1 to 256, corresponding to the column letter: 1 represents column A, 2 represents column B, and so on.
row	Any integer from 1 to 8192, corresponding to the row number.
absolute	Any integer from 1 to 8, specifying whether the cell reference is absolute, relative, or mixed, as follows: @COORD(2,2,2,1) returns $B:$B$2 @COORD(2,2,2,2) returns $B:B$2

ARGUMENT	DESCRIPTION
	@COORD(2,2,2,3) returns $B:$B2
	@COORD(2,2,2,4) returns $B:B2
	@COORD(2,2,2,5) returns B:$B$2
	@COORD(2,2,2,6) returns B:B$2
	@COORD(2,2,2,7) returns B:$B2
	@COORD(2,2,2,8) returns B:B2

NOTE

If the values entered for *worksheet, column, row,* and *absolute* are not integers, 1-2-3 will truncate them to integers.

For example, to return the relative address of cell AA11 in worksheet W, you could use the following function statement:

@COORD(23,27,11,8)

You can also use @COORD with @INDEX, @VLOOKUP, or @HLOOKUP to put together cell addresses from tables of values contained in the current file.

See Also @REFCONVERT

@DDELINK(*app-name,topic-name,item-name,[format],[max-rows],[max-cols],[max-sheets]*)

The @DDELINK function establishes a DDE link in the current cell. You can then adjust the link by altering the arguments for @DDELINK.

18

Info, Lookup Functions

The arguments for @DDELINK are as follows:

ARGUMENT	DESCRIPTION
app-name	The text name of a Windows application that can act as a DDE server: for example, "CorelDRAW" or "Winword" (including the " ", double quotation marks).
topic-name	The name of the application file including its path (for example, "D:\SHARING\FUNNYPIC.CDR" or "C:\WORD_DOX\HOTLINKS.DOC"— again, including the double quotation marks) to which the DDE link is to be made. You can use "system" to link to the system topic.
item-name	The name of the item to which you want to link in the server application. This is the item in the server application file to which you want to transfer data through the link.
format	Text, WK1, or WK3, representing the Clipboard formats that can be used for the link. The *format* argument is optional; if you omit it, 1-2-3 will use the Text Clipboard format.
max-rows	The maximum number of rows for the destination range to occupy. If you omit the *max-rows* argument, 1-2-3 will use as many rows as the destination range takes up.
max-cols	The maximum number of columns for the destination range to occupy. If you omit the *max-cols* argument, 1-2-3 will use as many columns as the destination range takes up.

ARGUMENT	DESCRIPTION
max-sheets	The maximum number of worksheets for the destination range to occupy. If you omit the *max-sheets* argument, 1-2-3 will use as many worksheets as the destination range takes up.

For example, Figure 18.1 shows a 1-2-3 spreadsheet named SALE-LINK.WK4 that contains three DDE links to the Word 6 for Windows document SALELINK.DOC shown in the window at the bottom of the screen. The Word document contains bookmarks defining the text to be carried over to 1-2-3. As you can see in the 1-2-3 spreadsheet, the DDE link shown below carries the information Quarter 4 into the 1-2-3 spreadsheet:

@DDELINK("Winword","C:\winword6\Salelink.doc","TimePeriod")

FIGURE 18.1

A 1-2-3 worksheet containing three DDE links to a Word 6 for Windows document

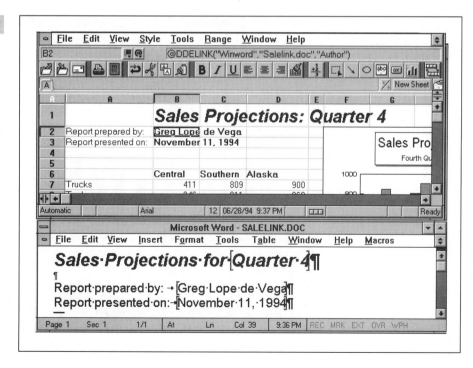

18

Info, Lookup Functions

Figure 18.2 illustrates a link the other way—between the 1-2-3 worksheet and a Word for Windows document. Specifically, the chart from the 1-2-3 worksheet is linked to the Word document, so that any changes made in the chart will appear in the linked copy in the Word document.

WARNING

When using multiple links, make sure you never create a *circular link*—a link in which information is constantly updating itself. This sounds like a no-brainer, but given the complexity of workbooks that 1-2-3 lets you create, it can be surprisingly easy to do. If this does happen, 1-2-3 will grind for a while and then produce an error message.

FIGURE 18.2

A Word 6 for Windows document containing a linked 1-2-3 chart

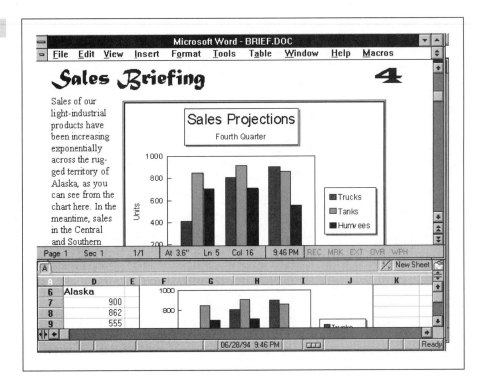

@ERR

The @ERR function returns the value ERR. Use @ERR to force an error condition in formulas when a certain result would be undesirable. For example, if you were calculating the profit margin on a product, you might use @ERR as an argument with @IF to return an error if the values you entered resulted in a negative profit margin (assuming you wanted to make money, of course). For example, the following function statement returns ERR if the value in cell C9 is less than 0:

    @IF(C9<0;@ERR;C9)

Another use of @ERR is to check whether a formula refers to a particular cell indirectly. For example, if you suspect that a value in cell B11 is throwing a wrench into your calculations, but you're not sure that the formula refers to cell B11, you could enter @ERR in cell B11, recalculate, and check to see whether the formula displayed ERR.

T I P   The Tools ➤ Audit command can sometimes be a simpler alternative for this kind of investigation, depending on the structure of the worksheet.

See Also @ISERR, @NA

@INFO(*attribute*)

The @INFO function returns system information for the current 1-2-3 session, such as the current directory path or the current operating system. *attribute* is a text string entered between double quotation marks (" ") and is one of the following:

ATTRIBUTE	DESCRIPTION
dbreturn-code	Returns the most recent error code returned by the external DataLens *driver*. For example, 0.

ATTRIBUTE	DESCRIPTION
dbdriver-message	Returns the most recent DataLens message from an external database driver. This will be blank if there has been no message.
dbrecord-count	Returns the number of records extracted, modified, or inserted from the last query (either in the worksheet or in an external database). For example, 5.
directory	Returns the current path, including the drive letter. For example, C:\123R4W\WORK\.
macro-step	Returns Yes if Step mode is on; returns No if Step mode is off.
macro-trace	Returns Yes if the Macro Trace window is open; returns No if it is not open.
memavail	Returns the amount of available memory (RAM and virtual memory) in bytes. For example, 12439040.
mode	1-2-3's current mode, indicated as one of the following numeric codes:

0   Wait

1   Ready

2   Label

3   Menu

4   Value

5   Point

6   Edit

7   Error

8   Find

9   Files

10   Help

ATTRIBUTE	DESCRIPTION
	11 Stat
	13 Names
	99 All other modes (for example, modes defined by the user with {INDICATE})
numfile	Returns the number of currently open files. For example, 1.
origin	Returns the absolute address of the top-left cell in the current worksheet. For example, $ZA:$A$1. This can be very useful for checking which worksheet a macro is operating on before anything disastrous happens.
osreturn-code	Returns the value returned by the most recent operating system command.
osversion	Returns the version of the current operating system. For example, DOS Version 6.20.
recalc	Returns the current recalculation mode for the worksheet as the label Automatic or the label Manual.
release	Returns the release number for the version of 1-2-3 for Windows you are using, in the following format: major release number, upgrade level, and version number. For example, 5.00.00.
setup-user-name	Returns your e-mail or network user name. If 1-2-3 cannot find an e-mail or network user name, it will return the registered user name.
screen-height	Returns the height of the screen as a value in pixels. For example, 480 if you're using 640 × 480 resolution.

ATTRIBUTE	DESCRIPTION
screen-width	Returns the width of the screen as a value in pixels. For example, 640 if you're using 640 × 480 resolution.
selection	Returns the address of the currently selected range, or the name of the currently selected chart, drawn object, or query table. For example, CHART 1.
selection-part	Returns the name of the selected part of a range or object. For example, 1-2-3 will display Legend labels if you have the legend labels of a chart selected.
selection-type	Returns the current selection type: Range, Draw, Query, or Chart.
system	Returns the name of the operating system. For example, pcdos.
totmem	Returns the total memory available, in bytes. This includes both memory currently available (which you can establish using the *memavail* argument, described above) and memory being used. For example, 12420704.

T I P Be sure to recalculate your worksheets before using @INFO to make sure you get the correct results.

The @INFO function can be crucial to writing successful macros. For example, you could use @INFO("directory") with @IF to change the directory if the user had selected the wrong directory. Alternatively, you might use @INFO("numfile") with @IF to see how many files were open and close extraneous files to conserve memory for the task at hand.

Figure 18.3 illustrates the most useful attributes for @INFO.

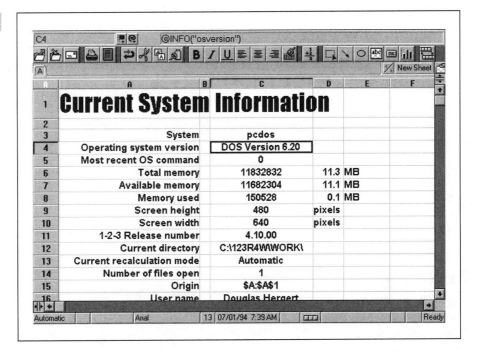

See Also @CELL, @CELLPOINTER

@NA

The @NA function returns the value NA ("not available") indicating that no value is available. The function has no arguments.

Use the @NA function when you're setting up a worksheet as a placeholder for key cells for which you do not yet have a valid entry. Any formulas that refer to the @NA in those cells will return NA, reminding you that the spreadsheet is not yet complete.

Figure 18.4 illustrates this use of the @NA function. In the figure, a record store uses 1-2-3 to track its inventory and keep quarterly totals to see which artists to stock and which to drop. To make sure that the results in column E, the Q1 column, are accurate, @NA is entered in each of the

18

Info, Lookup Functions

cells that will contain the monthly sales figures. The @SUM function is entered in column E to keep the quarterly totals. If any of the cells needed for that total contains NA, the @SUM cell also shows NA to indicate that the figure is not available.

You can also use the @NA function to make sure that a cell contains the type of information you want. For example, to make sure that you did not have a label in cell A1, you could use the following function statement:

```
@IF(@CELL("type";A1)="l",@NA,A1)
```

This would return NA if cell A1 contained a label. Another use for @NA is to check which formulas depend on a particular cell.

See Also @ERR, @ISNA

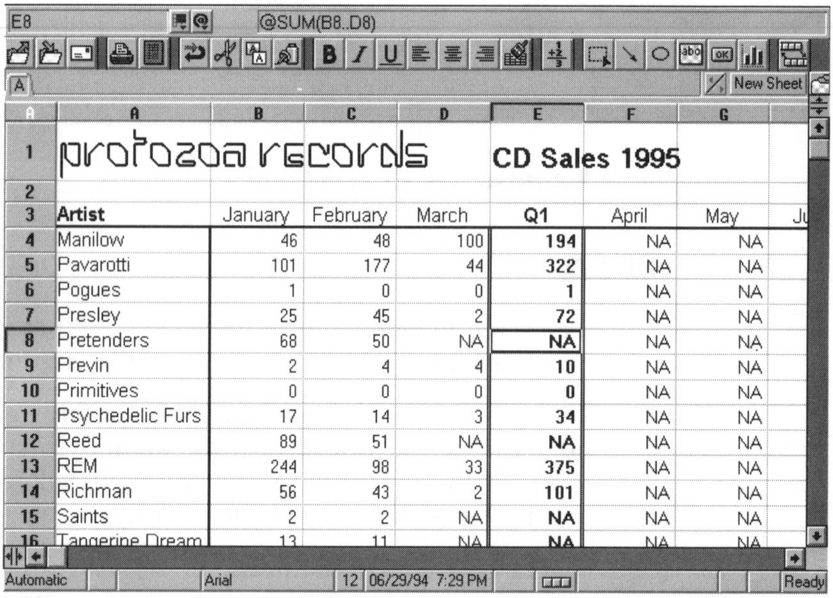

	A	B	C	D	E	F	G
3	Artist	January	February	March	Q1	April	May
4	Manilow	46	48	100	194	NA	NA
5	Pavarotti	101	177	44	322	NA	NA
6	Pogues	1	0	0	1	NA	NA
7	Presley	25	45	2	72	NA	NA
8	Pretenders	68	50	NA	NA	NA	NA
9	Previn	2	4	4	10	NA	NA
10	Primitives	0	0	0	0	NA	NA
11	Psychedelic Furs	17	14	3	34	NA	NA
12	Reed	89	51	NA	NA	NA	NA
13	REM	244	98	33	375	NA	NA
14	Richman	56	43	2	101	NA	NA
15	Saints	2	2	NA	NA	NA	NA
16	Tangerine Dream	13	11	NA	NA	NA	NA

FIGURE 18.4

Using the @NA function as a placeholder to remind you that key information is missing from a spreadsheet

@RANGENAME(*cell*)

The @RANGENAME function returns the name of the range in which *cell* is located, where *cell* is a cell address or the name of a single-cell range. The file containing *cell* must be loaded in memory when you use @RANGENAME.

For example, if cell Z280 is in the range NISSAN, the following function statement will return NISSAN:

    @RANGENAME(Z280)

To find out the name of the range containing the current cell, you could use @CELLPOINTER in conjunction with @RANGENAME:

    @RANGENAME(@CELLPOINTER("address"))

WARNING

Note that if you enter a *cell* that is in more than one range, @RANGENAME will return the first range name that it encounters. For example, if you have named the range A1..A10 TITLES and the range A1..F1 MONTHS, so that cell A1 is in both TITLES and MONTHS, @RANGE-NAME will return MONTHS, since it is alphabetically the first of the two. Note also that if *cell* is not in a named range, @RANGENAME will return ERR.

@REFCONVERT(*reference*)

The @REFCONVERT function returns the corresponding numbers (1–256) for the 1-2-3 column or worksheet letters (A–IV) to numbers from 1 through 256, and returns the corresponding column or worksheet letters for the numbers 1–256.

reference specifies a 1-2-3 column or worksheet and can be:

- a letter from A through IV entered as text in double quotation marks (" ")

18

Info, Lookup Functions

- an integer from 1 through 256

@REFCONVERT is not case-sensitive, so that both the following function statements return 11:

```
@REFCONVERT("k")
@REFCONVERT("K")
```

See Also @COLS, @COORD, @SHEETS

@ROWS(*range*)

The @ROWS function returns the number of rows in *range*, where *range* is a range address or a range name. For example, suppose you had a worksheet for keeping track of your prowess at baseball. If you had a range named RBI to which you added a new row after each baseball game with your number of runs batted in that day, you could use @ROWS to find out the number of rows in RBI in order to print the appropriate range by using the following function statement:

```
@ROWS(RBI)
```

T I P   Consider using @ROWS when using a {FOR} statement in a macro to determine on how many rows the macro should repeat the series of actions.

See Also @COLS, @SHEETS

@SCENARIOINFO(*option,name,* [*creator*])

The @SCENARIOINFO function returns information about a scenario. The arguments for the @SCENARIOINFO function are as follows:

ARGUMENT	DESCRIPTION
option	Any of the following text arguments inside double quotation marks (″ ″) to specify the information 1-2-3 is to return:
	"creator" returns the name of the person who created the scenario
	"modifier" returns the name of the person who last modified the scenario
	"created" returns the date and time the scenario was created, as a date and time number
	"modified" returns a date and time number indicating the date and time the scenario was last modified
	"comment" returns the comment for the scenario, up to a maximum of 512 characters; longer comments are truncated to 512 characters
	"hidden" returns 0 (FALSE) if the scenario is not hidden or 1 (TRUE) if it is hidden
	"protected" returns 0 (FALSE) if the scenario is not protected or 1 (True) if it is protected
name	The name of the scenario, entered as text enclosed within double quotation marks (″ ″). 1-2-3 will use the most recently created scenario if there are more than one with the same name.
creator	The name of the user who created the scenario, entered as text enclosed within double quotation marks (″ ″). *creator* is an optional argument that you can enter to help 1-2-3 determine which scenario to use.

For example, if you had scenarios named Best Case Harvest (for your Lotus-Drinkers vineyard), you could retrieve the name of the user who created the latest Best Case Harvest scenario by using the following function statement:

@SCENARIOINFO("Creator","Best Case Harvest")

Likewise, if your name were Hans Schleifenbaum, you could retrieve your latest comment on the Best Case Harvest scenario by using the following function statement:

@SCENARIOINFO("comment","Best Case Harvest","Hans Schleifenbaum")

See Also @VERSIONINFO

@SCENARIOLAST(*file-name*)

The @SCENARIOLAST function returns the name of the scenario that was last displayed in a file during the current 1-2-3 session. For *file-name*, enter the full name and extension of the file to test for within double quotation marks (" "); if the file is not (or will not be) in the current directory, include the path name as well in *file-name*.

For example, if the last-displayed scenario in your file named HARVEST in the directory Z:\APPS\123R5W\WORK\WINERY\ was Gewuerztraminer, entering the following function statement would return Gewuerztraminer:

@SCENARIOLAST("Z:\APPS\123R5W\WORK\WINERY\ HARVEST.WK4")

WARNING @SCENARIOLAST will return ERR if no scenarios have been displayed in file-name during the current 1-2-3 session.

See Also @SCENARIOINFO

@SHEETS(*range*)

The @SHEETS function returns the number of worksheets in *range*, where *range* is a range address or a range name.

For example, if your company kept its forecast in a file called FORECAST.WK4 that contained a growing number of worksheets featuring (among other ranges) a range named PERSONNEL, you could find out the number of worksheets that PERSONNEL spanned by using the following function statement:

@SHEETS(PERSONNEL)

T I P

The @SHEETS function also comes in useful with a {FOR} statement in a macro to determine on how many sheets the macro should repeat the series of actions.

See Also @COLS, @REFCONVERT, @ROWS

@SOLVER(*attribute*)

The @SOLVER function returns a value that gives information about the status of Solver. The attributes for the @SOLVER function are as shown in the following list. Enter the *attribute* in double quotation marks (" ").

consistent	Returns a value indicating whether all constraints are satisfied:
	1 indicates that all constraints are satisfied.
	2 indicates that at least one constraint is not satisfied.
	ERR indicates that Solver is not active or that there is no answer in the worksheet.

18

Info, Lookup Functions

done

Returns a value indicating whether Solver has finished solving:

1 indicates that Solver has finished solving.

2 indicates that Solver is still solving.

3 indicates that Solver is active but has not yet begun solving.

ERR indicates that Solver is not active.

moreanswers

Returns a value indicating whether Solver has found all the answers:

1 indicates that Solver has found all the answers.

2 indicates that Solver might be able to find more answers.

ERR indicates that Solver is not active.

needguess

Returns a value indicating whether Solver needs guesses to be supplied for it to find an answer:

1 indicates that Solver needs no guesses to find an answer.

2 indicates that Solver needs guesses to find an answer.

ERR indicates that Solver is not active or there is no answer in the worksheet.

numanswers

Indicates the number of answers that Solver found:

number (a number) indicates the number of answers or attempts that Solver found.

ERR indicates that Solver is solving or has not yet solved the problem.

optimal	Returns a value indicating whether Solver has found the optimal answer:
	1 indicates that Solver has found the optimal answer.
	2 indicates that Solver has found the best answer.
	3 indicates that the problem is unbounded.
	4 indicates that no optimization was requested or no answer found.
	ERR indicates that Solver is not active.
progress	Returns a value indicating the percentage of solving that Solver has completed:
	number (a number) indicates the percentage of solving that Solver has completed.
	ERR indicates that Solver is not active or solving has not begun.
result	Returns a value indicating the number of answers that Solver found:
	1 indicates that Solver found one or more answers.
	2 indicates that no answers were found but representative attempts are available.
	ERR indicates that Solver is not active or has not solved the problem yet.

The @SOLVER function is not recalculated every time 1-2-3 performs a recalculation. You need to recalculate manually using F9; in a macro, use either the {RECALC} command or the {RECALCCOL} command to recalculate the cells containing @SOLVER function statements.

@VERSIONCURRENT(*range*)

The @VERSIONCURRENT function returns the name of the current version in *range*, where *range* is the name or address of a range for which you need to find the version name.

For example, if you have a worksheet with a range named CD OUTPUT, the following function statement would return the name of the current version in the CD OUTPUT range:

@VERSIONCURRENT(CD OUTPUT)

If there were no current version, @VERSIONCURRENT would return ERR.

@VERSIONDATA(*option,cell, version-range,name,[creator]*)

The @VERSIONDATA function returns the contents of a specified cell in a version. The arguments for the @VERSIONDATA function are as follows:

ARGUMENT	DESCRIPTION
option	"formula" or "value", text entered in double quotation marks (" ") indicating the information for @VERSIONDATA to return from the cell, as follows:
	"formula" returns as a label the formula contained in the cell. If no formula is in the cell

ARGUMENT	DESCRIPTION
	"value" returns the result of a formula contained in the cell
cell	The name or address of the cell whose contents 1-2-3 returns. For @VERSIONDATA to work, *cell* must be located within *version-range*.
version-range	The name of the existing named range containing the version.
name	Text entered in double quotation marks (" ") indicating the name of the version. @VERSIONDATA will return the most recently created version if more than one version has the same name.
creator	Text entered in double quotation marks (" ") indicating the name of the user who created the version. *creator* is an optional argument that you can use to help @VERSIONDATA establish which version to use or delete. As with *name*, @VERSIONDATA will return the most recently created version if the same creator created more than one version with the same name.

For example, if users in your company, Mile-High Balloon Club, had versions named Stormy, you could retrieve the formula in cell B:C14 of the most recently created Stormy version in the range PROFIT by using

@VERSIONDATA("formula",B:C14,PROFIT,"Stormy")

Likewise, if your name were Chief Goldblum, you could retrieve the value or label in cell A:A1 of the version named Stormy most recently created by Chief Goldblum in the range PROFIT by using the following function statement:

@VERSIONDATA("value",A:A1,PROFIT,"Stormy","Chief Goldblum")

See Also @VERSIONINFO

18

Info, Lookup Functions

@VERSIONINFO(*option,name,* [*creator*])

The @VERSIONINFO function returns information about a version. The arguments for the @VERSIONINFO function are as follows:

ARGUMENT	DESCRIPTION
option	Any of the following text arguments inside double quotation marks (" ") to specify the information 1-2-3 is to return:
	"creator" returns the name of the person who created the version
	"modifier" returns the name of the person who last modified the version
	"created" returns the date and time the version was created, as a date and time number
	"modified" returns a date and time number indicating the date and time the version was last modified
	"comment" returns the comment for the version, up to a maximum of 512 characters; longer comments are truncated to 512 characters
	"hidden" returns 0 (FALSE) if the version is not hidden or 1 (TRUE) if it is hidden
	"protected" returns 0 (FALSE) if the version is not protected or 1 (True) if it is protected
name	The name of the version, entered as text enclosed within double quotation marks (" "). 1-2-3 will use the most recently created version if there are more than one with the same name.

ARGUMENT	DESCRIPTION
creator	The name of the user who created the version, entered as text enclosed within double quotation marks (" "). *creator* is an optional argument that you can enter to help 1-2-3 determine which version to use.
version-range	The name of the existing named range that contains the version.

For example, if you had versions named Strong Dollar (for Neuschwanstein Tours Inc.), you could retrieve the name of the user who created the latest Strong Dollar version by using the following function statement:

@VERSIONINFO("Creator","Strong Dollar")

Likewise, if your name were Ludwig the Mad of Bavaria, you could retrieve your latest comment on the Strong Dollar version by using the following function statement:

@VERSIONINFO("comment","Strong Dollar","Ludwig the Mad of Bavaria")

See Also @SCENARIOINFO

Overview of the Logical Functions

For quick reference, the logical functions are listed here in Table 18.2, with page numbers indicating their detailed discussions in the next section of this chapter, "Descriptions of the Logical Functions."

TABLE 18.2: Logical Functions Quick Reference

FUNCTION	RETURNS	SEE PAGE
@FALSE	The logical value 0 (FALSE), the opposite of the logical value 1 (TRUE).	853
@IF	The result given for *true* if the given condition evaluates as TRUE (not equaling zero) or the result given for *false* if condition evaluates as FALSE (equaling zero).	854
@ISAAF	1 (TRUE) if the given name is that of a defined add-in function for 1-2-3; 0 (FALSE) if it is not.	856
@ISAPP	1 (TRUE) if the given name is that of a defined add-in application for 1-2-3; 0 (FALSE) if it is not.	857
@ISEMPTY	1 (TRUE) if the specified location is a blank cell; 0 (FALSE) if it is not blank.	857
@ISERR	1 (TRUE) if the given value is the value ERR and 0 (FALSE) if *value* is not the value ERR.	858
@ISFILE	1 (TRUE) if the specified file-name exists and 0 (FALSE) if it does not exist.	859
@ISMACRO	1 (TRUE) if the specified name is a defined add-in macro command and 0 (FALSE) if it is not.	860
@ISNA	1 (TRUE) if the specified value is the value NA and 0 (FALSE) if *value* is not the value NA.	860
@ISNUMBER	1 (TRUE) if the specified value contains a value, NA, ERR, or a blank cell; 0 (FALSE) if the specified value is text or a cell containing a label or a formula that results in a label.	860

TABLE 18.2: Logical Functions Quick Reference (continued)

FUNCTION	RETURNS	SEE PAGE
@ISRANGE	1 (TRUE) if the specified range is a defined range name or valid range address; 0 (FALSE) if it is not.	861
@ISSTRING	1 (TRUE) if the specified value is text or a cell that contains a label or a formula that results in a label; 0 (FALSE) if the specified value is a value, ERR, NA, or a blank cell.	862
@TRUE	The logical value 1 (TRUE).	863

Descriptions of the Logical Functions

This section contains detailed descriptions of the logical functions that 1-2-3 offers.

NOTE See "Logical Functions" in Chapter 5 (starting on page 324) for a general-purpose discussion of these functions.

@FALSE

The @FALSE function returns the logical value 0 (FALSE), the opposite of the logical value 1 (TRUE). @FALSE has no arguments.

For example, the following function statement returns TRUE if the value in cell C11 is greater than that in cell D11 and FALSE if it is not:

    @IF(C11>D11,@TRUE,@FALSE)

18

Info, Lookup Functions

T I P While it might be easier to enter 0 than enter @FALSE when writing formulas for evaluating logical conditions, you'll probably find that having @FALSE in the formulas makes them easier to read later.

See Also @TRUE

@IF(*condition,true,false*)

The @IF function evaluates the specified *condition* and returns the result given for *true* if *condition* evaluates as TRUE (not equaling zero) or the result given for *false* if *condition* evaluates as FALSE (equaling zero). *condition* is typically a logical formula, but it can also be any formula, number, text within double quotation marks (" "), or the name or address of a cell.

T I P Note that blank cells, text, ERR, and NA all equal zero when used as a condition and thus equal FALSE.

true and *false* can be values, text within double quotation marks (" "), or the addresses or names of cells containing values or labels.

To prevent division by zero and the ERR values that result, you can use @IF with other functions, such as @SUM. For example, if you need to use @SUM in a spreadsheet that may not at any given point have values entered in all the cells you want to sum, you can use a function statement like the following:

    @IF(@SUM(Z20..Z28),@SUM(Z20..Z28)," ")

rather than a function statement like this:

    @SUM(Z20..Z28)

The first of these two function statements has the advantage that if there are no values in cells Z20..Z28, @IF will return a blank cell rather than 0. This is particularly useful if you need to perform a a further operation (such as division) with the result of the @SUM calculation.

Figure 18.5 shows the @IF function used for a basic small-business budget spreadsheet. Cell D5 contains a function statement to display *On Target* if the Actual expense in cell C5 is the same as or less than the Plan expense in cell B5 and *Overrun* if Actual is greater than Plan:

@IF(B5>C5,"On Target","Overrun")

Cell D11, which appears blank in the spreadsheet, shows the use of nested @IF functions. It contains the following function statement:

@IF(@IF(B11>C11,"On Target","Overrun"),@IF(B11>C11,"On Target","Overrun")," ")

This displays a blank cell if there are no entries in cells B11 and C11, or, if there are entries, it displays *On Target* or *Overrun* depending on whether the Actual expense is less than or equal to, or greater than, the Plan expense.

Using the @IF function to display different labels for a budget spreadsheet

Item	Plan	Actual	Evaluation
Lease	$50,000.00	$49,900.00	On Target
Salaries	$64,500.00	$67,550.00	Overrun
Stock	$200,000.00	$190,000.00	On Target
Sundries	$10,000.00	$6,500.00	On Target
Utilities	$5,000.00	$5,000.00	On Target
Entertainment	$2,000.00	$2,001.00	Overrun
Total	$331,500.00	$320,951.00	On Target

1995 Operating Expenses

D7 · @IF(B7>C7,"On Target" "Overrun")

18

Info, Lookup Functions

You can also use the @IF function in combination with the @ERR function to check for missing data or for errors. For example, in a payments spreadsheet, you might want 1-2-3 to reject entries with negative or zero values. A simple function statement would do the trick:

@IF(A1<=0,@ERR,A1)

If the amount entered in cell A1 is less than or equal to zero, the cell will display ERR; otherwise, it will display the amount entered in cell A1.

NOTE See page 324 for more about the @IF function.

@ISAAF(*name*)

The @ISAAF function tests to see if *name* is a defined add-in function for 1-2-3. *name* is the name of the add-in function and should be entered as text within double quotation marks (" ").

For example, if you have defined @BREAKEVEN as an add-in function, you can test for it by entering the following function statement:

@ISAAF("BREAKEVEN")

1-2-3 will return 1 (TRUE) if @BREAKEVEN is a defined add-in @function; otherwise, 1-2-3 will return 0 (FALSE). Note that the @ sign is omitted.

When testing for an add-in @function, omit the @ sign. When testing for an add-in macro command, omit the curly braces ({}).

WARNING Using @ISAAF on a 1-2-3 function (as opposed to an add-in function) will return an error. For example, @ISAFF("ISAFF") returns ERR.

See Also @ISAPP, @ISMACRO

@ISAPP(*name*)

The @ISAPP function tests to see if *name* is a defined add-in application for 1-2-3 currently loaded in memory. *name* is the name of the add-in application and should be entered as text within double quotation marks (" ").

For example, if you have defined @BUDGET as an add-in application and loaded it using Tools ➤ Add-in ➤ Load, you can test for it by entering the following function statement:

@ISAPP("BUDGET")

1-2-3 will return 1 (TRUE) if BUDGET is a defined add-in application and is loaded into memory; otherwise, 1-2-3 will return 0 (FALSE).

WARNING   @ISAPP will return 0 (FALSE) for add-in applications not loaded using Tools ➤ Add-in ➤ Load.

@ISEMPTY(*location*)

The @ISEMPTY function checks to see if *location* is a blank cell, where *location* is the name or address of one cell. If *location* is blank, @ISEMPTY returns 1 (TRUE); if location is not a blank, @ISEMPTY returns 0 (FALSE).

WARNING   @ISEMPTY will return 0 (FALSE) if you specify a range for *location*, even if all the cells in *location* are blank.

For example, if cell A1 contains the label Porcupines, cell B1 is blank, and cell C1 contains the value 3023, the following function statement will return 0 (FALSE):

@ISEMPTY(A1)

18

Info, Lookup Functions

@ISEMPTY(C1) will also return 0 (FALSE), but @ISEMPTY(B1) will return 1 (TRUE).

@ISERR(*value*)

The @ISERR function tests *value* for the value ERR. *value* can be any value, location, text, or condition. @ISERR returns 1 (TRUE) if *value* is the value ERR and returns 0 (FALSE) if *value* is not the value ERR.

One popular and practical use of @ISERR is to avoid division-by-zero errors, as shown in Figure 18.6. Column G of the First Grade Test Results worksheet contains a function statement to divide the sum of the results from the four tests (in columns B, C, D, and E) by the number of students in the class (in column F). The function statement is arranged to display "Missing Information" if the relevant cell in column F is empty, to provide a divide-by-zero error:

@IF(@ISERR(@SUM(B7..E7)/F7),"Missing Information",@SUM(B7..E7)/F7)

FIGURE 18.6

Using the @ISERR function to avoid a divide-by-zero error

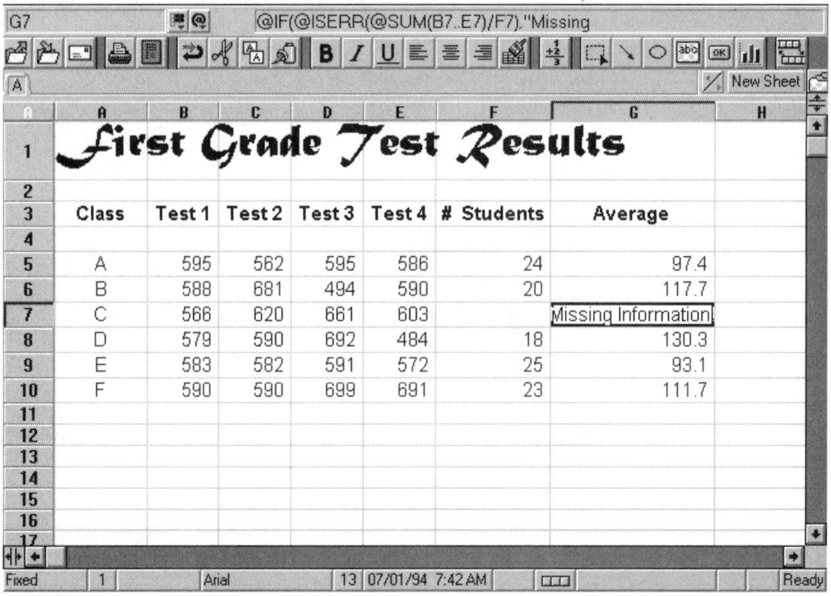

If a value does appear in cell F7, 1-2-3 will carry out the calculation, as it has for the other classes in the column.

See Also @ISNA

@ISFILE(*file-name*,*[type]*)

The @ISFILE checks to see if the file named *file-name* exists in memory or on disk, where *file-name* is the full name (including extension, and including path if the file is not in the current directory) of the file enclosed in double quotation marks (*" "*). *type* specifies whether 1-2-3 searches for *file-name* in memory or on disk:

- If *type* = 0, 1-2-3 searches in memory
- If *type* = 1, 1-2-3 searches on disk

0 is the default if you omit the *type* argument.

@ISFILE returns 1 (TRUE) if *file-name* exists and 0 (FALSE) if *file-name* does not exist.

For example, if the file OVERRUNS.WK4 is stored in the F:\FINANCE\123R5W\DATA directory, you could check for it by entering the following function statement:

@ISFILE("F:\FINANCE\123R5W\DATA\OVERRUNS.WK4",1)

This would return 1 (TRUE). To check to see if OVERRUNS.WK4 were in memory, you could use instead this function statement:

@ISFILE("F:\FINANCE\123R5W\DATA\OVERRUNS.WK4")

You could use @ISFILE in combination with @IF if you needed to make sure that, say, certain network files were available to one of your colleagues. Using a number of function statements such as the following to return Available for files that were available and Not Available for files that were not would be much quicker than checking manually for the files:

@IF(@ISFILE("Z:\PLANNING\BUDGET\1994_Q1.WK4",1), "Available","Not Available")

Alternatively, you might want to check to make sure particular files from which you needed to extract data were loaded into memory before running a particular macro.

@ISMACRO(*name*)

The @ISMACRO function checks to see if *name* is a defined add-in macro command, where *name* is entered as text within double quotation marks (″ ″) but without curly braces ({}).

@ISMACRO returns 1 (TRUE) if *name* is a defined add-in macro command and 0 (FALSE) if it is not. For example, if {REDEFINE} is a defined add-in macro command, the following function statement returns 1:

> @ISMACRO("REDEFINE"}

One use for @ISMACRO is to make sure that other macros that a macro needs to call are present before the macro starts running in earnest.

See Also @ISAAF, @ISAPP, @ISFILE

@ISNA(*value*)

The @ISNA function tests *value* for the value NA, where *value* is any value, location, text, or condition. @ISNA returns 1 (TRUE) if *value* is the value NA and 0 (FALSE) if *value* is not the value NA.

For example, if cell Z15 contains the value NA (produced by the @NA function), the following function statement returns 1 (TRUE):

> @ISNA(Z15)

You can use @ISNA in a similar way to the @ISERR function.

See Also @ISERR

@ISNUMBER(*value*)

The @ISNUMBER function checks to see if *value* contains a value, where *value* is any value, location, text, or condition. @ISNUMBER returns 1 (TRUE) if *value* contains a value, NA, ERR, or a blank cell; @ISNUMBER returns 0 (FALSE) if *value* is text or a cell containing a label or a formula that results in a label.

WARNING Be aware that NA and ERR are actually numeric values in 1-2-3—that is why they return 1 (TRUE) for @ISNUMBER. If your calculations will be thrown off by having NA or ERR instead of a value, consider using @ISNA and @ISERR to check for their presence. If a blank cell will upset matters, use @ISEMPTY to check for that too.

You can perform some calculations more reliably if you first check to see that a cell contains a number. Alternatively, you could stop a calculation or a macro and display an error message if a crucial cell is missing a value or contains a label instead.

WARNING Note that *value* must be a single cell. If *value* is a range consisting of more than one cell, @ISNUMBER will return 0 (FALSE) no matter what the first cell in the range (or, indeed, any of the cells in the range) contains.

For example, if cell H78 contains the value 999666, the following function statement returns 1 (TRUE):

@ISNUMBER(H78)

See Also @CELL, @CELLPOINTER, @ISEMPTY, @ISSTRING

@ISRANGE(*range*)

The @ISRANGE function checks to see if *range* exists as a defined range name or valid range address, where *range* can be any text or range address.

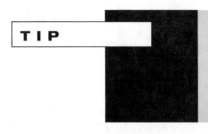

TIP

A valid range address is one with worksheet and column letters from A through IV and row numbers from 1 through 8192. For example, A:AB8190..AC8200 is not a valid range address. On the other hand, Z:A1 *is* a valid range address, even though it is a single cell.

@ISRANGE returns 1 (TRUE) if *range* is a defined range name or valid range address and 0 (FALSE) if it is not. For example, if the worksheet contains a range called EXECUTION, the following function statement returns 1 (TRUE):

@ISRANGE(EXECUTION)

By using @ISRANGE in combination with @IF, you can direct macros after checking whether an entry is a valid range name or not.

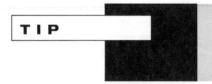

TIP

@ISRANGE works only with files in memory. Consider using @ISFILE to make sure that the relevant file is in memory before using @ISRANGE.

See Also @ISSTRING

@ISSTRING(*value*)

The @ISSTRING function checks to see if *value* contains text or a label, where *value* is any value, location, text, or condition. @ISSTRING returns 1 (TRUE) if *value* is text or a cell that contains a label or a formula that results in a label and 0 (FALSE) if *value* is a value, ERR, NA, or a blank cell.

When using @ISSTRING to check for a literal string, enclose *value* in double quotation marks (" "); when using @ISSTRING to check for a range name, there is no need for quotation marks. For example, you could run the following function statement for a worksheet that contains a range named NEW ORDER:

@ISSTRING("New Order")

This would return 1 (TRUE), as would the following function statement:

@ISSTRING(NEW ORDER)

See Also @CELL, @CELLPOINTER, @ISNUMBER

@TRUE

The @TRUE function returns the logical value 1 (TRUE). The function has no arguments.

The 1 that @TRUE returns is a valid 1 that you can use in calculations, as illustrated in the foolish personal finance worksheet in Figure 18.7.

In this worksheet, you have set up a simple budgeting spreadsheet to track income and expenses and keep a running total of what's left in your bank

FIGURE 18.7

Using the @TRUE function

	A	B	C	D	E	F	G
					@IF(B7>SAFETY NET,@TRUE,@FALSE)		
1	PERSONAL SPENDING PLAN						
2							
3		Safety Net	$1,000.00				
4							
5							
6	Date	Income	Outgoing	Balance	Over $1,000?	To spend	
7	10/01/94	$848.00		$848.00	0	$0.00	
8	10/05/94		$50.00	$798.00	0	$0.00	
9	10/09/94		$100.00	$698.00	0	$0.00	
10	10/13/94		$140.00	$558.00	0	$0.00	
11	10/17/94	$848.00		$1,406.00	1	$406.00	
12	10/21/94		$50.00	$1,356.00	0	$0.00	
13	10/25/94		$100.00	$1,256.00	0	$0.00	
14	10/29/94		$640.00	$616.00	0	$0.00	
15	11/02/94	$848.00		$1,464.00	1	$464.00	
16	11/06/94		$20.00	$1,444.00	0	$0.00	
17	11/10/94		$200.00	$1,244.00	0	$0.00	
18	11/14/94		$180.00	$1,064.00	0	$0.00	
19	11/18/94	$848.00		$1,912.00	1	$912.00	

E7 | @IF(B7>SAFETY NET,@TRUE,@FALSE)

Automatic | Arial | 12 | 06/29/94 8:43 PM | | Ready

18

Info, Lookup Functions

account. To give yourself an incentive, you've set up a mechanism to allow yourself to splurge on frivolities when the balance rises above your designated safety net of $1,000. Column E contains the following function statement in cell E7:

@IF(B7>SAFETY NET,@TRUE,@FALSE)

This will return 1 (TRUE) if your balance is above the safety net and 0 if it is not; this function statement is copied down the column. Column F contains the following function statement in cell F7:

(+D7–$SAFETY NET)*E7

This will calculate the amount of money you have to squander—the value of 1 (TRUE) or 0 (FALSE) multiplied by the amount over $1,000 in the account.

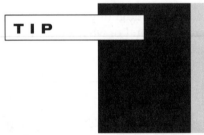

TIP

While it might be easier to enter 1 than enter @TRUE when writing formulas for evaluating logical conditions, you'll probably find that having @TRUE in the formulas makes them easier to read later. This applies in spades when you're working with formulas that somebody else wrote.

See Also @FALSE

Overview of the Lookup Functions

For quick reference, the Lookup functions are listed here in Table 18.3, with page numbers indicating their detailed discussions in the next section, "Descriptions of the Lookup Functions."

TABLE 18.3: Lookup Functions Quick Reference

FUNCTION	RETURNS	SEE PAGE
@@	The contents of the cell specified by means of a reference through the contents of another cell.	866
@CHOOSE	A value or label from a list or range of values.	867
@HLOOKUP	The contents of the cell indicated by a specified key in a specified row of a horizontal lookup table.	868
@INDEX	The contents of the cell located at the intersection of a specified column, row, and worksheet of a range.	871
@MATCH	The offset position in a range of the cell containing specified contents.	873
@MAXLOOKUP	An absolute reference to the cell containing the largest value in a list of ranges.	875
@MINLOOKUP	An absolute reference to the cell containing the smallest value in a list of ranges.	875
@N	The entry in the first cell of a specified range as a value.	876
@VLOOKUP	The contents of the cell indicated by a given key in a specified column of a vertical lookup table.	877
@XINDEX	The contents of the cell located at the intersection of a specified column_heading, row_heading, and worksheet_heading of a range.	879

18

Info, Lookup Functions

Descriptions of the Lookup Functions

This section of the chapter contains detailed descriptions of the lookup functions that 1-2-3 offers.

NOTE   See "Lookup Functions" in Chapter 5 (starting on page 335) for a general-purpose discussion of these functions.

@@(*location*)

The @@ function retrieves the contents of the cell specified in *location* by means of a reference through the contents of another cell. *location* can be the address or name of a cell containing a cell address or name, or a formula returning the address or name of a cell.

@@ is mysterious at first sight, but straightforward with an example. If cell D1 contains the value 44, and cell B1 contains the label 'D1 (note the apostrophe), you could enter the following function statement in cell A1:

    @@(B1)

This would return the contents of cell D1: 44. Note that *location* must be a valid cell address or range name for a single-cell range; otherwise, @@ will return ERR.

The @@ function is most useful for worksheets that contain several formulas that use the same argument—an argument that you need to change now and then. For example, in Figure 18.8, cell F5 contains the following function statement:

    +E5*@@(D$15)

This pulls the reference-cell information from cell D15 to calculate the commission for the salespeople. Since cell D15 contains 'G11, the value in cell G11—13.00%—is used in the calculation. You can easily change all the formulas in the Commission column at once by changing the label in cell D15.

TIP

Note that you will need to press F9 to recalculate an @@ formula if the *location* argument refers to a cell containing a formula; otherwise the @@ formula will return 0.

See Also @CHOOSE, @HLOOKUP, @INDEX, @VLOOKUP

FIGURE 18.8

Using the @@ function to change several formulas at once

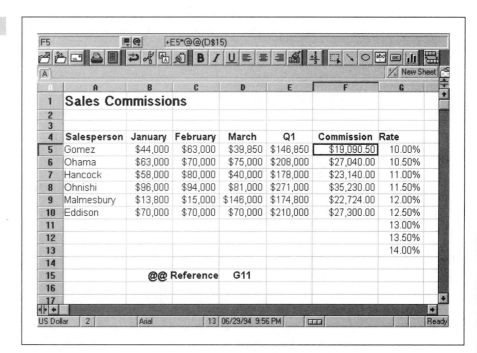

@CHOOSE(*value, list*)

The @CHOOSE function returns a value or label from a *list*, which is a group of values or the addresses or names of cells that contain values or labels. *value* indicates the offset number of the item's position in *list*.

For example, the worksheet shown in Figure 18.9 contains a list of labels in the range B1..E1 and a list of their offset numbers (0, 1, 2, 3) in the range B2..E2. To pull the label from D1, one could use the following function statement, since D2 contains 2, which is the offset number for D1 in *list*:

@CHOOSE(D2,B1,C1,D1,E1)

FIGURE 18.9

Using the @CHOOSE function to pull a label from a specified cell

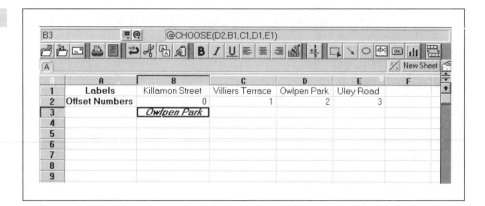

NOTE   See page 335 for more details about the @CHOOSE function.

See Also @HLOOKUP, @INDEX, @MATCH, @VLOOKUP, @XINDEX

@HLOOKUP(*key,range, row-offset*)

The @HLOOKUP function returns the contents of the cell indicated by *key* in a specified row of a horizontal lookup table, *range*. The horizontal lookup table is a range with either value information in ascending order or labels in the first row.

@HLOOKUP works by comparing *key* to the index values in each cell in the first row of the horizontal lookup table. When 1-2-3 finds the cell containing *key* (or, for a value entered for *key*, the value closest to but not larger than *key*), it moves down that column to the cell indicated by *row-offset* and returns the contents of that cell.

The arguments for the @HLOOKUP function are as follows:

ARGUMENT	DESCRIPTION
key	A value or text, depending on what the first row of the horizontal lookup table contains, as follows:
	Values. If the first row of the horizontal lookup table contains values, *key* can be any value greater than or equal to the first value in range. If *key* is smaller than the first value in range, @HLOOKUP returns ERR. If *key* is larger than the last value contained in the first row of *range*, @HLOOKUP will stop at the last cell in the row specified by row-offset and return the contents of that cell as the answer.
	Labels. If the first row of the horizontal lookup table contains labels, *key* can be text enclosed in double quotation marks (" "), a formula resulting in text, or the address or name of a cell that contains a label or a formula resulting in a label. @HLOOKUP will return ERR if *key* does not exactly match the contents of a cell in the first row of *range*.
range	A range address or range name indicating the location of the horizontal lookup table. Note that 1-2-3 will use only the first worksheet in a 3D range entered for range.
row-offset	A number indicating the offset position of the row in *range*.

For example, Figure 18.10 shows a company's Length of Service spreadsheet for employees of different salary grades. You could use @HLOOKUP to track how many employees of a particular grade have been at the company for a particular length of time. For example, you could use the following statement to find out how many Grade 2 employees have been at the company for five years:

@HLOOKUP("Grade 2",A3..G17,5)

This function statement returns 20.

N O T E See page 336 for more examples of using **@HLOOKUP**.

See Also @CHOOSE, @INDEX, @MATCH, @MAXLOOKUP, @MINLOOKUP, @VLOOKUP, @XINDEX

FIGURE 18.10

Using the @HLOOKUP function

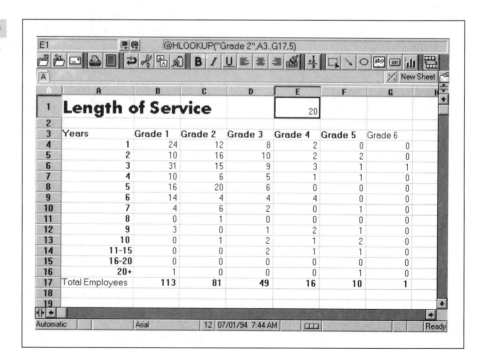

Years	Grade 1	Grade 2	Grade 3	Grade 4	Grade 5	Grade 6
1	24	12	8	2	0	0
2	10	16	10	2	2	0
3	31	15	9	3	1	1
4	10	6	5	1	1	0
5	16	20	6	0	0	0
6	14	4	4	4	0	0
7	4	6	2	0	1	0
8	0	1	0	0	0	0
9	3	0	1	2	1	0
10	0	1	2	1	2	0
11-15	0	0	2	1	1	0
16-20	0	0	0	0	0	0
20+	1	0	0	0	1	0
Total Employees	113	81	49	16	10	1

Length of Service — 20

@HLOOKUP("Grade 2",A3..G17,5)

@INDEX(*range,column,row,* [*worksheet*])

The @INDEX function returns the contents of the cell located at the intersection of a specified *column*, *row*, and *worksheet* of a *range*. (The *worksheet* argument is optional.)

The arguments for @INDEX are as follows:

ARGUMENT	DESCRIPTION
range	Any range address or range name.
column	The offset number of the column for @INDEX to use.
row	Either the offset number of the row for @INDEX to use, or the address or name of a cell containing 0 or a positive integer.
worksheet	The offset number of the worksheet for @INDEX to use. This is an optional argument; if you don't specify the worksheet, 1-2-3 will use the first worksheet in *range*.

For example, consider the Length of Service worksheet shown in Figure 18.11. In this figure, cell B19 contains the following function statement:

@INDEX(A3..G17,D19,F19)

This defines the range on which @INDEX operates and uses the values stored in cell D19 (representing the Grade of the employees) and cell F19 (representing the length of service of the employees) to quickly return the relevant value from the worksheet: 4. In the figure, cell D19 contains 4, specifying the fourth column offset from the beginning of the range, and cell F19 contains 6, specifying the sixth row offset from the top of the

18

Info, Lookup Functions

FIGURE 18.11

Using the @INDEX function to return the contents of a cell by specifying the relative positions of the rows and columns

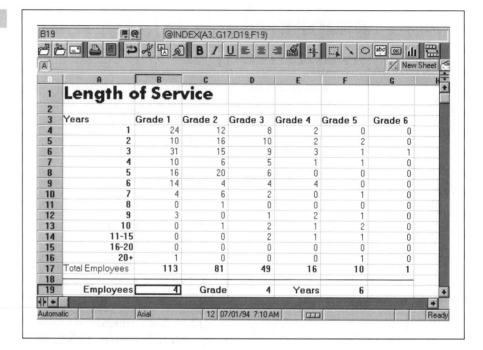

range. By changing the values in cells D19 and F19, you can easily look up information in other cells. For example, to look up the number of Grade 5 employees with 20 or more years of service at the company, you could enter 5 in cell D19 and 13 in cell F19.

For more about the @INDEX function, including some examples of its use, see page 336.

T I P

@INDEX is similar in use to three other 1-2-3 @ functions: @XINDEX, @HLOOKUP, and @VLOOKUP. The differences between these four functions are as follows: @XINDEX is for locating a cell using text or values in *column_heading, row_heading,* and *worksheet_heading* rather than specifying offset numbers for *column, row,* or *worksheet.* @HLOOKUP and @VLOOKUP are for locating cells by identifying the column or row in which they are located, then specifying an offset number from the row heading or column heading. @INDEX is for locating a cell in a lookup table by specifying its exact location without reference to the row heading or column heading.

See Also @CHOOSE, @HLOOKUP, @MATCH, @MAXLOOKUP, @MINLOOKUP, @VLOOKUP, @XINDEX

@MATCH (*cell-contents, range,[type]*)

The @MATCH function returns the offset position of the cell containing *cell-contents* in *range.* The arguments for the @MATCH function are as follows:

ARGUMENT	DESCRIPTION
cell-contents	The value or text to find. You can use wildcard characters if *cell-contents* is text.
range	Any range name or address.
type	0, 1, or 2 to specify how 1-2-3 compares *cell-contents* with the contents of the cells in *range,* as follows:
	0 If *type* = 0, @MATCH returns the first cell whose contents match cell-contents.

ARGUMENT	DESCRIPTION
	1 If *type* = 1, @MATCH returns the cell that contains the largest value less than or equal to *cell-contents*. 1 is the default setting if you omit the *type* argument. When *type* = 1, 1-2-3 sorts *range* in ascending order.
	2 If *type* = 2, @MATCH returns the cell that contains the smallest value greater than or equal to *cell-contents*. When *type* = 2, 1-2-3 sorts *range* in descending order.

TIP

The major difference between @MATCH and functions such as @HLOOKUP and @VLOOKUP is that @MATCH returns the position of the match item found rather than the item itself. Thus you could use @MATCH to find, say, an instance of a particular value or text and report its position, but not to bring that value or text into another calculation or string.

Note that @MATCH searches *range* from top to bottom in a column and from left to right. If *range* is a multisheet range, @MATCH searches the first worksheet in the range as described in the previous sentence before going to the second worksheet, and so forth. @MATCH stops the search when it encounters a match or reaches the end of *range*.

WARNING

@MATCH will return ERR if *range* does not include a match for *cell-contents*. @MATCH will also return ERR if *type* = 1 and the first cell in *range* contains a value greater than *cell-contents*, or if *type* = 2 and the first cell in *range* contains a value less than *cell-contents*.

See Also @CHOOSE, @HLOOKUP, @INDEX, @MAXLOOKUP, @MINLOOKUP, @VLOOKUP

@MAXLOOKUP(*range-list*)

The @MAXLOOKUP function returns an absolute reference to the cell containing the largest value in a list of ranges, *range-list*, which can be any combination of range names or addresses separated by argument separators. The absolute reference includes the file name.

> **N O T E**
>
> @MAXLOOKUP ignores labels and blank cells in the *range-list* argument and will return NA if none of the cells in *range-list* contains values.

For example, suppose you teach five classes and keep the scores for the students in the files YEAR_1.WK4, YEAR2_WK4, YEAR_3.WK4, YEAR_4.WK4, and YEAR_5.WK4 in your 1-2-3 \WORK\ directory. You built the files from the same template, so they have the same layout; each has a range named AVERAGE SCORE that contains the average scores for the students over all the tests in the year. To find the highest score for a student in any of the years, you could use

```
@MAXLOOKUP(<<YEAR_1.WK4>>AVERAGE
SCORE,<<YEAR2_WK4>>AVERAGE SCORE,<<YEAR_3.WK4>>
AVERAGE SCORE,<<YEAR_4.WK4>>AVERAGE
SCORE,<<YEAR_5.WK4>> AVERAGE SCORE)
```

See Also @CHOOSE, @HLOOKUP, @INDEX, @MATCH, @VLOOKUP, @XINDEX

@MINLOOKUP(*range-list*)

The @MINLOOKUP function returns an absolute reference to the cell containing the smallest value in a list of ranges, *range-list*, which can be any combination of range names or addresses separated by argument separators. The absolute reference includes the file name.

NOTE @MINLOOKUP ignores labels and blank cells in *range-list* and will return NA if none of the cells in *range-list* contain values.

For example, you keep the test scores for the students in the five classes you teach in the files YEAR_1.WK4, YEAR2_WK4, YEAR_3.WK4, YEAR_4.WK4, and YEAR_5.WK4 in your 1-2-3 \WORK\ directory. Since you built the files from the same template, they're laid out the same; each has a range named AVERAGE SCORE that contains the average scores for the students over all the tests in the year. To find the lowest score for a student in any of the years—perhaps for special tutoring—you could use this function statement:

```
@MINLOOKUP(<<YEAR_1.WK4>>AVERAGE
SCORE,<<YEAR2_WK4>>AVERAGE SCORE,<<YEAR_3.WK4>>
AVERAGE SCORE,<<YEAR_4.WK4>>AVERAGE
SCORE,<<YEAR_5.WK4>> AVERAGE SCORE)
```

See Also @CHOOSE, @HLOOKUP, @INDEX, @MATCH, @VLOOKUP, @XINDEX

@N(*range*)

The @N function returns the entry in the first cell of *range* as a value. @N returns the value 0 if the entry in the first cell of *range* is a label. *range* can be a cell address, a range address, or a range name. For example, if cell B100 contains 98.4, the this function statement returns 99.4:

```
@N(B100..B200)+1
```

Although at first sight the uses of @N may seem limited, the function has two common uses. First, you can use it to return a value from a cell containing a label, when returning a label would upset a calculation and return ERR. Second, you use @N in macros to check that a user enters a value where you need one. For example,

```
{IF @N(C1)=0}{BEEP}
```

would cause a macro to beep if a user entered a label in cell C1 (because @N returns 0 for a label).

See Also @ISNUMBER, @ISSTRING, @S

@VLOOKUP(*key,range, row-offset*)

The @VLOOKUP function returns the contents of the cell indicated by *key* in a specified column of a vertical lookup table, *range*. The vertical lookup table is a range with either value information in ascending order or labels in the first column.

@VLOOKUP works by comparing *key* to the index values in each cell in the first column of the vertical lookup table. When 1-2-3 finds the cell containing *key* (or, for a value entered for *key*, the value closest to but not larger than *key*), it moves across that row to the cell indicated by *column-offset* and returns the contents of that cell.

The arguments for the @VLOOKUP function are as follows:

ARGUMENT	DESCRIPTION
key	A value or text, depending on what the first column of the vertical lookup table contains, as follows: **Values.** If the first column of the vertical lookup table contains values, *key* can be any value greater than or equal to the first value in *range*. If *key* is smaller than the first value in *range*, @VLOOKUP returns ERR. If *key* is larger than the last value contained in the first column of *range*, @VLOOKUP will stop at the last cell in the column specified by *column-offset* and return the contents of that cell as the answer.

ARGUMENT	DESCRIPTION
	Labels. If the first column of the vertical lookup table contains labels, *key* can be text enclosed in double quotation marks (″ ″), a formula resulting in text, or the address or name of a cell that contains a label or a formula resulting in a label. @VLOOKUP will return ERR if *key* does not exactly match the contents of a cell in the first column of *range*.
range	A range address or range name indicating the location of the vertical lookup table. Note that 1-2-3 will use only the first worksheet in a 3D range entered for *range*.
column-offset	A number indicating the offset position of the column in *range*.

For example, Figure 18.12 shows a company's Length of Service spreadsheet for employees of different salary grades. You could use @VLOOKUP to track how many employees with a particular length of service have attained a specified salary grade. For example, you could use this function statement to find out how many 11–15-year employees have reached salary grade 5:

@VLOOKUP("11-15",A3..G17,5)

The answer is 1.

NOTE See page 336 for more examples of using @VLOOKUP.

See Also @CHOOSE,   @HLOOKUP,   @INDEX,   @MATCH, @MAXLOOKUP, @MINLOOKUP, @XINDEX

FIGURE 18.12

Using the @VLOOKUP
function

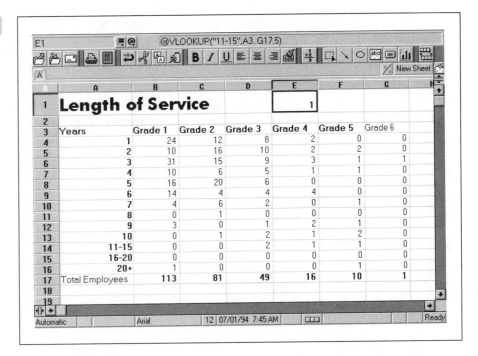

@XINDEX(*range,column,row,* [*worksheet*])

The @XINDEX function returns the contents of the cell located at the intersection of a specified *column_heading*, *row_heading*, and *worksheet_heading* of a *range*. (The *worksheet* argument is optional.)

The arguments for @XINDEX are as follows:

ARGUMENT	DESCRIPTION
range	Any range address or range name.
column_heading	A value or text representing the contents of a cell in the first row of *range*.

18

Info, Lookup Functions

ARGUMENT	DESCRIPTION
row_heading	A value or text representing the contents of a cell in the first column of *range*.
worksheet_heading	A value or text representing the contents of the first cell in *range*. This is an optional argument; if you don't specify the worksheet, 1-2-3 will use the first worksheet in *range*.

For example, consider the Length of Service worksheet shown in Figure 18.13. In this figure, cell B19 contains the following function statement:

@XINDEX(A3..G17,D19,F19)

This defines the range on which @INDEX operates (A3..G17). It uses the labels stored in cell D19 (Grade 3, representing the Grade of the employees) and cell F19 ('11-15, representing the length of service of the

FIGURE 18.13

Using the @XINDEX function to return the contents of a cell by specifying the column heading and row heading

Length of Service

Years	Grade 1	Grade 2	Grade 3	Grade 4	Grade 5	Grade 6
1	24	12	8	2	0	0
2	10	16	10	2	2	0
3	31	15	9	3	1	1
4	10	6	5	1	1	0
5	16	20	6	0	0	0
6	14	4	4	4	0	0
7	4	6	2	0	1	0
8	0	1	0	0	0	0
9	3	0	1	2	1	0
10	0	1	2	1	2	0
11-15	0	0	2	1	1	0
16-20	0	0	0	0	0	0
20+	1	0	0	0	1	0
Total Employees	113	81	49	16	10	1

Employees [2] Grade 3 11-15

employees; note the apostrophe to make this a label rather than letting it return −4) to quickly return the relevant value from the worksheet: 2. @XINDEX returns the contents of the cell referenced by Grade 3 in the column heading and '11-15 in the row heading. By changing the values in cells D19 and F19, you can easily look up information in other cells. For example, to look up the number of Grade 5 employees with 20 or more years of service at the company, you could enter Grade 5 in cell D19 and '20+ in cell F19.

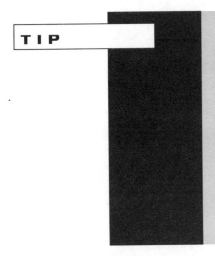

TIP

@XINDEX is similar in use to three other 1-2-3 @ functions: @INDEX, @HLOOKUP, and @VLOOKUP. The differences between these four functions are as follows: @INDEX is for locating a cell by specifying offset numbers for column and row rather than specifying text or values in a row-heading or column-heading cell. @HLOOKUP and @VLOOKUP are for locating cells by identifying the column or row in which they are located, then specifying an offset number from the row heading or column heading. @INDEX is for locating a cell in a lookup table by specifying its exact location without reference to the row heading or column heading.

See Also @CHOOSE, @HLOOKUP, @MATCH, @MAXLOOKUP, @MINLOOKUP, @VLOOKUP

18

Info, Lookup Functions

CHAPTER 19

Mathematical and Statistical Functions Reference

THIS CHAPTER looks at two of the most important groups of 1-2-3's functions—the mathematical and statistical functions.

The mathematical functions, which include functions such as @COS (for calculating the cosine of an angle), @DEGTORAD (for converting degrees to radians), and @EVEN (for returning the next even number), simplify a number of mathematical operations.

The statistical functions, which include functions such as @CHIDIST (for calculating a chi-distribution) and @WEIGHTAVG (for calculating weighted averages) perform calculations on lists of values.

Overview of the Mathematical Functions

1-2-3 provides a comprehensive set of mathematical functions that will take care of almost any basic or specialized mathematical operations. The mathematical functions fall into five categories:

- **Conversion functions.** For example, @DEGTORAD, which converts degrees to radians.

- **General mathematical functions.** For example, @RAND, which generates a random number.

- **Hyperbolic functions.** For example, @TANH, which calculates the hyperbolic tangent of a given angle.

- **Rounding functions.** For example, @TRUNC, which truncates a value to the number of decimal places requested.
- **Trigonometric functions.** For example, @SIN, which calculates the sine of a given angle.

For quick reference, the mathematical functions are listed here in Table 19.1, with page numbers indicating their detailed discussions in the next section of this chapter, "Descriptions of the Mathematical Functions."

TABLE 19.1: Mathematical Functions Quick Reference

FUNCTION	RETURNS	SEE PAGE
@ABS	The absolute value of the given number	890
@ACOS	The angle that is the arc cosine of the given number	890
@ACOSH	The arc hyperbolic cosine of the given angle	891
@ACOT	The arc cotangent of the given angle	891
@ACOTH	The arc hyperbolic cotangent of the given angle	891
@ACSC	The arc cosecant of the given angle	892
@ACSCH	The arc hyperbolic cosecant of the given angle	892
@ASEC	The arc secant of the given angle	892
@ASECH	The arc hyperbolic secant of the given angle	893
@ASIN	The arc sine of the given angle	893
@ASINH	The arc hyperbolic sine of the given angle	894
@ATAN	The arc tangent of the given angle	894
@ATAN2	The arc tangent of the given angle determined by the x and y coordinates using the tangent y/x ($n1/n$)	895

TABLE 19.1: Mathematical Functions Quick Reference (continued)

FUNCTION	RETURNS	SEE PAGE
@ATANH	The arc hyperbolic tangent of the given angle	896
@COS	The cosine of the given angle	896
@COSH	The hyperbolic cosine of the given angle	897
@COT	The cotangent of the given angle	898
@COTH	The hyperbolic cotangent of the given angle	898
@CSC	The cosecant (the reciprocal of the sine) of the given angle	899
@CSCH	The hyperbolic cosecant (the reciprocal of the hyperbolic sine) of the given angle	899
@DEGTORAD	The value in radians of the angle given in degrees	900
@EVEN	The nearest even integer to the number; positive values are rounded up and negative values are rounded down	900
@EXP	The value of the constant e (approximately 2.718282, the base of the natural logarithm) raised to the specified power	901
@EXP2	The value of the constant e (approximately 2.718282, the base of the natural logarithm) raised to the power (*numeric-value*^2)	902
@FACT	The factorial of the given number (the product of all positive integers from 1 to the number)	902

TABLE 19.1: Mathematical Functions Quick Reference (continued)

FUNCTION	RETURNS	SEE PAGE
@FACTLN	The natural logarithm of the factorial of a number	903
@INT	The integer value of the given number, disregarding any fractional portion	903
@LARGE	The *n*th largest value in the given range	904
@LN	The natural logarithm of the given value	905
@LOG	The common or base-10 logarithm (base 10) of the given value	906
@MOD	The *modulus* (remainder) after the given number is divided by the given divisor	906
@ODD	The given value rounded away from 0 to the nearest odd integer; positive values are rounded up and negative values are rounded down	908
@PI	The value of the mathematical constant π	908
@QUOTIENT	The integer result of the given number divided by the given divisor	909
@RAND	A random value between 0 and 1 calcutated to seventeen decimal places	909
@RADTODEG	The value in degrees of a value given in radians	910
@ROUND	The given number rounded to the nearest specified multiple of the power of 10	911
@ROUNDDOWN	The given value rounded down to the nearest multiple of the specified power	912

TABLE 19.1: Mathematical Functions Quick Reference (continued)

FUNCTION	RETURNS	SEE PAGE
@**ROUNDM**	The given value rounded to the nearest specified multiple	914
@**ROUNDUP**	The given value rounded up to the nearest multiple of the specified power	915
@**SEC**	The secant (the reciprocal of the cosine) of the given angle	917
@**SECH**	The hyperbolic secant (the reciprocal of the hyperbolic cosine) of the given angle	918
@**SEMEAN**	The standard error of the sample mean (or average) for the values in the given range	920
@**SIGN**	The sign of the given number	918
@**SIN**	The sine of the given angle	918
@**SINH**	The hyperbolic sine of the given angle	919
@**SMALL**	The nth smallest value in the given range	920
@**SQRT**	The positive square root of the given value	921
@**SQRTPI**	The square root of the given value multiplied by π	921
@**SUBTOTAL**	The total of the values in a list. @SUBTOTAL also indicates to @GRANDTOTAL which subtotals to include in the grand total	922
@**SUM**	The sum of the values in the given list	923
@**SUM-PRODUCT**	The sum of the products of values in corresponding cells in multiple ranges	924

TABLE 19.1: Mathematical Functions Quick Reference (continued)

FUNCTION	RETURNS	SEE PAGE
@SUMSQ	The sum of the squares of the values in the given list	925
@SUMXMY2	The sum of the squared differences after the values in one range have been subtracted from the corresponding cells in another range	925
@TAN	The tangent of the given angle	926
@TANH	The hyperbolic tangent of the given angle	927
@TRUNC	The given value truncated to the number of decimal places specified	927

Descriptions of the Mathematical Functions

This section contains detailed descriptions of the mathematical functions.

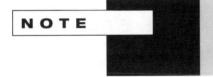

N O T E

See "Mathematical Functions" in Chapter 5 (beginning on page 298) for a general-purpose description of these functions.

@ABS(*number*)

The @ABS function calculates the absolute value of *number*, where *number* is any number. Absolute values are always positive. For example, the following function statement returns 33 if cell C119 contains −33 or 33:

@ABS(C119)

To return a negative value, use −@ABS instead of @ABS. For example, the following function statement returns −33 if cell C119 contains −33 or 33:

−@ABS(C119)

N O T E   See page 312 in Chapter 5 for more information about this function.

@ACOS(*number*)

The @ACOS function calculates the angle that is the arc cosine of *number*, where *number* is a value between −1 and 1. An arc cosine is an inverse cosine that produces its result as an angle in radians, between 0 and π, representing an angle between 0 and 180 degrees. For example, the following function statement returns 0.85 (rounded to two decimal places), the cosine of which is 0.66:

@ACOS(0.66)

See page 300 for more information about this and other inverse trigonometric functions.

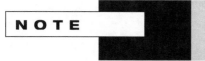

N O T E   You can convert the number in radians into an angle by using the @RADTODEG function.

See Also   @ACOSH, @COS, @RADTODEG

@ACOSH(*number*)

The @ACOSH function calculates the arc hyperbolic cosine using the hyperbolic cosine *number* of an angle, where *number* is a value of 1 or greater. An arc hyperbolic cosine is an inverse hyperbolic cosine; the result is in radians. For example, the following function statement returns 1.762747:

@ACOSH(3)

You can use @RADTODEG to convert the result of @ACOSH from radians to degrees—in this case, 101 degrees.

See Also @ACOS, @COS, @COSH, @RADTODEG

@ACOT(*number*)

The @ACOT function calculates the arc cotangent using the cotangent *number* of an angle, where *number* is the cotangent of an angle, a value between $-2*\pi$ and $2^{32}*\pi$. An arc cotangent is an inverse cotangent; the result is in radians from 0 to π, representing an angle between 0 and 180 degrees. For example, if the cotangent of angle *number* is 1.43, the following function statement returns 0.61:

@ACOT(1.43)

You can use @RADTODEG to convert the result in radians to degrees—in this case, @RADTODEG (0.61) gives a result of 34.97 degrees.

See Also @ACOTH, @COT

@ACOTH(*number*)

The @ACOTH function calculates the arc hyperbolic cotangent using the hyperbolic cotangent *number* of an angle, where *number* is a value less than -1 or greater than 1. An arc hyperbolic cotangent is an inverse hyperbolic cotangent; the result is in radians. For example, the following function statement produces -0.35:

@ACOTH(–3)

You can use @RADTODEG to convert the result in radians to degrees—in this case, @RADTODEG (–0.35) gives a result of –20 degrees.

See Also @ACOT, @COTH

@ACSC(*number*)

The @ACSC function calculates the arc cosecant using the cosecant *number* of an angle, where *number* is less than or equal to –1, or equal to or greater than 1. The result is an angle in radians from $-\pi/2$ through $\pi/2$, representing an angle between –90 and 90 degrees. For example, if the cosecant of angle *number* is 1.5, the following function statement returns 0.728 radians:

@ACSC(1.5)

You can use @RADTODEG to convert the result in radians to degrees—in this case, @RADTODEG(0.729728) returns a result of 41.8 degrees.

See Also @ACSCH, @CSC

@ACSCH(*numeric-value*)

The @ACSCH function calculates the arc hyperbolic cosecant using the hyperbolic cosecant *number* of an angle, where *number* is any value other than 0. An arc hyperbolic cosecant is an inverse hyperbolic cosecant; the result is in radians. For example, the following function statement produces 0.247:

@ACSCH(4)

You can use @RADTODEG to convert the result in radians to degrees—in this case, @RADTODEG (0.247) gives a result of 14.2 degrees.

See Also @ACSC, @CSCH

@ASEC(*numeric-value*)

The @ASEC function calculates the arc secant using the secant *number* of an angle, where *number* is less than or equal to –1 or equal to or greater than 1. (The arc secant is the inverse secant.) The result is an angle in radians from 0 to π, representing an angle between 0 and 180 degrees. For example, if the secant of angle *number* is 1, the following function statement returns 0 radians:

@ASEC(1)

You can use @RADTODEG to convert the result in radians to degrees, though in this case you hardly need to—as you might guess, @RADTODEG(0) gives a result of 0 degrees.

See Also @ASECH, @SEC

@ASECH(*numeric-value*)

The @ASECH function calculates the arc hyperbolic secant using the hyperbolic secant *number* of an angle, where *number* is a value greater than 0 and less than or equal to 1. An arc hyperbolic secant is an inverse hyperbolic secant; the result is in radians. For example, the following function statement returns 0.896:

@ASECH(0.7)

You can use @RADTODEG to convert the result in radians to degrees—in this case, @RADTODEG (0.896) gives a result of 51.3 degrees.

See Also @ASEC, @SECH

@ASIN(*numeric-value*)

The @ASIN function calculates the arc sine of *n*, where *number* is a value between −1 and 1. The arc sine is the inverse sine; the result is an angle in radians from −π/2 to π/2, representing an angle between −90 and 90 degrees. For example, to calculate the arc sine of 0.75, you could use the following function statement:

@ASIN(0.75)

This returns 0.8481. You can use @RADTODEG to convert the result in radians to degrees—in this case, @RADTODEG(0.8481) returns 43 degrees.

N O T E   See page 300 for more information about this and other inverse trigonometric functions.

See Also @ASINH, @SIN

@ASINH(*numeric-value*)

The @ASINH function calculates the arc hyperbolic sine using the hyperbolic sine *number* of an angle, where *number* is any value. An arc hyperbolic sine is an inverse hyperbolic sine; the result is in radians. For example, the following function statement produces 1.82:

@ASINH(3)

You can use @RADTODEG to convert the result in radians to degrees—in this case, @RADTODEG (1.82) gives a result of 104.25 degrees.

See Also @ASIN, @SINH

@ATAN(*numeric-value*)

The @ATAN function calculates the arc tangent of n, where *number* is the tangent of any angle and is any value. The arc tangent is the inverse tangent; the result is an angle in radians from $-\pi/2$ to $\pi/2$, representing an angle between −90 and 90 degrees. For example, if you know the tangent of angle *number* is 3/1 (i.e., 3), you can calculate the arc tangent of 3 by using the following function statement:

@ATAN(3)

This returns 1.249. You can then use @RADTODEG to convert the result in radians to degrees—in this case, @RADTODEG(1.249) returns 71.62 degrees.

See Also @ATAN2, @ATANH, @TAN

@ATAN2(*numeric-value1,* *numeric-value2)*

The @ATAN2 function calculates the arc tangent of the angle determined by the x and y coordinates (*numeric-value1* and *numeric-value2*) using the tangent y/x (*n1/n*). @ATAN2 produces a result of an angle in radians between −π and π, an angle between −180 and 180 degrees. For example, using coordinates with the same value, 50 degrees, the following function statement gives an angle of 45 degrees:

@RADTODEG(@ATAN2(50,50))

See page 300 for more information about this and other inverse trigonometric functions.

> **N O T E**
>
> @ATAN 2 returns 0 if y = 0 and returns ERR if both x = 0 and y = 0.

Depending on whether the values of the x and y coordinates are positive or negative, @ATAN2 can result in values for all four quadrants:

X	Y	VALUE RANGE	QUADRANT
Positive	Positive	0–π/2	I
Negative	Positive	π/2–π	II
Negative	Negative	−π– −π/2	III
Positive	Negative	−π/2–0	IV

> **N O T E**
>
> In quadrants I and IV, @ATAN2 produces the same results as @ATAN. For example, when x is positive (e.g., 4) and y is positive (e.g., 5), both @ATAN2(4,5) and @ATAN(5/4) produce 0.8961, which produces (using @RADTODEG) an angle of 51.34 degrees.

See Also @ATAN, @TAN

@ATANH(*numeric-value*)

The @ATANH function calculates the arc hyperbolic tangent using the hyperbolic tangent *number* of an angle, where *number* is a value between −1 and 1. An arc hyperbolic tangent is an inverse hyperbolic tangent; the result is in radians. For example, this function statement gives a result of −0.79281:

@ATANH(-0.66)

You can use @RADTODEG to convert the result in radians to degrees—in this case, @RADTODEG (−0.79281) gives an angle of −45.42 degrees.

See Also @ATAN, @ATAN2, @TANH

@COS(*numeric-value*)

The @COS function returns the cosine of *numeric-value*, which is an angle measured in radians and which is a value between $-2^{32}\ast\pi$ and $2^{32}\ast\pi$. @COS returns a value from −1 through 1.

NOTE The cosine is the ratio of the side adjacent an acute angle of a right triangle to the hypotenuse.

For example, to calculate the cosine of an angle of 6 radians, you would use the following function statement:

@COS(6)

This produces a result of 0.96017. You could then use @RADTODEG to convert this result to degrees, as in the following function statement:

@RADTODEG(0.96017)

This gives an angle of 55.014 degrees. Alternatively, you could combine @COS and @RADTODEG to produce this result rather more neatly:

@RADTODEG(@COS(6))

You can use @DEGTORAD to convert degrees to radians. To produce the cosine of an angle—for example, a 50-degree angle—use @COS in combination with @DEGTORAD:

@COS(@DEGTORAD(50))

NOTE See page 298 for more information about this and other trigonometric functions.

See Also @ACOS, @COSH, @DEGTORAD

@COSH(*numeric-value*)

The @COSH function returns the hyperbolic cosine of *numeric-value*, which can be any value from approximately −11355.1371 through 11355.1371. @COSH produces as a result a value greater than or equal to 1. For example, the following function statement returns 29937.07:

@COSH(11)

WARNING Using @COSH with large numbers is liable to produce numbers too large for 1-2-3 to store or display. If this happens, try using @COSH in combination with other @functions, such as @DEGTORAD, to return a value you can display and use. For example, use @COSH(@DEGTORAD(11111)) rather than @COSH(11111) to produce a displayable result.

See Also @ACOS, @COS

@COT(*numeric-value*)

The @COT function returns the cotangent of *numeric-value*, which is an angle measured in radians and which is a value between $-2^{32} \star \pi$ and $2^{32} \star \pi$.

For example, to calculate the cotangent of an angle of 4 radians, you would use the following function statement:

@COT(4)

This produces a result of 0.8637. You could then use @RADTODEG to convert this result to degrees:

@RADTODEG(0.8637)

This gives an angle of 49.49 degrees. Alternatively, you could combine @COT and @RADTODEG to produce this result rather more neatly:

@RADTODEG(@COT(4))

You can use @DEGTORAD to convert degrees to radians. To produce the cotangent of an angle—for example, a 50-degree angle—use @COT in combination with @DEGTORAD:

@COT(@DEGTORAD(50))

N O T E   The cotangent is the ratio of the side adjacent an acute angle of a right triangle to the opposite side. The contangent of an angle is the reciprocal of the tangent of the same angle.

See Also   @ACOT, @COTH, @TAN

@COTH(*numeric-value*)

The @COTH function returns the hyperbolic cotangent of *numeric-value*, which can be any value from approximately -11355.1371 through

11355.1371 except for 0. For example, the following function statement returns 1.00497:

@COTH(3)

To calculate the hyperbolic cotangent of a 45-degree angle, use @COTH combined with @DEGTORAD:

@COTH(@DEGTORAD(45))

This returns 1.525.

See Also @ACOTH, @COT, @TANH

@CSC(*numeric-value*)

The @CSC function returns the cosecant (the reciprocal of the sine) of angle *numeric-value*, where *numeric-value* is an angle measured in radians and is any value from $-2\wedge32\star\pi$ through $2\wedge32\star\pi$ except 0 and multiples of π. @CSC results in either a value greater than or equal to 1, or a value less than or equal to -1.

For example, the following function statement returns 7.086.

@CSC(3)

You can use @DEGTORAD with @CSC to determine the cosecant of an angle that you know in degrees:

@CSC(@DEGTORAD(45))

This returns 1.414, the cosecant of a 45-degree angle.

See Also @ACSC, @CSCH, @SIN

@CSCH(*numeric-value*)

The @CSCH function returns the hyperbolic cosecant (the reciprocal of the hyperbolic sine) of angle *numeric-value*, which is any value from approximately -11355.1371 through 11355.1371 with the exception of 0. For example, the following function statement returns 0.0366:

@CSCH(4)

WARNING Using @CSCH with large numbers is liable to produce numbers too large for 1-2-3 to store or display. If this happens, try using @CSCH in combination with other @functions, such as @DEGTORAD, to return a value you can display and use. For example, use @CSCH(@DEGTORAD (11111)) rather than @CSCH(11111) to produce a displayable result.

You can use @DEGTORAD with @CSCH to determine the hyperbolic cosecant of an angle that you know in degrees:

@CSCH(@DEGTORAD(45)) = 1.825306

This returns 1.1512, the hyperbolic cosecant of a 45-degree angle.

See Also @ACSCH, @CSC, @SINH

@DEGTORAD(*degrees*)

The @DEGTORAD function converts the value *degrees* to radians. For example, the following function statement returns 1.5708:

@DEGTORAD(90)

You can combine @DEGTORAD with other mathematical functions— for example, to calculate the sine of an angle:

@SIN(@DEGTORAD(75))

This returns 0.966, the sine of a 75-degree angle.

See Also @RADTODEG

@EVEN(*numeric-value*)

The @EVEN function rounds the value *numeric-value* away from zero to the nearest even integer. Positive values are rounded up; negative values are rounded down. *numeric-value* can be any value. For example, the following function statement returns 2:

@EVEN(1.0000001)

And the following function statement returns −6:

@EVEN(-4.4)

N O T E

If *numeric-value* is an even integer, @EVEN(*numeric-value*) will return the same integer: @EVEN(2) will return 2, while @EVEN(2.000000001) will return 4. Consider using @ROUND, @ROUNDUP, or @ROUNDDOWN before using @EVEN.

See Also @INT, @ODD, @ROUND, @ROUNDDOWN, @ROUNDM, @ROUNDUP, @TRUNC

@EXP(*numeric-value*)

The @EXP function returns the value of the constant e (approximately 2.718282, the base of the natural logarithm) raised to the power *numeric-value*. *Numeric-value* can be any value between approximately −11355.1371 and approximately 11356.5234; if *numeric-value* is outside this range of values, @EXP will return ERR because the calculation will be too big for 1-2-3 to store. If *numeric-value* is smaller than approximately −227.956 or larger than approximately 230.259, 1-2-3 will be able to calculate the result but will not be able to display it; you'll see a series of asterisks in the cell instead.

For example, the following function statement returns 66.686:

@EXP(4.2)

N O T E

See page 302 for more information about this function.

See Also @EXP2, @LN

@EXP2(*numeric-value*)

The @EXP2 function calculates the value of the constant *e* (approximately 2.718282, the base of the natural logarithm) raised to the power (*numeric-value*^2).

numeric-value can be a value from approximately −106.570 to approximately 106.570; if *numeric-value* is smaller than −106.570 or larger than 106.570, the @EXP2 calculation is too large for 1-2-3 to store, and you'll see ERR.

WARNING If *numeric-value* is outside the range −15.098 to 15.098 (i.e., between −106.570 and −15.098 or between 15.098 and 106.570), 1-2-3 will be able to calculate the result of @EXP2 but it will not be able to display it. You'll see a series of asterisks in the cell instead.

For example, this function statement returns 0.99005:

    @EXP2(0.1)

See Also @EXP

@FACT(*number*)

The @FACT function calculates the factorial of *number*. The factorial is the product of all positive integers from 1 to *number*—the factorial of 2 is 2 (1*2), the factorial of 3 is 6 (1*2*3), and so on. *number* can be 0 or any positive integer; if you enter a number that is not an integer, 1-2-3 will truncate it to an integer.

WARNING

1-2-3 cannot calculate or store the factorial for *number* greater than or equal to 1755, and will return ERR. 1-2-3 can calculate but not display the factorial for *number* greater than or equal to 70; you will see a series of asterisks in the cell to indicate that 1-2-3 cannot display the number.

19

Math, Stat Functions

For example, the following function statement returns 362880:

@FACT(9)

See Also @FACTLN, @PRODUCT

@FACTLN(*number*)

The @FACTLN function returns the natural logarithm of the factorial of *number*. The factorial is the product of all positive integers from 1 to *number*—the factorial of 2 is 2 (1*2), the factorial of 3 is 6 (1*2*3), and so on. *number* can be 0 or any positive integer; if you enter a number that is not an integer, 1-2-3 will truncate it to an integer.

For example, the following function statement returns 42.33562, the natural logarithm of the factorial of 20 [the same as @LN(@FACT(20)]:

@FACTLN(20)

See Also @FACT, @LN

@INT(*numeric-value*)

The @INT function returns the integer value of *numeric-value*, disregarding any fractional portion, where *numeric-value* can be any value.

WARNING Use @INT only when the fractional portion of a number is irrelevant to your purposes. *Do not* use @INT when you simply need to display only the integers from a calculation in a particular cell. Use Style ➤ Number Format instead, choose Fixed, and reduce the number of decimal places to zero.

For example, the boss gives you $75 to arrange a department party. If each gateau costs $6.63, how many can you get? (Let's ignore tax for the moment.) You could use the following function statement to produce the answer, which turns out to be 11:

@INT(75/6.63)

(If you simply divided 75 by 6.63, you'd get 11.31222—a difficult number of gateaux to buy exactly.)

See Also @EVEN, @ODD, @ROUND, @ROUNDDOWN, @ROUNDM, @ROUNDUP, @TRUNC

@LARGE(*range,number*)

The @LARGE function returns the *n*th largest value in *range*. *range* is the name or address of a range containing values. *number* is any positive integer but cannot be larger than the number of values in *range*, or @LARGE will return ERR.

For example, if you wanted to automatically track the largest deposits (or withdrawals) you made into (or from) your bank account, you could use the @LARGE function as illustrated in Figure 19.1.

In the Bank Account worksheet, cell F1 contains the function statement:

@LARGE(D4..D20,1)

This returns the first largest value from the range D4..D20. If the range D4..D20 were named EXPENDITURE, one could retrieve, say, the second largest value in the range by using the following function statement:

@LARGE(EXPENDITURE,2)

FIGURE 19.1

Using the @LARGE
function to return the
*n*th largest values from
a range

| F1 | @LARGE(D4..D20,1) | | | | | |

Bank Account — Most expensive purchase **$190.00**

	Check #	Date	Paid To	Amount	Balance
4	301	12-Nov-94	Gas Company	$14.44	$2,485.56
5	302	15-Nov-94	Electric Company	$26.12	$2,459.44
6	303	18-Nov-94	Target	$2.00	$2,457.44
7	304	21-Nov-94	Offline Services	$45.00	$2,412.44
8	305	24-Nov-94	Undertow Inc.	$190.00	$2,222.44
9	306	27-Nov-94	The Monster Lamp Co.	$85.00	$2,137.44
10	307	30-Nov-94	Offline Services	$45.00	$2,092.44
11	308	03-Dec-94	Fine Drain Cleaners	$66.66	$2,025.78
12	309	06-Dec-94	Buffalo Foods	$15.34	$2,010.44
13	310	09-Dec-94	Electric Company	$26.89	$1,983.55
14	311	12-Dec-94	Damaged Goods R Us	$10.00	$1,973.55
15	312	15-Dec-94	New Jersey Stakes	$36.39	$1,937.16
16	313	18-Dec-94	Offline Services	$55.00	$1,882.16
17	314	21-Dec-94	Wine Shops of Detroit	$66.43	$1,815.73
18	315	21-Dec-94	Lye Cleaners	$48.76	$1,766.97
19	316	21-Dec-94	All New and Improved	$59.00	$1,707.97

US Dollar | 2 | Arial | 12 | 07/07/94 3:43 PM | Ready

See Also @MAX, @MIN, @PUREMAX, @PUREMIN, @SMALL

@LN(*numeric-value*)

The @LN function returns the natural logarithm of *numeric-value*. *numeric-value* must be a value greater than 0; if *numeric-value* is less than 0, @LN will return ERR.

TIP

Natural logarithms are based on the constant *e*, which is approximately 2.718282. The @LN function is the inverse of the @EXP function.

For example, to calculate the natural logarithm of *e*, you could use the following function statement, which returns 1.098612:

@LN(3)

See page 302 for more information about this function.

See Also @EXP, @L, @LOG

@LOG(*numeric-value*)

The @LOG function returns the common or base-10 logarithm (base 10) of *numeric-value*, where *numeric-value* is a value greater than or equal to 0. (If *numeric-value* is a value less than or equal to 0, @LOG returns ERR. For example, to calculate the common logarithm of 3, you could use the following function statement, which returns 0.477121:

@LOG(3)

See Also @LN

@MOD(*number,divisor*)

The @MOD function returns the *modulus* (remainder) after the number *number* is divided by the divisor *divisor*. *number* is any value, and *divisor* is any value other than 0.

T I P

@MOD always returns a result with the same sign (+ or –) as the sign of *number*. For example, if *number* is negative, the modulus will also be negative. If *number* is 0, @MOD returns 0.

For example, the following function statement returns 2, because 2 is the remainder when 11 is divided by 3:

@MOD(11,3)

You can use the @MOD function to calculate the day of the week: Enter a date number as *number* in the @MOD function statement and 7 (days in the week) as the *divisor*. The remainder indicates the day of the week, from 0 (indicating Saturday) through 6 (indicating Friday). For example, to calculate the day of the week on which November 5, 1995 falls, you could use the following function statement:

@MOD(@DATE(95,11,5),7)

This returns 1, indicating that November 5, 1995 will fall on a Sunday.

See page 311 for more information about @MOD.

See Also @QUOTIENT

@MODULO(*number,divisor*)

The @MODULO function returns the *modulus* (remainder) after the number *number* is divided by the divisor *divisor*. *number* is any value, and *divisor* is any value other than 0.

TIP

@MODULO always returns a result with the same sign (+ or –) as the sign of *number*. For example, if *number* is negative, the modulus will also be negative. If *number* is 0, @MODULO returns 0. @MODULO differs from the @MOD function in that, while the result of @MOD is *number* – divisor * @INT(*number/divisor*), the result of @MODULO is *number* – divisor * @ROUNDDOWN-(*number/divisor*). @MODULO can produce substantially different results from @MOD, depending on the values of the number and the divisor.

For example, the first of the following function statements returns 4, while the second returns –3:

@MODULO(–45,7)
@MOD(–45,7)

See Also @MOD, @QUOTIENT

@ODD(*numeric-value*)

The @ODD function returns the value *numeric-value* rounded away from 0 to the nearest odd integer—positive values are rounded up; negative values are rounded down. *numeric-value* can be any value; if *numeric-value* is an odd integer, @ODD(*numeric-value*) returns *numeric-value*.

For example, the following function statement returns 5:

@ODD(3.03)

And this function statement returns −25:

@ODD(-25)

See Also @EVEN, @INT, @ROUND, @ROUNDDOWN, @ROUNDM, @ROUNDUP, @TRUNC

@PI

The @PI function returns the value of the mathematical constant π, the ratio of the circumference of a circle to its diameter. π is approximately 3.14159265358979324.

For example, to calculate the circumference of a circle that had a radius of 4, you could use the following function statement:

@PI*4^2

This returns 50.26548, the area of the circle.

NOTE See page 298 for more information about this and other trigonometric functions.

@QUOTIENT(*number,divisor*)

The @QUOTIENT function returns the integer result of *number* divided by *divisor*, where *number* is a value and *divisor* is a value other than 0.

For example, to divide 113 by 5 and ignore the remainder of the division, you could use the following function statement, which returns 22 rather than 22.6:

@QUOTIENT(113,5)

TIP @QUOTIENT returns 0 if *number* is 0, and ERR if *divisor* is 0.

See Also @MOD

@RAND

The @RAND function generates and returns a random value between 0 and 1 calculated to seventeen decimal places. For example, entering an @RAND function statement in a cell might return numbers such as the following:

0.4055564102742618
0.0685917209221942914
0.9325591693444453037

You can see from these examples that @RAND produces values with differing numbers of decimal places.

NOTE @RAND generates a new random value for each @RAND function statement each time 1-2-3 recalculates your work, whether the recalculation is automatic or manual. Each time you enter a new @RAND statement in a worksheet, all the other @RAND statements are recalculated.

To give yourself more flexibility when working with this @RAND function, you can use these three techniques:

- To return random values in different intervals, multiply @RAND by the size of the interval. For example, to produce numbers between 100 and 1,000, multiply @RAND by 99:

  @RAND*99

- To prevent @RAND from updating a particular random value when the worksheet is recalculated, press F2 and then F9 with the relevant cell selected to fix the value.

- To generate random whole numbers, use the @INT function or the @ROUND function in conjunction with @RAND:

  @ROUND(@RAND*9,1)
  @INT(@RAND)

N O T E   See page 303 for further examples of using the @RAND function.

@RADTODEG(*radians*)

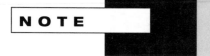

The @RADTODEG function converts radians to degrees, where *radians* is any value. For example, the following function statement returns 114.5916:

    @RADTODEG(2)

You can also use the @RADTODEG function together with other mathematical functions to return a value in degrees rather than in radians, which many of the mathematical functions return. The following list gives some examples of functions with which you can use @RADTODEG; look under the listing for each function for details of usage.

    @RADTODEG(@ACOS(0.45))
    @RADTODEG(@ACOT(3.1))
    @RADTODEG(@ACSC(2.8)

@RADTODEG(@ASEC(2))

@RADTODEG(@ASIN(0.5))

@RADTODEG(@ATAN(4))

@RADTODEG(@ATAN2(5,5))

@RADTODEG(@COS(85))

See Also @DEGTORAD

@ROUND(*numeric-value,number*)

The @ROUND function rounds the value *numeric-value* to the nearest multiple of the power of 10 specified by *number*. The arguments for the @ROUND function are as follows:

ARGUMENT	DESCRIPTION
numeric-value	Any value indicating the number to be rounded.
number	A value from −100 through 100 that specifies how to round the number, as per the following list:

Positive. If *number* is positive, @ROUND rounds the decimal portion of the number. If *number* is 1, @ROUND rounds *numeric-value* to the nearest tenth; if *number* is 2, @ROUND rounds *numeric-value* to the nearest hundredth; if *number* is 3, @ROUND rounds *numeric-value* to the nearest thousandth, etc.

ARGUMENT	DESCRIPTION
	Negative. If *number* is negative, @ROUND rounds the integer portion of the number. If *number* is −1, @ROUND rounds *numeric-value* to the nearest ten; if *number* is −2, @ROUND rounds *numeric-value* to the nearest hundred; if *number* is −3, @ROUND rounds *numeric-value* to the nearest thousand, etc.
	Zero. If *number* is 0, @ROUND rounds *numeric-value* to the nearest integer.

WARNING

Note that the @ROUND function actually changes the number, which in many cases is not desirable. If you simply want to change the display of a number to a given number of decimal places, change the number format of the cell rather than using @ROUND.

For example, if a function in cell A1 returned a decimal number that you needed to round to the nearest integer, you could use the following function statement:

```
@ROUND(A1,0)
```

See page 309 for a thorough discussion of @ROUND, including examples of its use.

See Also   @EVEN, @INT, @ODD, @ROUNDDOWN, @ROUNDM, @ROUNDUP, @TRUNC

@ROUNDDOWN(*numeric-value*, [*number*],[*direction*])

The @ROUNDDOWN function rounds the value *numeric-value* down to the nearest multiple of the power of 10 specified by *number*. The arguments for the @ROUNDDOWN function are as follows:

ARGUMENT	DESCRIPTION
numeric-value	Any value indicating the number to be rounded.
number	A value from −100 through 100 that specifies how to round the number, as per the following list. This is an optional argument; @ROUNDDOWN uses 0 if you omit it.

Positive. If *number* is positive, @ROUNDDOWN rounds the decimal portion of the number. If *number* is 1, @ROUNDDOWN rounds *numeric-value* to the nearest tenth; if *number* is 2, @ROUNDDOWN rounds *numeric-value* to the nearest hundredth; if *number* is 3, @ROUNDDOWN rounds *numeric-value* to the nearest thousandth, etc.

Negative. If *number* is negative, @ROUNDDOWN rounds the integer portion of the number. If *number* is −1, @ROUNDDOWN rounds *numeric-value* to the nearest ten; if *number* is −2, @ROUNDDOWN rounds *numeric-value* to the nearest hundred; if *number* is −3, @ROUNDDOWN rounds *numeric-value* to the nearest thousand, etc.

Zero. If *number* is 0, @ROUNDDOWN rounds *numeric-value* to the nearest integer.

direction	Zero or 1, indicating how to round negative values. This is an optional argument; @ROUNDDOWN uses 0 if you omit it. Note that the *direction* argument has no effect on positive numbers.

ARGUMENT   DESCRIPTION

0   If *direction* = 0, @ROUNDDOWN rounds negative values down.

1   If *direction* = 1, @ROUNDDOWN rounds negative values up.

For example, if you had a formula in cell Z280 that calculated a price, you could use @ROUNDDOWN to round it down to the nearest cent with the following function statement:

@ROUNDDOWN(Z280,2)

WARNING

Do not use the @ROUNDDOWN function if you simply want to change the display of a number—change the number format of the cell using the Format selector or Style ➤ Number Format. Use @ROUNDDOWN only when you want to round the number itself down.

See Also @EVEN, @INT, @ODD, @ROUND, @ROUNDM, @ROUNDUP, @TRUNC

@ROUNDM(*numeric-value, multiple,[direction]*)

The @ROUNDM function rounds the value *numeric-value* to the nearest *multiple*. *numeric-value* and *multiple* are any values that have the same sign; *direction* is an optional argument indicating whether to round *numeric-value* up or down as follows:

0   If *direction* = 0, @ROUNDM rounds *numeric-value* to the nearest multiple. This is the default setting if you omit the *direction* argument.

1   If *direction* = 1, @ROUNDM rounds *numeric-value* up.

−1   If direction = −1, @ROUNDM rounds *numeric-value* down.

Figure 19.2 illustrates the use of @ROUNDM. For example, cell B5 contains the following function statement:

@ROUNDM(987.654,0.05,1)

This rounds the numeric value 987.654 up to the nearest 0.05.

See Also @EVEN, @INT, @ODD, @ROUND, @ROUNDDOWN, @ROUNDUP, @TRUNC

FIGURE 19.2

Using the @ROUNDM function to round a numeric value to the nearest multiple

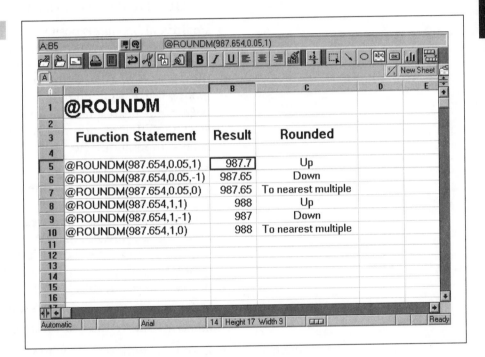

@ROUNDUP(*numeric-value*, [*number*],[*direction*])

The @ROUNDUP function rounds the value *numeric-value* up to the nearest multiple of the power of 10 specified by *number*. The arguments for the @ROUNDUP function are as follows:

ARGUMENT	DESCRIPTION
numeric-value	Any value indicating the number to be rounded.
number	A value from −100 through 100 that specifies how to round the number, as per the following list. This is an optional argument; @ROUNDUP uses 0 if you omit it.

Positive. If *number* is positive, @ROUNDUP rounds the decimal portion of the number. If *number* is 1, @ROUNDUP rounds *numeric-value* to the nearest tenth; if *number* is 2, @ROUNDUP rounds *numeric-value* to the nearest hundredth; if *number* is 3, @ROUNDUP rounds *numeric-value* to the nearest thousandth, etc.

Negative. If *number* is negative, @ROUNDUP rounds the integer portion of the number. If *number* is −1, @ROUNDUP rounds *numeric-value* to the nearest ten; if *number* is −2, @ROUNDUP rounds *numeric-value* to the nearest hundred; if *number* is −3, @ROUNDUP rounds *numeric-value* to the nearest thousand, etc.

Zero. If *number* is 0, @ROUNDUP rounds *numeric-value* to the nearest integer.

direction	Zero or 1, indicating how to round negative values. This is an optional argument; @ROUNDUP uses 0 if you omit it. Note that the *direction* argument has no effect on positive numbers.

0   If *direction* = 0, @ROUNDUP rounds negative values up.

1   If *direction* = 1, @ROUNDUP rounds negative values down.

For example, if you had a formula in cell Z280 that calculated a price, you could use @ROUNDUP to round it up to the nearest ten cents with the following function statement:

@ROUNDUP(Z280,1,0)

WARNING

The @ROUNDUP function changes the number itself, not its display. Do not use @ROUNDUP if you simply want to change the way a number appears in a cell—change the number format of the cell using the Format selector or Style ➤ Number Format instead.

See Also @EVEN, @INT, @ODD, @ROUND, @ROUNDDOWN, @ROUNDM, @TRUNC

@SEC(*numeric-value*)

The @SEC function returns the secant of the angle represented by *numeric-value*, where *numeric-value* is an angle measured in radians and is any value from $-2^{\wedge}32^{\star}\pi$ through $2^{\wedge}32^{\star}\pi$. The secant is the reciprocal of cosine and is the ratio of the hypotenuse to the side adjacent to an acute angle of a right triangle.

For example, to discover the secant of an angle of 24 radians, you could use the following function statement:

@SEC(24)

This returns 2.357495, the secant of an angle of 24 radians.

To find the secant of an angle measured in degrees, you can combine @SEC with @DEGTORAD, as in the following function statement, which finds the secant of a hundred-degree angle:

@SEC(@DEGTORAD(100))

See Also @ASEC, @ASECH, @COS, @DEGTORAD, @SECH

@SECH(*numeric-value*)

The @SECH function returns the hyperbolic secant (the reciprocal of the hyperbolic cosine) of the angle represented by *numeric-value*, where *numeric-value* is a value between approximately -1135.571 and approximately 1135.571. @SECH results in a value greater than 0 or less than or equal to 1.

For example, to calculate the hyperbolic secant of an angle of 3, you could use the following function statement:

@SECH(3)

This returns 0.09932792. To find the hyperbolic secant of an angle measured in degrees, you can combine @SECH with @DEGTORAD, as in the following function statement, which finds the hyperbolic secant of a 60-degree angle:

@SECH(@DEGTORAD(60))

See Also @ASECH, @DEGTORAD, @SEC

@SIGN(*numeric-value*)

The @SIGN function returns the sign of *numeric-value*, any number, as follows:

- @SIGN returns 1 if *numeric-value* is positive.
- @SIGN returns 0 if *numeric-value* is 0.
- @SIGN returns −1 if *numeric-value* is negative

For example, the following function statement returns 1 when cell AK47 contains a positive value:

@SIGN(AK47)

@SIN(*numeric-value*)

The @SIN function returns the sine of the angle represented by *numeric-value*, where *numeric-value* is an angle measured in radians and is any value from $-2^{\wedge}32\star\pi$ through $2^{\wedge}32\star\pi$. The sine is the ratio of the side opposite an acute angle of a right triangle to the hypotenuse.

For example, to calculate the sine of an angle of 2 radians, you could use the following function statement:

@SIN(2)

This returns 0.909297. Alternatively, you can use @SIN to find out the sine of an angle in degrees. For example, to calculate the sine of a 45-degree angle, you could combine @SIN with @DEGTORAD and use the following function statement:

@SIN(@DEGTORAD(45))

This returns 0.707107.

N O T E See page 298 for more information about this and other trigonometric functions.

See Also @ASIN, @DEGTORAD, @SINH

@SINH(*numeric-value*)

The @SINH function returns the hyperbolic sine of the angle represented by *numeric-value*, where *numeric-value* is a value between approximately −1135.571 and approximately 1135.571. For example, the following function statement returns 1.175201:

@SINH(1)

To establish the hyperbolic sine of an angle measured in degrees, use @SINH together with @DEGTORAD, as in the following function statement, which returns the hyperbolic sine of a 50-degree angle:

@SINH(@DEGTORAD(50))

See Also @ASINH, @DEGTORAD, @SIN

@SEMEAN(*range*)

The @SEMEAN function returns the standard error of the sample mean (or average) for the values in *range*, where *range* is a range name or address.

For example, if the range named DETROIT PARTS contains the values 10, 22, 6, 34, 17, and 44, you could use the following function statement to return the standard error of the sample mean:

@SEMEAN(DETROIT PARTS)

This returns 5.924056.

See Also @GEOMEAN, @HARMEAN, @PURESTD, @STD

@SMALL(*range,number*)

The @SMALL function returns the *n*th smallest value in *range*. *range* is the name or address of a range containing values. *number* is any positive integer but cannot be smaller than the number of values in *range*, or @SMALL will return ERR.

For example, if you wanted to automatically track the smallest deposits (or withdrawals) you made into (or from) your bank account, you could use the @SMALL function as illustrated in Figure 19.3.

In the Bank Account worksheet, cell F1 contains the function statement

@SMALL(D4..D20,1)

to return the first smallest value from the range D4..D20. If the range D4..D20 were named EXPENDITURE, one could retrieve, say, the second smallest value in the range by using this function statement:

@SMALL(EXPENDITURE,2)

See Also @LARGE, @MAX, @MIN, @PUREMAX, @PUREMIN

FIGURE 19.3

Using the @SMALL function to return the *n*th smallest values from a range

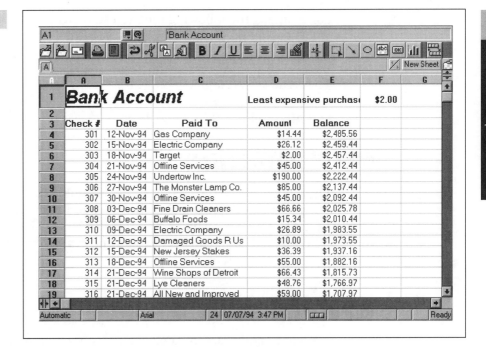

@SQRT(*numeric-value*)

The @SQRT function returns the positive square root of *numeric-value*, where *numeric-value* is a positive value. (If *numeric-value* is a negative value, @SQRT returns ERR.)

For example, to calculate the square root of the value in cell M61, you could use the following function statement:

@SQRT(M61)

If cell M61 contained the value 169, this function statement would return 13.

@SQRTPI(*numeric-value*)

The @SQRTPI function returns the square root of *numeric-value* multiplied by π, where *numeric-value* is any positive value or 0. (If *numeric-value* is a negative value, @SQRTPI returns ERR.)

For example, the following function statement calculates the square root of 20*π:

@SQRTPI(20)

The result is 7.926655.

See Also @PI, @SQRT

@SUBTOTAL(*list*)

The @SUBTOTAL function fulfills a double function: It adds together the values in a *list*, producing the total, and indicates to the @GRAND-TOTAL function which cells @GRANDTOTAL should sum. For @SUBTOTAL, *list* can be the following in any combination, separated by separator characters:

- numbers
- numeric formulas
- range addresses or range names containing numbers or numeric formulas

Figure 19.4 illustrates the use of the @SUBTOTAL function in a spreadsheet containing an output report for carved bears for the years 1985–1995. As you can see in the figure, cell B8 contains the following function statement to create a subtotal from the cells B5..B7:

@SUBTOTAL(B5..B7)

Cell A16 contains the following function statement to sum up all the subtotals into a grand total:

@GRANDTOTAL(B8..L13)

This adds together the subtotals in the range B8..L13 produced by the @SUBTOTAL function.

See Also @SUM, @SUMNEGATIVE, @SUMPOSITIVE

FIGURE 19.4

Using the @SUBTOTAL function to produce subtotals, which are then added together into a grand total by the @GRANDTOTAL function

| B13 | | @SUBTOTAL(B11..B12) | | | | | | | | | |

	A	B	C	D	E	F	G	H	I	J	K
1	**Output Report: Carved Bears**										
2											
3		1985	1986	1987	1988	1989	1990	1991	1992	1993	1994
4											
5	Northridge	4300	4000	3600	5800	5900	6000	7000	4400	7000	7000
6	Petaluma	1600	1500	1700	1900	2000	2000	2000	2000	2400	2200
7	Newcastle	7500	8000	8000	8000	8000	7500	6000	7500	8000	8500
8	Subtotals	13400	13500	13300	15700	15900	15500	15000	13900	17400	17700
9											
10		1985	1986	1987	1988	1989	1990	1991	1992	1993	1994
11	Vancouver	8000	7500	8000	8000	8500	8000	8700	8500	8900	8800
12	Twin Falls	2600	2300	2000	3000	2800	4000	4000	3300	3400	3500
13	Subtotals	10600	9800	10000	11000	11300	12000	12700	11800	12300	12300
14											
15	Grand total										
16	295300										
17											
18											

Automatic — Arial — 12 07/06/94 6:05 PM — Ready

@SUM(*list*)

The @SUM function returns the sum of the values in *list*, where *list* can be the following in any combination, separated by separator characters:

- numbers
- numeric formulas
- range addresses or range names containing numbers or numeric formulas

TIP The easiest way to add an @SUM function statement to a cell is to click on the Sum SmartIcon.

For example, to sum the values in the block A5..B13, you could use the following function statement:

@SUM(A5..B13)

See Also @DSUM, @GRANDTOTAL, @SUBTOTAL, @SUMNE-GATIVE, @SUMPOSITIVE

@SUMPRODUCT(*list*)

The @SUMPRODUCT function multiplies the values in corresponding cells in a *list* of multiple ranges and then sums the products. *list* is any combination of ranges containing values, provided that the ranges are the same shape. If the ranges in *list* are not the same shape, @SUMPRO-DUCT will return ERR.

@SUMPRODUCT multiplies the values in corresponding cells either by rows or by columns, as follows:

- If the ranges in *list* are columns, @SUMPRODUCT multiplies by rows.

- If the ranges in *list* are rows, @SUMPRODUCT multiplies by columns.

- If the ranges in *list* are more than one column wide, @SUMPRO-DUCT multiplies by rows.

For example, if cells A1..A10 contained values and made up the named range ACELLS, and cells B1..B10 contained values and made up the named range BCELLS, you could use the following function statement to calculate the sum of their products:

@SUMPRODUCT(ACELLS,BCELLS)

Since the ACELLS and BCELLS ranges are columns, @SUMPRO-DUCT will multiply by rows in this case and then calculate the sum of the products.

N O T E   See page 284 for another practical example of using this function.

See page 284 for another practical example of using this function.

See Also @SUMSQ

@SUMSQ(*list*)

The @SUMSQ function returns the sum of the squares of the values in *list*, where *list* can be the following in any combination, separated by argument separators:

- numbers
- numeric formulas
- range addresses or range names containing numbers or numeric formulas

For example, to calculate the sum of the squares of 3, 4, and 5, you could use the following function statement:

@SUMSQ(3,4,5)

This returns 50, or 9 + 16 + 25.

See Also @SUM, @SUMPRODUCT

@SUMXMY2(*range1, range2*)

The @SUMXMY2 function subtracts the values in *range2* from the corresponding cells in *range1*, squares the differences, and then sums the results. For @SUMXMY2, *range1* and *range2* are ranges identical in size and shape that contain values. (If *range1* and *range2* are different in size or shape, @SUMX2MY2 will return ERR.)

@SUMXMY2 handles subtraction either by rows or by columns, depending on the shape of *range1* and *range2*:

- If *range1* and *range2* are single-column ranges, @SUMXMY2 subtracts by row.

- If *range1* and *range2* are multicolumn ranges, @SUMXMY2 subtracts by columns.

For example, to find the sum of the squared differences between two ranges named Week1 and Week2 that occupied cells B5..C10 and D5..E10, respectively, you could use the following function statement:

@SUMXMY2(WEEK1,WEEK2)

Since Week1 and Week2 are multicolumn ranges, the subtraction in this case would be by columns.

See Also @SUMPRODUCT, @SUMSQ

@TAN(*numeric-value*)

The @TAN function returns the tangent of the angle represented by *numeric-value*, where *numeric-value* is an angle measured in radians and is any value from $-2^{32} * \pi$ through $2^{32} * \pi$. The tangent is the ratio of the side opposite an acute angle of a right triangle to the side adjacent the same acute angle.

For example, to calculate the tangent of an angle of 4 radians, you could use the following function statement:

@TAN(4)

This returns 1.157821. To work out the tangent of an angle measured in degrees, use @TAN with @DEGTORAD, as in the following function statement, which returns the tangent of an angle of 31 degrees:

@TAN(@DEGTORAD(31))

See Also @ATAN, @DEGTORAD, @TANH

@TANH(*numeric-value*)

The @TANH function returns the hyperbolic tangent of the angle represented by *numeric-value*, where *numeric-value* is a value between approximately −11355.1371 and approximately 11355.1371. The hyperbolic tangent is the ratio of the hyperbolic sine to the hyperbolic cosine. @TANH returns a value from −1 through 1.

For example, to calculate the hyperbolic tangent of an angle of 3, you could use the following function statement:

> @ATANH(3)

This returns 0.995054. To calculate the hyperbolic tangent of an angle measured in degrees, use @TANH together with @DEGTORAD, as in the following function statement, which calculates the hyperbolic tangent of an angle of 20 degrees:

> @TANH(@DEGTORAD(20))

See Also @ATANH, @DEGTORAD, @TAN

@TRUNC(*numeric-value, [decimal]*)

The @TRUNC function returns *numeric-value* truncated to the number of decimal places indicated by *decimal*. The arguments for the @TRUNC function are as follows:

ARGUMENT	DESCRIPTION
numeric-value	A numeric value.
decimal	A value between −100 and 100, indicating how to truncate *numeric-value*, as follows.

ARGUMENT	DESCRIPTION
	Positive. A positive value for *decimal* makes @TRUNC work on the decimal portion of the number, the portion to the right of the decimal point. For example, when *decimal* = 3, @TRUNC truncates *numeric-value* to the nearest thousandth.
	Negative. A negative value for *decimal* makes @TRUNC work on the integer portion of the number, the portion to the left of the decimal point. For example, when *decimal* = 3, @TRUNC truncates *numeric-value* to the nearest thousand.
	Zero. A value of 0 for *decimal* makes @TRUNC truncate *numeric-value* to the nearest integer. *decimal* is an optional value for this @TRUNC function; 0 is the default setting if you omit the *decimal* argument.

WARNING   Use the @TRUNC function only when you need to change a number by truncating it. For all formatting purposes— for example, to reduce the display to three decimal places—format the style of the relevant cell.

For example, you could use the following function statement to truncate a number to one decimal place:

@TRUNC(3.1415927)

This would return 3.1.

See Also @EVEN, @INT, @ODD, @ROUND, @ROUNDM, @ROUNDDOWN, @ROUNDUP

Overview of the Statistical Functions

1-2-3's statistical functions fall into five categories:

- **Forecasting functions.** For example, @REGRESSION, which performs multiple linear regression analysis.

- **General statistical functions.** For example, @GRANDTO-TAL, which calculates the sum of all cells that contain an @SUB-TOTAL function statement.

- **Probability functions.** For example, @POISSON, which calculates the Poisson distribution.

- **Ranking functions.** For example, @PRANK, which calculates percentile rank.

- **Significance-test functions.** For example, @ZTEST, which performs a z-test on the chosen population or populations.

For quick reference, the statistical functions are listed here in Table 19.2, with page numbers indicating their detailed discussions in the next section of this chapter, "Descriptions of the Statistical Functions."

TABLE 19.2: Statistical Functions Quick Reference

FUNCTION	RETURNS	SEE PAGE
@AVEDEV	The average of the absolute deviations of the values in the given list	933
@AVG	The average of the values contained in the given list	934
@BINOMIAL	The binomial probability mass function or the cumulative binomial distribution	935
@CHIDIST	The one-tailed probability of the chi-square distribution	937

TABLE 19.2: Statistical Functions Quick Reference (continued)

FUNCTION	RETURNS	SEE PAGE
@CHITEST	The independence on the data in a given range or the goodness of fit for the data in two given ranges	938
@COMBIN	The binomial coefficient for two specified values	940
@CORREL	The correlation coefficient of the values for two given ranges	940
@COUNT	The number of nonblank cells in the given list	941
@COV	Either the population or the sample covariance of the values in two given ranges	942
@CRITBI-NOMIAL	The largest integer for which the cumulative binomial distribution is less than or equal to alpha	943
@DEVSQ	The sum of squared deviations of the values in the given list from their mean (average)	944
@FDIST	The F-distribution of probability for the two given ranges (for determining the degree to which two samples vary)	945
@FTEST	The associated probability of an F probability test for the two given ranges (to test if two samples have different variances)	946
@GEOMEAN	The geometric mean of the values in the given list	947
@GRAND-TOTAL	The sum of all the cells in the given list that contain the function @SUBTOTAL	948
@HARMEAN	The harmonic mean of the values in the given list	948

TABLE 19.2: Statistical Functions Quick Reference (continued)

FUNCTION	RETURNS	SEE PAGE
@KURTOSIS	The kurtosis of the values in the given range—the concentration of a distribution around the mean of a range of values	950
@MAX	The largest value in the given list	950
@MEDIAN	The median value in the given list	952
@MIN	The smallest value in the given list	952
@NORMAL	The normal distribution function for the specific mean (average) and standard deviation	954
@PERCENTILE	The xth sample percentile among the values in the given range	956
@PERMUT	The number of permutations (ordered sequences) of objects that can be selected from a given number of objects	955
@POISSON	The Poisson distribution (for predicting the number of events that will occur over a specific period of time)	957
@PRANK	The percentile of the given value among the values in the given range	959
@PRODUCT	The product of the values in the given list	960
@PUREAVG	The average of the values contained in the given list, ignoring cells in the range that contain labels	961
@PURECOUNT	The number of nonblank cells in the given list, ignoring cells in the range that contain labels	961
@PUREMAX	The largest value	962
@PUREMIN	The smallest value in the given list, ignoring cells that contain labels	963

TABLE 19.2: Statistical Functions Quick Reference (continued)

FUNCTION	RETURNS	SEE PAGE
@PURESTD	The population standard deviation of the values in the given list, ignoring cells that contain labels	963
@PURESTDS	The sample standard deviation of the values in the given list, ignoring cells that contain labels	966
@PUREVAR	The population variance in the given list, ignoring cells that contain labels	968
@PUREVARS	The sample population variance in the given list, ignoring cells that contain labels	970
@RANK	The rank of the given value relative to other values in the range	971
@REGRESSION	The statistic specified from a multiple linear regression	973
@SKEWNESS	The skewness of the values in the given range—the symmetry of a distribution around its mean (average)	975
@STD	The population standard deviation of the values in the given list	976
@STDS	The sample standard deviation of the values in the given list	978
@SUM-NEGATIVE	The sum of the negative values in the given list	980
@SUM-POSITIVE	The sum of the positive values in the given list	980
@TDIST	The Student's t-distribution (the distribution of the ratio of a standardized normal distribution to the square root of the quotient of a chi-square distribution by the number of its degrees of freedom)	982

TABLE 19.2: Statistical Functions Quick Reference (continued)

FUNCTION	RETURNS	SEE PAGE
@TTEST	The associated probability of a Student's *t*-test on the data in two given ranges (to establish whether two samples are likely to have come from the same two underlying populations)	984
@VAR	The population variance in the given list of values	986
@VARS	The sample population variance in the given list of values	988
@WEIGHTAVG	The weighted average of values in a data range	990
@ZTEST	The associated probability of a *z*-test on one or two populations (for judging the likelihood that a particular observation is drawn from a particular population)	992

Descriptions of the Statistical Functions

This section contains detailed descriptions of the statistical functions.

N O T E   See "Statistical Functions" in Chapter 5 (beginning on page 284) for a general description of these functions.

@AVEDEV(*list*)

The @AVEDEV function returns the average of the absolute deviations of the values in *list*, where *list* contains any combination of any of the following.

ITEM	EXAMPLES
Numbers	$362000
Numeric formulas	+D22/17
Addresses of ranges containing numbers or numeric formulas	DD3..DD24
Names of ranges containing numbers or numeric formulas	HOUSES, MEN_LEFT

> **N O T E**   Separate the elements of your list with argument separators, such as semicolons (;).

See Also @DEVSQ, @PURESTD, @STD

@AVG(*list*)

The @AVG function returns the average of the values contained in the *list*, which can contain any combination of numbers, numeric formulas, and addresses or names of ranges that contain numbers or numeric formulas. For example, the following function statement returns 4, the average of the seven numbers:

    @AVG(5,2,2,1,4,6,8)

You can also use @AVG with addresses, with numeric formulas, with ranges, or with named ranges, as shown here:

    @AVG(A7, A44, B101)
    @AVG($1200/A47)
    @AVG(A7..A44, C11..C13)
    @AVG(TO_SELL)

You can also use @AVG with combinations of numbers, numeric formulas, addresses, and ranges:

    @AVG(4000, A12/5, B34..C56, AB80, UNPAID)

See @PUREAVG if you need to calculate the average of a list of values that includes labels; @PUREAVG ignores cells that have labels.

See Also @DAVG, @GEOMEAN, @HARMEAN, @MEDIAN, @PUREAVG

@BINOMIAL(*trials,successes, probability,[type]*)

The @BINOMIAL function calculates the binomial probability mass function or the cumulative binomial distribution, where the arguments are as follows:

ARGUMENT	DESCRIPTION
trials	The number of independent trials. The *trials* value must be positive integer, but you can enter it as a decimal number. If *trials* is not an integer, 1-2-3 will automatically truncate it to an integer.
successes	The number of successes from the trials, a positive integer that must be less than or equal to *trials*. *successes* can be 0 but (needless to say) not less than 0. As with *trials*, if you enter *successes* as a number other than an integer, 1-2-3 will truncate it to an integer for you.
probability	A value from 0 through 1 expressing the probability of success on each trial. For example, a probability of 0.5 represents a 1 in 2 chance.

ARGUMENT	DESCRIPTION
type	An optional argument that you can use to specify whether 1-2-3 calculates the probability mass function or the cumulative binomial distribution:
	0 (the default setting if you omit the *type* argument) results in the probability of the trials producing exactly *successes* number of successes—that is, of the trials succeeding exactly the number of times you predict.
	1 results in the probability of the trials producing at most *successes* number of successes—that is, of the trials succeeding the same number of times as or fewer than you predict.
	2 results in the probability of the trials producing at least *successes* number of successes—that is, of the trials succeeding the same number of times as or more than you predict.

As an example of @BINOMIAL, say that you decide on a trip to Vegas to bolster your sagging fortunes following a disastrous decade on the stock market. Assuming that the dice may be loaded and that the table looks rigged, you decide that roulette will be your best bet. Assuming that the wheel isn't weighted and that the house hasn't yet managed to add a third zero to it, what are your chances of winning big by having the ball land on red seven times out of ten?

Well, pretty poor, as @BINOMIAL can tell you. The probability of the ball not landing on zero should be 36/38, and of it landing on red should be half that—18/38, or 0.4737. So you could use the following formula to determine the probability of red winning exactly 7 times out of 10:

@BINOMIAL(10,7,0.4737)

This produces a pathetic 0.09363. Still, you'd be more interested in the probability that you'd win *at least* 7 times out of 10:

@BINOMIAL(10,7,0.4737,2)

This produces 0.1321, which looks a fraction better but still isn't as good as your chance of throwing a 6 at dice straight off. Maybe craps would be a better choice? But really the most revealing @BINOMIAL figure for you is the probability that you would win *at most* 7 times out of 10:

@BINOMIAL(10,7,0.4737,1)

This produces 0.9615—a high probability. And the probability of winning at most 5 times out of 10 is 0.6858—also uncomfortably high. Seeing this, you might consider the stock market instead...

See Also @COMBIN, @CRITBINOMIAL, @PERMUT

@CHIDIST(*numeric-value, degrees_freedom,[type]*)

The @CHIDIST function calculates the one-tailed probability of the chi-square distribution and can be used to test the validity of a hypothesis by comparing the observed values with the values expected.

The arguments for @CHIDIST are as follows:

ARGUMENT	DESCRIPTION
numeric-value	The value at which to evaluate the chi-square distribution. *numeric-value* is affected by the value you enter for *type*:
	0 If *type* is 0, the critical value or upper bound for the value of the chi-square cumulative distribution random variable, expressed as a value greater than or equal to 0; this is the default if the argument is omitted.
	1 If type is 1, a probability (significance level), expressed as a value between 0 and 1.

ARGUMENT	DESCRIPTION
degrees_freedom	The number of degrees of freedom for the sample, expressed as a positive integer (1-2-3 will truncate a value that is not an integer to an integer).
type	An optional argument that determines how 1-2-3 calculates @CHIDIST:

0   If *type* is 0, the significance level corresponds to *numeric-value*; this is the default if *type* is omitted.

1   If *type* is 1, the critical value corresponds to the significance level *numeric-value*.

For example, the following function statement returns 0.004995:

@CHIDIST(40,20)

The following function statement returns 1.3863:

@CHIDIST(0.5,2,1)

WARNING

1-2-3's @CHIDIST approximates the chi-square cumulative distribution to within ±3*10^-7, but if it cannot approximate the result to within 0.0000001 after one hundred iterations, it will throw out an ERR—so if you receive an ERR when using @CHIDIST in a sequence, try adjusting your figures a little before concluding that your whole approach is flawed.

See Also @CHITEST, @FDIST, @TDIST

@CHITEST(*range1*,[*range2*])

The @CHITEST function performs a chi-square test for independence on the data in *range1*, or a chi-square test for goodness of fit on the data in *range1* and *range2*, where *range1* and *range2* are ranges of the same size.

WARNING

Range1 and *range2* must be the same size and must not contain labels, text formulas, or blank cells. (If they're different sizes, or contain any of the above, @CHITEST will return ERR.)

For example, Figure 19.5 shows the results of a taste test for different colors of cola. Cell E7 contains the following function statement:

    @CHITEST(B5..C9)

This tests for independence, as does the function statement in cell E17:

    @CHITEST(B14..C18)

FIGURE 19.5

Using the @CHITEST function to test for independence

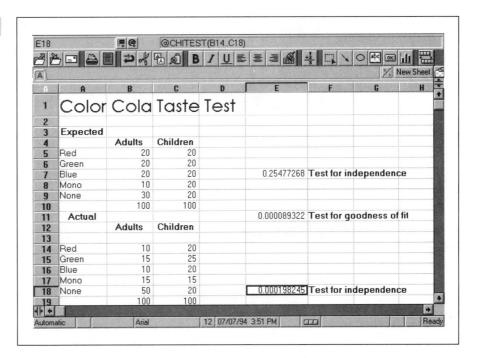

Cell E11 contains the following function statement to test for goodness of fit:

@CHITEST(B5..C9,B14..C18)

See Also @CHIDIST, @FTEST, @TTEST, @ZTEST

@COMBIN(*number, number_chosen*)

The @COMBIN function calculates the binomial coefficient for *number* and *number_chosen*—the number of ways that *number_chosen* can be selected from *number*, without regard for order, where *number* is the total number of objects and *number_chosen* is the number of objects in each combination. *number* can be 0 or any positive integer; *number_chosen* can be 0 or any positive integer, but must be less than or equal to *number*. (If *number* and *number_chosen* are not integers, 1-2-3 will truncate them to integers.)

For example, if a Lucky Dip at a rodeo contains one bill of each of six denominations of U.S. currency—$1, $5, $10, $20, $50, and $100—you could use @COMBIN to work out the number of possible different combinations of bills pulled out in two dips like this:

@COMBIN(6,2)

This returns 15.

See Also @BINOMIAL, @CRITBINOMIAL, @PERMUT

@CORREL(*range1,range2*)

The @CORREL function returns the correlation coefficient of values in *range1* and *range2*, where *range1* and *range2* are range names or range addresses of ranges that are the same size. 1-2-3 orders ranges from top to bottom, left to right, first sheet through last. Correlation measures the relationship between two sets of data independently of the unit of measure; for measuring the relationship between two sets of data depending on the unit of measure, use @COV instead.

WARNING	If *range1* and *range2* are not the same size, @CORREL will return ERR.

For example, if cells A2..A14 contained the named range MONTHS and cells B2..B14 contained the named range INCOME, you could compare the two by using either of the two following function statements:

```
@CORREL(A2..A14,B2..B14)
@CORREL(MONTHS,INCOME)
```

See Also @COV

@COUNT(*list*)

The @COUNT function returns the number of the nonblank cells in *list*, where *list* is any combination of range addresses or names separated by commas. @COUNT counts any kind of entry; @COUNT ignores only blank cells unless you enter a single cell address. For example, if cell A1 contains the label Plates of Shrimp, cell A2 contains the value 1, and cell A3 is blank, the following function statement returns 2, since cells A1 and A2 are not blank:

```
@COUNT(A1..A3)
```

However, the following function statement returns 1, even though cell A3 is blank:

```
@COUNT(A3)
```

To avoid returning a count of 1 for a single blank cell, refer to the cell as a block rather than as an individual cell and make part of the reference absolute:

```
@COUNT($A3..A3)
```

This will return 0 rather than 1.

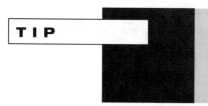

T I P

Use the @PURECOUNT function to exclude cells that contain labels. When using @COUNT, avoid including extra cells (for example, those containing separator lines) in your blocks, as they will be counted too.

Use @COUNT to stop or branch a macro that performs actions on a series of ranges when the cell pointer enters a range that contains no entries:

{IF @COUNT(PROJECTIONS_95)=0}{QUIT}

If the range PROJECTIONS_95 does not yet contain any entries, the macro is instructed to stop.

See Also @DCOUNT, @DPURECOUNT, @PURECOUNT

@COV(*range1,range2,[type]*)

The @COV functions returns either the population or sample covariance of the values in *range1* and *range2*, where *range1* and *range2* are names or addresses of ranges that are the same size. If *range1* and *range2* are different sizes, 1-2-3 will return an error. 1-2-3 orders ranges from top to bottom, left to right, first sheet through last.

N O T E

Covariance is the average of the products of deviations of corresponding values in lists. For measuring the relationship between two sets of data independently of the unit of measure, use @CORREL instead of @COV.

type is an optional argument that determines whether @COV returns the population covariance or the sample covariance. If *type* is set at 0 (the default if *type* is omitted), @COV returns population covariance; if *type* is set to 1, @COV returns sample covariance.

For example, you could calculate the population covariance of the ranges A1..A5 and B1..B5 by using the following function statement:

@COV(A1..A5,B1..B5)

(@COV(A1..A5,B1..B5,0) would produce the same result.) Or you could calculate the sample covariance by using the following function statement:

@COV(A1..A5,B1..B5,1)

See Also @CORREL, @PUREVAR, @PUREVARS, @VAR, @VARS

@CRITBINOMIAL(*trials, probability,alpha*)

The @CRITBINOMIAL function returns the largest integer for which the cumulative binomial distribution is less than or equal to alpha.

The arguments for @CRITBINOMIAL are as follows:

ARGUMENT	DESCRIPTION
trials	Any positive integer or 0 indicating the number of Bernoulli trials
probability	A value from 0 through 1 representing the probability of success for a single Bernoulli trial
alpha	A value from 0 through 1 representing the criterion probability

For example, say that your company manufactures ball bearings in consignments of 1,000. Four bearings out of every hundred are liable to have defects—a 96 percent chance that the bearings are free from defects. Your boss wants to be 99 percent sure that a certain number of bearings are not defective. To work this out, you would enter the following function statement:

@CRITBINOMIAL(1000,0.94,0.1)

This would produce 930, the number of bearings free from defects in each batch.

WARNING

The @CRITBINOMIAL function is what's euphemistically known as "processor-intensive"—that is, running it involves spectacular amounts of chip-thrashing from your PC and thumb-twiddling from you. Before you assume that your computer has hung, look for the Calc indicator on the right side of the status bar to confirm that it's still working. Then go take an early lunch break or badger your boss for that Pentium you've long wanted but never been able to justify.

See Also @BINOMIAL, @COMBIN, @PERMUT

@DEVSQ(*list*)

The @DEVSQ function calculates the sum of squared deviations of the values in *list* from their mean (average). *list* can contain any combination of numbers, numeric formulas, or addresses or names of ranges containing numbers or numeric formulas. As usual, multiple arguments need to be separated by commas or other separators (e.g., semicolons).

For example, the following function statement returns 166.875:

    @DEVSQ(11,14,15,11,19,9,4,6)

Alternatively, you could use ranges or numeric formulas in *list*:

    @DEVSQ(42,A11/B12,ENGINES,101)

In this example, ENGINES is a named range.

See Also @PURESTD, @STD

@FDIST(*numeric-value,degrees-freedom1,degrees-freedom2,* [*type*])

The @FDIST function calculates the F-distribution of probability. The F-distribution, used to determine the degree to which two samples vary, is a continuous distribution obtained from the ratio of two chi-square distributions, each divided by its number of degrees of freedom.

WARNING

@FDIST approximates the cumulative F probability distribution to within $\pm 3*10^{-7}$. @FDIST will return ERR if it cannot approximate the result to within 0.0000001 after 100 calculation iterations, the result is ERR.

The arguments for @FDIST are as follows:

ARGUMENT	DESCRIPTION
numeric-value	The value at which to evaluate the F-distribution. The *numeric-value* value depends on the value given for type as follows:
	0 If *type* is 0, *numeric-value* is a value greater than or equal to 0 representing the critical value or upper bound for the value of the cumulative F-distribution. This is the default setting if you omit the argument *type*.
	1 If *type* is 1, *numeric-value* is a value from 0 to 1 that represents probability.
degrees-freedom1	A positive integer representing the first sample (the numerator degrees of freedom).

ARGUMENT	DESCRIPTION
degrees-freedom2	A positive integer representing the second sample (the denominator degrees of freedom).
type	An optional argument used to specify how 1-2-3 calculates @FDIST:

0   Calculates the significance level corresponding to the critical value *numeric-value*. This is the default setting if you omit the argument.

1   Calculates the critical value that corresponds to the significance level *numeric-value*.

For example, the following function statement returns 0.465119:

@FDIST(1,5,10)

See Also @CHIDIST, @FTEST, @TDIST

@FTEST(*range1,range2*)

@FTEST returns the associated probability of an F probability test—to test if two samples have different variances—where *range1* and *range2* are ranges containing the data to be tested.

T I P   *range1* and *range2* do not have to be the same size— they can be different sizes, as illustrated in the example in Figure 19.6.

Figure 19.6 illustrates the use of the @FTEST function. The spreadsheet contains the results of two tests, one in the range A5..A8 and the other in the range B5..B11. To calculate the variance, cell A15 contains the following function statement:

@FTEST(A5..A8,B5..B11)

This returns 0.5299669.

See Also @CHITEST, @FDIST, @TTEST, @ZTEST

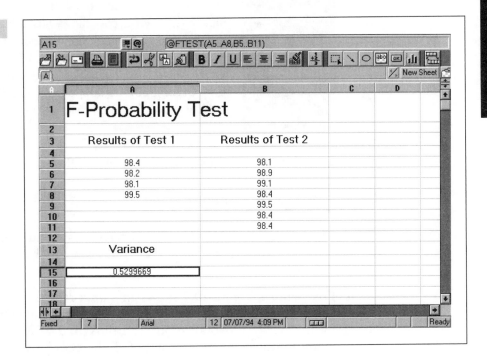

@GEOMEAN(*list*)

The @GEOMEAN function calculates the geometric mean of the values
in *list*. The geometric mean is the *n*th root of the product of the values in
list, where *number* is the number of values in *list*. *list* can include numbers,
numeric formulas that result in numbers, and addresses or names of
ranges containing numbers, or numeric formulas that result in numbers.
Note that all the values in *list* must be greater than zero.

For example, if cells B1, C1, D1, and E1 contain the values 100, 200, 300,
and 400, respectively, the following function statement returns 221.3364.

@GEOMEAN(A,B1,C1,D1)

TIP

The difference between @GEOMEAN and @AVG is that @AVG returns the arithmetic mean rather than the geometric mean. The geometric mean returns a result less than the arithmetic mean unless all the values in *list* are the same, in which case the results of the geometric mean and the arithmetic mean are the same. For example, @AVG(100,200,300,400) returns 250, while @GEOMEAN(100,200,300,400) returns 221.3364; but @AVG(500,500,500,500) and @GEOMEAN-(500,500,500,500) both return 500.

See Also @AVG, @HARMEAN, @MEDIAN, @PUREAVG

@GRANDTOTAL(*list*)

The @GRANDTOTAL function calculates the sum of all cells in *list* that contain the function @SUBTOTAL. *list* can be any combination of ranges.

For example, Figure 19.7 shows an output report for five factories manufacturing carved bears, with subtotals for the group of three locations and for the group of two locations. In cell A16, the following function statement produces the grand total of all the cells in the range B8..L13 that contain the @SUBTOTAL function:

@GRANDTOTAL(B8..L8)

The grand total is 295300.

See Also @DSUM, @SUM, @SUMNEGATIVE, @SUMPOSITIVE

@HARMEAN(*list*)

The @HARMEAN function calculates the harmonic mean of the values in *list*. The harmonic mean is the reciprocal of the arithmetic mean of the reciprocals of *list*. *list* can include numbers, numeric formulas that result in numbers, and addresses or names of ranges containing numbers, or

FIGURE 19.7

Using the @GRANDTOTAL function to produce a grand total from all cells in a range that contain the @SUBTOTAL function

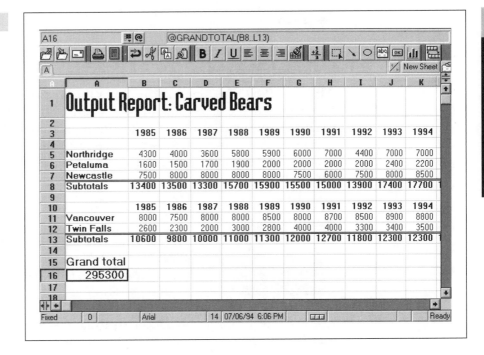

| A16 | | @GRANDTOTAL(B8..L13) |

Output Report: Carved Bears

	A	B	C	D	E	F	G	H	I	J	K
1											
2											
3		1985	1986	1987	1988	1989	1990	1991	1992	1993	1994
4											
5	Northridge	4300	4000	3600	5800	5900	6000	7000	4400	7000	7000
6	Petaluma	1600	1500	1700	1900	2000	2000	2000	2000	2400	2200
7	Newcastle	7500	8000	8000	8000	8000	7500	6000	7500	8000	8500
8	Subtotals	13400	13500	13300	15700	15900	15500	15000	13900	17400	17700
9											
10		1985	1986	1987	1988	1989	1990	1991	1992	1993	1994
11	Vancouver	8000	7500	8000	8000	8500	8000	8700	8500	8900	8800
12	Twin Falls	2600	2300	2000	3000	2800	4000	4000	3300	3400	3500
13	Subtotals	10600	9800	10000	11000	11300	12000	12700	11800	12300	12300
14											
15	Grand total										
16	295300										
17											
18											

| Fixed | 0 | Arial | 14 | 07/06/94 6:06 PM | | Ready |

numeric formulas that result in numbers. Note that all the values in *list* must be greater than zero.

For example, the following function statement produces 55.21405:

@HARMEAN(25,99,78,105)

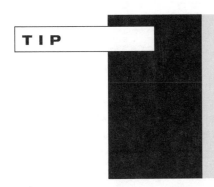

TIP

For the same *list*, the result of @HARMEAN is less than the result of @GEOMEAN (which in turn is less than the result of @AVG) unless all the values in *list* are equal. For example, @HARMEAN(100,200,300) produces 163.6363, @GEOMEAN(100,200,300) produces 181.7121, and @AVG(100,200,300) produces 200; @AVG(100,100,100), @GEOMEAN(100,100,100), and @HARMEAN(100,100,100) all produce 100.

See Also @AVG, @GEOMEAN, @MEDIAN, @PUREAVG

@KURTOSIS(*range*,[*type*])

The @KURTOSIS function calculates the kurtosis of the values in *range*, where *range* is the name or address of a range containing values. Kurtosis measures the concentration of a distribution around the mean of a range of values. A positive kurtosis indicates a relatively peaked distribution around the mean, while a negative kurtosis indicates a relatively flat distribution around the mean.

WARNING — Note that *range* must contain at least four values for the @KURTOSIS function to work. @KURTOSIS returns ERR if *range* contains fewer than four values.

type is either 0 (for a population kurtosis; this is the default if you omit the argument *type*) or 1 (for a sample kurtosis).

For example, if the range named RESULTS contains the values 1, 30, 1, and 1, the following function statement produces a population kurtosis of −0.66667:

    @KURTOSIS(RESULTS)

And this function statement produces a sample kurtosis of 4:

    @KURTOSIS(RESULTS,1)

See Also @SKEWNESS

@MAX(*list*)

The @MAX function finds and returns the largest value in *list*, where *list* can be the following in any combination, separated by argument separator characters:

- numbers
- numeric formulas
- range addresses or range names containing numbers or numeric formulas

For example, in the worksheet in Figure 19.8, cell C12 contains the following function statement to return the largest value from the range E4..E8:

    @MAX(E4..E8)

TIP   If your range contains labels, use the @PUREMAX function instead of the @MAX function.

FIGURE 19.8

Using the @MAX function to return the largest value from a range that does not contain labels

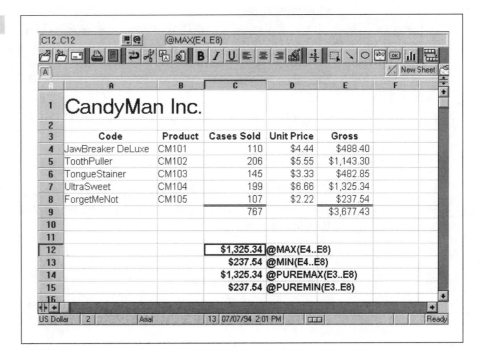

See Also @DMAX, @LARGE, @MIN, @PUREMIN

@MEDIAN(*list*)

The @MEDIAN function returns the median value in *list*, where *list* can be the following in any combination, separated by argument separator characters:

- numbers
- numeric formulas
- range addresses or range names containing numbers or numeric formulas

For example, if the range MEDIATE contains the values 6, 5, 4, and 7, the following function statement returns 5.5:

    @MEDIAN(MEDIATE)

TIP　　@MEDIAN returns the middle value if *list* contains an odd number of values and the arithmetic average of the two middle values if *list* contains an even number of values.

See Also @AVG, @GEOMEAN, @HARMEAN, @PUREAVG

@MIN(*list*)

The @MIN function finds and returns the smallest value in *list*, where *list* can be the following in any combination, separated by argument separator characters:

- numbers
- numeric formulas
- range addresses or range names containing numbers or numeric formulas

For example, in the worksheet in Figure 19.9, cell C12 contains the following function statement to return the largest value from the range E4..E8:

@MAX(E4..E8)

> **TIP**
>
> If your list contains labels, use @PUREMIN instead of @MIN; @PUREMIN ignores labels in *list*.

See Also @DMAX, @DMIN, @MAX, @PUREMAX

FIGURE 19.9

Using the @MIN function to return the smallest value from a range that does not contain labels

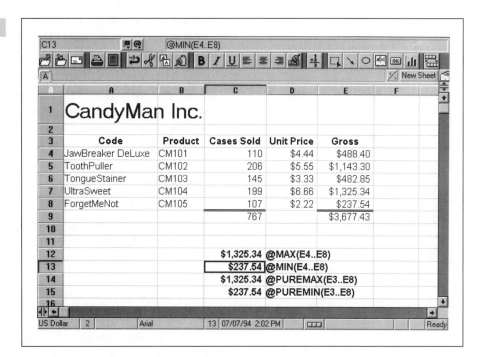

@NORMAL(*numeric-value,* [*mean*],[*std*],[*type*])

The @NORMAL function calculates the normal distribution function for the specific mean (average) and standard deviation. The arguments for the @NORMAL function are as follows:

ARGUMENT	DESCRIPTION
numeric-value	Any value indicating the upper boundary for the value of the cumulative normal distribution. *numeric-value* can be negative, but if it is, @NORMAL converts it to its absolute (positive) value.
mean	Any positive value or 0 indicating the mean of the distribution. *mean* is an optional argument; if you omit *mean*, @NORMAL uses 0.
std	Any positive value or 0 indicating the standard deviation of the distribution. *std* is an optional argument; if you omit *std*, @NORMAL uses 1.
type	Zero, 1, or 2, indicating the function for @NORMAL to calculate, as per the following list:

0   If *type* = 0, @NORMAL calculates the cumulative function distribution. This is the default setting if you omit the *type* argument.

1   If *type* = 1, @NORMAL calculates the inverse cumulative distribution.

2   If *type* = 2, @NORMAL calculates the probability density function.

19

Math, Stat Functions

WARNING   Note that you cannot use an optional argument unless you use those that precede it. For example, you cannot use *type* in @NORMAL if you do not specify *std*, and you cannot use *std* if you do not specify *mean*.

For example, to calculate the probability density function for 0.88, with a *mean* of 1 and a standard deviation of 0.5, you could use the following function statement:

@NORMAL(0.88,1,0.5,2)

This returns 0.775233.

See Also @CHIDIST, @FDIST, @POISSON, @TDIST

@PERMUT(*number-object, number-chosen*)

The @PERMUT function returns the number of permutations (ordered sequences) of objects that can be selected from *number-object*.

The arguments for the @PERMUT function are as follows:

ARGUMENT	DESCRIPTION
number-object	Zero or any positive integer indicating the number of objects. If *number-object* is not an integer, @PERMUT will truncate it to one.
number-chosen	Zero or any positive integer indicating the number of objects in each permutation. If *number-object* is not an integer, @PERMUT will truncate it to one. *number-chosen* cannot be greater than *number-object*; @PERMUT returns ERR if it is.

For example, suppose Lord Cardigan had had seven brigades at his command that fateful day in the Crimea and had been able to commit three of them to charging the wrong guns instead of just the poor old Light Brigade. Had he had 1-2-3 running on his OmniBook or Newton, he could have calculated the number of possible different ways of committing the brigades by using the following function statement:

@PERMUT(7,3)

This returns 210 possible permutations. But you still have the feeling he'd have sent in the Light Brigade anyway…

See Also @COMBIN

@PERCENTILE(*numeric-value, range*)

The @PERCENTILE function calculates the *x*th sample percentile among the values in *range*, where *numeric-value* (*x*) is a value between 0 and 1 indicating the percentile to find, and range is the name or address of a range containing values.

NOTE The @PERCENTILE function ignores any blank cells in *range* but includes any labels, to which it gives the value 0.

Figure 19.10 illustrates the use of the @PERCENTILE function for establishing a threshold of acceptance. The Fourth Grade Test Results spreadsheet contains the following function statement in cell E12 to determine the score at the eighty-fifth percentile for the average scores (column G):

@PERCENTILE(0.85,G5..G10)

This returns 91.25.

See Also @PRANK

FIGURE 19.10

Using the @PERCENTILE function to establish a determine the score at a percentile.

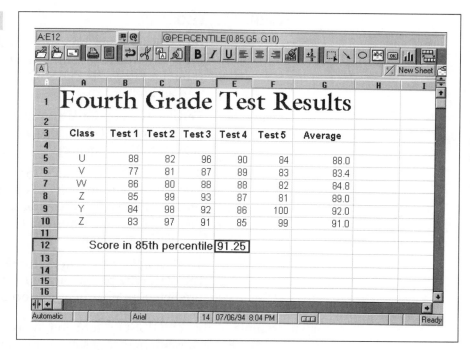

@POISSON(*number,mean,* [*cumulative*])

The @POISSON function calculates the Poisson distribution, which is mostly used for predicting the number of events that will occur over a specific period of time, using data collected from observation of similar events.

The arguments for the @POISSON function are as follows:

ARGUMENT	DESCRIPTION
number	Zero or an integer indicating the number of observed events. If you enter a number that is not an integer, @POISSON will truncate it to an integer.

ARGUMENT	DESCRIPTION
mean	A positive integer indicating the number of expected events. If you enter a number that is not an integer, @POISSON will truncate it to an integer.
cumulative	Zero or 1, an optional argument to determine how 1-2-3 calculates @POISSON, as follows:

0   If *cumulative* = 0, @POISSON calculates the probability of exactly the predicted *number* of events occurring. 0 is the default setting if you omit the *cumulative* argument.

1   If *cumulative* = 1, @POISSON calculates the probability of *at most* the predicted number of events occurring.

As an example of the @POISSON function, consider a company with 100 workers, all of whose punctuality slips from an impressive Monday high—everyone in by the 8:30 A.M. starting time—to an acceptable Friday low. Last Friday morning you observed 40 employees entering the building between 8:30 and 8:45; what is the probability that exactly 50 employees will enter the building between those times this Friday? You could use the following function statement to find out:

@POISSON(40,50)

This returns 0.0215. But a more realistic question might be how high the probability is that at most 50 employees will enter the building between 8:30 and 8:45. Use this function statement instead:

@POISSON(40,50,1)

This returns 0.08607, a much higher probability.

@PRANK(*numeric-value,range,* [*places*])

The @PRANK function returns the percentile of *numeric-value* among the values in *range*. The arguments for the @PRANK function are as follows:

ARGUMENT	DESCRIPTION
numeric-value	Any value indicating the percentile to find.
range	The name or address of a range containing values. *range* does not have to contain *numeric-value*, but if it does not, @PRANK assigns the 0th percentile position to the lowest value in *range*, assigns the 100th percentile position to the highest value in *range*, and then interpolates.
places	0 to 100, indicating the number of decimal places to which to round the result; the default setting is 2.

Figure 19.11 illustrates the use of @PRANK. In this Second Grade Test Results worksheet, cell C12 contains the following function statement to calculate the percentile rank of the score 94 among the averages in column G:

@PRANK(94,G5..G10)

This returns 0.6 (60 percent). Note the difference when you use @PRANK on a value that is not included in the *range*—cell C13 contains the following function statement:

@PRANK(93,G5..G10)

This returns 0, because the value 93 is not an item in the range.

See Also @PERCENTILE

FIGURE 19.11

Using the @PRANK function to return the percentile rank of an item in a range

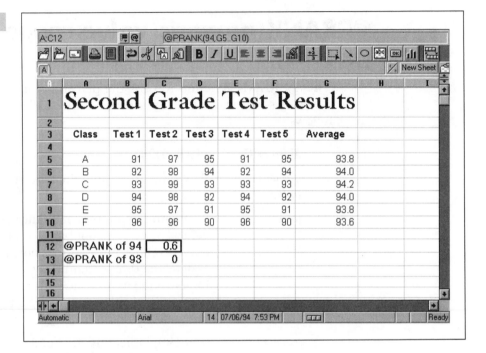

@PRODUCT(*list*)

The @PRODUCT function multiplies the values in *list*, where *list* can be the following in any combination, separated by separator characters:

- numbers
- numeric formulas
- range addresses or range names containing numbers or numeric formulas

For example, if a worksheet contains a range named ANTENNAE with the values 1, 2, 3, and 4 entered in the cells, the following function statement returns 24, the product of those four values:

    @PRODUCT(ANTENNAE)

See Also @FACT, @SUM, @SUMPRODUCT

@PUREAVG (*list*)

The @PUREAVG function returns the average of the values contained in a *list*, which can contain any combination of numbers, numeric formulas, and addresses or names of ranges that contain numbers or numeric formulas. @PUREAVG ignores cells in the range that contain labels.

For example, the following function statement returns 4, the average of the seven numbers:

@PUREAVG(5,2,2,1,4,6,8)

You can also use @PUREAVG with addresses, with numeric formulas, with ranges, or with named ranges, not to mention with combinations of numbers, numeric formulas, addresses, and ranges:

@PUREAVG(4000, A12/5, B34..C56, AB80, UNPAID)

See Also @DAVG, @GEOMEAN, @HARMEAN, @MEDIAN

@PURECOUNT(*list*)

The @PURECOUNT function returns the number of the nonblank cells in *list*, where *list* is any combination of range addresses or names separated by commas. @PURECOUNT ignores cells containing labels and does not include them in the number it returns. For example, if cell A1 contains the label Plate of Shrimp, cell A2 contains the value 1, and cell A3 is blank, the following function statement returns 1, since only one cell (cell A2) contains a value:

@PURECOUNT(A1..A3)

You can use @PURECOUNT to stop or branch a macro that performs actions on a series of ranges when the cell pointer enters a range that contains no entries:

{IF @PURECOUNT(PROJECTIONS_95)=0}{QUIT}

If the range PROJECTIONS_95 does not yet contain any entries, the macro is instructed to stop.

See Also @COUNT, @DCOUNT, @DPURECOUNT

@PUREMAX(*list*)

The @PUREMAX function finds and returns the LARGEST value in a *list* that contains labels that you want to exclude from the calculation, where *list* can be the following in any combination, separated by argument separator characters:

- numbers
- numeric formulas
- range addresses or range names containing numbers or numeric formulas

For example, in the worksheet in Figure 19.12, cell C14 contains the following function statement to return the largest value from the range E3..E8:

    @PUREMAX(E3..E8)

See Also @DMAX, @LARGE, @MIN, @PUREMIN

@PUREMIN(*list*)

The @PUREMIN function finds and returns the smallest value in a *list* that contains labels that you want to exclude from the calculation, where *list* can be the following in any combination, separated by argument separator characters:

- numbers
- numeric formulas
- range addresses or range names containing numbers or numeric formulas

For example, in the worksheet in Figure 19.13, cell C15 contains the following function statement to return the smallest value from the range E3..E8:

    @PUREMIN(E3..E8)

See Also @MAX, @DMIN, @PUREMAX

@PURESTD(*list*)

The @PURESTD function returns the population standard deviation of the values in a *list* containing labels that you want to exclude from the calculation, where *list* can be the following in any combination, separated by separator characters:

- numbers
- numeric formulas
- range addresses or range names containing numbers or numeric formulas

FIGURE 19.13

Using the @PUREMIN function to return the smallest value from a range that contains labels

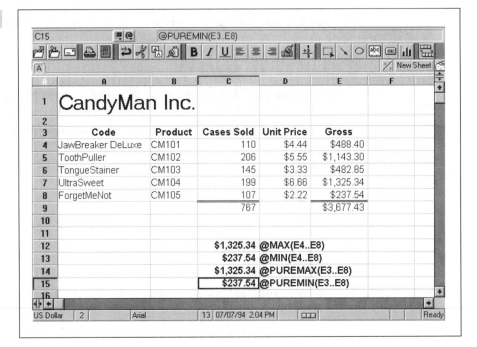

NOTE

While the @STD, @STDS, @PURESTD, and @PURESTDS functions work in similar ways, they produce significantly different results. @STD calculates the population standard deviation, while @STDS calculates the sample standard deviation. @PURESTD calculates the population standard deviation, ignoring cells that contain labels that would throw off the @STD calculation; and @PURESTDS calculates the sample standard deviation, likewise ignoring cells with labels that would throw off the @STDS calculation.

N O T E

Population standard deviation assumes that the selected values represent the entire population, while sample standard deviation assumes that the selected values represent only a sample of the population. To compensate for errors in the sample, sample standard deviation produces a standard deviation larger than the population standard deviation.

As an example of the @PURESTD function, consider Figure 19.14, which uses an @PURESTD function statement to calculate the population standard deviation on the figures in the Cases Sold column (column C):

@PURESTD(C3..C8)

This function statement returns 42.3159544. Note that the range C3..C8 includes the label in cell C3, since @PURESTD ignores labels included in the range, whereas @STD does not. While selecting the range without

FIGURE 19.14

Using the @PURESTD function to return the population standard deviation from a range that includes labels

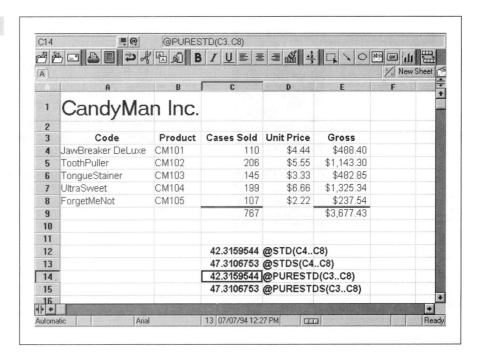

the label is no great chore in a small worksheet like this one, when you are working with larger worksheets that include many labels, the @PURESTD function can be very useful indeed.

See Also @DSTD, @DSTDS, @PUREVAR, @PUREVARS, @VAR, @VARS

@PURESTDS(*list*)

The @PURESTDS function returns the sample standard deviation of the values in a *list* containing labels that you want to exclude from the calculation, where *list* can be the following in any combination, separated by separator characters:

- numbers
- numeric formulas
- range addresses or range names containing numbers or numeric formulas

NOTE

While the @STD, @STDS, @PURESTD, and @PURESTDS functions work in similar ways, they produce significantly different results. @STD calculates the population standard deviation, while @STDS calculates the sample standard deviation. @PURESTD calculates the population standard deviation, ignoring cells that contain labels that would throw off the @STD calculation; and @PURESTDS calculates the sample standard deviation, likewise ignoring cells with labels that would throw off the @STDS calculation.

N O T E

Population standard deviation assumes that the selected values represent the entire population, while sample standard deviation assumes that the selected values represent only a sample of the population. To compensate for errors in the sample, sample standard deviation produces a standard deviation larger than the population standard deviation.

As an example of the @PURESTDS function, consider Figure 19.15, which uses an @PURESTDS function statement to calculate the sample standard deviation on the figures in the Cases Sold column (column C):

@STD(C3..C8)

This function statement returns 47.3106753. Note that the range C3..C8 includes the label in cell C3, which would interfere with the @STDS calculation but which @PURESTDS ignores. In larger worksheets that

FIGURE 19.15

Using the @PURESTDS function to return the sample standard deviation from a range that does not contain labels

contain multiple rows of labels among blocks of values, this function can prove handy.

See Also @DSTD, @DSTDS, @PUREVAR, @PUREVARS, @VAR, @VARS

@PUREVAR(*list*)

The @PUREVAR function calculates the population variance in a *list* of values, where *list* can be the following in any combination, separated by separator characters:

- numbers
- numeric formulas
- range addresses or range names containing numbers or numeric formulas

N O T E

Population variance assumes that the selected values are the entire population, while sample variance assumes that the selected values represent only a sample of the population. To compensate for errors in the sample, sample variance produces a variance larger than the population variance.

Figure 19.16 illustrates the @PUREVAR function. In this worksheet, cell C14 calculates the population variance of range C3..C8 by using the following function statement:

@PUREVAR(C3..C8)

This function statement returns 1790.64. Note the difference between this function statement and that for @VAR: When using @PUREVAR, you do not have to exclude from the range any labels that would interfere with the @VAR calculation if included in the range. In this case, the difference between the ranges C3..C8 and C4..C8 is mostly academic; but

19

FIGURE 19.16

Using the @PUREVAR function to calculate the population variance of a range that includes labels

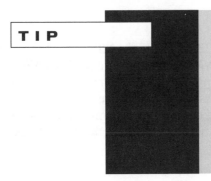

in a more complicated worksheet, where rows of labels are interspersed in blocks of values, @PUREVAR can be most useful.

TIP

The functions @VAR, @VARS, @PUREVAR, and @PURE-VARS all work in similar ways but produce substantially different results. While @VAR calculates population variance, @VARS calculates sample population variance. @PUREVAR calculates population variance but ignores cells that contain labels rather than values; and @PURE-VARS calculates sample population variance ignoring cells that contain labels rather than values.

See Also @DVAR, @DVARS, @PUREVARS, @VAR, @VARS

@PUREVARS(*list*)

The @PUREVARS function calculates the sample population variance in a *list* of values, where *list* can be the following in any combination, separated by separator characters:

- numbers
- numeric formulas
- range addresses or range names containing numbers or numeric formulas

N O T E Sample population variance assumes that the selected values represent only a sample of the population, while population variance assumes that the selected values comprise the entire population. To compensate for errors in the sample, sample variance produces a variance larger than the population variance.

Figure 19.17 illustrates the @PUREVARS function. In this worksheet, cell C15 calculates the population variance of range C3..C8 by using the following function statement:

@PUREVARS(C3..C8)

This function statement returns 2238.3. Note the difference between this function statement and that for @VARS: When using @PUREVARS, you do not have to exclude from the range any labels that would interfere with the @VARS calculation. In this case, the difference between the ranges C3..C8 and C4..C8 is barely significant; but in a complex worksheet with many rows of labels identifying blocks of values, @PUREVAR really comes into its own.

Math, Stat Functions

19

FIGURE 19.17

Using the @PUREVARS function to calculate the sample population variance of a range that includes labels

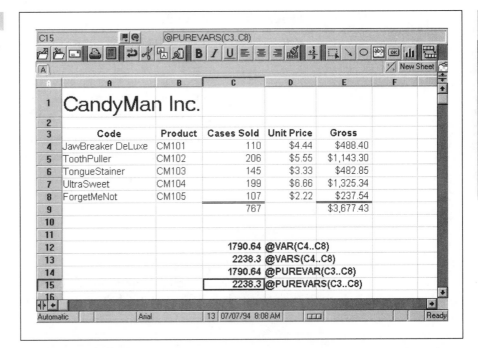

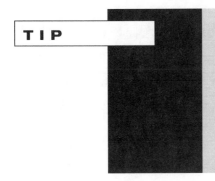

TIP

The functions @VAR, @VARS, @PUREVAR, and @PURE-VARS all work in similar ways but produce substantially different results. While @VAR calculates population variance, @VARS calculates sample population variance. @PUREVAR calculates population variance but ignores cells that contain labels rather than values; and @PUREVARS calculates sample population variance ignoring cells that contain labels rather than values.

See Also @DVAR, @DVARS, @PUREVAR, @VAR, @VARS

@RANK(*item,range,*[*order*])

The @RANK function calculates the rank of a value, *item,* relative to other values in a *range.* The arguments for the @RANK function are as follows.

ARGUMENT	DESCRIPTION
item	The value whose rank you want to establish.
range	The address or name of a range containing values and containing *item*; if *range* does not contain *item*, @RANK will return ERR.
order	Zero or 1, an optional argument indicating how to rank *item* in *range*, as follows:

0 The default setting for *order* and specifies descending order (9 to 1, z to a, etc.).

1 Specifies ascending order (1 to 9, a to z, etc.).

As an example of the @RANK function, consider Figure 19.18, which shows a Frequently Accessed Newsgroups worksheet. Column E contains the range named TOTAL ACCESS, and column G contains function

FIGURE 19.18

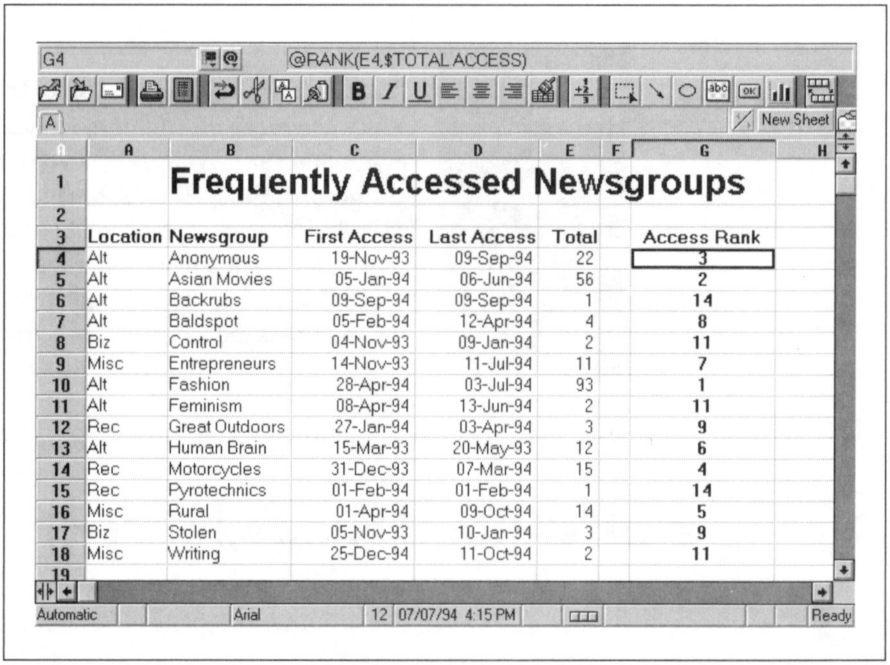

Using the @RANK function to establish the rank of items within a range

statements similar to the following one to establish the rank of the different newsgroups among those accessed:

@RANK(E10,TOTAL ACCESS)

N O T E

If *range* contains two items with the same value, @RANK assigns them the same rank. For example, in the Frequently Accessed Newsgroups worksheet, the newsgroups Control, Feminism, and Writing share eleventh place, and no twelfth or thirteenth place appears.

@REGRESSION(*x-range,y-range, attribute,*[*compute*])

The @REGRESSION function performs multiple linear regression and returns the statistic specified. The arguments for the @REGRESSION function are as follows:

ARGUMENT	DESCRIPTION
x-range	The name or address of a range containing the independent variables. *x-range* can contain up to 75 columns and 8,192 rows.
y-range	The name or address of a single-column range containing the set of values for the dependent variable. *y-range* must have the same number of rows as *x-range*.
attribute	1, 2, 3, 4, 5, 01–175, or 201–275, indicating which regression output value @REGRESSION is to calculate, as follows:

1   If *attribute* = 1, @REGRESSION calculates constant calculation.

2   If *attribute* = 2, @REGRESSION calculates the standard error of Y estimate constant calculation.

ARGUMENT	DESCRIPTION
3	If *attribute* = 3, @REGRESSION calculates the R squared constant calculation.
4	If *attribute* = 4, @REGRESSION calculates the number of observations calculation.
5	If *attribute* = 5, @REGRESSION calculates the degrees of freedom calculation.
01–175	If *attribute* = 01 to 175, @REGRESSION calculates the x coefficient (slope) for the independent variable specified by *attribute*. @REGRESSION numbers the independent variables in *x-range*, starting with the number 1, from top to bottom in a column and from left to right. For example, to find the x-coefficient for the independent variable in column A, use the attribute 100; to find the x-coefficient for the independent variable in column F, use 105.
201–275	If *attribute* = 201 to 275, @REGRESSION calculates the standard error of coefficient for the independent variable specified by *attribute*. @REGRESSION numbers the independent variables in *x-range*, starting with the number 1, from top to bottom in a column and from left to right. For example, to find the standard error of coefficient for the independent variable in column A, use 201 as the *attribute*; to find the standard error of coefficient for the independent variable in column D, use 203 as the *attribute*.

ARGUMENT	DESCRIPTION
compute	Zero or 1, indicating the Y intercept, as follows:
	0 If *compute* = 0, @REGRESSION uses 0 as the Y intercept.
	1 If *compute* = 1, @REGRESSION calculates the Y intercept; this is the default if you omit the optional *compute* argument.

@SKEWNESS(*range*,[*type*])

The @SKEWNESS function calculates the skewness of the values in *range*. Skewness measures the symmetry of a distribution around its mean (average). Positive skewness indicates a drawn-out tail to the left while negative skewness indicates a drawn-out tail to the right.

The arguments for the @SKEWNESS function are as follows:

ARGUMENT	DESCRIPTION
range	The name or address of a range containing at least three values. If *range* contains fewer than three values, @SKEWNESS will return ERR.
type	Zero or 1, indicating whether @SKEWNESS is to calculate population skewness or sample skewness, as follows:
	0 If *type* = 0, @SKEWNESS calculates the population skewness. This is the default setting if you omit the optional *type* argument.
	1 If *type* = 1, @SKEWNESS calculates the sample skewness.

For example, if the range APPRECIATE contained the values 1, 2, 4, 6, and 8, you could calculate the population skewness by using the following function statement:

@SKEWNESS(APPRECIATE)

This returns 0.205692. To calculate the sample skewness, you could use the following function statement, which returns 0.306628:

@SKEWNESS(APPRECIATE,1)

See Also @KURTOSIS, @PURESTD, @PUREVAR, @STD, @VAR

@STD(*list*)

The @STD function returns the population standard deviation of the values in *list*, where *list* can be the following in any combination, separated by separator characters:

- numbers
- numeric formulas
- range addresses or range names containing numbers or numeric formulas

NOTE

While the @STD, @STDS, @PURESTD, and @PURESTDS functions work in similar ways, they produce significantly different results. @STD calculates the population standard deviation, while @STDS calculates the sample standard deviation. @PURESTD calculates the population standard deviation, ignoring cells that contain labels that would throw off the @STD calculation; and @PURE-STDS calculates the sample standard deviation, likewise ignoring cells with labels that would throw off the @STD calculation.

NOTE

Population standard deviation assumes that the selected values represent the entire population, while sample standard deviation assumes that the selected values represent only a sample of the population. To compensate for errors in the sample, sample standard deviation produces a standard deviation larger than the population standard deviation.

As an example of the @STD function, consider Figure 19.19, which uses an @STD function statement to calculate the population standard deviation on the figures in the Cases Sold column (column C):

@STD(C4..C8)

This function statement returns 42.3159544. Note that the range C4..C8 excludes the label in cell C3, which would interfere with the @STD calculation. If the range includes labels, use the @PURESTD function instead.

FIGURE 19.19

Using the @STD function to return the population standard deviation from a range that does not contain labels

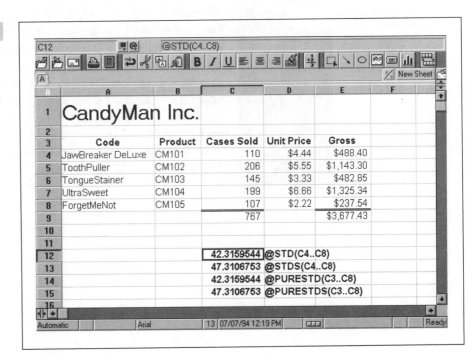

As an aside, if all the values in the @STD calculation are the same, the average will equal that value, and the standard deviation will be 0.

See Also @DSTD, @DSTDS, @PUREVAR, @PUREVARS, @STD, @VAR, @VARS

@STDS(*list*)

The @STDS function returns the sample standard deviation of the values in *list*, where *list* can be the following in any combination, separated by separator characters:

- numbers
- numeric formulas
- range addresses or range names containing numbers or numeric formulas

N O T E

While the @STD, @STDS, @PURESTD, and @PURESTDS functions work in similar ways, they produce significantly different results. @STD calculates the population standard deviation, while @STDS calculates the sample standard deviation. @PURESTD calculates the population standard deviation, ignoring cells that contain labels that would throw off the @STD calculation; and @PURE-STDS calculates the sample standard deviation, likewise ignoring cells with labels that would throw off the @STD calculation.

N O T E

Population standard deviation assumes that the selected values represent the entire population, while sample standard deviation assumes that the selected values represent only a sample of the population. To compensate for errors in the sample, sample standard deviation produces a standard deviation larger than the population standard deviation, as shown in the example in Figure 19.20.

As an example of the @STDS function, consider Figure 19.20, which uses an @STDS function statement to calculate the sample standard deviation on the figures in the Cases Sold column (column C):

@STDS(C4..C8)

This function statement returns 47.3106753. Note that the range C4..C8 excludes the label in cell C3, which would interfere with the @STDS

FIGURE 19.20

Using the @STDS function to return the population standard deviation from a range that does not contain labels

calculation. If the range includes labels, use the @PURESTDS function instead.

See Also @DSTD, @DSTDS, @PUREVAR, @PUREVARS, @STD, @VAR, @VARS

@SUMNEGATIVE(*list*)

The @SUMNEGATIVE function sums only the negative values in *list*, where *list* can be the following in any combination, separated by argument separator characters:

- numbers
- numeric formulas
- range addresses or range names containing numbers or numeric formulas

For example, if you keep track of your finances in an underdeveloped PDA and port them via the ether to your desktop PC and 1-2-3, you could use @SUMNEGATIVE as illustrated in Figure 19.24 to calculate your total expenditure without having to divide the income and expenditure figures into separate ranges. In Figure 19.21, cell D8 contains the following function statement to calculate total expenditure from the range CASHFLOWS:

    @SUMNEGATIVE(CASHFLOWS)

See Also @DSUM, @GRANDTOTAL, @SUBTOTAL, @SUM, @SUMPOSITIVE

@SUMPOSITIVE(*list*)

The @SUMPOSITIVE function sums only the positive values in *list*, where *list* can be the following in any combination, separated by argument

FIGURE 19.21

Using the @SUMNEGATIVE function to return only the negative values from a list

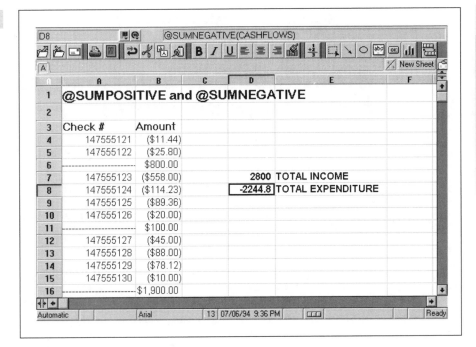

separator characters:

- numbers

- numeric formulas

- range addresses or range names containing numbers or numeric formulas

For example, if you keep track of your finances in an underdeveloped PDA and port them via the ether to your desktop PC and 1-2-3, you could use @SUMPOSITIVE as illustrated in Figure 19.21 (in the previous entry) to calculate your total income without having to divide the income and expenditure figures into separate ranges. In Figure 19.21, cell D7 contains the following function statement to calculate total income from the range CASHFLOWS:

@SUMPOSITIVE(CASHFLOWS)

See Also @DSUM, @GRANDTOTAL, @SUBTOTAL, @SUM, @SUMNEGATIVE

@TDIST(*numeric-value,degrees-freedom, [type],[tails]*)

The @TDIST function calculates and returns the Student's *t*-distribution. The Student's *t*-distribution is the distribution of the ratio of a standardized normal distribution to the square root of the quotient of a chi-square distribution by the number of its degrees of freedom.

The arguments for the @TDIST function are as follows:

ARGUMENT	DESCRIPTION
numeric-value	The value at which to evaluate the *t*-distribution. *numeric-value* depends on the *type* argument, which can be 0 or 1, as follows:
	0 If *type* = 0, *numeric-value* is the critical value (the upper bound) for the value of the cumulative t-distribution random variable. In this case
	1 If *type* = 1, *numeric-value* is a probability; enter *numeric-value* as a value from 0 to 1.
degrees-freedom	Any positive integer indicating the number of degrees of freedom for the sample.
type	Zero or 1, an optical argument indicating the direction of the *t*- distribution, as follows:
	0 If *type* = 0, @TDIST calculates the significance level that corresponds to the critical value, *numeric-value*. This is the default value if you omit the *type* argument.

ARGUMENT	DESCRIPTION
1	If *type* = 1, @TDIST calculates the critical value that corresponds to the significance level, *numeric-value*.
1	If *tails* = 1, 1-2-3 performs a one-tailed *t*-test.
2	If *tails* = 2, 1-2-3 performs a two-tailed *t*-test. *tails* is an optional argument; 2 is the default setting if you omit *tails*.

WARNING

You cannot use an optional argument unless you use those that precede it. For example, you cannot use *tails* in @TDIST if you do not specify *type*. Also be aware that @TDIST approximates the cumulative *t*-distribution to within $\pm 3*10^{\wedge}-7$; and if @TDIST cannot approximate the result to within 0.0000001 after 100 calculation iterations, it returns ERR.

Figure 19.22 shows an example of calculating a *t*-distribution with the @TDIST function. Cell B4 contains 0.75 as *numeric-value*, and cell B5 contains 8 as *degrees-freedom1*. Cells B7 through B10 contain four @TDIST function statements, illustrating the different permutations possible. For example, cell B9 contains the following function statement, which returns ERR for these values because @TDIST cannot approximate the result to within 0.0000001 after 100 calculation iterations:

@TDIST(B4,B5,1,1)

See Also @CHIDIST, @FDIST, @TTEST

FIGURE 19.22

Using the @TDIST function to calculate a *t*-distribution

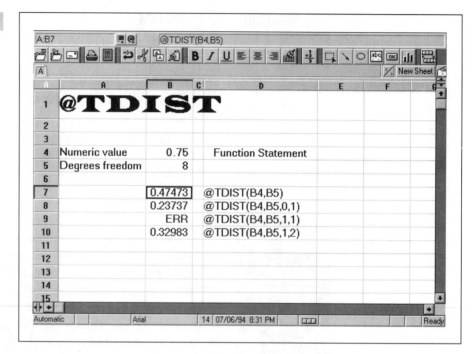

@TTEST(*range1*,*range2*,[*type*], [*tails*])

The @TTEST function calculates the associated probability of a Student's *t*-test on the data in *range1* and *range2*. The purpose of @TTEST is to establish whether two samples are likely to have come from the same two underlying populations.

The arguments for the @TTEST function are as follows:

ARGUMENT	DESCRIPTION
range1	The first data set, a range containing values.
range2	The second data set, a range containing values.

ARGUMENT	DESCRIPTION
type	0, 1, or 2, indicating what type of *t*-test to perform, as follows:
	0 If *type* = 0, 1-2-3 performs a *homoscedastic* *t*-test—a *t*-test for samples drawn from populations with the same variance. For a homoscedastic *t*-test, *range1* and *range2* do not have to contain the same number of cells. *type* is an optional argument; @TTEST uses 0 as the default if you omit *type*.
	1 If *type* = 1, 1-2-3 performs a heteroscedastic *t*-test—a *t*-test for samples drawn from populations with unequal variances. For a heteroscedastic test, *range1* and *range2* do not have to contain the same number of cells.
	2 If *type* = 2, 1-2-3 performs a *paired* *t*-test. For a paired *t*-test, *range1* and *range2* must contain the same number of cells.
tails	1 or 2, indicating the direction of the *t*-test, as follows:
	1 If *tails* = 1, 1-2-3 performs a one-tailed *t*-test.
	2 If *tails* = 2, 1-2-3 performs a two-tailed *t*-test. *tails* is an optional argument; 2 is the default setting if you omit *tails*.

WARNING

Note that you cannot use an optional argument unless you use those that precede it. For example, you cannot use *tails* in an @TTEST function statement if you do not specify *type*.

Figure 19.23 provides an illustration of the @TTEST function. Column A contains First Result, the result from the first test; column B contains Second Result, the result from the second test. Column C calculates the variance according to the different combinations that @TTEST offers; and column D contains the text of the function statements in column C.

Thus, cell C4 contains the following function statement to calculate a homoscedastic *t*-test with two tails:

@TTEST(A4..A11,B4..B11)

See Also @CHITEST, @FTEST, @TDIST, @ZTEST

FIGURE 19.23

Using the @TTEST function to return the Student's *t*-test probability

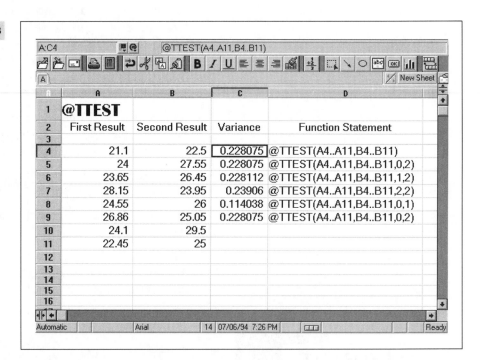

@VAR(*list*)

The @VAR function calculates the population variance in a *list* of values, where *list* can be the following in any combination, separated by separator characters:

- numbers
- numeric formulas
- range addresses or range names containing numbers or numeric formulas

NOTE Population variance assumes that the selected values are the entire population, while sample variance assumes that the selected values represent only a sample of the population. To compensate for errors in the sample, sample variance produces a variance larger than the population variance.

Figure 19.24 illustrates the @VAR function. In this worksheet, cell C12 calculates the population variance of range C4..C8 by using the following function statement:

@VAR(C4..C8)

This function statement returns 1790.64. Note that the range used here is C4..C8, excluding the label in cell C3, which would interfere with the @VAR calculation if included in the range.

TIP The functions @VAR, @VARS, @PUREVAR, and @PUREVARS all work in similar ways but produce substantially different results. While @VAR calculates population variance, @VARS calculates sample population variance. @PUREVAR calculates population variance but ignores cells that contain labels rather than values; and @PUREVARS calculates sample population variance ignoring cells that contain labels rather than values.

See Also @DVAR, @DVARS

FIGURE 19.24

Using the @VAR
function to calculate
the population
variance of a range

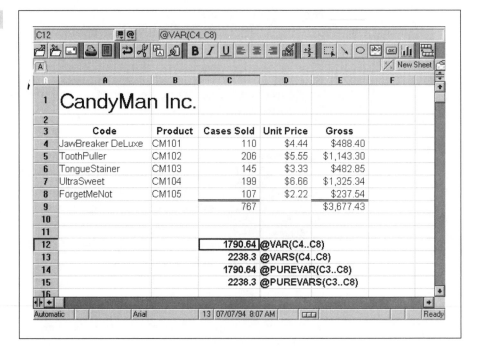

@VARS(*list*)

The @VARS function calculates the sample population variance in a *list* of values, where *list* can be the following in any combination, separated by separator characters:

- numbers

- numeric formulas

- range addresses or range names containing numbers or numeric formulas

19

Math, Stat Functions

NOTE

Sample population variance assumes that the selected values represent only a sample of the population, while population variance assumes that the selected values comprise the entire population. To compensate for errors in the sample, sample variance produces a variance larger than the population variance.

Figure 19.25 illustrates the @VARS function. In this worksheet, cell C13 calculates the sample population variance of range C4..C8 by using the following function statement:

    @VARS(C4..C8)

This function statement returns 2238.3. Note that the range used here is C4..C8, excluding the label in cell C3, which would interfere with the @VARS calculation if included in the range.

FIGURE 19.25

Using the @VARS function to calculate the sample population variance of a range

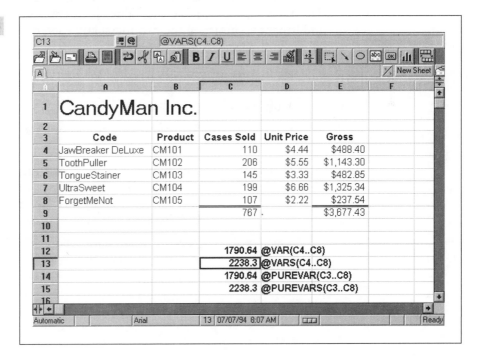

TIP

The functions @VAR, @VARS, @PUREVAR, and @PURE-VARS all work in similar ways but produce substantially different results. While @VAR calculates population variance, @VARS calculates sample population variance. @PUREVAR calculates population variance but ignores cells that contain labels rather than values; and @PUREVARS calculates sample population variance ignoring cells that contain labels rather than values.

See Also @DVAR, @DVARS, @PUREVAR, @PUREVARS, @VAR

@WEIGHTAVG(*data-range, weights-range,[type]*)

The @WEIGHTAVG function returns the weighted average of values in *data-range* by multiplying the values in corresponding cells of *data-range* and weight *r*, summing the products, and then dividing by the number of values in the list.

The arguments for the @WEIGHTAVG function are as follows:

ARGUMENT	DESCRIPTION
data-range	The name or address of a range containing values.
weights-range	The name or address of a range containing values. *weights-range* must be the same size and shape as *data-range*; otherwise, @WEIGHTAVG will return ERR.
type	Zero or 1, indicating how @WEIGHTAVG should calculate the weighted average, as follows.

ARGUMENT	DESCRIPTION
0	If *type* = 0, @WEIGHTAVG divides by the sum of the values in *weights-range*. This is the default setting if you omit the optional *type* argument.
1	If *type* = 1, @WEIGHTAVG divides by the number of values in *data-range*.

As an example of the @WEIGHTAVG function, consider the AutoMates! car dealership worksheet shown in Figure 19.26, in which cells C6..C8 contain the range named TOTAL SALES and cells E6..E8 contain the range named COMMISSION. To calculate the weighted average of sales and commission, cell D12 contains the following function statement:

@WEIGHTAVG(TOTAL SALES,COMMISSION)

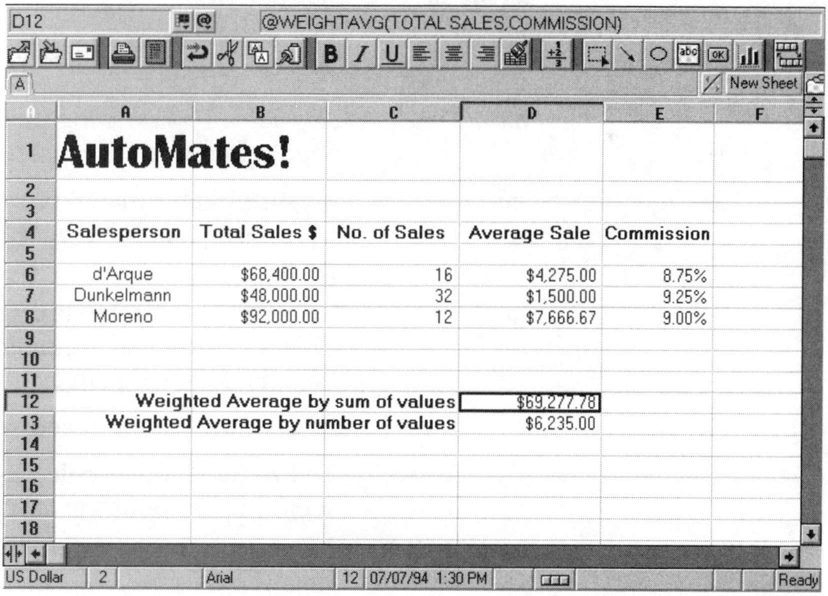

FIGURE 19.26

Using the @WEIGHTAVG function to calculate a weighted average

This function statement returns $69,277.78. Cell D13 contains the following function statement to return the weighted average by the number of values, which evaluates at $6,235.00:

@WEIGHTAVG(TOTAL SALES,COMMISSION,1)

See Also @SUMPRODUCT

@ZTEST(range1,mean1 std1, [tails],[range2],[mean2],[std2])

The @ZTEST function performs a z-test on one or two populations and returns the associated probability. A *z*-test is used to judge the likelihood that a particular observation is drawn from a particular population.

The arguments for the @ZTEST function are as follows:

ARGUMENT	DESCRIPTION
range1	The range containing the first (or only) set of data to be tested.
mean1	Any value representing the known population mean of *range1*.
std1	A value greater than 0 representing the known population standard deviation of *range1*.
tails	1 or 2, to specify the direction of the *z*-test. This is an optional argument; the values have the following effect:
	1 Produces a one-tailed *z*-test.
	2 Produces a two-tailed *z*-test (this is the default if you omit the *tails* argument).
range2	The range containing the second set of data to test.

19

Math, Stat Functions

ARGUMENT	DESCRIPTION
mean2	Any value representing the known population mean of *range2*; can be any value. This is an optional argument; 1-2-3 uses the default value of 0 if you do not specify another.
std2	A value greater than 0 representing the known population standard deviation of *range2*; 1-2-3 uses the default value of 1 if you do not specify a value for *std2*.

WARNING You cannot use an optional argument unless you use those that precede it. For example, you cannot use *tails* in @ZTEST if you do not specify *range2*.

For example, suppose you have a range called SPECIMEN that contains the values 49, 47, 55, 48, 56, and 51; and the population mean of these values is 51; and the population standard deviation of these values is 3.41565. You could use this function statement to calculate the z-test for these values and return the associated probability:

@ZTEST(SPECIMEN,51,3.41565)

See Also @CHITEST, @FTEST, @TTEST

20

Text
Functions
Reference

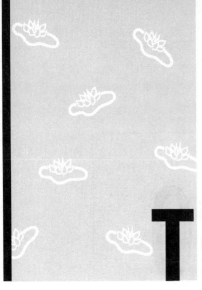

THIS chapter examines 1-2-3's text functions, which fall into two categories:

- Functions that provide information about text in cells. For example, the @CHAR function returns the character of the Lotus Multibyte Character Set (LMBCS) that corresponds to a number code, and the @S function returns the entry in the first cell in a range as a label.

- Functions that perform operations on text. For example, the @CLEAN function removes nonprinting characters from text, and the @LEFT function returns the specified number of left-most characters in a text string.

Overview of the Text Functions

For quick reference, the text functions are listed here in Table 20.1, with page numbers indicating their detailed discussions in the next section of this chapter, "Descriptions of the Text Functions."

TABLE 20.1: Text Functions Quick Reference

FUNCTION	RETURNS	SEE PAGE
@CHAR	The character of the Lotus Multibyte Character Set (LMBCS) that corresponds to the number code specified.	999
@CLEAN	The specified text string with all nonprinting characters removed from it.	1000
@CODE	The code for the Lotus Multibyte Character Set (LMBCS) code that corresponds to the first character in a text string.	1000
@EXACT	1 (TRUE) if the two specified sets of characters match exactly; 0 (FALSE) if the two sets do not match exactly.	1001
@FIND	The position in a given text string at which 1-2-3 finds the first occurrence of the specified search text, the search beginning at the given position.	1002
@LEFT	The specified number of the first (leftmost) characters in a given text string.	1003
@LENGTH	The number of characters in a string.	1005
@LOWER	The given string with all letters converted to lowercase.	1006
@MID	The specified number of characters from a text string, beginning with the character at the offset specified.	1008
@PROPER	The given string with all the letters converted to initial capital style (i.e., the first letter of each word in uppercase and the remaining letters all lowercase).	1010

20

Text Functions

TABLE 20.1: Text Functions Quick Reference (continued)

FUNCTION	RETURNS	SEE PAGE
@REPEAT	The specified string repeated the specified number of times.	1012
@REPLACE	The specified text string with the given replacement text added or appended.	1013
@RIGHT	The specified number of characters last (rightmost) in a text string.	1015
@S	The entry in the first cell of a given range as a label. If the entry is a value, @S returns a blank cell.	1017
@SETSTRING	A label the specified number of characters long consisting of the specified text string and enough blank spaces to align the text string with the chosen alignment.	1018
@STRING	The specified value converted to a label using the format specified.	1020
@TRIM	The specified text string with all leading, trailing, and consecutive space characters stripped from it.	1021
@UPPER	The specified string with all its letters converted to uppercase.	1021
@VALUE	The value corresponding to a number entered as a text string in one of the four formats 1-2-3 recognizes.	1023

Descriptions of the Text Functions

This section explains all the text functions in alphabetical order.

NOTE

See Chapter 5 (page 326) for a general description of the text functions and how they work.

@CHAR(*code*)

The @CHAR function returns the character of the Lotus Multibyte Character Set (LMBCS) that corresponds to the number *code*. *code* must be an integer—if it is not, 1-2-3 will truncate it to an integer. *code* must also correspond to a character in the Lotus Multibyte Character Set; if it does not, @CHAR will return ERR.

WARNING

Some of the LMCS characters are pretty weird. If your monitor can't display an LMCS character, 1-2-3 will do its best to display a similar character. Failing that, 1-2-3 will show a solid rectangle. Bear in mind that your printer also needs to be able to print the LMCS characters you use in your spreadsheets.

For example, to insert £ (the British pound sign), use this function statement:

    @CHAR(156)

To insert ¥ (the Japanese yen sign), use this one:

    @CHAR(190)

You can also refer to cell addresses. For example, to insert ® (the registered symbol) into cell A22, you could refer to the value in another cell:

@CHAR(D45)

This would return ® in cell A22 if cell D45 contained 169, the LMCS code for ®.

See Also @CODE

@CLEAN("text")

The @CLEAN function removes nonprinting characters from *text*, where *text* can be text enclosed in quotation marks (" "), the address or name of a cell containing a label, or a formula or function resulting in text. For example, this function statement would remove nonprinting characters from cell A34:

@CLEAN(A34)

TIP

Consider using the @CLEAN function after importing data into 1-2-3 from another program—for example, a word-processing application may leave in text codes that 1-2-3 cannot read and displays as gibberish.

See Also @CHAR, @TRIM

@CODE(text)

The function @CODE returns the code for the Lotus Multibyte Character Set (LMBCS) that corresponds to the first character in *text*, where *text* is

- text enclosed in double quotation marks (" "),
- the address or name of a cell containing a label, or
- a formula or @ function statement resulting in text.

For example, if cell A1 contains the label "X-modem," the function statement

@CODE(A1)

would return 88, since 88 is the LMBCS code for *X*, the first character of the label "X-modem."

See Also @CHAR

@EXACT(*text1,text2*)

The @EXACT function compares two sets of characters, *text1* and *text2*. @EXACT returns 1 (TRUE) if the two sets match exactly; if the two sets do not match exactly, @EXACT returns 0 (FALSE). Enter *text1* and *text2* inside double quotation marks (*" "*). Alternatively, you can enter formulas that result in text or the addresses or names of cells containing labels or formulas that result in labels.

T I P

The main difference between @EXACT and = (the equals sign) is that @EXACT is case-sensitive and also distinguishes between letters with and without accent marks. This makes @EXACT much more suitable than = for testing user input for correct passwords (including upper- and lowercase letters) and other critical input.

For example, while the statement Life = life equates to TRUE, the following statement equates to false because the difference in capitalization between the two strings means they are not exactly alike:

@EXACT("Life","life")

Using @EXACT with @IF, you could set a password check like the following to check that the user had entered the words *Running Man* in cell A8:

@IF(@EXACT("Running Man",A8),"Access granted. Perimeter deactivated.","Access denied. Perimeter activated.")

20

Text Functions

If users have entered the phrase with the correct spacing and capitalization, they get the *Access granted...* message; if they have entered the phrase wrongly or have entered the wrong phrase, they'll see the *Access denied...* message instead. (If they haven't entered anything in cell A8, @IF will return ERR.)

@FIND(*search-text,text, start-number*)

The @FIND function returns the position in the string *text* at which 1-2-3 finds the first occurrence of the string *search-text*, the search beginning at the *start-number* position.

search-text and *text* should be entered as text enclosed in double quotation marks (" "), as formulas that result in text, or the address or name of a cell that contains text or a formula that results in a label. *start-number* indicates the number of the character (offset from the beginning of the *text* string) at which to begin the search.

WARNING

You can generate an ERR in several ways by using @FIND. @FIND will return ERR if 1-2-3 does not find the *search-text* string in the *text* string, if *start-number* is a number larger than the number of characters in the *text* string, or if you enter a negative *start-number* (for example, by using a formula to produce the number without using @ABS to make sure it is positive). Note that @FIND is case-sensitive—@FIND("p","Philadelphia",0) will return 9 rather than 1 because it will find the lowercase *p* rather than the uppercase *P*.

@FIND can be particularly useful to extract information from a spreadsheet entered into one column that you would normally enter into two columns for flexibility. For example, if one of your colleagues built a spreadsheet of employee names but put both first name and last name into the same field in column B, you could extract the last name from column B to column C by using the following function statement, as shown in Figure 20.1:

@MID(B5,0,@FIND(",",B5,0))

FIGURE 20.1

Using the @FIND function to extract information from a text string in a spreadsheet

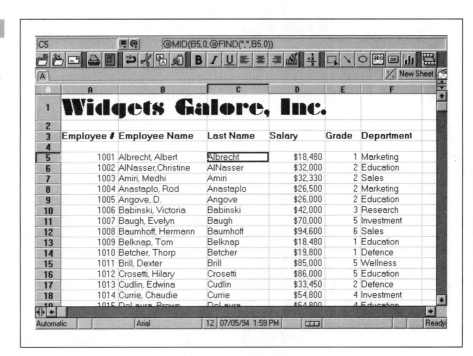

@LEFT(*text,number*)

The @LEFT function returns the first (leftmost) *number* of characters in *text*, where *text* is text enclosed in double quotation marks (" "), a formula resulting in text, or the address or name of a cell containing a label or a formula resulting in a label. *number* indicates the number of characters to return and can be a positive integer or 0 (in which case @LEFT will return an empty string).

WARNING Note that @LEFT will return all of *text* if *number* is greater than the length of the string *text*. If you run @LEFT on an empty cell, @LEFT returns an empty cell. Consider using the @ISEMPTY function before using @LEFT if it is important for you to retrieve a text string with at least some contents.

Use @LEFT when you need to copy part of a label into another cell—for example, to truncate phone numbers into area codes, as shown in the example in Figure 20.2. In the figure, cell E4 contains this function statement to retrieve the first three characters from cell D4:

@LEFT(D4,3)

TIP When using @LEFT, bear in mind that it will count spaces and punctuation as one character each. Note also that in Figure 20.2 the telephone numbers were entered as labels rather than as values—each is prefaced by a single quote (').

TIP If you're not sure how many characters you need to extract from a string, you can use @LEFT in combination with @FIND. For example, if you wanted to return the first name from a cell named BOTHNAMES that contained a first name and a last name separated by a space (for example, Paulette Jones), you could use @LEFT(BOTHNAMES,@FIND("*",BOTHNAMES,0)) to return the first name, Paulette. (The * makes @FIND search for one space.)

See Also @MID, @RIGHT

FIGURE 20.2

Using the @LEFT function to copy part of a label from one cell to another

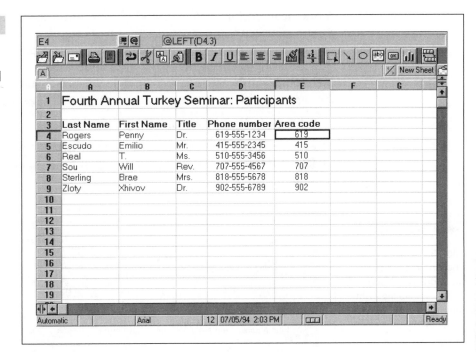

E4		@LEFT(D4,3)					
	A	**B**	**C**	**D**	**E**	**F**	**G**
1	Fourth Annual Turkey Seminar: Participants						
2							
3	Last Name	First Name	Title	Phone number	Area code		
4	Rogers	Penny	Dr.	619-555-1234	619		
5	Escudo	Emilio	Mr.	415-555-2345	415		
6	Real	T.	Ms.	510-555-3456	510		
7	Sou	Will	Rev.	707-555-4567	707		
8	Sterling	Brae	Mrs.	818-555-5678	818		
9	Zloty	Xhivov	Dr.	902-555-6789	902		

Automatic   Arial   12 07/05/94 2:03 PM   Ready

@LENGTH(*text*)

The @LENGTH function returns the number of characters in a string, *text*, where *text* is text entered in double quotation marks (" "), a formula resulting in text, or the address or name of a cell containing a label or a formula resulting in a label. When using @LENGTH, bear in mind that it will count spaces and punctuation as one character each.

For example, the following function statement returns 10, the number of characters in the string:

@LENGTH("Chapter 20")

TIP

To strip unwanted spaces from a text string, use the @TRIM function in conjunction with the @LENGTH function.

A practical use for the @LENGTH function is to check that the entry for a particular cell is the right length. For example, if you divided telephone numbers into area codes and local numbers in a database, you could use @LENGTH to check that each area code was three digits long and that each local number was seven digits long, as illustrated in Figure 20.3. In the figure, cell E4 contains the following function statement:

@IF(@LENGTH(D4)=3,"","ERROR!")

This returns nothing if the area code is three digits long, but returns ERROR! if it is not three digits long. Cell F4 contains a similar function statement.

FIGURE 20.3

Using the @LENGTH function to check that area codes and local numbers have the right number of digits apiece

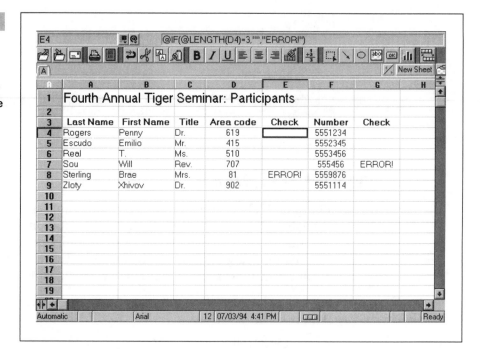

@LOWER(*text*)

The @LOWER function converts all the letters in a string, *text*, to lower-case, where *text* is text entered in double quotation marks (" "), a formula resulting in text, or the address or name of a cell containing a label or a formula resulting in a label.

For example, the following function statement returns the word *serpentine* in lowercase:

@LOWER("SERPENTINE")

To return the first letter of a word or string as a lowercase letter—for example, if you wanted to extract the first letter of a word for alphabetical filing —you can combine the @LOWER function with the @LEFT function, as in the following function statement:

@LOWER(@LEFT("Employee Policies",1)

This returns *e*, the first letter of Employee Policies.

If you run @LOWER on a number, 1-2-3 will return an error. For example, the following function statement will return ERR:

@LOWER(987654)

But if you enclose the number in double quotation marks (" "), @LOWER will return it as a label. For example, the following function statement returns 987654:

@LOWER("987654")

Figure 20.4 illustrates the use of the @LOWER function. In this worksheet containing customer occupations pulled unsatisfactorily in all uppercase from a database, cell E2 contains the following function statement to lowercase the occupation:

@LOWER(B2)

WARNING Because capitalization will affect the sort order of labels, it is often a good idea to use @LOWER (or @UPPER or @PROPER, whichever seems more appropriate) to establish consistent capitalization before using Range ➤ Sort or Query ➤ Sort.

See Also @PROPER, @UPPER

Using the @LOWER
function to lowercase
labels

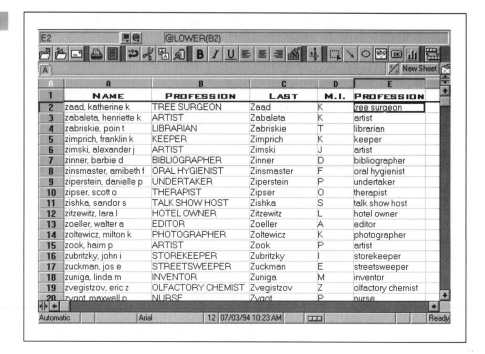

@MID(*text,start-number, number*)

The @MID function returns the specified *number* of characters from a *text* string, beginning with the character at the offset specified by *start-number*.

The arguments for the @ function are as follows:

ARGUMENT	DESCRIPTION
text	Text entered in double quotation marks (""), a formula resulting in text, or the address or name of a cell containing a label or a formula resulting in a label.

ARGUMENT	DESCRIPTION
start-number	The offset number at which @MID is to start. @MID will return an empty string if *start-number* is larger than the length of *text*.
number	Any positive integer or 0, indicating the number of characters for @MID to return. @MID will return all the characters from *start-number* to the end of *text* if *number* is larger than the length of *text* from *start-number* to its end.

Figure 20.5 illustrates the power of the @MID function. In this human resources worksheet for the MidString Corporation, the employee number, last name, and first name share a cell. To break the information out into its three component parts, the worksheet uses the following three

FIGURE 20.5

Using the @MID function to extract information from strings

B5   @MID(A5,@FIND(" ",A5,1),20)

	A	B	C	D	E	F	G
1	MIDSTRING CORPORATION						
2							
3	Employee # and Name	Name	Last	First	Salary	Grade	Departm
4							
5	#1001 Albrecht, Albert	Albrecht, Albert	Albrecht	Albert	$18,480	1	Marketing
6	#1002 AlNasser, Christine	AlNasser, Christine	AlNasser	Christine	$32,000	2	Education
7	#1003 Amiri, Medhi	Amiri, Medhi	Amiri	Medhi	$32,330	2	Sales
8	#1004 Anastaplo, Rod	Anastaplo, Rod	Anastaplo	Rod	$26,500	2	Marketing
9	#1005 Angove, D.	Angove, D.	Angove	D.	$26,000	2	Education
10	#1006 Babinski, Victoria	Babinski, Victoria	Babinski	Victoria	$42,000	3	Research
11	#1007 Baugh, Evelyn	Baugh, Evelyn	Baugh	Evelyn	$70,000	5	Investmen
12	#1008 Baumhoff, Hermann	Baumhoff, Hermann	Baumhoff	Hermann	$94,600	6	Sales
13	#1009 Belknap, Tom	Belknap, Tom	Belknap	Tom	$18,480	1	Education
14	#1010 Betcher, Thorp	Betcher, Thorp	Betcher	Thorp	$19,800	1	Defence
15	#1011 Brill, Dexter	Brill, Dexter	Brill	Dexter	$85,000	5	Wellness
16	#1012 Crosetti, Hilary	Crosetti, Hilary	Crosetti	Hilary	$86,000	5	Education
17	#1013 Cudlin, Edwina	Cudlin, Edwina	Cudlin	Edwina	$33,450	2	Defence
18	#1014 Currie, Chaudie	Currie, Chaudie	Currie	Chaudie	$54,800	4	Investmen
19	#1015 DeLaura, Brown	DeLaura, Brown	DeLaura	Brown	$54,800	4	Education

Automatic   Arial   12 07/03/94 5:19 PM   Ready

@MID function statements:

@MID(A5,@FIND(" ",A5,1),20)

This first function statement (in cell B5) finds the space after the employee number in cell A5 and returns the remainder of the contents of cell A5. Then, in cell C5, the following function statement returns the contents of cell B5 up to the comma:

@MID(B5,0,@FIND(",",B5,0))

Finally, in cell D5, the following function statement returns the contents of cell B5 after the space:

@MID(B5,@FIND(" ",B5,2),20)

WARNING

Remember that the @MID function counts punctuation and spaces as characters. If you're not sure how many characters you want to retrieve, enter a suitably large number to retrieve all of the *text* from *start-number* onward.

See Also @LEFT, @RIGHT

@PROPER

The @PROPER function converts all the letters in a string, *text*, to initial capital style, where *text* is text entered in double quotation marks (" "), a formula resulting in text, or the address or name of a cell containing a label or a formula resulting in a label. In initial capital style, the first case of each word is uppercase and the rest of each word is lowercase.

For example, the following function statement returns Rattlesnake City in initial capital style:

@PROPER("RATTLESNAKE city")

If you run @PROPER on a number, 1-2-3 will return an error. For example, the following function statement will return ERR:

@PROPER(987654)

But if you enclose the number in double quotation marks (" "), @PROPER will return it as a label. For example, the following function statement returns 987654:

@PROPER("987654")

Figure 20.6 illustrates the use of the @PROPER function. In this worksheet containing customer occupations pulled unsatisfactorily in all uppercase from a database, cell C2 contains the following function statement to return the last name in initial capital style:

@PROPER(@LEFT(A2,@FIND(",",A2,1)))

For example, the label in cell A2 is returned as Zaad in cell C2 by this function statement.

FIGURE 20.6

Using the @PROPER function to return labels in initial-capital style

	A	B	C	D	E
1	**NAME**	**PROFESSION**	**LAST**	**M.I.**	**PROFESSION**
2	zaad, katherine k	TREE SURGEON	Zaad	K	tree surgeon
3	zabaleta, henriette k	ARTIST	Zabaleta	K	artist
4	zabriskie, poin t	LIBRARIAN	Zabriskie	T	librarian
5	zimprich, franklin k	KEEPER	Zimprich	K	keeper
6	zimski, alexander j	ARTIST	Zimski	J	artist
7	zinner, barbie d	BIBLIOGRAPHER	Zinner	D	bibliographer
8	zinsmaster, amibeth f	ORAL HYGIENIST	Zinsmaster	F	oral hygienist
9	ziperstein, danielle p	UNDERTAKER	Ziperstein	P	undertaker
10	zipser, scott o	THERAPIST	Zipser	O	therapist
11	zishka, sandor s	TALK SHOW HOST	Zishka	S	talk show host
12	zitzewitz, lara l	HOTEL OWNER	Zitzewitz	L	hotel owner
13	zoeller, walter a	EDITOR	Zoeller	A	editor
14	zoltewicz, milton k	PHOTOGRAPHER	Zoltewicz	K	photographer
15	zook, haim p	ARTIST	Zook	P	artist
16	zubritzky, john i	STOREKEEPER	Zubritzky	I	storekeeper
17	zuckman, jos e	STREETSWEEPER	Zuckman	E	streetsweeper
18	zuniga, linda m	INVENTOR	Zuniga	M	inventor
19	zvegistzov, eric z	OLFACTORY CHEMIST	Zvegistzov	Z	olfactory chemist
20	zygot, maxwell n	NURSE	Zygot	P	nurse

A:C2 @PROPER(@LEFT(A2,@FIND(",",A2,1)))

Automatic | Arial | 12 | 07/03/94 10:25 AM | | Ready

20

Text Functions

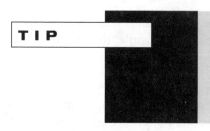

TIP

Because capitalization will affect the sort order of labels, it is often a good idea to use @PROPER (or @UPPER or @LOWER, whichever seems more appropriate) to establish consistent capitalization before using Range ➤ Sort or Query ➤ Sort.

See Also @PROPER, @UPPER

@REPEAT(*text,number*)

The @REPEAT function repeats a string, *text*, the number of times specified by *number*, where *text* is text entered in double quotation marks (""), a formula resulting in text, or the address or name of a cell containing a label or a formula resulting in a label; and *number* is any positive integer.

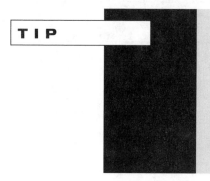

TIP

The main difference between the @REPEAT function and the repeating label-prefix character \ (the backslash) is that the @REPEAT function does not stop when the column is full but continues repeating the label up to the *number* specified. This can be handy if you need to fill in a row across a specific number of columns quickly—entering an @REPEAT function statement in the first cell can be quicker than entering \– and then copying it across the row.

For example, the following function statement produces **INVALID RESULTS** stretching across the worksheet:

    @REPEAT("**INVALID RESULTS**",20)

@REPLACE(*original-text,start-number,number,new-text*)

The @REPLACE function replaces the specified *number* of characters in the string *original-text* with the characters in *new-text*, starting at *start-number*.

The arguments for the @ function are as follows:

ARGUMENT	DESCRIPTION
original-text	The text to be replaced or added to, entered in double quotation marks (" "), a formula resulting in text, or the address or name of a cell containing a label or a formula resulting in a label.
start-number	Any positive value or 0, indicating the offset number of the character in *original-text* for @REPLACE to start at. Note that @REPLACE will append *new-text* to *original-text* if *start-number* is greater than the length of *original-text*.
number	Any positive integer or 0, indicating the number of characters in *original-text* that @REPLACE is to replace with *new-text*. A value of 0 for *number* indicates that @REPLACE should insert *new-text* without replacing any characters of *original-text*.
new-text	The text for @REPLACE to insert at *start-number* in the *original-text* string, text entered in double quotation marks (" "), a formula resulting in text, or the address or name of a cell containing a label or a formula resulting in a label.

20

Text Functions

TIP

Remember that punctuation and spaces count as characters for text functions such as @REPLACE, and include them in your calculations.

For example, consider the worksheet shown in Figure 20.7, which contains the Annual Crime Statistics for Anytown PD. For speed of assembly, column C contains @REPLACE function statements to change the labels in column A. For example, cell C3 contains the following function statement to replace the three letters of DUI in cell A3 with the word Assault:

@REPLACE(A3,5,3,"Assault")

The five-character offset takes care of the four characters of the year and the space following it.

FIGURE 20.7

Using the @REPLACE function to replace a text string

	A	B	C	D	E	F	G	H
C10			@REPLACE(A10,@FIND("DUI",A10,0),3,"Assault")					
1	**Anytown PD: Annual Crime Statistics**							
2								
3	1991 DUI	98	1991 Assault	23	1991 Battery	6	1991 Manslaughter	1
4	1992 DUI	101	1992 Assault	26	1992 Battery	4	1992 Manslaughter	0
5	1993 DUI	111	1993 Assault	44	1993 Battery	7	1993 Manslaughter	1
6	1994 DUI	94	1994 Assault	11	1994 Battery	8	1994 Manslaughter	2
7	1995 DUI	NA	1995 Assault	NA	1995 Battery	NA	1995 Manslaughter	NA
8								
9	**1995**		**1995**		**1995**		**1995**	
10	January DUI	4	January Assault	4	January Battery	0	January Homicide	0
11	February DUI	11	February Assault	3	February Battery	0	February Homicide	0
12	March DUI	8	March Assault	5	March Battery	1	March Homicide	1
13	April DUI	23	April Assault	2	April Battery	0	April Homicide	0
14	May DUI	4	May Assault	1	May Battery	0	May Homicide	0
15	June DUI	NA	June Assault	NA	June Battery	NA	June Homicide	NA
16	July DUI	NA	July Assault	NA	July Battery	NA	July Homicide	NA
17	August DUI	NA	August Assault	NA	August Battery	NA	August Homicide	NA
18	September DUI	NA	September Assault	NA	September Battery	NA	September Homicide	NA
19	October DUI	NA	October Assault	NA	October Battery	NA	October Homicide	NA
20	November DUI	NA	November Assault	NA	November Battery	NA	November Homicide	NA

Automatic | Arial | 12 | 07/03/94 2:48 PM | | | Ready

But in many cases, you won't know a consistent *start-number* to use with @REPLACE. In such cases, you can use the @FIND function to search for the relevant label, as in the following function statement contained in cell C10:

> @REPLACE(A10,@FIND("DUI",A10,0),3,"Assault")

The @FIND function finds DUI, which is then replaced by Assault.

@RIGHT(*text,number*)

The @RIGHT function returns the last (rightmost) *number* of characters in *text*, where *text* is text enclosed in double quotation marks (" "), a formula resulting in text, or the address or name of a cell containing a label or a formula resulting in a label. *number* indicates the number of characters to return and can be a positive integer or 0 (in which case @RIGHT will return an empty string).

WARNING Note that @RIGHT will return all of *text* if *number* is greater than the length of the string *text*. If you run @RIGHT on an empty cell, @RIGHT returns an empty cell. Consider using the @ISEMPTY function before using @RIGHT if it is important for you to retrieve a text string with at least some contents.

Use @RIGHT when you need to copy part of a label into another cell—for example, to shear phone numbers of their area codes, as shown in the example in Figure 20.8. Cell F4 contains this function statement to retrieve the last eight characters from cell D4:

> @RIGHT(D4,8)

FIGURE 20.8

Using the @RIGHT function to copy part of a label from one cell to another

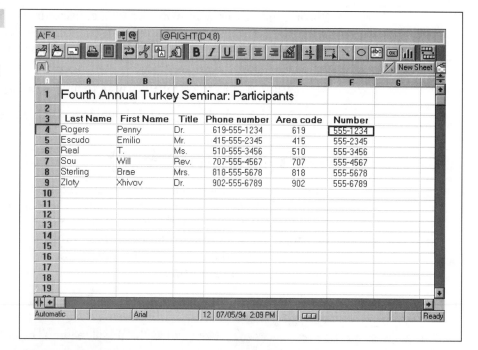

```
A:F4                  @RIGHT(D4,8)
```

	A	B	C	D	E	F	G
1	Fourth Annual Turkey Seminar: Participants						
2							
3	Last Name	First Name	Title	Phone number	Area code	Number	
4	Rogers	Penny	Dr.	619-555-1234	619	555-1234	
5	Escudo	Emilio	Mr.	415-555-2345	415	555-2345	
6	Real	T.	Ms.	510-555-3456	510	555-3456	
7	Sou	Will	Rev.	707-555-4567	707	555-4567	
8	Sterling	Brae	Mrs.	818-555-5678	818	555-5678	
9	Zloty	Xhivov	Dr.	902-555-6789	902	555-6789	
10							
11							
12							
13							
14							
15							
16							
17							
18							
19							

```
Automatic          Arial          12  07/05/94  2:09 PM                Ready
```

TIP

When using @RIGHT, bear in mind that it will count spaces and punctuation as one character each—that's why the function statement is @RIGHT(D4,8) rather than @RIGHT(D4,7), as D4 contains hyphens to separate the groups of numbers. Note also that in Figure 20.8 the telephone numbers were entered as labels rather than as values—each is prefaced by a single quotation mark (').

TIP

If you're not sure how many characters you need to extract from a string, you can use @RIGHT in combination with @FIND. For example, if you wanted to return the last name from a cell named BOTHNAMES that contained a first name and a last name separated by a space (for example, Paulette Jones), you could use @RIGHT(BOTHNAMES,@FIND("*",BOTHNAMES,0) to return the last name, Jones. (The * makes @FIND search for one space.)

See Also @LEFT, @MID

20

Text Functions

@S(*range*)

The @S function returns the entry in the first cell in *range* as a label, where *range* is a cell address or a range name. If the entry in the first cell of the range is a value, @S returns a blank cell.

For example, consider the Pandora's Ponies worksheet shown in Figure 20.9. Cell A12 contains the following function statement:

@S(A5..A8)

This returns Ponies, since Ponies is the label in the first cell of the range A5..A8. If the range were A3..A8, the function statement would return a blank cell because cell A3 contains a value (1995).

The @S function can be very useful in macros to check that a user enters a label where you need one. For example, you could use the following function statement:

{IF @S(C1)=""}{BEEP}

This would cause a macro to beep if a user entered a value in cell C1 (because @S returns a blank cell for a value).

See Also @ISSTRING, @N

@SETSTRING(*text,length,* [*alignment*])

The @SETSTRING function returns a label consisting of the number of characters specified by the *length* argument. The label consists of the *text* string and enough blank spaces to align *text* as specified by the *alignment* option.

The arguments for the @SETSTRING function are as follows:

ARGUMENT	DESCRIPTION
text	Any text.
length	An integer between 1 and 512 indicating the length of the string to be returned. If *length* is smaller than the number of characters in *text*, 1-2-3 returns *text*.

ARGUMENT	DESCRIPTION
alignment	0, 1, or 2, an optional argument specifying how to align *text*, as follows:

0   Specifies that *text* be aligned to the left of the extra spaces in *length*. 0 is the default setting if you omit the *alignment* argument.

1   Specifies that *text* be aligned in the center of the extra spaces in *length*. One leftover space is added to the left of *text* if there is an odd number of extra spaces.

= 2   Specifies that *text* be aligned to the right of the extra spaces in *length*.

Figure 20.10 demonstrates the use of the @SETSTRING function to align text. Cell A3 contains a function statement that aligns the phrase at

20

Text Functions

FIGURE 20.10

Using the
@SETSTRING function
to align text

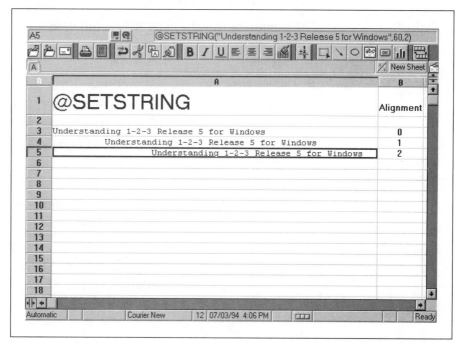

A5			@SETSTRING("Understanding 1-2-3 Release 5 for Windows",60,2)	

	A	B
1	@SETSTRING	Alignment
2		
3	Understanding 1-2-3 Release 5 for Windows	0
4	Understanding 1-2-3 Release 5 for Windows	1
5	Understanding 1-2-3 Release 5 for Windows	2
6		
7		
8		
9		
10		
11		
12		
13		
14		
15		
16		
17		
18		

Automatic   Courier New   12 07/03/94 4:06 PM   Ready

the left of the cell with the extra spaces to its right:

> @SETSTRING("Understanding 1-2-3 Release 5 for Windows",60)

This centers the phrase in the spaces:

> @SETSTRING("Understanding 1-2-3 Release 5 for Windows",60,1)

This aligns the phrase at the right of the cell with the extra spaces to its left:

> @SETSTRING("Understanding 1-2-3 Release 5 for Windows",60,2)

See Also @TRIM

@STRING(*numeric-value, decimal*)

The @STRING function converts the value *numeric-value* and returns it as a label using the format specified by *decimal*.

The arguments for the @STRING function are as follows:

Argument	Description
numeric-value	Any value.
decimal	An integer from the following list that determines the format in which @STRING returns the label:
	0–116 Fixed format, with *decimal* decimal places
	1000–116 Comma format, with decimal minus 1,000 decimal places
	−18 to −1 Scientific format, with @ABS (*decimal*) digits
	10001–10512 General format, up to decimal minus 10,000 characters

For example, the following function statement returns the label 1:

@STRING(1.31415927,0)

See page 333 in Chapter 5 for another example of how to use @STRING.

WARNING

The @STRING function does not convert formatting characters used on a cell, whether you add them to a cell or whether 1-2-3 adds them as a result of your having applied formatting. For example, both 45.67% and $45.67 would be returned by @STRING as 45.67.

See Also @VALUE

@TRIM(*text*)

The @TRIM function strips leading, trailing, and consecutive space characters from a *text* string, where *text* is text entered in double quotation marks (" "), a formula resulting in text, or the address or name of a cell containing a label or a formula resulting in a label.

For example, the following function statement strips extra spaces from the string and returns Wide-Eyed and Electric:

@TRIM(" Wide-Eyed   and Electric   ")

The @TRIM function is especially useful for ensuring regular presentation and sorting of information imported from other formats.

See Also @SETSTRING

@UPPER(*text*)

The @UPPER function converts all the letters in a string, *text*, to uppercase, where *text* is text entered in double quotation marks (" "), a formula resulting in text, or the address or name of a cell containing a label or a formula resulting in a label.

For example, the following function statement returns ANACONDA in uppercase:

@UPPER("anaconda")

To return the first letter of a word as an uppercase letter—for example, if you wanted to reduce a name to an initial—you can combine the @UPPER function with the @LEFT function, as in the following function statement:

@UPPER(@LEFT("gordon shumway",1)

This returns G, the first letter of Gordon.

If you run @UPPER on a number, 1-2-3 will return an error. For example, the following function statement will return ERR:

@UPPER(123456)

But if you enclose the number in double quotation marks (" "), @UPPER will return it as a label. For example, the following function statement returns 123456:

@UPPER("123456")

Figure 20.11 illustrates the use of the @UPPER function. In this worksheet containing customer names pulled clumsily in all uppercase from a database with the last name, first name, and middle initial all in one cell, cell D2 contains the following function statement to pull out and change the middle initial to lowercase:

@UPPER(@RIGHT(A2,1))

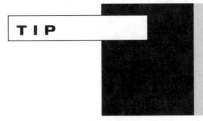

TIP Because capitalization will affect the sort order of labels, it is often a good idea to use @UPPER (or @PROPER or @ LOWER, whichever seems more appropriate) to establish consistent capitalization before using Range ➤ Sort or Query ➤ Sort.

See Also @LOWER, @PROPER

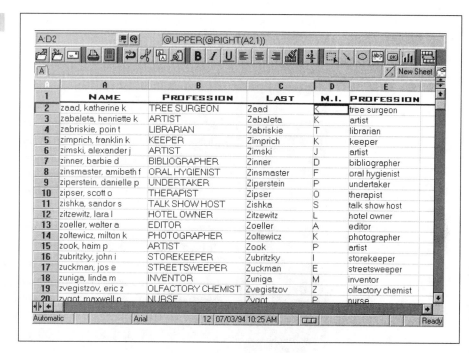

@VALUE(*text*)

The @VALUE function converts a number entered as a *text* string to its corresponding value, where *text* is text in double quotation marks (" ") or a label that contains numbers only.

text must be in one of the four recognized formats:

- Fixed format: 111.99
- Scientific format: 1.11 E2
- Mixed number format: 1 1/4
- Formatted number: 11.99%

See page 333 in Chapter 5 for more examples of using the @VALUE function.

For example, the following function statement returns the value .1199:

@VALUE("11.99%")

WARNING

While the @VALUE function ignores leading and trailing spaces, it will return ERR if the *text* string contains spaces between symbols and numbers (e.g., 11.99%) or if the *text* string contains any non-numeric characters. @VALUE returns 0 if *text* is a blank cell or an empty string.

TIP

You can replace a @VALUE function statement with the value it produces by pressing F2 and then F9 in the relevant cell. To assemble a formula using @VALUE, you need to repeat @VALUE. For example, @VALUE("100"+"500") is not valid and returns 0, but @VALUE("100")+@VALUE("500") returns 600.

See Also @STRING

Macro

Commands

Reference

THIS chapter provides a detailed reference to 1-2-3's macro language, which provides you with commands sufficient to automate almost any task you'll need to undertake in 1-2-3. If you need to resize the 1-2-3 window every time you start the application, load groups of four files at once, or create table upon table in an external database, the 1-2-3 macro language can make your life much easier.

The macro language includes more than three hundred macro commands; these commands fall into the following categories:

MACRO COMMANDS	PURPOSE	SEE PAGE
Chart	Create, modify, and manipulate charts.	1061
Data-Manipulation	Append data ranges, erase cells, store values, and recalculate.	1078
Database	Create, modify, and query databases.	1085
DDE and OLE	Create and maintain links and objects.	1105
Edit	Perform Edit menu commands (e.g., insert and delete; cut and move; search and replace).	1120
File	Perform File menu commands (e.g., opening, saving, and printing files).	1132

MACRO COMMANDS	PURPOSE	SEE PAGE
Flow-of-Macro	Control macros and subroutines.	1150
Keystroke Equivalents	Replicate the effect of certain keystrokes.	1160
Navigation	Move to locations or select items.	1163
Range	Perform Range menu commands (e.g., filling and sorting).	1171
SmartIcons	Perform the functions of popular SmartIcons (e.g., SmartSum and SortAscending).	1187
Solver	Perform the Range ➤ Analyze ➤ Backsolver and Solver commands.	1188
Style	Perform Style menu commands (e.g., changing column width, formatting styles).	1194
Text-File Manipulation	Perform operations with text files (e.g., open, close, read, and write).	1211
Tools	Perform Tools menu commands (e.g., audit, spell-checking).	1217
User Environment	Control macros (e.g., allowing user input) and create custom menus.	1225

21

Macro Commands

MACRO COMMANDS	PURPOSE	SEE PAGE
Version Manager	Perform the Range ➤ Version Manager commands (controlling scenarios and versions).	1250
Window and Screen Display	Control the screen display and size windows.	1260

The next section of this chapter, "Overview of the Macro Commands," contains an alphabetical list of all the macro commands, with a brief description of each and a reference to the page on which to find a detailed discussion of the command. In the section after that, "Using Macro Commands," you will find a brief reminder of the structure of macros and how to enter them in your worksheets. The rest of the chapter provides discussions of the macro commands.

Overview of the Macro Commands

For quick reference, the macro commands are listed in alphabetical order in Table 21.1, together with page numbers indicating where to find the detailed descriptions of the macro commands.

TABLE 21.1: Macro Commands Quick Reference

MACRO COMMAND	ACTION	SEE PAGE
{ -- comment}	Puts a comment into a macro	1220
{?}	Suspends macro execution until the user presses ↵	1225
{ADDIN-INVOKE}	Starts an add-in application	1217

TABLE 21.1: Macro Commands Quick Reference (continued)

MACRO COMMAND	ACTION	SEE PAGE
{ADDIN-LOAD}	Reads the specified add-in module into memory	1217
{ADDIN-REMOVE}	Removes the specified add-in from memory	1218
{ADDIN-REMOVE-ALL}	Removes all add-ins from memory	1218
{ALERT}	Displays a message box with the specified message and icon	1225
{APP-ADJUST}	Moves and scales the 1-2-3 window	1260
{APP-STATE}	Minimizes, maximizes, or restores the 1-2-3 window	1261
{APPENDBELOW}	Copies the contents of the specified source-location to the rows immediately below the specified target-location	1078
{APPENDRIGHT}	Copies the contents of the specified source-location to the columns immediately to the right of the specified target-location	1079
{AUDIT}	Highlights or produces a report of all formulas, or the relationships of values and formulas, or on circular references, file links, or DDE links	1106, 1219
{BACKSOLVE}	Finds values for one or more cells that make the result of a formula equal to a value specified	1188

21

Macro Commands

TABLE 21.1: Macro Commands Quick Reference (continued)

MACRO COMMAND	ACTION	SEE PAGE
{BEEP}	Sounds the Windows beep	1226
{BLANK}	Erases the contents of the specified location without changing the formatting of the cells or forcing recalculation	1079
{BRANCH}	Transfers macro control from the current macro instruction to the specified location and does not return to the calling macro	1150
{BREAK}	Clears the edit line when data is being entered or edited, or leaves the current dialog box during selection of a 1-2-3 command, and returns 1-2-3 to READY mode	1261
{BREAKOFF}	Disables the Ctrl+Break key combination while a macro is running	1227
{BREAKON}	Reactivates the Ctrl+Break key combination	1228
{CELL-ENTER}	Enters the specified data in the specified target-location	1163
{CHART-ASSIGN-RANGE}	Assigns all data ranges for the current chart	1061
{CHART-AXIS-INTERVALS}	Changes the intervals between X-axis, Y-axis, or 2nd Y-axis tick marks in the current chart	1062
{CHART-AXIS-LIMITS}	Creates a scale for the X-axis, Y-axis, or 2nd Y-axis for the current chart	1063

TABLE 21.1: Macro Commands Quick Reference (continued)

MACRO COMMAND	ACTION	SEE PAGE
{CHART-AXIS-SCALE-TYPE}	Indicates the type of scale to use for an axis in the current chart	1064
{CHART-AXIS-TICKS}	Specifies major and minor tick marks for an axis in the specified chart	1064
{CHART-AXIS-TITLE}	Changes an axis title in the current chart	1065
{CHART-AXIS-UNITS}	Changes the magnitude of the axis units and the axis-unit titles for the current chart	1066
{CHART-COLOR-RANGE}	Sets the color for each value in a data series in the current chart	1067
{CHART-DATA-LABELS}	Creates labels for data points or bars in the current chart	1067
{CHART-FOOTNOTE}	Adds chart footnotes to the current chart	1068
{CHART-GRID}	Displays or hides grid lines for an axis in the current chart	1069
{CHART-LEGEND}	Creates legend labels that identify the colors, symbols, or patterns of the current chart's data series	1070
{CHART-NEW}	Draws a chart using data from the currently selected range	1071
{CHART-PATTERN-RANGE}	Sets the pattern for each value in a data series in the current chart	1072

21

Macro Commands

TABLE 21.1: Macro Commands Quick Reference (continued)

MACRO COMMAND	ACTION	SEE PAGE
{CHART-PIE-LABELS}	Creates labels for the current pie chart	1072
{CHART-PIE-SLICE-EXPLOSION}	Explodes the chosen slices in the current pie chart	1073
{CHART-RANGE}	Sets the data range, series type, and 2nd Y-axis flag for a data series in the current chart	1073
{CHART-RANGE-DELETE}	Deletes the specified series from the current chart	1074
{CHART-RENAME}	Renames a chart	1074
{CHART-SET-PREFERRED}	Defines the current chart's type as the default chart type and defines the selected chart's grid settings as the default grid settings	1075
{CHART-TITLE}	Adds chart titles to the chosen position in the current chart	1075
{CHART-TYPE}	Changes the current chart to the type specified	1076
{CHART-USE-PREFERRED}	Changes the current chart to the default chart type and changes the current chart's grid settings to the default grid settings	1077
{CHOOSE-FILE}	Displays a Windows common dialog box containing a list of files	1228

TABLE 21.1: Macro Commands Quick Reference (continued)

MACRO COMMAND	ACTION	SEE PAGE
{CHOOSE-ITEM}	Displays a dialog box containing a list of data items	1229
{CHOOSE-MANY}	Displays a dialog box from which the user can select one or more check boxes (up to a maximum of eight check boxes)	1230
{CHOOSE-ONE}	Displays a dialog box and waits for the user to select an option button, then runs the associated macro	1231
{CLOSE}	Closes the text file opened with an {OPEN} command and saves any changes made to the file	1211
{COLUMN-WIDTH}	Adjusts columns in the given range to the width specified	1194
{COLUMN-WIDTH-FIT-WIDEST}	Adjusts columns in the given range to the width of the widest entries	1194
{COLUMN-WIDTH-RESET}	Resets the columns in the given range to the default column width	1195
{COMMIT}	Commits (finalizes) pending external database transactions	1085
{CONTENTS}	Copies the contents of the specified source-location to the specified target-location as a label without forcing recalculation	1080

MACRO COMMANDS REFERENCE

TABLE 21.1: Macro Commands Quick Reference (continued)

MACRO COMMAND	ACTION	SEE PAGE
{CROSSTAB}	Creates a cross-tabulation table for the database table indicated and places it on a new worksheet after the worksheet containing the database table	1086
{DATA-TABLE-1}	Substitutes values for one variable in one or more formulas and enters the results in the specified output-range	1172
{DATA-TABLE-2}	Substitutes values for two variables in one formula and enters the results in the specified output-range	1172
{DATA-TABLE-3}	Substitutes values for three variables in one formula and enters the results in the specified output-range	1173
{DATA-TABLE-RESET}	Clears the ranges and input-cell settings for all what-if tables in the current file	1175
{DATABASE-APPEND}	Adds new records to the specified database-table	1086
{DATABASE-CONNECT}	Connects the worksheet to an external database table	1087
{DATABASE-CREATE-TABLE}	Sets up the structure for and connects to a new table in an external database	1088
{DATABASE-DELETE}	Deletes the records from the specified database-table that meet the specified criteria	1090

TABLE 21.1: Macro Commands Quick Reference (continued)

MACRO COMMAND	ACTION	SEE PAGE
{DATABASE-DISCONNECT}	Disconnects an external table, ending all data exchange between 1-2-3 and the external table	1090
{DATABASE-FIND}	Locates and selects records in the specified database-table that meet the specified criteria	1091
{DATABASE-SEND-COMMAND}	Sends a command to an external database	1091
{DDE-ADVISE}	Specifies the macro to be executed when changes are made to data in the server application	1107
{DDE-CLOSE}	Terminates the specified DDE link with a Windows application	1108
{DDE-EXECUTE}	Sends a command string to a DDE server application	1108
{DDE-OPEN}	Opens a link to a running Windows server application	1109
{DDE-POKE}	Sends a range of data from 1-2-3 to a DDE server application during the current conversation	1110
{DDE-REQUEST}	Receives data from a Windows server application	1110
{DDE-TABLE}	Creates a table of all active DDE links in the active files	1111
{DDE-UNADVISE}	Ends a {DDE-ADVISE} command	1112

21

Macro Commands

TABLE 21.1: Macro Commands Quick Reference (continued)

MACRO COMMAND	ACTION	SEE PAGE
{DDE-USE}	Makes the specified conversation current, so that subsequent DDE macro commands refer to it	1112
{DEFINE}	Specifies where to store arguments passed to a subroutine in a {subroutine} command	1151
{DELETE-COLUMNS}	Deletes the whole of each column specified or the part of each column specified that falls within the specified range	1120
{DELETE-ROWS}	Deletes the whole of each row specified or the part of each row specified that falls within the specified range	1121
{DELETE-SHEETS}	Deletes the worksheets containing cells in the specified range	1121
{DIALOG}	Displays a custom dialog box created with the Lotus Dialog Editor and saved in a dialog-description table range	1234
{DIALOG?}	Displays the specified 1-2-3 dialog box	1233
{DISPATCH}	Branches indirectly to the cell specified, allowing you to branch the macro in various possible directions	1152
{DISTRIBUTION}	Creates a frequency distribution by counting how many values in the given values-range fall within each numeric interval bin	1175

TABLE 21.1: Macro Commands Quick Reference (continued)

MACRO COMMAND	ACTION	SEE PAGE
{EDIT-CLEAR}	Deletes selected data and formatting	1122
{EDIT-COPY}	Copies data and related formatting from the worksheet to the Clipboard	1122
{EDIT-COPY-FILL}	Copies the contents of the specified row, column, or worksheet in the specified range to all the other cells in the range	1123
{EDIT-CUT}	Cuts the specified data and its formatting from the worksheet to the Clipboard	1123
{EDIT-FIND}	Finds the first occurrence of specified text in labels, formulas, or both	1124
{EDIT-FIND?}	Displays the Edit Find and Replace dialog box	1125
{EDIT-GOTO}	Selects all or part of a range, query table, chart, or other drawn object, and then scrolls to it	1164
{EDIT-OBJECT}	Executes a verb for the currently selected OLE embedded object	1113
{EDIT-PASTE}	Pastes whatever data and related formatting is on the Clipboard into the active worksheet file at the specified location and in the specified format	1125

21

Macro Commands

TABLE 21.1: Macro Commands Quick Reference (continued)

MACRO COMMAND	ACTION	SEE PAGE
{EDIT-PASTE-LINK}	Creates a link between a worksheet file and the file referenced on the Clipboard	1113
{EDIT-PASTE-SPECIAL}	Pastes the contents of the Clipboard into the worksheet in the specified location and with the specified properties	1126
{EDIT-QUICK-COPY}	Copies data and its formatting from the specified source range to the specified destination range, without using the Clipboard	1126
{EDIT-QUICK-MOVE}	Moves data and its formatting from the specified source range to the specified destination range, without using the Clipboard	1127
{EDIT-REPLACE}	Finds the first occurrence of specified text in labels, formulas, or both, and replaces it with the specified text	1127
{EDIT-REPLACE-ALL}	Finds and replaces all instances of specified characters in labels, formulas, or both	1128
{FILE-CLOSE}	Closes the current file, allowing you to discard any unsaved changes	1132
{FILE-COMBINE}	Combines data from a 1-2-3 worksheet file on disk with data in the current file, starting in the current cell	1133

TABLE 21.1: Macro Commands Quick Reference (continued)

MACRO COMMAND	ACTION	SEE PAGE
{FILE-EXIT}	Ends the 1-2-3 session, giving you the option to discard any unsaved changes in the open files	1133
{FILE-EXTRACT}	Saves the specified range to another file	1134
{FILE-GET-RESERVATION}	Gets the network reservation for the current file	1135
{FILE-IMPORT}	Imports data from the specified text file into the current file	1136
{FILE-NEW}	Creates a new file on disk and in memory and displays the new file in a new and current window	1137
{FILE-OPEN}	Reads a file into memory, makes it the current file, and moves the cell pointer to the cell it was in when the file was last saved	1138
{FILE-OPEN?}	Displays the File Open dialog box	1139
{FILE-RELEASE-RESERVATION}	Releases the network reservation for the current file	1140
{FILE-RETRIEVE}	Opens the specified file and replaces the current file in memory, then moves the cell pointer to the cell it was in when the file was last saved	1140
{FILE-SAVE}	Saves changes to the current file	1141
{FILE-SAVE-ALL}	Saves all open files	1142

TABLE 21.1: Macro Commands Quick Reference (continued)

MACRO COMMAND	ACTION	SEE PAGE
{FILE-SAVE-AS?}	Displays the Save As dialog box so that the user can choose a name under which to save the file	1143
{FILE-SEAL}	Seals the current file so that no changes can be made to it	1143
{FILE-SEAL-NETWORK-RESERVATION}	Seals the network reservation setting of the current file	1143
{FILE-UNSEAL}	Unseals the current file and releases its network reservation setting	1144
{FILE-UPDATE-LINKS}	Recalculates all formulas in the current file that are linked to other files	1129
{FILESIZE}	Counts the number of bytes in an open text file and enters the number in the specified location	1212
{FILL}	Enters a sequence of values in a specified range	1176
{FILL-BY-EXAMPLE}	Fills the specified range with a sequence of data patterned on the data include in the range	1177
{FOR}	Creates a FOR loop that repeatedly performs a subroutine call to a subroutine until the specified number of loops is reached	1152
{FORBREAK}	Cancels a FOR loop created by a {FOR} command	1153

TABLE 21.1: Macro Commands Quick Reference (continued)

MACRO COMMAND	ACTION	SEE PAGE
{FORM}	Suspends the execution of a macro temporarily so that the user can enter and edit data in the unprotected cells in the specified input-location	1234
{FORMBREAK}	Ends a {FORM} command, resuming macro execution with the command after the {FORM} command	1235
{FRAMEOFF}	Has no effect in 1-2-3 Release 4 or later but is included for compatibility with macros created in previous versions of 1-2-3. Use {SET} instead	1262
{FRAMEON}	Has no effect in 1-2-3 Release 4 or later but is included for compatibility with macros created in previous versions of 1-2-3. Use {SET} instead	1262
{GET}	Suspends macro execution to allow the user to enter a keystroke, which it records as a left-aligned label in the specified location	1235
{GET-FORMULA}	Displays a dialog box so that the user can enter a formula	1236
{GET-LABEL}	Displays a dialog box so that the user can enter a label	1237
{GET-NUMBER}	Displays a dialog box so that the user can enter a number or a numeric formula	1238

21

Macro Commands

TABLE 21.1: Macro Commands Quick Reference (continued)

MACRO COMMAND	ACTION	SEE PAGE
{GET-RANGE}	Displays a dialog box so that the user can enter a range name or address or a numeric formula	1239
{GETPOS}	Enters in the specified location the current byte-pointer position in an open text file	1212
{HIDE-COLUMNS}	Hides all columns in the specified range	1195
{HIDE-SHEETS}	Hides all sheets in the specified range	1196
{IF}	Evaluates the specified condition as TRUE or FALSE and executes the appropriate instruction	1154
{INDICATE}	Displays text in the 1-2-3 title bar	1263
{INSERT-COLUMNS}	Inserts blank whole columns or blank partial columns at the specified location	1129
{INSERT-OBJECT}	Starts or activates the selected application, creates an OLE object in it, and embeds the object in the worksheet, closing the server application if it was not already open	1114
{INSERT-ROWS}	Inserts blank whole rows or blank partial rows at the specified location	1130

TABLE 21.1: Macro Commands Quick Reference (continued)

MACRO COMMAND	ACTION	SEE PAGE
{INSERT-SHEETS}	Inserts one or more blank worksheets in the current file at the specified location	1131
{LAUNCH}	Starts the specified Windows application and (optionally) switches to it or to any other running application	1154
{LET}	Enters a number or left-aligned label in the specified location	1081
{LINK-ASSIGN}	Specifies a destination range for an OLE link or a DDE link	1115
{LINK-CREATE}	Creates a link between the current worksheet file and a Windows DDE or OLE server application without using the Clipboard	1115
{LINK-DEACTIVATE}	Deactivates a DDE or OLE link in the current worksheet so that it is not updated	1117
{LINK-DELETE}	Deletes the specified DDE or OLE link	1117
{LINK-REMOVE}	Removes the currently used destination range for a DDE or OLE link but leaves the data in the range	1118
{LINK-TABLE}	Builds a table of all DDE and OLE links associated with the current file	1118
{LINK-UPDATE}	Updates active DDE and OLE links, or activates and updates deactivated links	1119

TABLE 21.1: Macro Commands Quick Reference (continued)

MACRO COMMAND	ACTION	SEE PAGE
{LOOK}	Checks the typeahead buffer for keystrokes and records the first keystroke (if there is one) as a left-aligned label in the specified location	1240
{LOTUS-LAUNCH}	Starts a Lotus Windows application and optionally switches to it	1155
{MAP-NEW}	Draws a map of the specified type at the specified location, using data from the currently selected range	1220
{MAP-REDRAW}	Redraws all maps in the current file	1221
{MATRIX-INVERT}	Inverts a square matrix	1177
{MATRIX-MULTIPLY}	Multiplies the first specified matrix by the second specified matrix and produces a third matrix containing the results	1178
{MENU-COMMAND-ADD}	Adds a command to the specified pull-down menu	1243
{MENU-COMMAND-DISABLE}	Disables a command in a custom menu so that the command appears dimmed	1244
{MENU-COMMAND-ENABLE}	Enables a custom-menu command disabled with {MENU-COMMAND-DISABLE}	1244
{MENU-COMMAND-REMOVE}	Removes the specified command from the specified pull-down menu	1245

TABLE 21.1: Macro Commands Quick Reference (continued)

MACRO COMMAND	ACTION	SEE PAGE
{MENU-CREATE}	Replaces the current 1-2-3 menu bar with the specified customized menu bar	1245
{MENU-INSERT}	Adds the specified custom pull-down menu to the default 1-2-3 menu bar	1246
{MENU-RESET}	Displays the default 1-2-3 menu bar	1248
{MENUBRANCH}	Displays a dialog box containing customized menu for the user to make a choice, then branches to the macro instructions associated with that command	1241
{MENUCALL}	Displays a dialog box containing a customized menu for the user to make a choice, then performs a subroutine call to the associated macro instructions	1242
{MODELESS-DISMISS}	Closes the open modeless dialog box	1248
{MODELESS-DISPLAY}	Displays a modeless dialog box until 1-2-3 reaches another {MODELESS-DISPLAY} command, a {MODELESS-DISMISS} command, or the end of the macro	1248
{NAMED-STYLE-USE}	Applies the named style specified to the target range or query table	1196

21

Macro Commands

TABLE 21.1: Macro Commands Quick Reference (continued)

MACRO COMMAND	ACTION	SEE PAGE
{ONERROR}	Specifies where to branch for errors that occur while a macro is running	1156
{OPEN}	Opens a text file for read-only processing or for read-and-write processing, depending on the type of access specified	1213
{PAGE-BREAK-COLUMN}	Inserts or deletes a vertical page break to the left of the current column	1197
{PAGE-BREAK-ROW}	Inserts or deletes a horizontal page break above the current row	1197
{PANELOFF}	Freezes the control panel until 1-2-3 encounters a {PANELON} command or the macro ends	1263
{PANELON}	Unfreezes the control panel and the status line, restoring the display to normal	1264
{PARSE}	Parses long labels imported from a text file into separate columns of data of one or more types (values, dates, times, and labels)	1178
{PLAY}	Plays a .WAV file	1249
{PRINT}	Prints the current file with the current page settings	1144
{PRINT?}	Displays the File Print dialog box	1145

TABLE 21.1: Macro Commands Quick Reference (continued)

MACRO COMMAND	ACTION	SEE PAGE
{PRINT-NAME-ADD}	Saves the current page settings as named page settings with the specified name	1145
{PRINT-NAME-USE}	Retrieves the named page settings in the specified file and uses them as the current page settings	1145
{PRINT-RESET}	Returns the selected Margins, Print titles, and Header, Footer, Options, Compression, and Orientation settings to the default settings	1146
{PROTECT}	Turns protection back on for the specified range	1198
{PUT}	Enters a number or left-aligned label in a cell within the specified location	1082
{QUERY-ADD-FIELD}	Adds a field to the currently selected query table	1092
{QUERY-AGGREGATE}	Performs calculations on groups of data from a query table	1093
{QUERY-CHOOSE-FIELDS}	Specifies the fields to appear in the currently selected query table	1093
{QUERY-COPY-SQL}	Copies to the Clipboard the SQL command equivalent to the current query	1094
{QUERY-CRITERIA}	Specifies criteria to determine which records to display in a new or currently selected query table	1095

21

Macro Commands

TABLE 21.1: Macro Commands Quick Reference (continued)

MACRO COMMAND	ACTION	SEE PAGE
{QUERY-DATABASE-TABLE}	Changes the database table for the currently selected query table	1095
{QUERY-JOIN}	Enables you to query multiple database tables containing a common field	1096
{QUERY-NAME}	Renames the currently selected query table	1096
{QUERY-NEW}	Creates a query table containing the records specified from a database table	1097
{QUERY-OPTIONS}	Turns on and off options for manipulating data in the currently selected query table	1098
{QUERY-REFRESH}	Refreshes the currently selected query table after changes have been made to the database table, query options, criteria, or aggregate, so that the fields are accurate	1099
{QUERY-REMOVE-FIELD}	Removes the specified field from the currently selected query table and refreshes the query table	1099
{QUERY-SHOW-FIELD}	Creates an alias field name for the specified field in the currently selected query table	1100
{QUERY-SORT}	Sorts data in the currently selected query table in the specified order	1100

TABLE 21.1: Macro Commands Quick Reference (continued)

MACRO COMMAND	ACTION	SEE PAGE
{QUERY-SORT-KEY-DEFINE}	Defines the sort key for a {QUERY-SORT} command to use	1101
{QUERY-SORT-RESET}	Resets all sort keys that have been defined for the currently selected query table	1102
{QUERY-UPDATE}	Copies any changes made to records in the currently selected query table to the corresponding database table	1102
{QUERY-UPGRADE}	Upgrades a query from a previous version of 1-2-3 so that it works with the Query commands in 1-2-3 Release 5	1103
{QUIT}	Ends the current macro and returns keyboard control to the user	1157
{RANGE-NAME-CREATE}	Assigns a name to a range address	1179
{RANGE-NAME-DELETE}	Deletes a range name in the current file	1180
{RANGE-NAME-DELETE-ALL}	Deletes all range names contained in the current file	1180
{RANGE-NAME-LABEL-CREATE}	Names a single cell, using an existing label immediately adjacent to the cell	1180
{RANGE-NAME-TABLE}	Creates a two-column table containing the names of all defined ranges in the current file and their addresses	1181

21

Macro Commands

TABLE 21.1: Macro Commands Quick Reference (continued)

MACRO COMMAND	ACTION	SEE PAGE
{RANGE-TRANSPOSE}	Copies data from the specified origin to the specified destination, transposing the copied data and replacing any copied formulas with their current values	1182
{RANGE-VALUE}	Copies the contents and styles from the specified origin range to the specified destination range, replacing all copied formulas with their current values	1183
{RANGE-VERSION?}	Displays the Version Manager window in the form specified	1250
{READ}	Copies the specified number of bytes from the current byte-pointer position in the open text file to the specified location and increases the byte-pointer position by the relevant number of bytes	1213
{READLN}	Copies the rest of the current line of text in the open text file, starting from the current byte-pointer position, to the specified location	1214
{RECALC}	Recalculates the values in the specified location, one row at a time	1083
{RECALCCOL}	Recalculates the values in location, proceeding column by column	1084

TABLE 21.1: Macro Commands Quick Reference (continued)

MACRO COMMAND	ACTION	SEE PAGE
{REGISTER}	Registers a procedure in a Dynamic Link Library (DLL) as an add-in @function, and loads the DLL into memory	1221
{REGRESSION}	Performs multiple linear regression analysis and calculates the slope of the line that best fits the data	1183
{RESTART}	Clears the subroutine stack, ending the macro when the current subroutine ends	1158
{RETURN}	Returns macro control from a subroutine to the calling macro	1158
{ROLLBACK}	Cancels pending external database transactions	1104
{ROW-HEIGHT}	Adjusts each row in the specified range to the specified height in points	1198
{ROW-HEIGHT-FIT-LARGEST}	Adjusts each row in the specified range to the height of the largest font in that row	1198
{SCENARIO-ADD-VERSION}	Adds a version to a scenario	1251
{SCENARIO-CREATE}	Creates the specified scenario	1252
{SCENARIO-DELETE}	Deletes the specified scenario	1252
{SCENARIO-INFO}	Lets you modify the comment and sharing options for a scenario	1253

21

Macro Commands

TABLE 21.1: Macro Commands Quick Reference (continued)

MACRO COMMAND	ACTION	SEE PAGE
{SCENARIO-REMOVE-VERSION}	Removes the specified version from the specified scenario	1253
{SCENARIO-SHOW}	Displays the selected scenario in the worksheet	1254
{SCROLL-COLUMNS}	Scrolls horizontally by the specified number of columns in the current worksheet without changing the current cell	1165
{SCROLL-ROWS}	Scrolls vertically by the specified number of rows in the current worksheet without changing the current cell	1165
{SCROLL-TO-CELL}	Scrolls in the current worksheet so that the first cell of the specified location is displayed in the top-left corner of the worksheet window	1166
{SCROLL-TO-COLUMN}	Scrolls left or right in the current worksheet, displaying the leftmost column of the specified location in the leftmost column of the worksheet window, without changing the current cell	1166
{SCROLL-TO-OBJECT}	Scrolls to but does not select a range, query table, chart or other drawn object in the current worksheet, without changing the current cell	1167

TABLE 21.1: Macro Commands Quick Reference (continued)

MACRO COMMAND	ACTION	SEE PAGE
{SCROLL-TO-ROW}	Scrolls up or down in the current worksheet to make the top row of the location be displayed on the top row in the worksheet window, without changing the current cell	1167
{SELECT}	Selects all or part of a range, chart, query table, or other drawn object, without scrolling to it	1167
{SELECT-ALL}	Selects all sheets in the current file, all charts on the current worksheet, all drawn objects on the current worksheet, or the active area of the current worksheet	1168
{SELECT-APPEND}	Adds to the group of selected items; it selects all or part of a range, chart, or other drawn object without deselecting any items currently selected	1169
{SELECT-RANGE-RELATIVE}	Moves the cell pointer and then selects a range whose address is represented by offsets of the current cell (the current cell is 0)	1169
{SELECT-REMOVE}	Removes a range, chart, or other drawn object from the currently selected collection	1170
{SELECT-REPLACE}	Replaces the specified old range in a collection with the specified new range	1171

21

Macro Commands

TABLE 21.1: Macro Commands Quick Reference (continued)

MACRO COMMAND	ACTION	SEE PAGE
{SEND-MAIL}	Sends a mail message using a 1-2-3–compatible mail application	1146
{SEND-RANGE}	Sends a range of worksheet data to other 1-2-3 users who have electronic mail	1147
{SEND-RANGE-LOGIN}	Automatically logs on to your mail application	1149
{SEND-SQL}	Sends the specified SQL command to an external database driver, against the database containing the specified external database table	1104
{SET}	Sets the specified Info component to the specified value	1158
{SETPOS}	Moves the byte pointer in an open text file the number of bytes specified by the given offset-number from the first byte in the file	1215
{SHEET-NAME}	Names a 1-2-3 worksheet in the current file	1184
{SHEET-NAME-DELETE}	Deletes the name of a 1-2-3 worksheet in the current file	1185
{SHOW-COLUMNS}	Reveals all hidden columns in the specified range	1199

TABLE 21.1: Macro Commands Quick Reference (continued)

MACRO COMMAND	ACTION	SEE PAGE
{SHOW-SHEETS}	Reveals all hidden sheets in the specified range	1199
{SMARTICONS-USE}	Selects a set of SmartIcons to use with 1-2-3	1224
{SMARTSUM}	Sums values in the cells above or to the right of the current cell	1187
{SOLVER-ANSWER}	Displays in the worksheet the answers or attempts that the 1-2-3 Solver finds	1189
{SOLVER-ANSWER-SAVE}	Saves the current Solver answer or attempt as a scenario	1189
{SOLVER-DEFINE}	Analyzes data in a worksheet and returns a number of possible Solver answers to the problem	1190
{SOLVER-DEFINE?}	Displays the Solver Definition dialog box with the choice of showing defaults specified	1191
{SOLVER-REPORT}	Creates a new worksheet file containing a report based on the current answer	1192
{SORT}	Arranges data in the specified range in the order you indicate	1185
{SORT-ASCENDING}	Sorts a range or database table in ascending order, using the selected column of the range or database table as the sort key	1187

21

Macro Commands

TABLE 21.1: Macro Commands Quick Reference (continued)

MACRO COMMAND	ACTION	SEE PAGE
{SORT-DESCENDING}	Sorts a range or database table in descending order, using the selected column of the range or database table as the sort key	1187
{SORT-KEY-DEFINE}	Defines a sort key for a {SORT} command to use	1186
{SORT-RESET}	Clears all sort keys defined for sorting range data	1186
{SPELLCHECK?}	Displays the Spell Check dialog box	1224
{STYLE-ALIGN-HORIZONTAL}	Sets the horizontal alignment of labels and values in the specified range	1200
{STYLE-ALIGN-ORIENTATION}	Alters the orientation of data in the specified range	1201
{STYLE-ALIGN-VERTICAL}	Sets vertical alignment for text within a cell whose height is greater than that of the largest typeface	1201
{STYLE-BORDER}	Sets borders for the specified range	1202
{STYLE-EDGE}	Sets the color, style, and width of the edge of charts, chart elements, text blocks, drawn objects, OLE objects, and pictures created in other Windows applications	1203
{STYLE-FONT}	Sets the font for the specified range	1203
{STYLE-FONT-ALL}	Sets the font and attributes for the specified range	1204

TABLE 21.1: Macro Commands Quick Reference (continued)

MACRO COMMAND	ACTION	SEE PAGE
{STYLE-FONT-ATTRIBUTES}	Sets the font attributes for the specified range	1205
{STYLE-FONT-RESET}	Restores the worksheet default font, font size, attributes and color to the specified range	1206
{STYLE-FONT-SIZE}	Assigns the specified point size to the fonts in the specified range	1206
{STYLE-FRAME}	Sets a frame for the specified range	1207
{STYLE-GALLERY}	Autoformats the specified range with one of 1-2-3's fourteen style templates	1207
{STYLE-INTERIOR}	Sets colors and patterns for each cell of the specified range	1208
{STYLE-LINE}	Changes the color, style, and width of the selected line for drawn lines and chart lines	1209
{STYLE-NUMBER-FORMAT}	Sets the display of values in the specified range	1209
{STYLE-NUMBER-FORMAT-RESET}	Resets the format of the specified range to the current default format specified in the Worksheet Defaults dialog box	1210
{subroutine}	Performs a subroutine call	1159
{SYSTEM}	Temporarily halts the 1-2-3 session to execute the specified operating-system command before resuming the session	1264

21

Macro Commands

TABLE 21.1: Macro Commands Quick Reference (continued)

MACRO COMMAND	ACTION	SEE PAGE
{TOGGLE-OUTLINE}	Adds or removes a border to or from the selected cell or range	1187
{TOGGLE-SHADOW}	Draws a drop shadow on the selected cell or range or removes a drop shadow if there already is one	1188
{UNPROTECT}	Turns protection off for the specified range	1211
{UNREGISTER}	Unregisters the procedure indicated by the specified alias-name	1224
{UPDATE-OBJECT}	Updates a 1-2-3 OLE object embedded in an OLE client application file	1119
{VERSION-CREATE}	Creates the new version specified	1254
{VERSION-DELETE}	Deletes the specified version	1255
{VERSION-INDEX-COPY}	Copies the information in the Index of the selected version to the Clipboard	1256
{VERSION-INDEX-MERGE}	Copies versions and scenarios from the source-file into the current file	1256
{VERSION-INFO}	Lets you modify style retention and sharing options for the specified version	1257

TABLE 21.1: Macro Commands Quick Reference (continued)

MACRO COMMAND	ACTION	SEE PAGE
{VERSION-REPORT}	Creates reports showing selected versions and their effect on the outcome of a formula	1258
{VERSION-SHOW}	Displays the selected version in the worksheet	1259
{VERSION-UPDATE}	Updates an already existing version with new data you enter in its named range	1259
{VIEW-ZOOM}	Decreases or increases the display size of cells as specified, or restores the default display size of cells	1265
{WAIT}	Suspends macro execution and displays WAIT as the mode indicator until the time specified	1250
{WINDOW-ACTIVATE}	Makes the specified window active	1265
{WINDOW-ADJUST}	Moves and sizes the active window relative to the 1-2-3 window	1266
{WINDOW-ARRANGE}	Sizes open windows and tiles or cascades them	1267
{WINDOW-STATE}	Minimizes, maximizes, or restores the active window	1267
{WINDOWSOFF}	Freezes the screen while a macro is running, suppressing screen updates	1268

21

Macro Commands

TABLE 21.1: Macro Commands Quick Reference (continued)

MACRO COMMAND	ACTION	SEE PAGE
{WINDOWSON}	Unfreezes the screen after it has been frozen with a {WINDOWSOFF} command	1268
{WORKSHEET-TITLES}	Freezes (or unfreezes) columns along the top of the worksheet, rows along the left edge of the worksheet, or both	1269
{WRITE}	Copies the specified text to the open text file, starting at the current byte-pointer position and increasing the byte-counter position with each byte written	1216
{WRITELN}	Copies the specified text to the open text file at the current byte-pointer position, adding a carriage-return and linefeed	1216

Using Macro Commands

As discussed in Chapters 9 and Chapter 12, macro commands are enclosed in braces ({ }) and share a common syntax, where *keyword* represents the macro command itself and *argument-list* represents the list of required or optional arguments:

{keyword argument-list}

Arguments fall into the following four categories:

- **Value.** A number, a numeric formula, or a range name or address indicating a number or a numeric formula.

- **Text.** A string of characters enclosed in double quotation marks (" "), a text formula, or a range name or address indicating a text label or a text formula.

- **Location.** A range name or address, or a formula that produces a range name or address.

- **Condition.** A logical expression that evaluates as 1 (TRUE) or 0 (FALSE).

To create a macro, you enter macro instructions into consecutive cells of a worksheet column and assign a range name to the first cell of a macro.

N O T E See Chapters 9 and 12 for practical examples of using macros.

Chart Macro Commands

This section of the chapter discusses the 1-2-3 chart macros, which include commands to create charts from selected data, select and title data ranges, and perform assorted formatting on charts.

{CHART-ASSIGN-RANGE}

{CHART-ASSIGN-RANGE *range;method*}

The {CHART-ASSIGN-RANGE} command assigns all data ranges for the current chart. It takes the following arguments.

range The name or address of a range to be used to create all the desired data ranges.

method Text indicating how {CHART-ASSIGN-RANGE} assigns the data ranges: *by-row* or *by-column*.

by-row assigns the A–W data ranges by row. If the first row of the range contains labels or dates, {CHART-ASSIGN-RANGE} assigns it as the X data range. If the first column of the range contains labels, {CHART-ASSIGN-RANGE} assigns it as the legends range.

by-column assigns the A–W data ranges by column. If the first column of the range contains labels or dates, {CHART-ASSIGN-RANGE} assigns it as the X data range. If the first row of the range contains labels, {CHART-ASSIGN-RANGE} assigns it as the legends range.

You could use the following command to assign all data ranges for the current chart, by row, from the range LONE_RANGE:

{CHART-ASSIGN-RANGE LONE_RANGE;"by-row"}

In this case, {CHART-ASSIGN-RANGE} uses the first column of data in LONE_RANGE as the X-axis labels.

Equivalent commands   Chart ➤ Ranges

{CHART-AXIS-INTERVALS}

{CHART-AXIS-INTERVALS *axis*;[*major*];[*minor*];[*major-interval*]; [*minor-interval*]}

The {CHART-AXIS-INTERVALS} command changes the intervals between X-axis, Y-axis, or 2nd Y-axis tick-marks in the current chart. It takes the following arguments.

axis   X, Y, or 2Y, indicating the axis you want to work with.

major   Yes or No, indicating whether you specify the major interval; if Yes, include a *major-interval* argument; if No, {CHART-AXIS-INTERVALS} will automatically calculate the major interval.

minor   Yes or No, indicating whether you specify the minor interval; if Yes, include a *minor-interval* argument; if No, {CHART-AXIS-INTERVALS} will automatically calculate the minor interval.

major-interval   A value indicating the major interval (only needed if you chose Yes for the *major* argument).

minor-interval   A value indicating the minor interval (only needed if you chose Yes for the *minor* argument).

You could use the following commands to select the chart named RESIN and set the major intervals on the Y-axis to 1000 and 50, respectively:

```
{SELECT "resin";;"chart"}
{CHART-AXIS-INTERVALS "y";"yes";"yes";1000;50}
```

Equivalent commands Chart ➤ Axis ➤ X-Axis, Chart ➤ Axis ➤ Y-Axis, Chart ➤ Axis ➤ 2nd Y-Axis

{CHART-AXIS-LIMITS}

{CHART-AXIS-LIMITS *axis;[upper];[lower];[upper-limit];[lower-limit]*}

The {CHART-AXIS-LIMITS} command creates a scale for the X-axis, Y-axis, or 2nd Y-axis for the current chart, displaying only the data that falls between (and includes) *upper-limit* and *lower-limit*. It takes the following arguments.

axis   X, Y, or 2Y, indicating the axis you want to work with.

upper   Yes or No, indicating whether you specify the upper limit; if Yes, include an *upper-limit* argument; if No, {CHART-AXIS-INTERVALS} will automatically calculate the upper limit.

lower   Yes or No, indicating whether you specify lower limit; if Yes, include a *lower-limit* argument; if No, {CHART-AXIS-INTERVALS} will automatically calculate the lower limit.

upper-limit   A value indicating the upper limit (only needed if you chose Yes for the *upper* argument).

lower-limit   A value indicating the lower limit (only needed if you chose Yes for the *lower* argument).

You could use the following commands to select the chart named RESIN and set the X-axis upper and lower limits to 40 and −40, respectively:

```
{SELECT "resin";;"chart"}
{CHART-AXIS-LIMITS "x";"yes";"yes";40;-40}
```

Equivalent commands Chart ➤ Axis ➤ X-Axis, Chart ➤ Axis ➤ Y-Axis, Chart ➤ Axis ➤ 2nd Y-Axis

{CHART-AXIS-SCALE-TYPE}

{CHART-AXIS-SCALE-TYPE *axis;type*}

The {CHART-AXIS-SCALE-TYPE} command indicates the type of scale to use for an axis in the current chart. It takes the following arguments.

axis   X, Y, or 2Y, indicating the axis you want to work with.

type   *standard*, *log* or *100%*, text indicating the type of scale to use for the *axis* chosen. *standard* increases scale numbers linearly by a fixed number of units; *log* increases scale numbers logarithmically; and *100%* displays scale numbers ranging from 0 through 100% and representing percentages instead of absolute values. *100%* is not available for the X-axis.

You could use the following command to impose a logarithmic scale on the current chart's X-axis:

{CHART-AXIS-SCALE-TYPE "x";"log"}

Equivalent commands Chart ➤ Axis ➤ X-Axis ➤ Options, Chart ➤ Axis ➤ Y-Axis ➤ Options, Chart ➤ Axis ➤ 2nd Y-Axis ➤ Options

{CHART-AXIS-TICKS}

{CHART-AXIS-TICKS *axis*;[*major*];[*minor*];[*space*]}

The {CHART-AXIS-TICKS *axis*} command specifies major and minor tick marks for an axis in the specified chart. It takes the following arguments.

axis   X, Y, or 2Y, indicating the axis you want to work with.

major   Yes or No, indicating whether {CHART-AXIS-TICKS} displays tick marks at major intervals.

minor   Yes or No, indicating whether {CHART-AXIS-TICKS} displays tick marks at minor intervals.

space   An integer specifying how many ticks appear between labels. If you omit the *space* argument, {CHART-AXIS-TICKS} uses 1.

You could use the following commands to select the chart named STAK-HANOVITES, set the X-axis major intervals at 5, and display tick marks only at major intervals:

```
{SELECT "stakhanovites";;"chart"}
{CHART-AXIS-INTERVALS "x";"yes";"no";5}
```

Equivalent commands Chart ➤ Axis ➤ X-Axis, Chart ➤ Axis ➤ Y-Axis, Chart ➤ Axis ➤ 2nd Y-Axis

{CHART-AXIS-TITLE}

{CHART-AXIS-TITLE *axis*;[*title*];[*title-cell*]}

The {CHART-AXIS-TITLE} command changes an axis title in the current chart. It takes the following arguments.

axis   X, Y, or 2Y, indicating the axis you want to work with.

title   Text enclosed in double quotation marks (" ") indicating the axis title. Use the *title-cell* argument if you want to use the contents of a cell for the axis title.

title-cell   The name or address of a cell containing a label to use as the axis title. If you include both *title* and *title-cell* arguments, {CHART-AXIS-TITLE} ignores the *title* argument.

TIP   You can delete an existing axis title by specifying " " for the title argument.

You could use the following commands to select the chart named STAK-HANOVITE and change the X-axis title to "Coal (Tons)":

```
{SELECT "stakhanovite";;"chart"}
{CHART-AXIS-TITLE "x";"Coal (Tons)"}
```

21

Macro Commands

Equivalent commands Chart ➤ Axis ➤ X-Axis, Chart ➤ Axis ➤ Y-Axis, Chart ➤ Axis 2nd ➤ Y-Axis

{CHART-AXIS-UNITS}

{CHART-AXIS-UNITS *axis*;[*manual-calculate*];[*manual-title*];[*exponent*];[*title*];[*title-cell*]}

The {CHART-AXIS-UNITS} command changes the magnitude of the axis units and the axis-unit titles for the current chart. It takes the following arguments.

axis   X, Y, or 2Y, indicating the axis you want to work with.

manual-calculate   Yes or No, indicating whether you want to specify an order of magnitude for the axis scale; if Yes, include an exponent argument; if No, {CHART-AXIS-UNITS} calculates the exponent automatically.

manual-title   Yes or No, indicating whether you want to create the axis-units title; if Yes, include a title or title-cell argument; if No, {CHART-AXIS-UNITS} generates the axis units title automatically.

exponent   An integer from −95 through 95 indicating the order of magnitude for the axis scale (the power of 10 by which the numbers along the scale must be multiplied to reflect the values being charted).

title   Text entered in double quotation marks (″ ″) indicating the units title. Use a *title-cell* argument to use the contents of a cell for the units title.

title-cell   The name or address of a cell containing a label to use as the axis title. If you include both *title* and *title-cell* arguments, {CHART-AXIS-TITLE} ignores the *title* argument.

TIP   You can delete an existing axis title by specifying ″ ″ for the title argument.

You could use the following commands to select the chart named BENCH, change the magnitude of the Y-axis units to tens, and change the unit title to Kilograms (Kg).

```
{SELECT "bench";;"chart"}
{CHART-AXIS-UNITS "y";"yes";"yes";10;"Kilograms (Kg)"}
```

Equivalent commands Chart ➤ Axis ➤ X-Axis ➤ Options, Chart ➤ Axis ➤ Y-Axis ➤ Options, Chart ➤ Axis ➤ 2nd Y-Axis ➤ Options

{CHART-COLOR-RANGE}

{CHART-COLOR-RANGE *series*;[*color-range*]}

The {CHART-COLOR-RANGE} command sets the color for each value in a data series in the current chart, using values in the *color-range* specified. It takes the following arguments.

series   Text indicating a single data series (A–W) in the current chart.

color-range   The name or address of a range whose values determine the color for each value in a data range. If you omit the *color-range* argument, {CHART-COLOR-RANGE} uses the default color for *series*.

You could use the following command to set the color for each bar in the D data series of the current chart using the values in the range COLORS FOR D:

{CHART-COLOR-RANGE "D";COLORS FOR D}

Equivalent commands Chart ➤ Numeric Color

{CHART-DATA-LABELS}

{CHART-DATA-LABELS *series*;[*label-range*];[*position*]}

The {CHART-DATA-LABELS} command creates labels for data points or bars in the current chart, using data in the specified label-range as the labels. It takes the following arguments.

series   Text indicating a single data series or all data series in the current chart. Use a letter from A–W to assign data labels for a single data series; use "all" to assign data labels for all data series.

label-range The name or address of a range containing the data labels. {CHART-DATA-LABELS} removes the data label for series from the chart if you omit the *label-range* argument.

position *center, below, above, left,* or *right,* indicating the location of the data labels. *center* centers the data labels on the data points in a line chart and area chart and above the bars in a bar chart. *right* positions the data labels to the right of the data points in a line chart and area chart and above the bars in a bar chart. *below* positions the data labels below the data points in a line chart and area chart and below the bars in a bar chart. *above* positions the data labels above the data points in a line chart and area chart and above the bars in a bar chart. *left* positions the data labels to the left of the data points in a line chart and area chart and above the bars in a bar chart.

You could use the following commands to create data labels for the B series in the chart LOUISIANA from data in the range TEXT. {CHART-DATA-LABELS} places the data labels above the bars in the chart.

```
{SELECT "louisiana";;"chart"}
{CHART-DATA-LABELS "b";TEXT;"above"}
```

Equivalent commands Chart ➤ Data Labels

{CHART-FOOTNOTE}

{CHART-FOOTNOTE [*line1*];[*line2*];[*position*];[*cell1*];[*cell2*]}

The {CHART-FOOTNOTE} command adds chart footnotes to the current chart. It takes the following arguments.

line1 Text entered in double quotation marks (″ ″) indicating the first line of the chart footnote.

line2 Text entered in double quotation marks (″ ″) indicating the second line of the chart footnote. If you want to use the contents of a cell for the first or second line of a chart footnote, use the *cell1* or *cell2* arguments.

position *left, center,* or *right* indicating the alignment of the footnote. *center* is the default if you omit the *position* argument.

cell1   The name or address of a range containing a label to use as the first line of the chart title or footnote. {CHART-FOOTNOTE} ignores *line1* if you include both *line1* and *cell1*

cell2   The name or address of a range containing a label to use as the second line of the chart title or footnote. {CHART-FOOTNOTE} ignores *line2* if you include both *line2* and *cell2*.

TIP   If you want to delete the existing chart footnote lines, specify " " for *line1* or *line2*.

You could use the following commands to change the footnote in the chart named INCOME to the contents of the cell named NET:

```
{SELECT "income";;"chart"}
{CHART-FOOTNOTE;;;net}
```

Equivalent commands   Chart ➤ Headings

{CHART-GRID}

{CHART-GRID *axis*;[*major*];[*minor*]}

The {CHART-GRID} command displays or hides grid lines for an axis in the current chart. It takes the following arguments.

axis   X, Y, or 2Y, indicating the axis from which the grid lines originate. X displays or hides vertical grid lines that originate from the X-axis; Y displays or hides horizontal grid lines that originate from the Y-axis; and 2Y displays or hides Horizontal grid lines that originate from the 2nd Y-axis.

major   Yes or No, indicating whether to display or hide grid lines originating from major-interval tick marks.

minor   Yes or No, indicating whether to display or hide grid lines originating from minor-interval tick marks.

TIP The {CHART-GRID} command has no effect whatsoever if the current chart is a pie chart or radar chart.

You could use the following commands to select the chart named SUCCESS and add major-interval grid lines to the X-axis and major-interval and minor-interval grid lines to the Y-axis:

```
{SELECT "success";;"chart"}
{CHART-GRID "x";"yes";"no"}
{CHART-GRID "y";"yes";"yes"}
```

Equivalent commands Chart ➤ Grids

{CHART-LEGEND}

{CHART-LEGEND *series*;[*legend*];[*position*];[*legend-range*]}

The {CHART-LEGEND} command creates legend labels that identify the colors, symbols, or patterns of the current chart's data series. It takes the following arguments.

series Text indicating a single data series or all data series in the current chart. Use a letter from A–W to assign legend labels for a single data series; use "all" to assign legend labels for all data series.

legend Text entered in double quotation marks (" ") indicating the legend label for series. If you have chosen All for the *series* argument, omit the *legend* argument. If you want to use the contents of a cell for the legend label, use the *legend-range* argument.

position *right*, *below*, or *manual*, indicating the location of the legend label. *right* positions the legend label to the right of the chart; *below* positions the legend label below the chart; and *manual* leaves the setting unchanged.

legend-range The name or address of a cell or range specifying a single cell (if *series* specifies a single data series) or a range containing as many labels as there are data series in the current chart (if *series* specifies all data series). {CHART-LEGEND} ignores the *legend* argument if you have included both a *legend* argument and a *legend-range* argument.

You could use the following command to create legend labels for the K series in the current chart using the range named LABEL FOR K and placing the legend labels to the right of the chart:

```
{CHART-LEGEND "k";;"right";LABEL FOR K}
```

Equivalent commands Chart ➤ Legend

{CHART-NEW}

```
{CHART-NEW location;[type];[style];[name]}
```

The {CHART-NEW} command draws a chart at the specified *location*, using data from the currently selected range. It takes the following arguments.

location The name or address of a range in the current file at which you want the new chart to be drawn. If you specify a single cell for *location*, the chart will appear in that cell and will not be automatically placed and sized.

type Text indicating the type chart to draw: Line, Area, Bar, Pie, XY, HLCO, Mixed, Radar, 3D-Line, 3D-Area, 3D-Bar, or 3D-Pie. {CHART-NEW} uses the default chart type if you do not specify one.

style The offset number indicating the desired style for the given type of chart, counting from left to right and top to bottom in the Chart Type dialog box. {CHART-NEW} uses the first style if you omit the *style* argument.

name The name for the chart; if you do not specify one, {CHART-NEW} will name the chart CHART 1, CHART 2, or the next default number.

You could use the following commands to create a default pie chart named PORK FAT in cells A:B2..A:E18 from the data in the range LARD:

```
{SELECT LARD}
{CHART-NEW A:B2..A:E18;"pie";;"pork fat"}
```

Equivalent commands Tools ➤ Chart

{CHART-PATTERN-RANGE}

{CHART-PATTERN-RANGE *series*; [*color-range*]}

The {CHART-PATTERN-RANGE} command sets the pattern for each value in a data series in the current chart, using values in the given *pattern-range*. It takes the following arguments.

series   Text indicating a single data series (A–W) in the current chart.

color-range   The name or address of a range whose values determine the pattern for each value in a data range. If you omit the *pattern-range* argument, {CHART-PATTERN-RANGE} uses the default pattern for *series*.

You could use the following command to set the pattern for each bar in the A data series of the current chart using the values in the range PATTERNS FOR A:

{CHART-PATTERN-RANGE "A";PATTERNS FOR A}

Equivalent commands   Chart ➤ Numeric Color

{CHART-PIE-LABELS}

{CHART-PIE-LABELS [*values*];[*percentage*];[*x-range*];[*c-range*]}

The {CHART-PIE-LABELS} command creates labels for the current pie chart. It takes the following arguments.

values   Yes or No, indicating whether to display the values in the A data range as pie-slice labels.

percentages   Yes or No, indicating whether to display each value in the A data range as a percentage of 100.

x-range   Yes or No, indicating whether to display the contents of the X data range.

c-range   Yes or No, indicating whether {CHART-PIE-LABELS} uses values you enter in the C data range to show or hide percentages.

You could use the following commands to select the pie chart named MARKET SEGMENTS and display the values in the A data range as labels and label the slices with the contents of the X data range:

```
{SELECT "market segments";;"chart"}
{CHART-PIE-LABELS "yes";"no";"yes";"no"}
```

Equivalent commands Chart ➤ Data Labels

{CHART-PIE-SLICE-EXPLOSION}

{CHART-PIE-SLICE-EXPLOSION *explosion-type*;[*all-by-%*]}

The {CHART-PIE-SLICE-EXPLOSION} command explodes the chosen slices in the current pie chart by the amount indicated in the *all-by-%* argument. It takes the following arguments.

explosion-type *None*, *All*, or *using-b*, indicating how {CHART-PIE-LABELS} explodes slices. *None* explodes no slices; *all* explodes all slices by the percent specified by the *all-by-%* argument; and *using-b* explodes slices based on data in the B data range.

all-by-% An integer from 1 through 100 indicating the percentage by which to explode the slices if *explosion-type* is All.

You could use the following commands to explode all slices of the current pie by 33 percent:

```
{CHART-PIE-SLICE-EXPLOSION "all";33}
```

Equivalent commands Chart ➤ Data Labels

{CHART-RANGE}

{CHART-RANGE *series*;[*series-range*];[*series-type*];[*2Y-axis*]}

The {CHART-RANGE} command sets the data range, series type, and 2nd Y-axis flag for a data series in the current chart. It takes the following arguments.

series A letter from A through Z (not Y), entered in double quotation marks (" "), indicating a data series in the current chart. If *series* is Z,

21

Macro Commands

{CHART-RANGE} uses the contents of *series-range* as the legend range.

series-range The name or address of the data range for *series*.

series-type *Area*, *Line*, or *Bar*, entered in double quotation marks (″ ″), indicating the type of series for mixed charts.

2Y-axis Yes or No, indicating whether this series should be plotted on the 2nd Y-axis.

You could use the following command to set the values in the range TO_CHART for the D data series of the current chart:

    {CHART-RANGE "d";TO_CHART}

Equivalent commands Chart ➤ Ranges

{CHART-RANGE-DELETE}

    {CHART-RANGE-DELETE *series*}

The {CHART-RANGE-DELETE} command deletes the specified series from the current chart. It takes the following argument.

series A letter from A through Z, (not Y), entered in double quotation marks (″ ″), indicating a data series in the current chart.

You could use the following command to remove the M data series from the current chart:

    {CHART-RANGE-DELETE "m"}

Equivalent commands Chart ➤ Ranges

{CHART-RENAME}

    {CHART-RENAME *old-name;new-name*}

The {CHART-RENAME} command renames a chart. It takes the following arguments.

old-name Text indicating the current name of the chart.

new-name Text indicating the new name for the chart.

You could use the following command to rename the chart INTEREST RATE with the name EXTORTION:

{CHART-RENAME "interest rate";"extortion"}

Equivalent commands Chart ➤ Name

{CHART-SET-PREFERRED}

{CHART-SET-PREFERRED}

The {CHART-SET-PREFERRED} command defines the current chart's type as the default chart type and defines the selected chart's grid settings as the default grid settings. The {CHART-SET-PREFERRED} command works on the current chart and has no arguments.

You could use the following commands to select the chart named EX-TORTION and define its settings as the default chart type:

{SELECT "extortion";;"chart"}
{CHART-SET-PREFERRED}

Equivalent commands Chart ➤ Set Preferred

{CHART-TITLE}

{CHART-TITLE [*line1*];[*line2*];[*position*];[*cell1*];[*cell2*]}

The {CHART-TITLE} command adds chart titles to the chosen position in the current chart. It takes the following arguments.

line1 Text entered in double quotation marks (" ") indicating the first line of the chart title.

line2 Text entered in double quotation marks (" ") indicating the second line of the chart title. If you want to use the contents of a cell for the first or second line of a chart title, use the *cell1* or *cell2* arguments.

position left, center, or right, indicating the alignment of the title; center is the default if you omit the *position* argument.

21

Macro Commands

cell1 The name or address of a range containing a label to use as the first line of the chart title or title. {CHART-TITLE} ignores *line1* if you include both *line1* and *cell1*.

cell2 The name or address of a range containing a label to use as the second line of the chart title or title. {CHART-TITLE} ignores *line2* if you include both *line2* and *cell2*.

> **TIP**
>
> If you want to delete the existing chart title lines, specify *" "* for *line1* or *line2*.

You could use the following commands to change the title of the chart named "Success" to "Success or Failure" and right-align the title:

    {SELECT "success";;"chart"}
    {CHART-TITLE "Success or Failure";;"right"}

Equivalent commands Chart ➤ Headings

{CHART-TYPE}

{CHART-TYPE *type;[style];[orientation];[value-tables];[auto-position]*}

The {CHART-TYPE} command changes the current chart to the type specified. It takes the following arguments.

type Text indicating the type chart to draw: Line, Area, Bar, Pie, XY, HLCO, Mixed, Radar, 3D-Line, 3D-Area, 3D-Bar, or 3D-Pie. {CHART-TYPE} uses the default chart type if you do not specify one.

style The offset number indicating the desired style for the given type of chart, counting from left to right and top to bottom in the Chart Type dialog box. {CHART-TYPE} uses the first style if you omit the *style* argument.

orientation *vertical* or *horizontal*, entered in double quotation marks (*" "*), indicating the orientation of the chart. *vertical* orients the X-axis across the bottom of the chart, the Y-axis along the left edge of the chart, and the 2nd Y-axis along the right edge of the chart (this is the default if you omit the *orientation* argument). *horizontal* orients the X-axis along the left edge of the chart, the Y-axis across the top of the chart, and the 2nd Y-axis along the bottom of the chart.

value-tables Yes or No, indicating whether to display data values under the chart. {CHART-TYPE} does not display the values if you omit *value-tables*, and ignores *value-tables* if the chart *type* is Pie, HLCO, Radar, or XY, or if *orientation* is Horizontal.

auto-position Yes or No, indicating whether 1-2-3 automatically places the plot within the chart.

You could use the following command to change the chart named CHART 23 from its current format to a vertical stacked bar chart:

    {CHART-TYPE "bar";1;"vertical"}

Equivalent commands Chart ➤ Type

{CHART-USE-PREFERRED}

    {CHART-USE-PREFERRED}

The {CHART-USE-PREFERRED} command changes the current chart to the default chart type and changes the current chart's grid settings to the default grid settings. The {CHART-USE-PREFERRED} command works on the current chart and has no arguments.

You could use the following commands to select the chart named Resin 1995 and change it to the default chart type:

    {SELECT "Resin 1995";;"chart"}
    {CHART-USE-PREFERRED}

Equivalent commands Chart ➤ Use Preferred

21

Macro Commands

Data-Manipulation Macro Commands

This section of the chapter discusses 1-2-3's data-manipulation macro commands, which include commands to store labels in cells, erase the contents of cells, and perform assorted recalculations.

{APPENDBELOW}

{APPENDBELOW *target-location;source-location*}

The {APPENDBELOW} command copies the contents of *source-location* to the rows immediately below *target-location*. It takes the following arguments.

target-location   A range of any size

source-location   A range of any size

NOTE

Make sure that you have enough blank and unprotected rows below the *target-location* for the number of rows in *source-location* to be added, or the macro will fail. If *source-location* contains formulas, their current values will be copied to *target-location*, not the formulas themselves. Note also that if you use named ranges, the rows or columns that contain the appended data will be included in the range name for target-location.

For example, if you import data from your PDA into a range named CONTACTS, where you organize it, you could use the following command to append data from CONTACTS into the range named COLDCALL, which would be expanded to include the records:

{APPENDBELOW COLDCALL;CONTACTS}

{APPENDRIGHT}

{APPENDRIGHT *target-location;source-location*}

The {APPENDRIGHT} command copies the contents of *source-location* to the columns immediately to the right of *target-location*. It takes the following arguments.

target-location   A range of any size

source-location   A range of any size

NOTE

Make sure that you have enough blank and unprotected rows to the right of the *target-location* for the number of rows in *source-location* to be added, or the macro will fail. If *source-location* contains formulas, their current values will be copied to *target-location*, not the formulas themselves. Note also that if you use named ranges, the rows or columns that contain the appended data will be included in the range name for target-location.

You could use the following command to append the information in your CONTACTS named range to the range named EX CLIENTS, which would be expanded to include the extra cells:

{APPENDRIGHT EX CLIENTS;CONTACTS}

{BLANK}

{BLANK *location*}

21

Macro Commands

The {BLANK} command erases the contents of *location*, but without changing the formatting of the cells in *location* and without forcing recalculation. To reset the formatting of cells in *location*, you can use the {STYLE-NUMBER-FORMAT-RESET} command; to force recalculation, you can use the {RECALC} command. The {BLANK} command takes the following argument.

location   The name or address of a cell or range. By using an @CELLPOINTER statement for *location*, you can erase the contents of the current cell.

You could use the following command to erase the contents of the range named MANAGEMENT:

> {BLANK MANAGEMENT}

{CONTENTS}

> {CONTENTS *target-location;source-location;[width];[format]*}

The {CONTENTS} command copies the contents of *source-location* to *target-location* as a label without forcing recalculation. To force recalculation, use the {RECALC} command. {CONTENTS} takes the following arguments.

target-location   The address or name of a cell or a range. If *target-location* is a range, {CONTENTS} uses the first cell.

source-location   The address or name of a cell or a range. If *source-location* is a range, {CONTENTS} uses the first cell.

width   An integer value between 1 and 240 indicating the width of the label {CONTENTS} should create. This is an optional argument; if you do omit *width*, the label created in *target-location* will have the same width as *source-location*.

format   An integer value between 0 and 127 indicating the format of the label {CONTENTS} creates. This is an optional argument; if you do omit *format*, the label created in *target-location* will have the same format as *source-location*. Here is what the values specify:

> 0 to 15 specifies Fixed format with 0 to 15 decimal places.
>
> 16 to 31 specifies Scientific format with 0 to 15 decimal places.

32 to 47 specifies Currency format with 0 to 15 decimal places.

48 to 63 specifies Percent format with 0 to 15 decimal places.

64 to 79 specifies Comma format with 0 to 15 decimal places.

112 specifies +/- format.

113 specifies General format.

114 specifies the following date format: 31-Dec-95.

115 specifies the following date format: 31-Dec.

116 specifies the following date format: Dec-95.

117 specifies Text format.

118 specifies Hidden format.

119 specifies the following time format: 11:59:59 AM.

120 specifies the following time format: 11:59 AM.

121 specifies the following date format: 12/31/93.

122 specifies the following date format: 12/31.

123 specifies the following time format: 23:59:59.

124 specifies the following time format: 59:59.

127 specifies the worksheet's default number format (chosen with Style ➤ Worksheet ➤ Defaults ➤ Number Format).

You could use the following command to return the contents of cell K9 in cell B4 and format it in currency format with two decimal places at the source width:

{CONTENTS B4;K9;;34}

{LET}

{LET *location;entry*}

The {LET} command enters a number or left-aligned label in the specified location. If you specify a formula as the entry for {LET}, the *location* will show the result of the formula. {LET} does not trigger automatic recalculation, but you can run a {RECALC} command after {LET} if you need to recalculate. It takes the following arguments.

location   The name or address of a cell or a range. If *location* is a range, {LET} enters the *entry* in the first cell of the range.

entry   A number, text, or a formula, or the name or address of a cell containing a number, a label, or a formula.

TIP You can add the suffix *:value* (or *:v* for short) to the *entry* argument to store the value as a number, or the suffix *:string* (*:s* for short) to store the value as a label.

You could use the following command to calculate the value of the formula RPM*SKID/SKILL and store it in DANGER:

```
{LET DANGER;RPM*SKID/SKILL}
```

{PUT}

{PUT *location;column-offset;row-offset;entry*}

The {PUT} command enters a number or left-aligned label in a cell within the specified location. If you specify a formula as the entry for {PUT}, the *location* will show the result of the formula. {PUT} does not trigger automatic recalculation, but you can run a {RECALC} command after {PUT} if you need to recalculate. It takes the following arguments.

location   The name or address of any range containing the cell in which to enter data.

column-offset   An offset number indicating the column position of a cell within *location*.

row-offset   An offset number indicating the row position of a cell within *location*.

entry   A number, text, formula, or name or address of a cell containing a number, label, or formula. Precede a text formula with a plus sign (+).

T I P

You can add the suffix *:value* (or *:v* for short) to the *entry* argument to store the value as a number, or the suffix *:string* (*:s* for short) to store the value as a label.

You could use the following command to store the value from cell EP45 in the cell in the fourth column (from left) and fifth row down (from top) of the range named DISCOUNT:

{PUT DISCOUNT;4;5;EP45}

{RECALC}

{RECALC *location;[condition];[iterations]*}

The {RECALC} command recalculates the values in the specified location, one row at a time. Use {RECALC} only when you have recalculation set to Manual in the User Setup dialog box. Note that {RECALC} does not recalculate formulas outside the range specified; if you need to get all formulas up to date at the end of a macro, use a {CALC} command. The {RECALC} command takes the following arguments.

location The name or address of the cell or range to recalculate.

condition A logical formula (or the name or address of a cell containing one), a numeric formula, a text formula, a number, or the name or address of a cell. {RECALC} repeats the recalculation until *condition* is TRUE (does not equal 0). If the *condition* depends on the recalculation, you'll need to make sure that the *location* specified includes cells referred to in the condition.

iterations A value indicating the number of times to repeat the recalculation. *iterations* is an optional argument; if you omit *iterations* or enter 0, {RECALC} will recalculate *once*. If you include both *condition* and *iterations* arguments, {RECALC} will recalculate until *condition* is true or until it finishes the specified number of iterations, whichever comes first.

21

Macro Commands

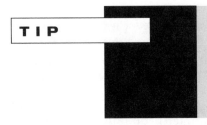

TIP Remember that 1-2-3 considers a numeric formula or number to be 1 (TRUE) unless its value is 0; a text formula is always 1 (TRUE); and a reference to a cell containing ERR or NA, a text formula, or a label, is always a TRUE. A reference to a blank cell is always FALSE.

You could use the following command to recalculate the formulas in the range named TESTS row-by-row until the value of the cell named DIVERGENCE is less than 0.4:

{RECALC TESTS;+DIVERGENCE<0.4}

{RECALCCOL}

{RECALCCOL *location*;[*condition*];[*iterations*]}

The {RECALCCOL} command recalculates the values in location, proceeding column by column. Use {RECALCCOL} only when you have recalculation set to Manual in the User Setup dialog box. Note that {RECALCCOL} does not recalculate formulas outside the range specified; if you need to get all formulas up to date at the end of a macro, use a {CALC} command. {RECALCCOL} takes the following arguments.

location The name or address of the cell or range to recalculate.

condition A logical formula (or the name or address of a cell containing one), a numeric formula, a text formula, a number, or the name or address of a cell. {RECALCCOL} repeats the recalculation until *condition* is TRUE (does not equal 0). If the *condition* depends on the recalculation, you'll need to make sure that the *location* specified includes cells referred to in the condition.

iterations A value indicating the number of times to repeat the recalculation. *iterations* is an optional argument; if you omit *iterations* or enter 0, {RECALCCOL} will recalculate *once*. If you include both *condition* and *iterations* arguments, {RECALCCOL} will recalculate until *condition* is true or until it finishes the specified number of iterations, whichever comes first.

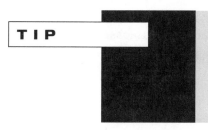

TIP

Remember that 1-2-3 considers a numeric formula or number to be 1 (TRUE) unless its value is 0; a text formula is always 1 (TRUE); and a reference to a cell containing ERR or NA, a text formula, or a label is always a TRUE. A reference to a blank cell is always FALSE.

You could use the following command to recalculate the formulas in the named range REVENUES column-by-column until either 25 iterations are complete or the contents of the cell RESULT are greater than 250:

{RECALCCOL REVENUES;RESULT>250;25}

Database Macro Commands

This section discusses the database macro commands, which are used for creating and working with internal and external databases.

{COMMIT}

{COMMIT [*driver-name*];[*database-name*]}

The {COMMIT} command commits—finalizes—pending external database transactions. If both arguments are specified, {COMMIT} commits the specified database transactions. If no arguments are specified, {COMMIT} commits all pending external database transactions. {COMMIT} (and its counterpart macro command, {ROLLBACK}) work only with the SQL Server driver. {COMMIT} takes the following arguments.

driver-name   Text indicating the name of the driver.

database-name   Text indicating the name of the external database.

21

Macro Commands

You could use the following command to commit the transactions pending for the driver SQL_SERVER and the database named FINANCE:

{COMMIT "SQL_SERVER";"FINANCE"}

{CROSSTAB}

{CROSSTAB *database-table;row-headings;col-headings;summary-field;summary-method*}

The {CROSSTAB} command creates a cross-tabulation table for the database table indicated and places it on a new worksheet after the worksheet containing the database table. It takes the following arguments.

database-table   The location of a database table.

col-headings   Text indicating the name of the field containing the entries to use as column headings.

summary-field   Text indicating the name of the field containing values to be summarized in the cells of the crosstab table.

summary-method   Text indicating the method used to summarize in the cross tabulation: *sum* (which adds the values), *avg* (which averages the values), *count* (which counts the values), *min* (which finds the smallest value), or *max* (which finds the largest value).

You could use the following command to create a cross-tabulation table from the database table named RETURNS. The table provides the total value for the 1994 database field, tabulated by the "Books" database field and the "Store" database field.

{CROSSTAB RETURNS;"Books";"Store";"1994";"max"}

Equivalent commands   Tools ➤ Database ➤ Crosstab

{DATABASE-APPEND}

{DATABASE-APPEND *source-range;database-table*}

The {DATABASE-APPEND} command adds new records to the specified database-table. It takes the following arguments.

source-range The name or address of the range (either a 1-2-3 range on an external database table) containing the records to append to *database-table*. The first row of *source-range* must contain field names that match those in the database table.

database-table The location of a database table.

You could use the following command to append records from the range named SCOTLAND to the database table EUROPE:

{DATABASE-APPEND SCOTLAND;EUROPE}

Equivalent commands Tools ➤ Database Append Records

{DATABASE-CONNECT}

{DATABASE-CONNECT *driver-name*;[*driver-user-id*];[*driver-password*];[*connection-string*];*db-name*;[*db-user-id*];[*db-password*];[*owner-name*];*table-name*;[*range-name*]}

The {DATABASE-CONNECT} command connects the worksheet to an external database table so you can use the table with other 1-2-3 commands. It takes the following arguments.

driver-name Text indicating the name of the database driver for the external database containing the table to be connected.

driver-user-id Text indicating the user ID for the specified driver. {DATABASE-CONNECT} will prompt you for a driver-user-ID if you omit one and the driver needs one.

driver-password Text in double quotation marks (" ") indicating the driver password. {DATABASE-CONNECT} will prompt you for a password if you omit one and the driver needs one.

connection-string Text in double quotation marks (" ") giving additional information needed to connect to a driver.

range-name Text in double quotation marks (" ") indicating the range name of the table. If you omit *range-name*, {DATABASE-CONNECT}

db-name Text in double quotation marks (" ") indicating the name of the external database containing the table to which you want to connect.

21

Macro Commands

db-user-id   Text in double quotation marks (" ") indicating the database user ID. {DATABASE-CONNECT} will prompt you for the database user ID if you omit one and the database needs one.

db-password   Text in double quotation marks (" ") indicating the database password. {DATABASE-CONNECT} will prompt you for the database password if you omit one and the database needs one.

owner-name   Text in double quotation marks (" ") indicating the name of the owner of the specified table.

table-name   Text in double quotation marks (" ") indicating the name of the external table to connect to.

range-name   Text in double quotation marks (" ") indicating the range name of the table. If you omit *range-name*, {DATABASE-CONNECT} will use the table name as *range-name*.

You could use the following command to connect 1-2-3 to the table named PROJECTG in the external database Z:\DB\PUBLIC\PLAN-NING with the driver SQL_SERVER. Note that the *db-user-id* is given as "vwells," while no password is given; if a password is necessary, the user will be prompted for one:

> {DATABASE-CONNECT "SQL_SERVER";;;;"Z:\DB\PUBLIC\PLAN-NING";"vwells";;"projectg"}

Equivalent commands Tools ➤ Database ➤ Connect to External

{DATABASE-CREATE-TABLE}

> {DATABASE-CREATE-TABLE *driver-name*;[*driver-user-id*];[*driver-password*];*db-name*;[*db-user-id*];[*db-password*];[*owner-name*];*table-name*;[*range-name*];[*creation-string*];*model-table*}

The {DATABASE-CREATE-TABLE} command sets up the structure for and connects to a new table in an external database. It takes the following arguments.

db-password   Text indicating the database password. {DATABASE-CREATE-TABLE} will prompt you for the database password if you omit one and the dtabase needs one.

driver-name   Text indicating the name of the database driver for the external database containing the table to be connected.

driver-user-id   Text indicating the user ID for the specified driver. {DATABASE-CREATE-TABLE} will prompt you for a driver-user-ID if you omit one and the driver needs one.

driver-password   Text indicating the driver password. {DATABASE-CREATE-TABLE} will prompt you for a password if you omit one and the driver needs one.

db-name   Text indicating the name of the external database containing the table to which you want to connect.

db-user-id   Text indicating the database user ID. {DATABASE-CREATE-TABLE} will prompt you for the database user ID if you omit one and the database needs one.

owner-name   Text indicating the name of the owner of the specified table.

table-name   Text indicating the name of the external table to connect to.

range-name   Text indicating the range name of the table. If you omit *range-name*, {DATABASE-CREATE-TABLE} will use the table name as *range-name*.

model-table   The name or address of a 1-2-3 database table or the name of an external table on which to model the new external table.

creation-string   Text giving additional information about the table. Some external databases (such as Paradox) let you give additional information; others do not.

You could use the following command to create a table named ANALYSIS in the external database named PROJECTG with the driver SQL_SERVER. The new table will be modeled on the table named CUSTOMER in the current file. In this case, no user ID or password is specified, so 1-2-3 will prompt the user for them if necessary.

```
{DATABASE-CREATE-TABLE "SQL_SERVER";;;;"Z:\DB\PUB-
LIC\PLANNING";;;;"analysis";;;"customer"}
```

Equivalent commands Tools ➤ Database Create Table

{DATABASE-DELETE}

{DATABASE-DELETE *database-table;criteria*}

The {DATABASE-DELETE} command deletes the records from the specified database-table that meet the specified criteria. {DATABASE-DELETE} does not work with external database tables. It takes the following arguments.

database-table   The name or address of a database table.

criteria   Text that specifies a criteria formula, entered in double quotation marks (" ").

You could use the following command to delete the records entered on April 1, 1994 from the database table INDUSTRY:

{DATABASE-DELETE INDUSTRY;"Date=@DATE(94,4,1)"}

Equivalent commands Tools ➤ Database ➤ Delete Records

{DATABASE-DISCONNECT}

{DATABASE-DISCONNECT *range-name*}

The {DATABASE-DISCONNECT} command disconnects an external table, ending all data exchange between 1-2-3 and the external table. To refer to the range name of the specified table again, you will need to reconnect it by using {DATABASE-CONNECT}.

WARNING   After you disconnect from an external table, any data queries or external commands referring to that table will generate errors.

{DATABASE-DISCONNECT} takes the following argument.

range-name Text indicating the range name of the table from which to disconnect. If you omit *range-name*, {DATABASE-DISCONNECT} will use the table name as *range-name*.

You could use the following command to disconnect 1-2-3 from the external table named INDUSTRY:

{DATABASE-DISCONNECT "industry"}

Equivalent commands Tools ➤ Database ➤ Disconnect

{DATABASE-FIND}

{DATABASE-FIND *database-table;criteria*}

The {DATABASE-FIND} command locates and selects records in the specified *database-table* that meet the specified *criteria*. {DATABASE-FIND} does not work with external databases. It takes the following arguments.

database-table The name or address of a database table.

criteria Text that specifies a criteria formula, entered in double quotation marks (" ").

You could use the following command to find the records of all the employees over age 59 who work in Station 4 by searching the database table HR:

{DATABASE-FIND HR;"Station=4";"Age">"59"}

Equivalent commands Tools ➤ Database ➤ Find Records

{DATABASE-SEND-COMMAND}

{DATABASE-SEND-COMMAND *driver-name;[driver-user-id];[driver-password];[connection-string];db-name;[db-user-id];[db-password]; command*}

db-name Text indicating the name of the external database containing the table to which you want to connect.

The {DATABASE-SEND-COMMAND} instruction sends a command to an external database. It takes the following arguments.

driver-name   Text indicating the name of the database driver for the external database containing the table to be connected.

driver-user-id   Text indicating the user ID for the specified driver. {DATABASE-CREATE-TABLE} will prompt you for a driver-user-ID if you omit one and the driver needs one.

driver-password   Text indicating the driver password. {DATABASE-CREATE-TABLE} will prompt you for a password if you omit one and the driver needs one.

connection-string   Text enclosed in double quotation marks (" ") that specifies any extra information needed to connect to a driver.

db-user-id   Text indicating the database user ID. {DATABASE-CREATE-TABLE} will prompt you for the database user ID if you omit one and the database needs one.

db-password   Text indicating the database password. {DATABASE-CREATE-TABLE} will prompt you for the database password if you omit one and the database needs one.

command   Text indicating the command to send.

You could use the following command to encrypt the table named 1995 in the external database G:\HR\MANAGERS\SALARIES. The user will have to enter the password "poiuytre" to perform the command.

```
{DATABASE-SEND-COMMAND "paradox";;;;"g:\hr\managers\sala-
ries";;;"encrypt=1995;poiuytre"}
```

Equivalent commands Tools ➤ Database ➤ Send Command

{QUERY-ADD-FIELD}

{QUERY-ADD-FIELD *field*}

The {QUERY-ADD-FIELD} command adds a field to the currently selected query table. The field is displayed as the last field in the query table.

After adding the field, 1-2-3 updates the query table. It takes the following argument.

field   Text entered in double quotation marks (″ ″) indicating the name of a field to add to the database table.

You could use the following commands to select the query table named RETURNS and add the field Quarter 1:

    {SELECT "Returns";;""query"}
    {QUERY-ADD-FIELD "Quarter 1"}

Equivalent commands   Query ➤ Add Fields

{QUERY-AGGREGATE}

    {QUERY-AGGREGATE *function;field-name*}

The {QUERY-AGGREGATE} command performs calculations on groups of data from a query table. It takes the following arguments.

function   Text indicating the aggregate function to be performed: *sum* (which adds the values); *avg* (which averages the values); *count* (which counts the values); *max* (which finds the largest value); *min* (which finds the smallest value); or *reset* (which resets the values).

field-name   Text indicating the name of a field in the selected query table.

You could use the following commands to display the total cost of phone calls in the query table named Expenses, which contains the fields Calls and Samples:

    {SELECT "Phone_Calls";;"query"}
    {QUERY-AGGREGATE "sum";"Calls"}

Equivalent commands   Query ➤ Aggregate

{QUERY-CHOOSE-FIELDS}

    QUERY-CHOOSE-FIELDS [*field1*];[*field2*];...;[*field15*]}

The {QUERY-CHOOSE-FIELDS} command specifies the fields to appear in the currently selected query table. The fields are displayed in the

21

Macro Commands

same left-to-right order as you specify in {QUERY-CHOOSE-FIELDS}. After performing the {QUERY-CHOOSE-FIELDS} command, 1-2-3 refreshes the query table. {QUERY-CHOOSE-FIELDS} takes the following argument.

field   Text entered in double quotation marks (" ") indicating the name of a field from the database table. You can specify up to fifteen fields to be displayed.

TIP

To choose all the fields in the source database table, enter no field in the {QUERY-CHOOSE-FIELDS} command.

You could use the following command to select the fields "Hired" and "Fired" from the currently selected query table:

{QUERY-CHOOSE-FIELDS "Hired";"Fired"}

Equivalent commands   Query ➤ Choose Fields

{QUERY-COPY-SQL}

{QUERY-COPY-SQL}

The {QUERY-COPY-SQL} command copies to the Clipboard the SQL command equivalent to the current query. Use this command with SQL servers after connecting with {DATABASE-CONNECT}; it has no arguments. If you send this command to an external database that does not support SQL, the database will return an Invalid Command error.

You could use the following command to create the SQL command equivalent to the current query and copy it to the Clipboard:

{QUERY-COPY-SQL}

Equivalent commands   Query ➤ Show SQL

{QUERY-CRITERIA}

{QUERY-CRITERIA [criteria]}

The {QUERY-CRITERIA} command specifies criteria to determine which records to display in a new or currently selected query table. It takes the following argument.

criteria Text that specifies a criteria formula, entered in double quotation marks (" "). {QUERY-CRITERIA} includes all records in the query table if you do not specify *criteria*.

You could use the following command to display the records of all employees who are under 21 and earn more than $75,000:

{QUERY-CRITERIA "AGE<21"#AND#"SALARY>75000"}

Aha! That's who's been hacking the payroll system...

Equivalent commands Query ➤ Set Criteria

{QUERY-DATABASE-TABLE}

{QUERY-DATABASE-TABLE *database-table*}

The {QUERY-DATABASE-TABLE} command changes the database table for the currently selected query table. Provided that the new database table specified contains the same fields as the current table, the current criteria, sort settings, aggregates, and location of the query table do not change; if the new table does not contain the same fields, {QUERY-DATABASE-TABLE} returns an error. It takes the following argument.

database-table The name or address of a database table.

You could use the following command to make the database table BOGUS the currently selected database table:

{QUERY-DATABASE-TABLE BOGUS}

Equivalent commands Query ➤ Set Database Table

21

Macro Commands

{QUERY-JOIN}

{QUERY-JOIN [*join-criteria*]}

The {QUERY-JOIN} command enables you to query multiple database tables containing a common field. It takes the following argument.

join-criteria   Text specifying a join formula for joining two tables, as follows:

+table1.field1=table2.field2

Here *table1* and *table2* are range names for two database tables you want to query and *field1* and *field2* are the names of fields containing similar entries in both tables. The field names must be entered exactly as they appear in the database tables but do not have to match exactly, though the two fields must contain the same type of data. Entries in one field must match entries in the other field, and one field should not contain duplicate entries.

WARNING   If you omit the *join-criteria* argument, 1-2-3 deletes all joins, leaving you with just the original database table.

You could use the following command to join the field LASTNAME in the database table RESPONSES with the field LASTNAME in the database table COLDCALLS:

{QUERY-JOIN "+RESPONSES.LASTNAME=COLDCALLS.LAST-NAME"}

Equivalent commands   Query ➤ Join

{QUERY-NAME}

{QUERY-NAME *new-name*}

The {QUERY-NAME} command renames the currently selected query table. It takes the following argument.

new-name   Text indicating the new name of the query table.

You could use the following command to rename the current query table EXPANSION:

    {QUERY-NAME EXPANSION}

Equivalent commands Query ➤ Name

{QUERY-NEW}

    {QUERY-NEW database-table;output-range;[criteria];[query-
    name];[record-limit];[field1];[field2];...;[field10]}

The {QUERY-NEW} command creates a query table containing the records specified from a database table. It takes the following arguments.

database-table   The name or address of a database table.

output-range   The name or address of the range in which to create the query table. Be aware that {QUERY-NEW} will overwrite any existing data in that range; that *output-range* cannot overlap *database-table* {QUERY-NEW}; and that if you specify a range, {QUERY-NEW} will display only as many records and fields as fit in that range (limited by the number of columns and rows; you can resize the query table afterwards if necessary to display more fields and records). If *output-range* is the top-left corner of a range, it is limited only by the boundaries of your worksheet.

criteria   Text that specifies a criteria formula, entered in double quotation marks (" "). You can omit *criteria* to have {QUERY-NEW} select all the records in *database-table*.

query-name   The name for the query table, entered as text. {QUERY-NEW} a default name (Query 1, Query 2, etc.) if you do not specify a name.

record-limit   An integer indicating the maximum number of records to be displayed in the query table; you can omit *record-limit* to display all records that match *criteria*.

field1...field10   The names of fields, entered in double quotation marks (" "), from *database-table* to display in the query table. Omit the *field* arguments to have {QUERY-NEW} display all the fields in *database-table*.

Arrange the *field* arguments in the order in which you want to have {QUERY-NEW} display them.

You could use the following command to create a new query table starting in cell U2 of sheet IC from the database table INVENTORY. The new table will be named REMAINDER, consisting of those records whose designation is "Perfume", and will include the "EDT" and "KLP" fields form INVENTORY:

> {QUERY-NEW INVENTORY;IC:U2;"Designation=""Perfume""";
> "Remainder";;"EDT";"KLP"}

Equivalent commands Tools ➤ Database ➤ New Query

{QUERY-OPTIONS}

> {QUERY-OPTIONS *option;on-off;[record-limit]*}

The {QUERY-OPTIONS} command turns on and off options for manipulating data in the currently selected query table. It takes the following arguments.

option Text indicating an option to set, from the following list: *allow-updates* allows you to copy any changes made in the query table to the database table; *unique-only* includes only unique records in the query table; *limit-output* lets you use the *record-limit* argument to limit the number of records that appear in the query table; *show-samples* lets you select from a list of unique values to indicate criteria for the query table; and *auto-refresh* refreshes the query table results when you change any criteria, sort settings, options, fields, or aggregation methods.

on-off On or Off, indicating whether to turn the given option on or off.

record-limit An integer from 1 through 8191 determining how many records appear in the query table. *record-limit* applies only if you turn on the *limit-output* option.

WARNING Avoid turning on the limit-output and allow-updates options for the same query table.

You could use the following command to refresh the current query table whenever criteria, sort settings, options, fields, or aggregation methods were changed:

{QUERY-OPTIONS "auto-refresh";"on"}

Equivalent commands Query ➤ Set Options

{QUERY-REFRESH}

{QUERY-REFRESH}

The {QUERY-REFRESH} command refreshes the currently selected query table after changes have been made to the database table, query options, criteria, or aggregate, so that the fields are accurate. {QUERY-REFRESH} has no arguments.

TIP Make sure that a database table can be refreshed by running a {QUERY-OPTIONS "allow updates";"on"} command before running a {QUERY-REFRESH} command.

You could use the following commands to refresh the query table HORNETS:

{SELECT "Hornets";;"query"}
{QUERY-OPTIONS "allow updates";"on"}
{QUERY-REFRESH}

Equivalent commands Query ➤ Refresh Now

{QUERY-REMOVE-FIELD}

{QUERY-REMOVE-FIELD *field*}

The {QUERY-REMOVE-FIELD} command removes the specified field from the currently selected query table; 1-2-3 automatically refreshes the query table after executing this command. {QUERY-REMOVE-FIELD}

21

Macro Commands

takes the following argument.

field   The name of a field from the database table, entered in double quotation marks (" ").

You could use the following command to remove the field named Address3 from the current database:

    {QUERY-REMOVE-FIELD "Address3"}

Equivalent commands   Query ➤ Choose Fields

{QUERY-SHOW-FIELD}

    {QUERY-SHOW-FIELD *field*; *field-alias*}

The {QUERY-SHOW-FIELD} command creates an alias field name for the specified field in the currently selected query table. This does not change the field name in the database itself, only in the query table. This is particularly useful for displaying more comprehensible names in your query tables than your database permits. It takes the following arguments.

field   The name of a field from the database table, entered in double quotation marks (" ").

field-alias   The alias (alternate name) that you want to appear for the field in the query table.

You could use the following command to specify the alias "Estimated Time to Completion" for the field named D_REM in the currently selected query table:

    {QUERY-SHOW-FIELD "D_REM";"Estimated Time to Completion"}

Equivalent commands   Query Show Field As

{QUERY-SORT}

    {QUERY-SORT [*key1*];[*order1*];[*key2*];[*order2*];[*key3*];[*order3*]}

The {QUERY-SORT} command sorts data in the currently selected query table in the specified order. It takes the following arguments.

key1   The first sort key.

order1   *ascend* or *descend*, the sort order for *key1* (*ascend* sorts alphabetically and from smallest to largest; *descend* sorts in reverse-alphabetical order and from largest to smallest).

key2   The second sort key.

order2   *ascend* or *descend*, the sort order for *key2*.

key3   The third sort key.

order3   *ascend* or *descend*, the sort order for *key3*.

T I P   Use the {QUERY-SORT-KEY-DEFINE} command (described next) if you need to sort with more than three keys.

You could use the following command to sort the records in the currently selected query table first by the LastName field, then by the FirstName field, and thirdly by the Initial field, all in alphabetical (ascending) order:

    {QUERY-SORT "LastName";"ascend";"FirstName";"ascend";
    "Initial";"ascend"}

Equivalent commands   Query ➤ Sort

{QUERY-SORT-KEY-DEFINE}

    {QUERY-SORT-KEY-DEFINE *key-number;key-field;key-order*}

The {QUERY-SORT-KEY-DEFINE} command defines the sort key for a {QUERY-SORT} command to use. {QUERY-SORT-KEY-DEFINE} does not actually perform the sort; you'll need to run {QUERY-SORT} after it. It takes the following arguments.

key-number   An integer value from 1 through 255 indicating the sort key. The smallest-numbered sort key is used first.

21

Macro Commands

key-field   Text indicating the field name to sort.

key-order   Text indicating the sort order for *key-field*, *ascend* or *descend* (*ascend* sorts alphabetically and from smallest to largest; *descend* sorts in reverse-alphabetical order and from largest to smallest).

You could use the following commands to select the query table ELECTION, define the sort key 1 to sort by the value of the "Votes" field, and sort in descending order:

```
{SELECT ELECTION;;"query"}
{QUERY-SORT-KEY-DEFINE 1;"Votes";"descend"}
{QUERY-SORT}
```

Equivalent commands   Query ➤ Sort

{QUERY-SORT-RESET}

```
{QUERY-SORT-RESET}
```

The {QUERY-SORT-RESET} command resets all sort keys that have been defined for the currently selected query table. It has no arguments.

Equivalent commands   Query ➤ Sort Reset

{QUERY-UPDATE}

```
{QUERY-UPDATE}
```

The {QUERY-UPDATE} command copies any changes made to records in the currently selected query table to the corresponding database table. This command has no arguments. To make sure that a database table is open for updates, consider running a {QUERY-OPTIONS "allow updates";"on"} command before a {QUERY-UPDATE} command.

You could use the following command to update changes made to the currently selected query table:

```
{QUERY-UPDATE}
```

Equivalent commands   Query ➤ Update ➤ Database Table

{QUERY-UPGRADE}

{QUERY-UPGRADE *input-range;output-range;criteria-range;*[*query-name*]}

The {QUERY-UPGRADE} command upgrades a query from a previous version of 1-2-3 so that it works with the Query commands in 1-2-3 Release 5. {QUERY-UPGRADE} creates a new query table that contains the same fields as those in the old *output-range* and displays the new query table on top of *output-range*. It takes the following arguments.

input-range   The name or address of the input range for queries from previous versions of 1-2-3.

output-range   The name or address of the output range for queries from previous versions of 1-2-3.

criteria-range   The name or address of the criteria range for queries from previous versions of 1-2-3.

query-name   The new name for the new query table, entered as text in double quotation marks (" "). You can omit *query-name*, and {QUERY-UPGRADE} will give the query table a default name (Query 1, Query 2, etc.).

WARNING   {QUERY-UPGRADE} adds a computed column to the query table for each criterion containing a formula on the left side of the operator [e.g., @ROUND(PROFIT-TAX)], and writes over any existing data in the query table location.

TIP   You can upgrade a join query from a previous version of 1-2-3 by using a {QUERY-UPGRADE} command with the join criteria as the criteria-range argument.

21

Macro Commands

You could use the following command to create a new query table named "Computers" from information contained in the old input range STOCK_BOUGHT and criteria range STOCK_CRIT, and locate the table on the old output range STOCK_SOLD:

{QUERY-UPGRADE STOCK-
BOUGHT;STOCK_SOLD;STOCK_CRIT;"Computers"}

{ROLLBACK}

{ROLLBACK [*driver-name*];[*database-name*]}

The {ROLLBACK} command cancels pending external database transactions. If both arguments are specified, {ROLLBACK} cancels the specified database transactions. If no arguments are specified, {ROLL-BACK} cancels all pending external database transactions. {ROLLBACK} (and its counterpart macro command, {COMMIT}) work only with the SQL Server driver. {ROLLBACK} takes the following arguments.

driver-name   Text indicating the name of the driver.

database-name   Text indicating the name of the external database.

You could use the following command to cancel the transactions pending for the driver SQL_SERVER and the database named FINANCE:

{ROLLBACK "SQL_SERVER";"FINANCE"}

{SEND-SQL}

{SEND-SQL *range*;*command*;[*output-range*];[*error-code-location*]}

The {SEND-SQL} command sends the specified SQL command to an external database driver, against the database containing the specified external database table.

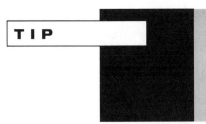

You need to connect to the external database before you can use the {SEND-SQL} command. Use the {DATABASE-CONNECT} command to connect to an external database. Make sure the external database supports SQL, or {SEND-SQL} will return an error.

{SEND-SQL} takes the following arguments.

range   The range name of an external database table.

command   Text that specifies an SQL command. You can enter a range as *command*, in which case {SEND-SQL} concatenates the labels in the range from left to right in a row and from top to bottom to produce the label.

output-range   The name or address of the destination range for data received from the SQL command. Be aware that {SEND-SQL} will overwrite any existing data in *output-range*.

error-code-location   The cell in which to display the SQL command return code.

You could use the following command to send the command "LOCK TABLE" to the range BENEFITS in the external database named HR:

    {SEND-SQL "BENEFITS";"LOCK TABLE"}

Equivalent commands Tools ➤ Database ➤ Send Command

DDE and OLE Macro Commands

This section discusses the DDE (Dynamic Data Exchange) and OLE (Object Linking and Embedding) macro commands. DDE commands are used to create and update links between 1-2-3 and other Windows applications, while OLE commands create and maintain OLE embedded objects.

NOTE See Chapter 11 (starting on page 613) for complete explanations of OLE and DDE.

{AUDIT}

{AUDIT *audit*;[*files*];[*result*];[*report-range*];[*audit-range*]}

The {AUDIT} command lets you identify or create a report of all formulas or the relationships of values and formulas in the current file or in all active files. You can also use {AUDIT} to identify or create a report of circular references, file links, or DDE links. It takes the following arguments.

audit   What to audit, entered as text: *formulas* to audit all cells that contain formulas; *precedents* to audit all cells that are referred to by a formula; *dependents* to audit all cells that contain a formula that refers to the cells; *circular* to audit the first cell involved in a circular reference; 1-2-3 also automatically uses the default settings for all arguments that follow audit; *file-links* to audit all cells that contain a formula that links to other 1-2-3 files; *dde-links* to audit all cells that contain a link between the current file and other Windows applications.

files   Text indicating which files to audit: Either *current-file*, which edits the current file and is the default setting if you omit the *files* argument, or *all-open-files*, which edits all open files.

result   Text indicating how 1-2-3 shows you the results of the audit: *selection* highlights the cells found in the audit and is the default if you omit the *result* argument; *report* produces a list of all cells found in the audit, one item per cell from top to bottom, left to right, in *report-range*.

report-range   The name or address of a blank cell or a blank range where 1-2-3 produces an audit report, if you specify *report* for *result*. {AUDIT} produces a list of all cells found in the audit, one item per cell from top to bottom, left to right.

audit-range The name or address of a range to audit for formula precedents or cell dependents. *audit-range* does not apply to other *audit* options. {AUDIT} audits the current selection if you omit *audit-range* and specify *precedents* or *dependents* for *audit*.

You could use the following command to produce an audit report of DDE links in the current file, starting in cell B2 of worksheet O:

    {AUDIT "dde-links";"current-file";"report";Z:B2}

Equivalent commands Tools ➤ Audit

{DDE-ADVISE}

    {DDE-ADVISE [*branch-location*];*item-name*;[*format*];
    [*destination*];[*acknowledge*]}

The {DDE-ADVISE} command specifies the macro to be executed when changes are made to data in the server application. It takes the following arguments.

branch-location The name or address of a cell or range containing macro instructions or the name of another macro or subroutine. If you specify a range, {DDE-ADVISE} branches to the first cell in the range. *branch-location* is optional if you include a *destination* argument.

item-name Text indicating the name of the linked item that {DDE-ADVISE} monitors.

format Text indicating which Clipboard format to use for incoming data: use *Text* (the default) for text format, *WK3* for worksheets in WK3 format, or *WK1* for worksheets in WK1 format.

destination The name or address of the range in which {DDE-ADVISE} is to put updated data.

acknowledge Yes or No, indicating whether to acknowledge data messages. The default setting (if you omit the *acknowledge* argument) is to acknowledge messages.

You could use the following command to execute the macro in the range named HOTLYNX if the linked item named "Flame_Chart" changes in the server application:

{DDE-ADVISE HOTLYNX;"Flame_Chart"}

{DDE-CLOSE}

{DDE-CLOSE [*conversation-number*]}

The {DDE-CLOSE} command terminates the specified DDE link with a Windows application. It takes the following arguments.

conversation-number   The number of the conversation to terminate. Windows assigns a unique identification number to each conversation taking place; the {DDE-OPEN} macro command receives this number and (if you use the *location* argument) stores it in the worksheet.

NOTE   You can omit the *conversation-number* argument. This causes {DDE-CLOSE} to close the current conversation. If there is no current conversation, {DDE-CLOSE} has no effect; you can use {DDE-USE} to make a conversation current. You can specify –1 for *conversation-number* if you want to close all the open conversations at once.

You could use the following command to close the third DDE link:

{DDE-CLOSE 3}

{DDE-EXECUTE}

{DDE-EXECUTE *execute-string*}

The {DDE-EXECUTE} command sends a command string to a DDE server application. Make sure that a conversation is open before running {DDE-EXECUTE}; otherwise, it will return an error. {DDE-EXECUTE} takes the following argument.

execute-string Any command supported by the server application, including macros, entered as text.

NOTE If the {DDE-EXECUTE} command is successful, 1-2-3 goes to the next cell in the macro, without carrying out any macro instructions after {DDE-EXECUTE} in the cell. If the {DDE-EXECUTE} command fails, 1-2-3 continues in the same cell. Plan your macros in case {DDE-EXECUTE} fails.

You could use the following command to close all the Word for Windows documents that were open, where Word was the server application:

    {DDE-EXECUTE "FileCloseAll 1"}

{DDE-OPEN}

    {DDE-OPEN *app-name*;*topic-name*;[*location*]}

The {DDE-OPEN} command opens a link to a running Windows server application. You can have {DDE-OPEN} make that link the current conversation and enter the conversation identification number in a given location in the worksheet. It takes the following arguments.

app-name The name of an open Windows application that supports DDE, entered as text in double quotation marks (" ").

topic-name The name of the application file to link to, including the complete path where necessary, entered as text in double quotation marks (" "). To link to the system topic, use "system".

location A range name or address to hold the conversation identification number. If you specify a range, 1-2-3 uses the first cell. *location* is optional but highly useful, especially if you use several {DDE-OPEN} commands in the same macro. If {DDE-OPEN} fails to open the conversation, *location* will display 0.

N O T E

If the {DDE-OPEN} command is successful, 1-2-3 goes to the next cell in the macro, without carrying out any macro instructions after {DDE-OPEN} in the cell. If the {DDE-OPEN} command fails, 1-2-3 continues in the same cell. Plan your macros in case {DDE-OPEN} fails.

You could use the following command to open Ami Pro and the Ami Pro file E:\AMIPRO\123LINK\SALES.SAM:

{DDE-OPEN "AMIPRO";"E:\AMIPRO\123LINK\SALES.SAM"}

{DDE-POKE}

{DDE-POKE *range;item-name;[format]*}

The {DDE-POKE} command sends a range of data from 1-2-3 to a DDE server application during the current conversation. Make sure that the server application supports this functionality; many do not. {DDE-POKE} takes the following arguments.

range   The name or address of the 1-2-3 range containing the data to send to the server application.

item-name   The name of the linked item in the server application to transfer the data to.

format   Text indicating which Clipboard format to use for incoming data: use *Text* (the default) for text format, *WK3* for worksheets in WK3 format, or *WK1* for worksheets in WK1 format.

You could use the following command to send the data in the range MARCH to the linked item "Results":

{DDE-POKE MARCH;"Results"}

{DDE-REQUEST}

{DDE-REQUEST *range;item-name;[format]*}

The {DDE-REQUEST} command receives data from a Windows server application. {DDE-REQUEST} returns an error if no conversation is in progress. Since {DDE-REQUEST} does not clear data or formatting from the specified range before entering data received from the server application, you may want to use an {EDIT-CLEAR} command on the range first to clear data or formatting. {DDE-REQUEST} takes the following arguments.

range The name or address of the range in which to enter the requested data.

item-name The name of the linked item in the server application, entered as text in double quotation marks (" "), from which to transfer data.

format Text indicating which Clipboard format to use for incoming data: use *Text* (the default) for text format, *WK3* for worksheets in WK3 format, or *WK1* for worksheets in WK1 format.

NOTE If the {DDE-REQUEST} command is successful, 1-2-3 goes to the next cell in the macro, without carrying out any macro instructions after {DDE-REQUEST} in the cell. If the {DDE-REQUEST} command fails, 1-2-3 continues in the same cell. Plan your macros in case {DDE-REQUEST} fails.

You could use the following command to request the current value from the linked item named "Author" and place it in cell B2 in the current worksheet:

    {DDE-REQUEST B2;"Author"}

{DDE-TABLE}

    {DDE-TABLE location;[type]}

The {DDE-TABLE} command creates a table of all active DDE links in the active files. It takes the following arguments.

21

Macro Commands

location   The address or name of the upper-left cell of the range in which to put the table of links.

type   *long* or *short*, entered as text in double quotation marks (" "). *long* includes both DDE conversation information (conversation number, application, and topic) and link information (item, format, status, data location, and branch location), and is the default setting if you omit the *type* argument. *short* includes DDE conversation information only (conversation number, application, and topic). A *long* table occupies eight columns; a *short* table occupies three columns; each is as many rows deep as there are links, plus one row for headings and one blank row.

You could use the following command to create a short-format table of links in the range LINKS:

    {DDE-TABLE LINKS;"short"}

{DDE-UNADVISE}

    {DDE-UNADVISE *item-name*;[*format*]}

The {DDE-UNADVISE} command ends a {DDE-ADVISE} command. It takes the following arguments.

item-name   Text indicating the name of the linked item that {DDE-ADVISE} monitors.

format   Text indicating which Clipboard format to use for incoming data: *Text* (the default) for text format, *WK3* for worksheets in WK3 format, or *WK1* for worksheets in WK1 format. *format* is an optional argument but is necessary when the {DDE-ADVISE} command that you are turning off contained a *format* argument, in which case the {DDE-UNADVISE} command must contain the same *format* argument.

You could use the following command to end the DDE command for the linked item named "Flame_Chart":

    {DDE-UNADVISE;"Flame_Chart"}

{DDE-USE}

    {DDE-USE *conversation-number*}

The {DDE-USE} command makes the specified conversation current, so that subsequent DDE macro commands refer to it. {DDE-USE} returns an error if given an invalid conversation number. It takes the following argument.

conversation-number   The unique identification number for the conversation. The easiest way to retrieve this is to use the *location* option in {DDE-OPEN}, which stores the identification number in the worksheet.

You could use the following command to make conversation number 3 current:

    {DDE-USE NUM_3}

{EDIT-OBJECT}

    {EDIT-OBJECT [*verb*]}

The {EDIT-OBJECT) command executes a verb for the currently selected OLE embedded object. It takes the following argument.

verb   *primary* or *secondary*, entered as text in double quotation marks (" "), indicating the verb to be executed. If you specify *secondary* and there is no secondary verb, {EDIT-OBJECT} executes the primary verb. If you omit the *verb* argument, the server application executes the edit verb, whether or not it is the primary verb.

You could use the following command to execute the primary verb for an OLE embedded object:

    {EDIT-OBJECT}

Equivalent commands   Edit ➤ Insert Object

{EDIT-PASTE-LINK}

    {EDIT-PASTE-LINK [*destination*];[*format*];[*reference*]}

The {EDIT-PASTE-LINK} command creates a link between a worksheet file and the file referenced on the Clipboard. The Clipboard needs to contain data copied from an application that supports OLE or DDE before you run the {EDIT-PASTE-LINK} command. {EDIT-PASTE-LINK} sets up links that update automatically. It takes the following arguments.

destination   The name or address of the range to which to send updated data.

format   Text indicating which Clipboard format to use for incoming data: *Text* (the default) for text format, *WK3* for worksheets in WK3 format, or *WK1* for worksheets in WK1 format.

reference   *absolute* or *relative* (the default), entered as text in double quotation marks (" "), indicating whether 1-2-3 creates absolute or relative cell references when linking to 1-2-3 cell data. (The *reference* argument does not apply to links with another application.)

You could use the following command to paste-link the contents of the Clipboard into the range DOCTEXT with the default format:

    {EDIT-PASTE-LINK DOCTEXT}

Equivalent commands   Edit ➤ Paste Link

{INSERT-OBJECT}

    {INSERT-OBJECT *object-type*;[*location*]}

The {INSERT-OBJECT} command starts or activates the selected application, creates an OLE object in it, and embeds the object in the worksheet, closing the server application if it was not already open. It takes the following arguments.

object-type   Text indicating the name of the OLE server object.

location   The name or address of the cell in which to put the upper-left corner of the OLE object. You can omit *location* if you want {INSERT-OBJECT} to use the current selection.

You could use the following command to create an OLE object with Word 6 for Windows and insert it in the range named WORDLINK:

    {INSERT-OBJECT "Microsoft Word 6.0 Document";WORDLINK}

Equivalent commands Edit ➤ Insert Object

{LINK-ASSIGN}

{LINK-ASSIGN *link-name;range;[clear-styles]*}

The {LINK-ASSIGN} command specifies a destination range for an OLE link or a DDE link. If the specified link is active, {LINK-ASSIGN} updates data even if the link-update mode is manual. It takes the following arguments.

link-name Text indicating the name of the existing link specified in {LINK-CREATE}. *link-name* must exist, or {LINK-ASSIGN} will return an error.

range The name or address of the destination range for the OLE link. Make sure that *range* is large enough for the incoming data, or else the incoming data will be clipped to fit the range.

clear-styles Yes or No, indicating whether to delete styles in *range* whenever the client data is updated. The default setting if you omit the *clear-styles* argument is not to delete the styles; and {LINK-ASSIGN} ignores the *clear-styles* argument if the link is not for range data.

You could use the following command to specify the range named LEASED PROPERTY for the link "Rent":

{LINK-ASSIGN "Rent";LEASED PROPERTY}

{LINK-CREATE}

{LINK-CREATE *link-name;app-name;topic-name;item-name;*
[format];[mode];[branch-location]}

The {LINK-CREATE} command creates a link between the current worksheet file and a Windows DDE or OLE server application without using the Clipboard. 1-2-3 tries to create an OLE link whenever possible, but if it cannot (e.g., for formats such as Text or WK1), it creates a DDE link instead. {LINK-CREATE} takes the following arguments.

21

Macro Commands

link-name   The link name, entered as text in double quotation marks (" "). {LINK-CREATE} returns an error if the link specified is already active.

app-name   The name of an open Windows DDE or OLE server application, entered as text in double quotation marks (" ") *without* a path and extension.

topic-name   The name of the application file to link to, entered as text in double quotation marks (" "). You can link to the system topic by using "system" as *topic-name*.

item-name   The name of the item to link to, entered as text in double quotation marks (" ").

format   Text indicating which Clipboard format to use for incoming data: *Text* (the default) for text format, *WK3* for worksheets in WK3 format, or *WK1* for worksheets in WK1 format.

mode   *automatic* or *manual*, indicating when data is to be updated. *automatic* (the default) provides automatic updating; *manual* provides updating only when the user chooses it. Note that some server applications do not support automatic and manual update modes; in such case, {LINK-CREATE} updates data in whichever mode is supported.

branch-location   The name or address of the cell where macro execution will start when the data from the link is updated. Note that {LINK-CREATE} ignores the *branch-location* argument for OLE links.

NOTE   If the {LINK-CREATE} command is successful, 1-2-3 goes to the next cell in the macro, without carrying out any macro instructions after {LINK-CREATE} in the cell. If the {LINK-CREATE} command fails, 1-2-3 continues in the same cell. Plan your macros in case {LINK-CREATE} fails.

You could use the following command to create a link to the bookmark named BLURB in the Word for Windows document PUBLISH:

{LINK-CREATE "LINK2";"Winword";"D:\WINWORD\ODDITIES\PUB-LISH.DOC";"BLURB"}

{LINK-DEACTIVATE}

{LINK-DEACTIVATE [*link-name*]}

The {LINK-DEACTIVATE} command deactivates a DDE or OLE link in the current worksheet so that it is not updated. The link remains in place, but is inactive; you can resuscitate it by using {LINK-UPDATE} or delete it forever by using {LINK-DELETE}. {LINK-DEACTIVATE} takes the following argument.

link-name The name of the existing link to deactivate, entered as text in double quotation marks (" "). (If the link does not exist, {LINK-DEACTIVATE} will return an error.) You can make 1-2-3 deactivate all existing links by omitting the *link-name* argument.

You could use the following command to deactivate the link named "LINK4":

{LINK-DEACTIVATE "LINK4"}

{LINK-DELETE}

{LINK-DELETE *link-name*}

The {LINK-DELETE} command deletes the specified DDE or OLE link. It dissociates any existing destination range from the link but leaves the values obtained through the link in the range. It takes the following argument.

link-name The name of the existing link to delete, entered as text in double quotation marks (" "). (If the link does not exist, {LINK-DELETE} will return an error.)

21

Macro Commands

> **NOTE** If you delete the last link in a conversation, the conversation will be closed.

You could use the following command to delete the link named "LINK4":

{LINK-DELETE "LINK4"}

{LINK-REMOVE}

{LINK-REMOVE *link-name*}

The {LINK-REMOVE} command removes the currently used destination range (specified by {LINK-ASSIGN}) for a DDE or OLE link but leaves the data in the range. For example, if you had linked a Freelance chart to a 1-2-3 spreadsheet, the link would be removed, leaving the Freelance chart as an embedded object.

{LINK-REMOVE} does not delete a link; use {LINK-DELETE} to delete a link. You can use {LINK-REMOVE} with {LINK-ASSIGN} to change the destination range for a link. {LINK-REMOVE} takes the following argument.

link-name The name of the existing link to deactivate, entered as text in double quotation marks (" "). (If the link does not exist, or if no destination range was assigned to the link with a {LINK-ASSIGN} command, {LINK-REMOVE} will return an error.)

You could use the following command to remove the destination link for the link named "LINK4":

{LINK-REMOVE "LINK4"}

{LINK-TABLE}

{LINK-TABLE *location*}

The {LINK-TABLE} command builds a table of all DDE and OLE links associated with the current file. The table contains the link name, application, topic, item, format, update mode, link status, and destination range. {LINK-TABLE} takes the following argument.

location   The name or address of the upper-left cell of the range in which to put the table. The table will take up eight columns, and one row for each link associated with the file plus one blank row. Leave enough space for the table in *location*, or it will overwrite existing data.

You could use the following command to create a table of links in cell Z280:

    {LINK-TABLE Z280}

{LINK-UPDATE}

    {LINK-UPDATE [*link-name*]}

The {LINK-UPDATE} command updates active DDE and OLE links, or activates and updates deactivated links. (To deactivate a link, use {LINK-DEACTIVATE}.) {LINK-UPDATE} takes the following argument.

link-name   The name of the existing link to be reactivated or updated. ({LINK-UPDATE} will return an error if the specified link does not exist.) To update all existing links for the current file, omit the *link-name* argument.

You could use the following command to update all the links in the current file:

    {LINK-UPDATE}

{UPDATE-OBJECT}

    {UPDATE-OBJECT}

The {UPDATE-OBJECT} command updates a 1-2-3 OLE object embedded in an OLE client application file. This command has no arguments.

21

Macro Commands

You could use the following command to update a 1-2-3 object embedded in a CorelDRAW! layout:

{UPDATE-OBJECT}

Equivalent commands   Edit ➤ Links ➤ Update, Edit ➤ Links ➤ Update All

Edit Macro Commands

This section of the chapter discusses the edit macro commands, which correspond to the commands on the Edit menu.

{DELETE-COLUMNS}

{DELETE-COLUMNS [*range*];[*delete-selection*]}

The {DELETE-COLUMNS} command deletes the whole of each column specified or the part of each column specified that falls within the specified range. It takes the following arguments.

range   The name or address of a range that contains at least one cell in each column to be deleted. If you do not specify a range, {DELETE-COLUMNS} deletes columns containing cells in the currently selected range or collection.

delete-selection   Yes or No, indicating whether to delete only the cells in *range* and move existing data to the left. If you omit *delete-selection*, {DELETE-COLUMNS} deletes entire columns.

You could use the following command to delete columns AA and AB in worksheet D:

{DELETE-COLUMNS D:AA1..AB2}

Equivalent commands   Edit ➤ Delete

{DELETE-ROWS}

{DELETE-ROWS [*range*];[*delete-selection*]}

The {DELETE-ROWS} command deletes the whole of each row specified or the part of each row specified that falls within the specified range. It takes the following arguments.

range   The name or address of a range that contains at least one cell in each row to be deleted. If you do not specify a range, {DELETE-ROWS} deletes rows containing cells in the currently selected range or collection.

delete-selection   Yes or No, indicating whether to delete only the cells in *range* and move existing data up. If you omit *delete-selection*, {DELETE-ROWS} deletes entire rows.

You could use the following command to delete the part of the rows contained in the range named ANALYSTS:

{DELETE-ROWS ANALYSTS;"yes"}

The cells below the deleted range will move up to fill those cells.

Equivalent commands   Edit ➤ Delete

{DELETE-SHEETS}

{DELETE-SHEETS [*range*]}

The {DELETE-SHEETS} command deletes the worksheets containing cells in the specified range. It takes the following argument.

range   The name or address of a range containing at least one cell in each worksheet to delete. If you do not specify a range, {DELETE-SHEETS} deletes all the worksheets containing cells in the currently selected range or collection.

You could use the following command to delete all worksheets included in the range named RECORDS:

{DELETE-SHEETS RECORDS}

Equivalent commands   Edit ➤ Delete

21

Macro Commands

{EDIT-CLEAR}

{EDIT-CLEAR [*selection*];[*property*]}

The {EDIT-CLEAR} command deletes selected data and formatting. It does not cut the selected data to the Clipboard.

WARNING {EDIT-CLEAR} does not work on cells that have been protected. Use an {UNPROTECT} command if you need to clear the contents of protected cells.

{EDIT-CLEAR} takes the following arguments.

selection   The name or address of the range whose contents you want to delete. If you do not specify a *selection*, {EDIT-CLEAR} clears the current selection.

property   *contents*, *styles*, or *both*, specifying what to clear. *contents* clears the contents of cells without affecting formatting; *styles* clears all style formatting except alignment without affecting the cell contents; and *both* clears both contents and style formatting.

You could use the following command to remove the contents of the range DELRANGE without changing any formatting applied to the cells:

{EDIT-CLEAR DELRANGE;"contents"}

Equivalent commands   Edit ➤ Clear

{EDIT-COPY}

{EDIT-COPY [*selection*];[*format*]}

The {EDIT-COPY} command copies data and related formatting from the worksheet to the Clipboard. It takes the following arguments.

selection   The name or address of the range to copy to the Clipboard. If you do not specify a selection, {EDIT-COPY} copies the current selection.

format   Text indicating which Clipboard format to use for incoming data: *Text* (the default) for text format, *WK3* for worksheets in WK3 format, or *WK1* for worksheets in WK1 format.

You could use the following command to copy the contents of the range FLIGHT SIMS to the Clipboard in WK3 format:

    {EDIT-COPY FLIGHT SIMS;"WK3")

Equivalent commands   Edit ➤ Copy

{EDIT-COPY-FILL}

    {EDIT-COPY-FILL *direction*;[*range*]}

The {EDIT-COPY-FILL} command copies the contents of the specified row, column, or worksheet in the specified range to all the other cells in the range. It takes the following arguments.

direction   *up*, *down*, *right*, *left*, *back*, or *forward*, entered as text in double quotation marks (" "), indicating the direction to copy the data: *down* copies the top row of *range* to all rows in *range*; *right* copies the leftmost column of *range* to all columns in *range*; *up* copies the bottom row of *range* to all rows in *range*; *left* copies the rightmost column of *range* to all rows in *range*; *back* copies the first worksheet of *range* to all worksheets in *range*; and *forward* copies the last worksheet of *range* to all worksheets in *range*.

range   The name or address of the range to fill. If you do not specify a range, {EDIT-COPY-FILL} uses the current selection.

You could use the following command to copy the formulas in the first column of the range named CASES SHIPPED to all the columns in that range:

    {EDIT-COPY-FILL "right";CASES SHIPPED}

Equivalent commands   Edit ➤ Copy ➤ Down, Edit ➤ Copy ➤ Right

{EDIT-CUT}

    {EDIT-CUT [*selection*];[*format*]}

21

Macro Commands

The {EDIT-CUT} command cuts the specified data and its formatting from the worksheet to the Clipboard, removing the data from the worksheet. It takes the following arguments.

selection The name or address of the range to cut to the Clipboard. If you do not specify a selection, {EDIT-CUT} cuts the current selection.

format Text indicating which Clipboard format to use for incoming data: Text (the default) for text format, *WK3* for worksheets in WK3 format, or *WK1* (for worksheets in WK1 format).

You could use the following command to cut the contents of the range named LABRADOR to the Clipboard in text format:

    {EDIT-CUT LABRADOR}

Equivalent commands Edit ➤ Cut

{EDIT-FIND}

    {EDIT-FIND [*search-for*];[*look-in*];[*search-through*]]}

The {EDIT-FIND} command finds the first occurrence of specified text in labels, formulas, or both. {EDIT-FIND} starts its search in the upper-left cell of the range or spreadsheet, then searches down columns, and searches worksheets front to back. If {EDIT-FIND} does not find the text sought, it displays a message box, ending the macro. The command takes the following arguments.

search-for The text to search for. You can search for the last text you searched for by not specifying a new *search-for* argument. *search-for* is not case-specific: It makes no distinction between uppercase and lowercase letters.

look-in *formulas* (cells containing formulas), *text* (cells containing text), or *both* (cells containing text or formulas), specifying the types of cell entries {EDIT-FIND} should search. You can search through the same type of cell entries you last searched by not specifying a new *look-in* argument.

search-through   The name or address of the range to search. To search through the whole of the current file, specify a single cell for the *search-through* argument; to search the current selection (of more than one cell), omit the *search-through* argument.

You could use the following command to find the text "Raptor" among those cells containing labels in the range A:A1..C:Z40:

    {EDIT-FIND "Raptor";"text";A:A1..C:Z40}

Equivalent commands   Edit ➤ Find & Replace

{EDIT-FIND?}

    {EDIT-FIND?}

The {EDIT-FIND?} command displays the Edit Find and Replace dialog box, allowing the user to perform an interactive search. The {EDIT-FIND?} command has no arguments.

You could use the following command to display the Edit Find and Replace dialog box so that the user could perform an interactive search:

    {EDIT-FIND?}

Equivalent commands   Edit ➤ Find & Replace

{EDIT-PASTE}

    {EDIT-PASTE [*selection*];[*format*]}

The {EDIT-PASTE} command pastes whatever data and related formatting is on the Clipboard into the active worksheet file at the specified location and in the specified format. It takes the following arguments.

selection   The name or address of the range into which to paste the contents of the Clipboard. To use the current selection, omit the *selection* argument.

format   Text indicating which Clipboard format to use for incoming data: *Text* (the default) for text format, *WK3* for worksheets in WK3 format, or *WK1* for worksheets in WK1 format.

You could use the following command to paste the contents of the Clipboard into the range LEVEL_5 in WK1 format:

{EDIT-PASTE LEVEL_5;"WK1"}

Equivalent commands Edit ➤ Paste

{EDIT-PASTE-SPECIAL}

{EDIT-PASTE-SPECIAL [*destination*];[*property*]}

The {EDIT-PASTE-SPECIAL} command pastes the contents of the Clipboard into the worksheet in the specified location and with the specified properties. It takes the following arguments.

destination The name or address of the range into which to paste the contents of the Clipboard. To paste into the current selection, omit the *destination* argument.

property Text indicating what to paste: *cell-contents* pastes in cell contents without changing the styles in the destination range; *styles* pastes all formatting from the Clipboard except label alignment, without affecting the contents of the destination range; *both* (the default if you omit the *property* argument) pastes both cell contents and styles into the destination range; *values* pastes both cell contents and formatting into the destination range, but converts all formulas to values; and *query* pastes a query table into the destination range.

You could use the following command to paste data into the range named SALARIES without affecting the formatting of the range:

{EDIT-PASTE-SPECIAL SALARIES;"cell-contents"}

Equivalent commands Edit ➤ Paste Special

{EDIT-QUICK-COPY}

{EDIT-QUICK-COPY *destination*;[*source*]}

The {EDIT-QUICK-COPY} command copies data and its formatting from the specified source range to the specified destination range, without using the Clipboard. {EDIT-QUICK-COPY} is the command equivalent of moving items with the mouse and is especially useful when you need to copy items without overwriting the current contents of the Clipboard. {EDIT-QUICK-COPY} takes the following arguments.

destination   The name or address of the range to copy to.

source   The name or address of the range to copy from. Omit the *source* argument to copy the current selection.

You could use the following command to copy data from the range REC ACCESS to the range INTERNET ACCESS:

    {EDIT-QUICK-COPY INTERNET ACCESS;REC ACCESS}

{EDIT-QUICK-MOVE}

    {EDIT-QUICK-MOVE *destination*;[*source*]}

The {EDIT-QUICK-MOVE} command moves data and its formatting from the specified source range to the specified destination range, without using the Clipboard. {EDIT-QUICK-MOVE} is the command equivalent of moving items with the mouse and is especially useful when you need to move items without overwriting the current contents of the Clipboard. It takes the following arguments.

destination   The name or address of the range to move to.

source   The name or address of the range to move from. Omit the *source* argument to move the current selection.

You could use the following command to move data from the range REC ACCESS to the range INTERNET ACCESS:

    {EDIT-QUICK-MOVE INTERNET ACCESS;REC ACCESS}

{EDIT-REPLACE}

    {EDIT-REPLACE [*search-for*];[*look-in*];[*replacement*];[*search-through*]}

The {EDIT-REPLACE} command finds the first occurrence of specified text in labels, formulas, or both. {EDIT-REPLACE} starts its search in the upper-left cell of the range or spreadsheet, then searches down columns, and searches worksheets front to back. If {EDIT-REPLACE} does not find the text sought, it displays a message box, ending the macro. The command takes the following arguments.

search-for   The text to search for. You can search for the last text you searched for by not specifying a new *search-for* argument.

look-in   *formulas* (cells containing formulas), *text* (cells containing text), or *both* (cells containing text or formulas), specifying the types of cell entries {EDIT-FIND} should search. You can search through the same type of cell entries you last searched by not specifying a new *look-in* argument.

replacement   The replacement text. You can reuse your last replacement text by not specifying a new *replacement* argument.

search-through   The name or address of the range to search. To search through the whole of the current file, specify a single cell for the *search-through* argument; to search the current selection (of more than one cell), omit the *search-through* argument.

You could use the following command to replace "Takeovers" with "Mergers and Acquisitions" in the range named ACTIVITY:

> {EDIT-REPLACE "Takeovers";"text";"Mergers and Acquisitions";ACTIVITY}

Equivalent commands   Edit ➤ Find & Replace

{EDIT-REPLACE-ALL}

> {EDIT-REPLACE-ALL [*search-for*];[*look-in*];[*replacement*];[*search-through*]}

The {EDIT-REPLACE-ALL} command finds and replaces all instances of specified characters in labels, formulas, or both, and replaces them. It takes the following arguments.

search-for   The text to search for. You can search for the last text you searched for by not specifying a new *search-for* argument. *search-for* is not case-specific: It makes no distinction between uppercase and lowercase letters.

look-in *formulas* (cells containing formulas), *text* (cells containing text), or *both* (cells containing text or formulas), specifying the types of cell entries {EDIT-FIND} should search. You can search through the same type of cell entries you last searched by not specifying a new *look-in* argument.

replacement The replacement text. You can reuse your last replacement text by not specifying a new *replacement* argument.

search-through The name or address of the range to search. To search through the whole of the current file, specify a single cell for the *search-through* argument; to search the current selection (of more than one cell), omit the *search-through* argument.

You could use the following command to replace all instances of "Takeaway" with "Takeout" in the range named RESTAURANTS:

{EDIT-REPLACE-ALL "Takeaway";"text";"Takeout";RESTAURANTS}

Equivalent commands Edit ➤ Find & Replace

{FILE-UPDATE-LINKS}

{FILE-UPDATE-LINKS}

The {FILE-UPDATE-S} command recalculates all formulas in the current file that are linked to other files. This command has no arguments.

You could use the following command to recalculate all linked formulas in the current file:

{FILE-UPDATE-LINKS}

Equivalent commands Edit ➤ Links ➤ File Links

{INSERT-COLUMNS}

{INSERT-COLUMNS [*range*];[*number*];[*insert-selection*]}

21

Macro Commands

The {INSERT-COLUMNS} command inserts blank whole columns or blank partial columns at the specified location. It takes the following arguments.

range   The name or address or name of the range to the left of which {INSERT-COLUMNS} is to insert columns. Omit the *range* argument to use the current selection.

number   An integer value indicating how many columns to insert. {INSERT-COLUMNS} inserts the same number of columns as *range* contains if you omit number.

insert-selection   Yes or No, indicating whether to insert partial columns (and move cells to the right to accommodate them) or whole columns (the default).

You could use the following command to insert another five whole columns to the left of the five-column range named WESTERN SALES:

     {INSERT-COLUMNS WESTERN SALES}

Equivalent commands   Edit ➤ Insert

{INSERT-ROWS}

     {INSERT-ROWS [*range*];[*number*];[*insert-selection*]}

The {INSERT-ROWS} command inserts blank whole rows or blank partial rows at the specified location. It takes the following arguments.

range   The name or address or name of the range above which {INSERT-ROWS} is to insert rows. Omit the *range* argument to use the current selection.

number   An integer value indicating how many rows to insert. {INSERT-ROWS} inserts the same number of rows as *range* contains if you omit number.

insert-selection   Yes or No, indicating whether to insert partial rows (and move cells to the down to accommodate them) or whole rows (the default).

You could use the following command to insert another five whole rows above the five-row range named EASTERN SALES:

{INSERT-ROWS EASTERN SALES}

Equivalent commands Edit ➤ Insert

{INSERT-SHEETS}

{INSERT-SHEETS [*where*];[*number*];[*range*]}

The {INSERT-SHEETS} command inserts one or more blank worksheets in the current file at the specified location. It takes the following arguments.

where Text indicating where to insert blank worksheets: *before* inserts worksheets before the first worksheet in *range*; *after* inserts worksheets after the first worksheet in *range*. *after* is the default setting if you omit the *where* argument.

number An integer value indicating how many worksheets to insert. {INSERT-SHEETS} inserts the same number of worksheets as *range* contains if you omit the *number* argument.

range The name or address or name of the range before or after which to insert the worksheets, depending on the *where* argument. Omit *range* to use the current selection.

You could use the following command to insert thirteen worksheets after the first worksheet in the range named MONITOR:

{INSERT-SHEETS "after";13;MONITOR}

Equivalent commands Edit ➤ Insert

21

Macro Commands

File Macro Commands

This section of the chapter discusses the file macro commands, which correspond to the commands on the File menu.

{FILE-CLOSE}

{FILE-CLOSE [*discard*]}

The {FILE-CLOSE} command closes the current file. You can choose to discard any unsaved changes, including updates to embedded OLE objects. {FILE-CLOSE} takes the following argument.

discard   Yes or No, indicating whether to discard any unsaved changes to the current file.

WARNING

Specifying Yes for the *discard* argument closes the file ignoring any unsaved changes in it. Specifying No for the *discard* argument closes a file that has no unsaved changes but leaves open a file that has unsaved changes. Often the best option is to omit the *discard* argument, in which case {FILE-CLOSE} will prompt you to save any unsaved changes in the file or simply close the file if there are no changes.

You could use the following command to close the current file and prompt you to save any unsaved changes:

{FILE-CLOSE}

Equivalent commands   File ➤ Close

{FILE-COMBINE}

{FILE-COMBINE [*how*];*file-name*;[*password*];[*source*]}

The {FILE-COMBINE} command combines data from a 1-2-3 work-sheet file on disk with data in the current file, starting in the current cell. {FILE-COMBINE} also works with Symphony files and Graph files. It takes the following arguments.

how Text indicating how to combine data: *add* adds numbers and formula results from the other file to numbers or blank cells in the current file; *replace* replaces data in the current file with data copied from the file on disk (this is the default if you omit the *how* argument); *subtract* subtracts numbers and formula results in the other file from numbers or blank cells in the current file. You can only use the *how* argument when combining data from 1-2-3 files.

file-name Text indicating the name of the worksheet file containing data to combine with data in the current file. Include the path if necessary.

password Text indicating a password for accessing the file. If you omit this argument, {FILE-COMBINE} will display a password dialog box if a password is necessary.

source The name or address of the range in the other file containing the data to combine with data in the current file. Enter *source* in double quotation marks (" "). Omit the *source* argument to have {FILE-COMBINE} combine all the data in the other file with data in the current file.

You could use the following command to replace data at the current location with data from the range named TEMPERATURE in the file C:\LOTUS\WEATHER\TEMPS.WK4:

{FILE-COMBINE "replace";" C:\LOTUS\WEATHER\
TEMPS.WK4";;TEMPERATURE}

Equivalent commands Combine ➤ 1-2-3 File

{FILE-EXIT}

{FILE-EXIT [*discard*]}

The {FILE-EXIT} command ends the 1-2-3 session. You can choose to discard any unsaved changes in the open files, including updates to embedded OLE objects. It takes the following argument.

discard   Yes or No, indicating whether to discard any unsaved changes to the open files.

WARNING

Specifying Yes for the *discard* argument closes all files, ignoring any unsaved changes in them, and exits 1-2-3. Specifying No for the *discard* argument closes files that have no unsaved changes and exits 1-2-3, but leaves open files that have unsaved changes. Often the best option is to omit the *discard* argument, in which case {FILE-CLOSE} will prompt you to save any unsaved changes in files or simply exit if there are no changes.

You could use the following command to exit 1-2-3 file and prompt you to save any unsaved changes:

    {FILE-EXIT}

Equivalent commands   File ➤ Exit

{FILE-EXTRACT}

    {FILE-EXTRACT *file-name*;[*file-type*];[*password*];[*backup*];[*extract-range*];[*properties*]}

The {FILE-EXTRACT} command saves the specified range to another file. It takes the following arguments.

file-name   Text indicating the name of the file to save. This can be an existing file or a new file; {FILE-EXTRACT} creates a new file if a file named *file-name* does not exist.

file-type   Text indicating the format of the file to be saved, from the following list: *1-2-3* for WK4 format (this is the default if you omit the *file-type* argument); *1-2-3 (wk3)* for WK3 format with formatting information in FM3 format; *1-2-3 (wk1)* for WK1 format with formatting information in FMT format; *dbase (dbf)* for a dBASE file; *paradox (db)* for a Paradox file; or *text (txt)* for a text file (TXT).

password Text indicating a password with which to save the file. If you omit the *password* argument, any existing password for *file-name* will remain in effect. Passwords do not work for text files.

backup Text indicating whether to create a backup file if a file named *file-name* already exists: *backup* saves the existing file with a .BAK extension and saves the current file as *file-name*; *replace* replaces the existing file with the current file, saved as *file-name*. If you do not enter a *backup* argument and a file named *file-name* already exists, {FILE-EXTRACT} will prompt you with the familiar Backup, Replace, Cancel dialog box.

extract-range The name or address of a range in the current file from which to extract data. Omit this argument if you want {FILE-EXTRACT} to use the currently selected range.

properties *formulas* or *values*, indicating how to save values from *extract-range*, as follows: *formulas* saves formulas without converting them to values (this is the default setting); *values* converts formulas to values.

You could use the following command to extract the contents of the named range PROJECTION_95 in the file STRATEGY.WK4, returning values for formulas:

```
{FILE-EXTRACT "STRATEGY.WK4";;;"backup";
PROJECTION_95;"values"}
```

Equivalent Commands File ➤ Save, File ➤ Save As

{FILE-GET-RESERVATION}

{FILE-GET-RESERVATION}

The {FILE-GET-RESERVATION} command gets the network reservation for the current file provided that it is available and that no one has saved the file since you opened it. Once you have the reservation, no one else can save changes to the file until you release the reservation. This command has no arguments.

21

Macro Commands

You could use the following commands to open the file BUDGET.WK4 and get the network reservation for it:

```
{FILE-OPEN "budget.wk4"}
{FILE-GET-RESERVATION}
```

Equivalent commands File ➤ Protect File ➤ Reservation

{FILE-IMPORT}

{FILE-IMPORT [*read-text-as*];*file-name*;[*character-set*]}

The {FILE-IMPORT} command imports data from the specified text file into the current file. You can choose from many different delimiter characters and code pages if necessary.

WARNING When importing numbers from a comma-delimited text file, make sure that the numbers are not formatted with commas. For example, 1,234,567,890 would be read as four different numbers, which might have unfortunate effects upon delicate calculations.

{FILE-IMPORT} takes the following arguments.

read-text-as Text in double quotation marks (" ") indicating how {FILE-IMPORT} is to combine data from a text file: any delimiter symbol (e.g., # or |) or *text* for nondelimited text (one line per cell in successive cells in a column, and up to 512 characters per cell and 8,192 lines of data per worksheet); *numbers* for text and numbers from a delimited text file, or just numbers from a nondelimited text file, one item per cell and one line per row; *tab* for tab-delimited text files; *comma* for comma-delimited text files; *space* for space-delimited text files; *semicolon* for semicolon-delimited text files; or *autoparse* for text and numbers based on the layout of the file.

file-name Text indicating the name of the text file on disk containing the data to import into the current file.

character-set Text indicating the code page to use for interpreting the data in the text file, as per the following list: *windows* for Windows ANSI (this is the default if you omit the argument); *oem* for DOS or OS/2; *cp580* for Multilingual; *cp932* for Japanese; *kanji* for Kanji; *big5* for Taiwanese; *ks* for Korean; *gb* for Chinese; *cp1252* for US Windows; *cp437* for US DOS; *cp860* for Portuguese; *cp863* for French Canadian; *cp865* for Norwegian/Danish; *cp1250* for Eastern European Windows; *cp852* for Eastern European DOS; *cp1251* for Cyrillic Windows; *cp866* for Cyrillic DOS; *cp1253* for Greek Windows; *cp851* for Greek DOS; *cp1254* for Turkish Windows; *cp857* for Turkish DOS; *cp1255* for Hebrew Windows; *cp862* for Hebrew DOS; *cp1256* for Arabic Windows.

You could use the following command to import data from the vertical-bar–delimited text file named PDAVALUE.TXT (that is, a text file using the | delimiter) into the current file, starting from the current cell:

    {FILE-IMPORT "|";"PDAVALUE.TXT"}

Equivalent commands File ➤ Open ➤ Combine

{FILE-NEW}

    {FILE-NEW [*file-name*];[*where*];[*smartmaster*]}

The {FILE-NEW} command creates a new file on disk and in memory and displays the new file in a new and current window. It takes the following arguments.

file-name The name of the file to create, entered as text in double quotation marks (" "). {FILE-NEW} will name your file for you if you omit *file-name*—FILE0001.WK4, FILE0002.WK4, etc.

where *before* or *after*, indicating where in memory (relative to the current file) to place the new file. This can be important when using a macro to move between worksheets. *before* is the default.

smartmaster Text indicating the name of the SmartMaster (WT4) file with which to create the new file. The path and extension of the SmartMaster are not necessary. If you do not specify a SmartMaster, {FILE-NEW} creates a new blank file.

You could use the following command to create a new file named 1994LAST.WK4 immediately after the current file using the Track Sales and Associated Costs SmartMaster (SALESPAK.WT4):

{FILE-NEW 1994last.wk4;"after";"salespak"}

Equivalent commands File ➤ New

{FILE-OPEN}

{FILE-OPEN *file-name*;[*password*];[*read-only*];[*where*];[*read-text-as*];[*character-set*]}

The {FILE-OPEN} command reads a file into memory, makes it the current file, and moves the cell pointer to the cell it was in when you last saved the file. It takes the following arguments.

file-name   The name of the file to open, entered as text in double quotation marks (" "). {FILE-OPEN} returns an error if that file does not exist or is already open.

password   Text indicating a password for opening the file. If you omit the *password* argument, you will be prompted for any existing password.

read-only   Yes or No, indicating whether {FILE-OPEN} should open the file as read-only if the network reservation is not available, or not open the file. If you specify Yes and the reservation is available, you still get the reservation. If you omit the *read-only* argument and the reservation is not available, {FILE-OPEN} will prompt you whether to open the file as read-only or not to open it.

where   *before* or *after*, indicating where in memory (relative to the current file) to open the file. This can be important when using a macro to move between worksheets. *before* is the default.

read-text-as   Text in double quotation marks (" ") indicating how {FILE-OPEN} is to handle data from a text file: *read-text-as* can be any delimiter symbol (e.g., # or |); or *text* for nondelimited text (one line per cell in successive cells in a column, and up to 512 characters per cell and 8192 lines of data per worksheet); *numbers* for text and numbers from a delimited text file, or just numbers from a nondelimited text file (one item per cell and one line per row); *tab* for tab-delimited text files; *comma* for comma-delimited text files; *space* for space-delimited text files; *semicolon* for semicolon-delimited text files; or *autoparse* for text and numbers based on the layout of the file.

character-set   Text indicating the code page to use for interpreting the data in the text file, as per the following list: *windows* for Windows ANSI (this is the default if you omit the argument); *oem* for DOS or OS/2; *cp580* for Multilingual; *cp932* for Japanese; *kanji* for Kanji; *big5* for Taiwanese; *ks* for Korean; *gb* for Chinese; *cp1252* for US Windows; *cp437* for US DOS; *cp860* for Portuguese; *cp863* for French Canadian; *cp865* for Norwegian/Danish; *cp1250* for Eastern European Windows; *cp852* for Eastern European DOS; *cp1251* for Cyrillic Windows; *cp866* for Cyrillic DOS; *cp1253* for Greek Windows; *cp851* for Greek DOS; *cp1254* for Turkish Windows; *cp857* for Turkish DOS; *cp1255* for Hebrew Windows; *cp862* for Hebrew DOS; *cp1256* for Arabic Windows.

NOTE   The {FILE-OPEN} command will open the following files: dBASE (.DBF), Excel Worksheet (.XLS), Excel Workbook (.XLW), Paradox (.DB), Text (.TXT, .PRN, .CSV, .DAT, .OUT, .ASC), Shared (.NS4), and SmartMaster template (.WT4).

You could use the following command to open the file named PAYMENTS.WK4 only if the network reservation is available:

    {FILE-OPEN "payments.wk4";;;"no"}

Equivalent commands   File ➤ Open

{FILE-OPEN?}

    {FILE-OPEN?}

The {FILE-OPEN?} command displays the File Open dialog box so that the user can choose a file to open. This command has no arguments.

You could use the following command to display the File Open dialog box so that the user could choose a file to open:

{FILE-OPEN?}

Equivalent commands File ➤ Open

{FILE-RELEASE-RESERVATION}

{FILE-RELEASE-RESERVATION}

The {FILE-RELEASE-RESERVATION} command releases the network reservation for the current file. This command has no arguments.

You could use the following command to release the reservation for the current file:

{FILE-RELEASE-RESERVATION}

Equivalent commands File ➤ Protect File ➤ Reservation

{FILE-RETRIEVE}

{FILE-RETRIEVE *file-name*;[*password*];[*read-only*];[*read-text-as*]}

The {FILE-RETRIEVE} command opens the specified file and replaces the current file in memory, then moves the cell pointer to the cell it was in when the specified file was last saved.

WARNING {FILE-RETRIEVE} does not save changes to the current file, nor does it prompt the user before closing it. If the current file may contain changes, use a {FILE-SAVE} command or a {FILE-SAVE-ALL} command before running a {FILE-RETRIEVE} command.

{FILE-RETRIEVE} takes the following arguments.

file-name The name of the file to open, entered as text in double quotation marks (" "). {FILE-RETRIEVE} returns an error if that file does not exist or is already open.

password Text indicating the password for opening the file. If you omit the *password* argument, you will be prompted for any existing password.

read-only Yes or No, indicating whether {FILE-RETRIEVE} should open the file as read-only if the network reservation is not available, or not open the file. If you specify Yes and the reservation is available, you still get the reservation. If you omit the *read-only* argument and the reservation is not available, {FILE-RETRIEVE} will prompt you whether to open the file as read-only or not to open it.

read-text-as Text in double quotation marks (" ") indicating how {FILE-IMPORT} is to combine data from a text file: any delimiter symbol (e.g., # or |) or *text* for nondelimited text (one line per cell in successive cells in a column, and up to 512 characters per cell and 8192 lines of data per worksheet); *numbers* for text and numbers from a delimited text file, or just numbers from a nondelimited text file (one item per cell and one line per row); *tab* for tab-delimited text files; *comma* for comma-delimited text files; *space* for space-delimited text files; *semicolon* for semicolon-delimited text files; or *autoparse* for text and numbers based on the layout of the file.

You could use the following command to replace the current file with the file named PLAN_95.WK4, using the default settings:

    {FILE-RETRIEVE "plan_95.wk4"}

Equivalent commands File ➤ Open

{FILE-SAVE}

    {FILE-SAVE [*file-name*];[*file-type*];[*password*];[*backup*]}

The {FILE-SAVE} command saves changes to the current file. It takes the following arguments.

file-name The name of the file to save, entered as text in double quotation marks (" "). Enter the full path if necessary. If *file-name* does not exist, {FILE-SAVE} will create it; if you do not specify *file-name* and the file has never been saved, the user will be prompted for a name. If *file-name* exists, the *backup* argument comes into effect.

file-type   Text indicating the format of the file to be saved, from the following list: *1-2-3* for WK4 format (this is the default if you omit the *file-type* argument); *1-2-3 (wk3)* for WK3 format with formatting information in FM3 format; *1-2-3 (wk1)* for WK1 format with formatting information in FMT format; *dbase (dbf)* for a dBASE file; *paradox (db)* for a Paradox file; or *text (txt)* for a text file (TXT).

password   Text indicating the password for saving the file. If you omit the *password* argument, you will be prompted if one is necessary.

backup   Text indicating whether to create a backup file if a file named *file-name* already exists: *backup* saves the existing file with a .BAK extension and saves the current file as *file-name*; *replace* replaces the existing file with the current file, saved as *file-name*. If you do not enter a *backup* argument and a file named *file-name* already exists, {FILE-EXTRACT} will prompt you with the familiar Backup, Replace, Cancel dialog box.

You could use the following command to save the current file with the name BITUMEN.WK4 and replace any existing file of the same name:

> {FILE-SAVE "Bitumen";;;"replace"}

Equivalent Commands   File ➤ Save, File ➤ Save As

{FILE-SAVE-ALL}

> {FILE-SAVE-ALL}

The {FILE-SAVE-ALL} command saves all open files. This command has no arguments.

You could use the following command to save changes to all the files currently open:

> {FILE-SAVE-ALL}

Equivalent commands   File ➤ Save

{FILE-SAVE-AS?}

{FILE-SAVE-AS?}

The {FILE-SAVE-AS?} command displays the Save As dialog box so that the user can choose a name under which to save the file. This command has no arguments.

Equivalent commands File ➤ Save As

{FILE-SEAL}

{FILE-SEAL [*password*]}

The {FILE-SEAL} command seals the current file so that no changes can be made to it. The file can still be opened and viewed. It takes the following arguments.

password The password for sealing or unsealing the current file, entered as text in double quotation marks (" "). If you omit the *password* argument, {FILE-SEAL} displays a dialog box demanding a password.

You could use the following command to seal the current file with the password "Goethe":

{FILE-SEAL "Goethe"}

Equivalent commands File ➤ Protect

{FILE-SEAL-NETWORK-RESERVATION}

{FILE-SEAL-NETWORK-RESERVATION [*password*]}

The {FILE-SEAL-NETWORK-RESERVATION} command seals the network reservation setting of the current file. It takes the following argument.

password The password for sealing or unsealing the network reservation of the current file, entered as text in double quotation marks (" "). If you omit the *password* argument, {FILE-SEAL-NETWORK-RESERVATION} displays a dialog box demanding a password.

21

Macro Commands

You could use the following command to seal the network reservation of the current file with the password "Schiller":

{FILE-SEAL-NETWORK-RESERVATION "Schiller"}

Equivalent commands File ➤ Protect

{FILE-UNSEAL}

{FILE-UNSEAL [*password*]}

The {FILE-UNSEAL} command unseals the current file and releases its network reservation setting. It takes the following argument.

password The password for sealing or unsealing the current file, entered as text in double quotation marks (" "). If you omit the *password* argument, {FILE-UNSEAL} displays a dialog box demanding a password.

You could use the following command to unseal the current file provided the user could provide the correct password:

{FILE-UNSEAL}

Equivalent commands File ➤ Protect

{PRINT}

{PRINT [*what*];[*from*];[*to*];[*start*];[*copies*]}

The {PRINT} command prints the current file with the current page settings. It takes the following arguments.

what *all*, *current*, or *selection*, entered as text in double quotation marks (" "), specifying what to print. *all* prints the current file; *current* prints the current worksheet; and *selection* prints the current selection. To print the range specified by the Print-Range Info setting, omit the *what* argument.

from An integer value indicating the page number of the first page to print.

to An integer value indicating the page number of the last page to print.

start An integer value indicating the page number at which to start numbering pages.

copies An integer value indicating the number of copies to print.

You could use the following command to print five copies of pages 1 and 2 of the current worksheet, without page numbers:

    {PRINT "current";1;2;;5}

Equivalent commands File ➤ Print

{PRINT?}

    {PRINT?}

The {PRINT?} command displays the File Print dialog box so that the user can choose interactive printing options. This command has no arguments.

Equivalent commands File ➤ Print

{PRINT-NAME-ADD}

    {PRINT-NAME-ADD *page-setting-name*}

The {PRINT-NAME-ADD} command saves the current page settings as named page settings with the specified name. It takes the following argument.

page-setting-name Text indicating the name of the file to save the settings to. {PRINT-NAME-ADD} adds the extension .AL3 to a file containing named page settings unless you specify a different extension.

You could use the following command to save the current page settings to the file PENGUINS.AL3:

    {PRINT-NAME-ADD "penguins"}

Equivalent commands File ➤ Page Setup

{PRINT-NAME-USE}

    {PRINT-NAME-USE *page-setting-name*}

21

Macro Commands

The {PRINT-NAME-USE} command retrieves the named page settings in the specified file and uses them as the current page settings. It takes the following argument.

page-setting-name   Text indicating the name of the named-page-settings file to retrieve. {PRINT-NAME-USE} assumes the extension .AL3 unless you specify another extension.

You could use the following command to apply the named page settings in the file QMS2200.AL3 to the current file:

    {PRINT-NAME-USE "QMS2200"}

Equivalent commands File ➤ Page Setup

{PRINT-RESET}

    {PRINT-RESET}

The {PRINT-RESET} command returns the selected Margins, Print titles, and Header, Footer, Options, Compression, and Orientation settings to the default settings. This command has no arguments.

You could use the following command to reset the current file's print settings to the default settings:

    {PRINT-RESET}

Equivalent commands File ➤ Page Setup ➤ Restore

{SEND-MAIL}

    {SEND-MAIL [to];[cc];[subject];[body];[clipboard];[file]}

The {SEND-MAIL} command sends a mail message using a 1-2-3–compatible mail application. The mail message can include text, the contents of the Clipboard, and the current file. It takes the following arguments.

to Either text entered in double quotation marks (" ") indicating the single recipient of the mail message, or a range of up to 100 cells in one row or column indicating multiple recipients. {SEND-MAIL} ignores cells that do not contain labels or text formulas. If you omit the *to* argument, {SEND-MAIL} displays a mail dialog box.

cc Either text entered in double quotation marks (" ") indicating the single recipient of a copy of the mail message, or a range of up to 100 cells in one row or column indicating multiple recipients of copies. {SEND-MAIL} ignores cells that do not contain labels or text formulas.

subject Text entered in double quotation marks (" ") indicating the subject of the mail message.

body Text entered in double quotation marks (" ") indicating the body of the message, or a range of up to 100 cells in one row or column. {SEND-MAIL} ignores cells that do not contain labels or text formulas. The labels from multiple cells are followed by a carriage-return/linefeed in the mail message.

clipboard Yes or No, indicating whether to attach the contents of the Clipboard to the mail message. The default is No. Attaching the contents of the Clipboard to the mail message will only work if you are using Lotus Notes.

file Yes or No, indicating whether to attach the current file to the mail message. The default is No.

You could use the following command to send the message contained in the range CLIPPER to Al with a copy to Bill, and with the subject line "Skip SkipJack now!":

    {SEND-MAIL "Al";"Bill";"Skip SkipJack now!";CLIPPER}

Equivalent commands File ➤ Send Mail

{SEND-RANGE}

{SEND-RANGE *range*;*to*;[*subject*];[*body*];[*return-receipt*];[*route*];
[*priority*];[*return-to-originator*];[*properties*]}

21

Macro Commands

The {SEND-RANGE} command sends a range of worksheet data to other 1-2-3 Release 5 users who have electronic mail. {SEND-RANGE} allows you to broadcast the range to all recipients at once or route it from one recipient to the next. It takes the following arguments.

range   The name or address of the range to send.

to   Either text entered in double quotation marks (″ ″) indicating the single recipient of the mail message, or a range of up to 100 cells in one row or column indicating multiple recipients. {SEND-MAIL} ignores cells that do not contain labels or text formulas. If you omit the *to* argument, {SEND-MAIL} displays a mail dialog box so that you can enter the recipient or recipients.

subject   Text entered in double quotation marks (″ ″) indicating the subject of the mail message.

body   Text entered in double quotation marks (″ ″) indicating the body of the message, or a range of up to 100 cells in one row or column. {SEND-MAIL} ignores cells that do not contain labels or text formulas. The labels from multiple cells are followed by a carriage-return/linefeed in the mail message.

return-receipt   1 or 0, indicating whether to send a delivery confirmation to each sender in a route list when the next person in the list receives the mail. The default is 0.

route   1 or 0, indicating whether to route the range from one recipient to the next or send it to all recipients at once. The default is 0, i.e., to send the range to all recipients at once.

priority   1, 2, or 3, specifying low, normal (the default), and urgent priority, respectively.

return-to-originator   1 or 0, indicating whether to add your name to the end of the list of recipients so that the item sent returns to you. The default is 0.

properties   *formulas* or *values*, indicating how to save values from *extract-range*, as follows: *formulas* saves formulas without converting them to values (this is the default setting); *values* converts formulas to values.

T I P

For the ultimate in Big-Brotherliness, use Yes for both *route* and *return-receipt,* as this will return a copy of the file to you each time the person currently at bat on the file forwards it to the next person.

You could use the following command to route the range named SALA-RIES and the message contained in the cell named MESSAGE to the group of VPs, one at a time, sending a confirmation to each sender, and returning the range to you (the originator) after it has passed through everyone's hands, all at an urgent priority:

{SEND-RANGE SALARIES;"VPs";;message;0;1;3;1}

Equivalent commands File ➤ Send Mail

{SEND-RANGE-LOGIN}

{SEND-RANGE-LOGIN [*mail-application-path*];[*user-name*];[*password*]}

The {SEND-RANGE-LOGIN} command automatically logs on to your mail application. It takes the following arguments.

mail-application-path Text indicating the path to your mail application. Include the drive letter. If you omit *mail-application-path*, {SEND-RANGE-LOGIN} will look for it in the [LOTUSMAIL] or [MAIL] section of your WIN.INI file.

user-name Text indicating your user name for your mail application. If you omit *user-name*, {SEND-RANGE-LOGIN} will look for it in the [LOTUSMAIL] or [MAIL] section of your WIN.INI file.

password Text indicating your password for your mail application. If you are leery about entering this in plain view, put it in some inaccessible corner of the worksheet, hide the relevant cell, name the cell something innocuous, and use the name in the {SEND-RANGE-LOGIN} statement.

You could use the following command to log into Lotus Notes automatically, assuming your user name is Ramon McDonald and your password

21

Macro Commands

is stored in the range named CROMWELL:

> {SEND-RANGE-LOGIN "f:\notes\notes.exe";"ramon mcdonald";cromwell}

Equivalent commands   File ➤ Send Mail

Flow-of-Macro Commands

This section of the chapter discusses the 1-2-3 flow-of-macro commands, which control macro execution.

{BRANCH}

> {BRANCH *location*}

The {BRANCH} command transfers macro control from the current macro instruction to *location* and does not return to the calling macro.

{BRANCH} is a flexible macro command that is particularly useful in the following circumstances:

- Combine {BRANCH} with {IF} for if-then-else processing or to transfer control to another macro.
- Construct a loop with {BRANCH} to create a loop by branching to a cell earlier in the macro than the {BRANCH} command until certain conditions are met.

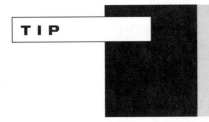

TIP

{BRANCH} is significantly different from the {EDIT-GOTO} command, in that {EDIT-GOTO} moves the cell pointer to the specified cell whereas {BRANCH} transfers macro execution to the commands that begin in the *location* specified.

{BRANCH} takes the following argument.

location The name or address of a cell or range containing macro in-structions—for example, the name of another macro or subroutine. Note that if you specify a range, {BRANCH} branches to the first cell in the range.

You could use the following commands to branch to a macro named LEVEL1 for orders over $10,000 (the value in the cell named ORDER) or to the macro named LEVEL2 for orders under $10,000:

```
{IF ORDER>10000}{BRANCH LEVEL1}
{BRANCH LEVEL2}
```

{BRANCH} is also discussed on page 649.

{DEFINE}

{DEFINE *location1;location2;...;location*n}

The {DEFINE} command specifies where to store arguments passed to a subroutine in a {subroutine} command. You must include a {DEFINE} command in any subroutine to which you pass arguments before the point in the subroutine at which the arguments are used.

1-2-3 does not automatically recalculate after a {DEFINE} command; use a {CALC} command if necessary. {DEFINE} should be the first command in all subroutines that include it. It takes the following argument.

location The name or address of a cell or range. {DEFINE} uses the first cell of a given range as the storage location. Include a *location* argument for each argument in the {subroutine} command, or else the {DEFINE} command will produce an error and crash the macro.

T I P

You can add the suffix *:value* (or *:v* for short) to the *location* argument to evaluate and store the value as a number, or the suffix *:string* (*:s* for short) to store the value as a label.

You could use the following command to specify the locations for the four arguments ARG1, ARG2, ARG3, and ARG4 that are passed by the subroutine named SUB1. Note that this command appears in the cell named SUB1.

{DEFINE ARG1;ARG2;ARG3;ARG4}

{DISPATCH}

{DISPATCH *location*}

The {DISPATCH} command branches indirectly to the cell specified in *location*. By changing the contents of *location*, you can branch the macro in various possible directions. It takes the following argument.

location   A single cell containing the name or address of the cell to which control of the macro is to be transferred. Beware that if *location* is a multicell range rather than a single cell, {DISPATCH} branches to *location*.

You could use the following command to branch the macro to the cell specified in the contents of the cell TRIGGER:

{DISPATCH TRIGGER}

{FOR}

{FOR *counter;start;stop;step;subroutine*}

The {FOR} command creates a FOR loop that repeatedly performs a subroutine call to a subroutine until the specified number of loops is reached. It takes the following arguments.

counter   The name or address of the cell in which to count the number of executions of the FOR loop. *counter* should be blank, as its contents will be overwritten.

start   The beginning value for *counter*.

stop   The value for terminating the FOR loop.

step   The value added to *counter* each time {FOR} executes the subroutine.

subroutine   The range name or address of the subroutine to be executed in the for loop.

> **WARNING**
>
> 1-2-3 runs a {FOR} command by entering the *start* value in the *counter* location, then comparing the number in *counter* with the *stop* value. If the number in *counter* is less than *stop*, 1-2-3 calls the subroutine, increases *counter* by *step*, and repeats the process; if the number in *counter* is greater than *stop*, 1-2-3 does not call the subroutine but continues the macro with the next instruction. Make sure that *step* is never 0, or you will produce an endless loop that can only be stopped by pressing Ctrl+Break.

You could use the following command to perform the subroutine GET-INPUT five times:

    {FOR COUNT;1;5;1;GETINPUT}

{FOR} is also discussed on page 645.

{FORBREAK}

    {FORBREAK}

The {FORBREAK} command cancels a for loop created by a {FOR} command. This command has no arguments. After a {FORBREAK} command, 1-2-3 continues with the next macro command after the {FOR} command.

> **WARNING**
>
> Do not use {FORBREAK} outside a {FOR} loop; it will produce an error and end the macro.

You could use the following command to terminate the FOR loop if the current cell contains "End":

    {IF @CELLPOINTER("contents")="End"}{FORBREAK}

{IF}

{IF *condition*}

The {IF} command evaluates the specified condition as TRUE or FALSE. If the condition is TRUE, 1-2-3 executes the instruction after the {IF} command in the same cell; if the condition is FALSE, 1-2-3 executes the instructions in the next cell in the column, ignoring any further instructions in the same cell as the {IF} command. {IF} takes the following argument.

condition   Often a logical formula or the name or address of a cell containing a logical formula; alternatively, any formula, number, text, or cell name or address. 1-2-3 evaluates any condition that does not equal 0 as false; blank cells, text, and ERR and NA values all equal 0 when used as the *condition* argument.

You could use the following command to branch to HOT if the value in the named cell CELSIUS is over 40:

{IF CELSIUS>40}{BRANCH HOT}

Turn to page 650 for more about {IF}.

{LAUNCH}

{LAUNCH *command*;[*window*];[*switch-to*]}

The {LAUNCH} command starts the specified Windows application and (optionally) switches to it. You can also choose to switch to any other application that is running. {LAUNCH} takes the following arguments.

command   Text entered in double quotation marks (" ") indicating the command string for starting the Windows application: drive, path, filename, and any optional parameters.

window   An integer value from 0 through 9 specifying how to handle the application's window, from the list below. Note that some Windows applications do not support all these values.

0 hides the application window and activates another window.

1 activates and displays the application window at its previous size and position.

2 activates and minimizes the application window.

3 activates and maximizes the application window.

4 displays the application window in its most recent size and position but leaves 1-2-3 as the active application.

5 activates the application window and displays it in its current size and position.

6 minimizes the application window and activates the top-level window in the window-manager's list.

7 minimizes the application window and leaves 1-2-3 as the active application. This is the default value.

8 displays the application window in its current state, leaving 1-2-3 as the active application.

9 activates and displays the application window at its original size and position.

switch-to   The text that appears in the title bar of an application: either the entire title, or just the beginning of it. For example, to switch to Word for Windows, you can specify "Microsoft Word" for the *switch-to* argument.

You could use the following command to launch the Notepad application, open the file C:\WAOL\BOBBITT.TXT, maximize Notepad, and switch to it:

{LAUNCH "C:\WINDOWS\NOTEPAD C:\WAOL\BOBBITT.TXT";3}

{LOTUS-LAUNCH}

{LOTUS-LAUNCH *name*;[*window*];[*switch-to*]}

The {LOTUS-LAUNCH} command starts a Lotus Windows application and optionally switches to it. It takes the following arguments.

name   Text entered in double quotation marks (" ") indicating the name of the Lotus application to start. The name needs to be entered as it appears in the Lotus Applications section of the file LOTUS.INI: ORGAN-IZE for Lotus Organizer, AMIPRO for Ami Pro, NOTES for Notes, etc.

21

Macro Commands

window   An integer value from 0 through 9 specifying how to handle the application's window, from the list below. Note that some Windows applications do not support all these values.

0 hides the application window and activates another window.

1 activates and displays the application window at its previous size and position.

2 activates and minimizes the application window.

3 activates and maximizes the application window.

4 displays the application window in its most recent size and position but leaves 1-2-3 as the active application.

5 activates the application window and displays it in its current size and position.

6 minimizes the application window and activates the top-level window in the window-manager's list.

7 minimizes the application window and leaves 1-2-3 as the active application. This is the default value.

8 displays the application window in its current state, leaving 1-2-3 as the active application.

9 activates and displays the application window at its original size and position.

switch-to   The text that appears in the title bar of an application: either the entire title, or just the beginning of it. For example, to switch to Ami Pro, you can specify simply "Ami" for the *switch-to* argument.

You could use the following command to start and maximize Lotus Organizer:

    {LOTUS-LAUNCH "ORGANIZE";3}

{ONERROR}

    {ONERROR *branch-location*;[*message-location*]}

The {ONERROR} command specifies where to branch for errors that occur while a macro is running. By using the {ONERROR} command, you can avoid having 1-2-3 display an error message and stop a macro. By using the optional *message-location* argument, you can record the error message for your edification after the macro has finished running.

{ONERROR} takes the following arguments.

branch-location   The name or address of the cell or range to branch to after an error occurs. If *branch-location* is a range, 1-2-3 branches to the first cell in the range.

message-location   The name or address of the cell or range in which to store the error message. If *message-location* is a range, 1-2-3 uses the first cell in the range.

TIP

Since each {ONERROR} command can trap only one error, you'll probably want to include a new {ONERROR} command in *branch-location* to reset the error trapping. The {ONERROR} command can trap all types of errors except macro syntax errors; these latter will crash a macro, no matter how many {ONERROR} commands it contains.

You could use the following command to branch to the subroutine named HITERROR if an error occurs and to store the error message generated in a cell named FIRST ERROR:

{ONERROR HITERROR;FIRST ERROR}

{QUIT}

{QUIT}

The {QUIT} command ends the current macro and returns keyboard control to the user. 1-2-3 never executes any instructions that follow a {QUIT} command.

WARNING

{QUIT} ends the entire macro even if the command is in a subroutine.

21

Macro Commands

You could use the following command to stop a macro if the value in the cell named YEAR was greater than 1995:

{IF YEAR>1995}{QUIT}

{RESTART}

{RESTART}

The {RESTART} command clears the subroutine stack, ending the macro when the current subroutine ends, so that the macro does not return to the calling program. This command has no arguments.

You could use the following command to stop the subroutine from returning to the calling program:

{RESTART}

{RETURN}

{RETURN}

The {RETURN} command returns macro control from a subroutine to the calling macro. If used in a subroutine called by a {FOR} command, it ends the current repetition of the loop and starts the next repetition. If used in the main body of a macro (rather than in a subroutine), {RETURN} ends the macro immediately, like {QUIT}. The {RETURN} command has no arguments.

You could use the following command to end the current subroutine and return control to the macro:

{RETURN}

{SET}

{SET *info-id;info-value*}

The {SET} command sets the specified Info component to the specified value. It takes the following arguments.

info-id Text indicating the name of the Info component whose value you want to set.

info-value The value to which to set the Info component. Depending on the component identified by *info-id*, the *info-value* argument can be a value, text, or a location.

You could use the following commands to set the default number format to Percent with one decimal place:

```
{SET "worksheet-format";"percent"}
{SET "worksheet-format-decimals";1}
```

{subroutine}

{subroutine [*arg1*];[*arg2*];...;[*argn*]}

The {subroutine} command performs a subroutine call. Use subroutines to break macros up into more manageable sections and to create reusable modules. You can nest subroutines as necessary. {subroutine} takes the following arguments.

subroutine The range name of the subroutine for the macro to call. (You can use a range address for the *subroutine* argument rather than a range name, but this may cause problems if you insert cells that move the subroutine.)

arg1,arg2,...,argn Up to 31 optional arguments to be passed to the subroutine. Arguments can be values or text, including formulas and the names or addresses of cells.

NOTE The subroutine must begin with a {DEFINE} command if arguments are specified.

21

Macro Commands

{SET}

{SET *info-id;info-value*}

The {SET} command sets the specified Info component to the specified value. It takes the following arguments.

info-id   Text indicating the name of the Info component whose value you want to set.

info-value   The value to which to set the Info component. Depending on the component identified by *info-id*, the *info-value* argument can be a value, text, or a location.

You could use the following commands to set the default number format to Percent with one decimal place:

```
{SET "worksheet-format";"percent"}
{SET "worksheet-format-decimals";1}
```

{subroutine}

{subroutine [*arg1*];[*arg2*];...;[*argn*]}

The {subroutine} command performs a subroutine call. Use subroutines to break macros up into more manageable sections and to create reusable modules. You can nest subroutines as necessary. {subroutine} takes the following arguments.

subroutine   The range name of the subroutine for the macro to call. (You can use a range address for the *subroutine* argument rather than a range name, but this may cause problems if you insert cells that move the subroutine.)

arg1,arg2,...,argn   Up to 31 optional arguments to be passed to the subroutine. Arguments can be values or text, including formulas and the

TABLE 21.2: Keystroke Equivalent Macro Commands

ACTION	MACRO INSTRUCTION
POINTER MOVEMENT MACRO COMMANDS	
DOWN	{DOWN} or {D}
UP	{UP} or {U}
LEFT	{LEFT} or {L}
RIGHT	{RIGHT} or {R}
PG DN	{PGDN}
PG UP	{PGUP}
CTRL+LEFT	{BACKTAB} or {BIGLEFT}
CTRL+RIGHT	{BIGRIGHT}
HOME	{HOME}
END	{END}
END CTRL+HOME	{LASTCELL} or {LC}
CTRL+END	{FILE}
CTRL+END CTRL+PG DN	{PREVFILE}, {PF}, or {FILE}{PS}
CTRL+END CTRL+PG UP	{NEXTFILE}, {NF}, or {FILE}{NS}
CTRL+END END	{LASTFILE}, {LF}, or {FILE}{END}
CTRL+END HOME	{FIRSTFILE},{FF}, or {FILE}{HOME}
CTRL+HOME	{FIRSTCELL} or {FC}
CTRL+PG UP	{NEXTSHEET} or {NS}
CTRL+PG DN	{PREVSHEET} or {PS}
FUNCTION KEY MACRO COMMANDS	
F1 (HELP)	{HELP}
F2 (EDIT)	{EDIT}

TABLE 21.2: Keystroke Equivalent Macro Commands (continued)

ACTION	MACRO INSTRUCTION
F3 (NAME)	{NAME}
F4 in Ready mode	{ANCHOR}
F4 (ABS)	{ABS}
F5 (GOTO)	{GOTO}
F6 (PANE)	{WINDOW}
F7 (QUERY)	{QUERY}
F8 (TABLE)	{TABLE}
F9 (CALC)	{CALC}
EDITING KEY MACRO COMMANDS	
BACKSPACE	{BACKSPACE} or {BS}
DEL	{DELETE} or {DEL}
INS	{INSERT} or {INS}
SHIFT+CTRL+LEFT	{SELECT-BIGLEFT}
SHIFT+CTRL+RIGHT	{SELECT-BIGRIGHT}
SHIFT+DOWN	{SELECT-DOWN}
SHIFT+CTRL+HOME	{SELECT-FIRSTCELL}
SHIFT+HOME	{SELECT-HOME}
END SHIFT+CTRL+HOME	{SELECT-LASTCELL}
SHIFT+LEFT	{SELECT-LEFT}
SHIFT+CTRL+PG UP	{SELECT-NEXTSHEET}
SHIFT+PG DN	{SELECT-PGDN}
SHIFT+PG UP	{SELECT-PGUP}
SHIFT+CTRL+PG DN	{SELECT-PREVSHEET}

TABLE 21.2: Keystroke Equivalent Macro Commands (continued)

ACTION	MACRO INSTRUCTION
SHIFT+RIGHT	{SELECT-RIGHT}
SHIFT+UP	{SELECT-UP}
Assorted Keystroke Macro Commands	
~ (tilde)	{~}
{ (open brace)	{{}
} (close brace)	{}}
/ (slash) or < (less than)	/, <, or {MENU}
ALT+F6 (ZOOM)	{ZOOM}
ESC	{ESCAPE} or {ESC}
ESC in 1-2-3 Classic edit line	{CLEARENTRY} or {CE}
TAB	{TAB}

Navigation Macro Commands

This section discusses the navigation macro commands, which let you move to items or select items.

{CELL-ENTER}

{CELL-ENTER *data*;[*target-location*]}

The {CELL-ENTER} command enters the specified *data* in the specified *target-location*. {CELL-ENTER} has the same effect as entering the data manually would have: 1-2-3 determines whether data is text, a formula, or a number, and reacts accordingly. For example, if you use {CELL-ENTER} to enter a formula, the result of the formula rather than the text of the formula will appear in the *target-location*. {CELL-ENTER} takes the following arguments.

data　The text, number, or formula to enter in the worksheet, enclosed in double quotation marks (″ ″)

target-location　The name or address of the cell in which to enter data. If *target-location* is a range, {CELL-ENTER} enters data in the first cell in the range. (If you omit *target-location*, {CELL-ENTER} enters data in the current cell.)

You could use the following command to enter the label "Paragons of Virtue, Inc." in the current cell:

```
{CELL-ENTER "Paragons of Virtue, Inc."}
```

To fill in the range K9..K12, you could use the following commands:

```
{EDIT-GOTO K9}
{CELL-ENTER "Bogus Fish"}
{RIGHT}
{CELL-ENTER "Whales"}
{RIGHT}
{CELL-ENTER "Tunes"}
{RIGHT}
{CELL-ENTER "Friends"}
```

{EDIT-GOTO}

```
{EDIT-GOTO name;[part];[type]}
```

The {EDIT-GOTO} command selects all or part of a range, query table, chart, or other drawn object, and then scrolls to it. Any items previously selected in the same file become unselected. {EDIT-GOTO} takes the following arguments.

name　The name of the item to select. The item can be in the current file or in another open file. When using {EDIT-GOTO} to select a query table, chart, or drawn object, enter the name in double quotation marks (″ ″).

part   The part of the item to select, such as the title in a chart. {EDIT-GOTO} selects the entire item if you omit the *part* argument. If *name* indicates a range, *part* must be the name or address of a single cell. If *name* indicates a chart, *part* must be the name of a chart element, entered in double quotation marks (" "). If *name* indicates a query table, *part* must be a field name, entered in double quotation marks (" ").

type   Text indicating what type of item the *name* argument refers to: *chart*, *draw*, *query*, or *range*. *range* is the default if you omit the *type* argument.

You could use the following command to select the title of the chart named EXTRACTION COSTS:

> {EDIT-GOTO "Extraction Costs";"title box";"chart"}

{SCROLL-COLUMNS}

> {SCROLL-COLUMNS [*amount*]}

The {SCROLL-COLUMNS} command scrolls horizontally by the specified number of columns in the current worksheet. {SCROLL-COLUMNS} does not change the current cell, only the display. It takes the following argument.

amount   An integer that specifies how many columns to scroll. A positive *amount* scrolls right; a negative *amount* scrolls left.

You could use the following command to scroll the display 50 columns to the right:

> {SCROLL-COLUMNS 50}

{SCROLL-ROWS}

> {SCROLL-ROWS *amount*}

The {SCROLL-ROWS} command scrolls vertically by row in the current worksheet. {SCROLL-ROWS} does not change the current cell, just the display. It takes the following argument.

amount   An integer indicating how many columns to scroll. A positive *amount* scrolls right; a negative *amount* scrolls left.

You could use the following command to scroll up ten rows without changing the current cell:

{SCROLL-ROWS –10}

{SCROLL-TO-CELL}

{SCROLL-TO-CELL *location*}

The {SCROLL-TO-CELL} command scrolls in the current worksheet so that the first cell of the specified location is displayed in the top-left corner of the worksheet window. {SCROLL-TO-CELL} does not change the active cell, just the display, and returns an error if the specified location is not in the worksheet containing the current cell. It takes the following argument.

location   The name or address of the range to which to scroll.

You could use the following command to scroll the current worksheet so that cell FR77 is the top-left cell:

{SCROLL-TO-CELL FR77}

{SCROLL-TO-COLUMN}

{SCROLL-TO-COLUMN *location*}

The {SCROLL-TO-COLUMN} command scrolls left or right in the current worksheet, making the leftmost column of the specified location to be displayed the leftmost column of the worksheet window. {SCROLL-TO-COLUMN} does not change the current cell. It takes the following argument.

location   The name or address of the range to which to scroll.

You could use the following command to scroll so that the first column in the range MOTORCYCLES is the leftmost column displayed:

{SCROLL-TO-COLUMN MOTORCYCLES}

{SCROLL-TO-OBJECT}

{SCROLL-TO-OBJECT *name*;[*type*]}

The {SCROLL-TO-OBJECT} command scrolls to but does not select a range, query table, chart or other drawn object in the current worksheet. {SCROLL-TO-OBJECT} does not change the current cell and returns an error if the specified item is not on the worksheet containing the current cell. It takes the following arguments.

name   The name of the item to scroll to. To scroll to a range, enter a range name or address. To scroll to a query table, a chart, or another drawn object, enter the name of the item as text in double quotation marks (" ").

type   Text indicating what type of item the *name* argument refers to: *chart*, *draw*, *query*, or *range*. *range* is the default if you omit the *type* argument.

You could use the following command to scroll to a chart named Inflation in the current worksheet:

{SCROLL-TO-OBJECT "Inflation";"chart"}

{SCROLL-TO-ROW}

{SCROLL-TO-ROW *location*}

The {SCROLL-TO-ROW} command scrolls up or down in the current worksheet to display the top row of *location* on the top row in the worksheet window. {SCROLL-TO-ROW} does not move the current cell. It takes the following argument.

location   The name or address of the range to scroll to.

You could use the following command to scroll the current worksheet so that row 11 is the top row displayed:

{SCROLL-TO-ROW A11..C11}

{SELECT}

{SELECT *name*;[*part*];[*type*]}

The {SELECT} command selects all or part of a range, chart, query table, or other drawn object, without scrolling to it. Any previously selected items in the same file become unselected. It takes the following arguments.

name   The name of the item to select. The item can be in the current file or in another open file. When using {SELECT} to select a query table, chart, or drawn object, enter the name in double quotation marks (" ").

part   The part of the item to select, such as the title in a chart. {SELECT} selects the entire item if you omit the *part* argument. If *name* indicates a range, *part* must be the name or address of a single cell. If *name* indicates a chart, *part* must be the name of a chart element, entered in double quotation marks (" "). If *name* indicates a query table, *part* must be a field name, entered in double quotation marks (" ").

type   Text indicating what type of item the *name* argument refers to: *chart*, *draw*, *query*, or *range*. *range* is the default if you omit the *type* argument.

You could use the following command to select the title of the chart named Inflation:

    {SELECT "Inflation";"title box";"chart"}

{SELECT-ALL}

    {SELECT-ALL [type]}

The {SELECT-ALL} command selects all sheets in the current file, all charts on the current worksheet, all drawn objects on the current worksheet, or the active area of the current worksheet. {SELECT-ALL} does not let you select parts of all items. It takes the following argument.

type   Text indicating what type of item to select: *cells* selects the active area of the current worksheet (this is the default if you omit the argument); *charts* selects all charts in the current worksheet; *drawn-objects* selects all drawn objects in the current worksheet; or *sheets* selects all worksheets in the current file.

You could use the following command to select all the worksheets in the current file:

{SELECT-ALL "worksheets"}

{SELECT-APPEND}

{SELECT-APPEND *name;part*}

The {SELECT-APPEND} command adds to the group of selected items; it selects all or part of a range, chart, or other drawn object without deselecting any items currently selected. It takes the following arguments.

name　The name of the item to add to the currently selected collection or group of items. This must be an existing name for the type of item currently selected, or {SELECT-APPEND} returns an error. In other words, if the currently selected collection consists of ranges, *name* can be the name or address of any range in the current file; if the currently selected collection consists of charts or drawn objects, *name* must be the name of a chart or drawn object in the current worksheet, entered as text in double quotation marks (" ").

part　The part of the item to select, such as the title in a chart. {SELECT-APPEND} selects the entire item if you omit the *part* argument. If *name* indicates a range, *part* must be the name or address of a single cell. If *name* indicates a chart, *part* must be the name of a chart element, entered in double quotation marks (" ").

You could use the following command to append the range SHOES SALES to the collection of selected items:

{SELECT-APPEND SHOE SALES}

{SELECT-RANGE-RELATIVE}

{SELECT-RANGE-RELATIVE [*column*];[*row*];[*worksheet*];[*cp-col-off*];[*cp-row-off*];[*cp-sheet-off*]}

The {SELECT-RANGE-RELATIVE} command moves the cell pointer and then selects a range whose address is represented by offsets of the current cell (the current cell is 0). Any previously selected items in the same file become unselected. {SELECT-RANGE-RELATIVE} takes the following arguments.

column   An offset number from −255 to 255, indicating how many columns to extend the selection from the current cell. Positive values extend the range to the right; negative values extend the range to the left. The default setting is 0 if you omit this argument.

row   An offset number from −8191 to 8191, indicating how many rows to extend the selection from the current cell. Positive values extend the range downwards; negative values extend the range upwards. The default setting is 0 if you omit this argument.

worksheet   An offset number from −255 to 255, indicating how many worksheets to extend the selection from the current cell. Positive values extend the range forward; negative values extend the range backward. The default setting is 0 if you omit this argument.

cp-col-off   An offset number from −255 to 255, indicating how many columns to move the current cell before selecting the range. Positive values move the cell to the right; negative values move the cell to the left. The default setting is 0 if you omit this argument.

cp-row-off   An offset number from −8191 to 8191, indicating how many rows to move the current cell before selecting the range. Positive values move the current cell downwards; negative values move the current cell upwards. The default setting is 0 if you omit this argument.

cp-sheets-off   An offset number from −255 to 255, indicating how many worksheets to move the current cell before selecting the range. Positive values move the current cell forward; negative values move the current cell backward. The default setting is 0 if you omit this argument.

If the current cell is A:D25, you could select the range A:D25..Z:O40 by using the following command:

{SELECT-RANGE-RELATIVE 10,15,25}

{SELECT-REMOVE}

{SELECT-REMOVE *name*}

The {SELECT-REMOVE} command removes a range, chart, or other drawn object from the currently selected collection. It takes the following argument.

name The name of the item to remove from the currently selected collection or group of items. {SELECT-REMOVE} returns an error if you specify a name that does not exist for the type of item currently selected. Enter a range name or address for *name* if ranges are currently selected, or the name of a chart or drawn object in double quotation marks (" ") if charts or drawn objects are currently selected.

You could use the following command to remove the range named BLUE HERONS from the currently selected collection:

    {SELECT-REMOVE BLUE HERONS}

{SELECT-REPLACE}

    {SELECT-REPLACE *old-range;new-range*}

The {SELECT-REPLACE} command replaces the specified old range in a collection with the specified new range. It takes the following arguments.

old-range The name or address of a currently selected range in the current file to replace with *new-range*.

new-range The name or address of the replacement range in the current file.

You could use the following command to replace the range 1994 with the range 1995 in the currently selected collection:

    {SELECT-REPLACE 1994;1995}

21

Macro Commands

Range Macro Commands

This section examines the range macro commands, which correspond to the commands on the Range menu.

{DATA-TABLE-1}

{DATA-TABLE-1 [*output-range*];[*input-cell-1*]}

The {DATA-TABLE-1} command substitutes values for one variable in one or more formulas and enters the results in the selected output-range. It takes the following arguments.

output-range   The name or address of a range containing the formula, a list of input values that the formula uses in place of the variable, and blank cells where {DATA-TABLE-1} places the results.

input-cell-1   The name or address of the first cell in which {DATA-TABLE-1} temporarily enters values while performing the calculations required to create the table. *input-cell-1* must be unprotected and must be outside *output-range*; any data in it will be overwritten.

WARNING   If you omit any of the arguments for a {DATA-TABLE-1} command, {DATA-TABLE-1} will use the same information as you used in your last {DATA-TABLE} command during the current 1-2-3 session. This may well overwrite data you wanted to keep.

You could use the following command to create a table of results in the range COMMISSION, using cell K11 as the input cell:

{DATA-TABLE-1 COMMISSION;K11}

Equivalent commands   Range ➤ Analyze ➤ What-If Table

{DATA-TABLE-2}

{DATA-TABLE-2 [*output-range*];[*input-cell-1*];[*input-cell-2*]}

The {DATA-TABLE-2} command substitutes values for two variables in one formula and enters the results in the specified output-range. It takes the following arguments.

output-range   The name or address of a range containing the formula, a list of input values that the formula uses in place of the variable, and blank cells where {DATA-TABLE-2} places the results.

input-cell-1   The name or address of the first cell in which {DATA-TABLE-2} temporarily enters values while performing the calculations required to create the table. *input-cell-1* must be unprotected and must be outside *output-range*; any data in it will be overwritten.

input-cell-2   The name or address of the second cell in which {DATA-TABLE-2} temporarily enters values while performing the calculations required to create the table. *input-cell-2* must be unprotected and must be outside *output-range*; any data in it will be overwritten.

21

Macro Commands

WARNING

If you omit any of the arguments for a {DATA-TABLE-2} command, {DATA-TABLE-2} will use the same information as you used in your last {DATA-TABLE} command during the current 1-2-3 session. This may well overwrite data you wanted to keep.

You could use the following command to create a table of results in the range named TEST TABLE, using the input cells K9 and K10:

    {DATA-TABLE-2 TEST TABLE;K9;K10}

Equivalent commands   Range ➤ Analyze ➤ What-If Table

{DATA-TABLE-3}

{DATA-TABLE-3 [*output-range*];[*input-cell-1*];[*input-cell-2*];[*input-cell-3*];[*formula*]}

The {DATA-TABLE-3} command substitutes values for three variables in one formula and enters the results in the specified output-range. It takes the following arguments.

output-range   The name or address of a range containing the formula, a list of input values that the formula uses in place of the variable, and blank cells where {DATA-TABLE-1} places the results.

input-cell-1   The name or address of the first cell in which {DATA-TABLE-3} temporarily enters values while performing the calculations required to create the table. *input-cell-1* must be unprotected and must be outside *output-range*; any data in it will be overwritten.

input-cell-2   The name or address of the second cell in which {DATA-TABLE-3} temporarily enters values while performing the calculations required to create the table. *input-cell-2* must be unprotected and must be outside *output-range*; any data in it will be overwritten.

input-cell-3   The name or address of the second cell in which {DATA-TABLE-3} temporarily enters values while performing the calculations required to create the table. *input-cell-3* must be unprotected and must be outside *output-range*; any data in it will be overwritten.

formula   The name or address of a cell containing the formula that has the three variables to change. Like the *input-cell* arguments, *formula* must be outside *output-range*.

WARNING   If you omit any of the arguments for a {DATA-TABLE-3} command, {DATA-TABLE-3} will use the same information as you used in your last {DATA-TABLE} command during the current 1-2-3 session. This may well overwrite data you wanted to keep.

You could use the following command to create a table of results in the range named LAND VALUES, using the input cells C4, C7, and C11:

    {DATA-TABLE-3 LAND VALUES;C4;C7;C11}

Equivalent commands   Range ➤ Analyze ➤ What-If Table

{DATA-TABLE-RESET}

{DATA-TABLE-RESET}

The {DATA-TABLE-RESET} command clears the ranges and input-cell settings for all what-if tables in the current file. This command has no arguments.

You could use the following command to clear the ranges and input-cell settings for all what-if tables in the current file:

{DATA-TABLE-RESET}

Equivalent commands Range ➤ Analyze ➤ What-If Table

{DISTRIBUTION}

{DISTRIBUTION [*values-range*];[*bin-range*]}

The {DISTRIBUTION} command creates a frequency distribution by counting how many values in the given values-range fall within each numeric interval bin. It takes the following arguments.

values-range The address or name of a range containing the values to analyze. {DISTRIBUTION} ignores blank cells in *values-range* and cells containing labels.

bin-range The address or name of a single-column range containing values indicating the limits of numeric intervals of the bins of the frequency distribution. The values in *bin-range* must be unique and arranged in ascending order reading down the column. Labels in *bin-range* receive the value 0 and are included in calculations. {DISTRIBUTION} displays the frequency distribution in the column immediately to the right of *bin-range*.

You could use the following command to count how many values in the named range SALES TOTALS fall in each of the bins defined in the single-column range named TARGET SALES:

{DISTRIBUTION SALES TOTALS;TARGET SALES}

Equivalent commands Range ➤ Analyze ➤ Distribution

21

Macro Commands

{FILL}

{FILL [*range*];[*start*];[*step*];[*stop*];[*units*]}

The {FILL} command enters a sequence of values in a specified range. It takes the following arguments.

range   The name or address of the range to fill. Omit this argument if you want to work on the current selection, provided it is a multicell range; if it is not a multicell range, {FILL} will reuse the last range in which you performed a fill operation.

start   The first value for {FILL} to enter in the specified range. If you omit this argument, {FILL} will reuse the last value with which you performed a fill operation.

step   The increment between each of the values in the range. If you omit this argument, {FILL} will reuse the last value with which you performed a fill operation.

stop   The limit of the sequence. If *step* is negative, you will need to specify a stop value smaller than the start value. If you omit this argument, {FILL} will reuse the last value with which you performed a fill operation.

units   Text indicating what the step increment is, from the following list of numbers and units of time: *numeric* (an integer; this is the default setting if you omit the *units* argument); *day* (one day is the unit); *week* (one week of 7 days is the unit); *month* (one month of 30 or 31 days is the unit); *quarter* (one quarter of 90 days) is the unit); *year* (one year of 365 or 366 days is the unit); *hour* (one hour is the unit); *minute* (one minute is the unit); *second* (one second is the unit).

You could use the following command to fill the cells in the range YEARS with values starting at 1944 and ending at 1999:

{FILL YEARS;1944;1;1999;"year"}

Equivalent commands   Range ➤ Fill

{FILL-BY-EXAMPLE}

{FILL-BY-EXAMPLE [*range*]}

The {FILL-BY-EXAMPLE} command fills the specified range with a sequence of data patterned on the data include in the range. It takes the following argument.

range   The name or address of the range to fill. You can omit the *range* argument to have {FILL-BY-EXAMPLE} use the current range.

You could use the following command to fill the range WEEKDAYS with the days of the week in three-letter format, if the first cell in the range contains the label Wed:

{FILL-BY-EXAMPLE WEEKDAYS}

Equivalent commands   Range ➤ Fill by Example

{MATRIX-INVERT}

{MATRIX-INVERT [*matrix-to-invert*];[*output-range*]}

The {MATRIX-INVERT} command inverts a square matrix. It takes the following arguments.

matrix-to-invert   The name or address of the range containing the matrix to invert.

output-range   The name or address of a range in which to display the matrix in its inverted state. Make sure *output-range* contains nothing that you mind overwriting. If you omit *output-range*, {MATRIX-INVERT} uses the same output range as the last time the command was run. This can be disastrous.

WARNING   Bear in mind that not every matrix can be inverted, and that some may crash the macro with an error.

You could use the following command to invert the square matrix named JOHN and put the results in a range named BENNETT:

    {MATRIX-INVERT JOHN;BENNETT}

Equivalent commands   Range ➤ Analyze ➤ Invert Matrix

{MATRIX-MULTIPLY}

    {MATRIX-MULTIPLY [*matrix1*];[*matrix2*];[*output-range*]}

The {MATRIX-MULTIPLY} command multiplies the first specified matrix by the second specified matrix and produces a third matrix containing the results. It takes the following arguments.

matrix1   The name or address of the range containing the first matrix to multiply.

matrix2   The name or address of the range containing the second matrix to multiply.

output-range   The name or address of the range in which to display the results of the matrix multiplication. Note that {MATRIX-MULTIPLY} will overwrite any data in this range.

You could use the following command to multiply the matrix in the range named SALES by the matrix in the range named COMMISSION and display the results in a range named NET:

    {MATRIX-MULTIPLY SALES;COMMISSION;NET}

Equivalent commands   Range Analyze ➤ Multiply Matrix

{PARSE}

    {PARSE [*parse-range*];[*output-range*];[*format-line*]}

The {PARSE} command parses long labels imported from a text file into separate columns of data of one or more types (values, dates, times, and labels). It takes the following arguments.

parse-range The name or address of a single-column range containing the labels to parse.

output-range The name or address of a range into which to put the parsed data. You can specify either the entire range or only the first cell; {PARSE} will overwrite any existing data in the range.

format-line Text that tells 1-2-3 how to parse (separate) data and enter it in a worksheet. You can omit this argument if the first cell specified in the *parse-range* argument is a valid format line.

WARNING

You can omit the *parse-range* or *output-range* arguments if you want {PARSE} to reuse the last {PARSE} range you specified in the current 1-2-3 session. This can save you time entering commands, but you run the risk of overwriting important data.

21

Macro Commands

You could use the following command to parse the data contained in the range named TEXT IMPORT and put the parsed data in the output range beginning at the named cell OUTPUT:

{PARSE TEXT IMPORT;OUTPUT}

Equivalent commands Range ➤ Parse

{RANGE-NAME-CREATE}

{RANGE-NAME-CREATE *range-name*;[*range-location*]}

The {RANGE-NAME-CREATE} command assigns a name to a range address. It takes the following arguments.

range-name Text indicating the name to assign to the range.

range-location The address of the range to name. To rename the current range, omit the *range-location* argument.

You could use the following command to name the range A1..A111 with the name CHESTERFIELDS:

{RANGE-NAME-CREATE CHESTERFIELDS;A1..A111}

Equivalent commands Range ➤ Name

{RANGE-NAME-DELETE}

{RANGE-NAME-DELETE *range-name*}

The {RANGE-NAME-DELETE} command deletes a range name in the current file. It takes the following argument.

range-name Text indicating the range name to delete.

You could use the following command to delete the range name LIVE HORSES:

{RANGE-NAME-DELETE "live horses"}

Equivalent commands Range ➤ Name

{RANGE-NAME-DELETE-ALL}

{RANGE-NAME-DELETE-ALL}

The {RANGE-NAME-DELETE-ALL} command deletes all range names contained in the current file. This command has no arguments.

You could use the following command to delete all range names from the current file:

{RANGE-NAME-DELETE-ALL}

Equivalent commands Range ➤ Name

{RANGE-NAME-LABEL-CREATE}

{RANGE-NAME-LABEL-CREATE [*direction*];[*label-range*]}

The {RANGE-NAME-LABEL-CREATE} command names a single cell, using an existing label immediately above, below, to the right of, or to the left of the cell. It takes the following arguments.

direction   Text indicating the position of the single-cell range relative to *text-range*, as follows: *right* names cells to the right of the labels, so that the labels in column C become the names for the adjacent cells in column D (*right* is the default if you omit the argument); *left* names the cells to the left of the labels, so that the labels in column Z become the names for the adjacent cells in column Y; *up* names the cells above the labels, so that the labels in row 2 become the names for cells in row 1; *down* names the cells below the labels, so that the labels in row 44 become the names for the cells in row 45.

label-range   The name or address of the range containing the text to assign as range name for the adjacent cells. Omit this argument if you want to work on the current selection.

You could use the following command to assign the label in each cell of the range named FLEET CARS as the range name of its right-adjacent cell:

{RANGE-NAME-LABEL-CREATE "right";FLEET CARS}

Equivalent commands   Range ➤ Name

{RANGE-NAME-TABLE}

{RANGE-NAME-TABLE [*table-location*]}

The {RANGE-NAME-TABLE} command creates a two-column table with the names of all defined ranges in the current file listed alphabetically in the left column, and the corresponding range addresses listed in the right column. It takes the following argument.

table-location   The name or address of the range in which to create the table of range names and addresses. You can give either the entire range or only the address of the first cell. To have {RANGE-NAME-TABLE} create the table at the top-left cell of the current range, omit the *table-location* argument. Remember that the table will be two columns wide and will take up as many rows as there are range names plus one extra (blank) row, and that {RANGE-NAME-TABLE} will overwrite any existing data that gets in its way.

You could use the following command to create a range-name table for the current file, the table starting in the top-left corner of the range named KEEP FREE:

{RANGE-NAME-TABLE KEEP FREE}

Equivalent commands Range ➤ Name

{RANGE-TRANSPOSE}

{RANGE-TRANSPOSE *destination*;[*transpose*];[*origin*]}

The {RANGE-TRANSPOSE command copies data from the specified origin to the specified destination, transposing the copied data and replacing any copied formulas with their current values. It takes the following arguments.

destination   The name or address of the range to copy data to; you can specify either the entire range or just the first cell. Bear in mind that {RANGE-TRANSPOSE} will overwrite any existing data that gets in its way.

transpose   Text indicating how to transpose the data: *rows-to-columns* transposes rows of data in the specified *origin* to columns of data in the specified *destination* (this is the default setting if you omit the *transpose* argument); *columns-to-sheets* copies the first column in every worksheet of the specified *origin* to the first worksheet in the specified *destination* (the second column in every worksheet of origin to the second worksheet in destination and so on; *columns-to-sheets* works only for multi-sheet ranges); *sheets-to-rows* copies the first row in every worksheet of the specified origin to the first worksheet in the specified destination (the second row in every worksheet of the specified origin to the second worksheet in the specified destination, and so on; *sheets-to-rows* works only for 3D ranges).

origin   The name or address of the range containing the data to copy and transpose. To use the currently selected range, omit the *origin* argument.

You could use the following command to copy the contents and styles of the range A1..D4 to the range A6..D9, transpose the rows of data in A1..D4 to columns of data in A6..D9, and replace formulas with their current values:

{RANGE-TRANSPOSE A6..D9;"rows-to-columns";A1..D4}

Equivalent commands Range ➤ Transpose

{RANGE-VALUE}

{RANGE-VALUE *destination*;[*origin*]}

The {RANGE-VALUE} command copies the contents and styles from the specified origin range to the specified destination range, replacing all copied formulas with their current values. It takes the following arguments.

destination   The name or address of the destination range. You can specify either the entire range or just its first cell.

origin   The name or address of the range containing the data to copy. Omit this argument if you want to work on the current selection.

You could use the following command to copy the values from the range B:B1..B:B44 to the range C:C1..C:C44 and replace the copied formulas with their current values:

{RANGE-VALUE C:C1..C:C44;B:B1..B:B44}

Equivalent commands Edit ➤ Copy followed by Edit ➤ Paste Special

{REGRESSION}

{REGRESSION [*X-range*];[*Y-range*];[*output-range*];[*intercept*]}

The {REGRESSION} command performs multiple linear regression analysis and calculates the slope of the line that best fits the data. It takes the following arguments.

X-range   The name or address of a range containing the independent variables. This range can contain up to 75 columns and 8,192 rows. {REGRESSION} reuses the last location used for this argument if you omit the argument.

Y-range   The name or address of a single-column range that contains the set of values for the dependent variables. Y-range must have the same number of rows as X-range. {REGRESSION} reuses the last location used for this argument if you omit the argument.

21

Macro Commands

output-range   The name or address of a range to receive the results of the regression analysis. You can specify either the entire range or only the first cell. Any existing data in this range will be overwritten. *output-range* takes up nine rows by three columns, with an extra column for every independent variable. {REGRESSION} reuses the last location used for this argument if you omit the argument.

intercept   Text indicating whether {REGRESSION} calculates the Y-axis intercept or uses 0 as the Y-axis intercept: *compute* calculates the Y-axis intercept and is the default setting; *zero* uses 0 as the Y-axis intercept.

You could use the following command to perform a regression analysis on the independent variables in the range named INDEPENDENTS and the dependent variables in the range named DEPENDENTS (which two ranges contain the same number of rows), compute the Y-intercept, and have the results appear in the range starting from the named cell RESULTS:

> {REGRESSION INDEPENDENTS;DEPENDENTS;RESULTS;
> "compute"}

Equivalent commands   Range ➤ Analyze ➤ Regression

{SHEET-NAME}

> {SHEET-NAME *new-name*;[*old-name*]}

The {SHEET-NAME} command names a 1-2-3 worksheet in the current file. It takes the following arguments.

new-name   Text indicating the new name for the worksheet.

old-name   Text indicating the current name or letter of the worksheet. Omit this argument to have {SHEET-NAME} name the current worksheet.

You could use the following command to name worksheet CC with the name CANDYFLOSS:

> {SHEET-NAME "candyfloss";"cc"}

{SHEET-NAME-DELETE}

{SHEET-NAME-DELETE [*worksheet-name*]}

The {SHEET-NAME-DELETE} deletes the name of a 1-2-3 worksheet in the current file. It takes the following argument.

worksheet-name   Text indicating the worksheet name to delete, replacing it with the worksheet letter. To have {SHEET-NAME-DELETE} delete any existing name from the current worksheet, omit the *worksheet-name* argument.

You could use the following command to delete any existing name from the current worksheet:

{SHEET-NAME-DELETE}

{SORT}

{SORT [*range*];[*key1*];[*order1*];[*key2*];[*order2*];[*key3*];[*order3*]}

The {SORT} command arranges data in the specified range in the order you indicate. It takes the following arguments.

key1   The first sort key.

order1   *ascend* or *descend*, the sort order for *key1* (*ascend* sorts alphabetically and from smallest to largest; *descend* sorts in reverse-alphabetical order and from largest to smallest).

key2   The second sort key.

order2   *ascend* or *descend*, the sort order for *key2*.

key3   The third sort key.

order3   *ascend* or *descend*, the sort order for *key3*.

21

Macro Commands

T I P

Use the {SORT-KEY-DEFINE} command if you need to sort with more than three keys.

You could use the following command to sort the records in the currently selected range first by the range named VALUE, then by the range named ALPHA, both in alphabetical (ascending) order:

{SORT "VALUE";"ascend";"ALPHA";"ascend"}

{SORT-KEY-DEFINE}

{SORT-KEY-DEFINE *key-number;key-range;key-order*}

The {SORT-KEY-DEFINE} command defines a sort key for a {SORT} command to use. ({SORT-KEY-DEFINE} does not perform the sort itself.) It takes the following arguments.

key-number   An integer value from 1 through 255 indicating the sort key. The smallest-numbered sort key is used first.

key-field   Text indicating the field name to sort.

key-order   Text indicating the sort order for *key-field*, *ascend* or *descend* (*ascend* sorts alphabetically and from smallest to largest; *descend* sorts in reverse-alphabetical order and from largest to smallest).

You could use the following commands to define sort key 1 as the value of the HOME PHONE field, to be sorted from largest to smallest:

{SORT-KEY-DEFINE 1;"HOME PHONE";"descend"}

Equivalent commands   Tools ➤ Sort

{SORT-RESET}

{SORT-RESET}

The {SORT-RESET} command clears all sort keys defined for sorting range data.

Equivalent commands   Range ➤ Sort ➤ Reset

SmartIcons Macro Commands

1-2-3 includes five SmartIcons macro commands that fulfill the functions of the SmartSum, Sort Ascending, Sort Descending, Toggle Outline, and Toggle Shadow SmartIcons.

{SMARTSUM}

{SMARTSUM}

The {SMARTSUM} command sums values in the cells above or to the right of the current cell. This command has no arguments.

{SORT-ASCENDING}

{SORT-ASCENDING}

The {SORT-ASCENDING} command sorts a range or database table in ascending order (from A to Z and from smallest to largest values), using the selected column of the range or database table as the key for sorting. This command has no arguments.

{SORT-DECENDING}

{SORT-DECENDING}

The {SORT-DESCENDING} command sorts a range or database table in descending order (from Z to A and from largest to smallest values), using the selected column of the range or database table as the key for sorting. This command has no arguments.

{TOGGLE-OUTLINE}

{TOGGLE-OUTLINE}

The {TOGGLE-OUTLINE} command adds or removes a border to or from the selected cell or range. This command has no arguments.

{TOGGLE-SHADOW}

{TOGGLE-SHADOW}

The {TOGGLE-SHADOW} command draws a drop shadow on the selected cell or range if there is currently no drop shadow or removes a drop shadow from the selected cell or range if there already is one. This command has no arguments.

Solver Macro Commands

This section discusses the Solver macro commands, which correspond to the Range ➤ Analyze ➤ Backsolver and Range ➤ Analyze ➤ Solver commands. These commands are discussed in Chapter 10, beginning on page 572.

{BACKSOLVE}

{BACKSOLVE *formula-cell;target-value;adjustable-range*}

The {BACKSOLVE} command finds values for one or more cells that make the result of a formula equal to a value you specify. It takes the following arguments.

formula-cell   The name or address of a cell containing the formula for which to find a specific result. If you specify a multicell range for *formula-cell*, {BACKSOLVE} uses the first cell in the range.

target-value   The specific value for the formula in *formula-cell* to result in.

adjustable-range   The name or address of a range containing values that 1-2-3 can change. Note that the formula in *formula-cell* must depend directly or indirectly on the cells in *adjustable-range*.

You could use the following command to set the result of the formula in cell K9 to $100,000 and solve for the principal amount in cell K8:

    {BACKSOLVE K9;100000;K8}

Equivalent commands Range ➤ Analyze ➤ Backsolver

{SOLVER-ANSWER}

    {SOLVER-ANSWER *answer*}

The {SOLVER-ANSWER} command displays in the worksheet the answers or attempts that the 1-2-3 Solver finds. It takes the following argument.

answer Text indicating which answer or attempt to display, from the following list: *next* displays the next answer or attempt; *first* displays the optimal answer (if any), the best answer found, or the first answer or attempt; *original* displays the values present in the worksheet before the Solver was run; and *solve* looks for more solutions to the problem.

You could use the following command to tell Solver to display the optimal answer (if there is one):

    {SOLVER-ANSWER "first"}

Equivalent commands Solver ➤ Answer

{SOLVER-ANSWER-SAVE}

    {SOLVER-ANSWER-SAVE *scenario*;[*comment*]}

The {SOLVER-ANSWER-SAVE} command saves the current Solver answer or attempt as a scenario. It takes the following arguments.

scenario Text indicating the name for the scenario.

comment Text indicating any comment for the scenario. This is an optional argument; if you include no *comment*, {SOLVER-ANSWER-SAVE} enters the default comment (the contents of the information box in the Solver Answer dialog box).

You could use the following command to save the current Solver answer as the scenario named Odd Results and the comment "Try this with November's data as well.":

> {SOLVER-ANSWER-SAVE "Odd Results";"Try this with November's data as well."}

Equivalent commands Solver ➤ Answer ➤ Save As Scenario

{SOLVER-DEFINE}

> {SOLVER-DEFINE [*adj-cells*];[*constraint-cells*];[*optimize*];[*opt-cell*];[*opt-type*];[*answers*]}

The {SOLVER-DEFINE} command analyzes data in a worksheet and returns a number of possible Solver answers to a problem you define. It takes the following arguments.

adj-cells The names or addresses of the adjustable cells, entered as text in double quotation marks (" "). You can use multiple ranges for *adj-cells* by enclosing the ranges, with argument separators, within double quotation marks (" ")—for example, "J1..J3;LIFE;Z8..Z34". You can omit this argument if you want {SOLVER-DEFINE} to use the information you used last time you solved this problem.

constraint-cells The names or addresses of the constraint cells, entered as text in double quotation marks (" "). You can use multiple ranges for *constraint-cells* by enclosing the ranges, with argument separators, within double quotation marks (" "). You can omit this argument if you want {SOLVER-DEFINE} to use the information you used last time you solved this problem.

optimize Yes or No, indicating whether Solver should use the *opt-cell* argument. You can omit this argument if you want {SOLVER-DEFINE} to use the information you used last time you solved this problem.

opt-cell The name or address for which Solver is to find the highest or lowest value. *opt-cell* must depend directly or indirectly on the value of one or more cells in *adj-cells*. You can omit this argument if you want {SOLVER-DEFINE} to use the information you used last time you solved this problem.

opt-type   *max* or *min*, text indicating whether Solver is to find the highest (*max*) or lowest (*min*) value for *opt-cell*. You can omit this argument if you want {SOLVER-DEFINE} to use the information you used last time you solved this problem.

answers   An integer value from 1 through 999 indicating the approximate number of answers sought. You can omit this argument if you want {SOLVER-DEFINE} to use the information you used last time you solved this problem.

You could use the following command to have 1-2-3 try to minimize the value of the named cell LEAST by adjusting the values of the range named EXPENSES, subject to the conditions in the range named OVERHEADS:

    {SOLVER-DEFINE "EXPENSES";"OVER-
    HEADS";"yes";LEAST;"min";10}

Equivalent commands Range ➤ Analyze Solver

{SOLVER-DEFINE?}

    {SOLVER-DEFINE? [*adj-cells*];[*constraint-cells*];[*optimize*];[*opt-
    cell*];[*opt-type*];[*answers*]}

The {SOLVER-DEFINE?} command displays the Solver Definition dialog box, with the choice of showing defaults specified, so that the user can run Solver interactively. It takes the following arguments.

adj-cells   The names or addresses of the adjustable cells, entered as text in double quotation marks (" "). You can use multiple ranges for *adj-cells* by enclosing the ranges, with argument separators, within double quotation marks (" ")—for example, "J1..J3;LIFE;Z8..Z34". You can omit this argument if you want {SOLVER-DEFINE?} to use the information you used last time you solved this problem.

constraint-cells   The names or addresses of the constraint cells, entered as text in double quotation marks (" "). You can use multiple ranges for *constraint-cells* by enclosing the ranges, with argument separators, within double quotation marks (" "). You can omit this argument if you want

21

Macro Commands

{SOLVER-DEFINE?} to use the information you used last time you solved this problem.

optimize   Yes or No, indicating whether Solver should use the *opt-cell* argument. You can omit this argument if you want {SOLVER-DEFINE?} to use the information you used last time you solved this problem.

opt-cell   The name or address for which Solver is to find the highest or lowest value. *opt-cell* must depend directly or indirectly on the value of one or more cells in *adj-cells*. You can omit this argument if you want {SOLVER-DEFINE?} to use the information you used last time you solved this problem.

opt-type   *max* or *min*, text indicating whether Solver is to find the highest (*max*) or lowest (*min*) value for *opt-cell*. You can omit this argument if you want {SOLVER-DEFINE?} to use the information you used last time you solved this problem.

answers   An integer value from 1 through 999 indicating the approximate number of answers sought. You can omit this argument if you want {SOLVER-DEFINE?} to use the information you used last time you solved this problem.

You could use the following command to have 1-2-3 display the Solver Definition dialog box showing the entered arguments for the Solver calculation:

> {SOLVER-DEFINE? "EXPENSES";"OVER-
> HEADS";"yes";LEAST;"min";10}

Equivalent commands   Range ➤ Analyze ➤ Solver

{SOLVER-REPORT}

> {SOLVER-REPORT *type*;[*comp1*];[*comp2*];[*diff-value*]}

The {SOLVER-REPORT} command creates a new worksheet file containing a report based on the current answer. It takes the following arguments.

type   Text indicating the type of report to create, as per the following list:

answer reports about all the answers or attempts Solver found for a problem; the report appears in a new file with a unique name beginning with ANSWER (e.g., ANSWER01.WK4).

cells reports about the adjustable, constraint, and optimal cells used to solve the problem; the report appears in a new file with a unique name beginning with CELLS (e.g., CELLS001.WK4).

differences reports on two answers or two attempts in which the values of cells differ by at least the amount you specify; the report appears in a new file with a unique name beginning with DIFFS (e.g., DIFFS001.WK4).

how reports on the information used to find an answer or attempt; the report appears in a new file with a unique name beginning with HOW (e.g., HOW00001.WK4).

inconsistent reports on constraint cells that were not satisfied (returned a value of 0) for the current attempt; the report appears in a new file with a unique name beginning with INCONS (e.g., IN-CONS01.WK4).

nonbinding reports on the constraint cells that were not binding for the current answer or attempt; the report appears in a new file with a unique name beginning with NBIND (e.g., NBIND001.WK4).

what-if reports to what extent the adjustable cells can change and still satisfy all the constraints for the current answer; the report appears in a new file with a unique name beginning with LIMITS (e.g., LIMITS01.WK4).

comp1   A value indicating the first answer to compare. The default setting is 1. This argument is not necessary if *type* is other than *differences*.

comp2   A value indicating the second answer to compare. The default setting is 2. This argument is not necessary if *type* is other than *differences*.

diff-value   A value that specifies a significant difference. The default setting is 0. This argument is not necessary if *type* is other than *differences*.

You could use the following command to have Solver create a report on constraint cells whose conditions were not satisfied for the current attempt:

{SOLVER-REPORT "inconsistent"}

Equivalent commands   Range ➤ Analyze ➤ Solver

Style Macro Commands

This section examines the style macro commands, which correspond to the commands on the Style menu.

{COLUMN-WIDTH}

{COLUMN-WIDTH *width*;[*range*]}

The {COLUMN-WIDTH} command adjusts columns in the given *range* to the width specified. It takes the following arguments.

width   A value specifying the width of the column as a number of characters.

range   The name or address of the range of columns to adjust. {COLUMN-WIDTH} uses the currently selected range, collection, or query table if you omit the *range* argument.

You could use the following commands to adjust all columns in the range named GROSS to fifteen characters wide:

{COLUMN-WIDTH 15, GROSS}

Equivalent commands   Style ➤ Column Width

{COLUMN-WIDTH-FIT-WIDEST}

{COLUMN-WIDTH-FIT-WIDEST *width*}

The {COLUMN-WIDTH-FIT-WIDEST} command adjusts columns in the given *range* to the width of the widest entries. It takes the following argument.

range The name or address of the range of columns to adjust. {COLUMN-WIDTH-FIT-WIDEST} uses the currently selected range, collection, or query table if you omit the *range* argument.

You could use the following commands to recalculate the results in a range named GROSS and adjust the columns to fit the widest entries:

```
{SELECT GROSS}
{RECALC}
{COLUMN-WIDTH-FIT-WIDEST}
```

Equivalent commands Style ➤ Column Width

{COLUMN-WIDTH-RESET}

{COLUMN-WIDTH-RESET [*range*]}

The {COLUMN-WIDTH-RESET} command resets the columns in the given *range* to the default column width. It takes the following argument.

range The name or address of the range of columns to adjust. {COLUMN-WIDTH-RESET} uses the currently selected range, collection, or query table if you omit the *range* argument.

You could use the following commands to reset the widths of the columns in a range named SPLAYED to the default width:

```
{COLUMN-WIDTH-RESET SPLAYED}
```

{HIDE-COLUMNS}

{HIDE-COLUMNS [*range*]}

The {HIDE-COLUMNS} command hides all columns in the specified range. It takes the following argument.

range The name or address of a range that contains at least one cell in each column to be hidden. To have {HIDE-COLUMNS} hide any column that contains cells in the current range, you can omit the *range* argument.

You could use the following command to hide the columns in the range SECRETS:

{HIDE-COLUMNS SECRETS}

Equivalent commands Style ➤ Hide

{HIDE-SHEETS}

{HIDE-SHEETS [*range*]}

The {HIDE-SHEETS} command hides all sheets in the specified range. It takes the following argument.

range The name or address of a range that contains at least one cell in each sheet to be hidden. To have {HIDE-SHEETS} hide any sheet that contains cells in the current range, omit the *range* argument.

You could use the following command to hide the sheets in the range PAYROLL:

{HIDE-SHEETS PAYROLL}

{NAMED-STYLE-USE}

{NAMED-STYLE-USE *style-name*;[*range*]}

The {NAMED-STYLE-USE} command applies the named style specified to the target range or query table. It takes the following arguments.

style-name Text indicating the name of the style to apply.

range The name or address of the range to which to apply the style. To apply the style to the current selection, omit the *range* argument.

You could use the following command to apply the style named DIS-PLAY to the range named RESULTS:

{NAMED-STYLE-USE DISPLAY;RESULTS}

Equivalent commands Style ➤ Named Style

{PAGE-BREAK-COLUMN}

{PAGE-BREAK-COLUMN *on-off*}

The {PAGE-BREAK-COLUMN} command inserts or deletes a vertical page break to the left of the current column. It takes the following argument.

on-off *on* to insert a page break, *off* to delete a page break; the argument should be entered as text in double quotation marks (" ").

You could use the following commands to delete a vertical page break to the left of column C:

{SELECT C1}
{PAGE-BREAK-COLUMN "off"}

Equivalent commands Style ➤ Page Break

{PAGE-BREAK-ROW}

{PAGE-BREAK-ROW *on-off*}

The {PAGE-BREAK-ROW} command inserts or deletes a horizontal page break above the current row. It takes the following argument.

on-off *on* to insert a page break, *off* to delete a page break; the argument should be entered as text in double quotation marks (" ").

You could use the following commands to insert a horizontal page break above row P42:

{SELECT P42}
{PAGE-BREAK-ROW "on"}

Equivalent commands Style ➤ Page Break

21

Macro Commands

{PROTECT}

{PROTECT [*range*]}

The {PROTECT} command turns protection back on for the specified range. It takes the following argument.

range The name or address of the range to protect. Omit the *range* argument to protect the current range.

You could use the following command to protect the range ALL DATA:

{PROTECT ALL DATA}

Equivalent commands Style ➤ Protection

{ROW-HEIGHT}

{ROW-HEIGHT *height*;[*range*]}

The {ROW-HEIGHT} command adjusts each row in the specified range to the specified height in points. It takes the following arguments.

height An integer value from 1 through 255 indicating the row height in points.

range The name or address of the range to adjust. Omit this argument if you want to work on the current selection.

You could use the following command to set the row height of the range DISPLAY to a tasteful 48 points:

{ROW-HEIGHT 48;DISPLAY}

Equivalent commands Style ➤ Row Height

{ROW-HEIGHT-FIT-LARGEST}

{ROW-HEIGHT-FIT-LARGEST [*range*]}

The {ROW-HEIGHT-FIT-LARGEST} command adjusts each row in the specified range to the height of the largest font in that row. It takes the following argument.

range   The name or address of the range to adjust. Omit this argument if you want to work on the current selection.

You could use the following command to adjust the height of each row in the range named SMALL PRINT to the height of the largest font in that row:

    {ROW-HEIGHT-FIT-LARGEST SMALL PRINT}

Equivalent commands   Style ➤ Row Height

{SHOW-COLUMNS}

    {SHOW-COLUMNS [*range*]}

The {SHOW-COLUMNS} command reveals all hidden columns in the specified range. It takes the following argument.

range   The name or address of a range containing at least one cell in each column to redisplay. Omit this argument if you want to work on the current selection.

You could use the following command to reveal the hidden columns in the range named RECORD PRICES:

    {SHOW-COLUMNS RECORD PRICES}

Equivalent commands   Style ➤ Hide ➤ Show

{SHOW-SHEETS}

    {SHOW-SHEETS [*range*]}

The {SHOW-SHEETS} command reveals all hidden sheets in the specified range. It takes the following argument.

range   The name or address of a range containing at least one cell in each sheet to redisplay. Omit this argument if you want to work on the current selection.

You could use the following command to reveal the hidden sheets in the range named VP:

> {SHOW-SHEETS VP}

Equivalent commands   Style ➤ Hide ➤ Show

{STYLE-ALIGN-HORIZONTAL}

> {STYLE-ALIGN-HORIZONTAL *horizontal*;[*range*];[*over-cols*];[*wrap*]}

The {STYLE-ALIGN-HORIZONTAL} command sets the horizontal alignment of labels and values in the specified range. It takes the following arguments.

horizontal   Text that specifies how to align labels and values in the range, entered in double quotation marks (" "), as follows: *general* aligns labels to the left and values to the right; *left* aligns data to the left; center aligns data in the center; *right* aligns data to the right; *evenly* stretches text within the cell by expanding the space between words and between the letters in words. *evenly* does not work on labels that end with a period, an exclamation point, a question mark, or a colon.

range   The location for the labels to be aligned. Omit this argument if you want to work on the current selection.

over-cols   Yes or No, indicating whether to align the text in the leftmost cell over the columns in the range. The default is No if you omit this argument.

wrap   Yes or No, indicating whether labels should wrap to fit inside a single cell. The default is No if you omit this argument.

You could use the following command to right-align data in the range named PRESENTATION:

> {STYLE-ALIGN-HORIZONTAL "right";PRESENTATION}

Equivalent commands   Style ➤ Alignment

{STYLE-ALIGN-ORIENTATION}

{STYLE-ALIGN-ORIENTATION *orientation*;[*angle*];[*range*]}

The {STYLE-ALIGN-ORIENTATION} command alters the orientation of data in the specified range. It takes the following arguments.

orientation   0, 1, 2, 3, or 4, indicating the orientation style to apply, as follows: 0 specifies regular alignment; 1 specifies vertical unrotated text; 2 specifies text rotated 90 degrees counterclockwise; 3 specifies text rotated 90 degrees clockwise; and 4 specifies text rotated at a specified angle.

angle   An integer from 1 through 90 indicating the rotation angle desired when *orientation* is 4. The default is 45 degrees.

range   The name or address of the range or query table in which to orient the data. Omit this argument if you want to work on the current selection.

You could use the following command to display the named range SALES STAFF skewed at a 60-degree angle:

{STYLE-ALIGN-ORIENTATION 4;60;SALES STAFF}

Equivalent commands   Style ➤ Alignment

{STYLE-ALIGN-VERTICAL}

{STYLE-ALIGN-VERTICAL *vertical*;[*range*]}

The {STYLE-ALIGN-VERTICAL} command sets vertical alignment for text within a cell whose height is greater than that of the largest typeface. It takes the following arguments.

vertical   Text within double quotation marks (" ") that specifies how to align the data: *top* aligns data with the top of the cell; *center* centers data vertically within the cell; and *bottom* aligns data with the bottom of the cell.

range   The name or address of the range or query table in which to align data. Omit this argument if you want to work on the current selection.

21

Macro Commands

You could use the following command to center the headings in the range MAIN TITLE vertically in their cells:

{STYLE-ALIGN-VERTICAL "center";MAIN TITLE}

Equivalent commands Style ➤ Alignment

{STYLE-BORDER}

{STYLE-BORDER *border;display;*[*range*];[*color*];[*style*]}

The {STYLE-BORDER} command sets borders for the specified range. It takes the following arguments.

border Text within double quotation marks (" ") indicating the border to work with: *outline* sets the border around the entire range; *all* sets the border around each cell in the range; *left* sets the left border of each cell; *right* sets the right border of each cell; *top* sets the top border of each cell; and *bottom* sets the bottom border of each cell.

display Yes or No, indicating whether to turn the border on (Yes) or off (No).

range The name or address of the range to work on. Omit this argument if you want to work on the current selection.

color An offset number from 0 through 15 indicating a line color from the Line Color drop-down list in the Lines & Color dialog box (0 is black, 1 is white, 2 is red, and so on, down to the colors whose names no one can agree on because they look different on different PCs). *color* only applies when *display* is On.

style An offset number from 0 through 7 that specifies a line style from the Line Style drop-down list in the Lines & Color dialog box (0 is "solid thin," 7 is "advanced Morse code signaling," and so on). *style* only applies when *display* is On.

You could use the following command to draw a simple Morse-style line in the rusty color around the outside edge of the selected range:

{STYLE-BORDER "outside";"on";;8;6}

Equivalent commands Style ➤ Lines & Color

{STYLE-EDGE}

{STYLE-EDGE [*color*];[*style*];[*width*];[*arrowhead*]}

The {STYLE-EDGE} command sets the color, style, and width of the edge of charts, chart elements (plot frames, solid data series, titles, legends, and footnotes), text blocks, drawn objects, OLE objects, and pictures created in other Windows applications. It takes the following arguments.

color   An integer from 0 through 255 indicating the color from the color palette.

style   An offset number from 0 through 7 indicating a line style from the Line Style drop-down list in the Lines & Color dialog box (e.g., 1 specifies a solid double line).

width   An offset number from 0 through 7 indicating a line width from the Line Width drop-down list in the Lines & Color dialog box (e.g., 7 specifies a very heavy line).

arrowhead   An offset number from 0 through 3 indicating an arrowhead type from the Arrowhead drop-down list in the Lines & Color dialog box.

You could use the following command to render the edges of the selected object as lime-green, solid, wide single lines:

{STYLE-EDGE 34;0;7}

Equivalent commands   Style ➤ Lines & Color

{STYLE-FONT}

{STYLE-FONT *typeface*;[*range*];[*font-family*];[*character-set*]}

The {STYLE-FONT} command sets the font for the specified range. It takes the following arguments.

typeface   Text within double quotation marks (" ") indicating the font to assign.

range   The name or address of the range to receive the font formatting. Omit this argument if you want to work on the current selection.

font-family   Text within double quotation marks (" ") indicating the font family for the specified *typeface* to be mapped to in case the font specified is not available on the user's system: *dontcare* specifies a font that most closely matches *typeface* (this is the default if you omit the *font-family* argument); *decorative* specifies a decorative typeface; *modern* specifies a fixed font; *roman* specifies a serif font; *script* specifies a script font; and *swiss* specifies a sans-serif font.

character-set   Text that specifies a character set: *ansi*, *oem*, *symbol*, or *kanji*. *ansi* is the default.

You could use the following command to set the font for the named range EXTRAMURAL as WingDings and use a decorative font if WingDings were not available:

    {STYLE-FONT "WingDings";EXTRAMURAL;"decorative"}

Equivalent commands   Style ➤ Font & Attributes

{STYLE-FONT-ALL}

    {STYLE-FONT-ALL [*typeface*];[*size*];[*bold*];[*italic*];[*underline*];[*range*];[*underline-style*];[*font-family*];[*character-set*]}

The {STYLE-FONT-ALL} command sets the font and attributes for the specified range. It takes the following arguments.

typeface   Text within double quotation marks (" ") indicating the name of the font to assign.

size   A value indicating the point size to assign.

bold   Yes or No, indicating whether to add or remove boldface.

italic   Yes or No, indicating whether to add or remove italics.

underline   Yes or No, indicating whether to add or remove underline.

range   The name or address of the range to receive the font formatting. Omit this argument if you want to work on the current selection.

underline-style   An offset number from 0 through 2 that specifies an underline style from the Underline drop-down list in the Font & Attributes dialog box.

font-family   Text within double quotation marks (″ ″) indicating the font family for the specified *typeface* to be mapped to in case the font specified is not available on the user's system: *dontcare* specifies a font that most closely matches *typeface* (this is the default if you omit the *font-family* argument); *decorative* specifies a decorative typeface; *modern* specifies a fixed font; *roman* specifies a serif font; *script* specifies a script font; *swiss* specifies a sans-serif font.

character-set   Text that specifies a character set: *ansi, oem, symbol,* or *kanji. ansi* is the default.

You could use the following command to assign 12-point Wide Latin font to the range named HEADINGS, to assign italic but no bold or underline, and to have 1-2-3 apply any convenient similar font if the user's machine does not have Wide Latin:

    {STYLE-FONT-ALL "Wide Latin";12;"off";"on";"off";HEAD-
    INGS;;"dontcare"}

Equivalent commands   Style ➤ Font & Attributes

{STYLE-FONT-ATTRIBUTES}

{STYLE-FONT-ATTRIBUTES *attribute;on-off;*[*range*];[*underline-style*]}

The {STYLE-FONT-ATTRIBUTES} command adds bold, italic, or underlining to a range. It takes the following arguments.

attribute   Text within double quotation marks (″ ″) indicating the attribute to add or remove: *bold* indicates boldface; *italic* indicates italics; and *underline* indicates underlining.

on-off   Yes or No, indicating whether to add the attribute (Yes) or remove the attribute (No).

range   The name or address of the range on which to work. Omit this argument if you want to work on the current selection.

underline-style   An offset number from 0 through 2 that specifies an underline style from the Underline drop-down list in the Font & Attributes dialog box. The default is 0.

21

Macro Commands

You could use the following command to remove italics from the data in the range named RAPTOR:

{STYLE-FONT-ATTRIBUTES "italics";"off";RAPTOR}

Equivalent commands Style ➤ Font & Attributes

{STYLE-FONT-RESET}

{STYLE-FONT-RESET [*range*]}

The {STYLE-FONT-RESET} command restores the worksheet default font, font size, attributes and color to the specified range. It takes the following argument.

range The name or address of the range to reset the font for. Omit this argument if you want to work on the current selection.

You could use the following command to reset the font for the named range ALTITUDE to the default font:

{STYLE-FONT-RESET ALTITUDE}

Equivalent commands Style ➤ Font & Attributes

{STYLE-FONT-SIZE}

{STYLE-FONT-SIZE *size*;[*range*]}

The {STYLE-FONT-SIZE} command assigns the specified point size to the fonts in the specified range. It takes the following arguments.

size An integer value indicating the point size to assign.

range The name or address of the range to which to assign the point size. Omit this argument if you want to work on the current selection.

You could use the following command to make the labels in the range named ZAIRE 6-point type:

{STYLE-FONT-SIZE 6;ZAIRE}

Equivalent commands Style ➤ Font & Attributes

{STYLE-FRAME}

{STYLE-FRAME *display*;[*color*];[*style*];[*range*]}

The {STYLE-FRAME} command sets a frame for the specified range. It takes the following arguments.

display   Yes or No, indicating whether to turn the frame on (Yes) or off (No).

color   An offset number from 0 through 255 indicating a color from the color palette. *color* does not apply when *display* is *off* and when *style* is 0 through 7.

style   An offset number from 0 through 15 indicating the frame style, as shown in the Designer Frame box of the Lines & Color dialog box. *style* only applies when *display* is *on*.

range   The name or address of the range to work on. Omit this argument if you want to work on the current selection.

You could use the following command to add a blue photo-corner frame around the range named ALTITUDE:

{STYLE-FRAME "on";168;3;ALTITUDE}

Equivalent commands   Style ➤ Lines & Color

{STYLE-GALLERY}

{STYLE-GALLERY *template*; [*range*]}

The {STYLE-GALLERY} command autoformats the specified range with one of 1-2-3's fourteen style templates. It takes the following arguments.

template   An offset number from 0 through 13 indicating a template from the Template list box in the Gallery dialog box. For example, use 13 to indicate the B&W4 format.

range   The name or address of the range to format. Omit this argument if you want to work on the current selection.

21

Macro Commands

You could use the following command to apply the template "Computer" automatically to the range named RECEIVED:

    {STYLE-GALLERY 2;RECEIVED}

Equivalent commands Style ➤ Gallery

{STYLE-INTERIOR}

    {STYLE-INTERIOR [*background-color*];[*pattern*];[*pattern-color*];[*text-color*];[*negatives*];[*range*]}

The {STYLE-INTERIOR} command sets colors and patterns for each cell of the specified range. It takes the following arguments.

background-color   An integer from 0 through 255 indicating a color in the color palette. The default setting is 0 if you omit this argument.

pattern   An offset number from 0 through 63 indicating a pattern from the Pattern Color drop-down list in the Lines & Color dialog box. The default setting is 0 if you omit this argument.

pattern-color   An integer from 0 through 255 indicating a color in the color palette. The default setting is 0 if you omit this argument.

text-color   An integer from 0 through 255 indicating a color in the color palette. The default setting is 0 if you omit this argument.

negatives   Yes or No, indicating whether to display negative values in red. *negatives* only applies to a range or query table.

range   The name or address of the range to format. Omit this argument if you want to work on the current selection.

You could use the following command to format the cells in the current range with a dark-blue background and negative numbers appearing in red:

    {STYLE-INTERIOR 186;;;;"yes"}

Equivalent commands Style ➤ Lines & Color

{STYLE-LINE}

{STYLE-LINE [*color*];[*style*];[*width*];[*arrowhead*];[*symbol*]}

The {STYLE-LINE} command changes the color, style, and width of the selected line for drawn lines and chart lines including line data series, grid lines, and axes. It takes the following arguments.

color An integer from 0 through 255 indicating the color from the color palette.

style An offset number from 0 through 7 indicating a line style from the Line Style drop-down list in the Lines & Color dialog box (e.g., 1 specifies a solid double line).

width An offset number from 0 through 7 indicating a line width from the Line Width drop-down list in the Lines & Color dialog box (e.g., 7 specifies a very heavy line).

arrowhead An offset number from 0 through 3 indicating an arrowhead type from the Arrowhead drop-down list in the Lines & Color dialog box.

symbol An offset number from 0 through 23 indicating a data-point symbol from the Symbol drop-down list in the Lines & Color dialog box. *symbol* is only used if the current selection is a line data series.

You could use the following command to define the style for the currently selected line as lime green, double-line, heavy, two-headed arrowhead, with a filled-diamond symbol:

{STYLE-LINE 34;1;7;3;1}

Equivalent commands Style ➤ Lines & Color

{STYLE-NUMBER-FORMAT}

{STYLE-NUMBER-FORMAT [*format*];[*decimals*];[*parentheses*]; [*range*];[*currency*]}

The {STYLE-NUMBER-FORMAT} command sets the display of values in the specified range. It takes the following arguments.

format   Text indicating the format to assign to the values in *range*: *Automatic, Comma, Currency, Fixed, General, Hidden, Label, Percent, Scientific, Text, +/–,dd-mmm, dd-mmm-yy, mmm-yy, Date-Long-International, Date-Short-International, hh:mm AM/PM, hh:mm:ss AM/PM, Time-Long-International,* or *Time-Short-International.*

decimals   An integer from 0 through 15 indicating the number of decimal places. The default setting is 2.

parentheses   Yes or No, indicating whether or not to enclose values in parentheses.

range   The name or address of the range to format. Omit this argument if you want to work on the current selection.

currency   Text indicating the currency symbol to use if *format* is *currency*, entered as the name of a currency symbol from the Currency list box in the Number Format dialog box—e.g., "Taiwan Dollar" or "Thai Baht".

You could use the following command to format the range named SWITZERLAND with "Malaysian Ringgit" currency format and two decimal places:

{STYLE-NUMBER-FORMAT "currency";2;;SWITZERLAND;"Malaysian Ringgit"}

Equivalent commands   Style ➤ Number Format

{STYLE-NUMBER-FORMAT-RESET}

{STYLE-NUMBER-FORMAT-RESET [*range*]}

The {STYLE-NUMBER-FORMAT-RESET} command resets the format of the specified range to the current default format specified in the Worksheet Defaults dialog box. It takes the following argument.

range   The name or address of the range to format. Omit this argument if you want to work on the current selection.

You could use the following command to reset the number format of the range named SPECS to the default format:

{STYLE-NUMBER-FORMAT-RESET SPECS}

Equivalent commands Style ➤ Number Format

{UNPROTECT}

{UNPROTECT [*range*]}

The {UNPROTECT} command turns protection off for the specified range. It takes the following argument.

range The name or address of the range to unprotect. Omit this argument if you want to work on the current selection.

You could use the following command to turn protection off for the range MANAGERS:

{UNPROTECT MANAGERS}

Equivalent commands Style ➤ Protection

Text-File Manipulation Macro Commands

This section examines the text-file manipulation macro commands, which can open, close, read, and write text files.

{CLOSE}

{CLOSE}

The {CLOSE} command closes the text file opened with an {OPEN} command and saves any changes made to the file. The {CLOSE} command has no arguments.

You could use the following command to close a text file that a macro had opened:

> {CLOSE}

{FILESIZE}

> {FILESIZE *location*}

The {FILESIZE} command counts the number of bytes in an open text file and enters the number in the specified location. It takes the following argument.

location   The name or address of a cell or a range. If you specify a range, {FILESIZE} enters the number in the first cell of the range.

You could use the following command to count the number of bytes in the open text file and return that number in the first cell of the range named LENGTH, branching to the location NOFILE if no text file is open:

> {FILESIZE LENGTH}{BRANCH NOFILE}

{GETPOS}

> {GETPOS *location*}

The {GETPOS} command enters in the specified location the current byte-pointer position in an open text file. The current byte-pointer position is the place in the text file from which data is currently being read or two which data is currently being written. It takes the following argument.

location   The name or address of a cell or a range. If you specify a range, {GETPOS} enters the number in the first cell of the range.

You could use the following command to return the current byte-pointer position in the cell named CELLP, branching to the location NOFILE if no text file is open:

> {GETPOS CELLP}{BRANCH NOFILE}

{OPEN}

{OPEN *file-name;access-type*}

The {OPEN} command opens a text file for read-only processing or for read-and-write processing, depending on the type of access specified. You can also use this command to create a new text file with the specified name. You need to open a text file before you can perform any other text-file manipulation commands on it. {OPEN} takes the following arguments.

file-name   Text entered in double quotation marks (" ") indicating the full name of a text file (including directory path and extension) or the name or address of a cell containing a text file name. If the specified text file does not exist, {OPEN} creates it.

access-type   *r*, *w*, *m*, or *a*, or the name or address of a cell containing one of those characters, indicating the type of access to establish to the file, as follows: *r* specifies read-only access; *w* specifies write access, which also allows reading; *m* specifies modify access, which allows reading and writing and places the byte pointer at the beginning of the file; and *a* specifies append access, which allows reading and writing and places the byte pointer at the end of the file.

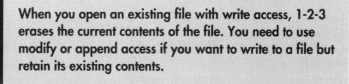

WARNING   When you open an existing file with write access, 1-2-3 erases the current contents of the file. You need to use modify or append access if you want to write to a file but retain its existing contents.

You could use the following command to open the existing text file RAWDATA.TXT to modify:

{OPEN "D:\SHARE\RAWDATA.TXT";m}

{READ}

{READ *byte-count;location*}

The {READ} command copies the specified number of bytes from the current byte-pointer position in the open text file to the specified location and increases the byte-counter position by the relevant number of bytes. It takes the following arguments.

byte-count   A value from 0 to 511 indicating the number of bytes to read from the text file. {READ} uses a value of 511 if you specify a negative number or a number greater than 511; if you specify more bytes than the text file contains from the current byte-pointer position, {READ} takes as many bytes as possible.

location   The name or address of a cell or range in which to enter the text from the text file. If you specify a range, {READ} enters the data in the first cell of the range.

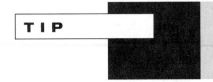

T I P   {READ} includes the carriage-return and linefeed characters at the end of text lines, while {READLN} does not.

You could use the following command to read 144 bytes from the open text file into the cell named TREATTEXT:

{READ 144;TREATTEXT}

{READLN}

{READLN *location*}

The {READLN} command copies the rest of the current line of text in the open text file, starting from the current byte-pointer position, to the specified location. {READLN} then moves the byte-pointer to the beginning of the next line in the file. It takes the following argument.

location   The name or address of a cell or range in which to enter the data from the text file. If you specify a range, {READLN} enters the data in the first cell of the range.

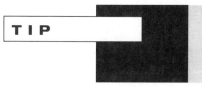

{READ} includes the carriage-return and linefeed characters at the end of text lines, while {READLN} does not.

You could use the following command to copy the remainder of the current line of text in the open text file into the range named LINE READ:

{READLN LINE READ}

{SETPOS}

{SETPOS *offset-number*}

The {SETPOS} command moves the byte pointer in an open text file the number of bytes specified by the given offset-number from the first byte in the file. The byte-pointer position is the place in the text file to which data is being written or from which data is being read. It takes the following argument.

offset-number　An offset number indicating the position in the file to which to move the byte pointer, starting from the first byte in the file.

Since 1-2-3 allows you to specify an offset number large enough to move the byte pointer past the end of a file, you'll probably want to run a {FILESIZE} command to establish the size of the text file before you issue a {SETPOS} command.

You could use the following command to place the byte pointer 220 bytes from the beginning of the currently open text file:

{SETPOS 220}

21

Macro Commands

{WRITE}

{WRITE *text*}

The {WRITE} command copies the specified text to the open text file, starting at the current byte-pointer position and increasing the byte-counter position with each byte written. The text file must have been opened with write (w), modify (m), or append (a) access. It takes the following argument.

text   The text to copy to the text file. {WRITE} evaluates any text formulas and writes their results to the file.

You could use the following command to write the text "Call FuturePerfect today on 1-800-328-7448." to the open text file:

{WRITE "Call FuturePerfect today on 1-800-328-7448."}

{WRITELN}

{WRITELN *text*}

The {WRITELN} command copies the specified text to the open text file at the current byte-pointer position, adding a carriage-return and linefeed. The text file must have been opened with write (w), modify (m), or append (a) access. {WRITELN} increments the byte-pointer position as it writes text to the text file. It takes the following argument.

text   The text to copy. {WRITELN} evaluates text formulas and enters their results in the text file.

You could use the following command to write the text "Time and again, style goes out of fashion." to the current text file and add a carriage-return and linefeed at the end:

{WRITELN "Time and again, style goes out of fashion."}

Tools Macro Commands

This section examines the Tools macro commands, which correspond to the commands on the Tools menu.

{ADDIN-INVOKE}

{ADDIN-INVOKE *add-in*}

The {ADDIN-INVOKE} command starts an add-in application. It takes the following argument.

add-in   The name of the add-in to invoke, entered as text in double quotation marks (" ").

If you had an add-in module named Product, you could invoke it with the following command:

{ADDIN-INVOKE "product.adw"}

Equivalent commands   Tools ➤ Add-in

{ADDIN-LOAD}

{ADDIN-LOAD *add-in*}

The {ADDIN-LOAD} command reads the specified add-in module into memory. It takes the following argument.

add-in   The name of the add-in you want to work with, entered as text in double quotation marks (" "). Note that you should include the path, as in the example below.

You could use the following command to load an add-in module named "Market" stored on your network drive F: in the \LOTUS\PUB-LIC\ADD-INS\ subdirectory into memory:

{ADDIN-LOAD "f:\lotus\public\add-ins\market.adw"}

21

Macro Commands

Equivalent commands Tools ➤ Add-in

{ADDIN-REMOVE}

{ADDIN-REMOVE *add-in*}

The {ADDIN-REMOVE} command removes the specified add-in from memory. It takes the following argument.

add-in The name of the add-in to remove, entered as text in double quotation marks (" ").

You could use the following command to remove the add-in module named "Market" from memory:

{ADDIN-REMOVE "market.adw"

N O T E   For {ADDIN-REMOVE}, you do not need to specify a path because the add-in module is already loaded into memory.

Equivalent commands Tools ➤ Add-in

{ADDIN-REMOVE-ALL}

{ADDIN-REMOVE-ALL}

The {ADDIN-REMOVE-ALL} command removes all add-ins from memory. This command has no arguments.

You could use the following command to remove all add-in modules currently loaded into memory:

{ADDIN-REMOVE-ALL}

Equivalent commands Tools ➤ Add-in

{AUDIT}

{AUDIT *audit*;[*files*];[*result*];[*report-range*];[*audit-range*]}

The {AUDIT} command highlights or produces a report of all formulas, or the relationships of values and formulas, in the current file or in all active files. {AUDIT} also highlights or produces a report on circular references, file links, or DDE links. It takes the following arguments.

audit   The items to audit, entered as text: *formulas* to audit all cells containing formulas; *precedents* to audit all cells referred to by a formula; *dependents* to audit all cells containing a formula that refers to the cells; *circular* to audit the first cell involved in a circular reference (1-2-3 also automatically uses the default settings for all arguments that follow audit); *file-links* to audit all cells that contain a formula that links to other 1-2-3 files; *dde-links* to audit all cells that contain a link between the current file and other Windows applications.

files   Text indicating which files to audit: Either *current-file*, which edits the current file and is the default setting if you omit the *files* argument, or *all-open-files*, which edits all open files.

result   Text indicating how 1-2-3 shows you the results of the audit: *selection* highlights the cells found in the audit and is the default if you omit the *result* argument; *report* produces a list of all cells found in the audit, one item per cell from top to bottom, left to right, in *report-range*.

report-range   The name or address of a blank cell or a blank range where 1-2-3 produces an audit report, if you specify *report* for *result*. {AUDIT} produces a list of all cells found in the audit, one item per cell from top to bottom, left to right.

audit-range   The name or address of a range to audit for formula precedents or cell dependents. *audit-range* does not apply to other *audit* options. {AUDIT} audits the current selection if you omit *audit-range* and specify *precedents* or *dependents* for *audit*.

You could use the following command to produce an audit report starting in cell B2 of worksheet Z of DDE links in the current file:

{AUDIT "dde-links";"current-file";"report";Z:B2}

Equivalent commands   Tools ➤ Audit

{ -- comment}

> { -- comment}

The { -- comment} command puts a comment into a macro—for example, for explaining what the macro does. 1-2-3 skips comments when running macros. { -- comment} takes the following arguments.

comment   The text of the comment to add. *comment* can contain any characters except a close brace (}) and does not have to be enclosed in double quotation marks (" ").

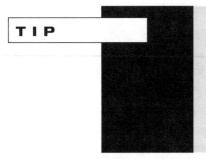

T I P   Comments can be a great help to others when it comes to understanding your macros—and to yourself, when you revisit old macros after a long time and have forgotten what you were doing. Since including a lot of long comments will slow down your macros, you may do better to document complicated macros by entering labels in the adjacent column to the commands.

You could use the following comment commands to keep track of a macro:

> { -- Track Inventory macro for Widgets Galore Inc.
> { -- written by Carlos Appletree, 11/28/94

{MAP-NEW}

> {MAP-NEW *location*;[*map-type*]}

The {MAP-NEW} command draws a map of the specified type at the specified location, using data from the currently selected range. It takes the following arguments.

location   The name or address of the range (in the current file) at which you want {MAP-NEW} to draw the new map. {MAP-NEW} does not automatically place and size the chart if *location* is a single cell.

map type   Text that identifies the geographic region.

You could use the following command to create a map of the currently selected range in the ranged named TO-MAP, using a map of Canada:

> {MAP-NEW TO-MAP;CANADA}

Equivalent commands   Tools ➤ Map

{MAP-REDRAW}

> {MAP-REDRAW}

The {MAP-REDRAW} command redraws all maps in the current file.

T I P   You can set map redrawing to automatic or manual by using a {SET "map-draw";"automatic"} or {SET "map-draw";"manual"} command.

Equivalent commands   Tools ➤ Map ➤ Redraw

{REGISTER}

> {REGISTER *module-name;procedure-name;alias-name;return-type;arg-count;arg-types*}

The {REGISTER} command registers a procedure in a Dynamic Link Library (DLL) as an add-in @function, and loads the DLL into memory. It takes the following arguments.

module-name   Text indicating the name of the DLL containing the procedure to register as an add-in @function.

21

Macro Commands

procedure-name   Text indicating the name of the procedure contained in *module-name* to register as an add-in @function.

alias-name   Text indicating the @function name to give the registered procedure. Omit the @ symbol.

return-type   Text indicating a letter code for the type of value returned from the registered function. The letters are given in the list below.

arg-count   An integer indicating the number of arguments that the function uses.

arg-types   Text indicating the type of value accepted for each argument for the @function. The letter codes for *arg-types* are given in the list below.

RETURN-TYPE/ ARG-TYPES	C DECLARATION	TYPE OF VALUE
A	Short int	Logical or Boolean.
B	Short int	Signed 2-byte integer.
C	Long int	Long 4-byte integer.
D	Double	IEEE 8-byte floating-point.
E	Char★	ANSI NULL terminated character string; maximum string length 255 characters.
F	Char★	Long LMBCS string pointer.
G	Unsigned char★	Byte-counted string pointer. The first byte contains the length of the string. The maximum string length is 255 characters.

RETURN-TYPE/ ARG-TYPES	C DECLARATION	TYPE OF VALUE
H	Double*	Pointer to IEEE 8-byte floating-point.
I	Long*	Pointer to a 4-byte integer.
J	Short int*	Pointer to a 2-byte integer.
K	Short int*	Pointer to a 2-byte logical.
L	Char*	ANSI NULL terminated character string; maximum string length is 255 characters. Modified in place.
M	Char*	Byte-counted string pointer. The first byte contains the length of the string. The maximum string length is 255 characters. Modified in place.

{SMARTICONS-USE}

> {SMARTICONS-USE *set-name*}

The {SMARTICONS-USE} command selects a set of SmartIcons to use with 1-2-3. It takes the following argument.

set-name   Text indicating the name of the SmartIcon set to use.

You could use the following command to select the Formatting SmartIcons set:

> {SMARTICON-USE "Formatting"}

Equivalent commands   Tools ➤ SmartIcons

{SPELLCHECK?}

> {SPELLCHECK?}

The {SPELLCHECK?} command displays the Spell Check dialog box so that the user can perform an interactive spell-check. The spell checker needs to have been installed for this command to work.

Equivalent commands   Tools ➤ Spell Check

{UNREGISTER}

> {UNREGISTER *alias-name*}

The {UNREGISTER} command unregisters the procedure indicated by the specified alias-name. It takes the following argument.

alias-name   Text indicating the name of the @function to unregister. Omit the @ symbol from the argument.

You could use the following command to unregister the add-in @function @REPHRASE:

> {UNREGISTER "REPHRASE"}

User Environment Macro Commands

This section examines the user environment macro commands, which suspend macro execution for user input, control macro execution, and create custom menus.

{?}

{?}

The {?} command suspends macro execution until the user presses ↵, which lets the user move the cell pointer or type any number of keystrokes (and enter them by clicking with the mouse).

WARNING

To enter data typed at the {?} command, you must include a ~ (a tilde) or a cursor-movement key (such as {LEFT} or {DOWN}) in the macro.

You could use the following commands to pause the macro at a cell named HELP CELL before continuing when the user pressed ↵:

{EDIT-GOTO HELP CELL}
{?}

{ALERT}

{ALERT *message*;[*buttons*];[*icon-type*];[*results-range*];[*x*];[*y*]}

The {ALERT } command displays a message box with the specified message and icon, and waits for the user to choose OK or Cancel (depending on which buttons the message box contains). It takes the following arguments.

message   The text of the message to appear in the box.

buttons   1 or 2. 1 is the default and displays only the OK button; 2 displays both the OK and Cancel buttons.

icon-type   The type of icon to display in the message box, entered as text: Note displays the Note icon (this is the default setting); Caution displays the Caution icon; Stop displays the Stop icon.

results-range   The name or address of the cell in which 1-2-3 stores the number of the button chosen by the user. (1 represents OK, 0 represents Cancel.) You can use the *results-range* to set the default button in the message box: 1 in the results range makes OK the default button, while 0 in the results-range makes Cancel the default button. You can omit *results-range*, in which case {ALERT} does not enter a result in the worksheet.

x   An optional value indicating the horizontal position, in pixels, from the left side of the screen to the left edge of the dialog box. If you omit *x*, the dialog box will appear in the middle of the screen (which is where the user usually expects it).

y   An optional value indicating the vertical position, in pixels, from the top of the screen to the top of the dialog box. If you omit *y*, the dialog box will appear in the middle of the screen.

You could use the following command to display a warning dialog box in the middle of the screen:

> {ALERT "You are destroying important government data. Remain in your seat till your supervisor arrives.";1;"stop"}

{BEEP}

> {BEEP}

The {BEEP} command sounds the Windows beep. This command has no arguments.

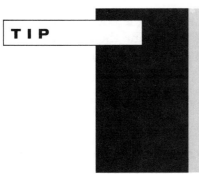

TIP

The {BEEP} command does not produce a tone if you have turned off the Beep on Error option in the User Setup dialog box (reached by selecting Tools ➤ User Setup) or if you have unchecked the Enable System Sounds check box in the Sound dialog box (reached from the Windows Control Panel). The Sound dialog box is also the place to choose a more interesting noise for the Default Beep event, as the beep is grandly titled.

{BREAKOFF}

{BREAKOFF}

The {BREAKOFF} command disables the Ctrl+Break key combination while a macro is running. This is a good way to stop users from terminating a macro while it is running, though you'd be well advised to inform them that Ctrl+Break will be disabled, lest they think their keyboard has locked up altogether and reboot their computer. The {BREAKOFF} command has no arguments.

WARNING

Once you've run a {BREAKOFF} command in a macro, the Ctrl+Break key combination will be disabled until either the end of the macro is reached or you run a {BREAKON} command in the macro. For this reason, add a {BREAKOFF} command at the end of the macro-writing process rather than at the beginning, as the Ctrl+Break key combination is the only way short of rebooting to escape from an infinite loop.

You could use the following commands to keep the secrets in your company's STRATEGY subroutine from prying eyes by preventing the user from stopping the macro (and possibly accessing the STRATEGY information) while the STRATEGY subroutine is running:

```
{BREAKOFF}
{STRATEGY}
{BREAKON}
```

21

Macro Commands

Note that the {BREAKON} command at the end is superfluous if the macro ends after the STRATEGY subroutine (because the Ctrl+Break key combination is turned back on at the end of a macro anyway).

{BREAKON}

> {BREAKON}

The {BREAKON} command reactivates the Ctrl+Break key combination, undoing a {BREAKOFF} command. This command has no arguments.

You could use {BREAKON} as in the following example to reactivate the Ctrl+Break key combination after the STRATEGY subroutine has stopped running, so the user can see what's happening for the rest of the macro:

> {BREAKOFF}
> {STRATEGY}
> {BREAKON}

{CHOOSE-FILE}

> {CHOOSE-FILE *file-type;results-range;title;[x];[y]*}

The {CHOOSE-FILE} command displays a Windows common dialog box containing a list of files so that the user can select one. The macro can then perform a series of actions on the file the user has selected. It takes the following arguments.

file-type Text indicating the type of files displayed in the dialog box. {CHOOSE-FILE} displays the names of files in the current directory; the user can change the path if necessary. You can enter the *worksheet*, *all*, or *text* to display 1-2-3 worksheet files, all the files in the directory, or text files (those with .TEXT and .PRN extensions), or enter the wildcard characters ? (for any single character) and * (for any number of consecutive characters).

results-range   The name or address of a cell in which {CHOOSE-FILE} stores the name of the file the user selected from the dialog box. (*results-range* is blank if the user chooses Cancel in the dialog box.).

title   Text that appears in the title bar of the dialog box to indicate the purpose of the file to be chosen.

x   A value indicating the horizontal position, in pixels, from the left side of the screen to the left side of the dialog box. If you omit the *x* argument, the dialog box will be centered horizontally on the screen.

y   A value indicating the vertical position, in pixels, from the top of the screen to the top of the dialog box. If you omit the *y* argument, the dialog box will be centered vertically on the screen—which is where the user will notice it most quickly.

You could use the following command to display a dialog box listing the .DOC files in your current directory—for example, if you were running a macro that installed DDE links in Microsoft Word documents:

{CHOOSE-FILE "*.DOC";A1;"Select the File to Be Linked to This Chart"}

The name of the file would be returned in cell A1 in this case.

{CHOOSE-ITEM}

{CHOOSE-ITEM *list-range;results-range;prompt;title;[x];[y]*}

The {CHOOSE-ITEM} command displays a dialog box containing a list of data items so that the user can select one. {CHOOSE-ITEM} then enters the index number for the user's choice in the specified range in the work-sheet. Use {CHOOSE-ITEM} when you need the user to choose an item other than a file; if you need the user to choose a file, use the {CHOOSE-FILE} macro command instead. It takes the following arguments.

list-range   The name or address of a single-column range containing the items to be displayed in the dialog box. The items must appear one per cell in the same order that you want them to appear in the list, and the list must end with a blank cell or a cell containing the value ERR or NA.

results-range   The name or address of a cell in which {CHOOSE-ITEM} returns the index number of the item that the user selects: 0 for the first item, 1 for the second, 2 for the third, etc. ({CHOOSE-ITEM} leaves *results-range* blank if the user chooses Cancel in the dialog box.)

prompt   Text that appears at the top of the dialog box (below the title bar of the dialog box) for telling the user what to choose and what will happen as a result.

title   The text for the title bar of the dialog box.

x   A value indicating the horizontal position, in pixels, from the left side of the screen to the left side of the dialog box. If you omit the *x* argument, the dialog box will be centered horizontally on the screen—probably the best position for it.

y   A value indicating the vertical position, in pixels, from the top of the screen to the top of the dialog box. If you omit the *y* argument, the dialog box will be centered vertically on the screen—which is where the user will notice it most quickly.

You could use the following command to display a dialog box inviting the user to indicate his or her choice of destination for the 1995 office trip:

> {CHOOSE-ITEM TRIPS;RESULT;"Please indicate your preferred destination for the 1995 office trip.";"Company Trip"}

This assumes that the possible destinations are stored in the range named TRIPS; the user's choice will be stored in the range named RESULT. Since {CHOOSE-ITEM} displays a list box, the first item in the list will be highlighted by default, so make sure that that is a reasonable choice.

{CHOOSE-MANY}

> {CHOOSE-MANY *choices-range;results-range;prompt;title;[x];[y]*}

The {CHOOSE-MANY} command displays a dialog box from which the user can select one or more check boxes (up to a maximum of eight check boxes). While {CHOOSE-MANY} does not perform further actions based on the results the user returns in the check boxes, you can check the row containing those results (the third row of the *choices-range*) and base further actions upon them. {CHOOSE-MANY} takes the following arguments.

choices-range   The name or address of the range containing descriptions of the check boxes. This range must have three rows and a column for each check box (up to the maximum of eight). Row 1 should contain the labels for {CHOOSE-MANY} to display to the right of the check boxes. Row 2 should specify the state in which the check box should be displayed in the dialog box: 0 for unchecked; 1 for checked, and NA for dimmed. Row 3 is where {CHOOSE-MANY} returns the state of the check box after the user has chosen OK; {CHOOSE-MANY} returns 0 for unchecked and 1 for checked.

results-range   The name or address of a cell where 1-2-3 stores the user's response to the dialog box: 0 for Cancel, 1 for OK.

prompt   Text to display at the top of the dialog box (below the title bar) to explain to users the purpose of the dialog box.

title   The text to display in the title bar of the dialog box.

x   A value indicating the horizontal position, in pixels, from the left side of the screen to the left side of the dialog box. If you omit the *x* argument, the dialog box will be centered horizontally on the screen.

y   A value indicating the vertical position, in pixels, from the top of the screen to the top of the dialog box. If you omit the *y* argument, the dialog box will be centered vertically on the screen.

You could use the following command to display a dialog box asking the user to choose all relevant budget constraints for economic forecasting from the list contained in the range named BUDGET PLAN:

> {CHOOSE-MANY budget plan,F1..H2,"Choose all relevant budget constraints.", Budget Constraints}

The dialog box is titled Budget Constraints, contains instructions, and returns *choices-range* information in the third row of BUDGET PLAN and *results-range* information in the range F1..H2.

{CHOOSE-ONE}

> {CHOOSE-ONE *choices-range*; *results-range*; *prompt*; *title*;[*x*];[*y*]}

The {CHOOSE-ONE} command displays a dialog box and waits for the user to select an option button with which a macro is associated. After the user chooses OK, {CHOOSE-ONE} runs the macro associated with the option button. If the user chooses Cancel, no macro associated with an option button is run, but the {CHOOSE-ONE} dialog box disappears and the initial macro continues to run. It takes the following arguments.

choices-range   The name or address of a range containing descriptions of the option buttons. This range must contain at least three rows and a column for each button (up to a maximum of eight buttons) Row 1 should contain the labels that {CHOOSE-ONE} is to display to the right of the buttons in the dialog box. Row 2 should specify the state in which the option button should be displayed in the dialog box: 0 for off, 1 for on, and NA for dimmed. Row 3 should contain macro commands (up to 511 characters per cell; then use subsequent rows as necessary) or the name of the subroutine for 1-2-3 to perform when the corresponding button in the dialog box is selected and the user chooses OK.

results-range   The address or range name of a cell in which {CHOOSE-ONE} returns 0 if the user chooses Cancel or 1 if the user chooses OK.

prompt   Text to display at the top of the dialog box (below the title bar) to explain to users the purpose of the dialog box.

title   The text to display in the title bar of the dialog box.

x   A value indicating the horizontal position, in pixels, from the left side of the screen to the left side of the dialog box. If you omit the *x* argument, the dialog box will be centered horizontally on the screen.

y   A value indicating the vertical position, in pixels, from the top of the screen to the top of the dialog box. If you omit the *y* argument, the dialog box will be centered vertically on the screen.

WARNING   Since only one button can be selected in the dialog box, only one cell in Row 2 can contain a 1; if more than one cell contains a 1, only the first of the buttons with ones will be selected. The first button will be selected if no cell contains 1.

You could use the following command to display a dialog box asking the user to choose one possible budget plan for economic forecasting from the list contained in the range named BUDGET PLAN:

{CHOOSE-MANY budget plan;thrust;"Choose the primary budget thrust."; Budget Constraints}

The dialog box is titled Budget Constraints, contains instructions, and returns *results-range* information in the range named THRUST. The option button chosen will run the relevant macro commands or subroutine named in the BUDGET PLAN range.

N O T E   {CHOOSE-ONE} is also discussed on page 636.

{DIALOG?}

21

Macro Commands

{DIALOG? *name*}

The {DIALOG?} command displays the specified 1-2-3 dialog box and waits for the user to choose OK or press ↵. It takes the following argument.

name   Text in double quotation marks (" ") indicating the name of the dialog box to display. The name should appear as it does in the title bar of the dialog box, with spaces in the title replaced by spaces and ampersands (&) replaced by the word *and*. For example, to display the Column Width dialog box, *name* would be "Column-Width", while the *name* for the Lines & Color dialog box would be "Lines-and-Color".

T I P   There are several special cases: Since the Range ➤ Sort and Query ➤ Sort commands both display Sort dialog boxes, use the names "range-sort" and "query-sort," respectively. Since the Range ➤ Name, Chart ➤ Name, and Query ➤ Name commands all display Name dialog boxes, differentiate them by using the names "range-name," "chart-name," and "query-name." Dialog boxes will only display if they apply to the current selection; for example, a macro will crash if you have a query table selected and try to display the (Range) Name dialog box.

You could use the following command to display the Page Setup dialog box and let the user enter information and choose OK to proceed:

{DIALOG? "page-setup"}

{DIALOG}

{DIALOG *range*}

The {DIALOG} command displays a custom dialog box created with the Lotus Dialog Editor and saved in a dialog-description table range.

WARNING

The {DIALOG} command will not display "real" 1-2-3 dialog boxes; use the {DIALOG?} command instead in such cases.

{DIALOG} takes the following argument.

range   The name or address of the first cell in the dialog-description table for the custom dialog box to display.

You could use the following command to display the custom dialog box stored in the dialog-description table named PIM:

{DIALOG PIM}

{FORM}

{FORM *input-location*;[*call-table*];[*include-list*];[*exclude-list*]}

The {FORM} command suspends the execution of a macro temporarily so that the user can enter and edit data in the unprotected cells in the specified input-location. The user can also run macros by using certain keystrokes. {FORM} takes the following arguments.

input-location   A range of any size containing unprotected cells in which to enter data. *input-location* cannot include any hidden columns or worksheets.

call-table   The name or address of a two-column range. The first column contains one macro keystroke in each cell; the cells in the adjacent column contain the macro instructions to perform for that keystroke. *call-table* is case-sensitive for letters typed at the keyboard.

include-list   A range containing a list of keystrokes that are allowed. *include-list* is case-sensitive for letters typed at the keyboard.

exclude-list   A range containing a list of keystrokes to ignore. The *exclude-list* argument only applies when no *include-list* argument is used. *exclude-list* is case-sensitive for letters typed at the keyboard.

N O T E

Use a {FORMBREAK} command to continue the macro after the {FORM} statement. Use a {QUIT} or {RESTART} command to end the macro.

21

Macro Commands

You could use the following command to enable the user to enter or edit data in the range named STRUCTURE, using keystrokes that run the macros defined in the range named EDITING:

{FORM STRUCTURE;EDITING}

{FORMBREAK}

{FORMBREAK}

The {FORMBREAK} command ends a {FORM} command, resuming macro execution with the command after the {FORM} command. {FORMBREAK} has no arguments.

You could use the following command to end the current form command:

{FORMBREAK}

{GET}

{GET *location*}

The {GET} command suspends macro execution to allow the user to enter a keystroke, which it records as a left-aligned label in the specified location. {GET} does not cause recalculation outside the specified location; use a {CALC} command if you need to force recalculation. {GET} takes the following argument.

location The name or address of a cell or range in which to store the keystroke input by the user. If you specify a range, {GET} uses its first cell to store the keystroke.

T I P

To record the keystrokes Ctrl+End Home, End Ctrl+Home, Ctrl+End End, Ctrl+End Ctrl+Pg Up, and Ctrl+End Ctrl+Pg Dn, you need to run two consecutive {GET} commands.

You could use the following command to suspend the macro, receive a keystroke from the user, and record it in the range named USER HIT:

    {GET USER HIT}

{GET-FORMULA}

    {GET-FORMULA [*prompt*];*result*;[*default*];[*title*];[*x*];[*y*]}

The {GET-FORMULA} command displays a dialog box so that the user can enter a formula. When the user chooses Cancel or OK, {GET-FORMULA} enters the formula in the worksheet and restarts execution of the macro at the next command. The formula can be up to 511 characters long. It takes the following arguments.

prompt Text that appears at the top of the dialog box to explain to the user what to do. You can omit this argument.

result The name or address of a range in which {GET-FORMULA} enters the formula that the user input. If *result* is a multicell range, {GET-FORMULA} uses the top-left cell.

default The default contents of the text box in the dialog box. To leave the text box blank, omit the *default* argument.

title   The text that appears in the title bar of the dialog box. If you do not specify a *title* argument, the title bar will be blank (which looks strange to many users).

x   An optional value indicating the horizontal position, in pixels, from the left side of the screen to the left edge of the dialog box. If you omit *x*, the dialog box will appear in the middle of the screen (a handy place to have it).

y   An optional value indicating the vertical position, in pixels, from the top of the screen to the top of the dialog box. If you omit *y*, the dialog box will appear in the middle of the screen.

You could use the following command to display a dialog box to get the formula the user needs for the current calculation:

> {GET-FORMULA "Enter the math formula to
> use:";MATH_22;;"Math Formula for Calculation 22"}

The title bar of the dialog box contains *Math Formula for Calculation 22*, the prompt is *Enter the math formula to use:*, the formula entered by the user will be recorded in the cell named MATH_22, and no default formula will appear in the text box.

{GET-LABEL}

> {GET-LABEL [*prompt*];*result*;[*default*];[*title*];[*x*];[*y*]}

The {GET-LABEL} command displays a dialog box so that the user can enter a label. When the user chooses Cancel or OK, {GET-LABEL} enters the label in the worksheet and restarts execution of the macro at the next command. The label can be up to 511 characters long. It takes the following arguments.

prompt   Text that appears at the top of the dialog box to explain to the user what to do. You can omit this argument.

result   The name or address of a range in which {GET-LABEL} enters the label that the user input. If *result* is a multicell range, {GET-LABEL} uses the top-left cell.

default   The default contents of the text box in the dialog box. To leave the text box blank, omit the *default* argument.

21

Macro Commands

title   The text that appears in the title bar of the dialog box. If you do not specify a *title* argument, the title bar will be blank.

x   An optional value indicating the horizontal position, in pixels, from the left side of the screen to the left edge of the dialog box. If you omit *x*, the dialog box will appear in the middle of the screen (which is where the user usually expects it).

y   An optional value indicating the vertical position, in pixels, from the top of the screen to the top of the dialog box. If you omit *y*, the dialog box will appear in the middle of the screen.

You could use the following command to get the user's phone number and store it in the range named USER_PHONE:

> {GET-LABEL "Please enter your phone number in the following format: (515) 555-1212:";USER_PHONE;;"Enter Phone Number"}

{GET-NUMBER}

> {GET-NUMBER [*prompt*];*result*;[*default*];[*title*];[*x*];[*y*]}

The {GET-NUMBER} command displays a dialog box so that the user can enter a number or a numeric formula. When the user chooses Cancel or OK, {GET-NUMBER} enters the number in the worksheet and re-starts execution of the macro at the next command. The number can be up to 511 characters long.

WARNING   {GET-NUMBER} returns an error if the user enters anything other than a number, a formula, or a reference to a cell containing a number or a formula, in the text box in the dialog box.

{GET-NUMBER} takes the following arguments.

prompt   Text that appears at the top of the dialog box to explain to the user what to do. You can omit this argument, but using it tends to be helpful.

result   The name or address of a range in which {GET-NUMBER} enters the value that the user input. If *result* is a multicell range, {GET-NUMBER} uses the top-left cell.

default   The default contents of the text box in the dialog box. To leave the text box blank, omit the *default* argument.

title   The text that appears in the title bar of the dialog box. If you do not specify a *title* argument, the title bar will be blank.

x   An optional value indicating the horizontal position, in pixels, from the left side of the screen to the left edge of the dialog box. If you omit *x*, the dialog box will appear in the middle of the screen (which is where the user usually expects it).

y   An optional value indicating the vertical position, in pixels, from the top of the screen to the top of the dialog box. If you omit *y*, the dialog box will appear in the middle of the screen.

You could use the following command to display a dialog box titled "Bottles Sold Today" that prompts the user for the number of bottles they sold and stores the result in the range named BOTTLES SOLD:

```
{GET-NUMBER "Please enter the number of bottles sold to-
day:";BOTTLES SOLD;;"Bottles Sold Today"}
```

{GET-RANGE}

```
{GET-RANGE [prompt];result;[default];[title];[x];[y]}
```

The {GET-RANGE} command displays a dialog box so that the user can enter a range name or address or a numeric formula. When the user chooses Cancel or OK, {GET-RANGE} enters the range name or address in the worksheet and restarts execution of the macro at the next command. The range name or address can be up to 511 characters long. It takes the following arguments.

prompt   Text that appears at the top of the dialog box to explain to the user what to do. You can omit this argument, but that may confuse the user.

21

Macro Commands

result The name or address of a range in which {GET-RANGE} enters the value that the user input. If *result* is a multicell range, {GET-RANGE} uses the top-left cell.

default The default contents of the text box in the dialog box. To leave the text box blank, omit the *default* argument.

title The text that appears in the title bar of the dialog box. If you do not specify a *title* argument, the title bar will be blank.

x An optional value indicating the horizontal position, in pixels, from the left side of the screen to the left edge of the dialog box. If you omit *x*, the dialog box will appear in the middle of the screen.

y An optional value indicating the vertical position, in pixels, from the top of the screen to the top of the dialog box. If you omit *y*, the dialog box will appear in the middle of the screen.

You could use the following command to display a dialog box titled *Free Range* with the prompt *Please enter the range to unprotect:* and storing the range entered by the user in the range named FREE:

> {GET-RANGE "Please enter the range to unprotect:";FREE;;"Free Range"}

{LOOK}

> {LOOK *location*}

The {LOOK} command checks the typeahead buffer for keystrokes and records the first keystroke (if there is one) as a left-aligned label in the specified location. (If the buffer is empty, {LOOK} enters a lonesome ' (an apostrophe label-prefix character) in the specified location. Since 1-2-3 does not recalculate automatically after a {LOOK} command, use a {CALC} command if you need to force recalculation.

N O T E   The *typeahead buffer* records keystrokes struck during noninteractive parts of a macro—parts that accept no user input.

{LOOK} takes the following argument.

location   The name or address of a cell or range in which to record the first keystroke from the typeahead buffer. If you specify a range, {LOOK} uses the first cell in the range.

You could use the following command to get a keystroke from the keystroke buffer and store it in the cell named STROKE:

{LOOK STROKE}

{MENUBRANCH}

{MENUBRANCH *location*;[*x*];[*y*]}

The {MENUBRANCH} command displays a dialog box containing customized menu for the user to make a choice, then branches to the macro instructions associated with that command. It takes the following arguments.

location   The name or address of the first cell of a row containing the items to appear in the menu in the dialog box.

x   An optional value indicating the horizontal position, in pixels, from the left side of the screen to the left edge of the dialog box. If you omit *x*, the dialog box will appear in the middle of the screen (which is where the user usually expects it).

y   An optional value indicating the vertical position, in pixels, from the top of the screen to the top of the dialog box. If you omit *y*, the dialog box will appear in the middle of the screen.

TIP   The {MENUBRANCH} function is mainly included in 1-2-3 Release 5 for compatibility with earlier releases of 1-2-3. Consider using the {MENU-CREATE} command instead of {MENUBRANCH}.

21

Macro Commands

You could use the following command to display a dialog box containing a custom menu drawn from the named range SALES MENU:

{MENUBRANCH SALES MENU}

{MENUCALL}

{MENUCALL *location*;[*x*];[*y*]}

The {MENUCALL} command displays a dialog box containing a customized menu for the user to make a choice, then performs a subroutine call to the macro instructions associated with that command. It takes the following arguments.

location The name or address of the first cell of a row containing the items to appear in the menu in the dialog box.

x An optional value indicating the horizontal position, in pixels, from the left side of the screen to the left edge of the dialog box. If you omit *x*, the dialog box will appear in the middle of the screen (which is where the user usually expects it).

y An optional value indicating the vertical position, in pixels, from the top of the screen to the top of the dialog box. If you omit *y*, the dialog box will appear in the middle of the screen.

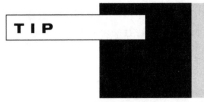

TIP

The {MENUCALL} function is mainly included in 1-2-3 Release 5 for compatibility with earlier releases of 1-2-3. Consider using the {MENU-CREATE} command instead of {MENUCALL}.

You could use the following command to display a dialog box containing a custom menu drawn from the named range PRODUCT LINES:

{MENUCALL PRODUCT LINES}

{MENU-COMMAND-ADD}

{MENU-COMMAND-ADD *menu-description-range;menu-index;command-index*}

The {MENU-COMMAND-ADD} command adds a command to the specified pull-down menu. It takes the following arguments.

menu-description-range   The name or address of a range containing a description of the command to add. This range requires five or more rows and one column.

NOTE   The first row of the menu description contains the name of the command to add. The second row contains a description of the command; this description appears in the title bar when you highlight the command. The third row contains *1, NA,* or a blank cell: *1* makes the command appear checked; *NA* makes the command appear dimmed; and a blank cell makes the command appear as normal (viz., neither dimmed nor checked). The fourth row remains blank. The fifth row contains macro commands (of up to 511 characters per cell) or the range name of the macro to perform when the command is chosen. (You can use further rows below the fifth row for more macro commands.)

21

Macro Commands

menu-index   An integer corresponding to the position of the menu in the menu bar, indicating which menu to add the command to. The first menu (e.g., the File menu) has the menu-index number 1.

command-index   An integer indicating where to position the command on the pull-down menu. The first command has a command-index number of 1.

You could use the following command to add the command stored in the range named PRINT DIRECTORY to the first pull-down menu as the eleventh command:

    {MENU-COMMAND-ADD PRINT DIRECTORY;1;11}

{MENU-COMMAND-DISABLE}

    {MENU-COMMAND-DISABLE *menu-index;command-index*}

The {MENU-COMMAND-DISABLE} command disables a command in a custom menu so that the command appears dimmed. {MENU-COMMAND-DISABLE} works only with custom menus; you cannot disable commands on the regular 1-2-3 menus, much though you might like to. It takes the following arguments.

menu-index An integer corresponding to the position of the menu in the menu bar, indicating which menu contains the command to be disabled. The first menu has the menu-index number 1.

command-index An integer indicating the position of the command on the pull-down menu. The first command has a command-index number of 1.

You could use the following command to disable the fifth command on the sixth pull-down menu:

    {MENU-COMMAND-DISABLE 6;5}

{MENU-COMMAND-ENABLE}

    {MENU-COMMAND-ENABLE *menu-index;command-index*}

The {MENU-COMMAND-ENABLE} command enables a command disabled with {MENU-COMMAND-DISABLE}. You can disable (and hence enable) only commands on custom menus—you cannot affect the regular 1-2-3 menus. {MENU-COMMAND-ENABLE} takes the following arguments.

menu-index An integer corresponding to the position of the menu in the menu bar, indicating which menu contains the command to enable. The first menu has the menu-index number 1.

command-index　An integer indicating the position of the command on the pull-down menu. The first command has a command-index number of 1.

You could use the following command to reenable the second command on the seventh pull-down menu:

    {MENU-COMMAND-ENABLE 7;2}

{MENU-COMMAND-REMOVE}

    {MENU-COMMAND-REMOVE *menu-index;command-index*}

The {MENU-COMMAND-REMOVE} command removes the specified command from the specified pull-down menu. It takes the following arguments.

menu-index　An integer corresponding to the position of the menu in the menu bar, indicating which menu contains the command to remove. The first menu has the menu-index number 1.

command-index　An integer indicating the position of the command on the pull-down menu. The first command has a command-index number of 1.

You could use the following command to remove the fourth command from the eight menu:

    {MENU-COMMAND-REMOVE 8;4}

{MENU-CREATE}

    {MENU-CREATE *menu-description-range*}

The {MENU-CREATE} command replaces the current 1-2-3 menu bar with the specified customized menu bar. It takes the following argument.

menu-description-range　The name or address of a range containing a description of the commands to add. This range requires five or more rows and one column, as described in the accompanying note.

NOTE The first row of the menu description contains the names of the commands in the menu bar, from left to right, up to a maximum of nine commands. The row of commands should end with either a blank cell or a cell containing ERR or NA. The second row contains a description of the command; this description appears in the title bar when you highlight the command. The third row contains 1, NA, or a blank cell: 1 makes the command appear checked; NA makes the command appear dimmed; and a blank cell makes the command appear as normal (viz., neither dimmed nor checked). The fourth row remains blank. The fifth row contains macro commands (of up to 511 characters per cell) or the range name of the macro to perform when the command is chosen. (You can use further rows below the fifth row for more macro commands.)

You could use the following command to display the menu described in the range named CUSTOM_12:

{MENU-CREATE CUSTOM_12}

{MENU-INSERT}

{MENU-INSERT *menu-description-range*;[*menu-index*]}

The {MENU-INSERT} adds the specified custom pull-down menu to the default 1-2-3 menu bar, placing it either where specified or between the Tools and Window menus. It takes the following arguments.

menu-description-range The name or address of a range containing a description of the command to add. This range requires five or more rows and one column, as described in the accompanying note.

NOTE

The first row of the menu description contains the name of the command to insert. The second row contains a description of the command; this description appears in the title bar when you highlight the command. The third row contains 1, NA, or a blank cell: 1 makes the command appear checked; NA makes the command appear dimmed; and a blank cell makes the command appear as normal (that is, neither dimmed nor checked). The fourth row contains the range name or address of a pull-down-menu–description range for the corresponding command. The fifth row contains macro commands (of up to 511 characters per cell) or the range name of the macro to perform when the command is chosen. (You can use further rows below the fifth row for more macro commands.)

NOTE

The pull-down-menu–description range is set up as follows. It consists of five or more rows and up to 25 columns (24 commands plus one blank row to end the list). The first row contains the name of the commands in the pull-down menu, from left to right; this list needs to end with a blank cell or a cell containing the value ERR or NA. The second row contains a description of the command; this description appears in the title bar when you highlight the command. The third row contains 1, NA, or a blank cell: 1 makes the command appear checked; NA makes the command appear dimmed; and a blank cell makes the command appear as normal (neither dimmed nor checked). The fourth row is left blank. The fifth row contains macro commands (of up to 511 characters per cell) or the range name of the macro to perform when the command is chosen. (You can use further rows below the fifth row for more macro commands.)

21

Macro Commands

menu-index   An integer corresponding to the position of the menu in the menu bar, indicating which menu to add the command to. The first menu has the menu-index number 1.

You could use the following command to display the menu specified in the range HACKER MENU as the fourth menu in the menu bar:

    {MENU-INSERT HACKER MENU;4}

{MENU-RESET}

    {MENU-RESET}

The {MENU-RESET} command displays the default 1-2-3 menu bar. This command has no arguments.

You could use the following command to reset your display to the default 1-2-3 menu bar:

    {MENU-RESET}

{MODELESS-DISMISS}

    {MODELESS-DISMISS}

The {MODELESS-DISMISS} command closes the open modeless dialog box. If no modeless dialog box is open, {MODELESS-DISMISS} has no effect. This command has no arguments.

You could use the following command to close the open modeless dialog box:

    {MODELESS-DISMISS}

{MODELESS-DISPLAY}

    {MODELESS-DISPLAY *message*;[*title*];[*on-top*];[*x*];[*y*]}

The {MODELESS-DISPLAY} command displays a modeless dialog box until 1-2-3 reaches another {MODELESS-DISPLAY} command, a {MODELESS-DISMISS} command, or the end of the macro. It takes the following arguments.

message Text of up to 512 characters to display in the dialog box.

title The text that appears in the title bar of the dialog box. This text can be up to 64 characters long. If you do not specify a *title* argument, the title bar will be blank.

on-top Yes or No, indicating whether the dialog box remains in the foreground even when it is not active. The default is Yes, leaving the dialog box in the foreground if you omit the *on-top* argument.

x An optional value indicating the horizontal position, in pixels, from the left side of the screen to the left edge of the dialog box. If you omit *x*, the dialog box will appear in the middle of the screen (which is where the user will usually expect it).

y An optional value indicating the vertical position, in pixels, from the top of the screen to the top of the dialog box. If you omit *y*, the dialog box will appear in the middle of the screen.

You could use the following command to display a modeless dialog box titled "Salary Information" in the on-top position, slap bang in the middle of the screen:

> {MODELESS-DISPLAY "The Payroll macro is updating the salary-information fields. Screen updating has been turned off until the macro ends.";"Salary Information";"yes"}

{PLAY}

> {PLAY *filename*}

The {PLAY} command plays a .WAV file. It takes the following argument.

filename The name of the .WAV file to play, including the path, entered as text in double quotation marks (" ").

You could use the following command to play the .WAV file UL-TRA.WAV, which is stored in the Z:\SYS:PUBLIC\SOUNDS directory:

> {PLAY "z:\sys:public\sounds\ultra.wav"}

21

Macro Commands

{WAIT}

{WAIT *time-number*}

The {WAIT} command suspends macro execution and displays WAIT as the mode indicator until the time specified by *time-number*. When the specified time arrives, 1-2-3 removes the WAIT indicator and continues the macro. You can interrupt a {WAIT} command by pressing Ctrl+Break. This ends the macro (unless you have run a {BREAKOFF} command. No other keystroke has any effect. It takes the following argument.

time-number   A time number representing a time that has not yet passed. (If the specified time has passed, {WAIT} has no effect.)

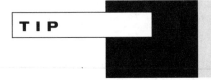

T I P

As you might expect, {WAIT} relies on your computer's date and time settings. Check them if necessary before issuing this command.

You could use the following command to pause a macro for 30 seconds:

{WAIT @NOW+@TIME(0;0;30}

Version Manager Macro Commands

This section of the chapter examines the Version Manager macro commands, which allow you to perform the Version Manager commands on the Range menu.

{RANGE-VERSION?}

{RANGE-VERSION? [*option*]}

The {RANGE-VERSION?} command displays the Version Manager window in the form specified. It takes the following argument.

option   Text indicating whether to close the Version Manager window or display it, and in which form to display it: *on* opens and activates the Version Manager window in the last form it was previously displayed, Manager or Index (*on* is the default if you omit the *option* argument). *off* closes the Version Manager window, if it is open. *manager* opens the Version Manager window and activates the Manager. *index* opens the Version Manager window and activates the Index.

You could use the following command to open the Version Manager window and activate the Index:

    {RANGE-VERSION? "index"}

Equivalent commands Range ➤ Version

{SCENARIO-ADD-VERSION}

    {SCENARIO-ADD-VERSION *scenario-name;[scenario-creator];version-range;version-name;[version-creator]*}

The {SCENARIO-ADD-VERSION} command adds a version to a scenario. It takes the following arguments.

scenario-name   Text indicating the name of the scenario. Note that this is case-sensitive.

scenario-creator   Text indicating the name of the creator of the scenario. Omit the *scenario-creator* argument to use the most recently created scenario specified by *scenario-name*.

version-range   The name of the existing named range containing the version to add.

version-name   Text indicating an existing version for the specified version-range. Note that this is case-sensitive.

version-creator   Text indicating the name of the creator of the version. Omit this argument to use the most recently created version.

You could use the following command to add the version Bad Harvest for the range named YIELD to the scenario named 1995:

{SCENARIO-ADD-VERSION "1995";"Papa Doc du Vin";YIELD;"Bad Harvest"}

{SCENARIO-CREATE}

{SCENARIO-CREATE *name*;[*share*];[*comment*]}

The {SCENARIO-CREATE} command creates the specified scenario. It takes the following arguments.

name   Text indicating the name to give the scenario. Note that this is case-sensitive.

share   Text indicating the sharing option for the version: *unprotected* applies no protection to the scenario (this is the default if you omit the *share* argument); *protected* prevents changes to the scenario; *hidden* prevents changes to the scenario and hides it.

comment   Text indicating a comment about the scenario. This is an optional argument.

You could use the following command to create a scenario named Positive Outlook, leave the scenario unprotected, and add the comment "A good year for the roses!" to the scenario:

{SCENARIO-CREATE "Positive Outlook";;"A good year for the roses!"}

{SCENARIO-DELETE}

{SCENARIO-DELETE *name*;[*creator*]}

The {SCENARIO-DELETE} command deletes a scenario. It takes the following arguments.

name   Text indicating the name of the scenario to delete. Note that this is case-sensitive.

scenario-creator   Text indicating the name of the creator of the scenario. Omit the *scenario-creator* argument to use the most recently created scenario specified by *name*.

You could use the following command to delete the scenario named Negative Eons created by Andy Nihilist:

{SCENARIO-DELETE "Negative Eons";"Andy Nihilist"}

{SCENARIO-INFO}

{SCENARIO-INFO *name*;[*share*];[*comment*]}

The {SCENARIO-INFO} command lets you modify the comment and sharing options for a scenario. It takes the following arguments.

name   Text indicating the name of the scenario. Note that this is case-sensitive.

share   Text indicating the sharing option for the version: *unprotected* applies no protection to the scenario (this is the default if you omit the *share* argument); *protected* prevents changes to the scenario; *hidden* prevents changes to the scenario and hides it.

comment   Text indicating a comment about the scenario. This is an optional argument.

You could use the following command to unprotect the scenario named Foreclosures:

{SCENARIO-INFO "Foreclosures";"unprotected"}

{SCENARIO-REMOVE-VERSION}

{SCENARIO-REMOVE-VERSION *name*;*version-range*}

The {SCENARIO-REMOVE-VERSION} command removes the specified version from the specified scenario. If the scenario is protected or hidden, or the version is hidden, the command will fail. It takes the following arguments.

name Text indicating the name of the scenario to remove. This is case-sensitive.

version-range The name of the existing named range containing the version to remove from the scenario. {SCENARIO-REMOVE-VERSION} removes the version currently displayed in *version-range*.

You could use the following command to remove the version currently displayed in the range named SLEDGES from the scenario named SouthWest:

{SCENARIO-REMOVE-VERSION "SouthWest";sledges}

{SCENARIO-SHOW}

{SCENARIO-SHOW *name*;[*creator*]}

The {SCENARIO-SHOW} command displays the selected scenario in the worksheet. It takes the following arguments.

name Text indicating the name of the scenario to display. Note that this is case-sensitive.

creator Text indicating the name of the creator of the scenario to display. Omit the *creator* argument to use the most recently created scenario specified by *name*.

You could use the following command to display the scenario named Unfounded Optimism created by Wilma White:

{SCENARIO-SHOW "Unfounded Optimism";"Wilma White"}

{VERSION-CREATE}

{VERSION-CREATE *version-range*;*name*;[*share*];[*retain-styles*]; [*comment*]}

The {VERSION-CREATE} command creates the new version specified. It takes the following arguments.

version-range The name of the existing named range from which to create the version.

name   Text indicating the name of the version to create. This is case-sensitive.

share   Text indicating the sharing option for the version: *unprotected* applies no protection to the scenario (this is the default if you omit the *share* argument); *protected* prevents changes to the scenario; *hidden* prevents changes to the scenario and hides it.

retain-styles   Yes or No, indicating whether to save style information with the new version. The default is to lose the style information.

comment   Text indicating a comment about the new version. This is an optional argument.

You could use the following command to create a version named Pentium from the range TIMES, save style information with the version, and add the comment "Adjust for DX4":

> {VERSION-CREATE TIMES;"Pentium";;"yes";"Adjust for DX4"}

{VERSION-DELETE}

> {VERSION-DELETE *version-range;name;[creator]*}

The {VERSION-DELETE} command deletes the specified version. It takes the following arguments.

version-range   The name of the existing named range containing the version to delete.

name   Text indicating the name of the version to delete. This is case-sensitive.

version-creator   Text indicating the name of the creator of the version to delete. Omit this argument to delete the most recently created version.

You could use the following command to delete the version named Unfounded Optimism created by Wilma White from the range PERFORMANCE:

> {VERSION-DELETE PERFORMANCE;"Unfounded Optimism";"Wilma White"}

{VERSION-INDEX-COPY}

{VERSION-INDEX-COPY}

The {VERSION-INDEX-COPY} command copies the information in the Index of the selected version to the Clipboard. Once you have copied this information to the Clipboard, you can paste it into a worksheet by using an {EDIT-PASTE} command. {VERSION-INDEX-COPY} has no arguments.

You could use the following command to copy the information in the Index of the selected version to the Clipboard:

{VERSION-INDEX-COPY}

{VERSION-INDEX-MERGE}

{VERSION-INDEX-MERGE *source-file*;[*date-filter*];[*user-filter*];[*table-location*]}

The {VERSION-INDEX-MERGE} command copies versions and scenarios from the source-file into the current file. It takes the following arguments.

source-file   The name of the file containing the versions and scenarios to merge. This file must be in memory. Include the path if *source-file* is not in the current directory.

date-filter   A date number (or text in day-month-year, day-month, or Long International Date format) specifying the cutoff date for versions to be merged. {VERSION-INDEX-MERGE} merges only versions created or modified on or after that date.

user-filter   Text indicating the name of the user by which to filter the versions and scenarios. {VERSION-INDEX-MERGE} merges only versions and scenarios created or last modified by that user.

table-location   The name or address of the range in which to create the table of merge results. You can specify either the entire range or just the first cell. Bear in mind that the table will be one column wide and as many rows deep as {VERSION-INDEX-MERGE} produces merge results, plus one blank row. Any existing data in *table-location* will be overwritten.

If there are not enough rows left in the worksheet to contain the table of merge results, the table will be truncated to fit.

You could use the following command to merge all scenarios and versions from the file VPAVERSE.WK5 created by user Merlin and create a table in the range named MERLIN MERGE:

> {VERSION-INDEX-MERGE "G:\PROJECT\VPAVERSE.WK5";;"Merlin";MERLIN MERGE}

{VERSION-INFO}

> {VERSION-INFO *version-range;name;[creator];[share];[retain-styles]*}

The {VERSION-INFO} command lets you modify style retention and sharing options for the specified version. It takes the following arguments.

version-range   The name of the existing named range containing the version to modify.

name   Text indicating the name of the version to modify. This is case-sensitive.

creator   Text indicating the name of the creator of the version to modify. Omit this argument to use the most recently created version.

share   Text indicating the sharing option for the version to modify: *unprotected* applies no protection to the scenario (this is the default if you omit the *share* argument); *protected* prevents changes to the scenario; and *hidden* prevents changes to the scenario and hides it.

retain-styles   Yes or No, indicating whether to save style information with the version. The default is to ignore style information if you omit the *retain-styles* argument.

You could use the following command to hide the version named Projected Takeovers:

> {VERSION-INFO HORNBLOWERS PLC;"Projected Takeovers";;" hidden"}

{VERSION-REPORT}

{VERSION-REPORT *version-range*;[*formulas-range*];[*include-data*];[*include-audit*];[*arrange-data*];*version1*;[*version2*];...;[*version10*]}

The {VERSION-REPORT} command creates reports showing selected versions and their effect on the outcome of a formula. {VERSION-REPORT} places the reports in a new file named REPORT*nn*.WK5. It takes the following arguments.

version-range   The name of the existing named range in the current file containing the version for which to create a report.

formulas-range   The name or address of a range in the current file containing formulas. This is an optional argument.

include-data   Yes or No, indicating whether to include the data for the selected versions. The default is Yes if you omit the *include-data* argument.

include-audit   Yes or No, indicating whether to include details of the creator and last modifier of the versions and the date at which they were created and last modified. The default is Yes if you omit the *include-audit* argument.

arrange-data   *rows* or *columns*, entered as text in double quotation marks (" "), indicating whether to arrange the data in the report by column (the default setting if you omit the *arrange-data* argument) or by row.

version1   Text indicating the name of a version to include in the report. Remember that version names are case-sensitive.

version2;...;*version10*.   The names of up to 9 additional versions to include in the report. Version names are case-sensitive.

You could use the following command to create a report on the versions named Low Interest, Medium Interest, and Pure Extortion for the range named HUNTERS VINEYARD, showing the effects of the two versions on the formula in the cell named TEST FORMULA, omitting the data and audit information for the versions, and arranging the data in the report by column:

> {VERSION REPORT HUNTERS VINEYARD;TEST FOR-
> MULA;"no";"no";"columns";"Low Interest";"Medium
> Interest";"Pure Extortion"}

{VERSION-SHOW}

> {VERSION-SHOW *version-range;name;[creator];[goto]*}

The {VERSION-SHOW} command displays the selected version in the worksheet. It takes the following arguments.

version-range   The name of the existing named range containing the version to display.

name   Text indicating the name of the version to display. This is case-sensitive.

version-creator   Text indicating the name of the creator of the version. Omit this argument to use the most recently created version.

goto   Yes or No, indicating whether to scroll to *version-range*. The default is No if you omit the *goto* argument.

You could use the following command to display the version named Pure Extortion for the range named HUNTERS VINEYARD and scroll to that version:

> {VERSION-SHOW HUNTERS VINEYARD;"Pure Extortion";;"yes"}

{VERSION-UPDATE}

> {VERSION-UPDATE *version-range;name;[creator]*}

The {VERSION-UPDATE} command updates an already existing version with new data you enter in its named range. It takes the following arguments.

version-range   The name of the existing named range containing the version to update.

version-name   Text indicating the existing version to update. Note that this is case-sensitive.

version-creator   Text indicating the name of the creator of the version. Omit this argument to use the most recently created version.

You could use the following command to update the Low Interest version of the HUNTERS VINEYARD range after a miraculous fall in interest rates:

{VERSION-UPDATE HUNTERS VINEYARD;"Low Interest"}

Window and Screen Display Macro Commands

This section of the chapter examines the window and screen display macro commands, which control the various parts of the screen display. By using these commands, you can make your copy of 1-2-3 much more friendly to use—or defy industrial espionage from your temporary workers.

{APP-ADJUST}

{APP-ADJUST *x;y;width;height*}

The {APP-ADJUST} command moves and scales the 1-2-3 window. {APP-ADJUST} places the upper-left corner of the window x pixels from the left of the screen and *y* pixels from the top corner of the screen, and sizes the 1-2-3 window to be *height* pixels high and width pixels wide. It takes the following arguments.

x   A value indicating the horizontal position, in pixels, from the left side of the screen to the left side of the 1-2-3 window.

y   A value indicating the vertical position, in pixels, from the top of the screen to the top of the 1-2-3 window.

width   A value indicating the window width, in pixels, from the left border to the right border.

height   A value indicating the window height, in pixels, from the top border to the bottom border.

WARNING

You can lose your 1-2-3 window partly or completely by using too large values for *x* and *y*. If you do this by accident, choose Window ➤ Tile in the Program Manager to make the window reappear, and adjust your macro. Bear in mind that users may use your macro with different screen resolutions, which can upset the best-laid plans of macros and men.

21

Macro Commands

You could use the following command to shrink the 1-2-3 window down to a little window in the bottom-right corner of a 640×480-pixel screen:

    {APP-ADJUST 440;330;200;150}

{APP-STATE}

> {APP-STATE *state*}

The {APP-STATE} command minimizes, maximizes, or restores the 1-2-3 window. It takes the following arguments.

state   *maximize*, *minimize*, or *restore*, entered as text between double quotation marks (" "). *maximize* maximizes the window; *minimize* minimizes the 1-2-3 window; and *restore* returns a maximized window to its previous state.

You could use the following commands to minimize the 1-2-3 window, then maximize it, then restore it to its previous state:

    {APP-STATE "minimize"}
    {APP-STATE "maximize"}
    {APP-STATE "restore"}

{BREAK}

> {BREAK}

The {BREAK} command clears the edit line when data is being entered or edited, or leaves the current dialog box during selection of a 1-2-3 command, and returns 1-2-3 to READY mode. {BREAK} has no effect in any other situation; {BREAK} does not terminate a macro (unlike the Ctrl+Break key combination, which does). This command has no arguments.

You could use the following command to ensure that 1-2-3 is in Ready mode when you start running a macro:

    {BREAK}

Alternatively, you could use the following command to rid the user of any current dialog box displayed and display the information in a range named INFO:

    {BREAK}{EDIT-GOTO INFO}

{FRAMEOFF}

    {FRAMEOFF}

The {FRAMEOFF} and {FRAMEON} commands have no effect in 1-2-3 Release 5 but are included for compatibility with macros created in previous versions of 1-2-3.

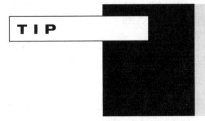

TIP The {FRAMEOFF} and {FRAMEON} commands have been taken over by the {SET} command: You can hide a worksheet frame by using {SET "window-display-frame";"no"} and redisplay it by using {SET "window-display-frame";"yes"}.

{FRAMEON}

The {FRAMEOFF} and {FRAMEON} commands have no effect in 1-2-3 Release 5 but are included for compatibility with macros created in previous versions of 1-2-3.

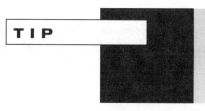

TIP The {FRAMEOFF} and {FRAMEON} commands have been taken over by the {SET} command: You can hide a work-sheet frame by using {SET "window-display-frame";"no"} and redisplay it by using {SET "window-display-frame";"yes"}.

{INDICATE}

{INDICATE [*text*]}

The {INDICATE} command displays text in the 1-2-3 title bar. The ti-tle-bar text remains unchanged until you run another {INDICATE} command or end the 1-2-3 session. It takes the following argument.

text Any text that fits in the title bar. You can fit in about 80–90 characters, depending on their width (the title bar uses a proportional sans-serif font). For that authentic Windows look, you'll need to experiment with a number of leading spaces to center your text in the title bar. (Left-aligned text in the title bar looks surprisingly odd. Microsoft has us conditioned…)

TIP To restore the standard title bar, use {INDICATE} without an argument. To display a blank title bar—the Bela Lugosi look—use {INDICATE" "}.

If you felt the urge to personalize your copy of 1-2-3 with the electronic equiva-lent of vanity plates, you could use something like the following command:

{INDICATE "The Text Butcher's customized spreadsheet for the GUI. Beware all imitations!"}

{PANELOFF}

{PANELOFF}

The {PANELOFF} command freezes the control panel until 1-2-3 en-counters a {PANELON} command or the macro ends. An {INDICATE} command also unfreezes the control panel.

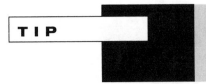

> **TIP**
>
> {PANELOFF} has two main uses—for turning off screen updating to speed up macros, and for hiding confidential information from snoops.

You could use the following command to freeze the display so that the user would not see the subsequent sequence of actions until a {PANELON} command or an {INDICATE} command was run, or the macro ended:

{PANELOFF}

{PANELON}

{PANELON}

The {PANELON} command unfreezes the control panel and the status line, restoring the display to normal.

You could use the following command to unfreeze the control panel and the status line after performing a sequence of actions you did not want the user to see:

{PANELON}

{SYSTEM}

{SYSTEM *command*}

The {SYSTEM} command temporarily halts the 1-2-3 session to execute the specified operating-system command before resuming the session. It takes the following argument.

command Any DOS command, including commands that run batch files or other programs. *command* is any text entered in double quotation marks (" "), a formula resulting in text, or the name or address of a cell containing a label or formula that results in a label.

> **WARNING** Don't be tempted to use the {SYSTEM} command to load TSRs; you might crash your 1-2-3 session.

You could use the following command to run the Print Console utility on a Novell network (for example, to determine which network printer was suffering least traffic before printing a monster document):

{SYSTEM "pconsole"}

{VIEW-ZOOM}

{VIEW-ZOOM *how*}

The {VIEW-ZOOM} command decreases or increases the display size of cells as specified. {VIEW-ZOOM} can optionally restore the default display size of cells. It takes the following argument.

how   Text indicating how to zoom: *in* increases the zoom in 10-percent increments, up to 400 percent; *out* decreases the zoom in 10-percent increments, down to 25 percent; and *custom* restores the display to the default size.

You could use the following command to restore cells to their default display size:

{VIEW-ZOOM "custom"}

Equivalent Commands   View ➤ Zoom In, View ➤ Zoom Out, View ➤ Zoom Custom

{WINDOW-ACTIVATE}

{WINDOW-ACTIVATE [*window-name*];[*reserved*];[*pane*]}

The {WINDOW-ACTIVATE} command makes the specified window active. It takes the following arguments.

21

Macro Commands

window-name   Text indicating the name of the open window to make active. Enter *window-name* as it appears in the title bar; include the file extension or path only if you have files open that share the same name but have different extensions or path names.

reserved   An argument reserved for use with 1-2-3 for the Macintosh. Omit this argument. Include an extra argument separator instead.

pane   An offset number indicating the pane to make current. Omit the *pane* argument to use the current pane. {WINDOW-ACTIVATE} returns an error if the specified pane does not exist in the window.

You could use the following command to activate the worksheet window named SWINDON.WK5:

> {WINDOW-ACTIVATE SWINDON.WK5}

Equivalent commands   Window ➤ *Window Name*

{WINDOW-ADJUST}

> {WINDOW-ADJUST *x;y;width;height*}

The {WINDOW-ADJUST} command moves and sizes the active window relative to the 1-2-3 window, placing the upper-left corner of the window *x* pixels from the left of the window and *y* pixels from its top corner, and sizing the active window to be *height* pixels high and *width* pixels wide. It takes the following arguments.

x   A value indicating the horizontal position, in pixels, from the left side of the 1-2-3 window to the left side of the window being adjusted.

y   A value indicating the vertical position, in pixels, from the top of the 1-2-3 window to the top of the window being adjusted.

width   A value indicating the width of the active window, in pixels, from the left border to the right border.

height   A value indicating the height of the active window, in pixels, from the top border to the bottom border.

You can lose your 1-2-3 window partly or completely by using too large values for *x* and *y*. If you do this by accident, choose Window ➤ Tile in Program Manager to make the window reappear, and adjust your macro. Bear in mind that users may use your macro with different screen resolutions.

You could use the following command to shrink the active window down to just its title bar at the top of the 1-2-3 window (below the SmartIcon set) on a 640~X480 screen:

{WINDOW-ADJUST 0;0;640;10}

{WINDOW-ARRANGE}

{WINDOW-ARRANGE *how*}

The {WINDOW-ARRANGE} command sizes open windows (either worksheets or Transcript windows) and arranges them as specified, either side by side or in a cascading stack with one on top of the other and just the title bars showing. It takes the following argument.

how Text indicating how to arrange the open windows: *stack* arranges the open windows in a cascading stack with just the title bars showing, and with the active window in front of the others; *vertical-tile* arranges the open windows side by side, with the active window in the top-left corner of the workspace.

You could use the following command to arrange all the open windows in a cascading stack with the title bars showing and with the active window in front:

{WINDOW-ARRANGE "stack"}

Equivalent commands Window ➤ Cascade, Window ➤ Tile

{WINDOW-STATE}

{WINDOW-STATE *state*}

The {WINDOW-STATE} command minimizes, maximizes, or restores the active window. It takes the following argument.

state   *maximize*, *minimize*, or *restore*, entered as text between double quotation marks (" "). *maximize* maximizes the active window; *minimize* minimizes the active window; and *restore* returns a maximized window to its previous state.

You could use the following command to minimize the active window:

{WINDOW-STATE "minimize"}

{WINDOWSOFF}

{WINDOWSOFF}

The {WINDOWSOFF} command freezes the screen while a macro is running, suppressing screen updates. You can use {WINDOWSOFF} to speed up execution of a macro or to hide sensitive information from inquisitive eyes. This command has no arguments.

You could use the following command to freeze the display during a macro:

{WINDOWSOFF}

{WINDOWSON}

{WINDOWSON}

The {WINDOWSON} command unfreezes the screen after it has been frozen with a {WINDOWSOFF} command. Normal worksheet display is restored.

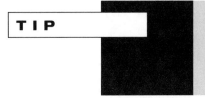

TIP

Since the end of a macro also unfreezes the screen, you don't need to run a {WINDOWSON} command to restore the worksheet display at the end of a macro—unless you need to restore the display before the end of a macro.

You could use the following command to unfreeze the screen during a macro:

{WINDOWSON}

{WORKSHEET-TITLES}

{WORKSHEET-TITLES *direction*}

The {WORKSHEET-TITLES} command freezes (or unfreezes) columns along the top of the worksheet, rows along the left edge of the worksheet, or both. It takes the following argument.

direction   Text indicating which titles to freeze; *horizontal* freezes all rows above the current cell; *vertical* freezes all columns to the left of the current cell; *both* freezes all rows above the current cell and all columns to the left of the current cell; and *none unfreezes all titles.*

You could use the following command to freeze the rows above the current cell:

{WORKSHEET-TITLES "horizontal"}

Equivalent commands View ➤ Freeze Titles, View ➤ Clear Titles

21

Macro Commands

INDEX

Note to the Reader: Throughout this index, **boldfaced** page numbers indicate primary discussions of a topic. *Italicized* page numbers indicate illustrations.

E

J

K

Q

W

X

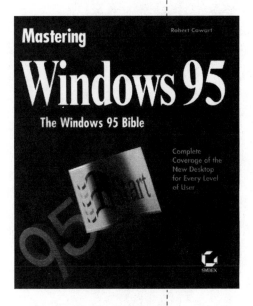

GET A FREE CATALOG JUST FOR EXPRESSING YOUR OPINION.

Help us improve our books and get a *FREE* full-color catalog in the bargain. Please complete this form, pull out this page and send it in today. The address is on the reverse side.

Name _____   Company _____

Address _____   City _____ State ____ Zip _____

Phone (___) _____

1. How would you rate the overall quality of this book?

❏ Excellent
❏ Very Good
❏ Good
❏ Fair
❏ Below Average
❏ Poor

2. What were the things you liked most about the book? (Check all that apply)

❏ Pace
❏ Format
❏ Writing Style
❏ Examples
❏ Table of Contents
❏ Index
❏ Price
❏ Illustrations
❏ Type Style
❏ Cover
❏ Depth of Coverage
❏ Fast Track Notes

3. What were the things you liked *least* about the book? (Check all that apply)

❏ Pace
❏ Format
❏ Writing Style
❏ Examples
❏ Table of Contents
❏ Index
❏ Price
❏ Illustrations
❏ Type Style
❏ Cover
❏ Depth of Coverage
❏ Fast Track Notes

4. Where did you buy this book?

❏ Bookstore chain
❏ Small independent bookstore
❏ Computer store
❏ Wholesale club
❏ College bookstore
❏ Technical bookstore
❏ Other _____

5. How did you decide to buy this particular book?

❏ Recommended by friend
❏ Recommended by store personnel
❏ Author's reputation
❏ Sybex's reputation
❏ Read book review in _____
❏ Other _____

6. How did you pay for this book?

❏ Used own funds
❏ Reimbursed by company
❏ Received book as a gift

7. What is your level of experience with the subject covered in this book?

❏ Beginner
❏ Intermediate
❏ Advanced

8. How long have you been using a computer?

years _____
months _____

9. Where do you most often use your computer?

❏ Home
❏ Work

❏ Both
❏ Other _____

10. What kind of computer equipment do you have? (Check all that apply)

❏ PC Compatible Desktop Computer
❏ PC Compatible Laptop Computer
❏ Apple/Mac Computer
❏ Apple/Mac Laptop Computer
❏ CD ROM
❏ Fax Modem
❏ Data Modem
❏ Scanner
❏ Sound Card
❏ Other _____

11. What other kinds of software packages do you ordinarily use?

❏ Accounting
❏ Databases
❏ Networks
❏ Apple/Mac
❏ Desktop Publishing
❏ Spreadsheets
❏ CAD
❏ Games
❏ Word Processing
❏ Communications
❏ Money Management
❏ Other _____

12. What operating systems do you ordinarily use?

❏ DOS
❏ OS/2
❏ Windows
❏ Apple/Mac
❏ Windows NT
❏ Other _____

13. On what computer-related subject(s) would you like to see more books?

_____

_____

_____

_____

14. Do you have any other comments about this book? (Please feel free to use a separate piece of paper if you need more room)

_____

_____

_____

_____

PLEASE FOLD, SEAL, AND MAIL TO SYBEX

SYBEX INC.
Department M
2021 Challenger Drive
Alameda, CA
94501

Elements of a Map

Map data   Map object

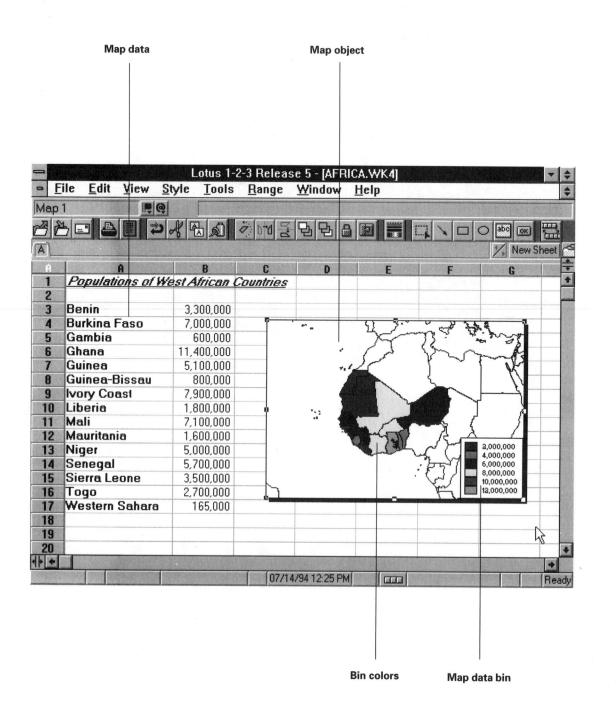

Bin colors   Map data bin